ADO.NET and XML:
ASP.NET On The Edge

ADO.NET and XML: ASP.NET On The Edge

Gregory A. Beamer
MCSD, MCSE, MCP+I, MVP

Wiley Publishing, Inc.

ADO.NET and XML: ASP.NET On The Edge

Published by
Wiley Publishing, Inc.
10475 Crosspoint Boulevard
Indianapolis, IN 46256
www.wiley.com

Copyright © 2002 by Wiley Publishing, Inc., Indianapolis, Indiana

Published simultaneously in Canada

ISBN: 0-7645-4849-2

Manufactured in the United States of America.

10 9 8 7 6 5 4 3 2 1

1O/SU/QX/QS/IN

For general information on our other products and services or to obtain technical support, please contact our Customer Care Department within the U.S. at 800-762-2974, outside the U.S. at 317-572-3993 or fax 317-572-4002.

Wiley also publishes its books in a variety of electronic formats. Some content that appears in print may not be available in electronic books.

Library of Congress Control Number: 2001092898

About the Author

Greg Beamer is a highly credentialed Microsoft developer with certifications in software development (MCSD), system engineering (MCSE), Internet (MCP+I), and database administration (MCDBA). Greg works as an Internet Architect for Robert Half Consulting, where he specializes in n-tier design and development with Microsoft technologies. Greg also spends time in the Microsoft Usenet groups, fulfilling his duties as a Microsoft Most Valuable Professional (MVP).

About the Contributor

Todd Meister is a developer specializing in Microsoft technologies. He has been a developer for over 10 years and has published articles for both ActiveWeb Developer and *MSDN Magazine*. Todd can be reached at `tmeister@tmeister.com`.

About the Series Editor

Michael Lane Thomas is an active development community and computer industry analyst who spends a great deal of time spreading the gospel of Microsoft .NET in his current role as a .NET Technology Evangelist for Microsoft. In working with over a half-dozen publishing companies, Michael has written numerous technical articles and authored/contributed to almost 20 books on numerous technical topics including Visual Basic, Visual C++, and .NET technologies. He is a prolific supporter of the Microsoft certification programs, having earned his MCSD, MCSE+I, MCT, MCP+SB, and MCDBA.

In addition to technical writing, Michael can also be heard over the airwaves from time to time, including two weekly radio programs on Entercom stations, most often in Kansas City on News Radio 980KMBZ. He is also occasionally found on the Internet doing an MSDN Webcast discussing .NET, the next generation of Web application technologies. Michael can be reached via e-mail at `mlthomas@microsoft.com`.

Credits

SENIOR ACQUISITIONS EDITOR
Sharon Cox

SENIOR PROJECT EDITOR
Jodi Jensen

DEVELOPMENT EDITOR
Maryann Steinhart

TECHNICAL EDITOR
Shervin Shakibi

COPY EDITORS
William A. Barton
Maryann Steinhart

EDITORIAL MANAGER
Mary Beth Wakefield

VICE PRESIDENT AND EXECUTIVE
GROUP PUBLISHER
Richard Swadley

VICE PRESIDENT AND EXECUTIVE
PUBLISHER
Bob Ipsen

VICE PRESIDENT AND PUBLISHER
Joseph B. Wikert

EXECUTIVE EDITORIAL DIRECTOR
Mary Bednarek

PROJECT COORDINATOR
Nancee Reeves

GRAPHICS AND PRODUCTION
SPECIALISTS
Kristin McMullan
Laurie Petrone
Jeremey Unger

QUALITY CONTROL TECHNICIANS
John Bitter
John Greenough
Andy Hollandbeck

PROOFREADING AND INDEXING
TECHBOOKS Production Services

I would like to dedicate this book to my grandfather, Edwin Reuben Hartz (1911–1997). It was your incredible passion for the written word that inspired me to write. And it was your faith and continued prayers that changed my life. I wish you had been able to stay on earth a bit longer to see your wonderful great-grandchildren grow up, but I know that God has a purpose for you, even now. Please forgive me for choosing a book that is not as befitting of your style . . . I may write that book one day. Thank you for your heart; I used to make fun of your crying towel, and now I need one of my own.

Preface

ASP.NET may well be the greatest leap a Microsoft product has taken since Microsoft opened its doors in the early '80s. More than just an upgrade to the existing Active Server Pages model, ASP.NET represents a completely different paradigm. For example:

- ◆ Code is now compiled, rather than interpreted.

- ◆ The entire core functionality of Windows is open to developers, without their having to work with the Windows API.

- ◆ Developers can write once and deploy to many different platforms. As of this writing, the Linux and BSD implementations of both C# and the .NET Framework are in the works. The UNIX implementation is likely to be just a short step behind.

- ◆ Developers have their choice of languages.

The .NET Framework, which changes the way people develop in the Microsoft world, comes with a new model for accessing data: ADO.NET. As with ASP.NET, ADO.NET is not simply an upgrade from ADO, either. The paradigm has changed from a connected model to a disconnected one, with XML as the underlying transfer mechanism.

XML has become a core technology for Microsoft. In the .NET Framework, you find a variety of XML implementations, including Simple Object Access Protocol (SOAP) and Universal Description, Discovery, and Integration (UDDI). The .NET Framework also uses XML to serialize objects, moving away from the cumbersome model used in Distributed Component Object Model (DCOM) objects.

Who Should Read This Book

This book is targeted for developers who want to use ASP.NET with Visual Basic .NET as their language of choice and ADO.NET and XML to create Internet applications. It is not written for beginners. Much of the material is introductory because ASP.NET is a new programming model, but I assume that the average reader has at least a few years of development experience under his or her belt and is familiar with either ASP or Visual Basic 6 development.

This book focuses on using ASP.NET to develop robust Internet applications. Along the way, I compare this new model to traditional ASP and Visual Basic 6 so that you can easily see the differences. I hope that this method will help current ASP and Visual Basic developers get up to speed quickly with this new technology. If you currently develop using Visual Basic, you'll enjoy learning about Visual

Basic .NET in Chapter 2. If you currently develop using ASP, you would do well to read both Chapters 2 and 3 before moving into the later sections of the book. I also encourage you to read Chapter 1 to get an idea of what .NET is all about.

Hardware and Software Requirements

The minimum hardware requirements are the same as those required to run the .NET Framework. I wrote this book on a computer with XP Professional, Visual Studio .NET, and SQL Server 2000 installed, but the code has been tested to run on the .NET Framework SDK on Windows 2000, as well. I am personally using 512MB of RAM, but I have tested the .NET Framework on machines with as little as 128MB of RAM. I suggest at least 256MB, especially if you are planning to use the Visual Studio .NET product for your development.

Most of the data-accessing code samples in the book are designed to use SQL Server 2000 as their data source. I have purposefully shied away from using the XML features of SQL Server 2000 to make it easier to use other databases as your data source. Although a couple of the code samples use Microsoft Access, it isn't necessary to have Access installed on your machine to run these samples.

How This Book Is Organized

Part I, "Introduction to .NET," presents the .NET Framework, ASP.NET, Visual Basic .NET, ADO.NET, and XML. At the end of this section, you build a simple ASP.NET application.

Part II, "Building Web Applications – ASP.NET and Visual Basic .NET," focuses on the core of ASP.NET, including how to configure your application and the controls at your disposal.

Part III, "Working with Data – ADO.NET," focuses on the method of data access you use with ASP.NET. This section quickly gets into real-world examples. I utilize Access and Oracle in some examples, but the majority of this section deals with SQL Server (SQL Server 2000 in particular) because Microsoft has developed a special provider in ADO.NET that works with SQL Server.

Part IV, "Collaboration and Presentation – XML," concentrates on the uses of XML in the .NET Framework. This section deals with many different forms of XML, including SOAP and UDDI.

In Part V, "Putting It All Together," I present the core of intranet, Internet, and extranet applications by developing them for a fictional company.

In addition to the chapters I just described, the companion Web site at www.wiley.com/extras includes three appendixes: An introduction to Visual Studio .NET, a comparison of C# and Visual Basic .NET, and a small compendium of .NET links for further information.

Companion Web Site

This book offers a companion Web site at `www.wiley.com/extras` from which you can get code examples, the sample applications used in the book, and three appendixes of additional information. On the site, you'll find download files for each chapter, and these download files are available in two flavors: the Visual Studio .NET version and the .NET Framework SDK version.

 When you unzip the downloaded files, be sure to use WinZip's default setting, Use Folder Names, which creates the directory structure for you. If you don't have this option set, all the files end up in a single folder and many of the applications may not run.

With the SDK downloads, I have included scripts, where applicable, to compile the code for you. I encourage you to download at least one of the SDK files, even if you are working with Visual Studio .NET, to familiarize yourself with the command-line compiler. The chapters that include some desktop code (Windows Forms applications) are probably the best to get a good introduction to the command-line compiler.

Conventions

Here are some conventions that I use throughout to help you use the book more efficiently:

- *Italics* indicate a new term that I'm defining, represent placeholder text (especially when used in code), or add emphasis.

- A special `monofont` typeface is used throughout the book to indicate code, a Visual Basic .NET keyword or an ASP.NET tag, a filename, or an Internet address.

- I use `bold monofont` and `shaded text` in code listings to point out particular parts of code that I'm focusing on in the surrounding discussion.

- A code continuation character (↵) at the end of a line of code indicates that the line won't fit on a single line due to the margin restrictions of the printed book. You should type it as a single line, however, when you type it into your application.

Navigating This Book

If you're completely new to ASP.NET and Visual Basic .NET, start at the beginning and work your way through to the end. Each chapter assumes that you're familiar with the contents of chapters before it. Intermediate to advanced developers can read the chapters and sections that appeal to them based on the table of contents and the introductory text in the chapters. Keep in mind, however, that some topics just don't stand well on their own, so the book includes a lot of information within the overall text. I suggest that you look through the table of contents or the index to find the appropriate bits of information in which you're interested.

Icons appear in the text to indicate important or especially helpful items. Here's a list of the icons and their functions:

Notes provide additional or critical information and technical data on the current topic.

Tips offer useful techniques and helpful hints.

Cross-Reference icons point you to another place in the book where you can find more information on a particular topic.

The Caution icon is your warning of a potential problem or pitfall.

The On the Web icon indicates that the companion Web site for the book contains a related file or additional information. Occasionally, this icon also points you to other Web resources.

Further Information

You can usually find me lurking around one of the Microsoft public Usenet groups, fulfilling my Microsoft MVP duties. I post under the moniker "cowboy." I spend some time in the .NET groups, but more time in the ASP groups, where I feel that I contribute more to solving real problems. Groups I regularly post to include:

- ◆ `microsoft.public.frontpage.client`

- ◆ `microsoft.public.inetserver.asp.general`

- ◆ `microsoft.public.sqlserver.xml`

I am also in the process of getting my own site up and running at `www.gbworld.com`. In the meantime, contact me at `BookAuthor@gbworld.com`.

Acknowledgments

Writing a book is a labor of love. It must be because so much time and effort go into ensuring that every little detail is in place. As it is such an arduous journey, there are a number of people who must be thanked.

I would like to thank my wife and children for understanding the time it takes to complete a book, especially when working from beta to product release on a new technology. I have to appreciate the love and patience of my wife, Tiffany, as I worked night after night, in addition to the many hours at my day job, to complete this tome. Even though my oldest daughter, Rebecca, thinks banging on a computer is "working," and my youngest, Emily, just smiles most of the time, I know that there were times when they wished daddy would work a bit less.

I also owe a great debt of gratitude to the people at Wiley for their continued support. Sharon Cox and Jodi Jensen have been the kindest editors a writer could ask for. I thank you for your continued patience over my missed deadlines. I am sure my schedule and need for perfection were maddening at times.

Thanks also go out to the technical editors who helped ensure that I had not missed something as we moved from beta to release. Although I sometimes disagreed with them on certain points, I have the utmost respect for Shervin Shakibi and Michael Lane Thomas.

I also owe a debt to many of my peers and colleagues. Although I would love to acknowledge all the Microsoft MVPs (Most Valuable Professionals) personally for their continued friendship and support (and occasional debate), I have limited space. You all know who you are. I will single out a few people who really helped me through this time:

- ◆ X (Xavier Pacheco), Bart Campbell, Antonio Ramirez Cobos, and Tony Campbell: Your continued faith in God has been a light in my life and has kept me on the path to completion. Thanks for holding me accountable.

- ◆ Tim Humphries and Bobby Stokes: The projects I worked on with you helped shape many of the ideas I used for this book. I know that a great many others also worked on these projects, and thanks goes out to them, as well.

- ◆ Tim Kinzer and Michael Simmons: The insight each of you has, not only in business, has been a welcome addition to my life and has shaped my work.

- Carsten Thomsen: Thanks for helping me through some of the early betas. Without your support, this would have been a very difficult road.

- Todd Meister: A special thanks to my contributing author for his dedication to the XML section of the book.

I also want to thank my church family and the men in my BSF study group. I am certain that it is your prayers that have kept me strong through the many late nights working on this book . . . and much more. Thank you for your continued support in my growth.

Most importantly, I would like to thank Christ for helping me learn to get a servant's heart. Without His sacrifice 2000 years ago, I would not have the perspective to understand that my troubles are very small, and I would focus on myself instead of others. I am reminded every time I watch my daughters sleep of what a miracle my life has been.

Finally, I need to thank you, the reader. I hope and pray that this book may be the work that helps you to have a better understanding of .NET.

Contents at a Glance

Contents

On the Companion Web Site

Part I

Introduction to .NET

Chapter 1

Introducing the .NET Framework and the CLR

I'VE BEEN WORKING WITH THE .NET FRAMEWORK for about a year and a half now. During this time, I have heard many misconceptions regarding the .NET Framework, the most common being that it is nothing more than a multilanguage object-oriented paradigm to build Web services. While this certainly describes a common use of .NET, it tells but a small part of the entire story. In this chapter, you are introduced to the underpinnings of the .NET Framework to better understand what .NET really is.

The .NET Framework

In its Microsoft Solution Framework (MSF), a complete set of guidelines for software projects, Microsoft defines a *framework* as a structure to help frame problems and facilitate effective decisions. The company contrasts a framework with a methodology, the latter of which includes predetermined tasks and deliverables. In other words, with a methodology, you know what you are building, while a framework is designed to help you build whatever you might want to build.

This definition inadequately explains what .NET is for developers, however, and a better definition is that a methodology becomes a framework if you move enough of the grunt work from a programmatic model to a declarative one. This means having more of the work falls on Microsoft's shoulders and less on your company's developers. Rather than have to write many lines of code to bring out new features in code, you need only point and click or run a simple tool.

Now that you have an understanding of a framework, you might wonder what the .NET Framework is. The .NET Framework is a structure or, more specifically, an environment for framing problems and facilitating effective decisions, which equates to building, deploying, and running applications. In this book, I am primarily concerned with Web applications, including Web services, but you are not limited to the Web by any means.

Figure 1-1 shows the parts of the .NET Framework. Notice that the framework divides neatly into the following three primary parts: the Common Language Specification (CLS) and .NET languages, the base class library, and the Common Language Runtime (CLR). In truth, most of the framework shown in Figure 1-1 can be thought of as a part of the CLR, so the illustration is more figurative than literal.

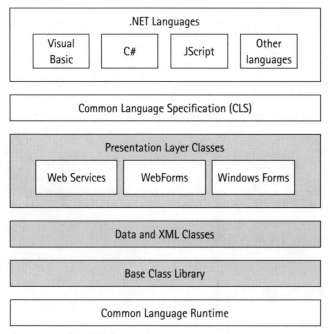

Figure 1-1: The .NET Framework.

◆ **Common Language Specification and .NET languages:** The *CLS* ensures that the various .NET languages can communicate with each other. As you find out, it also simplifies calling methods in portable executables (PEs) that you create in other .NET languages. If you're a Visual Basic developer who's tried to connect to a C++ DLL (dynamic link library), this feature may well prove worth the price of admission. The interoperability here is between .NET languages, not between .NET languages and traditional Windows programming language, which is more commonly known as COM Interop.

- **Base class library:** The *base class library* contains the central objects of the .NET Framework, most of which are contained in the System namespace. One of these items is `System.Object`. Every object you create ultimately derives from this object. The rest of the base class library deals with other core functionality that you use to create software in the .NET Framework. In essence, the base class library contains objects to do almost anything in Windows.

- **Common Language Runtime:** The *Common Language Runtime* is the core of the .NET Framework and is responsible for running all .NET-managed code on the chosen platform. I cover the CLR in much greater detail in the section "One Bytecode, Multiple Platforms," later in this chapter.

 You may have seen the term *Common Language Infrastructure* (CLI) tossed about. For this discussion, you should think of the CLI and the CLR as synonymous. In most Microsoft documentation, you see the CLR, while in ECMA (European Communications Manufacturers Association, a standards body) documentation, you see CLI. To view the documents submitted to ECMA, go to `http://msdn.microsoft.com/net/ecma`.

One of the most important features of this new paradigm is that you can extend or override any system object to alter the platform to best suit the applications that you create for your organization. You find out more about overriding base classes in Chapter 2.

N-tier development

Unless you've been in a coma for the past couple years, you've undoubtedly heard the term *n-tier development,* which is the concept of breaking software into layers, or tiers, that can act independently of other layers. The most common structure employed is to divide an application into three primary tier types: user interface, business rules, and data. The fact that you can have multiple user interfaces, business rules, or data layers is the reason this paradigm is called n-tier rather than three-tier.

The n-tier development movement gained a lot of ground at Microsoft with the advent of the Component Object Model (COM). COM has its roots in both OLE (Object Linking and Embedding) and ActiveX (a marketing term), so although it wasn't a new theory, it did finally put a firm set of rules to componentized software on the Windows platform. For the purposes of this discussion, know that COM worked through unique identifiers stored in the Windows registry.

N-tier development was further refined with MTS and the capability to easily make packages that work across multiple servers. Internet Information Server (IIS) and Active Server Pages (ASP), however, are what finally forced the tier issue, because interpreted script simply didn't scale as well as componentized software. I compare and contrast ASP, which is scripted, to ASP.NET, which is componentized and compiled, in Part II of this book.

Microsoft took COM to the next level, with COM+. COM+ added transactions and object brokering, which were formerly handled by MTS, and asynchronous processing, which was formerly handled by the Microsoft Message Queue (MSMQ), in one package.

The .NET Framework takes n-tier to a whole new level by moving a lot of the redundant plumbing to the .NET infrastructure and out of each object. This setup provides for smaller, more easily instantiated objects and makes object-oriented programming (OOP) a real possibility on the Windows platform, no matter what language you choose to program in. Combined with an underlying structure to create lightweight Web services, the .NET Framework may well make Internet-wide n-tier applications a common occurrence.

XML and SOAP

eXtensible Markup Language (XML) is a standardized method for structuring data, both internally and across the Internet. All the data objects in .NET use XML to move data from object to object. By combining it with SQL Server 2000, you can use XML all the way from the database to the user interface. Data transfer, however, isn't the most interesting part of the use of XML in .NET. You can now serialize objects into XML to more efficiently marshal objects across tiers.

Microsoft is committed to XML and uses quite a few XML applications like *Single Object Access Protocol (SOAP)* and *Universal Description and Discovery Interface (UDDI)* throughout .NET. Both SOAP and UDDI are types of XML documents used for specific purposes. UDDI is used to expose Web services, and SOAP is used to communicate between Web services and Web clients. I use the term Web here generically, to indicate any application that uses the TCP/IP protocol as its method of connecting clients.

Another important XML application is *Web Services Discovery Language (WSDL)*. While many of the specifics of WSDL are hidden from the developer, especially the developer who uses Visual Studio .NET, Web services will not work without the use of WSDL.

Multiple Languages, One Bytecode

At the core of .NET is the concept of using a variety of languages that compile down to the same bytecode, known as *Microsoft Intermediate Language* (*MSIL,* or *IL* for short). If you've worked with Visual Basic (VB) for any length of time, this concept may sound like a throwback to packed code (p-code), which was the only way to compile Visual Basic before version 5. While the methods of creating p-code applications and .NET MSIL might seem the same, they are very different, as you will see.

To facilitate this common Intermediate Language, .NET languages must follow a strict set of rules. I discuss some of the common rules in the sections "Common Functionality" and "One Bytecode, Multiple Platforms" a bit later in this chapter. Prior to discussing this subject, however, I need to explore the concept of *types*.

Everything in .NET is an *object,* but not all objects are the same *type*. No matter what language you work in, you need to become familiar with the concepts of *by reference* and *by value*. In Visual Basic, for example, you use the keyword `ByRef` to pass objects by reference and the word `ByVal` to pass them by value. The difference between the two is that `ByVal` passes the value and makes a copy in a new space in memory, while `ByRef` passes a pointer to the spot in memory where your object or variable sits. In other words, a variable will contain either the value of a variable or a reference to an object that holds that value.

When you pass variables by reference, or work with reference types, changing the value of the new variable also changes the value of the original variable. This is due to the fact you have passed a reference to a spot in memory. Both variables now point to the same spot, so any changes in one change the other.

Passing variables by value is safer than passing by reference if you need to alter the value of the new variable. This is due to the fact that you are only changing the new value, not the same spot in memory. On the downside, however, passing by value can get quite expensive if you're working with larger objects. Perhaps a few rules are in order:

- Pass variables by reference when you are passing them from one procedure to another inside the same object. The exception to this rule is when you are going to change the value of the variable inside of the procedure it is passed to. Unless there is a good reason, pass by value in this situation.

- Pass objects by value when you are passing them from one object to another.

Just as you have two methods to pass variables, or objects (remember that everything is an object in .NET), back and forth, you also have two basic types of objects. The smaller objects are generally *value types,* while the larger objects are generally *reference types*. Figure 1-2 shows the difference between value and reference types as they sit in memory.

I know I'm getting a bit advanced for an introductory chapter, but I think that seeing the difference between reference types and value types better illustrates the difference between the two. The value types (on the left in Figure 1-2) are placed directly on the memory stack. I use the word struct here, because a struct (or structure) is a value type that appears very much like a class. I discuss structs in Chapter 2. Most of the integral types (Integers and Longs, for example) are value types. Contrast the value type to the reference type (on the right in Figure 1-2), where a pointer is placed on the stack and the actual object is placed on the heap.

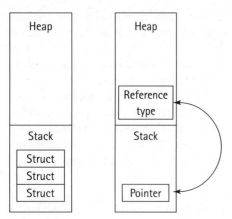

Figure 1-2: Value types (left) and reference types (right).

Reference types

As I mentioned in the preceding section, reference types are generally larger objects. In .NET, reference types are coded as classes and interfaces. In addition, Visual Basic .NET has a special type of class known as a `Module` that you will see if you create a console application. For simplicity, just remember that a `Module` is the starting point for creating applications that run from the command line.

As you find out in Chapter 2, the major benefit of using modules in Visual Basic .NET is maintainability of code, as Visual Studio .NET uses the module for its command line applications. For other application uses, use a class. When in doubt, follow the choices Visual Studio .NET makes. It will serve you well in most instances.

Reference types are located on the heap, which is the portion of memory set aside for program use. In addition, a pointer (or reference) to the reference type sits on the stack, which is a shared portion of memory. The CLR "garbage collector" watches these references to determine when it can free a particular instance of a reference type. When you create a variable of a specific type, you are creating an instance of this type. You can have multiple instances in one or many applications. I cover the garbage collector in the section "Other features of the CLR" a bit later in this chapter.

Value types

Values types are generally smaller than reference types, meaning that they occupy less memory. The most common forms of value types in .NET are enumerators (enums), which are named lists of values, and structures (structs), which are similar to classes in that they can have properties and methods. (Most developers will probably use a structure as a replacement for a user defined type (UDT) in Visual Basic 6.) All the integral types in .NET languages, with the exception of strings, are value types; these include integers, bytes, floating-point types (numbers that contain a decimal), and characters, to name a few. I cover integral types in the section "Common Language Specification," later in this chapter, along with the common type system (CTS).

You can temporarily turn a value type into a reference type. This is a concept known as *boxing*. The reverse, moving the object back from being a reference type, is known as *unboxing*. A good example of boxing comes when you split a string in Visual Basic .NET. The character you are splitting the string on becomes a reference type to complete the split. This is necessary to compare the value of the split character against a string, which is a reference object. Boxing is an implicit cast, because the user does not explicitly write code to create this conversion.

Source Code, Executables, Assemblies, and Applications

Within the .NET Framework, you work with source code, which compiles into *portable executables* (PEs). PEs rest in *assemblies,* and you deploy them to create applications. PE is a Microsoft term for a piece of compiled software that follows a well-defined set of rules. PEs have been a Microsoft standard since the late days of DOS. A discussion of all of the rules is outside the scope of this book, so I cover just the salient points in this chapter. Assemblies, as you will see, are the method of deploying software in .NET.

Source code

Source-code files sit at the core of your development effort. I am talking about the raw files you develop your code in. Working with ASP.NET, you become familiar with .ASPX (ASP.NET files) and .VB files, among others. These are your source code files. Unlike in Visual Basic 6, however, these source-code files don't represent individual objects.

In Visual Basic 5 and 6, you created a separate code module for each class in your DLL. To create three classes, you created three source code files. While you could compile multiple class files into a single DLL, you had to code them in separate .cls files. In contrast, you can place multiple classes in a single code module in .NET. This gives you a lot more flexibility, because you can create a single file for each class or multiple classes in a single file. I prefer multiple classes in one file when it is used as a type library (class library project in Visual Studio .NET), and leave a single class in each file when working with ASP.NET.

One of the most common uses of source code files is to organize code for ASP.NET applications, using one module for each page. Although not mandatory, using one .VB module per .ASPX page certainly helps maintain your code.

Those familiar with ASP may wonder why I call .ASPX files source-code files. After all, in ASP, IIS (or more correctly asp.dll and the scripting engine) interprets

ASP at runtime. ASP.NET is not, however, ASP. All code, even ASP.NET files, is compiled to IL prior to running in the CLR. I cover the topic of ASP.NET and compilation a bit more in depth in Chapter 3.

Modules

The first software concept to understand in .NET is the concept of the *module.* A module is a physical grouping of types. In many cases, you have a single module for each source code file. You may find, however, that you need to group your files a bit differently over time. For a simple application, you will most likely compile all your files to a single DLL or EXE. This is the default behavior of Visual Studio .NET, which a good number of you will use.

To be a bit more correct, the module is the part of IL, created from your source, without the assembly manifest. Figure 1-3 illustrates these concepts. To be complete, I have also included the next steps in the process, discussed further throughout this section, which is placing modules into assemblies and assemblies into applications.

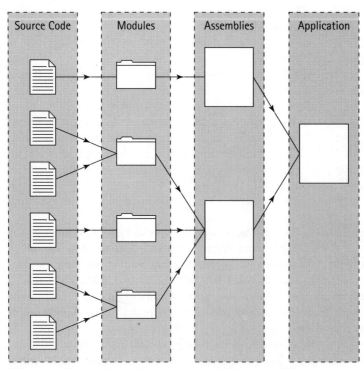

Figure 1–3: The relationship between source code and modules.

In .NET, each portable executable contains a certain amount of metadata (data about data) about the types that the module contains, along with Intermediate Language (IL or MSIL) for the Common Language Runtime (CLR). This metadata ultimately resides in the <u>assembly manifest</u>. The manifest gives you a complete description of its contents, as far as the types that it contains. Because of this manifest, <u>you can't deploy modules unless they're part of an assembly.</u> Assemblies and assembly manifests are covered in the next section.

Figure 1-4 shows a simple module. Notice that, as I just mentioned, a module, can't be deployed on its own outside of an assembly.

Figure 1–4: A simple module including types and metadata.

To put modules into perspective, remember that a module is the smallest unit of type deployment. You cannot create a class that does not compile into a module. Contrast the module to an assembly, the functional unit of code deployment, which is covered in the next section.

Assemblies

Assemblies are groupings of types that you deploy together as a unit of application functionality – a "<u>logical DLL</u>," if you will. Assemblies contain the IL code that the CLR executes, along with an assembly manifest, or metadata. An assembly isn't, however, the same thing as an application, since you can have an application that contains multiple assemblies. As a logical unit, a single assembly can contain multiple portable executables that you must to deploy as a single unit. Figure 1-5 shows a model of two assemblies.

In its simplest form, an assembly consists of a single module that contains all the assembly metadata as well as the type metadata in one portable executable. In this format, the assembly is synonymous with the portable executable. The example on the left in Figure 1-5 shows such a simple assembly, a single portable executable (PE) with all of the data and metadata in this single compiled file.

More complex assemblies contain multiple modules and possibly multiple PEs. Each module contains type metadata along with its own IL, as I cover in the preceding section about modules. One of the portable executables also contains the assembly metadata. The example on the right in Figure 1-5 shows such an assembly. This type of assembly may also contain a separate resource file.

I discuss metadata more in the section "One Bytecode, Multiple Platforms," but notice that you find assembly metadata in .NET in the portion of the assembly known as the *manifest,* as well as type metadata in each module. The manifest

♦ Establishes the identity of the assembly. This aspect of the manifest is extremely important when you start strongly typing an assembly, or adding a key that uniquely identifies your organization.

♦ Identifies the files that make up the assembly.

♦ Identifies the types and resources that make up the assembly.

♦ Identifies any dependencies on other assemblies that must be identified at compile time.

♦ Identifies all permissions necessary to run the assembly correctly.

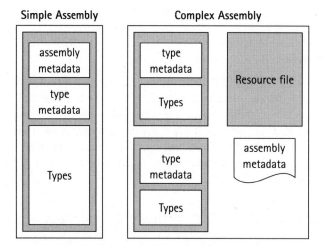

Figure 1-5: A simple assembly and a complex assembly.

You can store the manifest in many ways: in the file in a single PE assembly, in one of the files, or as a separate file. The default placement is different depending on how you create the assembly. If you use the Integrated Development Environment (IDE), or Visual Studio .NET, you place the manifest in a file; if you use the command-line tool AL.EXE, however, you place the manifest in its own file. (AL.EXE ships with the .NET Framework. It facilitates the linking of multiple modules into an assembly. It's a very interesting tool, but falls outside the scope of this book.)

Unlike in COM (Component Object Model), where a single portable executable is the functional unit of code deployment, an assembly is the functional deployment unit in .NET. This is a bit confusing at first. In COM you deploy a single DLL at a time. One project is one executable is one functional deployment unit. You cannot deploy parts of a DLL.

The Component Object Model (COM)

The Component Object Model (COM), which first appeared in the early 1990s, is, at its simplest level, a group of interfaces that allow communication between components. More specifically, COM is

- A binary standard for calling functions between objects. COM specifies how virtual function tables, or vtables, are set up in memory to facilitate calling functions in a component, no matter who the vendor is. The vtables used in COM are hidden from the Visual Basic developer.

- A standard way of setting up interfaces. In Visual Basic, all public methods are organized into a default interface without any work on the developer's part. The developer also has the opportunity to create additional interfaces, if the application dictates their use.

- A base interface called IUnknown, which contains the QueryInterface, contains a method to query the interfaces of the COM component, as well as methods to add and subtract from a reference counter (AddRef and Release). As long as at least one component contains a reference to your COM component, it won't be deleted from memory. This is why you should always set your objects to nothing in Visual Basic — to ensure that memory is released back to the system.

- A system of uniquely identifying each component, which is called a *Globally Unique Identifier* (GUID). A GUID is a 128-bit integer value, calculated using the MAC address of the computer's network card, along with date and time, that is statistically guaranteed to be unique across all computers.

What is DCOM?

The next step in the history of COM is the Distributed Component Object Model (DCOM), which describes how COM is used across machine boundaries, or from server to server. To a certain extent, DCOM is a bit of a misnomer, because COM had certain distributed characteristics prior to DCOM's first release in late 1996. Much of the hoopla was designed to make it seem like Microsoft was releasing a new version of COM specifically designed for distributed environments such as LANs, WANs, and even the Internet.

Continued

The Component Object Model (COM) *(Continued)*

The main thing that DCOM added to COM was a configuration tool (`dcomcnfg.exe`) for setting up distributed COM applications.

DCOM was most easily deployed using Microsoft Transaction Server (MTS), which became a starting point for the transition to COM+.

What is COM+?

COM+, as originally described, sounded more like .NET than COM. In practice, however, it was largely a blending of COM with MTS and the Microsoft Message Queue (MSMQ). In order to distinguish COM+ from MTS, packages were renamed applications and the MMC (Microsoft Management Console) plug-in was renamed Component Services. This is a bit simplistic, because there were other improvements behind the scenes, but it is a great starting point.

Much of the plus in COM+ came from MTS and MSMQ, including

- ◆ Role-based security: In MTS, you have the ability to assign roles to different packages. Packages run under a specific domain account, and roles allow you to map other domain users and groups to these packages. The main advantage of COM+ over MTS is the capability to restrict roles down to the ability to restrict specific methods.

- ◆ Object pooling: MTS contains the ability to pool objects so new instances can be pulled from a pool rather than instantiated from the class definition every time. With pooling, your applications run faster. The pooling model in COM+ is an improvement over MTS pooling.

- ◆ Queued components: Taken from MSMQ, the queuing model in COM+ is declarative rather than programmatic. What this means to you is that you no longer have to program your queue, as you did with MSMQ, but can use Component Services to indicate that a component on a different computer should be queued. If the computer with your COM+ application detects that the other computer is up and running, it makes a call to components on that computer; otherwise, it queues any calls to that computer until it is running.

COM+ events, however, are unique. COM+ enables you to design events using a publisher/subscriber model. You create a class that acts as a publisher to send out an event to any number of subscribers. (You use events in COM, as well, but all events are very tightly coupled from one component to another, making it very difficult to create an event that is consumed by a variety of components.)

In the same vein, you have to deploy an assembly as one unit, whether it contains multiple PEs or just one. The assembly metadata must be deployed with the assembly for the process to work, whether it is compiled with the modules or placed in a separate file.

If this all sounds confusing, don't worry too much. The Visual Studio .NET IDE handles this for you. If you don't use the IDE, you'll still find a great majority, if not all, of your projects will compile to a single module, in a single PE, which is your assembly.

VERSION CONTROL

COM worked with the concept of binary compatibility, which was a contract that no interface would change after you deployed it. This concept led to what was more commonly known as DLL hell, where new versions of DLLs often broke applications. You were very restricted on what you could change due to COM's concept of binary compatibility. If you've worked with COM and never experienced DLL hell, you're one of the lucky few. .NET solves DLL hell in a couple ways.

First, you can deploy and redeploy nonshared assemblies on the same machine in multiple folders. You can compile a new version of your application and easily install it to another directory without fear of conflict. This concept of installing in multiple directories for different applications is similar to side-by-side components in COM+ but is so much easier, as you can simply copy the application to a new folder and run it. This topic, however, is out of the scope of version control in an assembly.

The second method of version control applies to shared assemblies. Stored in the metadata with an assembly is a certain amount of version information. If your application contains multiple assemblies that rely on a certain version of an assembly, you can deploy a newer version of the assembly without fear of the application no longer working, even if you change interfaces. When your .NET application is compiled (I use the term application, but please realize that this applies to assembly as well), the exact version of the assemblies it relies on to work is saved in the assembly metadata. When your application is run, it looks for that version, even if a new version has been deployed.

The entire process is configurable on many levels. To override this behavior, you, as a developer, can place a configuration file in the application directory, telling the application to use a different version of the assembly. The publisher of an assembly can also create a publisher configuration file that ships with the assembly. (This is very useful for shared assemblies that have been updated to run more efficiently.) Finally, an administrator can create a configuration for the machine that overrides all of this behavior.

I'd like to tell you that this was magic that happened automatically, but there's a bit more to this story. It is still relatively simple, but you have to follow a few rules. To simplify these rules, I assume that you are deploying assemblies in a single PE (the more common scenario). The rules still apply with multiple PE assemblies, but the explanation is far more complex.

The first step to versioning in .NET is to strongly name your assemblies. When you create an assembly, using the default .NET setup, it is weakly named. To both the developer and to the CLR, the assembly is seen as the name of the file. For example, you create `myDLL.dll`, which is seen as `myDLL.dll`. If you compile a new version, it is still `myDLL.dll`. If it is incompatible, your application breaks. To strongly name your assemblies, you must do the following:

◆ Create an encryption key pair. The .NET Framework ships with a strong name tool, called sn.exe. By typing **sn.exe /k** on the command line, you create a key file. This file should be used for all of the assemblies created in your organization. Copy the file created to the application source directory in Visual Basic .NET.

◆ Either create an assembly programmatically, using the `System.Reflection` namespace (the hard way), like this:

```
objAssemblyKeyFile.keyfile = "myKey.snk"
objAssemblyVersionAttribute.version = "1.0.2"
```

Or specify attributes for your assembly, like this:

```
<Assembly: AssemblyKeyFileAttribute("nameofKey.snk")>
<Assembly:AssemblyVersionAttribute("1.1.0.1")>
```

◆ Place the assembly in the Global Assembly Cache (GAC). There are two ways to accomplish this. The easiest is to drag and drop in Windows explorer. The GAC is located at *rootDrive/Windows Root/*Assemblies, where *rootDrive* is the drive with your Windows folder, and *Windows Root* is the name of your Windows folder (normally Windows or WINNT). When you drag and drop, the .NET Framework takes over and versions the DLL for you. The more difficult method is to use the command-line tool GACUtil.exe. You can find more information about GACUtil.exe in the .NET Framework help file under the .NET Framework Tools folder. The full path in the help file is .NET Framework SDK/Tools and Debugger/.NET Framework Tools. You can also consult the index for the term GACUtil.exe.

There are four pieces of information in every strongly named assembly. The name of the assembly, of course, is first, and it is followed by the key used to sign the assembly (which you create with sn.exe), the version number, and the culture. Culture is used by many to indicate the language of the assembly. For example, you may have two versions of the same assembly, one for Spanish applications and another for English. I normally do not have this type of granularity, but it is nice to know it is there.

SECURITY

An assembly forms a *security boundary* for deployment. In human terms, this concept means that you set permissions for an assembly. You can set additional security with security policies (declaratively) and in your code (imperatively). An assembly is also the unit that you sign by using a *key pair* to sign the assembly manifest. This process is simple in an assembly containing only one portable executable, as you simply sign the single file. If you work with an assembly that contains multiple modules, you sign the file that contains the assembly manifest.

THE REST OF THE STORY

Another caveat comes with assemblies. Each assembly can have only one entry point, known most often as Main( ). Understand that this is an oversimplification, because there are other possible entry points. Keeping this idea in mind, along with the other information in this section, I give you the following simple suggestions for assemblies:

- ◆ If you need more than one entry point, you need more than one assembly.

- ◆ If you need different security settings, you need to create a new assembly.

- ◆ If you need to reuse a type name, you need to create a new assembly.

- ◆ If you need to restrict scope – for example, to create methods that you don't expose to your current types in your assembly – you need to create a new assembly.

Assemblies make up an integral part of this book. As such, you see assemblies pop up from time to time throughout most of the chapters that follow.

Putting it all together

You compile the source code files that you use into portable executables, which logically equate to modules; you place these modules into assemblies, which you deploy on the server. A group of assemblies creates an application. Figure 1-6 shows the deployment model in .NET.

The circle labeled "IL and metadata" in Figure 1-6 is closely related to the module. The module is composed of IL and metadata. The PE, or DLL or EXE, is created after the IL and metadata go through the linker. The assembly is not directly represented in this figure because it deals with the compilation process, which is far less conceptual than the ideas I have discussed thus far. The important point here is that the raw source goes through many steps before being deployed.

What about namespaces?

While I have covered a lot about how .NET works, there's still one important topic to discuss: the concept of namespaces.

If you've worked with XML, you're probably familiar with the concept of a *namespace*. A *namespace* is a logical concept that you use to group classes into a cohesive logical unit. You use namespaces primarily to simplify programming and separate classes into workable units. Figure 1-7 contains a model of the System namespace. I use many of the namespaces shown in this figure throughout the book.

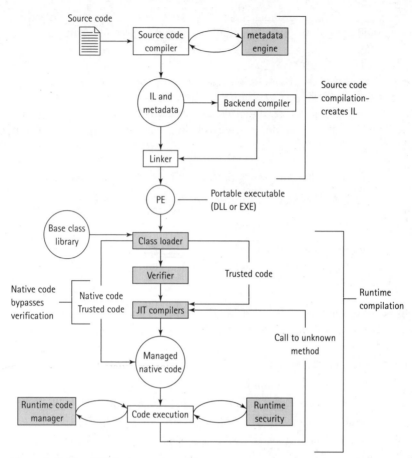

Figure 1-6: The .NET deployment model.

Namespaces simplify programming by allowing the developer to call methods in the namespace as if they were methods in your application. Rather than having to type System.Data.SQLClient.SQLAdapter (covered in Part III, "Working with Data — ADO.NET"), you can import the namespace System.Data.SQLClient and simply type SQLAdapter. This will make more sense when you get into some code in Chapter 2.

As you find out then, you can also alias namespaces to make code more maintainable and still retain the benefits of programming simplicity. Aliasing is the process of creating a typing shortcut for the namespace. For example, you can use SQLData as an alias for SQL.Data.SQLClient. Namespaces don't provide references for early binding, however, which may confuse many developers as they move to .NET. You still must add a reference to any namespaces that you import into your module. I cover the topic of imported namespaces and how you use them in Chapter 2.

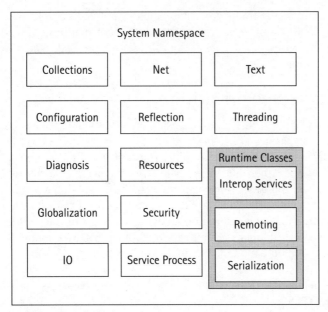

Figure 1-7: The System namespace.

As a namespace is a logical concept, no correlation exists between namespaces and source code files or assemblies. You can have multiple source code files or assemblies share a single namespace. By the same token, a single code module or assembly can contain multiple namespaces. If you develop in Visual Studio .NET, you will discover the most common method is a single namespace per assembly.

Common Functionality

The *Common Language Specification (CLS)* and the *Common Type System (CTS)* are the portions of the .NET Framework that enable language interoperability. Programmers often think of the CLS as a subset of the CTS, but this idea is a bit of a misnomer. Although the CLS does specify a subset of the types in the CTS, it also contains a set of usage conventions for these types.

Common Type System

The Common Type System (CTS) describes all the types that the Common Language Runtime (CLR) supports, how they interact with each other, and how you create them. This information is held in the manifest. As I discussed in the "Multiple Languages, One Bytecode" section earlier in this chapter, these types are reference types and value types. The CTS describes the rules that .NET language compilers must follow to interact with other .NET languages.

CTS establishes the portion of the framework that enables the integration of the various .NET languages. It also concerns type safety and helps manifest high-performance code execution. Think of the CTS as the rules set for the CLR, which I discuss in the following section.

Common Language Specification

The CLS is a subset of types that all .NET languages support. The challenge here is balancing the rich functionality necessary to make .NET easy to program while still maintaining a small enough set to remain manageable. The concern of the CLS isn't the internals of an assembly but rather the interoperability of managed code across assembly boundaries. As such, the CLS's only concern is with the public members of the types that the assembly contains. You can find a complete list of rules for the CLS in the .NET Framework SDK documentation under the topic Collected CLS Rules in the .NET Framework Developer's Specification. Table 1-1 shows some of the primitive types in the Common Language Specification.

TABLE 1-1 CLS PRIMITIVE TYPES

Type	Definition and size	Visual Basic 6 equivalent	Visual Basic .NET equivalent
System.Boolean	True or False (4 bytes)	Boolean	Boolean
System.Byte	1-byte unsigned integer	Byte	Byte
System.Char	2-byte unsigned integer representing a single Unicode character	—	Char
System.Int16	2-byte signed integer	Integer	Short
System.Int32	4-byte signed integer	Long	Integer
System.Int64	8-byte signed integer	—	Long
System.Single	4-byte floating point number	Single	Single
System.Double	8-byte floating point number	Double	Double
System.String	String of 0 or more characters or NULL	String	String
System.Object	The root of all classes in .NET	Object	Object

This is, by no means, an exhaustive list of all of the types you can access. I touch on the CLS primitive types a bit more in Chapter 2, because data types are important to building applications in Visual Basic .NET. If you're an old-time Visual Basic programmer, you probably just got a little shock over one of the changes from Visual Basic to Visual Basic .NET: the Integer to a Short and a Long to an Integer.

Before moving on, a brief explanation of signed and unsigned is in order. Signed types are those types that can contain negative and positive values, while unsigned types are those that contain only positive numbers. Integers are signed in Visual Basic .NET, while other types represented as integers, such as bytes and char, are not.

The .NET base classes

The .NET *base classes* contain most of the functionality of the .NET Framework. In the "What about namespaces?" section earlier in this chapter, I showed you an outline of the System namespace. In the last section, I showed you some of the primitive types that the System namespace contains. In the following section, I cover the System namespace in a bit more depth.

THE SYSTEM NAMESPACE

If you take a look at the .NET Framework SDK Reference (the help file that ships with the framework and Visual Studio .NET), you notice that almost all the namespaces that it covers start with *System*. In fact, the only other top-level namespace that it mentions is Microsoft. I discuss the Microsoft.VisualBasic namespace in Chapter 2, where I demonstrate how to create a command-line executable. There are also Microsoft.ComServices and Microsoft.Win32 namespaces. Everything else deals with the *System* namespace and the other namespaces that begin with *System*. These are the namespaces I cover in this section.

The rest of this section may look a little like a textbook, but it gives you a starting point toward understand the many namespaces that the .NET Framework contains.

SYSTEM   The *System Namespace* contains the base types that all other classes use, including those of the classes that you build. In addition to the types that I mention under the CLS, System is also responsible for handling exceptions as well as the base classes for enumerators, arrays, attributes, and versioning.

SYSTEM.CONFIGURATION   *System.Configuration* contains the classes that you use to aid the configuration of your application. I discuss the configuration of applications in ASP.NET in Chapter 12. In most of your work in ASP.NET, you'll use the web.config file, because the settings are contained in XML and more easily maintained. If you want to programmatically configure your application, you'll use the System.Configuration namespace objects.

SYSTEM.DATA   The *System.Data namespace* contains the classes that you use to interact with data. I cover these namespaces in great depth in Part III of this book. One thing to notice with System.Data is that SQL Server now offers its own set of classes, which you can use to get greater performance out of applications that use SQL Server. You still have the option of using a more generic OLEDB provider (in the System.Data.OLEDB namespace). The main advantage to using the OLEDB provider is the ability to quickly change databases without changing namespaces. This advantage is a small one, because it's almost as easy to switch to the SQLClient namespace.

SYSTEM.DIAGNOSTICS   You use the *System.Diagnostics* namespace to help debug and profile your applications. Although not many articles about .NET mention this namespace as of this writing, the capability to determine how your application is doing is very powerful and a much-needed improvement over what COM offers. I discuss System.Diagnostics a bit more as I cover tracing in Chapter 3. (Tracing, for those who have not yet touched .NET, is the CLR feature which tracks execution of code and outputs it for you to diagnose what is going on.)

In addition to tracing, the System.Diagnostics namespace also provides classes that allow you to debug your own applications, as well as interact with system processes, event logs, and performance counters.

SYSTEM.DRAWING   The *System.Drawing namespace* and its child namespaces (namely System.Drawing.Design, System.Drawing.Drawing2D, System.Drawing. Imaging, System.Drawing.Printing and System.Drawing.Text) deal with the user interface in particular WinForms. Because this book is about WebForms and Web services, I don't cover System.Drawing or any of its child namespaces in any detail.

SYSTEM.NET   *System.Net* deals with networking protocols, including Internet protocols. The System.Net namespace contains classes to handle cookies, IP addresses, and Web requests and responses.

SYSTEM.SECURITY   The *System.Security* namespace contains classes that deal with security policy, permissions, and encryption. I cover security in more detail in Chapter 13.

SYSTEM.WEB   Much of this book deals with the *System.Web* namespace and its children. In Chapter 3, you get your first real taste of the classes that this namespace contains, but the real meat of System.Web follows you throughout Part II of this book and in each of the sample applications in Part V.

The System.Web namespace contains all of the classes used in client/server applications that use HTTP (HyperText Transfer Protocol) as their protocol. This namespace has child namespaces for different types of Web controls, as well as security, session state, and Web services.

SYSTEM.WINDOWS.FORMS   I discuss Windows Forms briefly in both Chapters 4 and 7, but Windows Forms are more a concept of desktop applications. Because this book primarily concerns network-enabled applications, the discussion on Windows Forms is a brief one and primarily used to compare the similarities of creating desktop and Web applications.

SYSTEM.XML   XML is a very important part of .NET. Although I cover XML, including the System.XML namespace, in great detail in Part IV, you find that XML pops up occasionally in Part III as I discuss ADO.NET. XML is the underlying structure for all data in .NET, and you also use it to serialize objects. Serialization is the process of taking an object and representing it as text. XML is perfect for this, because it can contain nodes for each property and method.

EVERYTHING DERIVES FROM SYSTEM.OBJECT

In .NET everything is an object. System.Object (the core object in the System namespace), therefore, is the superclass for all classes in .NET. Although you're unlikely to explicitly show the derivation, unless you use aliases, you still need to know that every class and module that you build maintains its roots in System.Object. My assumption is that you have a fairly good idea of what a class is, having built your own classes in Visual Basic, I focus on the common elements of the Object class here, and I cover methods, properties, and events in Chapter 2.

The concept of a *constructor* may seem a little alien to you, mostly because you do not have to work with constructors in Visual Basic 6. Constructors enable you to, for lack of better words, construct an instance of a class. They are methods that are called when an object is created from a class. If you do not explicitly create a constructor, a default constructor is created for you.

As .NET is fully object-oriented, you can even create multiple constructors for a single class and use different types of arguments to determine which constructor gets fired as you create the object. For example, you may have a class that has constructors for both an ID, as an Integer, and a friendly name, as a String. When you create an instance of this class, you simply include the Integer or String and the CLR determines which constructor to use.

If you've never programmed in a language such as C++ or Java, you may not even realize that constructors exist, as Visual Basic doesn't use constructors in the true meaning of the word. To put the concept of a constructor in perspective, in Visual Basic 6, you can initialize certain values in an object by using the initialize event in class modules or, perhaps, the form-load event, but you can't pass variables into these events as you create your objects. In Visual Basic .NET, Sub New(), the Visual Basic .NET constructor, which can take arguments, extends this model. This feature, constructors, is really cool. I cover constructors in more depth in Chapter 2 as I discuss classes.

You can use a few methods in System.Object in your objects that make programming a bit easier: Equals, Finalize, GetHashCode, GetType, MemberwiseClone, and ToString. Of these methods, Equals, GetType and ToString are the most useful.

One Bytecode, Multiple Platforms

One of the benefits of .NET, is the capability to run your applications on multiple platforms. At present, you have only a Common Language Runtime (CLR) for the Windows platform. Now that Ximian is creating a CLR (called Mono) for Linux, and

Corel is developing a version for BSD, the CLR on Linux, UNIX, and Macintosh is just a matter of time.

The Common Language Runtime (CLR)

Before moving deeper into the CLR, let me take a moment to compare .NET to Java. Although much of the formatting is the same between Java and the .NET languages, especially when using C# where the syntax is very close, the differences are rather startling underneath the hood. In Java, you find the concept of a Virtual Machine (VM). Because of its safety regulations, firing off multiple applications in Java generally results in multiple instances of the VM. In .NET, however, the CLR serves as a complete virtual environment, and firing off multiple applications still results in only one CLR. This factor alone may help .NET win the performance battle. Since having multiple processes in one environment increases the likelihood of hung processes, the CLR is designed to release and renew after so many processes or so much time. This gives the best balance of safety and performance.

To understand the CLR a bit better, take a look at Figure 1-8. Although a bit technical, it provides a good starting point for discussing the CLR.

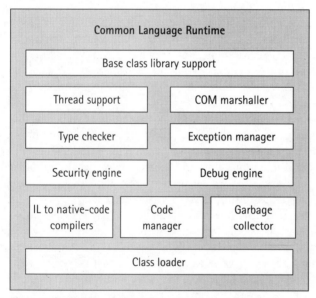

Figure 1-8: The Common Language Runtime architecture.

The source code compiler compiles your source code into IL and metadata with some help from the metadata engine. Metadata and IL are then linked together and compiled into an IL portable executable by the linker. At this point in time, it's basically an IL assembly. As an application runs, the verifier verifies the IL in the PE, the JIT compiler compiles it into native code, and the code execution module executes it; the CLR manages the object until the garbage collector collects it. The garbage collector is the piece of the CLR that manages the code by cleaning up objects that are no longer used.

The functionality of the CLR breaks down into various sections, as shown in Figure 1-9, which provides a simple analysis of the CLR. As you can see, the CLR is responsible for the functionality attributed to the Common Type System (CTS). In addition, the CLR contains all functionality relating to object lifetime management, type checking, security, exceptions and debugging, and profiling.

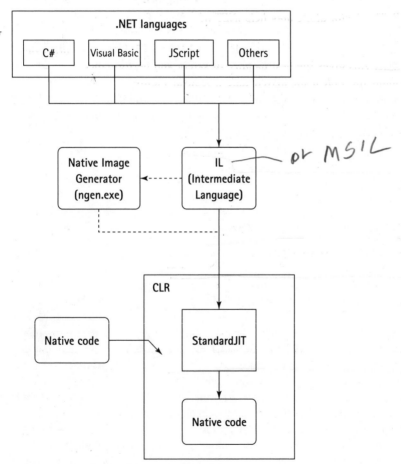

Figure 1-9: The core functionality of the CLR.

A NEW WAY TO CODE

From base classes to user applications, the CLR manages all code in .NET. This setup provides a lot of benefits for the .NET developer but also causes you to change the way that you code. The following list provides details of coding changes you need to note.

Handwritten margin notes: "Free memory", "Loss shift don't write free memory code"

◆ **Managed code:** You need worry no longer about destroying objects in your code because the CLR manages the entire lifetime of the objects under its control. The garbage collector portion of the CLR is also responsible for cleaning up any objects that the CLR no longer references. The consequence, however, is that that developer no longer controls when objects are cleaned up, which requires some changes for developers who normally clean up code in the terminate event.

Handwritten margin note: "Loss shift is not controlling security yourself ?"

◆ **Centralized security:** Creating secure applications without using huge amounts of code is now easier. You can check up the stack to ensure that users don't circumvent authentication. In addition, the CLR contains mechanisms to ensure that an administrator can exclude code from unknown development sources from running on the platform, which saves you time in programming security into your .NET applications but may also require a shift in your programming paradigm.

◆ **Common exception handling:** Programmers feel the benefit of this feature most deeply in environments that use multiple programming languages. In Visual Basic .NET, for example, the exception classes give you a lot more flexibility in handling errors than just running after error numbers, as is the case in other languages. You must, however, change your thinking to take full advantage of .NET exceptions. I cover the exception classes a bit more thoroughly in Chapter 2, in the section discussing overriding. I am not specifically dealing with Structured Error Handling (or the `Try ... Catch ... Finally` block).

Handwritten margin note: "Gain shift debug easier"

◆ **Centralizing debugging and profiling:** Thanks to this feature, you no longer need to switch debuggers every time that you switch languages – a great improvement for anyone who's ever debugged Visual Basic COM components by stepping through Active Server Page (ASP) code.

One thing that you want to notice as you examine the CLR is that most of the functionality built into the CLR and the .NET Framework is functionality that you formerly needed to code into each and every class that you built. In much the same way as COM and COM+ simplified programmers' lives by reducing the amount of code exposed to the Visual Basic developer, the CLR reduces the amount of code that all developers need to write. For Visual Basic developers, however, the pond just got bigger, because the entire functionality of the Windows API is exposed when using Visual Basic .NET, without complex coding. I cover coding in Visual Basic .NET in more detail in Chapter 2.

THE CLR VERSUS COM

Time now for a little history lesson. In the old days, before COM and certainly long before .NET, you built most applications as small, isolated pieces of code. To get your applications to communicate with each other was about as much fun as a trip to the dentist. Figure 1-10 illustrates the concept of such monolithic applications.

Notice the types shown inside of their individual applications. The types in the two illustrated applications could be identical, and a lot of code would be repeated from application to application.

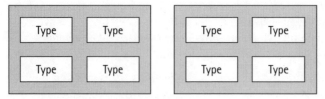

Figure 1–10: Early monolithic applications.

Microsoft created COM to help facilitate componentized software, and it proved very effective. Through a common set of interfaces, components could communicate with each other, and as a result, Microsoft finally implemented the concept of n-Tier development for developers. In Figure 1-11, I show the concept of COM and communication between COM objects.

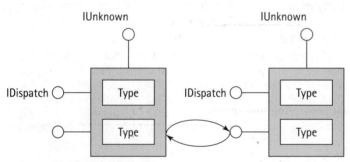

Figure 1–11: COM Applications.

COM was a strong technology, as it put forth a common set of rules for component development. It was, however, a bit more difficult to program, especially for C++ developers, who had to code each of the interfaces. If you have never touched C++, you have been shielded from this extra coding because Visual Basic set up the interfaces for you. One glaring feature missing from COM was the management of objects.

With IIS 4.0, on the NT platform, management of objects was added with Microsoft Transaction Server (MTS). This feature was added primarily for Web applications, but it was made available when MTS and COM were married finally in COM+ under Windows 2000.

As good as COM+ was, a few problems still needed tackling. Foremost was the fact that COM+ still required a lot of plumbing to make objects communicate. Additionally, COM compliance didn't necessarily mean that the COM objects you created in different languages could easily communicate. This communication problem is exactly what .NET is designed to solve. Figure 1-12 shows how objects run in .NET from a high level.

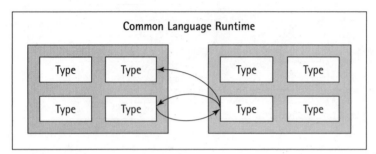

Figure 1-12: Objects running in .NET.

Pulling all the plumbing in .NET into the CLR removes the complexity of communication from the developer. It also facilitates cross-language type compatibility and puts Visual Basic .NET on a near-level playing field with .NET languages such as C#. When you compile a Visual Basic .NET project and a C# project that perform the same functionality, you end up with nearly identical Intermediate Languages (ILs).

Intermediate Language

Code from all .NET languages compile down to *Intermediate Language,* also known as *MSIL* or *IL.* IL is the simple bytecode that the CLR later compiles to native code for your platform through *Just-In-Time (JIT)* compilation. The term *just-in-time* indicates that the native compilation does not happen until the CLR reaches the first method call for the object. There are exceptions to this, for optimization. Just understand that the IL is not compiled in most instances until the object is used. The process that the CLR uses to compile from source code to IL to native code is shown in Figure 1-13.

The typical path for code is from your source files to IL, and then to the JIT compiler, which compiles it to native code.

The important point to understand is IL is compiled into native code when used. This is the reason the native code compilers are called JIT compilers (or Jitters), because the code is compiled when it is needed and not before.

Because IL is bytecode, breaking it down to see its signature is fairly easy. Although I cover this Hello World program in much more detail as the chapter progresses, a small snippet of code is useful at this juncture. Listing 1-1 is a simple Hello World command-line program in Visual Basic .NET.

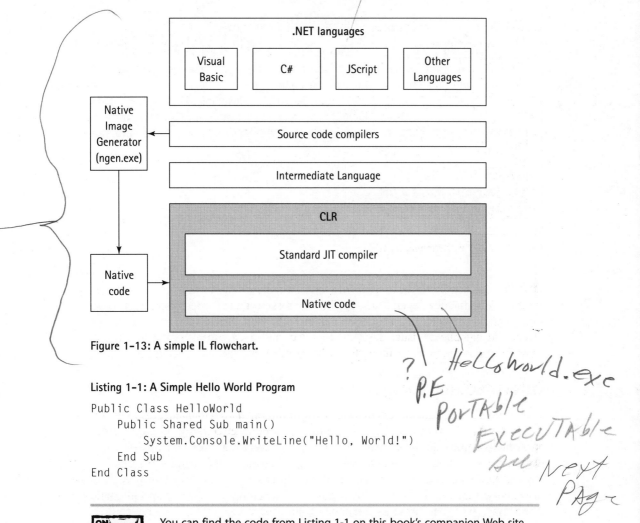

Figure 1-13: A simple IL flowchart.

Listing 1-1: A Simple Hello World Program

```
Public Class HelloWorld
    Public Shared Sub main()
        System.Console.WriteLine("Hello, World!")
    End Sub
End Class
```

You can find the code from Listing 1-1 on this book's companion Web site (www.wiley.com/extras) under Ch01SDK.zip (SDK version) or Ch01VS.zip. When you unzip the file, look for the HelloWorldSimple folder.

If you download the Visual Studio .NET file from this book's companion Web site, you'll notice that the code uses a Module. This is largely for simplicity, because the Visual Studio .NET IDE wants Visual Basic .NET Console applications to contain a Module. This also makes the IL look a bit different than it does in Figure 1-14.

Using the command-line compiler, I compiled this code into a Portable Executable (PE) that I call HelloWorld.exe. You can do the same by running the batch file, `HelloWorldSimple.bat`. Rather than focus on the actual code right now, however, I want to detail a bit about the MSIL for this application. (I promise to give you a full explanation of this code in Chapter 2.)

The .NET Framework ships with a tool known as ildasm.exe. Unlike most of the .NET Framework tools, this tool includes a graphical user interface (GUI). Figure 1-14 shows a screen of the IL disassembler breaking down the simple Hello World program that you'll put together in Chapter 2.

Figure 1-14: The .NET Framework's ildasm.exe tool takes apart the Hello World program.

To disassemble the code, you choose File → Dump from the menu (or press the Ctrl + D key combination). This action opens a dump screen similar to the one shown in Figure 1-15. In this example, I use all the features of the output to show my IL.

The important part of the dump is shown in Listing 1-2. It's a small portion of the actual IL contained in the metadata in the assembly manifest and type metadata. The portion shown represents the class.

Listing 1-2: HelloWorld Class in Intermediate Language

```
// =============== CLASS MEMBERS DECLARATION ===================
//   note that class flags, 'extends' and 'implements' clauses
//          are provided here for information only

.class /*02000002*/ public auto ansi HelloWorld
       extends [mscorlib/* 23000001 */]System.Object/* 01000001 */
{
```

```
.method /*06000001*/ public specialname rtspecialname
        instance void .ctor() cil managed
// SIG: 20 00 01
{
  // Method begins at RVA 0x2050
  // Code size       7 (0x7)
  .maxstack 8
  IL_0000: /* 02  |                      */ ldarg.0
  IL_0001: /* 28  | (0A)000001    */ call       instance void [mscorlib/* ↵
23000001 */]System.Object/* 01000001 */::.ctor() /* 0A000001 */
  IL_0006: /* 2A  |                      */ ret
} // end of method HelloWorld::.ctor


.method /*06000002*/ public static void
        main() cil managed
// SIG: 00 00 01
{
  .entrypoint
  .custom /*0C000001:0A000003*/ instance void [mscorlib/* 23000001 ↵
*/]System.STAThreadAttribute/* 01000003 */::.ctor() /* 0A000003 */ = ( 01 00 00 ↵
00 )
  // Method begins at RVA 0x2058
  // Code size       11 (0xb)
  .maxstack 8
  IL_0000: /* 72  | (70)000001       */ ldstr      "Hello, World!" /* ↵
70000001 */
  IL_0005: /* 28  | (0A)000002       */ call       void [mscorlib/* 23000001 ↵
*/]System.Console/* 01000002 */::WriteLine(string) /* 0A000002 */
  IL_000a: /* 2A  |                      */ ret
} // end of method HelloWorld::main

} // end of class HelloWorld
```

One thing that may seem a bit startling to you is the fact that you can see pretty much the entire implementation of your types, including the types methods, properties, and external dependencies. One of the reasons why compilation to native code is so appealing is that it hides the capability to see this much information about your code.

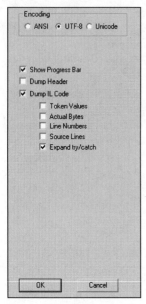

Figure 1–15: Dump output options for ildasm.exe.

This leads to a question about .NET. Will you ever be able to compile to native code and completely hide the metadata? The answer is no. Many of the features of the CLR, including the garbage collector, rely on the metadata to work properly.

TIP Since the release of .NET, a few third-party vendors have released obfuscators. While there is no 100% surefire method to protect your code from a clever code poker, an obfuscator hides your naming scheme from the curious by creating senseless variable names. If you want to protect your applications from decompiling, it's worthwhile investigating one of these obfuscators.

Other features of the CLR

Before wrapping up this chapter, I want take a few moments to cover the rest of the CLR. You may realize by this point that the CLR is the central nervous system for the .NET Framework. Every piece of code that runs on the .NET Platform runs under the CLR — period. The CLR even manages the code that you mark as unsafe in C#.

GARBAGE COLLECTION

Garbage collection is the process by which the CLR takes unreferenced reference types off the heap. The CLR runs the garbage collector at certain intervals or whenever it's running out of memory. The signal that an object is safe to remove is the fact that its last reference is gone. If the garbage collector finds an object that no longer has a reference, it calls the object's finalize method and destroys the object, removing it from the memory heap. As the garbage collector gets rid of all unreferenced objects, it ideally eliminates memory leaks and problems with circular references that come from certain types of recursion.

If you come from a Visual Basic background, you may be inclined to put some clean-up code in the finalize method and thus enable the garbage collector to clean up after your objects. You don't want to do this, however, because you don't know when the program actually calls the finalize method. The finalize method also adds time to the garbage collector's deallocation. I cover a creative way to use finalize in the override section of Chapter 2.

COM INTEROPERABILITY

When you began reading this chapter, you may have thought that COM was dead. After all, this stuff I'm discussing isn't compatible with COM. Although this fact is true, Microsoft realizes the problems involved in making .NET completely incompatible with COM. Microsoft has included some tools to interoperate with older COM applications, which enables you to capitalize on COM investments you have made in your company.

You have three command-line utilities for working with COM. The first is the *Type Library Importer* (tlbimp.exe), which enables you to create .NET metadata from a COM type library. The second is the *Type Library Exporter* (tlbexp.exe), which enables you to create a COM Type Library from .NET metadata. The third is the *ActiveX Control Importer* (aximp.exe), which enables you to import ActiveX Controls to use as Windows Forms controls.

You do face at least one caveat in the use of .NET with COM (and vice versa). Marshaling objects from one paradigm to another incurs a performance penalty. If you can simply build a new version of the application from scratch, you get tremendous performance benefits from a native .NET solution, as opposed to interoperating with legacy COM components.

Finding Information in the Framework SDK

One of the best sources of information about .NET is the various files that are released with the .NET Framework Software Development Kit (SDK), which you can download for free from Microsoft. In the following subsections I describe the resources shipped with the SDK that you can use to learn .NET.

Documents

In the directory where you install the .NET Framework (which is, by default, C:\Program Files\Microsoft Visual Studio .NET\Microsoft.NET), you find a variety of documents. The raw files for the SDK Framework Help files are in the Docs directory under FrameworkSDK (by default, C:\Program Files\Microsoft Visual Studio .NET\.FrameworkSDK\Docs); I detail these files in the following section. And, in the Tool Developers Guide docs directory (by default, C:\Program Files\Microsoft Visual Studio .NET\.FrameworkSDK\Tool Developers Guide\docs) you will find a few more low-level documents; you probably won't find these documents very interesting to begin with, but feel free to look around.

One of the more interesting documents is the Change document. While this is largely academic, if you have not played with any of the betas, it can be a real lifesaver.

The .NET Framework SDK documentation Help file

A variety of Help files ship with the .NET Framework. You access these files through the Start menu by choosing Start → Microsoft .NET Framework SDK, which loads the Help files into an MSDN-like interface. In the SDK Help files are explanations of the sample applications; an introduction to the framework, including the inner workings of the CLR; and a good reference of the .NET Framework classes.

Unlike previous versions of Microsoft development tools, which often had technical definitions and little more, the .NET documentation contains snippets of code for nearly every method, property, and event. This makes the documentation much easier to use as a learning tool.

Samples

TRY

A number of samples are included with the .NET SDK. To get to the start page for these samples, go to Start → Microsoft .NET Framework SDK and choose Samples and Quick Start Tutorials. Before you can use the samples, you have to install them. This is fairly simple to do from the HTML page that starts when you select this item. The quick-start tutorials, which comprise a large portion of the samples, can be found online at www.gotdotnet.com/quickstart.

Other sources

Microsoft offers a variety of information about the .NET Framework. Each contains some information that's useful as you develop .NET applications. Check out the following Web sites:

- ◆ http://msdn.microsoft.com/net: This URL takes you to the MSDN .NET Site.

- ◆ www.gotdotnet.com: Microsoft's site for the .NET Framework resides at this address. Click Community for links to a variety of .NET sites. This site also boasts a Visual Basic .NET section that's worthy of a look.

5/20

◆ www.asp.net: Microsoft's ASP.NET site resides at this address.

There some good links to other sites on the Internet from each of these sites. Following are a few more sites:

◆ www.asptoday.com: Wrox's premier ASP site features occasional articles on ASP.NET. Although this is now a pay site, I still recommend it because it has daily articles written by some of the leading experts in Enterprise development. Wrox has also launched www.csharptoday.com, a site for those who want to develop in C#.

◆ www.devx.com/dotnet: This site is run by Fawcette Technical Publications, the people who produce Visual Studio Magazine. Check out the .NET resources on this site for a variety of links to other .NET-related sites. The site has gotten a bit stale during the last few months, so many of the links are a bit older.

◆ www.aspfriends.com: While I am not a big fan of lists, this site, run by Charles Carroll, has some extremely focused lists in both ASP.NET and traditional ASP. You can view the lists through any news reader, but you have to join to post.

◆ www.dotnetbooks.com: Manohar Kamath, an ASP Microsoft Valuable Professional (MVP), has created this site to review the various .NET books.

Summary

I covered a lot of ground in this chapter. (Although the .NET Framework covers a lot more information, those topics are the subject of another book.) The chapter started with a quick look into the parts of the .NET Framework and how the layers stack up into three primary sections: the Common Language Runtime (CLR), the base class library and classes that derive from it, and the Common Language Specification (CLS) and the .NET Languages.

I showed you types in .NET and explained the differences between reference types (classes and interfaces) and value types (structures and enumerators). I then took you through the .NET paradigm for building applications out of these types and gave you a brief look at some of the .NET base classes.

The last section of this chapter dealt with the Common Language Runtime, just-in-time compilation, and the Microsoft Intermediate Language. I also provided a short look at some places to find additional information on the .NET Framework.

Chapter 2

Visual Basic .NET

IN THIS CHAPTER

- ◆ Examine reference and value types in Visual Basic .NET
- ◆ Work with classes in Visual Basic .NET
- ◆ Use object-oriented programming in Visual Basic .NET
- ◆ Set scope of routines and variables
- ◆ Learn new features of Visual Basic .NET

IF PROGRAMMING VISUAL BASIC .NET interests you, you may see Chapter 1 as a waste of time, because you can program in Visual Basic 6 without digging deep into the Windows API. This isn't the case with .NET. You either use the .NET Framework base classes in your Visual Basic .NET applications, or you must write a lot of code that repeats the functionality of the framework objects (the base class library).

From this point on, this book becomes a code-intensive experience. I'm assuming that you have some basic Visual Basic and/or ASP skills. Don't worry if you don't, however, because I believe that I include enough new material so that even a beginner can catch onto most of it. Many of the code listings in this chapter take some shortcuts in order to teach a particular concept, meaning that I do not always follow the best practices if they would cloud the concept I am trying to teach. As such, some of the examples may seem a bit disjointed. I advise you to take a look at the code and make sure that you understand the concepts being taught before moving on.

Everything Is an Object

As I mention in Chapter 1, everything in .NET is an *object*. Every language in .NET derives from the base classes, and Visual Basic .NET is no exception. For Visual Basic programmers, working with objects means saying goodbye to variants; if you code ASP instead, it means that everything has a type, but that type ultimately derives from System.Object, the base class for all .NET objects.

If you read Chapter 1, you know how to build a simple object in Visual Basic .NET. Listing 2-1 repeats the code in Chapter 1's Listing 1-1, which shows a simple HelloWorld object in Visual Basic .NET. If you are going to download the code, the code in Listing 2-1 is the SDK version.

Listing 2-1: A Simple Hello World Program

```
Public Class HelloWorld
    Public Shared Sub Main()
        System.Console.WriteLine("Hello, World!")
    End Sub
End Class
```

You can find the code from Listing 2-1 under `Ch02SDK.zip` (SDK version) or `Ch02VS.zip` (Visual Studio .NET version) on this book's companion Web site (`www.wiley.com/extras`). When you unzip the file, look for the HelloWorldSimple folder.

The class (`HelloWorld`) in this program is a reference type, so it sits on the memory heap with a pointer on the stack. The main thing to remember at this time is that the heap is the general section of memory shared by all programs, while the stack is a portion of memory set aside for a particular program (or set of programs).

Chapter 1 contains more information on the inner workings of the .NET Framework, including how memory in .NET maps to different types.

Notice a few things in this code. First, the coding of the class looks a bit more like a function (`Public Class HelloWorld`) than a class file in Visual Basic 6. Second, the only routine in the entire class is a shared routine called `Sub Main()`. This routine is the entry point into the application. While Visual Basic 6 allowed `Sub Main()` as an entry point for an application, it is *required* in Visual Basic .NET console applications; every console application you create must have a `Sub Main()`. Third, why are there so many dots in the line that writes "Hello, World!"?

Before I move a bit deeper into the subject of objects in Visual Basic .NET, helping you become more comfortable using the compiler from the command line is probably a good idea. Behind the scenes, the same compiler is used in each case, command line and Visual Studio .NET. With Visual Studio .NET, however, you will not set the options directly in most instances. If you are not interested in learning the command-line options, you can use the code that you find in the Visual Studio zip file for this chapter. I, however, believe that it is useful to learn how to use the compiler from the command line as you will better understand what is going on under the hood in Visual Studio .NET.

To compile the code in the preceding example, either type this code in an ASCII editor (Notepad does just fine) or download the zip file from the companion Web site. In the zip file I use a folder with the name Projects that contains subfolders for the various examples. After you copy the code to your hard drive, open a command prompt (the MS-DOS prompt in NT 4, Windows 9*x* or ME) and type **vbc**. The easiest way to do this in Windows 2000 and XP is to follow these steps:

1. Click on Start → Run, or (Windows Key) + R, then type **cmd** and click OK. (As an alternative, you can use Start → All Programs → Accessories → Command Prompt for XP or Start → Program Files → Accessories → Command Prompt for Windows 2000.)

   With NT and Windows 95/98/ME, use Start → Program Files → MS-DOS Prompt.

2. Type **vbc** or **vbc /?** and press the Enter key.

When you run the vbc command, you will see a screen much like the one shown in Figure 2-1, which displays the options in the Visual Basic .NET compiler.

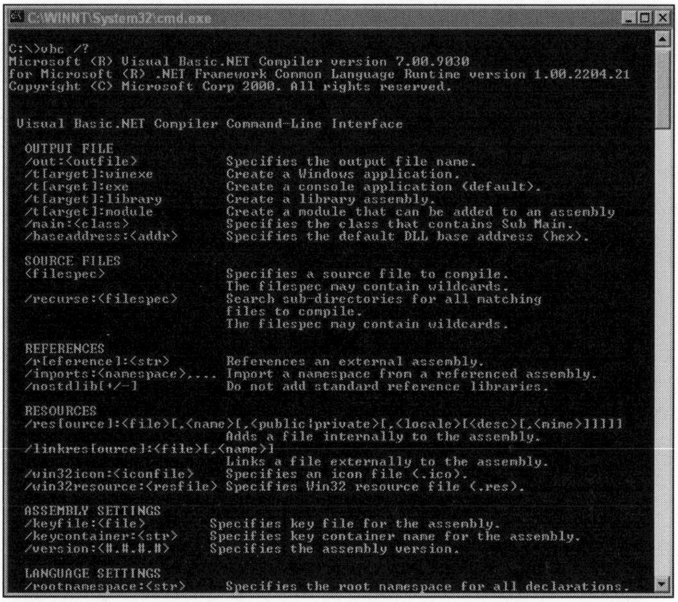

Figure 2-1: The Visual Basic .NET command–line compiler options.

To compile this code, you need to type only **vbc helloWorldSimple.vb.** To be a bit more explicit, however, you want to type the code as follows:

```
vbc /out:helloWorldSimple /t:exe /r:System.dll helloWorldSimple.vb
```

In the most recent builds of Visual Studio .NET and the .NET Framework, the install did not create a path to the .NET compilers. This leads you to a couple of choices:

◆ Add the path to the compilers to your application path. Since the version number changes with each build, this path statement may change. If this statement fails, open Windows Explorer and check the version number. I add the following line to each of the batch files; you can add it to the command line prior to running your compile statement.

```
Path c:\WINNT\Microsoft.NET\Framework\v1.0.3328;%PATH%
```

NOTE: The path will change slightly with different releases because the last directory in the path (v1.0.332) is the framework version number.

◆ Copy the file vbc.exe to your application directory. This is a bit of overkill, but it does make things simple.

I have set up batch files that will add the path to the compilers to your application path. As with the previous statement about adding the path, you may need to alter the numbers. If you are working with an older version of the SDK, you will have to do the same. The name of the file is addPath.bat. The batch file only needs to be run once per Windows session.

The following list describes the various parts of the vbc options that I present in this section (and you can expect to see a few more as we get deeper into Visual Basic .NET):

◆ /out:HelloWorld.exe: This compiler option enables you to choose the name of your output file. In a simple class, a *console app*, which takes on the name of the file, is the default. This option enables you to select a different name for your application than the source code file's name.

◆ /t:exe: This compiler option tells the compiler to create a console EXE file. If you change this option to /t:library, you create a DLL instead. If you change it to /t:winexe, it becomes a Windows executable. A class this simple runs, but it produces absolutely nothing useful. Finally, you can use /t:module, which creates a module that can be added to an assembly. It is unlikely you will use this option often; in fact, you cannot compile a module from Visual Studio .NET, but only from the command line.

◆ hellovb.vb: This compiler option identifies the source file you're compiling.

◆ /r:System.dll: This compiler option tells the compiler to include the file named as a reference in the assembly you are compiling. This example is a reference to the System type library. This particular call is unnecessary, because all .NET objects must reference this library, so the CLR takes care of this one for you. You will discover, however, that you must reference other libraries prior to using them. Importing a namespace (which I cover in the "Using Imports" section later in this chapter) isn't enough.

To run the Hello World file, open a command prompt, navigate to the proper directory, and run the executable.

If you choose to double-click the file `HelloWorld.exe`, it will also run, but it's unlikely that you'll see the "Hello, World!" output because there is no statement to pause the output long enough for it to be viewed. The easiest way to pause is to add a `Read()`, which causes the program to stop execution while it awaits input from you, the user. The line to add, beneath the `WriteLine()` is

```
System.Console.Read()
```

Reference types in Visual Basic .NET

To learn about reference types, you need to examine a more complex project. The code example in Listing 2-2 contains both a class and a module and is more akin to good object-oriented programming techniques. Because this code is illustrative in nature, much of it is unnecessary from a real-world standpoint. I add comments to make this example more readable.

Listing 2-2: A More Complex "Hello, World!" Application

```
'* Alias each Namespace
Imports msvb = Microsoft.VisualBasic
Imports SysCon = System.Console

Module Module1

    '* Entry point for the application
    Public Sub Main()
        '* Set up a string to hold our message
        Dim strMessage As String

        '* Pull from Command Line
        strMessage = msvb.Command()

        '* Make sure there is a message to print
        If strMessage = "" Then
            strMessage = "Hello, World!"
        End If

        '* Construct object from HelloWorldClass with constructor
        Dim objHelloWorld As New HelloWorldClass(strMessage)

        '* Print out the message from a method
        SysCon.WriteLine(objHelloWorld.GetMessage())

        '* Set the message with a property
```

Continued

Listing 2-2 *(Continued)*

```
        objHelloWorld.HelloMessage = "Hello World from Property!"

        '* Print out message from property
        SysCon.WriteLine(objHelloWorld.HelloMessage)

        '* Set from WriteOnly
        objHelloWorld.HelloMessage2b = "Hello World from WriteOnly!"

        '* Adding a parameter to a property - not a good idea
        SysCon.WriteLine(objHelloWorld.HelloMessage2a _
                        ("added ReadOnly!"))

        SysCon.Read()      End Sub

End Module

Public Class HelloWorldClass
    Inherits System.Object '* Line optional, but recommended

    '* Private - class level scope
    '* NOTE: I would normally have this as m_strMessage
    '*       this code is left this way to show the Me Keyword
    '*       in the New() subroutine.
    Private strMessage As System.String

    '* constructor for HelloWorld
    Public Sub New(ByVal strMessage As String)
        '* Set the message up
        Me.strMessage = strMessage
    End Sub

    '* Method to return the string
    Public Function GetMessage() As String
        '* Use return keyword
        Return strMessage
    End Function

    '* Public Property with Get and Set
    Public Property HelloMessage() As String
        Get
            Return strMessage
        End Get
        Set
            strMessage = Value
```

```
        End Set
    End Property


    '* Read Only Property - bad practice to set up two
    '* It is generally bad form to set up two properties where
    '* one would suffice.
    Public ReadOnly Property HelloMessage2a(ByVal _
anotherValue As String) As String
        Get
            HelloMessage2a = strMessage
        End Get
    End Property


    '* Write Only Property - see comment for read only property
    Friend WriteOnly Property HelloMessage2b() As String
        Set
            strMessage = Value
        End Set
    End Property

End Class
```

You can find the code from Listing 2-2 under `ChO2SDK.zip` (SDK version) or `ChO2VS.zip` (Visual Studio .NET version) on the companion Web site (www.wiley.com/extras). When you unzip the file, look for the HelloWorldComplex folder.

The entry point of this application is `Sub Main()`, which should be familiar to Visual Basic 6 developers, because Visual Basic 6 enables you to use `Sub Main()` as an entry point. In general, I recommend including both a `Sub Main()`, which is your entry point, and a `Sub New()`, which is a *constructor* (which I cover in the section "Working with Classes," later in this chapter), whenever you create a new command-line application.

Notice the use of the `Return` keyword in each `Property`. Although you can still set the value of a property or method by using `MethodName = Value`, the use of `Return` is more consistent with .NET best practices and the manner in which you code return values in other .NET languages. Both methods of returning values will compile to the same Intermediate Language (IL).

CLASSES

Classes are blueprints for objects. Much as an architect creates a blueprint for a house, which he can customize to his own specifications, you create classes to serve as the blueprints for your objects. When you set properties and run methods, you are altering the class to create your object. To state an oft-used analogy: You have a car class. When you look at the class code, you notice the car is a vehicle with four wheels, but you do not know if it is a Ferrari or a VW bug. When you create an object from this class is when it becomes a Ferrari.

If you're a Visual Basic coder, you're almost certainly already familiar with classes. The main difference between coding classes in Visual Basic and in Visual Basic .NET is that in Visual Basic .NET you can have multiple classes in one source code file.

Visual Basic 6 programmers are likely to notice the line `Inherits System.Object`. Including this line in your classes isn't mandatory, but I recommend doing so because it's clearer and more explicit. Since everything is an object, you inherit from this regardless of whether you include this line.

There is one exception to this rule. Do not include the `Inherits System.Object` line when you want to inherit from another class, because you can inherit from only one class. You can inherit as many interfaces as you desire, but only one class.

PROPERTIES   *Properties* describe the attributes of a class. To continue with the architect and house analogy, properties for a house include such items as the color of the brick. The class I use in the preceding example includes three properties: `HelloMessage`, `HelloMessage2a`, and `HelloMessage2b`.

Unlike in Visual Basic 6, in Visual Basic .NET you must create a `Get` and a `Set` for each property that you create unless you specify that it's a read-only or write-only property. For ASP developers, the `Get` retrieves values from an object, while the `Set` sets the property. In Visual Basic 6, there was also a `Let`, which set a property that was not an object, but this is no longer necessary, as everything is an object in .NET.

Listing 2-3 shows a property declaration in Visual Basic .NET. The routine is from the project HelloWorldComplex shown in Listing 2-2.

Listing 2-3: Property Declaration in Visual Basic .NET

```
'* Public Property with Get and Set
Public Property HelloMessage() As String
    Get
        Return strMessage
    End Get
    Set
        strMessage = Value
    End Set
End Property
```

As you look at the code, notice that I use the `Return` keyword to return the value of this property in the `Get` portion of the property. In the `Set` portion, you see the word `Value`. Where did that come from? `Value` is a keyword that represents the input for a property.

You may notice three differences between Visual Basic 6 and Visual Basic .NET. First are the properties Get and Set within the property declaration of the latter. Second, you find no Let in Visual Basic .NET. Third, Get and Set in Visual Basic .NET have the same scope. In Visual Basic 6, you could quite easily allow a Private Let and a Public Get, basically making a read-only property that could allow some input checking for internal setting of the property. In Visual Basic .NET, both the Get and Set are wrapped inside the property block, so they always share the same scope.

Unlike in Visual Basic 6, where you can set up a read-only property by dropping the Let or a write-only property by dropping the Get, in Visual Basic .NET you must explicitly state that a property is read-only or write-only, by using the ReadOnly and WriteOnly keywords. Listing 2-4 shows an example of a read-only and a write-only property in Visual Basic .NET. In this example, I use two properties of different scope to imitate something you could do in Visual Basic. I do not recommend this type of coding. The properties in the listing are taken from the HelloWorld complex project in Listing 2-2.

Listing 2-4: Read-Only and Write-Only Properties in Visual Basic .NET

```
'* Read-Only Property
Public ReadOnly Property HelloMessage2a(ByVal anotherValue _
        As String) As String
    Get
        HelloMessage2a = strMessage
    End Get
End Property


'* Write-Only Property
Friend WriteOnly Property HelloMessage2b() As String
    Set
        strMessage = Value
    End Set
End Property
```

You can no longer set different exposure for your Get and Set in Visual Basic .NET. Listing 2-4 shows a bit of a kludge (less than perfect way around a coding problem) to do something that's quite easy to accomplish in Visual Basic 6, which is to declare your Let differently than your Get. You now must work with two properties to mirror this effect.

The primary reason for setting a different scope for Property Get and Property Let is to enable you to retrieve a property from outside the library (DLL) but only set it (using Let) from another class within the library. To do so, you create a Friend Let and a Public Get. Listing 2-5 shows this technique. Once again, this is not something I would normally recommend.

Listing 2-5: Property Declaration in Visual Basic 6

```
Friend Property Let HelloMessage2(Value as String)
    m_strMessage = Value
End Property
Public Property Get HelloMessage2() As String
    HelloMessage2 = m_strMessage
End Property
```

You may notice in the preceding example that you use `Value as String` as input for the property `Let` in Visual Basic 6. In Visual Basic .NET, however, you may face the temptation to write something similar to the following example:

```
Public Property HelloMessage(ByVal Value As String) As String
```

This example, however, doesn't work in Visual Basic .NET because you can add a value to your property, as the following example shows:

```
Public ReadOnly Property HelloMessage2a(ByVal intIndex As Integer) As String
```

The primary reason for setting up a parameter for a property is to add an indexer. Indexers can prove useful, for example, if you want to create a property that's an indexed collection (or basically an array of objects).

The capability of adding parameters to a property isn't constrained to a single parameter or numeric parameters only. Listing 2-6 shows an example in which you use a single property to set all the properties in a class. This code sample is part of a program that I call BadCode, which you can find on the companion Web site for this book.

Listing 2-6: Using a Property To Set Private Variables

```
Private m_strMyString As String
Private m_strBadCode As String

Public Property BadCode(ByVal strInput As String) As String
    Set
        m_strBadCode = Value
        m_strMyString = strInput
    End Set
    Get
        Return m_strBadCode
    End Get
End Property

Public ReadOnly Property MyString() As String
    Get
```

```
        Return m_strMyString
    End Get
End Property
```

 You can find the code from Listing 2-6 under Ch02SDK.zip (SDK version) or Ch02VS.zip (Visual Studio .NET version) on the companion Web site (www.wiley.com/extras). When you unzip the file, look for the BadCode folder.

The code in Listing 2-6 is just bad code. If you were using the parameter to determine which item in an array should be returned, this example would be acceptable. To use a property to set other properties, however, is sloppy. If you need to set multiple properties in one routine, you want to use a method instead.

METHODS   *Methods* are routines that represent actions that your object performs, which you implement as subroutines or functions. For example, if we use building a house as an analogy to building our class in Visual Basic .NET, a routine such as OpenDoor() would be a method.

In Listing 2-7, I use a simple method in ASP, which may seem a bit strange to those of you who write inline code for all your ASP pages. Although less explicit than optimal for Visual Basic, this code runs under Visual Basic 6 without any editing.

Listing 2-7: A Simple Database Connection Method in ASP

```
Private Function ConnectToDatabase(strConn, objConn)
    On Error Resume Next

    Set objConn = Server.CreateObject("ADODB.Connection")
    Call objConn.Open(strConn)

    If Err.Number = 0 then
        ConnectToDatabase = True
    Else
        ConnectToDatabase = False
        Err.Clear
    End If
End Function
```

If you set Option Strict to on (Option Strict = on), which, unfortunately, is not the default in Visual Basic .NET, .NET requires you to add an output type for every function. There is no output type on this function, because it ends with the closing parenthesis of the parameter list. In Visual Basic 6, the default output type for a function is a variant, so you would not have to declare an output type to have the code run.

MODULES

For all practical purposes, a `Module` in Visual Basic .NET is a type of class. You normally use this type for creating command-line applications. Listing 2-8 shows a simplified `Module` that you can use to create a "Hello, World!" application.

Listing 2–8: A Simple "Hello, World!" Module

```
Module Module1
    Public Sub Main()
        System.Console.WriteLine("Hello, World!")
    End Sub
End Module
```

The code from Listing 2-8 is under `Ch02SDK.zip` (SDK version) on the companion Web site (`www.wiley.com/extras`). When you unzip the file, look for the FromVSNET folder. In the Visual Studio .NET zip file (`Ch02VS.zip`), this is HelloWorldSimple.

Compare this module to the class in Listing 2-9, which is our simple "Hello, World!" class from Chapter 1 again (Listing 1-1).

Listing 2–9: A Simple "Hello, World!" Class

```
Public Class HelloWorld
    Public Shared Sub Main()
        System.Console.WriteLine("Hello, World!")
    End Sub
End Class
```

You can find the code from Listing 2-9 on the companion Web site (`www.wiley.com/extras`) under `Ch02SDK.zip` (SDK version) in the folder HelloWorldSimple. The Visual Studio .NET version uses a module, so the code is slightly different. I have included a file `Module1.txt` to show this in the Visual Studio .NET download.

Through the rest of the book, I use modules in the same manner as they are used when you create an application in the Visual Basic .NET IDE. The manner employed by the IDE is to use a module as a container to hold the `Sub Main()` for a console (or command-line) application. Because this book focuses on ASP.NET, however, you won't find a lot of practice with modules after this chapter.

Value types in Visual Basic .NET

Value types sit on the stack, and the value of the object is passed rather than a reference to the type. Beyond the .NET primitive types, you have two major value types in Visual Basic .NET: structures and enumerators. Enumerators are a familiar concept to Visual Basic 6 developers, so I begin this section by discussing structures.

STRUCTURES

A *structure* is essentially a lightweight object. For Visual Basic 6 developers, a structure is the closest thing that you can find to a Visual Basic .NET replacement for a user-defined type (UDT). If you are not familiar with UDTs, they are simply a group of types passed as a single type. A simple student UDT, for example, might have the student's first name, last name, and Social Security number.

Look at the code in Listings 2-10 and 2-11 to see the similarities between a Visual Basic 6 UDT and a simple Visual Basic .NET structure.

Listing 2-10: A User-Defined Type (UDT) in Visual Basic 6

```
Public Type Customer
    Public LastName As String
    Public FirstName As String
    Public CustomerID As Integer
End Type
```

Listing 2-11: A Simple Structure in Visual Basic .NET

```
Structure MyStruct
    Public LastName As String
    Public FirstName As String
    Public CustomerID As Integer
End Structure
```

So structures are simply replacements for UDTs, right? Wrong. Although you can use structures as a UDT replacement, they're really much more than just a set of variables grouped under one name, as a UDT is. A structure, despite being a value type, is an object. Consider Listing 2-12 for a much more complex structure.

Listing 2-12: A Complex Structure

```
Structure Customer
    Private m_strLastName As String

    Public Property LastName() As String
```

Continued

Listing 2-12 *(Continued)*

```
        Get
            Return m_strLastName
        End Get
        Set
            m_strLastName = Value
        End Set
    End Property
End Structure
```

If structures are objects, why not just use structures in place of classes? The primary reason is one of performance, as passing a reference is less expensive with larger objects. Creating a large number of methods and properties in a structure passed from object to object will incur a performance penalty. Think before using a structure as much more than a UDT replacement and you will be fine.

You also want to note that structures require *shared constructors*. I cover constructors in the section "Working with Classes," a little later in this chapter. For now, remember that a shared constructor means that you can customize structures *after* instantiation but not as you instantiate. Visual Basic 6 programmers don't see customization after instantiation as a big drawback, as the Form_Load and Class_Initialize events carry the same caveat. With Visual Basic .NET, however, you can customize your objects in your constructor (at initialization), which is much more flexible and efficient.

Following is a simple rule: In general, use classes rather than structures for your objects. If you think you must use a structure instead, try to ensure that it follows these rules:

◆ The object that you're creating is very small. A replacement for a UDT is a prime example of a case in which you may want to use a structure instead of a class.

◆ The object that you're creating doesn't require custom construction, meaning that you don't need to set the properties or variables of the object during instantiation.

◆ The object that you're creating must pass by value instead of by reference. Be careful about using this rule as your only criterion, however, as breaking the other two rules for the sake of this one can lead to disastrous consequences.

ENUMERATORS

For those unfamiliar with the term, an *enumerator* is a distinct list of named constants. These constants map to a set of values of one of the primitive types. By default, this is a set of Long values. Because computers are more efficient with numbers and humans are more efficient with words, a gap needs bridging between the two. If you think about how URLs map to IP addresses, you may get a glimmer of the process. In the same vein, enumerators map numbers to friendly names to simplify programming for humans.

Perhaps the most well-known enumerators are those associated with ActiveX Data Objects, or ADO. Because most applications deal with data access, you've probably seen code similar to that shown in Listing 2-13. I have included part of the ADO CursorLocationEnum at the top to show how the values map to the constants.

Listing 2-13: Use of Enumerators in Visual Basic 6 and ASP

```
Public Enum CursorLocationEnum
    adUseNone = 1
    adUseServer = 2
    adUseClient = 3
End Enum

With objRS
    'CursorLocationEnum
    .CursorLocation = adUseServer
    .CursorLocation = 2

    'CursorTypeEnum
    .CursorType = adOpenDynamic
    .CursorType = 2

    'LockTypeEnum
    .LockType = adLockOptimistic
    .LockType = 3
End With
```

Each of the pairs of lines in Listing 2-13 shows the enumerator and then the numeric value that the particular enumerator item represents. You will code only the enumerator *or* the value. The enumerator is far less abstract than the numeric values that it represents. For example, using the enumerators, you can easily tell from this listing that the code uses a dynamic server-side cursor with an optimistic lock.

Although working with the numbers yields identical results, using these numbers is far less readable. The power of enumerators is code maintenance, especially with programmers who haven't had the time or inclination to memorize all the numbers that the common enumerators represent.

In Visual Basic 6, all enumerators have a data type of Long. In Visual Basic .NET, you have choices: You can use a data type of Byte, Short, Integer, or Long. The ability to use types other than just Long adds a lot of options to your coding. Listing 2-14 shows a small sample of an enumerator in Visual Basic .NET that's using a Byte data type.

Listing 2-14: An Enumerator in Visual Basic .NET

```
Public Enum ConnType As Byte
    ctNone = 0
    ctNetwork = 1
    ctInternet = 2
End Enum
```

Working with Classes

I believe that the most useful way to learn to code in a new language is to just get to it. You'll get more out of this section if you take the time to type in the code samples yourself. If you're already familiar with object-oriented programming, you may choose to simply look at the code.

For this section, I created a program that I call fileLister. This program takes a directory as an input and lists all the files in this directory and all subdirectories. Certain sections of the code aren't 100 percent "best practice" but I include them to cover as many concepts as possible. Listing 2-15 shows the entire program.

Listing 2-15: The fileLister Program

```
Imports SysCon = System.Console
Imports SysIO = System.IO

Module Module1

    Private m_strFolder As String

    Sub Main()
        m_strFolder = Trim$(Microsoft.VisualBasic.Command())

        If m_strFolder = "" Then
            'This will error if you do not have the SDK installed
            '     or if you have installed other than default.
            m_strFolder = "C:\Program Files\Microsoft Visual Studio" & _
                        ".NET\FrameworkSDK\GuiDebug"
        End If

        Dim objFileList As New fileList(m_strFolder)
        objFileList.SearchDirectory()
        SysCon.Read()
    End Sub

End Module
```

```vb
Public Class fileList

    Private m_strFolder As String
    Private m_intIndent As Integer

    Public Sub New(ByVal strFolder As String)
        m_strFolder = strFolder
    End Sub

    Public Sub SearchDirectory()

        'Done to use the folder set with constructor
        ProcessDirectory(m_strFolder, 0)

    End Sub

    Public Shared Sub ProcessDirectory(ByVal strDirectoryPath As String, _
                                       ByVal intIndent As Integer)

        'Create File System objects
        Dim objDirectoryInfo As New System.IO.DirectoryInfo(strDirectoryPath)
        Dim objFileInfo As System.IO.FileInfo
        Dim Directory As System.IO.DirectoryInfo

        'Write directory name
        SysCon.WriteLine(Space(intIndent) & objDirectoryInfo.Name)

        'Get info on each file in directory
        For Each objFileInfo In objDirectoryInfo.GetFiles
            SysCon.WriteLine(Space(intIndent + 5) & objFileInfo.Name)
        Next

        'increase indent for next set of directories
        intIndent = intIndent + 2

        'Recurse each directory
        For Each Directory In objDirectoryInfo.GetDirectories
            ProcessDirectory(Directory.FullName, intIndent)
        Next

    End Sub
End Class
```

You can find the code from Listing 2-15 under ChO2SDK.zip (SDK version) and ChO2VS.zip (Visual Studio .NET) on the companion Web site (www. wiley.com/extras). When you unzip the file, look in the FileLister folder.

Entry point

The entry point for our application is the Sub Main() in our module, which is the same point that I use for all command-line applications. The module is necessary in this particular application, as a constructor is on the fileList class. Listing 2-16 shows the important points of the entry point of our application.

Listing 2-16: The fileLister Entry Point

```
Sub Main()
    m_strFolder = Trim$(Microsoft.VisualBasic.Command())

    If m_strFolder = "" Then
        'This will error if you do not have the SDK installed
        '        or if you have installed other than default.
        m_strFolder = "C:\Program Files\Microsoft Visual Studio" & _
                    ".NET\FrameworkSDK\GuiDebug"
    End If

    Dim objFileList As New fileList(m_strFolder)
    objFileList.SearchDirectory()
    SysCon.Read()
End Sub
```

If you look at the line that declares the fileLister object, you see a couple things. First, I declare the object by using As New. In Visual Basic 6, declaring an object with As New isn't a good idea, because every call to a property or method on this class incurs overhead as Visual Basic checks to see whether the object is already instantiated. If you declare the object without the New keyword, this check is not made every time, which is much more efficient. The overhead of checking whether the object exists when using New doesn't occur in Visual Basic .NET. Second, notice that I add the argument to the instantiation of the object. The object takes this argument as a parameter for the constructor (Sub New()) of the fileList class.

Constructor

A *constructor* is a method that you use to help create, or construct, an instance of an object after you instantiate it from a class. In Visual Basic .NET, constructors take the form of a subroutine known as New(). In Visual Basic 6, the closest thing to a constructor is your `Form_Load` or `Class_Initialize` event. As with these Visual Basic 6 events, you use a constructor to add code that you need for your object to run. Unlike Visual Basic 6 events, however, constructors can take parameters. In Listing 2-17, I show the constructor that I use in the `fileList` class.

Listing 2-17: A Simple Constructor

```
Public Sub New(ByVal strFolder As String)
    m_strFolder = strFolder
End Sub
```

In a real-world application, I'd probably never use a constructor just to set a private variable, as I do this example. A simple example such as this one, however, is useful for illustrating how to use a constructor. The powerful part of constructors is that you can use them as a dynamic method for setting up an instance of a class. Those of you who set up classes that use a method to set properties may want to consider replacing these methods with constructors.

Constructors are very useful for data-tier classes that are property laden. Although I cover data access more thoroughly in Part III, Listing 2-18 shows a constructor for a data-tier object where you set all the properties at instantiation. The listing works with the Northwind database in SQL Server. If you don't have SQL Server, you can change the connection string to one that points to a Northwind Access database (which ships with Office and Visual Studio). The connection string looks something like the following example:

```
Provider=Microsoft.Jet.OLEDB.4.0;Data Source=C:\Program
    Files\Microsoft Visual Studio\VB\NWIND.MDB;
```

Listing 2-18: Constructor for a Data-Tier Object

```
Public Sub New(ByVal CustomerID As String)

    'Using Northwind Database: Can be SQL or ADO
    'This example is SQL Server
    Dim strConnectionString As String = _
        "Provider=SQLOLEDB.1;Server=(local);Database=Northwind;UID=sa;PWD=;"
    Dim strSQL As String = "SELECT * FROM Customers " & _
        "WHERE CustomerID ='" & CustomerID & "'"

    'Set up data objects
    Dim objConn As New SysADO.OleDbConnection(strConnectionString)
    Dim objCommand As New SysADO.OleDbCommand(strSQL, objConn)
    Dim objDataAdapter As New SysADO.OleDbDataAdapter(objCommand)
    Dim objDataSet As New System.Data.DataSet()
```

Continued

Listing 2-18 *(Continued)*

```
Dim objDataRow As System.Data.DataRow

'Open objects and populate DataSet and DataRow
objConn.Open()
objDataAdapter.Fill(objDataSet, "Customers")
objDataRow = objDataSet.Tables("Customers").Rows(0)

'* Set Properties
m_strCustomerID = CustomerID
m_strCompanyName = CStr(objDataRow("CompanyName"))
m_strContactName = CStr(objDataRow("ContactName"))
m_strContactTitle = CStr(objDataRow("ContactTitle"))
m_strAddress = CStr(objDataRow("Address"))
m_strCity = CStr(objDataRow("City"))

'* Test for a NULL value in the database
If Not IsDBNull(objDataRow("Region")) Then
    m_strRegion = CStr(objDataRow("Region"))
End If

m_strPostalCode = CStr(objDataRow("PostalCode"))
m_strCountry = CStr(objDataRow("Country"))
m_strPhone = CStr(objDataRow("Phone"))
m_strFax = CStr(objDataRow("Fax"))

'Close connection
objConn.Close()

End Sub
```

You can find the code from Listing 2-18 under `ChO2SDK.zip` (SDK version) or `ChO2VS.zip` (Visual Studio .NET) on the companion Web site (`www.wiley.com/extras`). When you unzip the file, look in the DataTier folder.

The code sample in Listing 2-18 has a constructor that uses `CustomerID` to load properties in a `Customer` object. I cover the ADO.NET objects in greater detail in Part III of this book. For now, just take a brief look at the code to get an idea of how to work with some of the objects in ADO.NET.

Working with Namespaces

If you work with some of the code samples that I use in the preceding sections, you may find the idea of typing a long string such as System.Console.WriteLine each time that you need to output to the command line a bit daunting. What if you could just type WriteLine instead? Fortunately, you can.

Using Imports

In .NET, you use namespaces to simplify typing methods and properties of objects. As you've seen in some of the exercises in this book, you use the keyword word Imports to use namespaces within your applications. What this means is that you type the full name of the namespace after the Imports keyword, and then you can use the namespace's objects without having to type the namespace in front of them. Listing 2-19 shows the simple Hello World application again but uses the System.Console namespace to simplify your program.

Listing 2-19: A Simple Hello World Program Using Namespaces

```
Imports System.Console

Public Class HelloWorld
    Public Shared Sub Main()
        WriteLine("Hello, World!")
    End Sub
End Class
```

 You can find the code from Listing 2-19 under ChO2SDK.zip (SDK version) or ChO2VS.zip (Visual Studio .NET) on the companion Web site (www.wiley.com/extras). When you unzip the file, look in the HelloWorldNamespace folder.

Importing the System.Console namespace solves the problem of typing long lines. You can now simply type in WriteLine instead of System. Console.WriteLine. Another problem, however, appears. Which object are you using to write lines to the command line? All you have is the keyword WriteLine, so you cannot tell which namespace this is from unless you memorize the objects. You solve the problem by using aliasing.

Aliasing namespaces

If you're sure that you're the only one who's ever going to maintain your code, not knowing which object your object is calling is a very small problem. In my professional life, however, I find very few situations in which the author of the code is the only person who ever maintains the code.

To solve this ambiguity problem (not knowing which namespace you are working with), you can add an alias to every namespace you import. An alias is simply a friendly name you use in your code to represent a .NET namespace.

To add an alias to a namespace in Visual Basic .NET, you simply add the name of the alias to the `Imports` line by typing the alias name, an equal sign (=), and then the name of the object you're aliasing.

Listing 2-20 shows the Hello World program yet again, this time with an alias for the `System.Console` namespace. The alias in this example is SysCon.

Listing 2-20: Aliasing Objects in Visual Basic .NET

```
Imports SysCon = System.Console

Public Class HelloWorld
    Public Shared Sub Main()
        SysCon.WriteLine("Hello, World!")
    End Sub
End Class
```

 The code from Listing 2-20 is under `Ch02SDK.zip` (SDK version) or `Ch02VS.zip` (Visual Studio .NET) on the companion Web site (`www.wiley.com/extras`). When you unzip the file, look in the HelloWorldAlias folder.

By using aliases, you no longer must type long lines to access objects, and you still have maintainable code. I advocate the use of aliases for all namespaces. This recommendation is likely to start a debate in programming circles, however, because you still have a bit more typing than you would by simply importing. But maintainability — or rather the lack thereof — costs business a ton of money in time each year, so I will continue to advocate using aliases with all namespaces.

As a little experiment, download the code for the SDK (`Ch02SDK.zip`) from the companion Web site, unzip the file, and open the FileLister folder. Delete the `.bat` file and compile the program. As a hint, you only need to reference the proper DLL that allows you to use the `Trim()` and `Space()` functions. While not exactly the same as not using aliases, the amount of time wasted finding this reference is very similar to the amount of time you will waste trying to find which namespace an object is in without aliases. Over time, you can memorize a lot of objects, but you will most likely never memorize all of them.

Namespaces and compiling programs

Although I mention the concept in the last section, I really need to reiterate the idea that importing a namespace doesn't create a reference to the object that contains that namespace. If you're working in Visual Studio IDE, you can create a reference to an assembly by right-clicking the reference folder and adding a new reference. If you use the command line, however, you must add each reference individually, using the /reference: command line flag (short version is /r:). If you have downloaded the SDK zip file, you can open any of the .bat files to see which assemblies are referenced.

If you played along with my game and deleted the .bat file from the FileLister program, you understand the difference between namespaces and assembly references. If you did not try this exercise, just look at the .bat file in this project and see how the file is compiled.

Visual Basic – Object-Oriented?

Although Visual Basic 6 is an object-based programming paradigm, Visual Basic .NET finally brings Visual Basic into the realm of truly object-oriented programming (OOP). In this section, I cover the newer object-oriented concepts in Visual Basic .NET, including inheritance, polymorphism, and the overriding and overloading of methods.

Inheritance

Inheritance is a feature of object-oriented programming in which a child class can inherit the behavior of a parent class. In Visual Basic 6, you can inherit the interface of an *abstract class,* which is a class with no code behind the methods and properties you're inheriting. In interface inheritance, you inherit the definitions of the methods and properties, but none of the code inside them. You must write code for every method and property inside a class inheriting that interface, even if the code's the same in each class that is inheriting this interface. This is not a very efficient way to code an application that has identical methods in multiple classes.

You can still use interface inheritance in Visual Basic .NET. In fact, if you want to inherit from multiple classes, you will have to use interface inheritance because Visual Basic .NET only supports single implementation inheritance, meaning you can only inherit from one parent class. While this may seem limiting, it is unlikely you will find many situations where multiple inheritance makes sense if you build your classes properly.

Unlike Visual Basic, in Visual Basic .NET, you can inherit the implementation of each method and property in the parent class. This feature is very powerful, as you now can write a method once in a parent class and use this same code in a variety of child classes without rewriting it.

When you choose to inherit, you should use the "kind of" rule: The child object should be a kind of the parent object. For example, a poodle is a kind of dog. If you have similar methods in multiple objects, but these objects do not follow this rule, consider inheriting from an interface.

There is a temptation to inherit from an object simply because most of the methods of the perceived parent object are the same as the child object. You should only use implementation inheritance when the child object is a kind of parent object. If you want to match methods, use an interface instead.

Listing 2-21 shows our simple Hello World program with two classes. In this program, the `HelloWorld2` class inherits from a `Hello` class.

Listing 2-21: Inheritance in Visual Basic .NET

```
Imports SysCon = System.Console

Module Module1

    Sub Main()
        Dim objHello As New HelloWorld2()
        objHello.PrintHello()
    End Sub

End Module

Public Class Hello
    Public Sub PrintHello()
        SysCon.WriteLine("Hello World!")
    End Sub
End Class

Public Class HelloWorld2
    Inherits Hello
End Class
```

You can find the code from Listing 2-21 under `ChO2SDK.zip` (SDK version) or `ChO2VS.zip` (Visual Studio .NET) on the companion Web site (www.wiley.com/extras). When you unzip the file, look in the HelloWorldInherit folder.

In Listing 2-21, you may notice that the object `HelloWorld2` prints out the line "Hello, World!" despite the fact that you don't explicitly create the `PrintHello()` method in the `HelloWorld2` class. Because `HelloWorld2` inherits `Hello`, all its methods (in this case, only one) are accessible through `HelloWorld2`.

What happens if you have a certain class that you don't want a developer to be able to inherit from? All you need to do is add the keyword `NotInheritable` in front of the class name. If you want to experiment, change the `Hello` class declaration to `Public NotInheritable Class HelloWorld2`. Your program should now throw an exception, or error, if you attempt to compile it.

 You can find the code from a non-inheritable Hello class under `Ch02SDK.zip` (SDK version) or `Ch02VS.zip` (Visual Studio .NET) on the companion Web site (`www.wiley.com/extras`). When you unzip the file, look in the HelloWorldInheritFail folder.

Inheritance applies to objects and not to methods. You can't stop inheritance of specific methods inside an object. You can, however, change the implementation of methods through overriding, which I discuss next.

Overriding

You must do two things to override a method or property in Visual Basic .NET. First, you must mark the methods that you're going to override by adding the keyword `Overridable` to the subroutine or function. You also must write an implementation of the `PrintHello()` method that includes the `Overrides` keyword. Listing 2-22 shows the Hello World program with an overridable method.

Listing 2-22: Overriding the PrintHello() Method

```
Imports SysCon = System.Console

Module Module1

    Sub Main()
        Dim objHello As New HelloWorld2()
        objHello.PrintHello()
    End Sub

End Module

Public Class Hello
    Public Overridable Sub PrintHello()
        SysCon.WriteLine("Hello World!")
    End Sub
```

Continued

Listing 2-22 *(Continued)*

```
End Class

Public Class HelloWorld2
    Inherits Hello

    Public Overrides Sub PrintHello()
        SysCon.WriteLine("A Different Hello!")
    End Sub
End Class
```

 You can find the code from Listing 2-22 under `ChO2SDK.zip` (SDK version) or `ChO2VS.zip` (Visual Studio .NET) on the companion Web site (`www.wiley.com/extras`). When you unzip the file, look in the HelloWorldOverride folder.

The capability to override is a very powerful tool in an application that mimics a real-world application. On the companion Web site, I include a program called DogMaker that contains different Dog classes that inherit from the class Dog. Some of the classes use the bark method from the Dog class, but others use the override to the bark method to output their own instinctive bark. I include a portion of the code for this project in Listing 2-23.

Listing 2-23: Additional Types of Overriding

```
Imports SysCon = System.Console

Module Module1

    Sub Main()
        SysCon.WriteLine("This is a poodle:")
        Dim objDog As New Poodle()

        SysCon.WriteLine("1. Bark")
        objDog.Bark()

        SysCon.WriteLine("2. Walk")
        objDog.Walk()

        SysCon.WriteLine("")
        SysCon.WriteLine("This is a teacup poodle:")
```

```
        objDog = New TeaCupPoodle()

        SysCon.WriteLine("1. Bark")
        objDog.Bark()

        SysCon.WriteLine("2. Walk")
        objDog.Walk()

        SysCon.Read()
    End Sub

End Module

Public MustInherit Class Dog

    Public Overridable Sub Bark()
        SysCon.WriteLine("   Generic Bark")
    End Sub

    Public Sub Walk()
        SysCon.WriteLine("   Walking the same as all other dogs.")
    End Sub

    Public MustOverride Property Color() As String

End Class

Public Class Poodle
    Inherits Dog
    Private m_strColor As String

    Public Sub New()
        m_strColor = "White"
    End Sub

    Public Overrides Sub Bark()
        SysCon.WriteLine("   Yip! Yip! I'm a poodle!")
        SysCon.WriteLine("   This is from the base class, Dog:")
        MyBase.Bark()
    End Sub

    Public NotOverridable Overrides Property Color() As String
        Set(ByVal Value As String)
            m_strColor = Value
```

Continued

Listing 2-23 *(Continued)*

```
        End Set
        Get
            Return m_strColor
        End Get
    End Property
End Class

Public Class TeaCupPoodle
    Inherits Poodle

    Public Overrides Sub Bark()
        SysCon.WriteLine(" Yip! I'm a teacup poodle!")
        SysCon.WriteLine(" This is from the base class, poodle:")
        MyBase.Bark()
    End Sub
End Class
```

 The code from a non-inheritable `Hello` class is in `Ch02SDK.zip` (SDK version) or `Ch02VS.zip` (Visual Studio .NET) on the companion Web site (`www.wiley.com/extras`). When you unzip the file, look in the DogMaker folder.

As you read through the preceding code, you notice quite a few new keywords that relate to overriding classes. The following list describes these keywords:

♦ `Overridable`: If you use a method or property that you either can or can't override, use the keyword `Overridable` to override it. You may override a method that you designate as `Overridable`, but nothing forces you to do so.

♦ `NotOverridable`: In some examples, you have methods or properties that must use the implementation in the parent class. In these cases, use the keyword `NotOverridable` to guarantee that you don't override this method or property in the child class.

♦ `MustOverride`: If you use a method or a property that you know must exist in all child objects, but you either don't know the implementation or know that the implementation varies with every child, you use the `MustOverride` keyword. This keyword functions similarly to how inheritance works in Visual Basic 6, because interfaces do not have an implementation for the methods and properties, only a definition.

- ◆ **MustInherit:** Every class with a method or property that you must override you must declare as MustInherit.

- ◆ **MyBase.Method( ):** Using MyBase enables you to call the parent's implementation to an overridden method. The example in Listing 2-23 is not the best use of this feature, but it illustrates the point. If you inherit a class with a constructor, you want to use MyBase.New( ) as you construct the child class. Because the Dog class does not have a constructor, this is not necessary.

 If you find that you are overriding the implementation of a great number of the methods from your parent class, you probably have a child object that does not fit the "kind of" rule. In this case, you may want to re-architect to use an interface for the methods that change.

Overloading

Another of the powerful new object-oriented features of Visual Basic .NET is the capability to overload a function. *Overloading* is the capability to declare a method more than once with a different set of parameters. In Listing 2-24, you find the last Hello World program of this book with an overloaded constructor.

Listing 2-24: Overloading a Constructor in Visual Basic .NET

```
Imports SysCon = System.Console
Imports VB = Microsoft.VisualBasic

Module Module1

    Sub Main()
        SysCon.WriteLine("Using an Integer with the constructor:")
        Dim objHello As New Hello(1)

        SysCon.WriteLine("Using a String with the constructor:")
        objHello = New Hello("Hello, World!")

        SysCon.Read()
    End Sub

End Module

Public Class Hello
```

Continued

Listing 2-24 *(Continued)*

```
    Public Sub New(ByVal strInput As String)
        SysCon.WriteLine(strInput)
    End Sub

    Public Sub New(ByVal intInput As Integer)
        SysCon.WriteLine(GetHello(intInput))
    End Sub

    Private Function GetHello(ByVal intInput As Integer) As String
        Select Case intInput
            Case 1
                GetHello = "Hello Number One!"
            Case 2
                GetHello = "Hello Number Two!"
            Case Else
                GetHello = "Hello Universe!"
        End Select
    End Function

End Class
```

 You can find the code from a non-inheritable `Hello` class under `Ch02SDK.zip` (SDK version) or `Ch02VS.zip` (Visual Studio .NET) on the companion Web site (`www.wiley.com/extras`). When you unzip the file, look in the HelloWorldOverload folder.

To overload a method, you simply make two versions of the method with different parameters. You can also use the keyword `Overloads` on each implementation of the method, if you want to be more explicit, but you must include the `Overloads` keyword on *each* method if you do this. Note, however, that you cannot use `Overloads` on your `Sub New()` (the constructor).

When you overload, you must use a different parameter list for each implementation. In functions, you can use a different data type as an output for each implementation of the method that you override, but you must also alter the parameter list in some manner to override the method. The following code snippet, which only changes the output of the function, is not legal:

```
Public Function MyFunction(ByVal intInput As Integer) As String
End Function
Public Function MyFunction(ByVal intInput as Integer) As Double
End Function
```

You have one exception to this rule, which is shown in Listing 2-25. If you are inheriting from a parent class, you must use the `Overloads` keyword in the child class, regardless of whether or not `Overloads` is used in the parent class. You can opt to use `Overloads` in the parent class if you have overloaded the method, but you are required to use `Overloads` in the child class. Understand that the original method in the parent class is still available. If you type in a new method in the child class with the same parameter list as the parent class, you will receive an error.

Listing 2-25: Overloading an Inherited Method

```
Imports SysCon = System.Console
Imports VB = Microsoft.VisualBasic

Module Module1

    Sub Main()
        Dim objHello As New HelloWorld()

        SysCon.WriteLine("As inherited from parent class:")
        objHello.PrintHello()

        SysCon.WriteLine("Overloaded with Integer parameter:")
        objHello.PrintHello(1)

        SysCon.WriteLine("Overloaded with String parameter:")
        objHello.PrintHello("Hello, World!")

        SysCon.Read()
    End Sub

End Module

Public Class Hello
    Public Sub PrintHello()
        SysCon.WriteLine("Hello World Normal")
    End Sub
End Class

Public Class HelloWorld
    Inherits Hello

    Public Overloads Sub PrintHello(ByVal intInput As Integer)
        SysCon.WriteLine("Hello From Integer Version: You input " & intInput)
```

Continued

Listing 2-25 *(Continued)*

```
    End Sub

Public Overloads Sub PrintHello(ByVal strInput As String)
    SysCon.WriteLine("Hello From String Version - Here is your message:")
    SysCon.WriteLine(strInput)
    End Sub
End Class
```

 You can find the code from a non-inheritable `Hello` class under `Ch02SDK.zip` (SDK version) or `Ch02VS.zip` (Visual Studio .NET) on the companion Web site (`www.wiley.com/extras`). When you unzip the file, look in the HelloWorldOverrideInherit folder.

If you run this program, it can use the implementations in the `HelloWorld` class or the implementation in the `Hello` class, depending on the parameters that you give it. Notice that no `Overloads` keyword is in the parent class, `Hello`, because the method isn't overloaded in this class.

You may be wondering, "Can I overload a method in a parent class and then further overload it in my child class?" The answer is yes. If you download the code, you'll find that I commented out a section of the parent class that does just that. Before you design your classes like this, however, take a good, hard look at what you are doing. Overloading methods at each level of your object inheritance tree is a practice that can lead to what I will call "OO Hell," because the developers who maintain your code will have to remember which parameter lists they can use at every level of your class hierarchy. If you find yourself overloading further in child objects, you might want to examine your application design to see if you have created the right methods.

 Be careful not to use overloading simply to make your methods more abstract. For example, you have a `GetCustomer()` method that can either use a `Long` (`CustomerID`) or a `String` (`strSSN`). You also have a `GetCompany()`, which can either use an `Integer` (`CompanyID`) or two `Strings` (`CompanyName` and `City`). To further abstract, you might think of just creating a `GetData()` method. While this level of abstraction might reduce the amount of code you write, it will also make the application less maintainable.

Interfaces

Although creating parent classes is a powerful tool, what if all your methods and properties are abstract? You can create a class with MustOverride methods, but you have a better way to inherit the definitions of methods without creating a complete class.

Listing 2-26 shows an interface built in Visual Basic .NET. If you currently code in Visual Basic 6, this should look somewhat familiar. The main difference is the fact that you are not creating an empty class file to create this interface, because there is an Interface keyword in Visual Basic .NET.

Listing 2-26: An Interface Declaration in Visual Basic .NET

```
Imports SysCon = System.Console

Module Module1

    Sub Main()
        SysCon.WriteLine("From English Method:")
        Dim objHello As New Hello()
        SysCon.WriteLine(objHello.HelloEnglish())

        SysCon.WriteLine("From French Method:")
        SysCon.WriteLine(objHello.HelloFrench())

        SysCon.WriteLine("From combined method:")
        Dim objHelloWorld As New HelloWorld()
        SysCon.WriteLine(objHelloWorld.Hello())

        SysCon.Read()

    End Sub

End Module

Public Interface IMyInterface
    Function HelloEnglish() As String
    Function HelloFrench() As String
End Interface

Public Class Hello
    Implements IMyInterface

    Public Function HelloEnglish() As String _
            Implements IMyInterface.HelloEnglish
```

Continued

Listing 2-26 *(Continued)*

```
        Return "Hello, World!"
    End Function

    Public Function HelloFrench() As String _
            Implements IMyInterface.HelloFrench
        Return "Bonjour, la monde!"
    End Function
End Class

Public Class HelloWorld
    Implements IMyInterface

    Public Function Hello() As String _
            Implements IMyInterface.HelloEnglish, _
            IMyInterface.HelloFrench
        Return "Bonjour, World!"
    End Function
End Class
```

 You can find the code from a non-inheritable `Hello` class under `Ch02SDK.zip` (SDK version) or `Ch02VS.zip` (Visual Studio .NET) on the companion Web site (`www.wiley.com/extras`). When you unzip the file, look in the HelloWorldInterface folder.

Notice that `Hello()` in the `HelloWorld` class implements two methods from the `Interface`, something that you can never do in Visual Basic 6. This is one of the advantages of coding interfaces in Visual Basic .NET. As in Visual Basic 6, you can inherit from as many interfaces as you want. Remember, however, that you can only inherit from one parent class.

As a rule, use `Interface` if you implement each of the methods, properties, and events in a different manner in the child classes; use inheritance from a parent class if the code inside the method or property is the same. If you know you are going to use the same method and property names, but you do not use the same code in most, if not all, of your child classes, it is better to use an interface. Otherwise, you are going to be writing a lot of code in a parent object only to override it in each of the children. Excessive overriding is not a very efficient coding practice.

Remember that Visual Basic .NET allows full implementation inheritance from only one class. If you want to inherit from multiple sources, you must use interface inheritance. There are developers who are pushing Microsoft to include multiple class inheritance in .NET. I personally would like to see a good case study before joining this group, because I see greater potential damage than good coming out of that.

Scope

Let's now look at a subject that's more familiar to Visual Basic programmers than to ASP programmers: the concept of scope. *Scope* is the visibility of your variables, methods, and properties from different places in your code. Although the concept is the same in ASP, those who've written only inline code know only page-level scope, where you can use the object anywhere in the page.

When you write code, where you place your variables limits both the scope of the variable and the keywords that you can use. If you place code inside a code block or a procedure, for example, you must use the keyword Dim, which indicates a variable that is only visible inside that block of code or procedure. Outside a code block but inside a class or structure, you use Public, Private, or Friend. In Visual Basic .NET, you no longer have a Global keyword, because global variables really have no place in object-oriented programming. You do have, however, the concept of shared scope, which applies to all instances of the same class. In the following sections, I show you different levels of scope, moving from the most restrictive to the least.

Block-level scope

If you place a variable inside a code block, you declare it by using the keyword Dim, and it has *block-level scope.* By *code block,* I'm talking about using a variable inside a conditional piece of code, such as an If...Then block. Although writing code similar to that in Listing 2-27 isn't a good programming practice in Visual Basic 6, doing so is perfectly legal.

Listing 2-27: Declaring a Variable Inside an If ... Then Block in Visual Basic 6

```
Private Function GetMessage(ByVal blnCreated As Boolean) As String
    If blnCreated Then
        Dim strMessage As String
        strMessage = "My Message"
    End If

    GetMessage = strMessage
End Function
```

If you try the same code in Visual Basic .NET, it fails at the point where you assign strMessage to the function. This failure is the way Visual Basic should've been all along. Using a variable that you declare inside of a block should limit it to the block. In Visual Basic, however, it is limited to the entire procedure that the code block resides in. This example would likely error out in Visual Basic 6 as well, because the variable would never be created if blnCreated were False. If the expected behavior is True, however, you may not find the error for many months. Fortunately, Visual Basic .NET doesn't permit you to make such an error.

Procedural-level scope

Variables that you declare inside a procedure (a function or a subroutine) have *procedural-level* scope. You also declare these variables by using the keyword Dim. Procedural level scope should be a familiar concept to both Visual Basic 6 developers and ASP developers who have coded procedures. Attempting to access procedural-level variables outside the procedure raises an exception.

For a more detailed description of exceptions and error handling, consult Chapter 10.

Listing 2-28 shows a procedural-level variable in Visual Basic .NET.

Listing 2-28: Procedural-Level Variables

```
Public Class MyClass
    Public Sub UseVariable()
        Dim MyVariable As String
        MyVariable = "My String"
    End Sub
    Public Sub TestVariable()
        'Will error out here
        SysCon.WriteLine(MyVariable)
    End Sub
End Class
```

As you do in Visual Basic 6, you can use the same variable name at both object-level (declared inside a class, but outside of all procedures) and procedural-level. You use the procedural-level variable as long as you're within the procedure, while you use the object-level variable throughout the rest of the code in the object. This concept is known as hiding. You can't, however, have a block-level variable and a procedural-level variable with the same name, as Visual Basic .NET doesn't enable you to hide the implementation of the procedural-level variable inside a block.

Object-level scope

To set a variable with *object-level* scope, you use the keyword Private. As it does in Visual Basic 6, this keyword makes the variable available to the object but not to any other objects, including child objects, whether they're in your source-code file or not. I use numerous object-level variables in the many samples in this chapter. I use the prefix m_ to indicate object-level variables; this designation comes from Visual Basic 6, where these variables are known as *module-level* variables.

Class- and subclass-level scope

Somewhere between object- and assembly-level scope is a scope that covers the object and all objects that use this object as a parent. For lack of a better term, I call this *class scope* because all objects created from a class, along with objects created from classes that inherit the original class, can use variables set with this scope. To set a variable so that it's available inside the class and its children, you use the keyword Protected. Listing 2-29 shows a Protected variable.

Listing 2-29: Protected Object Members

```
Public Class Parent
    Protected MyVariable As String = "Nothing"
End Class

Public Class Child
    Inherits Parent

    Public Function GetVariable() As String
        Return MyVariable
    End Function
End Class
```

Assembly-level scope

The next level of scope is the *assembly*. To make variables available to all classes in your assembly, you use the keyword Friend. This keyword is the same one that you use in Visual Basic 6 to create variables accessible to all objects in the type library. All variables that you declare by using the keyword Friend are accessible by all objects in your assembly in .NET. They aren't accessible, however, to outside applications that use the assembly. If you remember that the assembly is the smallest unit of deployment in .NET, just as the executable (DLL, EXE, OCX) is the smallest unit of deployment in Visual Basic 6, then this concept is much easier to grasp.

Public scope

As it does in Visual Basic 6, using the Public keyword makes a method or variable available to every object that uses the object. Although you normally declare methods and most properties as Public, you want to carefully evaluate all variables before setting them to Public. Think of programming as a pessimistic endeavor and try to limit exposure of your code as much as possible. Following this advice reduces mistakes and helps you write better code. If you need to have a public variable, consider a property instead; you can add some form of check in the code to prevent developers using your assemblies to set a variable with an incorrect value. You cannot check a Public variable until you use it, which gets very inefficient if you use it in a lot of places.

Shared

As I mention at the beginning of this "Scope" section, you have no global scope in Visual Basic .NET. The closest equivalent is *shared* scope, which isn't a scope at all (you can still add the `Public`, `Private` or `Friend` keyword to a `Shared` variable), although it can slightly alter the scope of a variable. If you use the keyword `Shared`, your variable is available to all instances of the same class. Listing 2-30 shows a `Shared` variable that you use as an incrementing counter to tell you the number of objects that you have create from the same class.

Listing 2-30: A Shared Variable

```
Public Class MyClass
    Private Shared m_intClassCount as Integer

    Public Sub IncrementCounter()
        m_intClassCount += 1
    End Sub
End Class
```

Here's a nice piece of information about `Shared` methods that can serve you well in the future: All constructors that you place inside `Modules` (meaning the `Module` keyword) are implicitly shared constructors. If you want to test this fact, simply place `Public Sub New()` inside a `Module` and read the resulting error. You want to be aware, too, that shared constructors can't take arguments, nor can you scope them as `Private`, `Public`, or `Friend`.

Error Handling

One of the nicest additions to Visual Basic .NET is structured error handling. If you work in Visual Basic, you know how weak the `On Error Goto` method can prove. If you're an ASP programmer, you no doubt pull your hair out every time you use `On Error Resume Next`. Although the procedure may take a bit of time to become familiar with, structure error handling is a much nicer way to handle an error.

You institute structured error handling by using the code block `Try...Catch...Finally`. Listing 2-31 shows a simple structured error handler. In this example, I purposefully raise an error to show both the error being handled in the `Catch` section of the block and the code that always runs in the `Finally` section of the block.

Listing 2-31: A Simple Error Handler

```
Imports SysCon = System.Console

Module Module1
```

```
   Sub Main()
     Try
       Err.Raise(1024)
     Catch e As Exception
       SysCon.WriteLine(e.ToString())
     Finally
       SysCon.WriteLine("This code runs every time!")
     End Try
   End Sub
End Module
```

Although I cover error handling in more detail in Chapter 10, for now you need to remember the following rules:

◆ Every `Try` block must contain a `Catch`, a `Finally`, or both. You can't try to do nothing.

◆ You can institute multiple `Catch` statements if you want to trap a specific type of exception. The most generic `Catch` must appear last because only one `Catch` section will run when an exception is raised. If you put the generic `Catch` first, the more specific `Catch` statement(s) never run.

◆ The code in the `Finally` portion of a block runs whether you throw an exception or not. Make sure that any code that you run here runs regardless of whether an exception is thrown.

The Good, the Bad, and the Ugly

Most of the rest of this chapter takes a quick look at some of the new features in Visual Basic .NET, along with some of the caveats that come along for the ride. Although I like the new language overall, I'm not going to pull any punches here. I include this section as a catalog of changes from Visual Basic 6 and divide it into "New features" (those features that don't break your Visual Basic 6 code), "Code breakers" (those features that do break your code), and "Behind the curtain" (features that enhance Visual Basic but have absolutely no effect on your code). I don't mean this section as an exhaustive list of all the new features in Visual Basic .NET, because I cover additional new features in other chapters.

New features

The following sections describe some additions to Visual Basic that can enhance your experience of the language. Most of these new features are simply changes in coding conventions. There were a few other new features when Visual Basic .NET debuted, but strong developer backlash got quite a few of them removed. This list is by no means exhaustive; for a more complete list, check the references in the summary section of this chapter.

OPERATIONS

Although your mathematical code from Visual Basic 6 still works in Visual Basic .NET, you have a couple new methods to use. Table 2-1 shows both the Visual Basic 6 method and the Visual Basic .NET methods for a variety of mathematical operations. Any of you who work with JavaScript, C++, Java, and so on are sure to recognize a lot of the new syntax. You can still use the old syntax with Visual Basic .NET; the new syntax is just a bit easier to type in.

TABLE 2-1 MATHEMATICAL OPERATIONS

Operation	Visual Basic 6 Syntax	Visual Basic .NET Syntax
Addition	`intAdd = intAdd + 1`	`intAdd += 1`
Subtraction	`intMinus = intMinus - 1`	`intMinus -= 1`
Multiplication	`intTimes = intTimes * 2`	`intTimes *= 2`
Division	`intDivide = intDivide/2`	`intDivide /= 2`
Integer Division	`intIDivide = intIDivide\2`	`intIDivide \= 2`
Exponent	`intExpo = intExpo ^ 2`	`intExpo ^= 2`

Although it's technically not a mathematical operation, you can also use the same methodology (operation plus equal sign) to concatenate strings, as in the following example:

```
strText &= " This text is added."
```

NEW DATA TYPES

For cases where you need a single character, you have a new data type: Char. In most of the examples I've seen using Char, you use the data type as part of an array rather than as a single character by itself. The Char data type is two bytes long to provide for the use of Unicode characters.

In the numeric field, you have a new data type known as a Short. It is 16 bits (two bytes) long, the same length as a Visual Basic 6 Integer. Integers are now 32 bits long.

INITIALIZERS

In Visual Basic .NET, you can now initialize a variable in the same line of code in which you declare it. Although I don't mention it there, Listing 2-29, earlier in this chapter, uses an initializer on the Protected variable in the Parent class.

```
Protected MyVariable As String = "Nothing"
```

USE KEYWORDS AS PROCEDURE NAMES

It is possible to create a method or property that is named the same as a keyword. In Listing 2-32, I show a property by the name of `Region`. Because `Region` is a Visual Basic .NET keyword, this property results in an error. Visual Basic .NET, however, permits you to use this keyword as a property if you use brackets around it. The I Buy Spy application (at `www.ibuyspy.com`), which was originally written in C#, uses keywords in some of its classes as well.

Listing 2-32: Creating a Property with the Same Name as a Keyword

```
Public ReadOnly Property [Region]() As String
    Get
        Return m_strRegion
    End Get
End Property
```

   While this feature might make your life easier when moving code from one language to another, I suggest that you don't use keywords from any language in your Visual Basic .NET code, and use this feature only as a backup when you have a routine you have already named with a keyword.

Code breakers

The following changes from Visual Basic 6 to Visual Basic .NET can break your Visual Basic 6 code if you port it directly to Visual Basic .NET. Some of these changes are unlikely to affect you if you use good coding practices, while others affect everyone.

NO MORE VARIANTS

Visual Basic .NET doesn't support variants. Although this change is likely to elicit a "good riddance" from many of you, the change also may well break some of your code. One of the more common uses of variants is along with parameters that are either strings or numerics. To work around the lack of variants, consider using an overloaded method instead. You can also take a generic object as a parameter, although that is far less efficient.

ARRAYS ARE 0-BASED

In Visual Basic 6, you can set your array base to 0 or 1 by using `Option Base`, which Visual Basic .NET doesn't support. (If you've used Visual Basic, you are familiar with `Option Base`, a phrase that allows you to set a different starting number for your arrays.) In addition, you can set the beginning and ending numbers in Visual Basic 6 for an array in a `Dim` statement. Visual Basic .NET doesn't support the following syntax, which sets the bounds of an array:

```
Dim strMyArray(1 to 10) As String
```

The only way to get around the fact that Visual Basic .NET supports only 0-based arrays is to use the `Microsoft.VisualBasic.Compatibility.VB6` namespace. The downside is a much slower array, so use with care. Be careful, as Microsoft has stated that this compatibility may not be supported in future versions of .NET.

CHANGES IN DEFAULT PROPERTIES

In Visual Basic .NET, you can create only a default property that uses parameters; there are no longer unparameterized default properties. Because I'm an advocate of explicit coding, however, I believe that default parameters are a pariah, so I did not use them. If you routinely use `frmMain = "Form Name"` to set your caption, the lack of default properties breaks your code.

The change in default properties affects more than just Forms code, however. If you write such code as `Response.Write objRS("LastName")`, you might face a shock in finding out that you must write the output out in long hand in Visual Basic .NET, as in the following example:

```
objRS.Fields("LastName").Value
```

CHANGES IN THE DATA TYPES

As you learned in Chapter 1 (Table 1-1 in the "Common Language Specification" section), an `Integer` is now 32 bits long instead of 16 bits, as it is in Visual Basic 6. In the same vein, `Long` is now 64 bits instead of 32 bits.

NO MORE FIXED-LENGTH STRINGS

If you like to constrain the size of your strings to match a `Char` field in a database, you're probably sad to hear that code such as `Dim strCustomerID As String * 7` has gone the way of the dinosaur. The `Microsoft.VisualBasic.Compatibility.VB6` namespace includes a type called `fixedlengthstring`, which does the same thing as the fixed-length string in Visual Basic 6. Once again, use the compatibility namespace sparingly, because Microsoft does not guarantee support in the future.

GRAVEYARD OF VISUAL BASIC PROJECTS

In Visual Basic 6, Microsoft included two project types that are now defunct. The first is the IIS Application, which created a special type of class file called a `webclass`. To enable DHTML development in Visual Basic, Microsoft also created an ActiveX document project. Both of these projects are now defunct in Visual Studio .NET, and their functionality is either discarded or partially folded into the .NET Framework.

YOU MUST INITIALIZE OPTIONAL VALUES

Because I consider initializing an optional value a good coding practice, this change doesn't affect my code. If you don't usually pass a variable, however, and then use `IsMissing()` to find out whether it passes, you need to rework your code a bit to initialize each optional value. (Oh, by the way, IsMissing() is gone, too.) The following code shows two functions with optional values. The first tests for IsMissing, while the other sets the optional value:

```
Public Function BadOpt(Optional varMyVar as Variant) as Boolean
    If IsMissing(varMyVar) then
        BadOpt = False
    Else
        BadOpt = True
    End If
End Function

Public Function GoodOpt(Optional intMyInt as Integer = 0) As Boolean
    If intMyInt = 0 then
        GoodOpt = False
    Else
        GoodOpt = True
    End If
End Function
```

CHANGES TO VARIABLE DECLARATION

In Visual Basic 6, you can Dim a variety of objects on the same line, even if their data types are different. If you have multiple variables on the same line, each one must specify a data type, even if they're all the same. If you fail to data-type a variable, it types as a variant. The following code shows how you could place multiple variable declarations on a single line:

```
Dim strMyString As String, intMyInteger As Integer
Dim lngMyLong1 as Long, lngMyLong2 As Long
```

In Visual Basic .NET, you can still declare multiple variables on a single line, but each one must have the same data type, as follow:

```
Dim lngMyLong1, lngMyLong2 as Long
```

I advocate putting each variable declaration on its own line to avoid confusion as to what type each variable is. The result is also a bit more readable, which helps preserve the maintainability of the code that you write.

WHILE ... WEND IS NOW WHILE ... END WHILE

The Do ...Loop isn't gone in Visual Basic .NET. While ...End While, however, seems to be the preferred method to code loops. This change seems a little strange to me, because Microsoft deprecated While...Wend in Visual Basic 6. While ...End While is likely to break some applications. The following example uses While ...End While to increment a counter:

```
While intCounter < 1000
    intCounter += 1
End While
```

NULL PROPAGATION IS DEAD

In Visual Basic 6, you can easily avoid errors in a database application by concatenating an empty string to a NULL value. In the following example, you add an empty string to ensure that the NULL values from the recordset are cast as a string and do not error out the application:

```
strMyField = "" & objRS.Fields("MyField").Value
```

In Visual Basic .NET, you must rewrite this code to handle the database NULL, as shown in the following snippet:

```
If Not IsDBNull(objDataRow("Region")) Then
    m_strRegion = CStr(objDataRow("Region"))
End If
```

Summary

In this chapter, I present the basic structure of a Visual Basic .NET program. I lead you through the task of creating programs with a variety of reference and value types and end with a list of changes in Visual Basic .NET. This list, although by no means exhaustive, gives you a good starting point in writing your own Visual Basic .NET programs.

If you want additional information about Visual Basic .NET, check out the following Web sites, many of which are critical of the changes from Visual Basic to Visual Basic .NET:

- ◆ http://home.earthlink.net/~butlerbob/VBNet/index.htm: Bob Butler's site contains an exhaustive list of the new features and changes in Visual Basic .NET, including a fairly detailed analysis of the changes and how they affect your programming.

- ◆ www.totalenviro.com/vb7: Bill McCarthy provides a shorter list than Bob's but also includes wish lists for Visual Basic .NET and some interesting code samples that you're not likely to see anywhere else.

- ◆ www.mvps.org/vb/rants/vfred.htm: Karl Peterson, a Visual Basic Most Valuable Professional (MVP), provides on his Visual Fred page a long list of changes that break your code.

◆ `www.dotnet101.com`: This site offers a few Visual Basic .NET samples, along with a variety of ASP.NET applications.

◆ `www.c-sharpcorner.com`: This site is dedicated to programming in C#. You find a couple really nice Visual Basic .NET examples to peruse, however, including an interesting database-explorer application.

◆ `www.gotdotnet.com/team/vb/`: This site has a new Visual Basic section. Check out the samples at the bottom of the page.

Chapter 3

ASP.NET

IN THIS CHAPTER

◆ Windows Forms and WebForms

◆ Web controls, HTML controls, and custom user controls

◆ Configuration of your Web application

◆ Debugging and tracing

WITH THE VISUAL BASIC .NET INFORMATION from Chapter 2 under your belt, you're ready to get into the meat of ASP.NET. In this chapter, I cover ASP.NET and the .NET Framework as it deals with the creation of Web applications.

ASP.NET and the .NET Framework

In many ways, the term ASP.NET is a misnomer, because the .NET version of Active Server Pages (ASP) is much more than a simple replacement for ASP. The first change is using compiled languages rather than interpreted languages. Developers who code strictly in ASP have long been considered pariahs by other developers. While this is unfair in many instances, there is no argument that ASP allows developers to break many of the rules of good programming practice. In some instances, ASP actually encourages or forces a developer to make some bad decisions.

One of the biggest points of contention with traditional ASP, is the fact that it uses weakly typed languages. To put this in simpler terms, when you declare a variable, you are unable to say whether or not it is a String, an Integer, or any other specific type. The language infers what type you have declared by how it is used. In traditional ASP, everything is a variant.

ASP.NET, on the other hand, uses strongly typed languages. While you can still generically declare your types by declaring them as an object (from the System. Object class), it is not the norm.

The presentation tier

ASP.NET, as was its predecessor, ASP, is designed primarily as a *presentation-layer* technology; that is, if you use ASP.NET correctly, you deal with displaying information to users and allowing them to interact with the system. ASP.NET migrates most of the code to .NET components. Although the separation of code and user

83

interface has been the push for ASP since the ASP 1.0 beta, the typical ASP Web application is mainly inline code containing presentation, business rules, and data-access tiers in one page.

One reason for this trend (placing code from the presentation, business, and data layers) is the amount of work necessary to migrate code from a variant-only, inline structure (ASP) to a data-typed, function-oriented structure (Visual Basic). While there are things you can do to make this easier, it is still a bit of a pain. Another reason is books and Web sites dedicated to ASP generally pushed an inline structure over functions and subroutines. And, finally, coding an inline ASP page is simply easier than building a Visual Basic COM component. As ASP.NET uses Visual Basic .NET, migration of code is no longer an issue, as you employ exactly the same structure for ASP.NET and the components that hold code your pages use.

Because the languages are the same in both your page and in the components that lie behind the page, separating the business rules (components) from the presentation logic (ASP.NET) is becoming easier. The primary benefit of this type of coding is the capability to create different user interfaces (UIs) for your desktop and Web applications but utilize the same code behind the scenes. I cover the reason for using the words *code behind* in the "CodeBehind" section later in this chapter.

WINDOWS FORMS

So this book is about ASP.NET, right? Then why am I covering Windows Forms? Aren't they a desktop-application construct? Okay, you caught me. But I have a very good reason for writing about Windows Forms in this chapter (and again in Chapter 7): The technology of ASP.NET really covers both Windows Forms and WebForms.

That's a bit of oversimplification, because the method of building each is a blend of the methodologies used in both Visual InterDev and Visual Basic. Although the deployment is quite different, you find a lot of common technology in Windows Forms and WebForms. Microsoft also put a great deal of effort into making the deployment of the application inconsequential to the coding structure. The idea is that the presentation layer should not have any bearing on the application that it drives. Although COM attempted to move developers into this paradigm (the n-tier paradigm), .NET pretty much forces it, unless you work hard to buck the system.

For those of you who come from a Visual Basic 6 background, working with Windows Forms in the Visual Studio .NET IDE is very familiar. (See Appendix A for more information about the Visual Studio .NET IDE.) The coding of the form, however, is very different. In Visual Basic 6, all the form code is hidden from the developer, while .NET exposes all the placement code to the developer.

While this book does not focus on Windows Forms, I cover the similarity between Windows Forms and WebForms a bit more in Chapter 7, where you will learn to code a Windows Forms application.

To illustrate the differences in the older Visual Basic 6 model and the .NET model, I'm going to create the form shown in Figure 3-1 in both languages. I visit this form again in the following section about WebForms to help compare Windows Forms and WebForms. Listings 3-1 and 3-2 show the code that I created from each of these forms. In Listing 3-1, you see the form code, which normally remains hidden from the developer. I use the default name Form1 in each to maintain consistency. If you would like to see this code in your applications, open the .frm file in Notepad or some other ASCII text editor. I show it here as a comparison to how all of the code is exposed in Visual Basic .NET.

Figure 3-1: A simple Windows desktop form.

Listing 3-1: A Simple Form in Visual Basic 6

```
VERSION 5.00
Begin VB.Form Form1
    Caption         =   "My Simple Form"
    ClientHeight    =   570
    ClientLeft      =   60
    ClientTop       =   345
    ClientWidth     =   4635
    LinkTopic       =   "Form1"
    ScaleHeight     =   570
    ScaleWidth      =   4635
    StartUpPosition =   3  'Windows Default
    Begin VB.Label Label1
        Caption         =   "Hello, World!"
        Height          =   495
        Left            =   0
        TabIndex        =   0
        Top             =   0
        Width           =   4575
    End
End
Attribute VB_Name = "Form1"
Attribute VB_GlobalNameSpace = False
Attribute VB_Creatable = False
Attribute VB_PredeclaredId = True
Attribute VB_Exposed = False

'This is the only line that shows up in the
```

Continued

Listing 3-1 *(Continued)*

```
'     code window for the form. All code above
'     hidden from the developer.
Option Explicit
```

 You can find the code from Listing 3-1 on the companion Web site (www.wiley.com/extras) under ChO3SDK.zip (SDK version) or ChO3VS.zip (Visual Studio .NET version). When you unzip the download, look for the VB6Form folder.

Compare Listing 3-1, the hidden portion of a Visual Basic form (.frm file), with the Visual Basic .NET example in Listing 3-2. The section between the #Region keywords contains the form setup information (the portion that was hidden in Visual Basic 6). You can edit this information in the Visual Studio .NET Integrated Development Environment (IDE); you no longer have to open the file in an ASCII editor to edit this. Note, however, that editing this section is discouraged, as was editing the .frm file in Visual Basic 6. The code in Listing 3-2 is exactly as it is produced in Visual Studio .NET.

Listing 3-2: A Windows Forms Application in Visual Basic .NET

```
Public Class Form1
   Inherits System.Windows.Forms.Form

#Region " Windows Form Designer generated code "

   Public Sub New()
     MyBase.New()

     'This call is required by the Windows Form Designer.
     InitializeComponent()

     'Add any initialization after the InitializeComponent() call

   End Sub

   'Form overrides dispose to clean up the component list.
   Protected Overloads Overrides Sub Dispose(ByVal disposing As Boolean)
     If disposing Then
       If Not (components Is Nothing) Then
         components.Dispose()
       End If
```

```vb
    End If
    MyBase.Dispose(disposing)
  End Sub

  'Required by the Windows Form Designer
  Private components As System.ComponentModel.IContainer

  'NOTE: The following procedure is required by the Windows Form Designer
  'It can be modified using the Windows Form Designer.
  'Do not modify it using the code editor.
  Friend WithEvents Label1 As System.Windows.Forms.Label
  <System.Diagnostics.DebuggerStepThrough()> Private Sub InitializeComponent()
    Me.Label1 = New System.Windows.Forms.Label()
    Me.SuspendLayout()
    '
    'Label1
    '
    Me.Label1.Name = "Label1"
    Me.Label1.Size = New System.Drawing.Size(216, 23)
    Me.Label1.TabIndex = 0
    Me.Label1.Text = "Hello, World!"
    '
    'Form1
    '.
    Me.AutoScaleBaseSize = New System.Drawing.Size(5, 13)
    Me.ClientSize = New System.Drawing.Size(304, 37)
    Me.Controls.AddRange(New System.Windows.Forms.Control() {Me.Label1})
    Me.Name = "Form1"
    Me.Text = "My Simple Form"
    Me.ResumeLayout(False)

  End Sub

#End Region

End Class
```

You can find the code from Listing 3-2 on the companion Web site (www.wiley.com/extras) under Ch03SDK.zip (SDK version) or Ch03VS.zip (Visual Studio .NET version). When you unzip, look for the WindowsFormVB folder.

As mentioned a moment ago, to see the Visual Basic 6 form code in your own projects, open your .frm file in an ASCII text editor such as Notepad. On the companion Web site, in the Chapter 3 folder of the Visual Studio section, you find three projects: VB6Form, WinFormVB, and WinFormCSharp. I use the same UI (from Figure 3-1) in each of these projects. I created the Visual Basic .NET and C# versions to illustrate the fact that ASP.NET is the underlying presentation layer technology in each of these forms.

WEBFORMS

WebForms may seem a bit familiar to both ASP and Visual Basic developers. The code structure is more like that of ASP in nature, but the IDE methodology (drag and drop) is more like the process of building a Visual Basic Standard Executable. The following example is a simple page that I designed in the same manner as the Windows Forms in the preceding section.

I talk more about building a .NET WebForm application in Chapter 6. This concept is built on throughout Part II of the book.

In Figure 3-2, I show a simple WebForm application with the default Visual Studio .NET name: WebForm1. In a real-world application, I'd rename this file to better fit the application. I've left the default name here to match your application if you want to build a WebForm application in Visual Studio .NET.

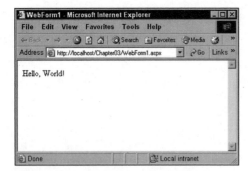

Figure 3-2: A simple Hello, World! WebForm.

According to the text in the preceding paragraph, this should be an application with the default Visual Studio .NET name WebForm1.

The code for the application in Figure 3-2 is shown in Listing 3-3. This particular form contains a simple label control that displays the words *Hello, World!*

Listing 3-3: WebForm Code in ASP.NET

```
<%@ Page Language="vb" AutoEventWireup="false"
Codebehind="WebForm1.aspx.vb" Inherits="Chapter03.WebForm1"%>
<!DOCTYPE HTML PUBLIC "-//W3C//DTD HTML 4.0 Transitional//EN">
<HTML>
  <HEAD>
    <title>WebForm1</title>
    <meta name="GENERATOR"
      content="Microsoft Visual Studio .NET 7.0">
    <meta name="CODE_LANGUAGE" content="Visual Basic 7.0">
    <meta name="vs_defaultClientScript"
      content="JavaScript">
    <meta name="vs_targetSchema"
      content="http://schemas.microsoft.com/intellisense/ie5">
  </HEAD>
  <body>
    <!-- A Web control -->
    <form id="Form1" method="post" runat="server">
      <asp:Label id="Label1" runat="server">
    Hello, World!
    </asp:Label>
    </form>
  </body>
</HTML>
```

You can find the code from Listing 3-3 under `Ch03SDK.zip` (SDK version) or `Ch03VS.zip` (Visual Studio .NET version) on the companion Web site (`www.wiley.com/extras`). When you unzip, look in the Chapter03 folder for `WebForm1.aspx`. There is an `.msi` file to install the Web application, as well as an `install.txt` file with instructions.

Building a single WebForm does have a downside if you're using the Visual Studio .NET IDE. By default, each solution creates a new Web application on your server, much as in Visual InterDev. For experimentation alone, the creation of a full solution can get unwieldy.

In the following sections, I discuss the types of controls that are available to you in creating WebForms. I cover *HTML controls,* which pretty much mimic the different elements available for forms in standard HTML, as well as *Web controls,* which render as HTML on the client, but are run server-side. You may see Web controls called *Server controls* in some documentation. I prefer not to use this nomenclature for two reasons. First, you can also run HTML controls on the server also;

this is done to preserve state. Second, the namespace for Web controls is `System.Web.UI.WebControls`; as such, using the name Server controls further abstracts these controls from their namespace.

Whether you use HTML controls or Web controls, the resulting HTML sent to the client is essentially the same. The main difference comes both in the code used to produce the control and the manner in which it is handled.

In the rest of this section on WebForms, I add new pages to the WebForm project (Chapter03.vbproj). I call the new pages WebFormHTML and WebFormWeb. The first uses HTML controls, while the second uses Web controls.

HTML CONTROLS   HTML controls are very similar to the tags that you use in your current ASP and HTML pages. You have controls for your form elements, such as text boxes, radio buttons, check boxes, and buttons, as well for as horizontal rules, tables, and images. In coding HTML controls in an ASCII text editor, you can see that these controls appear exactly the same as they do in normal HTML, with the exception of those controls that run on the server side, which will use `runat="server"`. The main reason for HTML controls running on the server is to maintain state (which item is chosen, what the text box contains, and so forth).

Figure 3-3 shows a WebForm with HTML controls. I've chosen a variety of controls for this example so that we can compare it to the Web controls version of the page, which I get to in the next section.

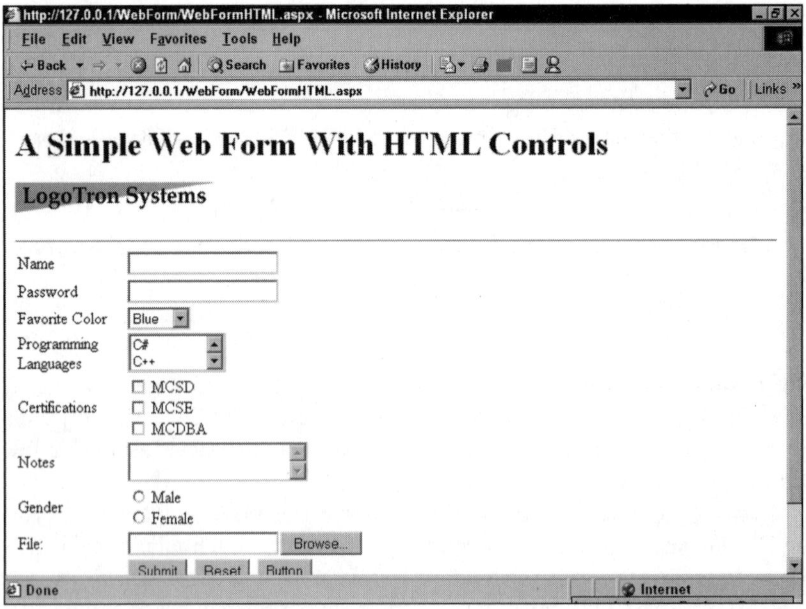

Figure 3-3: A WebForm with HTML controls.

Listing 3-4 shows the code for the WebForm in Figure 3-3. As you go through the code, pay attention to the fact that some controls have the attribute `runat="server"`.

Listing 3-4: A WebForm with HTML Controls

```
<%@ Page Language="vb" AutoEventWireup="false"
    Codebehind="WebFormHTML.aspx.vb" Inherits="Chapter03.WebFormHTML"%>
<!DOCTYPE HTML PUBLIC "-//W3C//DTD HTML 4.0 Transitional//EN">
<HTML>

<HEAD>
  <meta name="GENERATOR" content="Microsoft Visual Studio .NET 7.0">
  <meta name="CODE_LANGUAGE" content="Visual Basic 7.0">
  <meta name="vs_defaultClientScript" content="JavaScript">
  <meta name="vs_targetSchema"
        content="http://schemas.microsoft.com/intellisense/ie5">
</HEAD>

<body>

<form id="WebFormHTML" method="post" runat="server">
  <h1>A Simple Web Form with HTML Controls</h1>
  <p><img alt="Logo" src="images/logo.gif"></p>
  <hr width="100%" size="1">
  <table cellspacing="1" cellpadding="1" width="400" border="0">
   <tr>
    <td style="WIDTH: 107px">Name</td>
    <td><input type="text" name="strName" id="Text1" size="20"></td>
   </tr>
   <tr>
    <td style="WIDTH: 107px">Password</td>
    <td><input type="password" size="20"></td>
   </tr>
   <tr>
    <td style="WIDTH: 107px">Favorite Color</td>
    <td><select name="intCertifications" runat="server">
      <option value="1" selected>Blue</option>
      <option value="2">Green</option>
      <option value="3">Red</option>
      <option value="4">Purple</option>
     </select></td>
```

Continued

Listing 3-4 *(Continued)*

```
 </tr>
 <tr>
  <td style="WIDTH: 107px">Programming Languages</td>
  <td><select multiple size="2"
         name="intLanguages" runat="server">
    <option value="1">C#</option>
    <option value="2">C++</option>
    <option value="3">JScript</option>
    <option value="4">Visual Basic</option>
    <option value></option>
   </select></td>
 </tr>
 <tr>
  <td style="WIDTH: 107px">Certifications</td>
  <td>
   <p><input type="checkbox" name="chkMCSD" value="ON">
       MCSD<br>
      <input type="checkbox" name="chkMCSE" value="ON">
       MCSE<br>
      <input type="checkbox" name="chkMCDBA" value="ON">
       MCDBA</p>
  </td>
 </tr>
 <tr>
  <td style="WIDTH: 107px">Notes</td>
  <td><textarea name="strNotes" rows="2" cols="20" /><td>
 </tr>
 <tr>
  <td style="WIDTH: 107px">Gender</td>
  <td>
   <p><input type="radio" name="radGender"> Male<br>
    <input type="radio" name="radGender"> Female</p>
  </td>
 </tr>
 <tr>
  <td style="WIDTH: 107px">File:</td>
  <td><input type="file"> </td>
 </tr>
 <tr>
  <td style="WIDTH: 107px"></td>
  <td><input type="submit" value="Submit" id="Submit1">
       <input type="reset" value="Reset"> 
```

```
        <input type="button" value="Button"></td>
  </tr>
 </table>
</form>
<hr width="100%" size="1">
</body>
</HTML>
```

You can find the code from Listing 3-4 under ChO3SDK.zip (SDK version) or ChO3VS.zip (Visual Studio .NET version) on the companion Web site (www.wiley.com/extras). When you unzip, look for the Chapter03 folder and find WebFormHTML.aspx.

Most of the controls in this example run on the client side, which is the default. This is the same manner in which today's HTML forms run. When you submit a standard HTML form, you have to write code for each of the controls on the form if you want its state maintained. In the Microsoft world, this programming would likely be done in ASP.

In the form in Listing 3-4, I have made it so quite a few of the controls run server side, using runat="server". To see this in action, run the form in a browser and change the color, select some programming languages, or check some certifications. Now, submit the form by clicking the Submit button. You'll see that your choices are saved after you submit. If you are not 100% certain that the choices are being submitted, click the Reset button: if the form has been submitted, this has no effect; if the form has not been submitted, your choices will disappear. You can also examine the difference in the code by viewing the HTML source in your browser.

I discuss building WebForms with HTML controls in more detail in Chapter 7.

Table 3-1 shows the HTML controls available in ASP.NET, as well as the HTML that the control produces. The HTML shown in the table is the HTML sent to the client browser. This is the same HTML you encounter in the .aspx page. Older browsers will ignore the style formatting that some of the tags use, such as the Label control, so the HTML in the .aspx file will be the same as what you see when you view the source in your browser.

TABLE 3-1 HTML CONTROLS

HTML Control	HTML Equivalent
Label	`<DIV style="DISPLAY: inline; WIDTH: 70px; HEIGHT: 15px" ms_positioning="FlowLayout">Label</DIV>`
Button	`<input type="button" value="Button">`
Reset Button	`<input type="reset" value="Reset">`
Submit Button	`<input type="submit" value="Submit">`
Text Field	`<input type="text">`
Text Area	`<TEXTAREA rows="2" cols="20"></TEXTAREA>`
File Field	`<input type="file">`
Password Field	`<input type="password">`
Checkbox	`<input type="checkbox">`
Radio Button	`<input type="radio">`
Hidden Field	`<input type="hidden">`
Table	`<table><tr><td></td></tr></table>`
Linear Layout Panel	`<DIV style="WIDTH: 100px; HEIGHT: 100px" ms_positioning="FlowLayout"></DIV>`
Grid Layout Panel	`<DIV style="WIDTH: 100px; POSITION: relative; HEIGHT: 100px" ms_positioning="GridLayout"></DIV>`
Image	`<IMG alt="" src="images/logo.gif">`
Listbox	`<SELECT size="2"> <OPTION>Option 1</OPTION> </SELECT>`
DropDown	`<SELECT> <OPTION selected>Option 1</OPTION> </SELECT>`
Horizontal Rule	`<HR width="100%" SIZE="1">`

WEB CONTROLS   Web controls also go out to the client browser as simple HTML. The main difference is that you group Web controls by functionality, which means that a single Web control can map to multiple HTML tags. In addition, Web controls contain additional functionality to make them more dynamic. A prime example of this additional functionality is the `RadionButtonList` control, which enables you to create a group of radio buttons from a data source, an XML document, or an array.

Figure 3-4 shows a form that uses Web controls. Notice that the form is very similar in appearance to the form shown in Figure 3-3. The major differences take place behind the scenes. You can see the code differences in Listing 3-5.

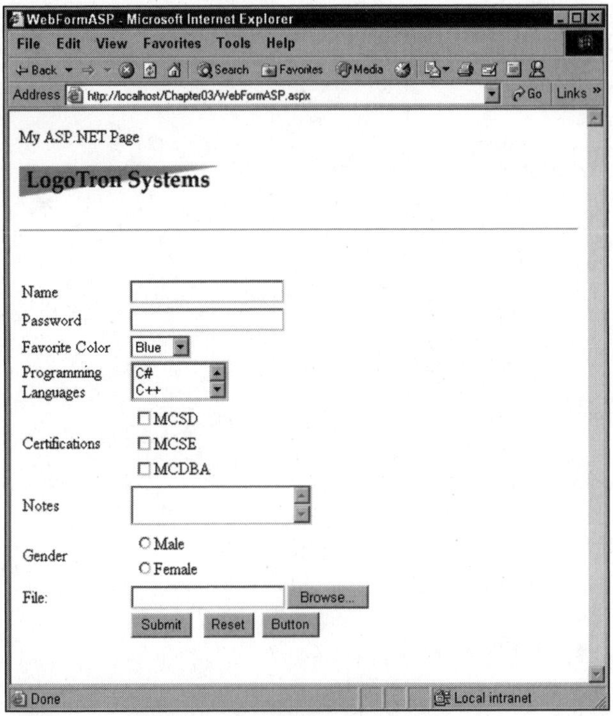

Figure 3-4: A WebForm with Web controls.

The code to create the page shown in Figure 3-4 is detailed in Listing 3-5. Notice that each of the Web controls have tags that begin with an XML namespace asp. Adding this namespace to the tag tells the CLR to preprocess this tag as a Web control. I've included only the body section of the code, because that's where the differences lie.

Listing 3-5: A WebForm with Web Controls

```
<%@ Page Language="vb" AutoEventWireup="false"
Codebehind="WebFormASP.aspx.vb"
Inherits="Chapter03.WebFormASP"%>
<!DOCTYPE HTML PUBLIC "-//W3C//DTD HTML 4.0 Transitional//EN">
<HTML>
  <HEAD>
    <title>WebFormASP</title>
```

Continued

Listing 3-5 *(Continued)*

```
  <meta name="GENERATOR"
   content="Microsoft Visual Studio .NET 7.0">
  <meta name="CODE_LANGUAGE" content="Visual Basic 7.0">
  <meta name="vs_defaultClientScript" content="JavaScript">
  <meta name="vs_targetSchema"
   content="http://schemas.microsoft.com/intellisense/ie5">
</HEAD>
<body>
  <form id="WebFormASP" method="post" runat="server">
    <p>
      <asp:label id="Label1" runat="server" Width="323" Height="19">
My ASP.NET Page</asp:label>
    </p>
    <p>
      <asp:Image id="Image1" runat="server"
        ImageUrl="images/logo.gif" />
    </p>
    <hr width="100%" size="1">
    <table cellspacing="1" cellpadding="1" width="400" border="0">
      <tbody>
        <tr>
          <td style="WIDTH: 107px">Name</td>
          <td>
            <asp:TextBox id="TextBox1" runat="server" />
          </td>
        </tr>
        <tr>
          <td style="WIDTH: 107px">Password</td>
          <td>
            <asp:TextBox id="TextBox2" runat="server" textmode="Password" />
          </td>
        </tr>
        <tr>
          <td style="WIDTH: 107px">Favorite Color</td>
          <td>
            <asp:DropDownList id="DropDownList1" runat="server">
              <asp:ListItem Value="Blue">Blue</asp:ListItem>
              <asp:ListItem Value="Green">Green</asp:ListItem>
              <asp:ListItem Value="Red">Red</asp:ListItem>
            </asp:DropDownList>
          </td>
        </tr>
        <tr>
          <td style="WIDTH: 107px">Programming Languages</td>
```

```
      <td>
        <asp:ListBox id="ListBox1" runat="server" Rows="2">
          <asp:ListItem Value="C#">C#</asp:ListItem>
          <asp:ListItem Value="C++">C++</asp:ListItem>
          <asp:ListItem Value="JScript">JScript</asp:ListItem>
          <asp:ListItem Value="Visual Basic">
      Visual Basic</asp:ListItem>
        </asp:ListBox>
      </td>
  </tr>
  <tr>
    <td style="WIDTH: 107px">Certifications</td>
    <td>
      <p>
        <asp:CheckBoxList id="CheckBoxList1" runat="server">
          <asp:ListItem Value="MCSD">MCSD</asp:ListItem>
          <asp:ListItem Value="MCSE">MCSE</asp:ListItem>
          <asp:ListItem Value="MCDBA">MCDBA</asp:ListItem>
        </asp:CheckBoxList></p>
    </td>
  </tr>
  <tr>
    <td style="WIDTH: 107px">Notes</td>
    <td>
      <asp:TextBox id="TextBox3" runat="server"
      TextMode="MultiLine" /></td>
  <tr>
    <td style="WIDTH: 107px; HEIGHT: 28px">Gender</td>
    <td style="HEIGHT: 28px">
      <p>
        <asp:RadioButtonList id="RadioButtonList1" runat="server">
          <asp:ListItem Value="Male">Male</asp:ListItem>
          <asp:ListItem Value="Female">Female</asp:ListItem>
        </asp:RadioButtonList></p>
    </td>
  </tr>
  <tr>
    <td style="WIDTH: 107px">File:</td>
    <td><input type="file"> </td>
  </tr>
  <tr>
    <td style="WIDTH: 107px"></td>
    <td>
      <asp:Button id="Submit" runat="server" Text="Submit" />
```

Continued

Listing 3-5 *(Continued)*

```
             
            <asp:Button id="Reset" runat="server" Text="Reset" />
             
            <asp:Button id="Button" runat="server" Text="Button" />
          </td>
          </TD></tr>
        </tbody>
      </table>
    </form>
  </body>
</HTML>
```

You can find the code from the page for Listing 3-5 under ChO3SDK.zip (SDK version) or ChO3VS.zip (Visual Studio .NET version) on the companion Web site (www.wiley.com/extras). When you unzip, look for the Chapter03 folder and find WebFormASP.aspx.

Each of these controls runs on the server side, which is the default. Running controls on the server is much different than in our current ASP applications and provides a lot of benefits, including maintaining the current state of the control. If this does not seem like a major benefit, picture doing the same thing in traditional ASP where you have to retrieve each value and place it in the control when the user inputs invalid data. Now, you only need to drop a control on a page and all of this additional work is handled for you.

You're likely to notice a few differences about the Web control version of this form as you work with it. The following list describes these differences:

♦ As you submit the form, the values of each of the controls are saved without any additional work on your part. The value is saved because of the attribute runat=server and not because this is a Web control. The only real difference between the Web control and an HTML control at this point is the fact that Web controls have to be run on the server, while you have a choice with most HTML controls.

♦ Multiple HTML tags share a single Web control. You use a TextBox control, for example, to create text, passwords, and multiline (or textarea) fields on your form. If you use Visual Studio .NET, you will see that you only have a TextBox control in the toolbox. You will set the TextMode attribute to change the type of text box.

♦ There are Web controls to represent a group of check boxes as a single item. The same is true for radio buttons. Having a single control for each of these cases makes binding data to the HTML much easier.

I left a couple of HTML controls in the form because

♦ There is no Web control version of the horizontal rule.

♦ The Web control buttons are designed to fire off events rather than just submit the page. I cover buttons in the "CodeBehind" section later in this chapter.

Table 3-2 shows the Web controls available in ASP.NET, as well as the HTML that the control produces. I also include some notes to help you use these controls in your own code.

TABLE 3-2 WEB CONTROLS IN ASP.NET

Web Control	HTML Equivalent	Notes
Label	\\	
TextBox	\<input type="text"> \<input type="password"> \<textaread>\</textarea>	
Button	\<input type="button"> \<input type="submit">	To change type to submit, you need to code a server-side event handler.
Link Button	\<a id="LinkButton1" href= "javascript:__doPostBack ('LinkButton1',''>	
\</a>	This hyperlink acts as a form submit button, differentiating it from the hyperlink control.	
Image Button	\<input type="image">	
Hyperlink	\<a>\</a> \<a href="">\</a>	Although you can use this control as an anchor, the real strength comes in that it's a dynamically controlled hyperlink.
DropDownList	\<select>\<option> \</option>\</select>	

Continued

TABLE 3-2 WEB CONTROLS IN ASP.NET *(Continued)*

Web Control	HTML Equivalent	Notes
ListBox	<select size="4"> <option></option> </select>	
DataGrid		You use this control with ADO.NET to create a data-driven table.
DataList		You use this control with ADO.NET to create a data-driven drop-down list.
Repeater		
CheckBox	<input type="checkbox">	
CheckBoxList	<table id="CheckBoxList1" border="0"><tr><td> <input type="checkbox">	
</td></tr></table>	This control creates a check-box list. You can attach it to a data source.	
RadioButtonList	<table id="RadioButtonList1" border="0"><tr><td> <input type="radio">	
</td></tr></table>	This control creates a radio-button list. You can attach it to a data source.	
RadioButton	<input type="radio">	
Image	<img src="">	
Panel	<div></div>	
Calendar	Varies	This control creates a table that contains a calendar.
AdRotator	Varies	This control is similar to the ad rotator component in ASP.
Table	<table><tr><td> </td></tr></table>	You use this control for more dynamic content than the HTML control version provides.

Web Control	HTML Equivalent	Notes
RequiredValidator	Varies based on the control being validated.	This control checks to make sure that a specified control isn't empty.
CompareValidator	Varies based on the control being validated.	This control compares the value of a specified control to a value or list of values.
RangeValidator	Varies based on the control being validated.	This control compares the value of a specified control to a set a range of values.
RegularExpressionValidator	Varies based on the control being validated.	This control compares the value of a specified control to a regular expression.
CustomValidator	Varies based on the control being validated.	This control uses a custom script to validate a specified control.
ValidationSummary	Varies based on the number of controls being validated.	This control creates a summary for the validation controls in a form. It's useful for forms that you want people to submit over the Internet.
CrystalReportsViewer	Varies based on the Crystal Report being viewed.	You use this control to place a report created in Crystal Reports into your Web page. (Crystal Reports is a third-party tool for creating reports.)

CREATING CUSTOM USER CONTROLS

One nice addition to ASP.NET is the capability to create your own custom controls. Although you could include files using an include tag and create pagelets in earlier versions of ASP, you have no traditional ASP equivalent to custom user controls.

User controls can consist of HTML, ASP.NET, or a mixture of ASP.NET and HTML. You create them just as you do any other ASP.NET page. You save your user controls with an ASCX extension (ASCX is an ASP.NET user control file; ASPX is an ASP.NET page). Listing 3-6 shows a simple user control that displays a common header. Listing 3-7 shows how to use this user control in your own page.

Listing 3-6: A Simple User Control (header.ascx)

```
<%@ Control Language="vb" AutoEventWireup="false"
Codebehind="header.ascx.vb"
Inherits="Chapter03.header"
TargetSchema="http://schemas.microsoft.com/intellisense/ie5" %>
<table width="100%">
<tr>
<td><a href="WebFormHTML.aspx">HTML Controls</a></td>
<td><a href="WebFormASP.aspx">ASP Controls</a></td>
<td><a href="WebFormBehind.aspx">CodeBehind</a></td>
</tr>
</table>
```

You can find the code from the page for Listing 3-6 under `ChO3SDK.zip` (SDK version) or `ChO3VS.zip` (Visual Studio .NET version) on the companion Web site (`www.wiley.com/extras`). When you unzip, look for the Chapter03 folder and find `header.ascx`.

Note that the user control uses a slightly different @ directive than an ASPX page. In this instance, the @ `Page` directive becomes an @ `Control` directive.

The @ directives, including @ `Page` and @ `Control` are covered later in this chapter, in the "CodeBehind" section.

The user control in this example creates a set of three hyperlinks to include in your pages. To use this control in another page, you have to add a line to the page to register the component, as well as a tag to place the control in the page. Listing 3-7 has a simple ASPX page that includes the control from Listing 3-6.

Listing 3-7: Calling the Header User Control from an ASP.NET Page

```
<%@ Page Language="vb" AutoEventWireup="false"
Codebehind="TestUserControl.aspx.vb"
Inherits="Chapter03.TestUserControl"%>

<%@ Register Tagprefix="uc1"
Tagname="header" Src="header.ascx" %>

<HTML>
```

```
<HEAD>
    <title>Test the User Control</title>
</HEAD>
<body
    <form id="Form1" method="post" runat="server">
        <uc1:header id="Header1" runat="server" />
    </form>
</body>
</HTML>
```

 You can find the code from the page for Listing 3-7 under ChO3SDK.zip (SDK version) or ChO3VS.zip (Visual Studio .NET version) on the companion Web site (www.wiley.com/extras). When you unzip, look for the Chapter03 folder and find TestUserConrol.aspx.

The two important sections here are the @ tag, which contains the directives to register the control, and the line that includes the control.

♦ **The @ Register tag:** This sits at the top of the page, just below the @ Page tag. You can register multiple user controls with the same tag prefix, but you must use a tag prefix other than asp, because that's the tag prefix (XML namespace) for Web controls. Here's the tag:

```
<%@ Register Tagprefix="uc1"
Tagname="header" Src="header.ascx" %>
```

♦ **The tag that includes the control:** Since the tag prefix was set to uc1 and the tag name to header, this tag has the format <uc1:header>. The entire tag is shown here:

```
<uc1:header id="Header1" runat="server" />
```

This example is very simplistic. In your own user controls, you can have any amount of code to render the control. You can also use CodeBehind (covered later in this chapter) to create complete objects as controls. In the ASP world, user controls are closest in nature to ActiveX controls, the main differences being that you can code a user control as HTML only (as in Listing 3-7) and that user controls are not restricted to Internet Explorer.

The business rules and data tiers

So far, I have been discussing the presentation tier, which is the primary focus of ASP.NET, at least as far as the ASPX page is concerned. Throughout most of this book, I leave the business rules and data access in the CodeBehind file (which is covered later in this chapter). By separating the code from the HTML, the page becomes easier to maintain than a traditional ASP page, but this is not true n-tier, object-oriented programming.

Let me run through a quick example of a multitiered application. To do this, I've created a presentation tier ASPX page, a business rules tier class, and a data access class. Because data access is the focus of Part III, "Working with Data — ADO.NET," I'll just create a stub class that always returns the same answer. The assumption here is that the stub class would be filled in with some form of database connectivity when the application is completed.

The basics of the application are as follows:

1. The ASPX page creates an object from the BusinessRules class and calls a method called `GetMessage()`.

2. The BusinessRules object creates an object from the `DataAccess` class and calls a method named `RetrieveHello()`.

3. The BusinessRules object ensures that the DataAccess object returns the answer "Hello, World!" and, if it doesn't, overrides the DataAccess object to return this famous phrase.

4. The ASPX page displays this message to the user.

The names of the methods used in this application are rather arbitrary and are used for illustrative purposes only. If this were a real-world application, I'd spend quite a bit more time creating method names that better fit their tasks.

THE ASPX PAGE

The ASPX page is the presentation layer in this exercise. The only code I include in the page is the Page_Load event. (If you are using Visual Studio .NET to code your own pages, remove the `Page_Load()` event from the CodeBehind file to avoid an error.)

Listing 3-8 shows the code for this ASPX page.

Listing 3–8: The Presentation Layer ASPX Page

```
<%@ Page Language="vb" AutoEventWireup="false"
Codebehind="Presentation.aspx.vb"
Inherits="Chapter03.Presentation"%>
<!DOCTYPE HTML PUBLIC "-//W3C//DTD HTML 4.0 Transitional//EN">
<HTML>
  <HEAD>
    <title>Presentation</title>
    <meta name="GENERATOR"
```

```
  content="Microsoft Visual Studio .NET 7.0">
 <meta name="CODE_LANGUAGE" content="Visual Basic 7.0">
 <meta name="vs_defaultClientScript" content="JavaScript">
 <meta name="vs_targetSchema"
  content="http://schemas.microsoft.com/intellisense/ie5">
 <script language="vb" runat="server">
   Private Sub Page_Load(ByVal sender As System.Object, _
     ByVal e As System.EventArgs) Handles MyBase.Load
     Dim objBusinessRules As New Chapter03.BusinessRules()
     Label1.Text = objBusinessRules.GetMessage()
   End Sub
 </script>
</HEAD>
<body>
  <form id="Form1" method="post" runat="server">
   <asp:Label id="Label1" runat="server">Label</asp:Label>
  </form>
</body>
</HTML>
```

You can find the code from the page for Listing 3-8 under ChO3SDK.zip (SDK version) or ChO3VS.zip (Visual Studio .NET version) on the companion Web site (www.wiley.com/extras). When you unzip, look for the Chapter03 folder and find Presentation.aspx.

The important line in this code is the one that sets the text property of Label1 to the string returned by the BusinessRules object through the GetMessage() method. Notice, please, that the BusinessRules object is created as Chapter03.BusinessRules. This isn't necessary with the same line in the CodeBehind file, because all of the CodeBehind files in the application already belong to this namespace. It won't hurt the code if you always include this namespace in the object declaration, but it's only necessary if you mix code with your HTML, a practice that I discourage.

BUSINESS RULES OBJECT

The primary purpose of a business rules object is to check and make sure that data does not break the rules of the organization. For example, one of the rules of your company could be that every retail customer has to be charged sales tax in the state of Tennessee. When you get an order, you input the customer and order information into the business rules component, which determines if the customer is a retail customer from Tennessee. If so, the sales tax is added to the order before it is sent to the database; if not, no sales tax is charged.

While something this simple could easily be performed in the ASPX page, or in the CodeBehind file for the ASPX page, doing so presents a problem. If your organization wants to move to a Windows Forms application, all of the business rules code has to be migrated from the ASPX page to the Windows Form. This is not the most efficient reuse of code.

There's a very simple business rules class in Listing 3-9. The business rule here is that the only message that can be returned from an object made from this class is "Hello, World!", plus a string stating where the message came from. Admittedly, this is not a very real-world example, but it does illustrate the how to get data from the business rules tier to the user interface (ASPX page).

Listing 3-9: The Business Rules Layer Class

```
Public Class BusinessRules
  Public Function GetMessage() As String
    Dim objDataAccess As New DataAccess()
    Dim strMessage As String = objDataAccess.RetrieveHello()

    'Ensure Hello, World is grammatically correct
    If strMessage <> "Hello, World!" Then
      strMessage = "Hello, World! <BR /> From business rules."
    Else
      strMessage = strMessage & " <BR /> From data access."
    End If

    Return strMessage
  End Function
End Class
```

 You can find the code from the page for Listing 3-9 under Ch03SDK.zip (SDK version) or Ch03VS.zip (Visual Studio .NET version) on the companion Web site (www.wiley.com/extras). When you unzip, look for the Chapter03 folder and find BusinessRules.vb.

DATA ACCESS OBJECT

The data access tier of an application is responsible for getting data in and out of a data source. I say data source here, because Microsoft has worked hard to ensure that, through ADO and ADO.NET, data access works with a variety of non-traditional data sources, such as Exchange Server.

I cover ADO.NET in great detail in Part III, so the data access component in this exercise contains stub code only. In a real-world application, stub code is used to give the developers on another tier the ability to continue coding their portion of the application with an answer formatted the same way as a real answer.

In Listing 3-10 is our simple data access component. I've added a TODO line to make sure I connect to a database when the application is finished. If you use Visual Studio .NET to work with this application, you'll see that the TODO line shows up in the task list.

Listing 3-10: The Data Tier Layer Class

```
Public Class DataAccess
    Public Function RetrieveHello() As String
        'TODO: Pull this from a database
        Return "Hello, World!"
    End Function
End Class
```

ASP.NET Built-in Objects

Calling the objects in this section ASP.NET built-in objects is a real misnomer, because they are simply additional classes in the .NET Framework, but there is a method to this madness. In traditional ASP, there's a built-in set of objects you use to code your applications. The built-in ASP objects are `Session`, `Application`, `Server`, `Response`, and `Request`. In addition, there's a top-level object called `Context` that you don't normally interact with directly, because it's an object that manages the process space in which your ASP application is running.

If your ASP application calls on COM+ components, the `ObjectContext` in your COM+ component is the same object as the ASP context object. This is due to the fact that IIS processes, including ASP applications, run in COM+. If you are using NT 4, this functionality is supplied by Microsoft Transaction Server (MTS), which was first introduced with Internet Information Server (IIS) 4.0.

For a bit of backward compatibility, you can still code against the "built-in" objects in ASP.NET using familiar syntax. In addition, there are a few other objects you can work with directly in ASP.NET. Table 3-3 shows the ASP.NET objects that correspond to the ASP built-in objects.

TABLE 3-3 ASP.NET OBJECTS

Object	Description

Application	The `Application` object contains an instance of the `HttpApplicationState` class, which contains a collection of application variables. Here's a bit of sample code using an Application variable:
	
	```\nApplication("MyVar") = MyValue\nResponse.Write Application("MyVar")\n```
	
	In ASP.NET, the following is a "more correct" method of setting and getting this property:
	
	```\nApplication.Set("MyVar", MyValue)\nApplication.Get("MyVar")\n```

Request	The `Request` object contains an instance of the `HttpRequest` class. You use the `Request` object to request information sent to the server from the client browser. The following code, which is very similar to traditional ASP, pulls an ID from the query string: ```\nDim strTest As String\nstrTest = Request.QueryString("ID")\n\nIf strTest <> "" then\n Response.Write("You entered an ID!")\nElse\n Reponse.Write("Please enter an ID!")\nEnd If\n```
Response	The `Response` object contains an instance of the `HttpResponse` class. You use the `Response` object to write items out to the HTTP stream in response to a client browser request. The coding for `Response.Write` is identical with the exception of parentheses. ```\nResponse.Write("Hello, World!")\n```
Server	The `Server` object contains an instance of the `HttpServerUtility` class. As with traditional ASP, you can use this object to URL encode a string, HTML encode a string, and map a path to the file directory of a specific page in an application. Here's a code example that maps a path to the Chapter03 application on my Web server: ```\nLabel1.Text = Server.MapPath("Chapter03")\n```

Object	Description

Session	The `Session` object contains an instance of the `HttpSessionState` class. While all of the other objects in this table come from the `System.Web` namespace, this object has its own namespace: `System.Web.SessionState`. The `Session` object, like the `Application` object is primarily used to store values.
	
	`Session("MySessionVar") = "Hello, World"`
	
	`Response.Write(Session("MySessionVar"))`

Trace	The `Trace` object contains an instance of the `TraceContext` class. Tracing is a new concept in ASP.NET that allows you to determine the exact location of an error in your page without extensive debugging. You'll learn more about tracing in Chapter 10, and there's also a section on setting up your own traces in Chapter 12.

These objects will appear throughout Part II. This section is designed solely to introduce these objects and to note that much of your legacy work still runs. If you migrate code from ASP to ASP.NET, you find that most of your code requires no changes. This is not because ASP.NET is identical in syntax, but rather because Microsoft has included a lot of backward-compatible syntax. If changes are required, you'll find that most are minor modifications, such as the addition of parentheses.

Choice of Languages

One of the nicer points about .NET is that the selection of language is now what Microsoft terms "a lifestyle choice." Although I'm not 100 percent in agreement with the terminology, the crux is that you can use any language that you choose to create your ASP.NET applications. The two most common languages that people use are Visual Basic .NET and C#. Microsoft also has J# (basically Java), JScript.NET, and Managed C++ as additional choices. Third-party vendors have created implementations for PERL, PYTHON, COBOL and a variety of other languages.

Visual Basic .NET or C#

The major debate going on in the .NET newsgroups is over which language developers need to know. Most C++ developers are already declaring a winner in C#, although Visual Basic developers are split between the two. In the long run, however,

I believe that you're likely to find more Visual Basic developers choosing Visual Basic .NET for most of their work. ASP developers are also split, although I find more of them moving toward C#. The primary reason for this choice seems the sheer number of C# examples available in comparison to a lack of Visual Basic .NET examples. The fact that C# is a new language has made it a hot commodity, so there are plenty of great examples on the Web.

Most developers who are familiar with C++, Java, or JavaScript have an easier time with C#, while most Visual Basic .NET and ASP developers have an easier go with Visual Basic .NET. Whichever route you choose, you find a lot of similarities in the programming paradigm for both languages. (I discuss this similarity in Appendix B, which compares C# to Visual Basic .NET.)

Why choose Visual Basic .NET?

I'm more inclined to move toward Visual Basic .NET. C# does offer a few advantages, but most applications don't need to stray into these areas to perform well. I sum up my reasons for choosing Visual Basic .NET over C# in the following list:

◆ **Easier code structure:** Although you find a lot of difference between Visual Basic 6 and Visual Basic .NET (or ASP), the code structure is still far more readable than that of C#. It's also easier to teach, especially if your company uses the Visual Studio .NET IDE.

◆ **Shorter learning curve:** In truth, the curve isn't that much shorter in Visual Basic .NET, but the *perceived* curve is much shorter, which is likely to influence many companies to decide in favor of a Visual Basic .NET coding standard.

◆ **Greater number of resources:** Even though many people pick up C# as a programming language, my contention is that most the VB developers are likely to choose Visual Basic .NET over C#. Some folks have a problem with classifying people as resources, but the reality is that employees *are* resources. When a company has to choose between languages, with all other things being equal, having more developers gives a language a slight advantage.

◆ **More maintainable:** I largely base my reasoning here on the reasons in the preceding points. Easier code structure and a greater number of resources make code more maintainable. Maintainability often costs businesses more than performance, and because you suffer no performance loss with Visual Basic .NET, the trade-off of performance versus maintainability isn't as cut and dried as it is in Visual Basic 6 versus C++. Visual Basic .NET and C# classes appear nearly identical in the IL.

◆ **It's what's in this book:** By itself, this isn't a very good reason for choosing Visual Basic .NET. But, because you did pick up this book, trying to shift all its examples to C# now isn't a wise investment in time.

The major advantage of C# over Visual Basic .NET is the ability to use unmanaged code in your applications. Since direct memory access is not necessary in most applications, and using unmanaged code takes you outside the realm of CLR, I don't see this as a major benefit in most applications. If you need this functionality, you can code an object in C# and use it (or inherit from it) with your Visual Basic .NET object.

CodeBehind

The push in .NET is to move all of your code — the methods, event handlers, and properties — to a language-specific file known as a *CodeBehind* file. You then put only the tags in your ASPX file. This separates the user interface logic from the user interface tags.

When you move all of your code into a CodeBehind file, you find it much easier to maintain your application. This isn't a new concept. In Visual Basic 6, you designed the form visually and added the code in a different window. Since the form code and your code were contained in the same file, the IDE easily hid the code from you. In other words, all of the form code was hidden from you unless you opened the file in an ASCII editor.

In ASP.NET, the concept is similar, but the code is fully exposed. If you use Visual Studio .NET, you see the `#Region` keyword used to block off sections of code that are controlled by the IDE.

 Be very careful when editing code blocks set aside by the Visual Studio .NET IDE. In editing these sections, you may change the page such that you can no longer edit it in Visual Studio .NET. Every item in this section can be edited through property pages.

The @ directive

The @ directive is a tag in the ASPX page. For those not familiar with ASP, the @ directive is the first tag at the top of the page, as shown in Listing 3-6. In traditional ASP, this tag generally contains only the scripting language for the page. It can, however, also contain directives for how the page handles transactions.

In Visual Basic .NET, the @ directive holds a lot more information than it does in ASP. The first line of Listing 3-11 is a typical @ directive for traditional ASP, while the second is an @ directive for ASP.NET. The comments are added here only to show which line is added to which file. Because the @ directive is the first line in an ASP or ASPX page, you should not add comments like this in your code.

Listing 3-11: Sample @ directive in ASP and ASP.NET

```
<!-- ASP -->
<%@ Language="VBScript" %>


<!-ASP.NET -->
<%@ Page Language="vb" AutoEventWireup="false"
Codebehind="WebFormBehind.aspx.vb" Inherits="WebForm.WebFormBehind"%>
```

The important part of the directive, from the perspective of this section, involves the last two attributes. As you create a page in the Visual Studio .NET IDE, the IDE automatically creates a code module for each page in your application. By default, the page is named the same as the ASPX page with an extension for the language with which the CodeBehind file is created. In my examples, the language is Visual Basic .NET, so the extension is .vb.

If you code the @ directive on your own, point the Codebehind attribute to your CodeBehind file and remember to inherit a class from the CodeBehind file for the page. You normally have only one class per CodeBehind file, so determining what to put there is not too difficult. In theory, you can place all of your classes into one CodeBehind file and point different pages to different classes in this file. I do not recommend doing this in your applications, because it runs contrary to Visual Studio .NET, which is probably the tool you'll use for most of your .NET coding.

Using CodeBehind in Visual Studio .NET

When you code your pages in Visual Studio .NET, a .vb file is created for every CodeBehind file. By default, the IDE doesn't show the .vb files. Instead, you choose to view code for the ASPX page to see the CodeBehind page. There are a few ways to do this:

◆ Click the View Code button at the upper right corner of the Solution Explorer when you have an ASPX page open. This opens the CodeBehind file for the ASPX page that's open.

◆ Choose View → Code from the menu bar.

◆ Press the F7 key.

◆ Double-click on any of the controls in the Design window for the ASPX page. As in Visual Basic 6, this adds the default event for this control.

You can also see the actual files by clicking on the Show All Files icon in Solution Explorer (second from the right). This places the .vb files in a hierarchy below the .aspx files they serve as CodeBehind for. If you show all files, you can double-click on the file in Solution Explorer to edit it.

Before moving on to the actual CodeBehind file, I want to discuss a couple of the attributes in the @ directive tag, namely `CodeBehind` and `Inherits`.

◆ `CodeBehind="WebFormBehind.aspx.vb"` — This directive points to the page that holds the code that runs events for this page.

◆ `Inherits="Chapter03.WebFormBehind"` — This particular directive tells you that you're inheriting the `WebFormBehind` class in the `Chapter03` namespace (as shown in Listing 3-7). The default namespace for a solution is the name of the solution.

There are additional @ directive tags besides than `Page`. I discuss the most important @ directive tags for your ASP.NET pages in the following sections.

PAGE (AND CONTROL)

While this is not an exhaustive list, the main @ `Page` directive tag attributes are as follows (those marked with an asterisk [*] also apply to the @ `Control` directive):

◆ `aspCompat` — When set to `true`, the aspx page is compatible with traditional ASP applications. The primary reason to set `aspCompat` to `true` is for applications that call COM+ components that use the ASP built-in objects. Using these components results in a performance penalty, so use this attribute wisely. The default setting is `false`.

◆ `AutoEventWireup*` — This attribute is set to `false` in Visual Studio .NET, and you should normally leave it this way. When it is set to `true`, you do not have to specify which event your event handles; you just have to name it the right name. The trade-off here is a bit less typing for less flexibility. In the following `Page_Load` event, you'd drop the `Handles MyBase.Load` portion of the code if you set `AutoEventWireup` to `true`.

```
Private Sub Page_Load(ByVal sender As System.Object,
        ByVal e As System.EventArgs) Handles MyBase.Load
```

◆ `Buffer` — Sets page buffering on and off. By default, this is set to `true`.

◆ `ClassName*` — Specifies the name of the class that will be dynamically compiled when this page is requested. Unlike many of the directives, you do not include the namespace with this attribute. If you use this attribute, you should also use the `Src` attribute.

◆ `ClientTarget` — This attribute is valuable when you need to set the application to work with downlevel browsers, which is a term for pre-4.0 browsers. You can set any valid client browser for this attribute. If you use this attribute, set it to the browser with the least capabilities for your application.

◆ `CodePage` — Sets up the code page for this ASP.NET page. This is useful for internationalization of applications.

◆ CompilerOptions* — Enables you to set compiler options in the same way you set up compiler options on the command line.

◆ ContentType — Enables you to set a different MIME type for the page. For example, to output a page as an XML document, you can use the following:

ContentType="text/XML"

◆ Debug* — Tells whether or not a page should be compiled with debug symbols. In general, this is set to false for production applications. If you use Visual Studio .NET for coding, you don't have to worry about this attribute.

◆ Description* — A text description of the page. This is for documentation purposes, because the ASP.NET parser ignores this attribute.

◆ EnableSessionState — Tells whether the page participates in the ASP.NET application session. Don't set this directive to false if you use mandatory Session_Start events in your global.asax file. The value can be set to true, false, or ReadOnly.

◆ EnableViewState* — Tells whether the state of the page, and especially server controls (those with runat=server), is maintained across requests. The default is true.

◆ EnableViewStateMac — ASP.NET contains a method of telling whether the string that stores state information was altered on the client. Because the string is encrypted, it is unlikely that setting this attribute to true will do anything but degrade performance. Of course, the encryption scheme may eventually be broken, so the addition of this attribute is a nice forethought. If EnableViewState is set to false, this should be set to false as well.

◆ ErrorPage — Sets a page for any unhandled exceptions.

◆ Explicit* — Indicates whether Option Explicit is turned on. By default, this is set to false. If you code inside your ASPX page, turn this to true.

◆ Inherits* — The class that your page inherits from. The method of setting this up is namespace.class.

◆ Language* — Sets the coding language for the page. For the most part, this book uses vb, which indicates the page is coded in Visual Basic .NET. In theory, you can override this on a block-by-block basis if you code in the ASPX file.

◆ Src* — Specifies the CodeBehind page to dynamically compile when this page is requested. This attribute allows you to edit your page and have the new code available as you save. It can be dangerous to use this attribute if you edit on your production server.

◆ Strict* — Signifies whether Option Strict is set to on. As with Explicit, I'd set this to true if you code in your ASPX page.

- ◆ `Trace` — Specifies whether tracing is turned on for this page. This attribute is useful if you need to set a trace for a particular page to catch a bug. Tracing is covered in more detail in Chapter 10.

- ◆ `Transaction:` — Determines whether your ASP.NET page handles transactions. Set this directive to `true` if you want to carry on transactions in your ASP.NET page. This is useful for data-driven applications that perform numerous changes to a database.

- ◆ `WarningLevel*` — Sets the warning level for compilation, and determines whether warnings are treated as compilation errors.

IMPLEMENTS

The `@ Implements` directive is used to implement an interface in your page. `interface` is the only attribute of this control:

```
<%@ Implements interface="MyNamespace.MyInterface" %>
```

ASSEMBLY

The `@ Assembly` tag directive is used to link an assembly to the current page. When you add an assembly, all of the classes and interfaces are available for use in your page. You use only one of the two attributes, `Name` or the `Src`, at one time.

- ◆ `Name` — A string that represents the friendly name of the assembly to link to the page.

  ```
  <%@ Assembly Name="MyAssembly" %>
  ```

- ◆ `Src` — A string representing the path to a source file.

  ```
  <%@ Assembly Src="MyAssembly.vb" %>
  ```

OUTPUTCACHE

The `@ OutputCache` tag directive is used to control the output caching of an ASPX page or an ASCX user control. Its attributes include the following:

- ◆ `Duration` — The amount of time that a page or user control is cached, in seconds.

- ◆ `Location` — The location where a control or page is cached. The possible values are `Any` (the default), `Client`, `Downstream`, `None`, or `Server`. The difference between `Downstream` and `Client` is the type of browser or device that caches the page. You can find more information about the `Location` attribute in the .NET help files that ship with the SDK and Visual Studio .NET.

- ◆ `VaryByCustom` — Used when you want to use custom criteria to determine caching. One possible value is `browser`, which varies the cache based on the type of browser.

- VaryByHeader — Used to cache based on different HTTP headers. One possibility is Accept-Language, which caches based on different languages that the page supports. The parameters in the list are separated by semicolons, as this code sample shows:

  ```
  VaryByHeader="LastName;FirstName"
  ```

- VaryByParam — Varies the cache by the parameters that the page accepts, either via the query string collection (GET) or form collection (POST). The parameters in the list are separated by semicolons. The following code sample shows a page that has a different cache when variables are passed through a form submission (POST) than when the variables are passed on the query string (GET):

  ```
  VaryByParam="GET;POST"
  ```

- VaryByControl — Varies the cache by the properties of a user control. The parameters in this list are separated by semicolons.

REFERENCE

The @ Reference directive is used to add a page or control that is to be dynamically compiled when the page is run. Specify a Page or a Control.

REGISTER

You use the @ Register directive to register user controls for your page. Of the following @ Register attributes, the Tagprefix is always mandatory. You then either link to a particular assembly and class or create a Tagname and point to a source file:

- Tagprefix — The prefix to use to identify this tag. This attribute is basically an alias for an XML namespace.

- Tagname — The name of the tag within the XML namespace that you named in the Tagprefix attribute. The Tagname is associated with a particular class in the namespace.

- Namespace — The namespace in which the control or controls reside. Used with Assembly.

- Assembly — The assembly where the user control(s) are found.

- Src — The source file of the user control. Uses the extension .ascx.

IMPORT

You use the @ Import directive to import a namespace into an ASPX page, as shown in the following code example:

```
<% @ Import Namespace="System.IO">
```

Namespace is the only attribute of the @ Import directive tag. It is synonymous to the Imports tags in a Visual Basic .NET file, like the CodeBehind file Imports line show here:

```
Imports System.IO
```

The CodeBehind file

The CodeBehind file is one of the most important new features in programming for Microsoft Internet applications. The basic idea is to put all of your tags in the ASPX page and all of the code in a CodeBehind file. This allows you to separate the actual user interface from any code that allows you to dynamically alter the page.

In this section, I use Visual Studio .NET to create the code. You can use CodeBehind without using Visual Studio .NET, it makes things a little more difficult. Remember that CodeBehind, by itself, does not dynamically compile your application when the page is accessed. You use the Src attribute of the @ Page directive to indicate that the CodeBehind file should be dynamically compiled. If you have added a user control, you should also have an @ Register directive in your page to indicate which user control should be compiled with the page.

Listing 3-12 displays the CodeBehind file for the WebFormBehind.aspx page, which is called WebFormBehind.aspx.vb. The class, as I mentioned previously, is WebFormBehind.

Listing 3-12: WebFormBehind.aspx.vb — a CodeBehind File

```
Public Class WebFormBehind
    Inherits System.Web.UI.Page
    Protected WithEvents Label1 As System.Web.UI.WebControls.Label
    Protected WithEvents Image1 As System.Web.UI.WebControls.Image
    Protected WithEvents TextBox1 As System.Web.UI.WebControls.TextBox
    Protected WithEvents TextBox2 As System.Web.UI.WebControls.TextBox
    Protected WithEvents DropDownList1 As _
     System.Web.UI.WebControls.DropDownList
    Protected WithEvents ListBox1 As System.Web.UI.WebControls.ListBox
    Protected WithEvents CheckBoxList1 As System.Web.UI.WebControls.CheckBoxList
    Protected WithEvents TextBox3 As System.Web.UI.WebControls.TextBox
    Protected WithEvents RadioButtonList1 _
     As System.Web.UI.WebControls.RadioButtonList
    Protected WithEvents Submit As System.Web.UI.WebControls.Button
    Protected WithEvents Reset As System.Web.UI.WebControls.Button
    Protected WithEvents Button As System.Web.UI.WebControls.Button

#Region " Web Form Designer Generated Code "

    'This call is required by the Web Form Designer.
```

Continued

Listing 3-12 *(Continued)*

```
<System.Diagnostics.DebuggerStepThrough()> _
Private Sub InitializeComponent()

End Sub

Private Sub Page_Init(ByVal sender As System.Object, _
 ByVal e As System.EventArgs) Handles MyBase.Init
    'CODEGEN: This method call is required by the Web Form Designer
    'Do not modify it using the code editor.
    InitializeComponent()
End Sub

#End Region

Private Sub Page_Load(ByVal sender As System.Object, _
 ByVal e As System.EventArgs) Handles MyBase.Load
    'Put user code to initialize the page here
 End Sub

Private Sub Submit_Click(ByVal sender As System.Object, _
 ByVal e As System.EventArgs) Handles Submit.Click

End Sub
End Class
```

 The code for this page can be downloaded from the companion Web site (www.wiley.com/extras) in the file CH03SDK.zip (SDK version) or Ch03VS.zip (Visual Studio .NET version). The file is located in the Chapter03 Web project, which can be installed with the Ch03.msi file (in the installer directory) or using the instructions in the install.txt file.

The ASPX page that I created for this exercise is a copy of the WebFormASP.aspx page in Listing 3-5. Because the code is now contained in the CodeBehind file, I need to focus on the button controls, which are shown in Listing 3-13. Note that there are absolutely no changes in the buttons from Listing 3-5.

Listing 3-13: Server-Side Buttons

```
<asp:Button id="Submit" runat="server" Text="Submit" />
 
<asp:Button id="Reset" runat="server" Text="Reset" />
```

```
 
<asp:Button id="Button" runat="server" Text="Button" />
```

To make the form interactive, I have to add event handles to the click events for each button. These link to the event handlers in Listing 3-14, which shows some simple event handlers for all three buttons. These events simply change the text of Label1 in the ASPX page. If you use Visual Studio .NET, you can simply double-click the buttons to create the event handlers.

Listing 3-14: Event Handlers

```
Private Sub Submit_Click(ByVal sender As System.Object, _
  ByVal e As System.EventArgs) Handles Submit.Click
  Label1.Text = "You clicked submit"
End Sub

Private Sub Reset_Click(ByVal sender As System.Object, _
  ByVal e As System.EventArgs) Handles Reset.Click
  Label1.Text = "You clicked reset"
End Sub

Private Sub Button_Click(ByVal sender As System.Object, _
  ByVal e As System.EventArgs) Handles Button.Click
  Label1.Text = "You clicked the button."
End Sub
```

Now when you open up the page and submit the form, you notice that a message appears at the top of the page. Although this code is not a very elegant example, it demonstrates the ease of coding in .NET and how separation of code and HTML is a good thing.

To put the simplicity of this coding in perspective, take a look at the steps that are necessary to accomplish the same thing in ASP and Visual Basic COM+. I choose COM+ over COM, because I can write directly to the HTTP stream through the COM+ type library. If you are using NT 4, MTS serves the same purpose as COM+. If I use COM instead of COM+, I must make my writeHTML() method return a string to response.write in the ASP page because I cannot output directly to the HTTP stream without using MTS or COM+.

Listing 3-15 shows a traditional ASP page that simply calls a COM+ component, which outputs its message to the HTTP stream.

Listing 3-15: ASP Page To Call a COM Component

```
<% @ Language="VBScript" %>
<%
Option Explicit
```

Continued

Listing 3-15 *(Continued)*

```
Private m_objASPWriter 'As ASPWrite.clsASPWriter

Set m_objASPWriter = Server.CreateObject("ASPWrite.clsASPWriter")
    Call m_objASPWriter.WriteHTML("Message to print from ASP page")
Set m_objASPWriter = Nothing
%>
```

 The code from Listing 3-15 can be found on the companion Web site (www.wiley.com/extras) in the COMPlus.asp page in the download file Ch03SDK.zip (SDK version) or Ch03VS.zip (Visual Studio .NET version). The page is included in the chapter03 Web project, which can be installed with the Ch03.msi file in the installer directory.

Listing 3-16 shows the COM+ component that writes out to the HTTP Stream after the ASP page calls the method WriteHTML(), which is shown in Listing 13-15. I've commented out some lines if you want to use this component in MTS (on NT 4) instead of COM+. You'll also have to add a reference to the MTS Type Library in your Visual Basic project and recompile. COM+ components won't run under MTS, so make sure you recompile if you want to use this component on an NT 4 system. If it were not for the ASP Type Library objects, this code could well run outside of COM+.

Listing 3-16: The ASPWrite.clsASPWriter Class Module

```
Option Explicit

    '* COM+, switch comments for MTS
      'Implements MTxAS.ObjectControl
      Implements COMSVCSLib.ObjectControl

    '* COM+, switch comments for MTS
      'Private m_objContext As MTxAS.ObjectContext
      Private m_objContext As COMSVCSLib.ObjectContext

Private m_blnMTS As Boolean
Private m_objResponse As ASPTypeLibrary.Response

Public Sub WriteHTML(ByVal strInput As String)
```

```vb
        Call m_objResponse.Write("<html>" & vbCrLf)
        Call m_objResponse.Write("<head><title>ASPWriter</title></head>" & vbCrLf)
        Call m_objResponse.Write("<body>" & vbCrLf)
        Call m_objResponse.Write("<h1>Written from ASPWriter</h1>" & vbCrLf)
        Call m_objResponse.Write("<p>" & strInput & "</p>" & vbCrLf)
        Call m_objResponse.Write("</html>" & vbCrLf)
End Sub


Private Sub ObjectControl_Activate()

    '* GAB:  Create Context for MTS and
    '*         and set boolean flag for MTS.
    Set m_objContext = GetObjectContext()
    m_blnMTS = Not (m_objContext Is Nothing)

    If m_blnMTS Then
        Set m_objResponse = m_objContext.Item("Response")
    End If

End Sub

Private Function ObjectControl_CanBePooled() As Boolean

    '* GAB:  This must be FALSE for VB 6 under MTS
    ObjectControl_CanBePooled = False

End Function

Private Sub ObjectControl_Deactivate()

    '* GAB:  Destroy object context
    Set m_objContext = Nothing

End Sub
```

The important point I'm trying to make here isn't how to write a COM+ component, but the lack of extensive plumbing code in the .NET version of the project. If you create a CodeBehind page by adding a CodeBehind file and an `Inherits` directive, .NET handles all the plumbing for you.

Configuration

Two areas of configuration reside in your Web applications: the Web server itself and the application. In ASP, you configure your application through `global.asa` and the Web server through the metabase, which you configure through the Internet Services Manager. The basic idea of separation of application settings and Web server settings carries forward into ASP.NET.

Some differences, however, do exist. In ASP.NET, you still set up your application and session events in a global file, known as `global.asax`. The Web settings, however, are a bit different. Although you can work with the settings of your application through the use of tools, you can also edit the file directly. The name of the configuration file where you place these settings is `web.config`.

Chapter 12 covers `web.config` and other configuration files in detail.

global.asax

You can use the `global.asax` file to set your session and application events, just as you use `global.asa` in earlier versions of ASP. The scripting in ASP and ASP.NET is very similar, with the major difference being the languages that each uses. As is the case with all .NET files, you can use such languages such as Visual Basic .NET, C#, and JScript.NET in your `global.asax` file. The `global.asax` file also has its own corresponding CodeBehind file; if you follow the .NET paradigm, you place all of your code in this file.

For more information on the `global.asax` file, as well as information how to use this file to set up your sessions and applications, see Chapter 11.

EVENTS

Most of your work in the `global.asax` file is through events that your application and individual sessions fire off, like `Session_Start`. The model, in this respect, is very similar to that of the `global.asa` file in traditional ASP. Table 3-4 highlights the major events that you can code for in your `global.asax` file.

TABLE 3-4 EVENTS AND METHODS TO USE IN THE GLOBAL.ASAX IN ASP.NET

Name	Description
Application_Start	This event fires at the start of the application and is global to every person using the application. It's equivalent to the Application_OnStart event in traditional ASP. The Application_Start event is global to all instances of an application. The basic change for the methods in ASP.NET is the addition of parameters, as shown here:

```
Sub Application_Start(ByVal sender As
Object,
                ByVal e As EventArgs)
    'Code to initialize the application
End Sub
```

Name	Description
Application_BeginRequest	This event fires with every request on the application. Here's the signature of this event:

```
Sub Application_BeginRequest(ByVal
sender As Object,
                ByVal e As EventArgs)
    'Request specific code here
End Sub
```

Name	Description
Application_End	This event fires after the application shuts down and is commonly used for clean-up code. It's equivalent to the Application_OnEnd event in traditional ASP. The Application_End event is global to all instances of an application, as in the following example:

```
Sub Application_End(ByVal sender As
Object,
                ByVal e As
EventArgs)
    'Code to cleanup at the end of an
application
End Sub
```

Continued

TABLE 3-4 EVENTS AND METHODS TO USE IN THE GLOBAL.ASAX IN ASP.NET
       (Continued)

Name	Description
Init	This is the method that you use as you create a specific instance of an application. Although very similar to the Application_Start event, Init works only on a single instance in the application instance pool. This method comes from the HttpApplication class (System.Web.HttpApplication) and must be overridden to include in your global.asax file:

```
Overrides Sub Init()
    'Code for initializing an instance
of an app
End Sub
```

| Dispose | You use this method when the CLR destroys a specific instance of an application. It's very similar to the Application_End event but works in a smaller scope. As with the Init method, the developer must override the Dispose method, as follows: |

```
Overrides Sub Dispose()
    'Code for the destruction of an
instance of an app
End Sub
```

| Session_Start | This event fires at the beginning of every session. It is equivalent to the Session_OnStart event in traditional ASP. |

```
Sub Session_Start(ByVal sender As
Object,
                ByVal e As EventArgs)
    'Code to initialize a session
End Sub
```

Name	Description
Session_End	This event fires at the end of every session. You traditionally use it for clean-up code at the session level. It's equivalent to the Session_End event in traditional ASP, as follows:

```
Sub Session_End(ByVal sender As Object,
            ByVal e As EventArgs)
   'Code to cleanup a session
End Sub
```

Name	Description
Authentication Events	Authentication is a very large topic, which I discuss in detail in Chapter 13. There is a different authentication event for each type of authentication. Here's an example of the WindowsAuthentication_OnAuthenticate event:

```
Public Sub _
     WindowsAuthentication_
OnAuthenticate(Source _
     As Object, e As
WindowsAuthenticationEventArgs)
  e.User = New MyPrincipal(e.Identity)
End Sub
```

This event assigns the user to a new Principal object. To use a different a different type of authentication, you change the event signature to one of the following:

For forms authentication:

```
Public Sub _
     FormsAuthentication_
OnAuthenticate(Source _
     As Object, e As
FormsAuthenticationEventArgs)
  e.User = New MyPrincipal(e.Identity)
End Sub
```

Continued

TABLE 3-4 EVENTS AND METHODS TO USE IN THE GLOBAL.ASAX IN ASP.NET
            (Continued)

Name	Description
	For Passport authentication:

```
Public Sub _
      PassportAuthentication_
OnAuthenticate(Source _
      As Object, e As
PassportAuthenticationEventArgs)
   e.User = New MyPrincipal(e.Identity)
End Sub
```

There is also a special form of authentication handler that is a bit more generic. If you are not sure whether your authentication event is going to stay the same throughout the lifetime of the application, you can use default authentication:

```
Public Sub _
      DefaultAuthentication_
OnAuthenticate(Source _
      As Object, e As
DefaultAuthenticationEventArgs)
   e.User = New MyPrincipal(e.Identity)
End Sub
```

Name	Description
Error	You can handle errors generically by using the Error event of your application. You can use this if you want to provide a friendly message for an unhandled exception in your application, as follows:

```
Sub Application_Error(sender as Object,
                      e As EventArgs)
      'Handle the error here
End Sub
```

Although this table may seem rather extensive, it doesn't even scratch the surface of the events and methods available to your application through the global.asax file. Here I touched on only the most useful events and methods for the majority of Web applications I can envision.

I cover `global.asax` events in greater detail in Chapter 11.

DIRECTIVES

I introduced you to @ directives for your ASP.NET pages in the section of that name earlier in this chapter. The `global.asax` file also contains directives. Table 3-5 shows the directives available for use at the application level in your `global.asax` file. The application directives reside at the top of the `global.asax` file.

TABLE 3-5 DIRECTIVES FOR USE IN GLOBAL.ASAX

Directive	Description

@ Application	The @ Application directive can take two attributes: Inherits and Description. You use Inherits in the same manner as the Inherits directive in your ASPX page; the main difference is that the entire application, not just a single page, inherits from this object. The Description attribute allows you to specify a friendly name for the application. You can place both directives in the same tag, as follows:
	
	`<@ Application Inherits="MyBusinessApp.`
	`PeopleFinder"`
	`Description="This application is used to find`
	`employees.">`

@ Import	Use this directive to import namespaces into your application. Remember that importing a namespace is used to help reduce typing. The benefit of using the @ Import directive is that you won't have to include the namespace in every page. The downside is you do not alias the namespace, which may hinder maintenance of the application. Use a single @ Import directive tag for each namespace, as shown here:
	
	`<@ Import Namespace = "System.XML">`
	`<@ Import Namespace = "System.IO">`

Continued

TABLE 3-5 DIRECTIVES FOR USE IN GLOBAL.ASAX *(Continued)*

Directive	Description
@ Assembly	Use this directive to link an assembly to the current application in order to use the classes from this assembly. Notice that all assemblies in your /bin directory are automatically available to the application and don't need the @ Assembly directive for you to use them. You specify a single assembly for each @ Assembly directive tag: `<@ Assembly Name = "MyDLL.dll">`

OBJECTS

You can store objects at the application or session level, both of which are largely frowned on in traditional ASP. Because the objects in ASP.NET generally display very small footprints, storing objects in this manner certainly isn't as big an issue as it is in traditional ASP. Listing 3-17 shows the code to use to declare an object in an application in ASP.NET, along with the code necessary to retrieve this object in your ASP.NET pages.

Listing 3-17: Setting and Using Objects at the Application Level

```
<Object Runat="Server" Scope="Application" ID="MyID"
ProgID="MyNS.MyID" />


<%
Response.Write(MyID.MyMethod())
%>
```

web.config

web.config is a new file that basically replaces the metabase settings for an ASP.NET Web application. You can also do inside the web.config file many of the things that you can do inside the global.asax file. In the web.config file, you set up items using XML tags, while you generally set items up programmatically in the global.asax file.

The web.config file is an XML file that contains a hierarchy of settings for your application. The various sections of the file are as shown in Table 3-6.

TABLE 3-6 WEB.CONFIG

Section	Description
appsettings	Use this section to create custom settings for your application. You can place a connection string here, for example, to make it available for all pages in your application.
browsercaps	Use this section of the file to create new additions to the Browser Capabilities object. This section can prove useful if you need to test for a specific custom browser.
compilation	Use the compilation section to set global settings that relate to compilation. You can, for example, set a custom compiler for use in compiling files of a certain language. You can also use this section to set up your application to maintain the temporary source files to aid with debugging.
customerrors	The customerrors section of the file enables you to define pages for custom HTTP errors. For example, you may want a special HTML page to appear if someone encounters a 500 (server) error.
globalization	Use the globalization section to set the encoding for responses and requests to your application. This section is useful for applications that you need to set up with a custom encoding scheme.
httphandlers	Use this section to map incoming requests to a specified IhttpHandler class. In short, you can define specific types of custom actions for your Web applications.
httpmodules	This section enables you to add HTTP modules to your application. These modules can fall within the .NET Framework or you can code your own custom modules.
location	Use this section to map any location in your Web to a specific group or set of users.
processmodel	This section contains the settings for the ASP.NET process model, including the timer settings to enable an ASP.NET process to shut down after remaining idle.
security	Use this section to configure security settings for the application. You can set the authentication method, set a list of authorized users, and create an identity for the application to run under, effectively enabling the application to impersonate a system or domain user.

Continued

TABLE 3-6 WEB.CONFIG *(Continued)*

Section	Description
sessionstate	This section contains attributes to set the session state for your application. Here you can set whether the application uses session cookies.
trace	This section is the most useful one for debugging your applications. By making a simple change here, you can set up your application to trace errors and print the results at the bottom of each of your pages. (I cover tracing in greater detail in Chapter 10.)
webcontrols	Use this section to identify the directory that contains client-side script libraries in your ASP.NET application.
webservices	This section deals with settings to Web services in your application. Because Web services are part of the core of Microsoft .NET, this section is very detailed. (I cover Web services at length in Chapter 14.)

The web.config file is covered in much greater detail in Chapter 12.

Finding the Problem

You have a couple ways to find problems in your ASP.NET application. As is the case with traditional ASP applications, you can use the debugger to find exceptions in your application. ASP.NET, however, offers a new method of finding errors in your code, which is known as *tracing*.

Debugging

You want to do most of your ASP.NET debugging in the Visual Studio .NET IDE, because the IDE makes debugging your applications much easier. If the IDE isn't available to you, however, the .NET Framework SDK ships with a GUI debugging tool called the CLR Debugger. It's much more lightweight than the IDE version and is really not the best tool for debugging ASP.NET, unless you have the solution file, which is created using Visual Studio .NET when you create your solution (remember that every project is part of a solution, even if it is the only project in the solution). If you have this file, then you probably have Visual Studio .NET. The main advantage of the CLR Debugger is that it consumes less memory than the Visual Studio .NET IDE.

You can find the CLR Debugger at <root>:\Program Files\Microsoft Visual Studio .NET\FrameworkSDK\GuiDebug\DbgCLR.exe. Figure 3-5 shows the CLR Debugger.

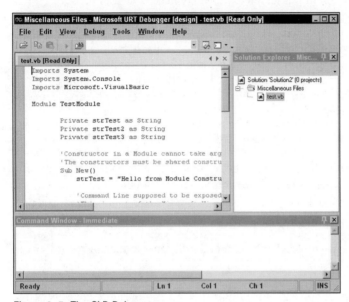

Figure 3-5: The CLR Debugger.

Tracing

I mentioned tracing briefly in the web.config section earlier in this chapter. When you set up tracing in web.config, the settings apply to the entire application. But what if you only want to trace errors for a specific page? No problem; this task is easy to accomplish. Listing 3-18 shows the directive that you use to add tracing to a specific page.

Listing 3-18: Setting Up Tracing in a Page

```
<% @ Page Trace="True" %>
```

I cover tracing in greater detail in Chapter 10. In the section about tracing in that chapter, I discuss a couple of scenarios that help you become familiar with the process of tracing errors in your applications.

Summary

I cover a lot of information in this chapter and barely make a dent in the subject. I do discuss a few key concepts that you need to remember, as the following list describes:

◆ As you code your ASP.NET page, you use compilable languages rather than scripting to do your server-side work. Using compiled languages is a major improvement on traditional ASP, but it's also a major change. If you've never worked in Visual Basic, most of your learning curve concentrates on this change.

◆ Despite the use of compilable languages, you still need to consider ASP.NET a presentation layer technology. As much as possible, you want to consider using CodeBehind to better separate code from content. Even following this rule, you still have additional components to handle business rules and data access.

◆ Everything is configurable in ASP.NET.

◆ Finding errors in your code is much easier if you use such additions as tracing.

You may notice that Chapter 2, "Visual Basic .NET," is a bit more code-intensive than this chapter. This variation is by design. I made the introduction to Visual Basic .NET code-intensive to accustom you to the language you're going to use to code your ASP.NET pages. This chapter shows you the many features of ASP.NET. You'll have plenty of opportunities to get deeper into ASP.NET code throughout the rest of the book.

 You get an opportunity to code some ASP.NET in Chapter 6, and I devote all of Part II of this book, Chapters 7 through 14, to building ASP.NET applications.

Chapter 4

XML

IN THIS CHAPTER

- ◆ Why to use XML in your own Internet applications

- ◆ The basics of XML structure and how you validate XML

- ◆ The use of XSLT to render HTML from XML

- ◆ XML objects that you use in .NET

I've worked with XML full time for the past few years. Although it's not a panacea for all the ills of Web development, XML is the best method I know of for representing data in Internet applications. In this chapter, I cover why XML is becoming so popular with the Web community, along with a short primer on using XML in your own applications. Most of this chapter doesn't focus on .NET in particular, so you can use this chapter to support your COM+ applications as well.

Why XML?

Before delving into the benefits of XML, getting a basic understanding of how XML came about is a good idea. The history of XML demonstrates why XML is an integral part of the World Wide Web as we know it today.

XML, like HTML before it, has its roots in a language known as SGML, or Standard General Markup Language. SGML is a subset of a language known as GML, which was created in 1969 as a metalanguage for data. In 1986, SGML became an adopted ISO standard (ISO 8879) for data storage, description, and exchange. Users have also utilized SGML to describe documents. The use of SGML for both documents and data made it a perfect language for government use.

In the early '90s, different groups made an effort to move SGML to the Internet to create an easy language for creating linked documents. Before this point, developers created linked documents by using a protocol known as GOPHER. GOPHER was very strong for creating large linked sites, but it was a bit unwieldy to pick up. The learning curve was just a bit too steep. Although the World Wide Web has eclipsed GOPHER, the last time that I checked, a few GOPHER sites were still operating in the educational community.

In 1993, Tim Bernars-Lee debuted the World Wide Web (what most people now mistakenly think of as the Internet) with an SGML subset known as HyperText

Markup Language, or HTML for short. HTML is a simple, easy-to-learn language for creating image-rich pages. Although early Web pages were very simple in comparison to their modern counterparts, they were still easier to build and more graphically rich than their GOPHER counterparts.

As the Internet expanded, people became aware that HTML alone wasn't enough to sustain an application-rich environment. In 1996, the World Wide Web Consortium (W3C), a recommendations organization based in Boston, started the process of creating an easily extended markup language to combine the data-definition capability of SGML with the simplicity of HTML. The result is the language known as *eXtensible Markup Language,* or XML.

XML is a simple way to set up text documents that describe data. This is probably the most well-known use of XML. Because it is easily extended, however, XML can be used to build new means of describing any form of data. The data in an XML document can easily be transformed using XSLT (eXtensible Style Language for Transformations). XML, in the form of XHTML, can also be used as a replacement for HTML. You can think of XHTML as a very rigidly structured, or well-formed, version of HTML. XML offers the following benefits:

◆ **XML is a standard:** Technically, it's only a recommendation, because the W3C isn't a standards board capable of forcing companies to use XML. The major computer software manufacturers, however, are employing XML in nearly all their Internet-aware applications, so it may as well be a standard.

◆ **XML is open:** No one owns a patent to XML, which means that every company is free to use XML as an open standard to communicate with any other vendor. The move from company standards to open standards is a good one. The XML DOM is now published on the W3C site (www. w3c.org), and Microsoft has worked hard to implement the latest version of the standard in all its products.

◆ **XML is extensible:** You can create tags to represent your data in any manner that befits your company. If you take the time to represent this data as a *Document Type Definition (DTD)* or *schema,* you can easily share this data with your partners and clients. In fact, by using products such as BizTalk, you can map your partners' and clients' data to your internal structure, eliminating the need for customized translation software. The other side to extensibility is the capability to create new "applications," such as XSLT and XPath – or even Simple Object Access Protocol (SOAP). XPath is used for creating paths (in most instances in a way similar to hyperlinks, but that just scratches the surface). SOAP (Simple Object Access Protocol) is used to access objects across the Internet. SOAP is the type of XML used in Web Services, which are covered in detail in Chapter 14.

◆ **XML is self-describing:** All your data resides between opening and closing tags that describe the data that they contain. This self-describing nature makes XML documents easy to read and understand.

◆ **XML is a perfect language for n-tier development:** While XML itself is used primarily to represent data, the combination of XML and XSLT, when used to create XHTML, is very well suited to an application in which you separate the user interface from your coded components.

◆ **XML is the underlying structure for object transfer in .NET:** This benefit is a new one but is worthy of mention since this book is about .NET. As you'll see in Chapter 5 and throughout Part III of this book, XML is the underlying method of transporting your ADO.NET objects. It's also the method that you use to more efficiently transfer objects from object to object in a process known as *serialization,* which entails creating a text stream that represents the current state of an object as it is moved from one object to another object, and perhaps even from one machine to another machine.

XML Structure

Although XML is very flexible, you must follow some very precise rules. I cover structure and syntax for XML documents in this section and leave validity to the section "Valid versus well-formed," later in this chapter. For now, I focus on the rules for creating a well-formed XML document.

In the browser market, Microsoft Internet Explorer's taken the lead in XML. Figure 4-1 shows a web.config document that I've saved as config.xml. I've closed down all the comments (notice the plus signs) to make seeing the XML structure a bit easier.

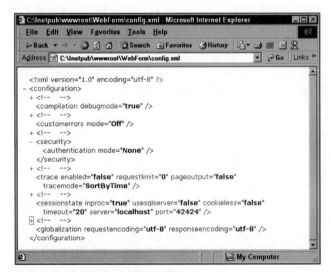

Figure 4-1: A simple .NET XML file.

Document structure

A well-formed XML document includes an optional prolog (at the beginning of the document), a body that contains one or more elements (with a single root element), and an optional epilog (at the end of the document), as the following list describes:

♦ **Prolog:** The prolog contains the XML tag and any number of comments and processing instructions (PIs). The prolog can also contain embedded DTDs and schemas, which I cover in the section "Valid versus well-formed" later in this chapter. Other than DTDs or schemas, you do not normally see much in the prolog; I have yet to work on many applications that utilize PIs. The prolog for an XML document should look something like the following example.

```
<?xml version="1.0" encoding="utf-8" ?>
<!-- Any number of comments -->
<!-- Processing instructions go here -->
```

♦ **Body:** The body of an XML document contains a single root tag, with a hierarchical structure of tags inside the root tag. The body section of the document looks something like the following XML example web.config taken from a `web.config` file, which is covered in Chapter 12.

```
<configuration>
    <security>
        <authentication mode="None" />
    </security>
    <sessionstate
            inproc="true"
            usesqlserver="false"
            cookieless="false"
            timeout="20"
            server="localhost"
            port="42424"
    />
</configuration>
```

♦ **Epilog:** This section is for comments and processing instructions. Because running processing instructions is not very common at this point, you don't see an epilog in many documents.

ELEMENTS AND ATTRIBUTES

Two important structures follow through the entire syntax of XML: elements and attributes. Elements are the tags themselves, while attributes modify these tags. Elements and attributes are a point of contention with a lot of developers, because most XML DOM parsing engines are more efficient at utilizing attributes. As such, many developers opt for using attributes everywhere. On the other hand, elements are more human readable and make code easier to maintain (and errors easier to find). As always, the performance-versus-maintainability argument rears its ugly head. Personally, I think of attributes as containing metadata, and elements as containing data. I've also used attributes for primary and foreign key fields from the database. I use elements for any data I intend to present to the user. Because they are more human readable, elements are easier to maintain.

Listing 4-1 shows a simple XML document. I name the elements and attributes according to their type, so navigating this code should prove very easy. The ID fields in the example represent the primary key for the parent and child elements. I broke my rule of separation of data and metadata here by using attribute2 in the child element to hold "ASP .NET" and "Visual Basic .NET"

Listing 4-1: Elements and Attributes in XML

```
<rootElement>
    <parentElement attribute1="value" ID="1">
        <childElement attribute2="ASP.Net" />
    </parentElement>
    <parentElement attribute1="value" ID="2">
        <childElement attribute2="Visual Basic.Net">
    </parentElement>
</rootElement>
```

A FEW RULES

Besides the rudimentary basics of XML that I just discussed, there are a few rules that XML documents must follow to be considered well formed. Here's a list of the more important rules for XML:

◆ **The XML declaration must come first:** While you don't have to have a prolog at all, much less an XML tag, if you *do* have an XML tag, it must be the first tag in the document. The XML tag looks like this:

```
<?xml version="1.0" encoding="utf-8" ?>
```

◆ **Every tag must have a closing tag:** This is different from HTML, where you could have a <P> tag without a corresponding </P> tag, or could use a <BR> tag (which has no closing tag) for a break. In XML a tag either has a separate closing tag or is self-closing. The two types are shown here:

```
<WithClosingTag>data or tags here</WithClosingTag>
```

```
<SelfClosingTag />
```

The <BR> tag in XHTML must follow this rule as well, so you often see it written as

◆ **XML is case-sensitive:** Unlike HTML, where a `<P>` and a `<p>` represent the same tag, you can have nested tags with the same name, as long as the tag is written with at least one letter in a different case. While not the best practice, the following snippet is perfectly legal:

```
<Book>
    <book>book name here</book>
</Book>
```

◆ **Your tags must be properly nested:** This caveat is present in HTML, as well. The main difference is that an XML parser is not supposed to "fix" your code, although I have encountered parsers that do. On the other hand, most browsers are designed to ignore some types of nesting errors. For example, here is an improperly nested piece of XHTML that will create an error in an XML parser:

```
<font face="Arial"><b>Hello, World!</font></b>
```

Here's the same snippet but with properly nested tags, which will render in an XML parser:

```
<font face="Arial"><b>Hello, World!</b></font>
```

◆ **Attribute values must be placed in quotes:** While it is considered bad form, you can drop the quotation marks around the values of attributes in HTML. A tag like `<script language=JavaScript>` renders in a browser without a problem. In XML, you must place attribute values in single or double quotes; so tags like the ones that follow cause errors:

```
<table width=150>
    <tr>
        <td width=100></td>
        <td width=50></td>
    </tr>
</table>
```

The correct form would be:

```
<table width="150">
    <tr>
        <td width="100"></td>
        <td width="50"></td>
    </tr>
</table>
```

◆ **XML ignores white space:** Although there are a few ways to preserve white space for formatting, the general rule is that XML ignores all white space in your document. You can use white space to make your document more readable, however, because you face no penalty for your extra carriage returns.

◆ **You must escape certain special characters:** In XML, there are two characters that must be escaped to be rendered: < and &. In the XML spec, there are entity references included to escape these characters: < is escaped as <, and & is escaped as &. The rule follows HTML, where you must escape these characters to have them appear where the user can read them. In HMTL, the browser ignores characters that are not properly escaped. In XML, the page causes an error.

IT LOOKS LIKE HTML

Many of the constructs of XML come from the same roots as those of HTML, so you may find that much of XML structure looks like HTML. (I cover the use of HTML inside of XML when I introduce transformations with XSLT in the "Rendering XML with XSLT" section later in this chapter.) Comments and entity references, for instance, are pretty much the same in both XML and HTML.

◆ **Comments:** Comments in both HTML and XML follow the structure `<!--` `Type comment here -->` for opening and closing brackets. The XML parser ignores anything that you place in a comment tag.

◆ **Entity references:** An entity reference is a set of characters to represent another string of characters. Although you can create your own entity references in XML, a few are the same as their HTML equivalents. These are & (ampersand, or &), < (less than, or <), > (greater than, or >), " (quotation mark, or "), and ' (apostrophe or single quote, or ').

You also find some differences between HTML and XML, including some coding standards that you must change slightly to make HTML fully compatible with XML. These changes prompted the adoption of XHTML, which is, in essence, well-formed HTML (that is, HTML that has an opening and closing tag for every tag pair). If you embed HTML in an XSLT stylesheet, you must make sure that it's well-formed HTML. Well-formed HTML, or XHTML, is covered a bit later in the section "Rendering XML with XSLT."

For more information about XSL and XSLT, you can read the specification on the W3C site, at www.w3c.org/Style/XSL. For more general information on Web style sheets, go to www.w3c.org/Style.

One of the rules that you must follow to make sure that your HTML is well formed is to always include a closing tag. Because some tags in HTML don't require closing tags and others don't even *have* closing tags, this requirement may seem a bit odd.

To illustrate a closing tag when there is none in HTML, consider the <br> tag. In standard HTML, the <br> tag is used to break a line and has no closing tag. In XHTML, however, it must be closed to be well formed. There are two solutions to this problem. First, I can add an arbitrary closing tag, ending up with
</br>. This is a bit strange looking, and some HTML editors will actually drop the </br> tag because it isn't in the HTML specification. A better solution is to self-close the tag like this: <br/>. This creates a problem with Netscape, which sees the tag as br/, not br. The easy solution is to add a space between the br and the /, so you end up with <br />. Listing 4-2 shows an example of HTML that's well formed.

Listing 4-2: Well-Formed HTML

```
<html>
<head>
<title>Sample Well-Formed HTML</title>
</head>
<body>
<img src="images/logo.gif" /><br />
</body>
</html>
```

As you look at the code in Listing 4-2, pay close attention to the image (<img>) and the line break (<br>) tags. This page renders (displays) in older browsers while remaining XML-compliant. In other words, this page will display if you are using Netscape 3, and it is still formatted properly to be used in an XSLT stylesheet. Once again, the important point is to add a space before the / at the end of the tag.

Valid versus well-formed

You must make sure that an XML document is well-formed if you want to parse it, whether you want to render it for a user or just transform it. Although the document must be well formed, it doesn't need to be *valid*.

A valid document is one that follows a set of rules created by an individual or organization and expressed as either a Document Type Definition (DTD) or an XML schema. This section explains how DTDs and schemas are used to ensure that an XML document is valid.

DOCUMENT TYPE DEFINITION (DTD)

A *Document Type Definition* (DTD) is a document that describes the expected layout of an XML document. DTDs are a bit of a leftover from the SGML standard, although you still use it in some cases. DTDs have a shortcoming: they don't define data types; everything is treated as a string, whether it is numeric or character data. Because one of the primary purposes of XML is to describe and transfer data, Microsoft is pushing away from DTDs in favor of schemas.

If you want to describe your documents in a way that's less bleeding edge, how-ever, you want to use DTDs. They're a bit unwieldy, but they're an adopted recom-mendation of the W3C. I don't dwell on DTDs in this book, however, because they're not the primary format of describing data in .NET. Listing 4-3 shows a sim-ple DTD that you can use to describe a typical farm.

Listing 4-3: A Simple Farm DTD

```
<?xml version="1.0" encoding="UTF-8"?>
<!ELEMENT Farm (Cow|Pig|Duck)* >
<!ELEMENT Cow (#PCDATA)>
<!ATTLIST sound(moo|grunt) "moo">
<!ELEMENT Pig (#PCDATA)>
<!ATTLIST sound(oink|snort) "oink">
<!ELEMENT Duck (#PCDATA)>
<!ATTLIST sound(quack|wail) "quack">
```

The DTD is Listing 4-3 tells us the root element of this XML document is Farm. Farm has Cow, Pig, and Duck elements. These elements are designated by the word ELEMENT. Each animal in this farm has a sound attribute, which is designated by the keyword ATTLIST. Each sound has a default, which is set by adding the value, in quotes, after the choices; for example, the cow's default sound is "moo." The XML document in List 4-4 uses the DTD in Listing 4-3.

Listing 4-4: An XML Farm

```
<?xml version="1.0" encoding="UTF-8"?>
<Farm>
<Cow sound="moo" />
<Pig sound="snort" />
<Duck sound="quack" />
</Farm>
```

In Listing 4-4, as in the DTD, we have a Farm element as the root element, and Cow, Pig, and Duck elements. I've set a sound for each animal; only the pig uses a sound other than its default.

 The tags in XML are case-sensitive. You cannot substitute <farm> for <Farm> in the XML document in Listing 4-4, for example. If you capitalize one tag, and not its mate, you get a parsing error.

SCHEMAS

Schemas are the direction the industry is heading with XML. A schema is a representation of your XML rules in a hierarchical format, rather than using the DTD shorthand. In a schema, each element is defined using an `ElementType` tag, with `element` tags representing the manner in which tags are nested.

Schemas are both easier to read and easier to create than DTDs, especially with the tools that Microsoft provides. One of the easiest tools to work with is the SQL Server 2000 Query Analyzer. In Listing 4-5, I issue the command to create an XML document with an attached schema. The most important part here, from a schema standpoint, is the keyword `XMLDATA`.

Listing 4–5: SQL XML Command

```
Use Northwind
SELECT * FROM Products
WHERE ProductID = 45
FOR XML AUTO, XMLDATA, ELEMENTS
```

Listing 4-6 shows the XML that returns from this query.

Listing 4–6: The XML that Returns from the SQL Query

```
<Schema name="Schema4" xmlns="urn:schemas-microsoft-com:xml-data"
    xmlns:dt="urn:schemas-microsoft-com:datatypes">
  <ElementType name="Products" content="eltOnly"
        model="closed" order="many">
    <element type="ProductID"/>
    <element type="ProductName"/>
    <element type="SupplierID"/>
    <element type="CategoryID"/>
    <element type="QuantityPerUnit"/>
    <element type="UnitPrice"/>
    <element type="UnitsInStock"/>
    <element type="UnitsOnOrder"/>
    <element type="ReorderLevel"/>
    <element type="Discontinued"/>
  </ElementType>
  <ElementType name="ProductID" content="textOnly" model="closed" dt:type="i4"/>
  <ElementType name="ProductName" content="textOnly" model="closed"
    dt:type="string"/>
  <ElementType name="SupplierID" content="textOnly" model="closed"
dt:type="i4"/>
  <ElementType name="CategoryID" content="textOnly" model="closed"
dt:type="i4"/>
  <ElementType name="QuantityPerUnit" content="textOnly" model="closed"
    dt:type="string"/>
  <ElementType name="UnitPrice" content="textOnly" model="closed"
```

```
        dt:type="fixed.14.4"/>
    <ElementType name="UnitsInStock" content="textOnly" model="closed"
        dt:type="i2"/>
    <ElementType name="UnitsOnOrder" content="textOnly" model="closed"
        dt:type="i2"/>
    <ElementType name="ReorderLevel" content="textOnly" model="closed"
        dt:type="i2"/>
    <ElementType name="Discontinued" content="textOnly" model="closed"
        dt:type="boolean"/>
</Schema>
<Products xmlns="x-schema:#Schema4">
    <ProductID>45</ProductID>
    <ProductName>Rogede sild</ProductName>
    <SupplierID>21</SupplierID>
    <CategoryID>8</CategoryID>
    <QuantityPerUnit>1k pkg.</QuantityPerUnit>
    <UnitPrice>9.5000</UnitPrice>
    <UnitsInStock>5</UnitsInStock>
    <UnitsOnOrder>70</UnitsOnOrder>
    <ReorderLevel>15</ReorderLevel>
    <Discontinued>0</Discontinued>
</Products>
```

The data type returns with each element in the schema. If you look closely, you notice that the basic format is as follows:

◆ `<Schema>` tags wrap the entire content of the schema. Note that the Schema tag is capitalized. Note that there is a namespace, `dt`, included in the tag. This namespace will be used in `ElementType` tags to define the data-type.

```
<Schema name="Schema1"
xmlns="urn:schemas-microsoft-com:xml-data"
xmlns:dt="urn:schemas-microsoft-com:datatypes">\
</Schema>
```

◆ `<ElementType>` tags contain the information about the tags in the schema, including the name, content, model, and datatype. The following element is an integer (in SQL Server) that occupies 4 bytes in memory. The data type is i4, which means a 4-byte integer. Note the capitalization in `ElementType`.

```
<ElementType name="ProductID" content="textOnly"
    model="closed" dt:type="i4"/>
```

◆ `<element>` tags represent the hierarchy in the schema. `<element type="ProductID" />`, for example, resides inside the `<ElementType>` tag for `Products`. This format shows that the `<ProductID>` tag is a child element to `<Products>`. Note that element is lowercase.

```
<element type="ProductID"/>
```

For each `<element>` tag, you will have a corresponding `<ElementType>` tag that defines the element.

 TIP If you use SQL Server 2000 as your database, you can reduce the amount of time it takes to produce a schema by using Query Analyzer, as I've done in the preceding example. The keyword of importance is `XMLDATA`; it is used in a `FOR XML` query. Here's an example:

`SELECT * FROM Customers FOR XML AUTO, XMLDATA, ELEMENTS`

Without the `XMLDATA` keyword, you'd simply get the XML data, and not the schema.

Rendering XML with XSLT

As I mentioned earlier in this chapter, many of the elements of HTML and XML are the same, which is why mixing XML and HTML syntax in an XSLT file is so easy.

What is XSLT?

XSLT is an XML subset, or application, that you use to transform data that's in the form of XML into HTML or more XML. It is the subset of the XSL specification that deals specifically with transforming XML. This explanation is a bit of an oversimplification, but it serves our purpose well enough at this point.

There are a couple good reasons to transform XML with XSLT:

- ◆ Your organization uses one data structure and a client or partner uses another. As long as you both use XML for data transport, you can use XSLT to change your data format to the data format used by your partner. This is the methodology behind BizTalk server, which has a mapping tool to transform documents from one format to another.

- ◆ You have a list of reports that are viewable as HTML. Rather than use a mixture of HTML tags and ASP to output your report, you can easily transform the XML data with an XSLT stylesheet and output your report as HTML. The upside to this methodology is it can easily be edited to produce a variety of reports without altering the application. The same is true for output as text or Rich Text Format (rtf).

If you think of XML primarily as a data transport, you can probably come up with other reasons to use XSLT to transform the XML from one format to another.

The basic idea is that you can either transform the data into another data format, or you can transform the document from XML to another document format.

Figure 4-2 shows the methodology behind XML and XSLT and the resulting output from XML transformations. You probably notice that the diagram includes SOAP and BizTalk, both of which use XML.

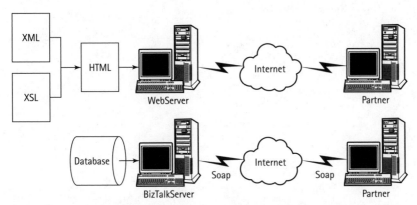

Figure 4-2: XSLT transformations and XML technologies: XSL and SOAP.

Transforming XML

Because this chapter is an introductory chapter, I'm just going to show you an example of transformation here. Chapter 20 covers transformations in detail (you want to understand transformations if you're going to use XML in your .NET applications). For now, I create a simple HTML table from an XML document with an XSLT stylesheet attached.

Listing 4-7 contains a simple XML document, which is a list of .NET languages. This document will be used to create an HTML table.

Listing 4-7: An ASP-Language XML Document (dotnet.xml)

```
<?xml version="1.0" encoding="utf-8" ?>
<?xml-stylesheet type="text/xsl" href="dotnet.xsl"?>
<DotNet>
    <language>C#</language>
    <language>JScript</language>
    <language>Managed C++</language>
    <language>Visual Basic.Net</language>
</DotNet>
```

The XSLT stylesheet used to create the HTML table is shown in Listing 4-8. Note that there are two template sections in this XSLT document. This is one way to format an XSLT document to make it more maintainable. Since the template that matches the DotNet section is separate from the rest of the document, I can choose to change my table without altering the rest of the document. If each section, or perhaps each type of node, has its own template, it's easy for a developer to search for the section that needs editing.

Listing 4–8: The XSLT Document (dotnet.xsl)

```
<?xml version="1.0" ?>
<xsl:stylesheet version="1.0"
xmlns:xsl="http://www.w3.org/1999/XSL/Transform">
  <xsl:template match="/">
    <html>
      <head>
        <title>A Basic Stylesheet</title>
      </head>
      <body>
        <h1>Dot Net Languages</h1>
        <xsl:apply-templates/>
      </body>
    </html>
  </xsl:template>

  <xsl:template match="DotNet">
    <table border="1">
    <xsl:for-each select="language">
       <tr><td>
       <xsl:value-of/>
       </td></tr>
    </xsl:for-each>
    </table>
  </xsl:template>

</xsl:stylesheet>
```

Figure 4-3 shows the result of this transformation. I'm using XML Spy here to display the browser output of the transformation. You can use Internet Explorer to display the output if you'd like to see this transformation on your own system.

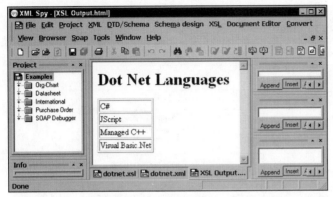

Figure 4-3: An XML/XSLT transformation in the browser view of XML Spy.

XML Objects in .NET

XML is an important part of the .NET Framework. Numerous objects in .NET help you work with XML documents. One of the reasons for XML's importance in .NET is Microsoft's dedication of so many resources to developing new interoperability standards, such as Universal Description, Discovery, and Integration (UDDI) and SOAP. The fact that the main data-transfer methodology of ADO.NET is XML however, doesn't hurt.

SOAP and UDDI are covered in greater detail in Part IV of the book. While you do not see it as SOAP unless you peek under the hood, Web Services use SOAP to package data for the Web service.

Objects that represent XML

The first set of XML objects in the .NET Framework contains those that you use to represent objects in the XML DOM. The one that you use the most is the `System.XML` namespace, although you need to become familiar with each of these objects.

SYSTEM.XML

`System.XML` is the parent of the other XML namespaces in the .NET Framework. Here you find XML documents, elements, attributes, and the reader and writer classes necessary to manipulate XML in the application stream. The object model for `System.XML` is shown in Figure 4-4.

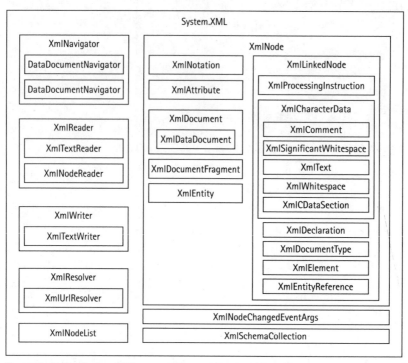

Figure 4-4: The System.XML namespace and its class hierarchy.

SYSTEM.XML.XSL

The `System.XML.XSL` namespace contains two objects. The first is the `XslTransform` class, which you use to transform XML documents. The second is the `XslException` class, which you use to handle XSL exceptions.

XSLT transformations are covered in greater detail in Chapter 20.

SYSTEM.XML.XPATH

The System.XML.XPath namespace is used to run XPath queries. There are five classes in the System.XML.XPath namespace: XPathDocument, XPathException, XPathExpression, XPathNavigator, and XPathNodeIterator. The names of the objects pretty well explain their purpose, but here is the run-through:

- **XPathDocument:** Unlike an XML document, the XPath document is a read-only cache for XML processing using XSLT with XPath queries.

- **XPathException:** If you have an error when processing an XPath query, you can catch it with this object. XPath exception should be placed ahead of the generic exception object in structure error handling.

- **XPathExpression:** This class is used to hold a compiled XPath expression.

- **XPathNavigator:** The navigator is used to navigate the XPath document, which can be queried with compiled XPath expressions.

- **XPathNodeIterator:** This object is used to iterate through a set of nodes in the XPath document.

Serialization

Serialization is the process of taking an object and turning it into a serial message, which, simply put, means breaking down the object into individual bytes of information to stream from one process to another. In .NET, this term means taking an object and breaking it down into XML. Because this process adds complexity to code, your first question may be, "Why do you want to do that?" The answer is very simple: a serialized object passes more efficiently than one that you marshal from application space to application space as an object. Serialization also enables you to easily create a new instance of an object rather than work with a reference to the original object.

The .NET Framework serializes objects into XML. As XML is a simple way to hierarchically represent data, you can easily adopt it to show classes, their methods and properties, as well as the values of any arguments that these methods and properties use.

For more information about arguments in properties in Visual Basic .NET, see Chapter 2.

SYSTEM.XML.SERIALIZATION

The System.XML.Serialization model is quite complex. Although you carry out the majority of the work with the writer and reader objects, delving into this topic a bit deeper is still worth your time.

Serialization of objects is covered in greater detail in Chapter 18.

Figure 4-5 shows the object model for the System.XML.Serialization namespace. Note that the XmlMembersMapping and XmlTypeMapping objects are contained inside of the base (parent) class from which they inherit.

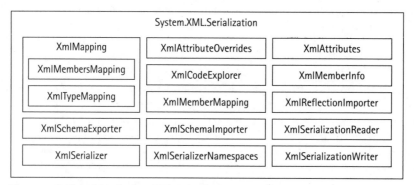

Figure 4-5: The major System.XML.Serialization namespace.

SYSTEM.XML.SERIALIZATION.SCHEMA

The System.XML.Serialization.Schema namespace is also quite complex. You use this model to create the schemas that represent your objects after you serialize them. The schema here is a data reduced schema, much like the schema produced by the SQL Server query that you saw in Listing 4-5 earlier in this chapter. Figure 4-6 shows the objects in the System.XML.Serialization.Schema object model.

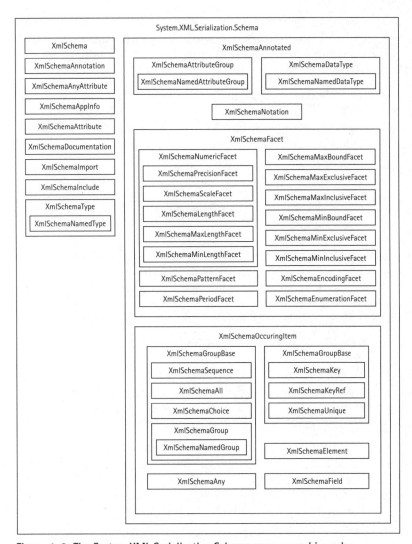

Figure 4-6: The System.XML.Serialization.Schema namespace hierarchy.

Other Microsoft XML Initiatives

In case you don't keep up with the MSDN site or any of the news items from the Microsoft Web site, Microsoft is very committed to using XML. In the past two years, Microsoft has moved wholeheartedly into XML and logged the following accomplishments:

◆ Development of the first browser that's XML capable. Although not fully compliant with all the W3C recommendations for XML, Internet Explorer 5.0 was the first browser to market that parses and validates XML documents.

◆ Development of SOAP (Simple Object Access Protocol) as a new standard up for consideration. SOAP is a method for accessing object methods by using XML. SOAP uses a two-part document consisting of a package wrapped inside an envelope.

◆ Work on UDDI or (Universal Description, Discovery, and Integration), an XML variant for use in the discovery of Web services. While SOAP's purpose is to contact known objects, UDDI's design enables it to query Web servers for available services. You can find out more about UDDI at www.uddi.org.

◆ Development of one of the best implementations of the XML DOM. Having worked with the MSXML DOM for the past few years, I can simply say, "Wow!" The first implementation was a bit slow but relatively solid. As the product matures, however, it just keeps getting faster and faster. As of this writing, Microsoft is up to version 4.0 of the MSXML DOM.

◆ Microsoft's spearheading of the BizTalk initiative with a server that it calls BizTalk Server. Although Microsoft touts this platform as a .NET Enterprise server, understand that it contains no .NET technology. BizTalk is a nice way to transform your documents into a format that a customer or a partner can use. Microsoft designed it primarily for B2B (business-to-business) commerce, but you can adapt it to other uses.

◆ XML as the underlying technology behind object and data transfer in .NET. You see this throughout the book: XML is core in the configuration of ASP.NET applications (Chapter 12), Web services (Chapter 14), and ADO.NET (all of part III), for example. You may not always be exposed to the XML, especially if you are using Visual Studio .NET, but it is there.

Summary

As you discover in this chapter, XML is very important to Microsoft's .NET vision. XML is a simple, straightforward language that you can use to describe and transport data. It uses open standards that are compatible with a variety of platforms and is now the main method of transferring content across the Web (other than HTML, of course). By using DTDs and schemas, you can easily describe the format of your data, and with tools such as BizTalk, you can easily transform your data into a format that one of your partners can use.

There are a variety of XML implementations of which you should be aware if you're going to develop in .NET. Part IV of this book explores XML further, including UDDI and SOAP.

In the next chapter, I introduce ADO.NET, particularly the objects used to access and utilize data, which reside in the namespaces `System.Data`, `System.Data.SQClient,` and `System.Data.OleDb`.

Chapter 5

ADO.NET

IN THIS CHAPTER

- ◆ Differences between ADO and ADO.NET

- ◆ The ease of creating distributed applications in ADO.NET

- ◆ The object model that you use in ADO.NET, including hierarchies
  for each of the ADO.NET namespaces

ADO.NET IS THE DATA ACCESS METHOD that you employ in the .NET platform. It is a major improvement over ADO, but may provide a major shock, as well.

I cover all this material in great detail in Part III, so much of this chapter may seem to be a technical reference to the objects in the `System.Data` namespace hierarchy. Because data is very important to all applications, though, focusing on the objects is time well spent.

More than ADO+

At the time that Microsoft first announced ADO.NET — as ADO+ — it sounded as though the company was simply releasing a version of ADO with some additional features. After all, COM+ was basically an update to COM, including the new features of Microsoft Transaction Server (MTS) and Microsoft Message Queue (MSMQ). Such a minor update isn't the case with ADO.NET. Microsoft's completely remanufactured data access in ADO.NET rather than just built on top of the old model. To illustrate this point, Table 5-1 shows some of the differences between ADO and ADO.NET.

TABLE 5-1 COMPARISON OF ADO AND ADO.NET

ADO	ADO.NET
Represents data in memory as a Recordset, which is like a single table.	Represents data in memory as DataSets, which can contain one or more DataTables.

Continued

TABLE 5-1 COMPARISON OF ADO AND ADO.NET *(Continued)*

ADO	ADO.NET
You must merge data from multiple tables into a single "table" through the use of joins. You can have multiple Recordset objects that you can access through a single Connection object.	Supports DataRelations to relate multiple DataTables in a single DataSet.
Sequential access of data only.	Can navigate data nonsequentially through the relations set up in the DataRelations object.
Normal method of communication is a connected paradigm, using the Connection object. You can set up disconnected Recordsets. Connection objects use OLE DB providers to communicate to the data source. Uses the Connection objects to issue commands to the data source.	Normal method of communication is a disconnected paradigm. Uses a DataSetCommand object to communicate with OLE DB providers (or directly to the data API, as in SQL Server). The DataSets, therefore, are completely disconnected from the data. Uses XML as the command mechanism, simplifying both communication and transport of data.
Uses COM to marshal disconnected Recordset objects between tiers in your application.	Uses XML to move data from object to object.
COM makes transferring data through firewalls difficult, as additional ports need to open to marshal COM objects.	XML can pass through HTTP on port 80, the same port that Web servers use, which is open on most firewalls to enable Web access.
ADO isn't as scalable, as locks and active database connections can limit available data resources.	ADO.NET's disconnected nature doesn't hold locks or connections with data sources, enabling you to use more scalable applications.

A robust object model

The underlying transport of data in the ADO.NET model is XML. If you've been holding off on learning XML, now may be a good time to start. Although you can program in ADO.NET without understanding XML, knowing at least a little about the technology is wise and helps you appreciate how revolutionary this new model is.

XML is a pivotal technology used throughout the .NET Framework, including ADO.NET, Web services, and configuration of your .NET applications. XML is the focus of Part IV of this book.

Table 5-2 shows the primary ADO.NET objects that you're likely to use in your applications, along with their closest ADO equivalent. The table is divided into core ADO.NET objects and ADO.NET managed provider objects. Core objects are used no matter what data source is used. The managed provider objects are ODBC-, OLEDB-, or SQL Server-specific objects. I discuss the managed provider objects more specifically as the chapter progresses.

TABLE 5-2 THE PRIMARY ADO.NET OBJECTS

Managed Provider Object	Purpose	Closest ADO Equivalent
Connection	Represents a Connection to a data source.	Connection
Command	Represents a command to execute. A command can be a table, a stored procedure or a SQL query.	Command
CommandBuilder	Builds INSERT, UPDATE, and DELETE statements from a SELECT command in a DataAdapter.	None
DataAdapter	Serves as a bridge between a data source and a DataSet. It stores the various SQL commands used to interact with the data source.	None
DataReader	A forward-only, read-only stream of data. While the DataReader is a very efficient means of displaying data, it doesn't support scrolling or updating of data.	Forward-only, Read-only, Recordset

Continued

TABLE 5-2 THE PRIMARY ADO.NET OBJECTS *(Continued)*

Core Object	Purpose	Closest ADO Equivalent
DataSet	A relational view of data containing one or more DataTables. The DataSet is more akin to a mini-relational database than a Recordset.	None
DataTable	A single table in a DataSet. This is the closest object to a Recordset in ADO.	Recordset
DataView	A specific view of a DataTable or DataTables, which is useful in data binding. You can set the sort order and even filter the data represented through a DataView. While a DataView has no equivalent in ADO, it is very much like a view in SQL Server	None
DataRelation	Used to describe a relation between two DataTables in a DataSet.	None

I put these objects in perspective as I progress through the chapter. Remember, when I talk about a managed provider, I mean the objects in the `System.Data.SqlClient` and `System.Data.OleDb` namespace; core objects are in the `System.Data` namespace.

ADO to ADO.NET: A paradigm shift

The shift from ADO to ADO.NET is more than a simple change in objects. While the separation of provider objects from core objects is certainly a modification, the more important change is the paradigm shift from a connected model (ADO) to a disconnected one (ADO.NET).

To better illustrate the differences, Figure 5-1 shows the traditional ADO method of accessing data. While you can disconnect a Recordset object from a Connection object, the norm is having the Recordset connected for its entire lifetime.

In contrast, Figure 5-2 shows the data access methodology of ADO.NET. You create a connection, and use a data adapter as a bridge from the core objects to the managed provider. In the data adapter, you can use one or more commands to fill data tables in a data set. You can then use the data table or a view of the table (data view object) to fill a data grid in your ASP.NET page. In addition, you can create a data reader object to move data directly from the connection to the data grid in your page (this reduces a lot of programming weight, but is a read-only data object).

In ADO, you populate a `Recordset` by using an OLE DB provider. Although you can also build `Recordsets` on-the-fly or even migrate data from XML into a `Recordset`, you have no easy way to facilitate this transformation, at least not with hierarchical data. The transformation is easy but largely unnecessary in ADO.NET, because the data is always represented as XML, if you choose to program using this paradigm. To clarify this point: You can transform data objects to XML, but you can also program using an XML model and leave the data in the data grid. I discuss this subject a bit more in the "XML and distributed applications" section later in this chapter.

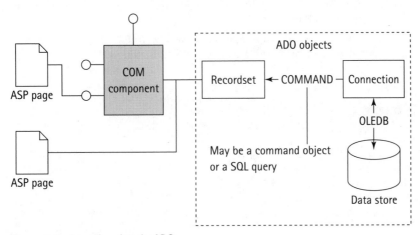

Figure 5-1: Accessing data in ADO.

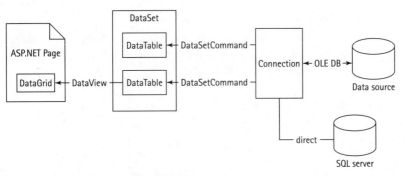

Figure 5-2: Accessing data in ADO.NET.

Working with data in ADO.NET

The core object in ADO.NET is the DataSet. A DataSet is, for lack of a more apt comparison, a mini-relational database held in memory. When you create a DataSet, you build tables, views, and relations, just like you do in a relational database. Because the data is held in memory, you should be prudent and limit the amount of data you place in a DataSet.

A DataSet persists as XML, which makes transfer of DataSets more robust than marshaling Recordsets in ADO. (Marshaling means moving across process boundaries; marshaling occurs when you use move data, especially objects, from object to object, when these objects are running in different process spaces or threads. Since objects are reference types, and this forces a copy, rather than a pointer, it is expensive, in terms of CPU cycles.) I cover DataSet persistence in greater detail in the following section, "XML and distributed applications."

Figure 5-3 shows an ADO.NET application in which you create a simple SQL query to pull data from the Northwind database in SQL Server.

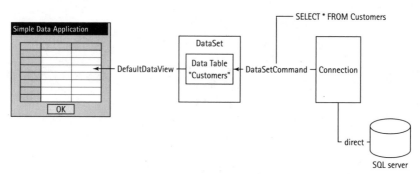

Figure 5-3: The model for a simple ADO.NET application.

The code for this simple application appears in Listing 5-1. Don't worry about understanding everything concerning this model right now; I cover ADO.NET in much more detail in Part III (Chapters 15 through 17).

Listing 5-1: A Simple ADO.NET Application

```
Imports SQLData = System.Data.SqlClient
Imports SysData = System.Data

Public Class Form1
   Inherits System.Windows.Forms.Form

#Region " Windows Form Designer generated code "
```

```vb
Public Sub New()
  MyBase.New()

  'This call is required by the Windows Form Designer.
  InitializeComponent()

  'Add any initialization after the InitializeComponent() call

End Sub

'Form overrides dispose to clean up the component list.
Protected Overloads Overrides Sub Dispose(ByVal disposing As Boolean)
  If disposing Then
    If Not (components Is Nothing) Then
      components.Dispose()
    End If
  End If
  MyBase.Dispose(disposing)
End Sub

'Required by the Windows Form Designer
Private components As System.ComponentModel.IContainer

'NOTE: The following procedure is required by the Windows Form Designer
'It can be modified using the Windows Form Designer.
'Do not modify it using the code editor.
Friend WithEvents DataGrid1 As System.Windows.Forms.DataGrid
Friend WithEvents btnDataTable As System.Windows.Forms.Button
<System.Diagnostics.DebuggerStepThrough()> Private Sub InitializeComponent()
  Me.DataGrid1 = New System.Windows.Forms.DataGrid()
  Me.btnDataTable = New System.Windows.Forms.Button()
  CType(Me.DataGrid1, System.ComponentModel.ISupportInitialize).BeginInit()
  Me.SuspendLayout()
  '
  'DataGrid1
  '
  Me.DataGrid1.DataMember = ""
  Me.DataGrid1.HeaderForeColor = System.Drawing.SystemColors.ControlText
  Me.DataGrid1.Name = "DataGrid1"
  Me.DataGrid1.Size = New System.Drawing.Size(456, 256)
  Me.DataGrid1.TabIndex = 0
  '
```

Continued

Listing 5-1 *(Continued)*

```
    'btnDataTable
    '
    Me.btnDataTable.Location = New System.Drawing.Point(8, 264)
    Me.btnDataTable.Name = "btnDataTable"
    Me.btnDataTable.Size = New System.Drawing.Size(88, 23)
    Me.btnDataTable.TabIndex = 1
    Me.btnDataTable.Text = "Submit"
    '
'Form1
    '
    Me.AutoScaleBaseSize = New System.Drawing.Size(5, 13)
    Me.ClientSize = New System.Drawing.Size(464, 301)
    Me.Controls.AddRange(New System.Windows.Forms.Control() {Me.btnDataTable, ↵
Me.DataGrid1})
    Me.Name = "Form1"
    Me.Text = "Form1"
    CType(Me.DataGrid1, System.ComponentModel.ISupportInitialize).EndInit()
    Me.ResumeLayout(False)


  End Sub

#End Region


  Private Sub btnDataTable_Click(ByVal sender As System.Object, ByVal e As ↵
System.EventArgs) Handles btnDataTable.Click
    'Declare objects
    Dim strConn As String = "Server=(local);" & _
        "Database=Northwind;UID=sa;PWD=;"
    Dim strSQL As String = "SELECT * FROM Customers"

    'managed provider objects
    Dim objConn As New SQLData.SqlConnection(strConn)
    Dim objCmd As New SQLData.SqlCommand(strSQL, objConn)
    Dim objDataAdapter As New SQLData.SqlDataAdapter(objCmd)

    'Core object(s)
    Dim objDataSet As New SysData.DataSet()

    'Fill Dataset with DataAdapter (bridge)
    objConn.Open()
    objDataAdapter.Fill(objDataSet, "Customers")
```

```
objConn.Close()

'Bind data to Dataset
DataGrid1.DataSource = objDataSet.Tables("Customers").DefaultView

  End Sub
End Class
```

 The code from Listing 5-1 can be downloaded from the companion Web site (www.wiley.com/extras) in the file Ch05VS.zip (Visual Studio .NET version) or Ch05SDK.zip (SDK version). After you unzip the file, look at the project SimpleWinForm.

In this application, you load a single table into a DataGrid control on a Visual Basic .NET form. Don't worry if you don't understand all the syntax right now; just pay attention to the flow. I cover ADO.NET in great detail in Part III, and some of the heavy-handed nature of this code starts to make sense there.

To better understand Listing 5-1 and how to use ADO.NET, let's step through the different objects used:

1. You instantiate a SQLConnection object by using a simple connection string, as follows:

```
Dim strConn As String = "Server=(local);" & _
                        "Database=Northwind;UID=sa;PWD=;"
Dim objConn As New SysSQL.SQLConnection(strConn)
objConn.Open()
```

   Note: If you're using an OLEDB managed provider, you have to add the provider attribute (provider=SQLOLEDB.1) to the connection string.

2. You instantiate a DataSet object, as follows:

```
Dim objDataSet As New DataSet()
```

3. You create a SQLCommand:

```
Dim strSQL As String = "SELECT * FROM Customers"
Dim objCmd As New SysSQL.SqlCommand(strSQL, objConn)
```

4. You create a DataAdapter to transfer data from the SQLConnection to the DataSet. One of the constructors of the Data Adapter object allows you to

specify a select command; in this instance, I use the SQLCommand object I created in the previous step.

```
Dim objDataAdapter As New SysSQL.SqlDataAdapter(objCmd)
```

5. You use the `Fill()` method of the DataAdapter to fill the DataSet. In this instance, you are creating a DataTable object called Customers in the DataSet:

```
objDataAdapter.Fill(objDataSet, "Customers")
```

6. You populate the DataGrid by using the default DataView of the "Customers" DataTable. The default view property is optional here; I include it because I lean toward more explicit code.

```
DataGrid1.DataSource = _
            objDataSet.Tables("Customers").DefaultView
```

XML and distributed applications

The problem with the ADO model becomes glaringly evident when you start to deal with remote data, because migrating Recordsets across the Internet isn't a good idea. Recordsets are objects, which means you must have some means of object transport; because serialization is not native to ADO, you have performance issues with ADO Recordsets when you need to transport these objects from server to server, or across the Web. ADO.NET utilizes XML to transfer data from one tier to another, so creating distributed applications is a lot easier. Figure 5-4 shows a distributed application utilizing ADO.NET.

In early 2000, I worked on a model very similar to the example shown in Figure 5-4 using ASP, Visual Basic COM, and XML. The application required quite a bit of work to create the XML on one end and to reconstitute it on the other end. A lot of effort went into the interface, because Visual Basic and ASP did not have many of the tools and objects available in .NET. I experimented with BizTalk, finding that the BizTalk server makes schema mapping very easy but that its price was prohibitive for a simple data transfer. I wish .NET had been around when I developed the application — it would have made my job a lot easier.

BizTalk is Microsoft's business-to-business server. One of BizTalk's primary purposes is mapping from one data transfer format, such as EDI, to another, such XML. BizTalk has many features, but schema mapping is the most important one for this chapter.

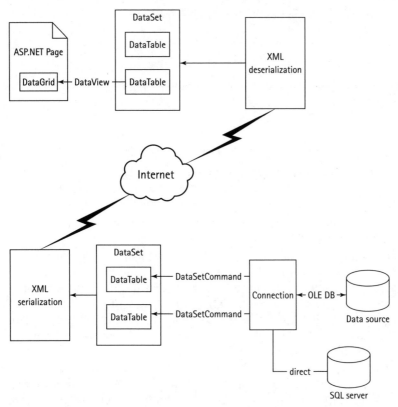

Figure 5-4: Distributed Internet application with ADO.NET.

Transferring from a Recordset to XML and back is fairly easy in ADO. It gets more difficult, however, if you're working with hierarchical data, because you need to employ a variety of Recordsets to represent the entire model. Following is a basic step-by-step guide for creating hierarchical XML from ADO. This process is fairly simplified, although the model can get much more complex, depending on the number of recordsets involved. The steps show how to create an XML document for an order and its details:

1. Create a recordset for the order from the order header table. This is the parent recordset.

2. Create a root node in an XML document called orders.

3. Create a node called order for one of the records in the parent recordset.

4. Create attribute nodes for fields in this record and give each attribute node the same name as the field name.

5. Assign the value of the field to the attribute node.

6. Create a child recordset for the order details.

7. Create a root node for one record in the child recordset.

8. Create an element node for a field in this record and give it the name of the field.

9. Create a text node.

10. Attach the text node (step 9) to the element node (step 8).

11. Repeat steps 8 through 10 for each field in this record.

12. Repeat steps 7 through 11 for each record in the child recordset.

13. Repeat steps 3 through 12 for each record in the parent recordset.

Not the easiest way to create XML, is it? You can simplify the process, but it requires using the XML capabilities of ADO, which basically force you to save off the XML as a file. Unfortunately, it tends to be hit or miss when dealing with hierarchical recordsets. Your other option is to use the XML capabilities of SQL Server 2000. If you are going to stick with ADO, the second option is preferable if you want to lighten up your objects. Either way, you need the same number of recordsets if you want to reconstitute the data on the client.

The .NET model simplifies the transfer from DataSets to XML and back. Listing 5-2 demonstrates the simplicity of creating hierarchical DataSets from XML and from a DataSet back to XML. In this example I use a file to load the XML. I have two versions of loading the DataSet here. The XMLReader is a bit more proper, especially if you intend on manipulating the XML. I could load the XML directly, but a URL is expected.

Listing 5-2: XML and DataSets

```
Private Sub btnExplicit_Click(ByVal sender As System.Object, _
    ByVal e As System.EventArgs) Handles Button1.Click
    'From XML file to DataSet (version 1)
    Dim objStreamReader As New SysIO.StreamReader("my.xml")
    Dim objXMLReader As New SysXML.XmlTextReader(objStreamReader)
    Dim objDataSet As New SysData.DataSet("MyDataSet")
    objDataSet.ReadXml(objXMLReader)
    DataGrid1.DataSource = objDataSet.Tables("Customers").DefaultView
End Sub

Private Sub btnSimple_Click(ByVal sender As System.Object, _
    ByVal e As System.EventArgs) Handles Button2.Click
    'From XML file to DataSet (version 2 - simlified, less explicit)
    Dim objStreamReader As New SysIO.StreamReader("my.xml")
```

```
    Dim objDataSet As New SysData.DataSet("MyDataSet")
    objDataSet.ReadXml(objStreamReader)
    DataGrid1.DataSource = objDataSet.Tables("Customers").DefaultView
End Sub

Private Sub btnXMLWriter_Click(ByVal sender As System.Object, _
  ByVal e As System.EventArgs) Handles Button1.Click
    'From XML file to DataSet (version 1)
    Dim objStreamReader As New SysIO.StreamReader("my.xml")
    Dim objXMLReader As New SysXML.XmlTextReader(objStreamReader)
    Dim objDataSet As New SysData.DataSet("MyDataSet")
    objDataSet.ReadXml(objXMLReader)
    DataGrid1.DataSource = objDataSet.Tables("Customers").DefaultView

    objDataSet.WriteXml("myxml2.xml")
End Sub
```

The code from Listing 5-2 can be downloaded from the companion Web site (www.wiley.com/extras) in the file Ch05VS.zip (Visual Studio .NET version) or Ch05SDK.zip (SDK version). After you unzip the file, look at the project DataFromXML.

The ADO.NET Object Models

The following namespaces contain the .NET Framework Data objects: System.Data, System.Data.OleDb, System.Data.Internal, System.Data.SQL, and System.Data.SqlTypes.

The rest of this chapter is the part that appears more like a catalog. Although the ADO.NET object model may not make a lot of sense right now, please take time to at least skim the material that I present here. You can use this chapter as a reference after you finish Part III of this book. .NET is very dependent on the base classes, so you need to understand which namespace contains the objects that you need. In most applications, you must import at least two namespaces (and add references to the underlying type libraries) to use data in your applications. The IDE handles part of the importation and referencing of objects.

System.Data

System.Data holds the objects that make up the ADO.NET architecture. The central object in this namespace is the DataSet, which, as I mentioned in Table 5-2, can hold multiple related `DataTables` to create a mini-relational database in memory. Table 5-3 covers the primary objects in the `System.Data` namespace.

TABLE 5-3 THE SYSTEM.DATA NAMESPACE

Object	Description
DataSet	An in-memory cache of data. Each `DataSet` can hold numerous `DataTables` that you can relate by using `DataRelations`.
DataTable	A single table of in-memory data. `DataSets` contain `DataTables`.
DataTableCollection	A collection of `DataTables` in a `DataSet`.
DataRelation	A parent-child relationship between two `DataTables`. Adding a `DataRelation` does not constrain the relationship (ensure a parent row before inserting a child row); you use a `ForeignKeyConstraint` for this.
RelationsCollection	A collection of `DataRelations` in a `DataTable`.
DataColumn	A single column within a `DataTable`.
DataColumnCollection	A collection of `DataColumns` in a `DataTable`.
Constraint	An object representing a constraint that you place on one or more `DataColumns` in a `DataTable`.
ConstraintCollection	A collection of constraints for a `DataTable`.
ForeignKeyConstraint	A constraint that you use to create referential integrity among `DataTables` in your `DataSet`. A `ForeignKeyConstraint` ensures that you cannot insert a new row in a child `DataTable` without a row using the ID in a parent table. For example, if the employee table is a child of the person table, I must insert a row in the person table before I can insert a row in the employee table.
DataRow	A single row within a `DataTable`.
DataRowCollection	A collection of `DataRows` in a `DataTable`.
DataView	A customizable, data-bindable of a `DataTable`, which enables you to sort, filter, search, edit, or navigate the data in the `DataTable`.
DataRowView	A customized view of a `DataRow`.

The System.Data namespace also offers a variety of exception objects, which can prove useful. These objects are shown in Table 5-4. All derive from System.Data. DataException, which ultimately derives from the base class System.Exception.

TABLE 5-4 THE SYSTEM.DATA DATAEXCEPTION OBJECTS

Exception Object	Description
ConstraintException	Exception thrown for actions that violate a DataConstraint.
DBConcurrencyException	Represents an exception thrown when the number of rows updated equals zero.
DeletedRowInaccessibleException	Represents the exception that is thrown when you attempt an action on a DataRow that is no longer present.
DuplicateNameException	Represents the exception thrown if you attempt to add an object with the same name to a DataSet, like a DataTable.. You can give different types of objects the same name, but not the same type of object.
EvaluateException	Represents an exception thrown when the Expression in the Expression property of a DataColumn cannot be evaluated.
InRowChangingEventException	Represents the exception thrown in the RowChanging event when you alter the data in a manner inconsistent with the data. This is normally due to concurrency issues. This exception is thrown during the EndEdit event.
InvalidConstraintException	Exception thrown if you try to create an improper relationship. The most normal reason for this exception is linking columns with different data types when you create a parent-child (foreign key) relationship between two DataTables.

Continued

TABLE 5–4 THE SYSTEM.DATA DATAEXCEPTION OBJECTS *(Continued)*

Exception Object	Description
InvalidExpressionException	Exception thrown if you attempt to add a DataColumn with an invalid expression to a DataColumnCollection. Expressions are used to aggregate or filter data. For example, you might want to create a column in your DataTable that contains the sum of all sales for a salesperson. If you fat-finger (mistype) the expression, you get this exception.
MissingPrimaryKeyException	Exception thrown when you try to access a specific row in a DataTable with no primary key.
NoNullAllowedException	Exception thrown when you insert a NULL into a DataColumn where AllowDBNull is set to false.
ReadOnlyException	Exception thrown if you attempt to update data on a ReadOnly DataColumn.
RowNotInTableException	Exception thrown if you attempt to perform an operation on a DataRow that is not in a DataTable. The most common reason for a missing row is a previous edit deleted it.
VersionNotFoundException	Exception thrown if you attempt to access a version of a DataRow that is deleted. This exception is a bit similar to the DeletedRowInaccesibleException, but deals with data that still exists in some version in the DataTable. Understand that a DataTable contains both the current condition of every row, along with the original data that was pulled from the database.
StrongTypingException	Represents an exception thrown when a user accesses a DBNull value in a strongly-typed DataSet.
SyntaxErrorException	Represents an exception thrown when the expression property of a DataColumn contains a syntax error.

Exception Object	Description
TypedDataSetGeneratorException	Represents an exception thrown when a naming conflict occurs during the creation of a typed DataSet.
VersionNotFoundException	Represents an exception thrown when you attempt to access a version of a DataRow that does not exist. You encounter this exception when you attempt to access a DataRow you deleted in a previous operation.

To put everything all together, Figure 5-5 shows the hierarchy of the classes in the System.Data namespace.

To use the System.Data objects to their fullest in distributed applications, add each of the tables that you use in one set of actions to your DataSet and make sure that the data types, relations, and other constraints are set up in the DataSet. If you follow these rules, you can throw exceptions on the client side rather than wait for a round trip to clean up any inconsistent data. There are, of course, items that cannot be cleaned up on the client side, but at the very least, you can minimize round trips to the database.

System.Data.OleDb

The System.Data.OleDb namespace deals with managed providers in ADO.NET. You can access a managed provider for your database through ADO.NET, and it is highly likely that any database you use will incorporate the objects of the System.Data.OleDb namespace. The fact that each provider is accessible through System.Data.OleDb objects ensures consistency of the object model no matter which managed provider you're using. In your applications, use the System.Data.OleDb namespace objects to populate the objects in the System.Data namespace.

In ADO.NET, as in ADO, a provider can access any data store, including non-traditional data stores such as WebDav and Exchange, as well as the more traditional databases such as Access, FoxPro, and Oracle. The rule is that you can access any database with an OLE DB provider through the System.Data.OleDb namespace by using the correct managed provider. Although access through System.Data.OleDb includes SQL Server, using the System.Data.SqlClient namespace for accessing SQL Server is preferable in most instances, because you eliminate the OLE DB provider from the equation. This is covered shortly, in the "SQL Server Has Its Own Objects" section.

Table 5-5 shows the objects in the System.Data.OleDb namespace.

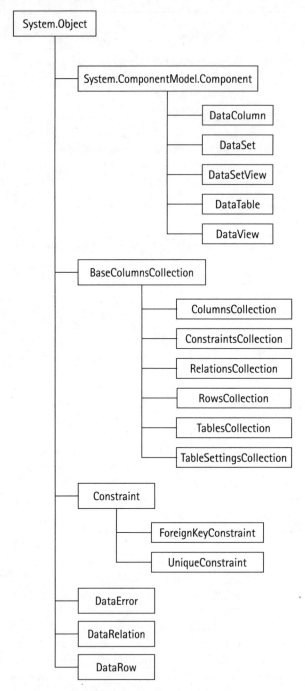

Figure 5-5: The System.Data object model.

TABLE 5-5 THE SYSTEM.DATA.OLEDB NAMESPACE

Object	Description
OleDbConnection	Represents an open connection to a data source. This is the top-level object in the System.Data.OleDb namespace.
OleDbCommand	Represents a command to make to a data source. You use OleDbCommand objects in an OleDbDataAdapter to populate a DataSet. You can also use OleDbCommand objects to populate an OleDbDataReader.
OleDbDataAdapter	Serves as a bridge between the data connection (OleDbConnection) and the DataSet. An OleDbDataAdapter can link to multiple commands to SELECT, INSERT, UPDATE, and DELETE data.
OleDbDataReader	Represents a read-only, forward-only stream of records from a data source. This object is useful in populating controls on the form where you have a known set of options.
OleDbError	Collects information about an error returning from a data source.
OleDbErrorCollection	A collection of all OleDbError objects.
OleDbException	Contains an exception thrown from a managed provider.
OleDbParameter	Represents a parameter in an OleDbCommandObject.
OleDbParameterCollection	A collection of OleDbParameter objects.
OleDbPermission	Provides the ability to ensure that a user has the proper security level to access the data store.
OleDbPermissionCollection	A collection of OleDbPermission objects.
OleDbTransation	Represents a SQL transaction for a data source.

The System.Data.OleDb namespace is the closest to the traditional ADO model, although you'll note a lot of changes. The System.Data.OleDb object model is shown in Figure 5-6.

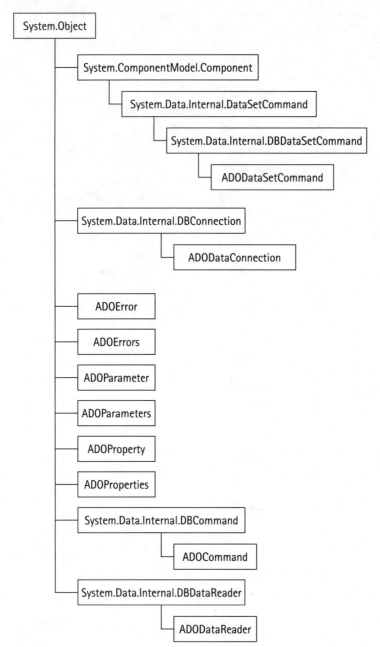

Figure 5-6: The System.Data.OleDb object model.

System.Data.Common

The `System.Data.Common` namespace contains the core objects from which all managed providers inherit. The most important object in this namespace is the `DataAdapter`, which serves as a base (or parent) class for the `OleDbDataAdapter` and the `SqlClientDataAdapter`. Because this particular namespace is of little importance in day-to-day data activities, I'm not going into a great deal of detail about it.

 You can find more information about the System.Data.Common namespace in the help files with both the .NET SDK and Visual Studio .NET.

SQL Server Has Its Own Objects

In ADO.NET, Microsoft finally decided to create a set of objects that work directly with SQL Server. The main advantage to using the SQL objects instead of the OleDb managed provider for SQL Server is the removal of the OLE DB layer. Removing this layer makes using the SQL objects with SQL Server a more efficient paradigm than using the OleDb managed provider.

System.Data.SqlClient

The `System.Data.SqlClient` namespace is very similar to the `System.Data.OleDb` namespace. For most of the objects, you use the prefix `Sql` in place of the prefix `OleDb`. From a coding standpoint, there is really no difference between the objects other than the name. Okay, if you push, you notice that there is `SchemaGuid` object in the `SqlClient` namespace, but it is not needed in SQL Server; and there's also a `SqlDebugging` object, but it's used in the .NET Framework infrastructure, so you will never use it.

So, the main difference is under the hood: There is no OleDb layer in the underlying architecture when you use the `System.Data.SqlClient` namespace objects to access SQL Server. To compare the similarities between the two managed providers, take a gander at Table 5-6 and compare it to Table 5-5.

The object model for the `System.Data.SqlClient` namespace is shown in Figure 5-7. Compare it to the `System.Data.OleDb` object model in Figure 5-6 and you'll see a small difference in the hierarchy for one of the objects: the `SchemaGuid` class is present in `OleDb`, but not `SqlClient`.

TABLE 5-6 THE SYSTEM.DATA.SQLCLIENT NAMESPACE

Object	Description
SqlClientPermission	Provides the ability to ensure that a user has the proper security level to access the data store.
SqlClientPermissionCollection	A collection of SqlClientPermission objects.
SqlConnection	Represents an open connection to a data source. This is the top-level object in the System.Data.SqlClient namespace.
SqlCommand	Represents a command to make to a data source. You use SqlCommand objects in a SqlDataAdapter to populate a DataSet. You can also use SqlCommand objects to populate a SqlDataReader.
SqlDataAdapter	Serves as a bridge between the data connection (SqlConnection) and the DataSet. A SqlDataAdapter can link to multiple commands to SELECT, INSERT, UPDATE, and DELETE data.
SqlDataReader	Represents a read-only, forward-only stream of records from a data source. This object is useful in populating controls on the form where you have a known set of options.
SqlError	Collects information about an error returning from a data source.
SqlErrorCollection	A collection of all SqlError objects.
SqlException	Contains an exception thrown from a managed provider.
SqlParameter	Represents a parameter in a SqlCommand object.
SqlParameterCollection	A collection of SqlParameter objects.
SqlTransaction	Represents a SQL transaction for a data source.

System.Data.SqlTypes

The System.Data.SqlTypes namespace contains objects for the native data types in SQL Server. The reason for using this namespace is type safety: It helps prevent type conversion errors that can occur if you're using the .NET Framework types. Table 5-7 shows the SqlTypes and their SQL Server equivalents. Notice that many of the SQL Server native datatypes map to the same object in the `System.Data.SqlTypes` namespace. The last part of the table shows System.Data.SqlTypes exception objects.

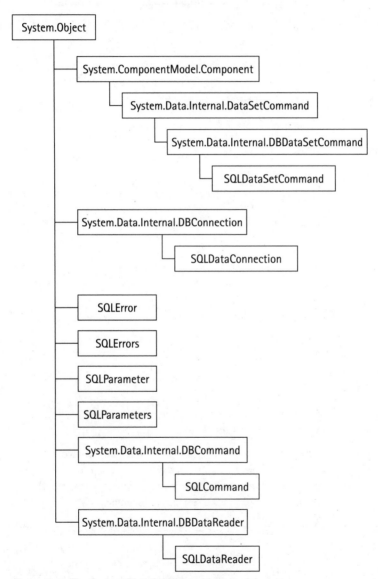

Figure 5-7: The System.Data.SqlClient object model.

TABLE 5-7 THE SQLTYPES AND THEIR SQL SERVER EQUIVALENTS

System.Data.SqlTypes Object	SQL Server Type
SqlBinary	binary, image, timestamp, and varbinary
SqlInt64	bigint
SqlBoolean	bit
SqlByte	tinyint
SqlDateTime	datetime and smalldatetime
SqlDecimal	decimal and numeric
SqlDouble	float
SqlGuid	uniqueidentifier
SqlInt16	smallint
SqlInt32	int
SqlInt64	bigint
SqlMoney	money and smallmoney
SqlSingle	real
SqlString	char, nchar, ntext, nvarchar, sysname, text, and varchar
Use System.Object, because there is no SqlTypes equivalent for sql_variant.	sql_variant
SqlNullValueException	Exception thrown when the value property of any of the SqlTypes objects is set to NULL.
SqlTruncateException	Exception thrown when setting the value property would require the object to truncate the value — if you put the string "13 characters" into a character object with a length of 10 (char(10) in SQL Server), for example.

System.Data.Odbc

As of this writing, `System.Data.Odbc` namespace objects require a separate download from Microsoft. While this may seem like a step back, consider that ODBC is not the access method of choice in the Windows environment. Don't worry; Microsoft is not going to abandon ODBC — it can't if it wants to port the .NET Framework to the Unix and Linux environments.

The `System.Data.Odbc` object model is virtually identical to both the `System.Data.OleDb` object model and the `System.Data.SqlClient` object model, and you're already familiar with them from this chapter.

You can find the ODBC.NET provider objects on the MSDN download site, `http://msdn.microsoft.com/download`. Type **ODBC.NET** in the search window to quickly find the page, or click the .NET Framework menu item (left-hand side) to expose the ODBC.NET link.

Summary

This chapter gave you a whirlwind look at the major objects in ADO.NET. Because data is important to all real-world applications, the data objects in ADO.NET are integral to creating robust .NET applications.

The major differences between data access in ADO and ADO.NET are the capability to disconnect data from a data source without a performance penalty and the capability to represent data in a relational manner in a distributed application. Although realizing the benefits of this new model may take some time, it's worth your effort.

XML is the underlying transfer method in ADO.NET, as I mention many times in this chapter. By using XML, relational data is as easy to use as a single table is in ADO. The cost of this flexibility is a bit of extra coding on your part for simple data access. You can eliminate much of the extra coding by using a `DataReader`. Remember, however, that the `DataReader` is forward-only. You get your first taste of the `DataReader` in Chapter 8, in the "Building Tables in the CodeBehind File" section. The `DataReader` is also the main subject of Chapter 15.

In the next chapter, you get the opportunity to build your first ASP.NET application, a simple phone list with a search page. The technology introduced in the next chapter is explained in more detail in Part II, which begins with Chapter 7.

Chapter 6

Your First .NET Application

IN THIS CHAPTER

- ◆ Working with a simple ASPX page

- ◆ Moving code to a component

- ◆ Adding data to the application

- ◆ Deploying the application

THE BEST WAY TO MASTER a new programming paradigm, as I mentioned in Chapter 2, is to build an application. I dedicate this entire chapter, therefore, to building a simple intranet application by using .NET. I don't fully explain some of the concepts introduced in this chapter, but I do my best to refer you to the appropriate chapter that can help you get a better understanding of what's going on in this chapter. I encourage you to think about how the techniques in this chapter may prove useful to your own application and in helping you alter the application to meet your needs. (I find that I get much more out of applications that relate to my job than I do building "Hello, World!" and other small examples.)

Before you begin, I need to caution you about one thing: As you go through this chapter, remember that the goal is just to get the basic flow of a simple application. You don't need to understand everything that I present in this chapter after you finish it, as I explain everything in more detail in later chapters of the book. The idea for now is just to understand how simple the code is in ASP.NET.

Overview

Book-O-Matic is a small company that sells *sleep books:* a type of book that you place underneath your pillow at night so that you gain new knowledge while you sleep. The company's product is a tremendous success both with the college-age market and among middle-aged business professionals. The company went public a few years ago and is looking for new financing to build a new product that customers can use while driving a car. As the stock market's recently taken a hit, Book-O-Matic must trim costs and increase profitability to gain sufficient financing to launch this new product.

Recently, the president of Book-O-Matic noticed the incredible amount of paper that the company was wasting by handing out employee lists. The current system is for Dorothy, the HR secretary (from Kansas, I suppose), to type up a new list and distribute it every time a change occurs among the company's employees. As Book-O-Matic is enjoying tremendous growth, these lists go out to all the employees every couple days.

Your task, then, is to create an application to reduce the amount of time and money going to waste on producing paper phone lists.

The HR employee phone list application

Your solution to the problem is to utilize Book-O-Matic's state-of-the-art intranet to disseminate the phone-list information. You have a simple Web page that displays a form for searching for employee information. After a user selects an employee's name, you want the person's employee information, including phone number, to appear on the page. In addition, you're going to produce a complete list of employees for those who feel more comfortable with such a list.

Selecting technologies

As Book-O-Matic keeps up with the latest in Microsoft technology, you have a new Windows .NET Server to work with, complete with the latest version of the .NET Framework. You have servers running SQL Server 2000 at your disposal for the application. You settle on the following platform:

◆ **Server:** Windows .NET Server running IIS 6.0.

◆ **Database:** Modeling in Access XP and deployment on SQL Server 2000.

◆ **Technology:** ASP.NET using Visual Basic .NET and Visual Basic .NET-complied components. Initial modeling of the application is done in ASP.NET.

You'll find the code for this chapter's application on the companion Web site (www.wiley.com/extras) in the file Ch06SDK.zip (SDK version) or Ch06VS.zip (Visual Studio .NET version).

Before going any further, download the code for this chapter from the book's companion Web site. As you unzip the files, make sure that you're using the option to create folders (this is the default if you are using WinZip to unpack the files). This option ensures that the directory structure is correct for the database. If you build your own application, you need to tweak the connection string to match your database location. The instructions for doing this are contained in the download.

Building the Page

To create the page for this ASP.NET application, use the simple HTML page `template.aspx` (in the zip file for this chapter) as a template. Copy the page and the entire Images folder to the folder that holds your Web Application. Figure 6-1 shows the page as it appears in Internet Explorer 6.0.

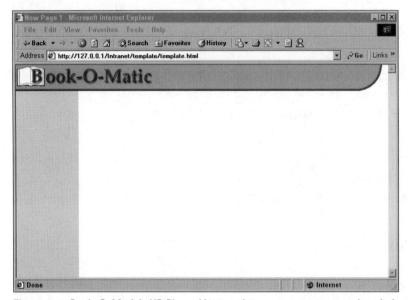

Figure 6-1: Book-O-Matic's HR Phone List template, an empty page used to design the site.

The Page_Load event

The `Page_Load` event fires every time the client browser requests a page. There are a couple ways this happens:

- The user clicks a link to the page, or enters a page address in address bar of his browser.

- The user clicks a Submit button in the page, or another control that allows posting back to the page.

The page's `IsPostBack` property is a Boolean value to indicate whether the page is being posted back to the server. When the user reaches the page via a hyperlink or entering the address in the address bar of his browser, the value of `IsPostBack` is false, because the page isn't being posted back. If the user clicks any control that posts back to the server, the value of `IsPostBack` is true. In most cases, you see this used in the Page_Load event, because it is guaranteed to fire on every page request, whether it is posted back, or not.

You can also handle posting back to the page with events on a server control. Chapter 8 covers events for server controls for most of the controls. To keep things simple right now, I just work with the Page_Load event.

 In ASP.NET, most controls that can be marked runat="server" can submit the form back to the server. If the control can submit back to the server, you can handle this event either with IsPostBack or with an event that handles the postback.

HTML controls are covered in greater detail in Chapter 7, while ASP.NET Web controls (also called server controls in Microsoft lingo) can be found in Chapter 8. In Chapter 8, I also deal with events rather than using the IsPostBack property of the Page object.

Listing 6-1 shows a simple Page_Load event in ASP.NET. Following the CodeBehind paradigm, all of the code is in the CodeBehind page, which is the default.aspx.vb.

Listing 6-1: The Page_Load Event

```
<script language=vb runat=server>
    Sub Page_Load(sender As System.Object, e As System.EventArgs)
        If (Page.IsPostBack <> True) Then
            'Code here for PostBack
        End If
    End Sub
</script>
```

You generally add this code to the head section of your page. After you add the data to your application, you use this event to control the postback of the form. At present, you don't need this event, as you have no code to work with. You populate this event in the section "Adding Data," later in this chapter.

Adding controls to the page

For this page, you add a drop-down list, three text boxes, and two buttons (Submit and Reset). The code for these changes is in Listing 6-2.

Listing 6-2: Controls on the Page

```
<form id="Form1" method="post" runat="server">
  <table border="0" cellpadding="0" cellspacing="0" width="100%">
    <tr>
```

```
  <td height="45" width="247" bgcolor="#33cc33" colspan="2">
  <img border="0" src="images/logo.gif" width="272" height="45"></td>
  <td height="45" bgcolor="#33cc33"> </td>
  <td width="51" height="45">
  <img border="0" src="images/rightCap_top.gif"
   width="51" height="45"></td>
</tr>
<tr>
  <td height="5" width="125" background="images/topTableBottom.gif">
  <img border="0" src="images/clear.gif" width="125" height="5"></td>
  <td height="5" width="122" background="images/topTableBottom.gif">
  <img border="0" src="images/clear.gif" width="1" height="5"></td>
  <td height="5" background="images/topTableBottom.gif">
  <img border="0" src="images/clear.gif" width="100%" height="5"></td>
  <td width="51" height="5">
  <img border="0" src="images/rightCap_bottom.gif"
   width="51" height="5"></td>
</tr>
<tr>
  <td width="125" height="100%" valign="top"></td>
  <td height="100%" valign="top" colspan="2">
    <table cellpadding="5" width="100%" ID="Table1">
      <TBODY>
        <tr>
          <td>
            <P>Department:  
              <asp:dropdownlist id="ddDept" runat="server" /></P>
            <P>Last name:
              <asp:textbox id="strLastName" runat="server" /><BR>
              First name:
              <asp:textbox id="strFirstName" runat="server" />
            <P>
            <P>
              <asp:Button id="Button1" runat="server"
               Text="Submit"></asp:Button></P>
            <asp:DataGrid id="DataGrid1" runat="server"
               ForeColor="Black">
              <ItemStyle BackColor="white" />
              <AlternatingItemStyle BackColor="Gainsboro" />
              <HeaderStyle BackColor="Navy" ForeColor="White"
               Font-Bold="True" />
            </asp:DataGrid>
          </td>
        </tr>
```

Continued

Listing 6-2 *(Continued)*

```
      </TBODY>
    </table>
  </td>
  <td width="51" height="100%"></td>
</tr>
<tr>
  <td height="1" width="125">
  <img border="0" src="images/clear.gif" width="125" height="1"></td>
  <td height="1" width="122">
  <img border="0" src="images/clear.gif" width="1" height="1"></td>
  <td height="1">
  <img border="0" src="images/clear.gif" width="100%" height="1"></td>
  <td width="51" height="1">
  <img border="0" src="images/clear.gif" width="51" height="1"></td>
</tr>
  </table>
</form>
```

 The file for Listing 6-2 can be downloaded from this book's companion Web site (www.wiley.com/extras) in the file Ch06VS.zip (Visual Studio .NET version) or Ch06SDK.zip (SDK version). The file to look at is nonCodeBehind.aspx.

If you're using the .NET IDE, create the table and drag the drop-down list, text boxes, and buttons onto your Web form. I cover the code to populate the drop-down list in the next section.

Adding Data

The next step is to add data to your form. I use a database called dbIntranet, which is included in the download file for this chapter.

To use ADO in your application, you must import a couple namespaces:

- ◆ System.Data — This namespace includes the core data classes used in .NET, such as the DataSet class.

- ◆ System.Data.OLEDB — This namespace is used with OLEDB managed provider. (In the "Porting to SQL Server" section later in this chapter, I show you a better namespace to use when coding against SQL Server.)

The tags to import the data namespaces are shown in Listing 6-3. You place these tags just below the main @ directive tag. Because I'm coding inside the ASPX page, rather than in a CodeBehind file, these tags are necessary if I don't want to type the entire namespace every time I create an object.

Listing 6-3: Importing Data Namespaces

```
<%@ Import Namespace=System.Data %>
<%@ Import Namespace=System.Data.OLEDB %>
```

Working with Microsoft Access

Our first run is with Access. You gain no real benefit from starting with Access under the .NET Framework if SQL Server is available, but I include this example to show how easily you can move to SQL Server if you start with Access as a database.

Listing 6-4 shows you how to use ADO.NET to bind data to a drop-down list. At this point, all of the code is contained in a script block in the page, rather than in a CodeBehind file. If you are using Visual Studio .NET, and you want to build this page from scratch, delete the Page_Load event in the CodeBehind file.

Listing 6-4: Binding the Department Table to the Drop-Down List

```
<script language="vb" runat="server" ID="Script1">
    Sub Page_Load(sender As System.Object, e As System.EventArgs) _
        Handles MyBase.Load
        'Make sure this is pointing at your database.
        Dim strConn As String = "PROVIDER=Microsoft.Jet.OLEDB.4.0;" & _
        "Data Source=" & Server.MapPath("dbIntranet.mdb")
        Dim strSQL As String = "SELECT intDepartmentID, " & _
            "strDepartmentName FROM tblDepartment " & _
            "ORDER BY intDepartmentID"

        'Create data objects
        Dim objConn As New OleDbConnection(strConn)
        Dim objCmd = New OleDbCommand(strSQL, objConn)
        Dim objDataSet As DataSet = New DataSet()
        Dim objDataAdapter As New OleDbDataAdapter(objCmd)

        'Create a Connection Object and Open
        objConn.Open()

        'Fill data set
        objDataAdapter.Fill(objDataSet, "tblDepartment")
```

Continued

Listing 6-4 *(Continued)*

```
        'Close Connection
        objConn.Close()

        'Bind to the Drop Down
        ddDept.DataSource = objDataSet.Tables("tblDepartment").DefaultView
        ddDept.DataValueField = "intDepartmentID"
        ddDept.DataTextField = "strDepartmentName"
        ddDept.DataBind()

        'Add IsPostBack from Listing 6-6 here
    End Sub
</script>
```

This example more or less follows the way you build the application in traditional ASP. One notable difference is the fact that all your data code is inside a subroutine. You fill the drop-down list by data-binding a server-side control, which is a much more efficient method than looping through a `Recordset` object, as you would with traditional ASP.

With ASP.NET, you can bind most of the controls to data with a few lines of code. Binding data is covered in great detail in Part III of this book, but let's take a brief look at the data binding in this page to understand what is going on:

```
ddDept.DataSource = objDataSet.Tables("tblDepartment").DefaultView
ddDept.DataMember = "intDepartmentID"
ddDept.DataTextField = "strDepartmentName"
ddDept.DataBind()
```

To bind to a drop-down list in ASP.NET, I have to set up a data source, a data member, and a data text field:

- ◆ `DataSource` – The DataReader, or DataTable in a DataSet, that contains the information you want to bind. In ASP.NET, you can also bind to XML, certain collections, and any type of array.

- ◆ `DataValueField` – The field that shows up in the `option` tag when the page is sent to the browser as HTML.

- ◆ `DataTextField` – What the user sees in the drop-down list.

One more little tidbit about the `Page_Load` event: Notice that the end of the function is `Handles MyBase.Load`. This is necessary due to the flexibility of .NET on the naming of events. You can name an event anything you want since you have the `Handles` keyword to link an event to the Load event in the underlying page class.

Although you have the capability to name events anything you want in .NET, be very wary of creating a different naming convention unless you absolutely have to, because this tends to make your code less maintainable.

You'll find a page called LoadingDaPage.aspx in the download file for this chapter. In it, I have renamed the Page_Load event LoadingDaPage. While it illustrates how easy it is to change event names, it also shows how this ability can easily be abused.

So you bind the drop-down list to data and fill it up. What about posting the form back to the server and returning data? This leads us to the next step, which is to create a container for the data. Although I could have also used a Repeater or DataList, I use a DataGrid control in this page because it is one of the easier controls to bind data to and end up with a nice looking page.

Listing 6-5 shows the additional code that you add to the page for the DataGrid. This code goes just below the drop-down list covered in Listing 6-4. I add a couple text boxes that are quite important in the next section.

Listing 6-5: DataGrid Control

```
<asp:DataGrid id="DataGrid1" runat="server" ForeColor="Black">
    <ItemStyle BackColor="white" />
    <AlternatingItemStyle BackColor="Gainsboro" />
    <HeaderStyle BackColor="Navy" ForeColor="White" Font-Bold="True" />
</asp:DataGrid>
```

As you can see in Listing 6-5, you don't have to write a lot of code to create a very nice looking DataGrid.

You use the DataGrid's properties to control the look of the table that appears after someone displays the page in a browser. The example produces a table with a dark blue header, which comes from the HeaderStyle property, and alternating white and light-blue table rows, which come from the ItemStyle and AlternatingItemStyle properties.

When I talk about the HeaderStyle, ItemStyle, and AlternatingItemStyle as properties, I am talking about the underlying objects that hold these styles. In the page, these "styles" are shown as tags. If you want to play with the underlying object, you can do something similar to the following code—just remember that the only style you can set this way is the style of the entire page.

```
Dim objTableStyle As New System.Web.UI.WebControls.TableStyle()
objTableStyle.BackColor = System.Drawing.Color.Red
DataGrid1.ApplyStyle(objTableStyle)
```

To use the grid, you simply bind it to your data. You do so by adding another DataTable to your DataSet and binding it to the DataGrid. Listing 6-6 shows the IsPostBack event with code necessary to return employee information from the database.

Listing 6-6: IsPostBack Event

```
If IsPostBack = True Then
    Dim blnWhere As Boolean
    Dim intDept As Integer = CInt(Request("ddDept"))
    strSQL = "SELECT strLastName as [Last Name], " & _
      "strFirstName as [First Name], " & _
      "intExtension as [Extension] FROM tblEmployee e"

    If intDept <> 0 Then
        CheckWhere(strSQL, blnWhere)
        strSQL = strSQL & "intDepartmentID = " & intDept
    End If

    If Request("strLastName") <> "" Then
        CheckWhere(strSQL, blnWhere)
        strSQL = strSQL & "strLastName LIKE '" & _
            CStr(Request("strLastName")) & "%'"
    End If

    '... repeat If for other postback events (see code)

    strSQL = strSQL & " ORDER BY strLastName, strFirstName"

    objCmd = New OleDbCommand(strSQL, objConn)
    objDataAdapter = New OleDbDataAdapter(objCmd)

    objConn.Open()
    objDataAdapter.Fill(objDataSet, "tblEmployee")
    objConn.Close()

    DataGrid1.DataSource = objDataSet.Tables("tblEmployee").DefaultView
    DataGrid1.DataBind()
End If

...
'Paste the following code outside of the Page_Load event
Private Sub CheckWhere(ByRef strSQL as String, ByRef blnWhere as Boolean)
  If blnWhere = True Then
    strSQL = strSQL & " AND "
  Else
```

```
    strSQL = strSQL & " WHERE "
    blnWhere = True
  End If
End Sub
```

The subroutine `CheckWhere` is placed outside of the `Page_Load` event. Add the `IsPostBack` section below the code that binds the drop-down list. I left a comment line in Listing 6-4 indicating where to add the IsPostBack section from Listing 6-6.

Now, run the page. If your database is in the correct location (that is, it's in the location specified in `strConnString`), everything should work fine. (If it doesn't work, you'll need to edit the variable `strConnString` and point it to the location where you placed the Access .mdb file.) Make sure the drop-down list is set to Marketing and then click the Submit button.

Porting to SQL Server

This section assumes that the prototype of your mini application receives the necessary approval and that you make the decision to move the data to SQL Server. You create a DTS package and move the data over to SQL Server, and you next need to switch the application over as well. To do so — assuming that you don't mind using the OLEDB managed provider instead of the SQL Server managed provider — you need to change only one line, as shown in Listing 6-7. In this listing, I also show the changes to the `IsPostBack` portion of the `Page_Load` event. Pay attention to the bold section in Listing 6-7, because it's the only change to the code.

In general, you want to use the SQL Server managed provider, which is found in the `System.Data.SQLClient` namespace. Other than the ease of changing a provider string, there is not much reason to use the OLEDB managed provider for SQL Server.

The main reason to use the SQL Server managed provider when attaching to a SQL Server database is performance. The SQL Server managed provider works directly against SQL Server, taking the OLEDB layer out of your application. There are additional advantages that will show up in the next version of SQL Server.

Listing 6-7: Changing the Connection String

```
Private Sub Page_Load(ByVal sender As System.Object, ByVal e As _
    System.EventArgs) Handles MyBase.Load
```

Continued

Listing 6-7 *(Continued)*

```
Dim strConn As String = "PROVIDER=SQLOLEDB.1;Server=(local);" & _
    "Database=dbIntranet;UID=sa;PWD=;"
Dim strSQL As String = "SELECT intDepartmentID, " & _
    "strDepartmentName FROM tblDepartment " & _
    "ORDER BY intDepartmentID"

'Create data objects
Dim objConn As New OleDbConnection(strConn)
Dim objCmd = New OleDbCommand(strSQL, objConn)
Dim objDataSet As DataSet = New DataSet()
Dim objDataAdapter As New OleDbDataAdapter(objCmd)

'Create a Connection Object and Open
objConn.Open()

'Fill data set
objDataAdapter.Fill(objDataSet, "tblDepartment")
'objDataAdapter = Nothing

'Close Connection
objConn.Close()

'Bind to the Drop Down
ddDept.DataSource = objDataSet.Tables("tblDepartment").DefaultView
ddDept.DataValueField = "intDepartmentID"
ddDept.DataTextField = "strDepartmentName"
ddDept.DataBind()

If IsPostBack = True Then
    Dim blnWhere As Boolean

    Dim intDept As Integer = CInt(Request("ddDept"))

    strSQL = "SELECT strLastName as [Last Name], " & _
             "strFirstName as [First Name], " & _
             "intExtension as [Extension] FROM tblEmployee e"

    If intDept <> 0 Then
        CheckWhere(strSQL, blnWhere)
        strSQL = strSQL & "intDepartmentID = " & intDept
    End If

    If Request("strLastName") <> "" Then
        CheckWhere(strSQL, blnWhere)
```

```
        strSQL = strSQL & "strLastName LIKE '" & _
            CStr(Request("strLastName")) & "%'"
    End If

    '... repeat If for other postback events (see code)

    strSQL = strSQL & " ORDER BY strLastName, strFirstName"

    objCmd = New OleDbCommand(strSQL, objConn)
    objDataAdapter = New OleDbDataAdapter(objCmd)

    objConn.Open()
    objDataAdapter.Fill(objDataSet, "tblEmployee")
    objConn.Close()

    DataGrid1.DataSource = objDataSet.Tables("tblEmployee").DefaultView
    DataGrid1.DataBind()
    End If

End Sub
```

You'll find the code for Listing 6-7 in the file Ch06SDK.zip (SDK version) or Ch06VS.zip (Visual Studio .NET version) on this book's companion Web site (www.wiley.com/extras). The SQL Server page is called PhoneListSQLOLEDB.aspx.

Managed provider objects are covered in great detail in Chapter 15, which touches on the OLEDB, ODBC, and SQLClient namespaces. In addition, Chapter 16 deals strictly with the SQL Server managed provider.

Using System.Data.SqlClient

Using the managed provider isn't the most efficient way to work with SQL Server, because you are adding an additional layer called OLEDB. If you want your application to perform a bit better, use the SQL Server .NET native provider, which is contained in the namespace System.Data.SqlClient.

To change from using a SQL Server managed provider for OLEDB to using the SQL native provider, you need to delete the "Provider=SQLOLEDB.1;" from the connection string, because the SQLClient predetermines the provider. Next, you need to change the word OLEDB in all the data objects to SQLClient.

Listing 6-8 shows the changes to the `Page_Load`. I've included the entire `Page_Load` event in this listing to show how few changes are necessary to move from the OLEDB managed provider to the SQL Server managed provider (native provider). The changes are shown in bold.

Listing 6-8: Changes Necessary to Use the SQL Objects

```
Private Sub Page_Load(ByVal sender As System.Object, ByVal e As _
    System.EventArgs) Handles MyBase.Load

    Dim strConn As String = "PROVIDER=SQLOLEDB.1;Server=(local);" & _
        "Database=dbIntranet;UID=sa;PWD=;"
    Dim strSQL As String = "SELECT intDepartmentID, " & _
        "strDepartmentName FROM tblDepartment " & _
        "ORDER BY intDepartmentID"

    'Create data objects
    Dim objConn As New SqlConnection(strConn)
    Dim objCmd = New SqlCommand(strSQL, objConn)
    Dim objDataSet As DataSet = New DataSet()
    Dim objDataAdapter As New SqlDataAdapter(objCmd)

    'Create a Connection Object and Open
    objConn.Open()

    'Fill data set
    objDataAdapter.Fill(objDataSet, "tblDepartment")
    'objDataAdapter = Nothing

    'Close Connection
    objConn.Close()

    'Bind to the Drop Down
    ddDept.DataSource = objDataSet.Tables("tblDepartment").DefaultView
    ddDept.DataValueField = "intDepartmentID"
    ddDept.DataTextField = "strDepartmentName"
    ddDept.DataBind()

    If IsPostBack = True Then
        Dim blnWhere As Boolean

        Dim intDept As Integer = CInt(Request("ddDept"))

        strSQL = "SELECT strLastName as [Last Name], " & _
                 "strFirstName as [First Name], " & _
                 "intExtension as [Extension] FROM tblEmployee e"
```

```
    If intDept <> 0 Then
        CheckWhere(strSQL, blnWhere)
        strSQL = strSQL & "intDepartmentID = " & intDept
    End If

    If Request("strLastName") <> "" Then
        CheckWhere(strSQL, blnWhere)
        strSQL = strSQL & "strLastName LIKE '" & _
                CStr(Request("strLastName")) & "%'"
    End If

    '... repeat If for other postback events (see code)

    strSQL = strSQL & " ORDER BY strLastName, strFirstName"

    objCmd = New SqlCommand(strSQL, objConn)
    objDataAdapter = New SqlDataAdapter(objCmd)

    objConn.Open()
    objDataAdapter.Fill(objDataSet, "tblEmployee")
    objConn.Close()

    DataGrid1.DataSource = objDataSet.Tables("tblEmployee").DefaultView
    DataGrid1.DataBind()
    End If

End Sub
```

You can find the code for Listing 6-8 in the file ChO6SDK.zip (SDK version) or ChO6VS.zip (Visual Studio .NET version) on this book's companion Web site (www.wiley.com/extras). The SQL Server page is called PhoneListSQLClient.aspx.

Migrating to CodeBehind

You can deploy the application that you build in the preceding sections as is. One of the strengths of .NET, however, is the capability to easily link your page to a compiled component from your ASP.NET page. If you build a new application in the Visual Studio .NET IDE, the default behavior is to place the working code into a component. In the example in the preceding sections, I have you build the application as a plain ASPX page. I do so largely to show you the similarities and differences between ASP and ASP.NET applications.

In an ASP application, you must do quite a few things to migrate your code to a Visual Basic COM component. In ASP.NET, this procedure is simply a matter of migrating your code to a CodeBehind file. Listing 6-9 shows how the code looks once moved into the CodeBehind file. To mix things up, I optimized the code a bit and removed the Request object; the changes are highlighted in bold.

Listing 6-9: A Simple Visual Basic .NET CodeBehind Component

```
Imports SysData = System.Data
Imports SqlData = System.Data.SqlClient

Public Class PhoneList
  Inherits System.Web.UI.Page
  Protected WithEvents ddDept As System.Web.UI.WebControls.DropDownList
  Protected WithEvents strLastName As System.Web.UI.WebControls.TextBox
  Protected WithEvents strFirstName As System.Web.UI.WebControls.TextBox
  Protected WithEvents Button1 As System.Web.UI.WebControls.Button
  Protected WithEvents strExtension As System.Web.UI.WebControls.TextBox
  Protected WithEvents DataGrid1 As System.Web.UI.WebControls.DataGrid

#Region " Web Form Designer Generated Code "

  'This call is required by the Web Form Designer.
  <System.Diagnostics.DebuggerStepThrough()> Private Sub InitializeComponent()

  End Sub

  Private Sub Page_Init(ByVal sender As System.Object, ByVal e As ⏎
System.EventArgs) Handles MyBase.Init
    'CODEGEN: This method call is required by the Web Form Designer
    'Do not modify it using the code editor.
    InitializeComponent()
  End Sub

#End Region

  Private Sub Page_Load(ByVal sender As System.Object, ByVal e As ⏎
System.EventArgs) Handles MyBase.Load
    'Make sure this is pointing at your database.
    Dim strConn As String = "Server=(local);" & _
      "Database=dbIntranet;UID=sa;PWD=;"

    Dim strSQL As String = "SELECT intDepartmentID, " & _
      "strDepartmentName FROM tblDepartment " & _
```

```
 "ORDER BY intDepartmentID"

'Create data objects
Dim objConn As New SqlData.SqlConnection(strConn)
Dim objCmd = New SqlData.SqlCommand(strSQL, objConn)
Dim objDataSet As SysData.DataSet = New SysData.DataSet()
Dim objDataAdapter As New SqlData.SqlDataAdapter(objCmd)

'Create a Connection Object and Open
objConn.Open()

'Fill data set
objDataAdapter.Fill(objDataSet, "tblDepartment")

'Close Connection
objConn.Close()

'Bind to the Drop Down
ddDept.DataSource = objDataSet.Tables("tblDepartment").DefaultView
ddDept.DataValueField = "intDepartmentID"
ddDept.DataTextField = "strDepartmentName"
ddDept.DataBind()

'Added from Listing 6-6
If IsPostBack = True Then
  Dim blnWhere As Boolean
  Dim intDept As Integer = ddDept.SelectedIndex
  strSQL = "SELECT strLastName as [Last Name], " & _
  "strFirstName as [First Name], " & _
  "intExtension as [Extension] FROM tblEmployee e"

  If intDept <> 0 Then
    CheckWhere(strSQL, blnWhere)
    strSQL = strSQL & "intDepartmentID = " & intDept
  End If

  If strLastName.Text <> "" Then
    CheckWhere(strSQL, blnWhere)
    strSQL = strSQL & "strLastName LIKE '" & _
    CStr(strLastName.Text) & "%'"
  End If

  If strFirstName.Text <> "" Then
```

Continued

Listing 6-9 *(Continued)*

```
            CheckWhere(strSQL, blnWhere)
            strSQL = strSQL & "strFirstName LIKE '" & _
            CStr(strFirstName.Text) & "%'"
        End If

        If strExtension.Text <> "" Then
            CheckWhere(strSQL, blnWhere)
            strSQL = strSQL & "intExtension = " & _
            CStr(strExtension.Text)
        End If

        strSQL = strSQL & " ORDER BY strLastName, strFirstName"

        objCmd = New SqlData.SqlCommand(strSQL, objConn)
        objDataAdapter = New SqlData.SqlDataAdapter(objCmd)

        objConn.Open()
        objDataAdapter.Fill(objDataSet, "tblEmployee")
        objConn.Close()

        DataGrid1.DataSource = objDataSet.Tables("tblEmployee").DefaultView
        DataGrid1.DataBind()
    End If

End Sub

Private Sub CheckWhere(ByRef strSQL As String, ByRef blnWhere As Boolean)
    If blnWhere = True Then
        strSQL = strSQL & " AND "
    Else
        strSQL = strSQL & " WHERE "
        blnWhere = True
    End If
End Sub

End Class
```

 You can download the code for Listing 6-9 from the companion Web site (www.wiley.com/extras) in the file Ch06SDK.zip (SDK version) or Ch06VS.zip (Visual Studio .NET version). The SQL Server page is called PhoneList.aspx and the CodeBehind file is PhoneList.aspx.vb.

I created this example in the Visual Studio .NET IDE and added the aliases. To migrate the code from the ASPX page, copy all code from the <script> block (including all code in the Page_Load event and the CheckWhere subroutine) into your CodeBehind file.

Remember that you must add aliases for each of the SqlClient objects to avoid errors. The result should look as follows:

```
Dim objConn As SQLData.SQLConnection
Dim objDataSet As DataSet = New Data.DataSet()
Dim objDataSetCmd As SQLData.SQLDataSetCommand
Dim objCmd As SQLData.SQLCommand
```

As you see from the preceding steps, migrating between ASP.NET and Visual Basic .NET is a simple copy-and-paste operation. The only thing that you really need to do other than copy and paste is to add aliases — if you're using aliases in your file, that is. If you're using the Visual Studio .NET IDE to code your application, you place the code in this CodeBehind file from the start.

Deploying the Application

Remember DOS applications? For some of you, I may be showing my age here, so perhaps I need to explain. In the age of MS-DOS, deploying an application was as simple as copying the executable to a new disk and running it. After Visual Basic came on the scene, the addition of a runtime DLL and an INI file complicated this task. In an effort to create greater interactivity, COM killed the INI file but muddied the waters with the concept of the registry (which actually started prior to COM). Microsoft Transaction Server (MTS) and COM+ simplified the deployment of Web applications by getting rid of the Web server reboot necessary to update DLL files, which are locked by the Web server. COM+, however, still required some registry entries and a rather complex deployment process.

Now, .NET brings back the simplicity of DOS with all the advanced features of COM. Although it may seem hard to believe, you can deploy and redeploy .NET Web applications with a simple drag-and-drop or copy-and-paste operation. Because you need to maintain at least part of the structure for the application to work, deploying a .NET application breaks down to a simple xcopy operation. (For those not familiar with xcopy, it's an application designed to copy directory structures along with the files that they contain.)

Creating the Web application

I'm going to show you four different methods of creating a new Web application:

◆ Internet Services Manager — This method offers the most options when creating a new application.

♦ FrontPage – This one-step method is the easiest way to create an application if you do not have Visual Studio .NET installed.

♦ Visual Interdev – This method is preferred for sites that contain both ASP and ASP.NET pages. You can use the same steps to attach to a current application if you have created one using any of the other methods. This is great for legacy ASP applications that are being upgraded to ASP.NET.

♦ Visual Studio .NET – This is by far the easiest method if you have Visual Studio .NET installed.

If you are using Visual Studio .NET, you can skip the next three subsections altogether, because you can easily deploy applications through the Visual Studio .NET IDE (Integrated Development Environment). I include these subsections largely for those of you who are developing applications using an ASCII text editor such as Notepad.

CREATING A WEB APPLICATION BY USING THE INTERNET SERVICES MANAGER

Because this book is aimed at Enterprise developers, I'm going to highlight the method that you employ to create a Web application on Internet Information Server. These steps apply if you're using Windows NT Server 4.0, Windows 2000, Windows .NET Server or Windows XP Professional. With Windows NT Workstation, the steps are slightly different; if you have any problems consult the Peer Web Services help file.

Before you construct a new Web site, you must create a directory for the site. The easiest way do so is to open Windows Explorer and create the directory by choosing File → New → Folder.

Next, open the Internet Services Manager from the Administrative Tools folder on the Start menu or in the Control Panel, and right-click Default Web Site. Choose New → Site or New → Virtual Directory from the pop-up menu.

TIP If you are using a server version of Windows, you have the option to create either a new site or a new virtual directory. In general, a virtual directory is fine for most applications.

Figure 6-2 shows the Internet Services Manager at the beginning of this process. After the New Web Site Wizard opens, work through the following steps:

1. Type in the Web Site Description textbox (see Figure 6-3) and click Next.

2. Type in the IP Address, Port, or Host Header. In most cases, you won't have to use a separate IP address on a development machine. On a production machine, this is normally up to your network administrator. Click Next.

3. Fill in the Path textbox. (You can use the browse button to find the directory in which this application resides.) After selecting a path, click Next.

4. Decide on permissions by clicking the check boxes. I'd stick with the defaults here unless you know you need additional permissions. Click Finish.

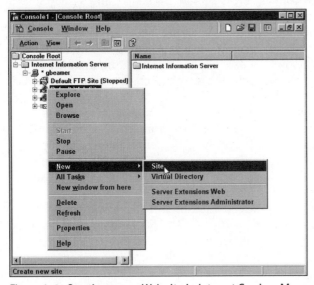

Figure 6-2: Creating a new Web site in Internet Services Manager.

You now have a place to which you can copy your directory structure, which is the final step in completing your Web application. The wizard's steps are as shown in Figure 6-3.

Figure 6-3: The steps in creating a new Web site by using the New Web Site Wizard.

CREATING A WEB APPLICATION BY USING FRONTPAGE

This section and the next provide options for creating a site when you are not going to use Visual Studio .NET to deploy your sites on other machines. I've chosen the FrontPage and Visual InterDev applications because they're fairly common on a Microsoft Web developer's desktop. These options are useful for creating the application on the server prior to copying the .NET site. If you're using Visual Studio .NET, though, you'd be wiser to deploy your application from Visual Studio .NET.

The server platform isn't important in working with FrontPage, because FrontPage uses the same steps to create a Web application in Windows 2000 Professional as it does in Windows 2000 Server. Since Internet Information Server (IIS) 4.0, you normally handle the underlying management of Web sites via FrontPage extensions.

FrontPage is Microsoft's premier Web design product, which comes with a variety of built-in applications such as Database Results Wizard (DRW in the FrontPage newsgroups), Web counters, and search capability. In order for these components to work without any programming knowledge on the part of the user, a set of components called the FrontPage extensions must reside on every server that runs a FrontPage Web site.

One part of the functionality of these extensions is Web site management. This is the portion used by FrontPage, Visual InterDev, and WebDAV to manipulate items in your Web site. It's actually very complicated, so just remember that FrontPage extensions are installed on most IIS servers and provide the ability to manage a site using programs like FrontPage and Visual Interdev.

Because the FrontPage extensions are present on most IIS servers, I'm comfortable recommending that you use FrontPage to set up your Web application, even if you have no intention of using FrontPage to design or manage your site. To create your Web application, follow these steps:

1. Choose File → New → Web from the FrontPage menu bar.

2. Click the Empty Web icon (see Figure 6-4). The default name for the new Web is myweb; highlight myweb in the Location text box, and type in the name of your application.

3. Click OK.

Import Web Wizard is another choice in the New dialog box. (It's to the right of Empty Web in Figure 6-4.) When you use this wizard, you grab the static content for the site, so it is a useful tool for maintaining a UI, not grabbing code. For an existing site that contains code, you would be wise to open the site in FrontPage and copy the content to your local machine instead.

CREATING A WEB APPLICATION BY USING VISUAL INTERDEV

Creating a Web site in Visual InterDev is a bit more involved than in FrontPage, largely because of the number of steps. The benefit of using Visual InterDev instead of FrontPage is that it enables you to hold the source files locally in a separate directory. The capability to maintain a local copy enables multiple developers to work on a single site — each developer edits a local copy rather than the copy on the development or production server.

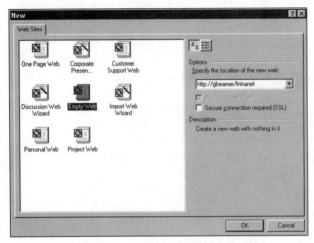

Figure 6-4: Choose Empty Web in the New dialog box.

 Be extremely cautious when editing files on a common server without some form of source control. While this goes without saying for most experienced developers, I've worked on numerous projects with multiple developers and no source control mechanism.

If you have a copy of Visual Studio or Visual Studio .NET, you have a copy of SourceSafe. I advise you to use this for your own projects, even those for which you are the only developer. From personal experience, I can attest that changing files without any form of source control is a risk that is not worth it.

If the site already exists, the steps are the same, with the exception of attaching to an existing application, rather than creating a new one (I cover this when we get to it in the list). To create a new Web application in Visual InterDev, follow these steps:

1. Start the new project by selecting File → New.

2. In the New Project dialog box, type a name for your project in the Name textbox. The new name is automatically added to the end of the path in the Location text box. (I normally alter the path, because I like my projects stored in a Project folder instead of in my profile.)

3. Leave the project site set on New Web Project, as shown in Figure 6-5, and click Open.

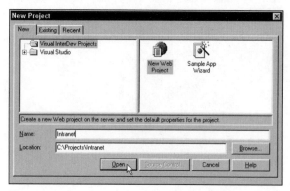

Figure 6-5: Creating a new project using the New Web Project Wizard.

4. In Step 1 of 4 of the Web Project Wizard (shown in Figure 6-6), select the server from the What Server Do You Want to Use drop-down list box, and then choose the mode in which you want to work. Working in Master Mode is a bit easier, but setting up in Local Mode is worth the time if you have a Web server on the development machine. When you're done, click Next.

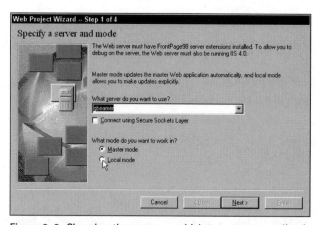

Figure 6-6: Choosing the server on which to run your application.

5. In Step 2 of 4 (see Figure 6-7) of the wizard, select whether to Create a New Web Application, for which you must type a name in the Name text box, or to Connect to an Existing Web Application. (Unless you've already created the Web site, you must create a new Web application.)

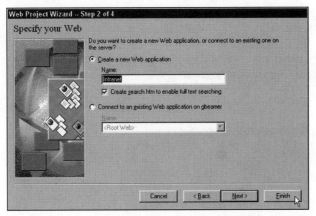

Figure 6-7: Creating a new Web application with the name of your application.

6. You have the option of clicking Next to add themes and layouts to your application, but that isn't necessary in .NET applications. Click Finish instead.

If you're attaching to an application that you've already created using one of the other methods, you get a screen asking whether you want to add the Script Library. Unless you see some overwhelming reason to use Design Time Controls (DTCs) with traditional ASP, click No on this one.

USING VISUAL STUDIO .NET

Visual Studio .NET makes it extremely easy to create a new Web application. You can either click the New Project button on the start page or select File → New. You can also use the shortcut Control + N. The New Project dialog box (see Figure 6-8) appears.

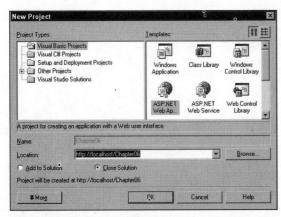

Figure 6-8: The New Project dialog box.

In order to create a new Web application, click the ASP.NET Web Application icon. Make sure the location for the application, the server, and the name are correct, and click the OK button.

If you already have an application that you need to attach to, select New Project in Existing Folder (see Figure 6-9) instead of ASP.NET Web Application in the dialog box.

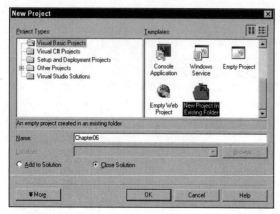

Figure 6-9: Using Visual Studio .NET to create a project from an existing application.

Select the folder or URL for the application you want to work on (see Figure 6-10), and click OK.

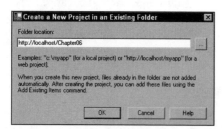

Figure 6-10: Selecting the URL for your existing Web application.

xcopy deployment

At this point, you have both ASPX pages and executables to deploy on your newly created Web application. To really understand the simplicity of the process in .NET, I now contrast it with the method that you use with COM+ and ASP. Table 6-1 shows the differences in deployment in COM+ and .NET.

TABLE 6-1 DEPLOYMENT OF COM+ AND .NET APPLICATIONS

COM+	.NET
Create a Web application on the server.	Create a Web application on the server.
Compile all your components by opening the projects (or Project Group) and building each of the DLLs.	Compile all your components by opening theWeb solution and then building the entire solution using Build → Build Solution.
Copy the entire Web application tree structure to your server. If using earlier versions of the FrontPage extensions, you're wise to use the Publish features of either FrontPage or Visual InterDev.	Copy the entire Web application tree structure to the new server.
Copy the components to a directory on the server.	*(That's it! You're done.)*
Create a COM+ Application in the Component Services (Microsoft Transaction Server). You can skip this step if you use regsvr32.exe.	
Add your COM+ components to the application that you build in the preceding step by right-clicking the components folder in the application and choosing New → Component. Alternatively, you can use regsvr32.exe to register the components on the server.	

The differences between COM+ and .NET are even more apparent if you're redeploying all or part of an application. In .NET, the steps are pretty much the same, but COM+ requires quite a few extra steps. Table 6-2 shows the difference between redeployment in COM+ and .NET.

TABLE 6-2 REDEPLOYMENT OF COM+ AND .NET APPLICATIONS

COM+	.NET
Compile all your components by opening the projects (or Project Group) and building each of the DLLs.	Compile all your components by opening the Web solution and building the solution using Build → Build Solution.
Copy the new pages to the Web application. Again, if using certain versions of the extensions, I recommend that you publish through FrontPage or Visual InterDev.	Copy the changed components and pages to the Web application on the server.
Open the Component Services and delete the components from the application. If you're using `regsvr32.exe`, shut down the Web server (which may require shutting down the entire IIS Service from the service manager).	*(That's it! You're done.)*
Right-click the application and shut it down; the application automatically restarts with the next page hit. If you're using `regsvr32.exe`, you now must run it again on each component with the `-u` flag:	

```
Regsvr32 -u MyDll.dll
```

The `-u` flag for the regsvr registration utility unregisters a previously registered component. Open a command prompt and type in **regsvr32 /?** to see all of flags available.

Copy the new versions of the components on top of the old versions.

Add the new versions of your COM+ components to the application you build in the preceding step by right-clicking the Components folder in the application and choosing New → Component. Alternatively, you can use regsvr32.exe to register the components on the server.

Although this book isn't about COM+, I feel obliged to mention the following couple caveats if you're using the older system:

◆ COM+ is always easier than registering components using regsvr32, even with nontransactional components. There are some performance caveats, so using COM+ is not a panacea. One of the purposes of COM+/MTS is object brokering, or allowing COM+ to pool instances of the objects created from your DLL. If you use regsvr32, IIS locks the components for the duration of the application. The best-case scenario is a shutdown of the Web application that uses the component that you want to change. Shutting down Web services on the machine, however, is more common. The worst-case scenario of regsvr32 is rebooting the machine to free up the components.

◆ If you're using COM+, get into the habit of running `regsvr32 -u` on each of the components that you delete from COM+ applications to make sure the registry entries for the DLL are erased, especially if you've broken binary compatibility by changing a public method or property. Deleting a COM+ component from an application doesn't clean up all the registry entries, as does using `regsvr32 -u`. Although not absolutely necessary if you maintain binary compatibility, a clean registry tends to make a happy Windows server. If binary compatibility becomes broken, a server may attempt to access an older version of the interface, which leads to nasty crashes.

Just to give you a rough idea of how long redeploying new versions of applications takes, I can perform all the steps necessary in COM+ in about 25 to 30 seconds. Using regsvr32, the same process generally takes a couple minutes, if the server doesn't require a reboot. In .NET, deploying the same application takes a fraction of a second on a good network, because deploying a .NET application is strictly a copy-and-paste operation.

USING XCOPY TO DEPLOY A .NET APPLICATION

In the old DOS days, it was quite common to move files from one location to another using the command line, an operation more commonly accomplished in the Windows world by dragging and dropping files in Windows Explorer. There were two commands for copying in the DOS world: `copy` and `xcopy`:

◆ `copy` – Used to copy any number of files from one directory to another. `copy` does not create an underlying directory structure.

◆ `xcopy` – Used to copy an entire directory structure from one location to another.

In the .NET world, `xcopy` is more useful than `copy` because you normally have a couple of folders underneath the main solution folder. The most important of these folders is the bin folder, which contains your compiled executable.

Listing 6-10 shows a simple `xcopy` routine to move code from the test folder (`c:\Inetpub\wwwroot\test`) to the Chapter06 folder (`c:\Inetpub\wwwroot\Chapter06`).

Listing 6-10: Using xcopy to Copy an Entire Solution from One Folder to Another

```
xcopy c:\Inetpub\wwwroot\test c:\Inetpub\wwwroot\Chapter06
```

MAPPING A NETWORK DRIVE AND COPYING AN APPLICATION

To move from one drive to another with `xcopy`, you must map the drive. You accomplish this task by using the Tools → Map Network Drive command from the Windows Explorer menu bar. You type the UNC (Universal Naming Convention) for the folder that you want to map to, and you may need to add credentials for the drive if your network logon doesn't work (if your credentials are not working, you'll get an access denied message). If you're using XP, you can change the access credentials by clicking Connect using a different user name.

You can also map by right-clicking any folder in the network and choosing Map Network Drive from the pop-up menu — or just use the `net use` command from the command line, as shown in Listing 6-11. Listing 6-11 also shows the `xcopy` command that you use to copy your application to this new drive.

Listing 6-11: Mapping a Network Drive from the Command Line

```
net use e: \\WebServer\inetpub\
xcopy c:\Inetpub\wwwroot\test e:\Chapter06
```

UNC (Universal Naming Convention) is a designation for a server and a path that can reside on any computer. It is basically the network equivalent of a URL (Universal Resource Locator).

In the Windows world, a UNC most commonly takes the form of a computer name and then a path. You can use an IP address instead of a computer name. Both of these options (machine name and IP address) are shown below:

```
\\ComputerName\MyPath
\\192.168.1.100\MyPath
```

Summary

In this chapter, you built a simple ASP.NET application, and I took you through the steps necessary to deploy the application to another folder. I also compared it to a COM+ application using traditional ASP.

In the next chapter, you'll see how to move the phone list application to a Windows Forms application, and how easy it is to migrate code in ASP.NET.

Part II

Building Web Applications – ASP.NET and Visual Basic .NET

Chapter 7

Windows Forms and WebForms

IN THIS CHAPTER

♦ Building a Windows Form

♦ Building a WebForm by using HTML controls

♦ Examining HTML controls

A GOOD PLACE TO START BUILDING Web applications is to learn about building WebForms. In this chapter, I focus on building WebForms by using HTML controls. This subject isn't as exciting as the use of Web controls (which I cover in Chapter 8), but each of these controls inherits directly from standard HTML (and ASP) and that is basic to your applications. Because each control uses the same syntax as standard HTML, HTML controls are the easiest to use if you need to port an ASP application to ASP.NET.

In addition to discussing WebForms that you build by using HTML Controls, I build a couple small Windows Forms applications. The first demonstrates the differences between Windows Forms and Visual Basic 6 Standard EXE applications. The second shows you how easily you can move code from a WebForm to a Windows Forms and vice versa. For the comparison of Windows Forms and WebForms, I port over the PhoneList application from Chapter 6.

Building a Windows Forms Application

One of the goals of the .NET Framework – and of the Windows Distributed iNternet Architecture (DNA), for quite some time now – is to make the user interface (the portion of the application the user interacts with, be it a browser or a standard executable, like Word) completely separate from the business rules and data of the application. But without the right tools, most real-world applications can't realize this goal. Although this book doesn't focus on Windows Forms, taking the time to understand the similarities between the code in both desktop and

Internet applications is a worthy investment. With .NET, the user interface, be it a Windows Form or a WebForm, should be inconsequential to the work being done behind the scenes.

Before I show you how simple porting code from a WebForm to a Windows Form is, you need to understand something of how Windows Forms work. Windows Forms are dramatically different from Visual Basic 6 standard executables, so take a deep breath and hang tight.

A simple Visual Basic 6 form

In Visual Basic 6, most of the code that defines your form is hidden from you. If you ever open the file in Notepad, you see code that initializes each of your controls and the form itself. You can't, however, edit this code inside the Visual Basic IDE. Figure 7-1 shows a simple form that uses a command button to change a label so that its caption equals the text property of a textbox.

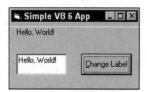

Figure 7-1: A simple Visual Basic 6
Hello, World application.

The application shown in Figure 7-1 allows you to type something in the text box and click the Change Label button. The label, shown just below the header bar, changes to whatever you have typed in the text box. When you open this in the Visual Basic IDE and go to Code View, you see the following:

```
Option Explicit

Private Sub cmdChange_Click()
  lblOutput.Caption = txtInput.Text
End Sub
```

When you click the Change Label (cmdChange) button, you access the click event that sets the label's caption property to the value of the textbox's text property. Fairly simple, right? As you look at the code, however, you notice that there is no way to set where the different controls sit on the form. This is all done in design time, using the IDE. The complete code for the form is shown in Listing 7-1. You have to open the frmVB6.frm file in Notepad or some other ASCII text editor to see the same code this listing shows.

Listing 7-1: The Entire Source Code for frmVB6.frm

```
VERSION 5.00
Begin VB.Form frmVB6
    Caption         =   "Simple VB 6 App"
    ClientHeight    =   1485
    ClientLeft      =   60
    ClientTop       =   345
    ClientWidth     =   3045
    LinkTopic       =   "Form1"
    ScaleHeight     =   1485
    ScaleWidth      =   3045
    StartUpPosition =   3  'Windows Default
    Begin VB.CommandButton cmdChange
        Caption         =   "&Change Label"
        Height          =   495
        Left            =   1680
        TabIndex        =   2
        Top             =   720
        Width           =   1215
    End
    Begin VB.TextBox txtInput
        Height          =   495
        Left            =   120
        TabIndex        =   1
        Top             =   720
        Width           =   1215
    End
    Begin VB.Label lblOutput
        Height          =   375
        Left            =   120
        TabIndex        =   0
        Top             =   120
        Width           =   2775
    End
End
Attribute VB_Name = "frmVB6"
Attribute VB_GlobalNameSpace = False
Attribute VB_Creatable = False
Attribute VB_PredeclaredId = True
Attribute VB_Exposed = False
Option Explicit

Private Sub cmdChange_Click()
    lblOutput.Caption = txtInput.Text
End Sub
```

You can find the code for this example on this book's companion Web site (www.wiley.com/extras) in the Ch07SDK.zip (SDK version) or Ch07VS.zip (Visual Studio .NET version) file. After you unzip the file, find the HelloWorldVB folder, which contains the project files. This example requires Visual Basic 6 or Visual Studio 6 to compile.

In all likelihood, you won't ever want to mess with this file outside the Visual Basic IDE, because the IDE gives you much easier tools for handling changing elements. You also have to compile the file to get it to work, and compiling outside the IDE is not a realistic option in Visual Basic 6. In Visual Basic .NET, you probably don't want to code all your form elements either, because it is easier to design forms by dragging controls onto them, but you can if you want to. In Visual Basic .NET, all the initialization code for the form opens up to you right in the IDE, so you don't need to open the file in Notepad as you did in Visual Basic.

The .NET version of the same application opens up the code. You can now access all your code and even program Visual Basic .NET without the IDE. In Listing 7-2, I introduce you to a Windows Form that does the same thing as the application in Listing 7-1.

Listing 7-2: The Hello, World Label Application in Visual Basic .NET

```
Public Class Form1
    Inherits System.Windows.Forms.Form

#Region " Windows Form Designer generated code "

    Public Sub New()
      MyBase.New()
      InitializeComponent()
    End Sub

    Protected Overloads Overrides Sub Dispose(ByVal disposing As Boolean)
      If disposing Then
        If Not (components Is Nothing) Then
          components.Dispose()
        End If
      End If
      MyBase.Dispose(disposing)
    End Sub

    'Required by the Windows Form Designer
    Private components As System.ComponentModel.IContainer
```

```vb
'NOTE: The following procedure is required by the Windows Form Designer
'It can be modified using the Windows Form Designer.
'Do not modify it using the code editor.
Friend WithEvents cmdChange As System.Windows.Forms.Button
Friend WithEvents lblOutput As System.Windows.Forms.Label
Friend WithEvents txtInput As System.Windows.Forms.TextBox
<System.Diagnostics.DebuggerStepThrough()> _
Private Sub InitializeComponent()
  Me.lblOutput = New System.Windows.Forms.Label()
  Me.txtInput = New System.Windows.Forms.TextBox()
  Me.cmdChange = New System.Windows.Forms.Button()
  Me.SuspendLayout()
  '
  'lblOutput
  '
  Me.lblOutput.Location = New System.Drawing.Point(8, 8)
  Me.lblOutput.Name = "lblOutput"
  Me.lblOutput.Size = New System.Drawing.Size(184, 23)
  Me.lblOutput.TabIndex = 0
  '
  'txtInput
  '
  Me.txtInput.Location = New System.Drawing.Point(8, 56)
  Me.txtInput.Name = "txtInput"
  Me.txtInput.Size = New System.Drawing.Size(96, 20)
  Me.txtInput.TabIndex = 1
  Me.txtInput.Text = ""
  '
  'cmdChange
  '
  Me.cmdChange.Location = New System.Drawing.Point(120, 40)
  Me.cmdChange.Name = "cmdChange"
  Me.cmdChange.Size = New System.Drawing.Size(75, 48)
  Me.cmdChange.TabIndex = 2
  Me.cmdChange.Text = "Change Label"
  '
  'Form1
  '
  Me.AutoScaleBaseSize = New System.Drawing.Size(5, 13)
  Me.ClientSize = New System.Drawing.Size(200, 101)
  Me.Controls.AddRange(New System.Windows.Forms.Control() _
     {Me.cmdChange, Me.txtInput, Me.lblOutput})
  Me.Name = "Form1"
```

Continued

Listing 7-2 *(Continued)*

```
    Me.Text = "Simple VB.NET App"
    Me.ResumeLayout(False)

End Sub

#End Region


Private Sub cmdChange_Click(ByVal sender As System.Object, _
  ByVal e As System.EventArgs) Handles cmdChange.Click
    lblOutput.Text = txtInput.Text
End Sub
End Class
```

 The code for this project is available in the file ChO7SDK.zip (SDK version) or ChO7VS.zip (Visual Studio .NET version) on the companion Web site (www.wiley.com/extras). After you unzip the file, open the project folder HelloWorldVB.NET. I've included a version that was created by the upgrade wizard, in case you are curious: HelloWorldUpgrade.

I want to take you through the code in the Windows Forms version (Listing 7-2):

1. At the top of your source code file, you import any namespaces that you intend to use in your form. If you're using Visual Studio .NET, you may not see the need to import with aliases, because Visual Studio .NET creates the controls with the full namespace. I, however, choose to use aliases for all namespaces in this project.

   ```
   Imports SysDraw = System.Drawing
   Imports WinForms = System.Windows.Forms
   Imports CompModel = System.ComponentModel
   ```

2. The code for the form sits in a class with the same name as the form file. You have to inherit System.Windows.Forms.Form as your base class, because this is a Windows Forms application. In the following example, I use the alias WinForms, which is covered in step 1. There are three methods that are placed in this Windows Form: New(), which is the constructor; InitializeComponent(), where the form controls will be placed in the next steps; and Dispose, which is where you code to dispose of this application when the CLR is finished with it.

```
Public Class frmVBNET
    Inherits WinForms.Form

    Public Sub New()
        MyBase.New()
        InitializeComponent()
    End Sub

    Protected Overloads Overrides Sub
      Dispose(ByVal disposing As Boolean)
        If disposing Then
            If Not (components Is Nothing) Then
                components.Dispose()
            End If
        End If
        MyBase.Dispose(disposing)
    End Sub
    <System.Diagnostics.DebuggerStepThrough()>
     Private Sub InitializeComponent()
     End Sub
End Class
```

3. The next step is to declare the variables for the label, text box, and button that are placed on the form. Each control is declared `WithEvents` to ensure that you can code against the `Click` event of the button in a later step:

```
Friend WithEvents lblOutput As WinForms.Label
Friend WithEvents txtInput As WinForms.TextBox
Friend WithEvents cmdChange As WinForms.Button
Private components As CompModel.IContainer
```

4. You now create an `InitializeComponent()` subroutine, which is used to instantiate each of the components you have placed on your form. Note that Visual Basic .NET still uses the `Me` keyword to indicate the form you are working on.

```
<System.Diagnostics.DebuggerStepThrough()>↵
Private Sub InitializeComponent()
    Me.lblOutput = New System.Windows.Forms.Label()
    Me.txtInput = New System.Windows.Forms.TextBox()
    Me.cmdChange = New System.Windows.Forms.Button()
    Me.SuspendLayout()
    '
    'lblOutput - the Label conrol
```

```
        '
        Me.lblOutput.Location = _
            New System.Drawing.Point(8, 8)
        Me.lblOutput.Name = "lblOutput"
        Me.lblOutput.Size = _
            New System.Drawing.Size(184, 23)
        Me.lblOutput.TabIndex = 0
        '
        'txtInput - the Textbox
        '
        Me.txtInput.Location = _
            New System.Drawing.Point(8, 56)
        Me.txtInput.Name = "txtInput"
        Me.txtInput.Size = _
            New System.Drawing.Size(96, 20)
        Me.txtInput.TabIndex = 1
        Me.txtInput.Text = ""
        '
        'cmdChange
        '
        Me.cmdChange.Location = _
            New System.Drawing.Point(120, 40)
        Me.cmdChange.Name = "cmdChange"
        Me.cmdChange.Size = _
            New System.Drawing.Size(75, 48)
        Me.cmdChange.TabIndex = 2
        Me.cmdChange.Text = "Change Label"
        '
        'Form1
        '
        Me.AutoScaleBaseSize = _
            New System.Drawing.Size(5, 13)
        Me.ClientSize = _
            New System.Drawing.Size(200, 101)
        Me.Controls.AddRange(New System.Windows.Forms.Control() _
            {Me.cmdChange, Me.txtInput, Me.lblOutput})
        Me.Name = "Form1"
        Me.Text = "Simple VB.NET App"
        Me.ResumeLayout(False)
    End Sub
```

5. You now have a form created that matches the Visual Basic 6 application from Listing 7-1. To complete the application, you need to add a cmdChange_Click() method to handle the Click event for the button control. There are only three differences here between Visual Basic 6 and

Visual Basic .NET: the `Caption` property of the Visual Basic 6 label is now a `Text` property, the `Click` event handler now has arguments, and the event handler specifically states which event it handles.

```
Private Sub cmdChange_Click(ByVal sender As System.Object, _
                            ByVal e As System.EventArgs)
                            Handles cmdChange.Click
    lblOutput.Text = txtInput.Text
End Sub
```

PhoneList, part two — the Windows Forms version

To put the changes from Visual Basic 6 to Visual Basic .NET in perspective, you want to see a real-world implementation. For this reason, I created a PhoneList application that uses the same functionality as the PhoneList WebForm application from Chapter 6 (Listing 6-9). To get a little practice, build the form yourself and migrate the code from the WebForm version. Figure 7-2 shows how the Form for the PhoneList desktop application looks.

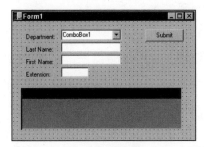

Figure 7-2: The PhoneList desktop application as a Windows Form.

The code for Windows Forms application is shown in Listing 7-3.

Listing 7-3: The PhoneList Application as a Windows Form

```
Private Sub cmdSubmit_Click(ByVal sender As System.Object, _
  ByVal e As System.EventArgs) Handles cmdSubmit.Click
    Dim strConn As String = "Server=(local);" & _
     "Database=dbIntranet;UID=sa;PWD=;"
    Dim objConn As New SqlConnection(strConn)
    Dim objDataSet As DataSet = New DataSet()
    Dim blnWhere As Boolean
    Dim intDept As Integer = CInt(ddDept.SelectedIndex)
    Dim strSQL As String = "SELECT strLastName as [Last Name], " & _
     "strFirstName as [First Name], " & _
     "intExtension as [Extension] FROM tblEmployee e"
```

Continued

Listing 7-3 *(Continued)*

```vb
If intDept <> 0 Then
     CheckWhere(strSQL, blnWhere)
     strSQL = strSQL & "intDepartmentID = " & intDept
   End If

   If strLastName.Text <> "" Then
     CheckWhere(strSQL, blnWhere)
     strSQL = strSQL & "strLastName LIKE '" & _
     CStr(strLastName.Text) & "%'"
   End If

   '... repeat If for other postback events (see code)

   strSQL = strSQL & " ORDER BY strLastName, strFirstName"

   Dim objCmd As New SqlCommand(strSQL, objConn)
   Dim objDataAdapter As New SqlDataAdapter(objCmd)

   objConn.Open()
   objDataAdapter.Fill(objDataSet, "tblEmployee")
   objConn.Close()

   DataGrid1.DataSource = objDataSet.Tables("tblEmployee").DefaultView
End Sub

Private Sub Form1_Load(ByVal sender As System.Object, _
  ByVal e As System.EventArgs) Handles MyBase.Load
   'Make sure this is pointing at your database.
   Dim strConn As String = "Server=(local);" & _
     "Database=dbIntranet;UID=sa;PWD=;"

   Dim strSQL As String = "SELECT intDepartmentID, " & _
     "strDepartmentName FROM tblDepartment " & _
     "ORDER BY intDepartmentID"

   'Create data objects
   Dim objConn As New SqlConnection(strConn)
   Dim objCmd = New SqlCommand(strSQL, objConn)
   Dim objDataSet As DataSet = New DataSet()
   Dim objDataAdapter As New SqlDataAdapter(objCmd)

   'Create a Connection Object and Open
```

```
    objConn.Open()

    'Fill data set
    objDataAdapter.Fill(objDataSet, "tblDepartment")

    'Close Connection
    objConn.Close()

    'Bind to the Drop Down
    ddDept.DataSource = objDataSet.Tables("tblDepartment").DefaultView
    ddDept.ValueMember = "intDepartmentID"
    ddDept.DisplayMember = "strDepartmentName"
End Sub


Private Sub CheckWhere(ByRef strSQL As String, _
        ByRef blnWhere As Boolean)
    If blnWhere = True Then
        strSQL = strSQL & " AND "
    Else
        strSQL = strSQL & " WHERE "
        blnWhere = True
    End If
End Sub
```

 You can download the code for Listing 7-3 from the companion Web site (www.wiley.com/extras): Ch07VS.zip (Visual Studio .NET version) or Ch07SDK.zip (SDK version). Open the project named HelloWorldUpgrade.

This code looks pretty much the same as the code in Listing 6-9, with the most notable changes being the placement of code (which event it is placed in) and slightly different properties of some of the controls. Let's look at the sections that have changed:

◆ To initially load the combo box (ddDept), you place the Windows Forms code in the Form1_Load() method, which is the constructor. In the WebForm application, the code is placed in Page_Load() outside of the Page.IsPostBack property section.

◆ The code contained in the New() method is very similar to the code from the WebForm application, with the exception of the binding of the

combo-box (drop-down selection box). Here's that code, with lines that
are different marked with '***:

```
'In ASP.NET
cboDepartment.DataSource = objDataSet.Tables("tblDepartment")
cboDepartment.DataValueField = "strDepartmentName"   '***
cboDepartment.DataMember = "intDepartmentID"          '***
cboDepartment.SelectedIndex = 0
cboDepartment.DataBind()                                  '***


'In Visual Basic .NET
cboDepartment.DataSource = objDataSet.Tables("tblDepartment")
cboDepartment.DisplayMember = "strDepartmentName"   '***
cboDepartment.ValueMember = "intDepartmentID"        '***
cboDepartment.SelectedIndex = 0
```

◆ The code to load the `DataGrid` is placed in the `cmdSubmit_Click()` event.
Technically, this is where I should have placed it in the WebForm application in Chapter 6, but I was illustrating the `IsPostBack` property of the
`Page` object. There is no equivalent to `IsPostBack` in Windows Forms.
You have to add a few objects; I have bolded the additions in Listing 7-3.

◆ There is no method to explicitly bind the `DataGrid` once its `DataSource` is
established. I have left the `DataGrid` visible on the Windows Form; it's hidden to start on the WebForm. This is shown in the following code snippets:

```
'In ASP.NET
DataGrid1.DataSource = _
     objDataSet.Tables("tblEmployee").DefaultView
DataGrid1.DataBind()
DataGrid1.Visible = True


'In Visual Basic .NET
DataGrid1.DataSource = _
     objDataSet.Tables("tblEmployee").DefaultView
```

◆ Any properties placed in code will either have to be set in the Visual
Studio .NET IDE design properties, or you have to set them in code. For
example, `datatextfield` and `datavaluefield` were set in a tag in our
ASP.NET application. Here they are set in code. In the following comparison, I show both an HTML control and an ASP.NET Web control to create
the drop-down:

```
'In ASP.NET (HTML Control - this chapter)
<select ID="cboDepartment" datatextfield="strDepartmentName"
datavaluefield="intDepartmentID" runat="server">
```

```
'In ASP.NET (Web control - Chapter 8)
<asp:DropDownList ID="cboDepartment"
    DataTextField="strDepartmentName"
    DataValueField="intDepartmentID" Runat="server"/>

'In Visual Basic .NET
cboDepartment.DisplayMember = "strDepartmentName"
cboDepartment.ValueMember = "intDepartmentID"
```

 You'll find the code for the PhoneList application on the companion Web site (www.wiley.com/extras) in the file ChO7SDK.zip (SDK version) or ChO7VS.zip (Visual Studio .NET version). After you unzip the file, look in the folder PhoneListWinForm.

This separation of code and interface is the way Web programming should have been for quite some time. Attempting to migrate code from ASP to Visual Basic 6, however, is more akin to pulling teeth. I'd prefer to see all the controls map 100 percent, of course, but having the same language in which to program both desktop and Internet applications makes switching from a Web interface to a desktop interface, much easier, because you can migrate most of your code, without change, during the transition.

Building a WebForm

As you discovered in Chapter 6, building a WebForm application is fairly simple. In this section, I focus on building WebForms by using HTML controls. HTML controls (whose names map directly to the HTML they represent) can be run on the server (to maintain state, for example), but there is no requirement that they be anything other than static HTML. You can use Web controls, which are often called server controls, for the same purpose, although they are programmatic and must run on the server.

 ASP.NET Web controls (also known as server controls) are very important, and I cover them in Chapter 8. HTML controls are the focus of the rest of this chapter. I suggest that you familiarize yourself with both HTML and Web controls.

Figure 7-3 shows the object model for the HTML controls.

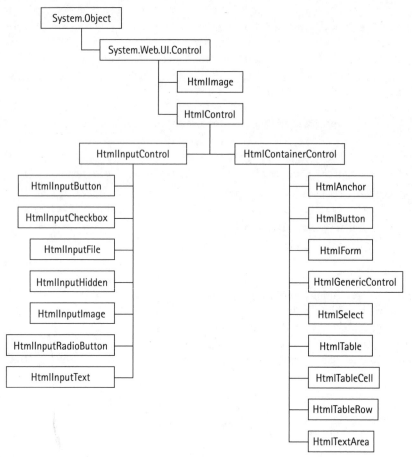

Figure 7-3: The HTML controls object model hierarchy.

HTML controls

HTML controls, for the most part, mirror their HTML counterparts; in other words, they use the same tags. You do find one slight difference: By using HTML controls, you can indicate that the code runs on the server side. For most controls, this change alone makes the control maintain state after a postback. What this means is the text box that you have filled in will still contain the same value after you click on a submit button.

Because ASP.NET Web controls also run on the server and maintain state, why even use HTML controls? Because you can't run Web controls on the client, which means that you maintain state unless you either add code to lose the state or use HTML controls. In most instances, you want to maintain state, so this is not a problem.

To use HTML controls in your application, you can either drag-and-drop them from the toolbox onto the page, using the IDE, or hand-code the HTML in your favorite ASCII text editor. The HTML controls must run on the server, using `runat=server` to access the properties, methods, and events in your application code, or to maintain state after the user clicks the submit button.

 Much of the rest of this chapter details classes in the `System.Web`, `System.Web.UI` and `System.Web.UI.HtmlControls` namespaces. In these sections, you may see the words object, class, and control used interchangeably. Just remember: A class is a blueprint for an object. An object is an instance of a class (that is, it's used by your program at this very moment when it is an object). A control is a class or object that ultimately inherits from the `Control` class. These objects (or classes) are called controls because they have a user-interface aspect.

As you continue through the chapter, notice that I use both a friendly name as well as the .NET Framework class name for each control. The friendly name is the main part of the section title, and the class name is in parentheses.

CONTROL CLASS (CONTROL)

The `Control` class is the granddaddy of the HTML controls and the Web controls programming model. Although you seldom program directly against a `Control` object, you do use the methods of this class because they're implemented in the various classes that inherit this class. To help you chew on this mouthful, take another look at Figure 7-3. Any class lower in the hierarchy can use the properties and methods of classes higher in the hierarchy as long as you can link them in a parent-child relationship. Thus, the `HtmlTextArea` class can use all of the methods and properties of `HtmlContainerControl` (its immediate parent, or base class), `HtmlControl`, `Control`, and `Object` classes.

Following is a list of the most important properties of this class. Other controls, further down the hierarchy, inherit each of the following properties.

- ◆ ID: Use this property to set the programmatic ID for the control. In HTML, you use `ID=""` to set this property. You use `ID` with all controls if you plan to access the controls programmatically. The first example that follows works for JavaScript but not for DHTML and ASP.NET; the second works for DHTML and ASP.NET but not for JavaScript. The third is optimal for all three.

  ```
  <input type="text" name="strFirstName" runat="server">
  ```

  ```
  <input type="text" id="txtFirstName" runat="server">
  ```

```
<input type="text" name="strFirstName" id="txtFirstName"
runat="server">
```

◆ **Visible:** The default for this property is true. If you set this property to false, you can access only the values on the server side, because the control doesn't even appear in the HTML. Its primary use is for items that you need to access programmatically on the server side but need no client implementation. Don't attempt to use the `visible` property of the text controls to make a hidden `<input>` tag for regular form submission, because the value is on only the server side. While it may seem a bit unorthodox, if you come from a traditional ASP background, you can use the `Visible` property to hide elements to create a multipart form. The following example shows a textbox that gets filled with the value of `ID`, when the form is posted, but is not visible. After it is the tag in the page.

```
<script language="vb" runat=server>
    'Yes, this will still work.
    txtHidden.value = Request("ID")
    txtHidden.visible = False
</script>
...
<input type="text" id="txtHidden">
```

◆ **Parent:** Use this property to get the parent control for the control that you're accessing. To better understand this, you must realize that all form controls (those that represent items in an HTML form) have the form as a parent. In the same manner, a table cell has a table row as a parent, which has a table as a parent. If you picture how tags are nested in HTML, this makes more sense. The use of the word control is due to the fact that the programming model of ASP.NET sees these items as controls, or objects, rather than tags. In the following snippet of code, I pull the Parent of the textbox control named `txtHidden`:

```
strParent = txtHidden.Parent
```

◆ **Page:** Use this property to get the page that contains the current control. Here's an example:

```
strPage = txtHidden.Page
```

`DataBind` is a `Control` class method that you use to bind data to a particular control and all its child controls. I touched on this method in Chapter 6, where I discussed the PhoneList drop-down control (or combo box) that holds department names. Here's an example of its use:

```
cboDepartment.DataBind()
```

CONTAINER CONTROLS (HTMLCONTAINERCONTROL)

`Container` controls represent HTML tags that have other tags nested inside of them. For example, a table contains rows and cells, and individual cells in a table can contain other controls. As such, table, row, and cell are all container controls. Each of these controls derives from the `HtmlContainerControl` class. The two most important properties of the `HtmlContainerControl` class are `InnerHtml` and `InnerText`. If you've worked with DHTML before, these properties are sure to appear familiar to you.

◆ `InnerHtml`: This property replaces the content inside a container control with HTML. It applies all HTML tags prior to displaying the new content. In the following example, line 1 shows the `<p>` tag to change; line 2 shows the line of code to change the `InnerHtml`; and line 3 is the result:

```
<p id="myPara">Original text!</p>

myPara.innerHtml = "<i>Text after innerHtml change!</i>"

Text after innerHtml change!
```

◆ `InnerText`: This property replaces the content inside a container control with text. Any HTML tags show up as tags when the new content is displayed. In the following example, line 1 shows the `<p>` tag to change; line 2 shows the of code to change the `InnerText`; and line 3 is the result:

```
<p id="myPara">Original text!</p>

myPara.innerHtml = "<i>Text after innerText change!</i>"

<i>Text after innerText change!</i>
```

FORM (HTMLFORM)   The `HtmlForm` control class matches up to the `<form>` tag in HTML. The `HTMLForm` control class uses five properties that directly relate to the control: `action`, `enctype`, `method`, `name`, and `target`. Each of these properties has a direct correlation to an attribute of the HTML form tag.

Table 7-1 shows the different properties and how to use them. If you have experience with traditional ASP or HTML, you're certainly familiar with the properties of the `HtmlForm` control, because they're the same as the HTML `<form>` tag properties.

TABLE 7-1 THE FORM CONTROL

Control Property	HTML	Description
action	action="myurl.asp"	Sets the page that handles the form.
enctype	enctype="applicaton/ x-www-form- urlencoded"	Sets the form encoding type. Valid values include "application/ x-www-form-urlencoded" (shown in the HTML column), "multipart/ form-data", "text/plain", and "image/jpeg".
method	method="POST"	Sets the method for the form submission. The default value is "POST", which uses the form collection. You can also use "GET", which uses the query string to pass all arguments.
name	name="MyForm1"	Sets the name for the form. This property is useful for accessing the element from custom JavaScript routines.
target	target="MyFrame"	Sets a target frame or window to which to redirect the form. This property is useful for pop-up forms that submit back to a parent window or for forms that are used in a Web site that utilizes frames.

As you experiment with the Form control, realize that Microsoft discourages changing the default values for most of these properties, because doing so changes the default method of posting back to the same page. There is a great temptation to post to another page, but I discourage succumbing to it. It's better to learn the new paradigm as it works, even if it seems a bit strange.

ANCHOR (HTMLANCHOR)   You use the HtmlAnchor control class to create anchor tags, or <a>, which you can as bookmarks or hyperlinks. Table 7-2 shows the properties of the HtmlAnchor control class and Listing 7-4 shows a sample script demonstrating its use. For hyperlinks, you have a more robust Web control, known as the Hyperlink control.

TABLE 7-2 HTMLANCHOR CLASS PROPERTIES

Property	Description
Href	Sets a URL for the anchor tag.
Target	Sets the frame or window for the new content.
Title	Sets the title that the browser displays in the status bar as the mouse hovers over the link.

Listing 7-4: Anchor Tags in ASP.NET

```
<script language="vb" runat="server">
  Private Sub Page_Load(Sender As Object, _
               e As EventArgs) _
               Handles MyBase.Load
    If Request.QueryString("UserID") = "" then
      EnterLink.InnerText = "No Entry Allowed!"
      EnterLink.Href = "http://www.wiley.com"
      EnterLink.Title = "You cannot enter!"
    End If
  End Sub
</script>
...
<a href="enter.aspx" ID="EnterLink" runat="server">Enter</a>
```

BUTTON (HTMLBUTTON)   You use the `HtmlButton` control class to create a button control in your form. Only Internet Explorer (4.0 or higher) supports the `<button>` tag, so you don't want to implement this object on Web sites that you're targeting toward Netscape browsers or lower-level browsers. In HTML, this tag enables you to embed HTML content in your button; a common use is to place italicized or bold text on a button. The `button` object has no unique properties and no direct relation in the Web controls. Listing 7-5 shows the usage of the `button` object in code.

Listing 7-5: Using Button controls in ASP.NET

```
  Private Sub btnCheck_Click(Sender As Object, _
               e As EventArgs) _
               Handles btnCheck.Click
    prettyButton.InnerHtml = "<i>You clicked me!</i>"
  End Sub
...
<button ID="prettyButton">Click Me</button>
```

SELECT OR DROP-DOWN (HTMLSELECT)   You use the `HtmlSelect` control class to create a select control in your page. Most of the unique properties of this item are used for data binding. One event also is usable by this object to cause a server post back: `ServerChange`. Table 7-3 shows the unique properties of the `select` object. You could use this object in Chapter 6 with the drop-down list that you create for the PhoneList application. A more robust Web control equivalent is the `DropDownList` control.

TABLE 7-3 THE PROPERTIES OF THE HTMLSELECT CLASS

Property	Description
DataSource	Sets the data source used to populate the drop-down list.
DataTextField	Sets the field for the text appearing in the drop-down list.
DataValueField	Sets the field that populates the value for each item in the drop-down list. Normally, the field you use here is a primary key field from the database.
Items	Presents a list of items in the drop-down list. The `Items` property returns a variable as a `ListItemsCollection`.
Multiple	Determines whether someone can select multiple items from the list.
Size	Sets the number of lines visible at one time.
Value	Gets or sets the value of the currently selected item in the drop-down list. When data bound, this item does not affect the values in the database — it just changes the text that the user sees as selected.
ServerChange	Used in HTML as "OnServerChange=", this event fires as "ControlName_Change". It fires when you change the selected item in the drop-down list and the form is submitted back to the server.

Listing 7-6 is an example of using the `HtmlSelect` class in an application. The code is assumed to sit in the CodeBehind file, although you could place it in a script block (`<script></script>`) and place it directly in with the HTML tags.

Listing 7-6: Working with the HtmlSelect Class

```
Private Sub Page_Load(Sender As Object, _
                e As EventArgs)
    Dim objConn As SQLConnection = New SQLConnection("Server=(local);" & _
                "Database=dbIntranet;UID=sa;PWD=;")
    Dim objDataSet As DataSet = New DataSet()
```

```
    Dim objCmd as New SQLCommand("SELECT * FROM Department", objConn)
    Dim objDataAdapter as New SQLDataAdapter(objCmd)
    objConn.Open()
        objDataAdapter.Fill(objDataSet,"tblDepartment")
    objConn.Close()

    lstMyList.DataSource = _
        objDataSet.Tables("tblDepartment").DefaultView
    lstMyList.DataBind()
  End Sub
...
<select ID="lstMyList" datatextfield="strDepartmentName"
datavaluefield="intDepartmentID" runat="server"></select>
```

Listing 7-6 places some of the properties in the HTML and some in the code. If I wanted to place the fields to bind in my code, instead of in the tag, I would write something more like the following:

```
lstMyList.DataValueField = "intDepartmentID"
lstMyList.DataTextField = "strDepartmentName"
```

TABLE (HTMLTABLE)   You use the `HtmlTable` control class in conjunction with the `HtmlTableRow` and the `HtmlTableCell` controls to build tables in your ASP.NET applications. The properties of the `HtmlTable` controls are shown in Table 7-4. More robust Web controls are available for each of the table-building HTML controls.

 ASP.NET Web controls for creating tables are covered in more detail in Chapter 8.

TABLE 7-4 THE TABLE CONTROL IN ASP.NET

Property	Description
Align	Gets or sets the alignment of the content contain in an HtmlTable object. You can override the alignment by setting it at the row or cell level.
BgColor	Gets or sets the background color of the table. You can override the table background color by setting it at the row or cell level.

Continued

TABLE 7-4 THE TABLE CONTROL IN ASP.NET *(Continued)*

Property	Description
Border	Gets or sets the border width in pixels.
BorderColor	Gets or sets the color of the border. You can set this property in hexadecimal or by using HTML color constants. You can override the table border color by setting it at the row or cell level.
CellPadding	Gets or sets the amount of padding (the space between the border and the content of the cells).
CellSpacing	Gets or sets the amount of spacing between cells.
Height	Gets or sets the height of the table.
Rows	Gets a collection of row objects for the table. This property returns as an HtmlTableRowCollection object.
Width	Gets or sets the width of the table.

TABLE ROW (HTMLTABLEROW)   The HtmlTableRow control class is used to create a single row inside an HtmlTable. A single HtmlTableRow object represents each row in a table, and the HtmlTableRowCollection object contains *all* the rows. The properties of the HtmlTableRow object are shown in Table 7-5.

TABLE 7-5 THE TABLE ROW CONTROL IN ASP.NET

Property	Description
Align	Gets or sets the alignment of the content that an HtmlTableRow object contains. You can override the row alignment by setting it at the cell level.
BgColor	Gets or sets the background color of the row. You can override the row background color by setting it at the cell level.
BorderColor	Gets or sets the color of the border for a row. You can set this property in hexadecimal or by using HTML color constants. You can override the row border color by setting it at the cell level.
Cells	Gets a collection of cell objects for the row. This property returns as an HtmlTableCellCollection object.

Property	Description
Height	Gets or sets the height of the row.
Valign	Gets or sets the vertical alignment of the row. You can override the row vertical alignment by setting it at the cell level.

TABLE CELL (HTMLTABLECELL) You use the `HtmlTableCell` control class to create a single cell inside an `HtmlTableRow` control. A single `HtmlTableCell` object represents each cell in a table, and the `HtmlTableCellCollection` object contains *all* the cells. The properties of the `HtmlTableCell` object are shown in Table 7-6.

TABLE 7-6 THE TABLE CELL CONTROL IN ASP.NET

Property	Description
Align	Gets or sets the alignment of the content that an `HtmlTableCell` object contains.
BgColor	Gets or sets the background color of the table cell.
BorderColor	Gets or sets the color of the border for a cell. You can set this property in hexadecimal or by using HTML color constants.
ColSpan	Gets or sets the number of columns that a cell spans.
Height	Gets or sets the height of the cell.
NoWrap	Gets or sets a value to indicate whether any text inside of a table cell wraps.
RowSpan	Gets or sets the number of rows that a cell spans.
Valign	Gets or sets the vertical alignment of the cell.
Width	Gets or sets the width of a table cell.

TEXTAREA (HTMLTEXTAREA) The `HtmlTextArea` control class is used to create multiline text boxes in ASP.NET. To make it consistent with other container classes, you dimension the `TextArea` object in columns (cols) and rows. There is no direct Web control equivalent to the `HtmlTextArea` control. Table 7-7 shows the properties of the `HtmlTextArea` class.

TABLE 7-7 THE TEXTAREA CONTROL IN ASP.NET

Property	Description
Cols	Gets or sets the width of the text area, in characters. The property is name cols (columns) to maintain consistency with other container controls.
Name	Gets or sets the name of the text area. Remember that ID can be set, as well, as it is inherited from Control.
Rows	The height of the text area, in lines. You state it in rows to maintain consistency with other container controls.
Value	Gets or sets the text inside of a text area.

INPUT CONTROLS (HTMLINPUTCONTROL)

The input controls are those that you use as form elements in HTML. They are the controls with which the user interacts. These controls derive from the HtmlInputControl class, which derives from the Control class. The important properties are name, type, and value, as shown in Table 7-8.

TABLE 7-8 HTMLINPUTCONTROL CLASS

Property	HTML Usage	Programmatic Usage
type	`<input type="button" id="btnSubmit">`	`btnSubmit.type="submit"`
value	`<input type="text" value="My Text" id="txtLastName">`	`txtLastName="Smith"`
name	`<input type="checkbox" id=" chkFootball" name="chkFootball" checked`	`chkFootball.name = "chkFB"`

The name property is very important, because you often use it to program with client-side JavaScript if you're not using Dynamic HTML (DHTMl). In most examples, I set the name and the ID properties to the same value, which makes programming elements on the page easier. This is not a requirement, however, so you can set them to different names, if you want, although I discourage this practice because it leads to confusion.

BUTTON (HTMLINPUTBUTTON) The `HtmlInputButton` control class is used to create buttons, submit buttons, and reset buttons. The Web control equivalent is the `Button` class. Listing 7-7 shows the HTML code for the different types of `HtmlInputButton` controls, along with a brief code sample that uses an event to submit the form on the Check button.

Listing 7-7: Buttons in ASP.NET

```vb
<script language="vb" runat="server">
  Private Sub btnCheck_Click(Sender As Object, _
              e As EventArgs)
              Handles btnCheck.Click
    'Need button code here
  End Sub
</script>
...
<input type="submit" ID="btnSubmit" name="btnSubmit" runat="server">
<input type="reset" ID="btnReset" name="btnReset" runat="server">
<input type="button" ID="btnCheck" runat="server"
OnServerClick="btnCheck_Click" name="btnCheck">
```

CHECKBOX (HTMLINPUTCHECKBOX) The `HtmlInputCheckbox` control class is used to create short lists of nonexclusive choices, usually about three to four items; use a list box (a multiline text box) if you want to offer more choices. The Web equivalent is the `Checkbox` class, but a better version for data binding in Web controls is the `CheckboxList` class, which automatically creates multiple check boxes for you. The HTML code for an `HtmlInputCheckbox` control class is shown in Listing 7-8, along with code to determine whether the resulting check box is checked.

Listing 7-8: Checkbox in ASP.NET

```vb
<script language="vb" runat="server">
  Private Sub btnCheck_Click(Sender As Object, _
              e As EventArgs)
    If (chkSocialCommitee.Checked = True) Then
      'Run social committee only code
    Else
      'Run all non social committee code
    End If
  End Sub
</script>
...
<input type="checkbox" id="chkSocialCommitee" runat="server">
```

The only property of the `HtmlInputCheckbox` control class that isn't part of one of the parent objects it derives from is the `checked` property. You use this property to determine whether the user has selected, or checked, this box on the form.

FILE (HTMLINPUTFILE)   The `HtmlInputFile` control class is used to create a text box that stores a filename. You use this control for uploading files to a server. There's no direct equivalent in Web controls. Listing 7-9 shows the use of an input file control.

Listing 7-9: An HtmlInputFile Control in ASP.NET

```
<script language="vb" runat="server">
  Private Sub Page_Load(Sender As Object, _
                 e As EventArgs)
    If (Page.IsPostBack = True) Then
      If Not IsNull(txtFile.PostedFile) then
         txtFile.PostedFile.SaveAs(strPath & _
txtFileName.Text)
      End If
    End If
  End Sub
</script>
...
<input type="text" ID="txtFileName" runat="server">
<input type="file" ID="txtFile" runat="server">
```

HIDDEN (HTMLINPUTHIDDEN)   The `HtmlInputHidden` control class is used to create a hidden input, seen in HTML as `<input type="hidden">`. All its members derive from parent classes, so there are no unique properties. The main use for this control in ASP.NET is to dynamically add hidden values to a field at runtime. Since you can create a control and hide it, yet still maintain state from page view to page view (or form submission), this particular control is a bit less useful than it is in traditional ASP. As with the hidden field in HTML, the text can be viewed by anyone who chooses to view source in his browser, and that is something to consider when you're deciding between hiding a control that runs on the server and using the `HtmlInputHidden` control.

IMAGE (HTMLINPUTIMAGE)   The `HtmlInputImage` control class creates an `<input type="image">` HTML element. This is a more useful control than an `HtmlInputButton` control is for making custom buttons, because more browsers support this image tag (`<input type="image">`) than support the button tag `<input type="button">`. The downside here is you have to create graphics for your buttons. There is no direct equivalent available in Web controls, although you can use an `Image` control with events to mimic the behavior of this HTML control by creating an `Image` control with a click event and using it to submit your form in the same manner as the `HtmlInputImage` control.

RADIO BUTTON (HTMLINPUTRADIOBUTTON)   The `HtmlInputRadioButton` control class is used to create short lists of exclusive choices (in contrast to check boxes, which allow multiple selections). You usually limit a list of radio buttons to about three to four items; use a drop-down list if you want a user to choose from among more items. The Web control equivalent is the RadioButton class, but a better version for data binding in Web controls is the RadioButtonList class, which automatically creates all of the radio buttons by binding to a data source. The HTML code for an HtmlInputRadioButton control class is shown in Listing 7-10, along with code to determine which radio button someone chooses. Notice that you need to keep the same name for your entire group of radio buttons (another advantage to using a RadioButtonList Web control).

Listing 7-10: Radio Buttons in ASP.NET

```vb
<script language="vb" runat="server">
  Private Sub Page_Load(Sender As Object, _
               e As EventArgs)
    If (Page.IsPostBack = True) Then
      If full.Checked = True Then
        'Run full member code
      ElseIf associate.Checked = True Then
        'Run associate member code
      Else
        'Run non-member code
      End If
    End If
  End Sub
</script>
<input type="radio" name="radMember" ID="full" runat="server" />
Full member<br />
<input type="radio" name="radMember" ID="associate" runat="server" />
Associate member<br />
<input type="radio" name="radMember" ID="non-member" runat="server" />
Non member<br />
```

TEXT (HTMLINPUTTEXT)   The HtmlInputText control class is used to create text and password fields. To code with Web controls, use the TextBox class as an equivalent. Table 7-9 shows the properties of the HtmlInputText class.

TABLE 7-9 PROPERTIES OF THE HTMLINPUTTEXT CLASS

Property	Description
MaxLength	Gets or sets the maximum number of characters that someone can type into a text box.
Size	Gets or sets the physical size (width) of a text box.
Value	Gets or sets the text inside a text box.

Listing 7-11 shows a practical way to use the `HtmlInputText` control.

Listing 7-11: Text Fields in ASP.NET

```vb
<script language="vb" runat="server">
  Private Sub Page_Load(Sender As Object, _
              e As EventArgs)
    If (Page.IsPostBack = True) Then
      If (strLogon.Value="User") And
         (strPassword.Value="Password") Then
        'Authenticate the User
      End If
    End If
  End Sub
</script>
...
<input type="text" id="strLogon" runat="server">
<input type="password" id="strPassword" runat="server">
```

Summary

In this chapter, you learned about building a Windows Form and how similar the Windows Form code and WebForm code are. To illustrate, you moved some code from the WebForm sample application from Chapter 6 into the Windows Form version of the same form in this chapter. The main objective is to realize how few lines need to be changed if you switch to a new user interface.

You also learned about HTML controls, which are the closest equivalent in ASP.NET to regular HTML elements. To code each of the HTML controls in ASP.NET, you write them as plain HTML. The major difference between HTML controls and traditional HTML elements is the capability to maintain state after form submission through the use of the `runat="server"` property of each HTML control.

In the next chapter, you expand on this knowledge by learning how to use ASP.NET Web controls. These powerful controls help you build dynamic forms with ease.

Chapter 8

Adding Interactivity with ASP.NET Web Controls

IN THIS CHAPTER

◆ The `Control` and `WebControl` classes

◆ The AdRotator and Calendar controls

◆ Other Web controls in ASP.NET and how they map to HTML

YOU CAN BUILD TRADITIONAL FORMS in ASP.NET by using normal HTML syntax, but the real strength of ASP.NET is that it enables you to build forms with completely dynamic controls. This chapter focuses on the dynamic controls known as Web controls.

Working with Web Controls

ASP has long been considered a kludge in the world of Web development. Although you can develop complete applications, the scripting paradigm leaves many developers cold, especially those working with CGI or Java. Considering the notable shortcomings of ASP (such as every variable being a variant, the ability to implicitly cast almost anything, and the lack of any formal error-handling structure), you probably won't be surprised to hear that as their skill level increases, many serious Web developers migrate most of their code to MTS/COM+ components.

ASP.NET changes this paradigm. With ASP.NET, Web developers can program with a variety of full-fledged object-oriented languages. Unfortunately, as a result, programming in ASP.NET is more complicated. The first trip out is often extremely frustrating, as you fight a whole series of errors made in ignorance. To combat the sharp learning curve, Microsoft has added a whole new series of Web controls to your arsenal. Although the syntax is more difficult to grasp, the new controls greatly simplify dynamic Web programming.

Although Web controls are also called server controls in Microsoft lingo, I don't use that terminology because HTML controls can be set up to run on the server as well.

The Control class

The Control class is the object from which all HTML control and Web control objects are derived. Chapter 7 covers this concept, as the root of HTML controls. I cover the important aspects of the Control class, as it applies to Web controls, in Table 8-1. You can use each of these properties with the Web controls you use in your application.

TABLE 8-1 THE CONTROL CLASS

Property, Method, or Event	Description
Controls	Property that returns a ControlsCollection object that represents all of the child controls for this particular control.
EnableViewState	Property to get or set whether a control and its child controls should maintain state when the current page request is finished.
ID	Property to get or set the programmatic ID for the control. This is the same ID that is used with DHTML, if you choose to use DHTML on the client side.
Page	Read-only property to get the Page object that contains the current control.
Parent	Read-only property to get the parent control in the UI hierarchy. For a TableRow, for example, a Table object would be returned.
Site	Read-only property to get the site information for a control.
Visible	Gets or sets a property that tells whether the control should be rendered on the client side. A creative use of this property would be to set hidden properties that are not accessible on the client side.
DataBind	Method to cause the control, and its children, to bind to a data source.
HasControls	Method to determine whether the current control has children controls. This method of determining whether an object has children is more efficient than accessing the count property of the ControlsCollection object.
RenderControl	Method to output the content of the control to an HtmlTextWriter output stream.
ResolveUrl	Method to return an absolute URL for the page when a relative URL for the control is supplied.
DataBinding	Event that occurs when a control is bound to data.

Property, Method, or Event	Description
Init	Event fired when a control is initialized. This event allows you to dynamically alter a control at runtime.
Load	Event fired when a control is added to the hierarchy under a page object.
PreRender	The last event fired when a control is instantiated. Using this event is your last chance to alter the behavior of a control before rendering it for the user.
Unload	This event occurs when a control is unloaded from memory. It offers a chance to write clean-up code.

You can apply all the properties, methods, and events described in Table 8-1 to HTML controls, although you probably won't use them very often, which is the reason I present them in this chapter. Listing 8-1 shows a couple properties (bolded in the code so you can see them better) used with the AdRotator control, which is the first extended control I cover in this chapter.

Listing 8-1: Using Properties of the Control Class

```
<script language="vb" runat="server">
  Sub arMyAds_Load(source as object, e as EventArgs)
    If Page.IsPostBack then
      ArMyAds.visible = "False"
    End If
  End Sub
</script>
...
<asp:AdRotator id="arMyAds" runat="server">
</asp:AdRotator>
```

The WebControl class

Web controls also derive from the WebControl class, which offers us a more robust programming model than that of the HTML controls. Table 8-2 shows the most important properties of the WebControl Class.

Most of the properties in the WebControls class are fairly straightforward for anyone who has ever worked with HTML.

Listing 8-2 shows how to add an image programmatically to a page. I add a panel control to place the image. (I could have added directly to the page's control collection, as well, but the image would appear outside of the <HTML> tags if I did not build the entire page dynamically.)

TABLE 8-2 THE WEBCONTROL CLASS

Property, Method or Event	Description
AccessKey	Property to get or set the keyboard shortcut key to access a control.
Attributes	Property to get the non-rendering attributes of a control. Examples of this type of attribute are OnClick, OnFocus, and OnBlur.
BackColor	Property to get or set the background color of the control.
BorderColor	Property to get or set the border color of a control.
BorderWidth	Property to get or set the border width of a control.
CssClass	Property to get or set the class used by Cascading Style Sheets (CSS) with the control.
Enabled	Property to get or set whether the control is currently enabled.
Font	Read-only property to get font information for a control.
ForeColor	Property to get or set the foreground color of the control. This property generally applies to text in the control.
Height	Property to get or set the height of a control.
Style	Property to get or set the style for a control.
TabIndex	Property to get or set the tab index for a control. This is useful on forms to ensure that the controls are accessed in the correct order.
ToolTip	Property to get or set the text displayed during a mouseover.
Width	Property to get or set the width of the control.
CopyBaseAttributes	Method used to copy the base properties from one control to another. The base properties are AccessKey, Enabled, ToolTip, TabIndex, and Attributes.
GetAttribute	Method to get the value of a single attribute from the attributes collection.
SetAttribute	Method used to set a single attribute from the attributes collection. This would be the place, for example, to set an OnClick, OnFocus, or OnBlur client-side event.

Listing 8-2: Programmatically Working with the WebControl Properties in an Image Control

```
If Page.IsPostBack Then
    Dim Image1 As New WebControl.Image()
    Dim unitBorderWidth = New WebControl.Unit(1)
    Dim unitHeight = New WebControl.Unit(48)
    Dim unitWidth = New WebControl.Unit(80)

    With Image1
      .BorderWidth = unitBorderWidth
      .Height = unitHeight
      .Width = unitWidth
      .ResolveUrl("images/logo.gif")
    End With

    Panel1.Controls.Add(Image1)
End If
```

The code for Listing 8-2 can be downloaded from the companion Web site (www.wiley.com/extras) in the file Ch08VS.zip (Visual Studio .NET) or Ch08SDK.zip (SDK version). The file is named AddControl.aspx.

The AdRotator control

If your background includes ASP programming, you have run into an AdRotator control before. This control is used to randomly pick an "ad," which is represented by a Web graphic. With each hit on the page, the ad file is consulted, and a graphic is displayed.

THE TRADITIONAL ASP ADROTATOR

In ASP 2.0 and 3.0, the AdRotator control was in its infancy. Other than to add weight to a particular ad (as a percentage of the time the ad should be displayed), you could not do a whole lot with the control. Listing 8-3 shows the code necessary to use an AdRotator in traditional ASP.

Listing 8-3: Coding the AdRotator in ASP 2/3

```
<%Set ad = Server.CreateObject("MSWC.AdRotator")%>
<%= ad.GetAdvertisement("RandomAd.txt") %>
```

Listing 8-4 shows the file that holds the ads that will be used. The first section details the size and border of the image, as well as the page for redirection, while the last section contains individual ads.

Listing 8-4: Ad File in ASP 2/3

```
REDIRECT AdRedir.asp
WIDTH 468
HEIGHT 60
BORDER 1
*
../images/rollover.gif
http://www.microsoft.com/frontpage
Free Beta Copy of Microsoft FrontPage 98
2
```

Listing 8-5 shows the code contained in the ad redirector file. From Listing 8-4, you know that the name of this page is AdRedir.asp.

Listing 8-5: The Ad Redirector File

```
<% Response.Redirect(Request.QueryString("url")) %>
```

Unfortunately, AdRotator hasn't developed too much in ASP.NET. Few differences exist between the ASP and the ASP.NET versions of this control. The main differences are

- ◆ The ad file is an XML file.

- ◆ The weight for the ads comes in impressions rather than percentages.

- ◆ You can use multiple rotators out of one file by using keywords to filter the ads.

- ◆ You do not have to code a redirector file.

ASP.NET ADROTATOR

Listing 8-6 shows the method of using the AdRotator control in ASP.NET. The control here is set to the proper width for standard banner ads.

Listing 8-6: Using the AdRotator in ASP.NET

```
<asp:AdRotator id="arMyRotator" runat="server"
    AdvertisementFile="MyAds.xml"
    KeywordFilter="books"
    Borderwidth="0"
    Height="468"
    Width="60"
    Target="_blank" />
```

Notice the KeywordFilter; it'll be important as we go forward. It's linked to the Keyword tag in the XML file, which is shown in Listing 8-7.

Listing 8-7: The XML Ad File

```
<Advertisements>
    <Ad>
        <ImageUrl>images/hungryminds.gif</ImageUrl>
        <NavigateUrl>http://www.hungryminds.com</NavigateUrl>
        <AlternateText>Hungry Minds</AlternateText>
        <Keyword>books</Keyword>
        <Impressions>100</Impressions>
    </Ad>
    <Ad>
        <ImageUrl>images/Amazon.gif</ImageUrl>
        <NavigateUrl>http://www.wiley.com</NavigateUrl>
        <AlternateText>Wiley</AlternateText>
        <Keyword>books</Keyword>
        <Impressions>50</Impressions>
    </Ad>
    <Ad>
        <ImageUrl>images/microsoft.gif</ImageUrl>
        <NavigateUrl>http://www.microsoft.com</NavigateUrl>
        <AlternateText>Microsoft</AlternateText>
        <Keyword>software</Keyword>
        <Impressions>100</Impressions>
    </Ad>
</Advertisements>
```

Table 8-3 lists the unique properties and methods of the `AdRotator` class. Although this probably goes without saying, you can also use the properties and methods of the classes from which this class is derived, namely the `Control` and `WebControl` classes.

TABLE 8-3 THE ADROTATOR CLASS PROPERTIES AND METHODS

Property or Event	Description
AdvertisementFile	Property to get or set the XML file that contains the ads for the control. Note that you can have multiple rotators on a single ad file if you use keyword filters.
KeywordFilter	Property to get or set the keyword filter. This is used when you want to get ads of a certain type (as with personalization) or you want to have multiple pages reading from a single file.

Continued

TABLE 8-3 THE ADROTATOR CLASS PROPERTIES AND METHODS *(Continued)*

Property or Event	Description
Target	Property to get or set the target frame or browser window to direct the content URL to.
AdCreated	Event that fires after an ad is created, but before it is rendered. You can use this event to track views on ads.

The lack of an ad redirection file and the XML nature of the ad file are nice, but the control itself has not changed very much. Unfortunately, the programmability, at least as it applies to real-world applications, has not advanced that much either. The AdCreated event, which I use in a moment, is fine if you want to track the number of views on an ad. No event exists, however, to handle the click. This means you still have to use the old-fashioned redirect on the querystring if you want to track clickthroughs.

AN ADROTATOR APPLICATION

In this section, I show you a simple application that tracks both views and click-throughs. For this application, you will have an ad that points back to the same page and redirects after registering the clickthrough. Listing 8-8 shows the AdRotator, the event that tracks the view, and the event that tracks the click.

Listing 8-8: Ad Tracking Application

```
'CodeBehind file
Private Enum enmLogType
    ltAdCreated = 1
    ltAdClicked = 2
End Enum

Private Sub Page_Load(ByVal sender As System.Object, ByVal ⏎
e As System.EventArgs) Handles MyBase.Load

    Dim intRedir As Integer = CInt(Request("redir"))

    If intRedir = 1 Then
        Dim strURL As String = Request("url")
        LogURL(strURL, enmLogType.ltAdClicked)
        Response.Redirect(strURL)
    End If
```

```
End Sub

Private Sub arMyRotator_AdCreated(ByVal sender As System.Object, _
  ByVal e As System.Web.UI.WebControls.AdCreatedEventArgs) _
  Handles arMyRotator.AdCreated

    Dim strURL As String = e.NavigateUrl

    'Log ad creation
    LogURL(strURL, enmLogType.ltAdCreated)

    Dim strURLHead As String = ↵
"http://localhost/Chapter08/AdRotator.aspx?redir=1&url="

    'Add to URL to navigate to
    e.NavigateUrl = strURLHead & strURL

End Sub

Private Sub LogURL(ByVal strURL As String, _
  ByVal lngAdClick As enmLogType)
    'TODO: Add logging mechanism here to track ads
End Sub

...

<!-- ASP.NET file -->
<asp:AdRotator id="arMyRotator"
runat="server"
Width="468px" Height="60px"
AdvertisementFile="myAds.xml"
KeywordFilter="books"
Target="_blank" />
```

 You can download the code for Listing 8-8 from this book's companion Web site (www.wiley.com/extras) in the file Ch08VS.zip (Visual Studio .NET) or Ch08SDK.zip (SDK version). The file to look at is AdRotator. aspx, and its CodeBehind file, AdRotator.aspx.vb.

In order to track these ads, I pull the NavigateUrl and add a redirect page. In this instance, to make things simple, I redirect to the same page, although I could use any page.

If you aren't comfortable altering the `NavigateUrl`, you can hardcode the redirect URL into the XML ad file. I show this methodology in Listing 8-9.

Listing 8-9: Ad Tracking XML Ad File

```
<Advertisements>
    <Ad>
        <ImageUrl>images/hungryminds.gif</ImageUrl>
        <NavigateUrl>
            AdRotator2.aspx?url=http://www.hungryminds.com
        </NavigateUrl>
        <AlternateText>Hungry Minds</AlternateText>
        <Keyword>books</Keyword>
        <Impressions>100</Impressions>
    </Ad>
    <Ad>
        <ImageUrl>images/hungryminds.gif</ImageUrl>
        <NavigateUrl>
            AdRotator2.aspx?url=http://www.wiley.com
        </NavigateUrl>
        <AlternateText>Wiley</AlternateText>
        <Keyword>books</Keyword>
        <Impressions>100</Impressions>
    </Ad>
    <Ad>
        <ImageUrl>images/microsoft.gif</ImageUrl>
        <NavigateUrl>
            AdRotator2.aspx?url=http://www.microsoft.com
        </NavigateUrl>
        <AlternateText>Microsoft</AlternateText>
        <Keyword>software</Keyword>
        <Impressions>100</Impressions>
    </Ad>
</Advertisements>
```

The advantage of this system is that the XML file is easier to edit than the CodeBehind file because it can be altered by a salesperson rather than a programmer. You can also code a simple ad file tool to alter the XML, which makes it more flexible.

The Calendar control

Microsoft shipped a Calendar control with FoxPro and Visual J++, so it's had a calendar control available for quite some time. Yet in traditional ASP, you had to embed an ActiveX control or Java Applet to get that kind of functionality. ASP.NET, however, does ship with a Calendar control. The ASP.NET Calendar control is largely derived from the Web Foundation Classes used in Visual J++. If you have ever worked with WFC, you should have a slight idea of the capabilities of this control. Figure 8-1 shows the Calendar control in its default configuration.

Figure 8-1: The Calendar control.

Most of the properties of the Calendar control are format properties and affect the manner in which the control is displayed in the browser. Rather than list each of the properties, I've grouped them according to their functions:

◆ CellPadding sets the space between cell borders and the content of a cell, CellSpacing sets the space between cells, and ShowGridlines determines whether the border shows. These properties are much like their counterparts in an HTML table, which is how the Calendar control is displayed for the client.

◆ SelectionMode determines how a user can make a selection. The options are Day (user can select days only), DayWeek (select either day or week), or DayWeekMonth (can also select entire months).

◆ DayHeaderStyle, DayStyle, OtherMonthDayStyle, SelectedDayStyle, TitleStyle, and TodayDayStyle are read-only properties to pull styles set in the control.

◆ The SelectedDate and SelectedDates properties are used to get the date or dates selected. You can also set the SelectedDate property to have the control default to a date other than the current date.

Other Web Controls

The remaining Web controls are designed to simplify common tasks, such as building forms and tables and data access. Unlike the AdRotator or the Calendar control, they do not add additional cool functionality, but they greatly simplify the creation of Web pages. The general method of showing how to use these controls is to show sample code and then show the HTML code produced by the control. At this time, I only data bind the data controls. I cover data binding of other controls in Part III, "Working with Data — ADO.NET," of this book.

Controls to build forms

You can use the first set of controls to create forms. These controls are the most like the HTML controls covered in Chapter 7. As I go through the use of these controls, I focus on how to extend the functionality of the HTML controls by using the Web control equivalent.

For each of the controls in this section, I show how to use the control, and I show the HTML output that is generated for the control when it is finally rendered. So that you can easily see the various elements, the control itself is highlighted as **bold**, additional HTML produced is in *italic,* and the portion produced by programmatically working with the control is highlighted with a background highlight.

In this section and the section that covers tables and other container controls, I place the code inside the ASP.NET page in order to show the similarity between ASP and ASP.NET. Every snippet of code is designed to sit in the CodeBehind file, although you can easily place the code in a <SCRIPT> block instead.

BUTTON

You use the Button control to create buttons on your page. This includes HTML <input> tags of the type button, submit, and reset. In traditional HTML, buttons are the only way to submit a form without using client-side scripting. This is still true, but you can use many other Web controls to submit a form because the Web control creates the client-side script for you.

Table 8-4 presents the Button control, how to program against it, and the HTML that results from using this control.

TABLE 8-4 THE BUTTON CONTROL

Setting Up the Control

```
<form runat="server" ID="Form1">
    <asp:Button id="Button1" Text="Click Me" runat="server" />
    <p><asp:label id="Label1" runat="server" /></p>
</form>
```

Working with the Control Programmatically

```
Private Sub Button1_Click(ByVal sender As System.Object, _
  ByVal e As System.EventArgs) Handles Button1.Click
    Label1.Text = "You just clicked the button and changed it."
    Button1.Text = "Don't Click Me!"
    Button1.BackColor = System.Drawing.Color.Beige
End Sub
```

Resulting HTML

```
<form name="Form1" method="post" action="Button.aspx" id="Form1">
  <input type="hidden" name="__VIEWSTATE"
   value="dDwxMDA3MzE2Mz...I03HPds=" />
  <input type="submit" name="Button1"
   value="Don't Click Me!" id="Button1"
   style="background-color:Beige;" />
  <p><span id="Label1">
    You just clicked the button and changed it.
  </span></p>
</form>
```

CHECKBOX

The CheckBox control creates an input where type is "checkbox". You use this control to create non-exclusive lists. A check box works best with short lists; you'd use a list box if the list of choices were larger. It is preferable to use a check box for limited size lists. In Table 8-5, the check box used has the AutoPostBack attribute, which corresponds to the AutoPostBack property of the control, set to true, which causes this control to submit the form.

Table 8-5 shows how to use a CheckBox control both in the ASP.NET page and in code.

TABLE 8-5 THE CHECKBOX CONTROL

Setting Up the Control

```
<form id="Form1" method="post" runat="server">
    <p><asp:CheckBox id="CheckBox1" runat="server"
```

Continued

TABLE 8-5 THE CHECKBOX CONTROL *(Continued)*

Working with the Control Programmatically

```
    TEXT="Test checkbox" AutoPostBack="True" /></p>
    <p><asp:label id="Label1" runat="server" /></p>
</form>

Private Sub CheckBox1_CheckedChanged(ByVal sender As System.Object,
_
  ByVal e As System.EventArgs) Handles CheckBox1.CheckedChanged
    CheckBox1.BorderStyle = BorderStyle.Dashed
    CheckBox1.BorderWidth = New System.Web.UI.WebControls.Unit(2)
    Label1.Text = "You click the checkbox and the state is: " & _
      CheckBox1.Checked
End Sub
```

Resulting HTML

```
<form name="Form1" method="post" action="Checkbox.aspx" id="Form1">
<input type="hidden" name="__EVENTTARGET" value="" />
<input type="hidden" name="__EVENTARGUMENT" value="" />
<input type="hidden" name="__VIEWSTATE" value="dDwxM...wC7UK" />

<script language="javascript">
<!--
    function __doPostBack(eventTarget, eventArgument) {
        var theform = document.Form1;
        theform.__EVENTTARGET.value = eventTarget;
        theform.__EVENTARGUMENT.value = eventArgument;
        theform.submit();
    }
// -->
</script>
  <p><span style="border-width:2px;border-style:Dashed;">
    <input id="CheckBox1" type="checkbox" name="CheckBox1"
     checked="checked" onclick="__doPostBack('CheckBox1','')"
     language="javascript" />
    <label for="CheckBox1">Test checkbox</label></span></p>
  <p><span id="Label1">You click the checkbox and
    the state is: True</span></p>
</form>
```

Take a look at all the JavaScript code in the resulting HTML in Table 8-5. The Web control produces this code to aid in submitting the form back to the server. ASP.NET saves the developer a bunch of time in this area. Note that JavaScript is produced every time the `AutoPostBack` property is set to `True`.

CHECKBOXLIST

The CheckBoxList control creates a group of check boxes based on a list. This list can be hand-coded, as in the example, or can come from databinding to an array or a data source. Part III of this book covers the databinding capabilities of ADO.NET.

Table 8-6 shows a CheckBoxList control. Once again the `AutoPostBack` attribute is set to `True`, which causes this form to submit when any of the check boxes in the CheckBoxList control is checked or unchecked. Note that the event to handle the postback is `SelectedIndexChanged`. The user of this page gets the answer right only if all three correct items are selected.

TABLE 8-6 THE CHECKBOXLIST CONTROL

Setting Up the Control

```
<form id="Form1" method="post" runat="server">
  <P>What are the colors of the American flag (choose all that
apply)?</P>
  <P><asp:CheckBoxList id="CheckBoxList1" runat="server"
      AutoPostBack="True" RepeatDirection="Vertical"
      RepeatLayout="Flow" TextAlign="Right">
      <asp:ListItem Value="1">Red</asp:ListItem>
      <asp:ListItem Value="2">White</asp:ListItem>
      <asp:ListItem Value="3">Blue</asp:ListItem>
      <asp:ListItem Value="4">Green</asp:ListItem>
  </asp:CheckBoxList></P>
  <P><asp:Label id="Label1" runat="server" /></P>
</form>
```

Working with the Control Programmatically

```
Private Sub CheckBoxList1_SelectedIndexChanged(ByVal _
  sender As System.Object, ByVal e As System.EventArgs) _
  Handles CheckBoxList1.SelectedIndexChanged
    If CheckBoxList1.Items(0).Selected = True _
      And CheckBoxList1.Items(2).Selected = True _
```

Continued

TABLE 8-6 THE CHECKBOXLIST CONTROL *(Continued)*

```
        And CheckBoxList1.Items(2).Selected = True Then
          Label1.Text = "Correct! The colors of the " & _
            "American flags are red, white and blue!"
      End If
End Sub
```

Resulting HTML

```
<form name="Form1" method="post" action="Checkboxlist.aspx"
id="Form1">
<input type="hidden" name="__EVENTTARGET" value="" />
<input type="hidden" name="__EVENTARGUMENT" value="" />
<input type="hidden" name="__VIEWSTATE" value="dDw4...ET9Mw==" />

<script language="javascript">
<!--
function __doPostBack(eventTarget, eventArgument) {
  var theform = document.Form1;
  theform.__EVENTTARGET.value = eventTarget;
  theform.__EVENTARGUMENT.value = eventArgument;
  theform.submit();
}
// -->
</script>

<P>What are the colors of the American flag (choose all that
apply)?</P>
<P>
  <span id="CheckBoxList1">
  <input id="CheckBoxList1_0" type="checkbox"
    name="CheckBoxList1:0" checked="checked"
    onclick="__doPostBack('CheckBoxList1:0','')"
    language="javascript" />
  <label for="CheckBoxList1_0">Red</label><br>
  <input id="CheckBoxList1_1" type="checkbox"
    name="CheckBoxList1:1" checked="checked"
    onclick="__doPostBack('CheckBoxList1:1','')"
    language="javascript" />
  <label for="CheckBoxList1_1">White</label><br>
```

```
    <input id="CheckBoxList1_2" type="checkbox"
      name="CheckBoxList1:2" checked="checked"
      onclick="__doPostBack('CheckBoxList1:2','')"
      language="javascript" />
    <label for="CheckBoxList1_2">Blue</label><br>
    <input id="CheckBoxList1_3" type="checkbox"
      name="CheckBoxList1:3"
      onclick="__doPostBack('CheckBoxList1:3','')"
      language="javascript" />
    <label for="CheckBoxList1_3">Green</label>
    </span>
</P>
<P><span id="Label1">
  Correct! The colors of the American flag are
  red, white and blue!
</span></P>
</form>
```

This is not the best example, as the form submits every time a check box is checked. As the CheckBoxList control is a bit more complex, a couple of notes are in order. Table 8-7 shows some of the parameters you can add to your control and explains how they change your CheckBoxList.

TABLE 8-7 PARAMETERS OF THE CHECKBOXLIST CONTROL

Parameter	Description
RepeatColumns	Adding this parameter lays out the check boxes in rows. When RepeatLayout is set to flow, the check boxes don't line up. You need to set it to table to have everything align.
RepeatLayout	If you set this parameter to flow, the check boxes flow one after another. When you set it to table, the check boxes are placed in a table. You also need to apply the CellPadding, CellSpacing, BorderStyle, BorderWidth, and BorderStyle.

Continued

TABLE 8-7 PARAMETERS OF THE CHECKBOXLIST CONTROL *(Continued)*

Parameter	Description
Font parameters	A variety of parameters are available for fonts: ForeColor (sets the font color), Font-Bold, Font-Italic, Font-Name, Font-Overline, Font-Underline, Font-Size, and Font-Strikeout. To set the properties in script, use the following syntax. The font parameters are inherited from the Web control class.

```
<script language="vb" runat="server">
  Sub Page_Load(sender as Object, e as EventArgs)
    Checkboxlist1.font.underline = True
  End Sub
</script>
```

DROPDOWNLIST

The DropDownList control creates a <SELECT> HTML tag with each of its items presented as an <OPTION>. The drop-down list, like the check box list, can be hard-coded or data-bound. You use the drop-down list to create a list where the user can select only one item. If you want a drop-down list in which the user can select multiple items, use a list box instead.

The DropDownList sample, shown in Table 8-8, is a bit more real world than some of the samples so far. Using a drop-down list to forward a user to another page is a common task on a Web site. Because this is another list control, the event is the SelectedIndexChanged. Note that AutoPostBack is set to true to ensure that the form is submitted as soon as the selected item is changed.

TABLE 8-8 THE DROPDOWNLIST CONTROL

Setting Up the Control

```
<form id="Form1" method="post" runat="server">
  <asp:DropDownList id="DropDownList1"
    runat="server" AutoPostBack="True">
    <asp:ListItem Value="http://localhost/Chapter08/DropDownList.aspx">
      Choose one</asp:ListItem>
    <asp:ListItem Value="http://www.microsoft.com">
      Microsoft</asp:ListItem>
    <asp:ListItem Value="http://www.cnn.com">
      CNN</asp:ListItem>
```

```
    <asp:ListItem Value="http://www.foxnews.com">
        Fox News</asp:ListItem>
 </asp:DropDownList></form>
```

Working with the Control Programmatically

```
Private Sub DropDownList1_SelectedIndexChanged(ByVal _
  sender As System.Object, ByVal e As System.EventArgs) _
  Handles DropDownList1.SelectedIndexChanged
    Dim strURL As String = DropDownList1.SelectedItem.Value
    Response.Redirect(strURL)
End Sub
```

Resulting HTML

```
<form name="Form1" method="post" action="DropDownList.aspx"
id="Form1">
<input type="hidden" name="__EVENTTARGET" value="" />
<input type="hidden" name="__EVENTARGUMENT" value="" />
<input type="hidden" name="__VIEWSTATE" value="dDw3M...zUkQ==" />

<script language="javascript">
<!--
  function __doPostBack(eventTarget, eventArgument) {
  var theform = document.Form1;
  theform.__EVENTTARGET.value = eventTarget;
  theform.__EVENTARGUMENT.value = eventArgument;
  theform.submit();
}
// -->
</script>
  <select name="DropDownList1"
```

Resulting HTML

```
id="DropDownList1" onchange="__doPostBack('DropDownList1','')"
  language="javascript">
<option value="http://localhost/Chapter08/DropDownList.aspx">
```

Continued

TABLE 8-8 THE DROPDOWNLIST CONTROL *(Continued)*

```
  Choose one</option>
<option value="http://www.microsoft.com">
  Microsoft</option>
<option value="http://www.cnn.com">
  CNN</option>
<option value="http://www.foxnews.com">
  Fox News</option>
</select>
</form>
```

IMAGE

You use the Image control to display an image on the page. This control offers very little advantage over its HTML counterpart, because the HTML control is programmable enough to accomplish all the items necessary for most developers.

Table 8-9 shows how to use the Image control. You can set different properties at runtime, but most of your work with the Image control will be design time, as shown in Table 8-9.

TABLE 8-9 THE IMAGE CONTROL

Setting Up the Control

```
<form id="Form1" method="post" runat="server">
  <asp:Image id="Image1" runat="server"
    AlternateText="MyImage" ImageAlign="Left"
    Height="69" Width="87" ImageUrl="images/myLogo.gif" />
</form>
```

Resulting HTML

```
<form name="Form1" method="post" action="Image.aspx" id="Form1">
  <input type="hidden" name="__VIEWSTATE" value="dDw5...4Ums=" />
  <img id="Image1" src="/Chapter08/images/myLogo.gif"
    alt="MyImage" align="Left" border="0"
    style="height:69px;width:87px;" />
</form>
```

IMAGEBUTTON

You use the ImageButton control to create an input of the type image: `<input type="image">`. You use the ImageButton control when you want to create custom graphics for your Submit and Reset buttons. The example in Table 8-10 uses the ImageButton control to create a banner ad (much like the AdRotator). I have included a TODO comment to make sure I go back and add code to log the click.

TABLE 8-10 THE IMAGEBUTTON CONTROL

Setting Up the Control

```
<form id="Form1" method="post" runat="server">
    <asp:ImageButton id="ImageButton1" runat="server"
      AlternateText="Logo" ImageAlign="Left"
      ImageUrl="images/Microsoft.gif" />
</form>
```

Working with the Control Programmatically

```
Private Sub ImageButton1_Click(ByVal sender As System.Object, _
  ByVal e As System.Web.UI.ImageClickEventArgs) _
  Handles ImageButton1.Click
    Response.Redirect("http://www.microsoft.com")
End Sub
```

Resulting HTML

```
<form name="Form1" method="post"
  action="ImageButton.aspx" id="Form1">
    <input type="hidden" name="__VIEWSTATE" value="dDw...Q==" />
    <input type="image" name="ImageButton1"
     id="ImageButton1" src="/Chapter08/images/Microsoft.gif"
     alt="Logo" align="Left" border="0" />
</form>
```

LABEL

The Label control is used to create a label for displaying text on a Web page. The term "label" is familiar to Visual Basic desktop application developers. Because

Microsoft has made creating ASP.NET applications in Visual Studio .NET as simple as Windows forms applications in Visual Studio 6, the name *label* fits.

For those of you more versed in Web development, the Label control is rendered as a <SPAN> and shows up as text when rendered in a browser. The label in the example in Table 8-11 takes its input from the TextBox control on the page when the user clicks the Submit button.

TABLE 8-11 THE LABEL CONTROL

Setting Up the Control

```
<form id="label" method="post" runat="server">
  <P><asp:TextBox id=TextBox1 runat="server"
  Text="Click to put this in the label" /></P>
  <P><asp:Label id=Label1 runat="server" /></P>
  <P><asp:Button id=Button1 runat="server"
  Text="Button" /></P>
</form>
```

Working with the Control Programmatically

```
Private Sub Button1_Click(ByVal sender As System.Object, _
  ByVal e As System.EventArgs) Handles Button1.Click
    Label1.Text = TextBox1.Text
End Sub
```

Resulting HTML

```
<form name="Form1" method="post" action="Label.aspx" id="Form1">
  <input type="hidden" name="__VIEWSTATE" value="dDw...XQ==" />
  <P><input name="TextBox1" type="text"
    value="Click to put this in the label"
    id="TextBox1" /></P>
  <P><span id="Label1">Click to put this in the label</span></P>
  <P><input type="submit" name="Button1"
    value="Button" id="Button1" /></P>
</form>
```

LINKBUTTON

You use the LinkButton control to create a hyperlink that acts as a button. This is useful when you need to make a link that submits a form. In Table 8-12 has a very simple LinkButton that submits the form back to the page. Most likely, you would not have a page this simple unless you were tracking clicks, so I added a TODO comment to go back and add code to track this click in my database.

TABLE 8-12 THE LINKBUTTON CONTROL

Setting Up the Control

```
<form id="Form1" method="post" runat="server">
  <asp:LinkButton id="LinkButton1" runat="server">
  Click to Visit a Random Site
  </asp:LinkButton>
</form>
```

Working with the Control Programmatically

```
Private Sub LinkButton1_Click(ByVal sender As System.Object, _
  ByVal e As System.EventArgs) _
  Handles LinkButton1.Click

  Randomize()
  Dim intRandom As Integer = CInt(Rnd() * 4) + 1
  Dim strURL As String

  Select Case intRandom
    Case 1
      strURL = "http://www.microsoft.com"
    Case 2
      strURL = "http://www.worldnetdaily.com"
    Case 3
      strURL = "http://www.cnn.com"
    Case 4
      strURL = "http://www.wiley.com"
    Case Else
      strURL = "http://www.hungryminds.com"
```

Continued

TABLE 8-12 THE LINKBUTTON CONTROL *(Continued)*

```
End Select

Response.Redirect(strURL)

End Sub
```

Resulting HTML

```
<form name="Form1" method="post" action="LinkButton.aspx"
id="Form1">
  <input type="hidden" name="__EVENTTARGET" value="" />
  <input type="hidden" name="__EVENTARGUMENT" value="" />
  <input type="hidden" name="__VIEWSTATE"
value="dDwyMDIyOTgwODAyOzs+64GJCsQKw3EzYhHxdsy1yCVSHIo=" />

<script language="javascript">
<!--
  function __doPostBack(eventTarget, eventArgument) {
    var theform = document.Form1;
    theform.__EVENTTARGET.value = eventTarget;
    theform.__EVENTARGUMENT.value = eventArgument;
    theform.submit();
  }
// -->
</script>

<a id="LinkButton1"
href="javascript:__doPostBack('LinkButton1','')">
Click to Visit a Random Site
</a>
</form>
```

LISTBOX

You use the ListBox control to create a single- or multiple-line list box, which you can render as either a drop-down list or a text box. In addition, you can program-matically set the control to allow a user to select one or multiple items. In Table 8-13, a ListBox control submits back to the server when the drop-down selected item is changed.

TABLE 8-13 **THE LISTBOX CONTROL**

Setting Up the Control

```
<form id="Form1" method="post" runat="server">
    <P>
    <asp:ListBox id="ListBox1" runat="server"
      SelectionMode="Single" AutoPostBack="True">
        <asp:ListItem>FOX News</asp:ListItem>
        <asp:ListItem>USA Today</asp:ListItem>
        <asp:ListItem>CNN</asp:ListItem>
        <asp:ListItem>World Net Daily</asp:ListItem>
    </asp:ListBox></P>
    <P><asp:Label id="Label1" runat="server" /></P>
</form>
```

Working with the Control Programmatically

```
Private Sub ListBox1_SelectedIndexChanged(ByVal _
  sender As System.Object, _
  ByVal e As System.EventArgs) _
  Handles ListBox1.SelectedIndexChanged
    Label1.Text = "You chose " & ListBox1.SelectedItem.Text
End Sub
```

Resulting HTML

```
<form name="Form1" method="post" action="ListBox.aspx" id="Form1">
    <input type="hidden" name="__EVENTTARGET" value="" />
    <input type="hidden" name="__EVENTARGUMENT" value="" />
    <input type="hidden" name="__VIEWSTATE" value="dF..U=" />

<script language="javascript">
<!--
  function __doPostBack(eventTarget, eventArgument) {
    var theform = document.Form1;
    theform.__EVENTTARGET.value = eventTarget;
    theform.__EVENTARGUMENT.value = eventArgument;
```

Continued

TABLE 8-13 THE LISTBOX CONTROL *(Continued)*

```
    theform.submit();
  }
// -->
</script>

  <P>
    <select name="ListBox1" id="ListBox1" size="4"
onchange="__doPostBack('ListBox1','')" language="javascript">
      <option selected="selected" value="FOX News">FOX News</option>
      <option value="USA Today">USA Today</option>
      <option value="CNN">CNN</option>
      <option value="World Net Daily">World Net Daily</option>
    </select>
  </P>
  <P><span id="Label1">You chose FOX News</span></P>
</form>
```

RADIOBUTTON

You use the RadioButton control to create a single radio button. You use this control with other radio buttons to create a list in which the user can select a single item. Radio buttons are useful for small lists of items. For larger lists of items, use a drop-down list instead. In Table 8-14, I use two RadioButton controls and then determine which one is selected. As you will discover in the next section, this is not the most efficient way to build this type of control.

TABLE 8-14 THE RADIOBUTTON CONTROL

Setting Up the Control

```
<form id=radiobutton method=post runat="server">
<P><asp:radiobutton id=RadioButton1 runat="server"
  Checked="True" Text="male" GroupName="gender" /></P>
<P><asp:radiobutton id=RadioButton2 runat="server"
  Text="female" GroupName="gender" /></P>
<P><asp:Label id=Label1 runat="server" /></P>
<P><asp:Button id=Button1 runat="server"
  Text="Submit" OnClick="Button_Click" /></P>
</form>
```

Working with the Control Programmatically

```
Private Sub Button1_Click(ByVal sender As System.Object, _
    ByVal e As System.EventArgs) Handles Button1.Click
  If radiobutton1.checked then
        label1.text = "male"
    Else
        label1.text = "female"
    End if
  End Sub
</SCRIPT>
```

Resulting HTML

```
<form name="Form1" method="post" action="RadioButton.aspx"
id="Form1">
    <input type="hidden" name="__VIEWSTATE" value="dDwt...sA==" />
    <P><input id="RadioButton1" type="radio" name="gender"
      value="RadioButton1" />
        <label for="RadioButton1">male</label></P>
    <P><input id="RadioButton2" type="radio" name="gender"
      value="RadioButton2" checked="checked" />
        <label for="RadioButton2">female</label></P>
    <P><span id="Label1">female</span></P>
    <P><input type="submit" name="Button1"
      value="Submit" id="Button1" /></P>
</form>
```

RADIOBUTTONLIST

The RadioButtonList control is identical to the RadioButton control, except that it can bind to a list of items. These items can be hard-coded or come from databinding to an array or a data source. The RadioButtonList control in this example creates the same page as the RadioButton control example. Using a RadioButtonList control is far easier than using individual radio buttons.

Table 8-15 shows the RadioButtonList control. In this example, I do not have the RadioButtonList set to AutoPostBack. You do have this capability, as you do with any list control; however, I don't think that it is extremely useful to submit the form when a radio button is clicked. If you want to create a page that submits the form when one of the radio buttons is clicked, add an OnSelectedIndexChanged attribute and the AutoPostBack="True" attribute, and then code a routine to handle the index changed click event.

TABLE 8-15 THE RADIOBUTTONLIST CONTROL

Setting Up the Control

```
<form id="radiobuttonllist" method="post" runat="server">
<asp:RadioButtonList id=RadioButtonList1 runat="server"
AutoPostBack="True">
<asp:listitem Selected=True Text="male" />
<asp:listitem Text="female" />
</asp:RadioButtonList>
</form>
```

Working with the Control Programmatically

```
Private Sub Button1_Click(ByVal sender As System.Object, _
  ByVal e As System.EventArgs) Handles Button1.Click
    Label1.text = RadioButtonList1.SelectedItem.Text
End Sub
```

Resulting HTML

```
<form name="Form1" method="post" action="RadioButtonList.aspx"
id="Form1">
  <input type="hidden" name="__VIEWSTATE" value="dDw...33Sw==" />
  <table id="RadioButtonList1" border="0">
    <tr>
      <td><input id="RadioButtonList1_0" type="radio"
          name="RadioButtonList1" value="male" />
          <label for="RadioButtonList1_0">male</label></td>
    </tr><tr>
      <td><input id="RadioButtonList1_1" type="radio"
          name="RadioButtonList1" value="female" checked="checked"
/>
          <label for="RadioButtonList1_1">female</label></td>
    </tr>
  </table>
  <P><span id="Label1">female</span></P>
  <P><input type="submit" name="Button1"
    value="Submit" id="Button1" /></P>
</form>
```

TEXTBOX

You use the TextBox control to create either a text box (one line) or text area (multiple line) box for text entry on a form. You can also use it to create a password input box. The example in Table 8-16 has a text box that the user must fill in with the word *yes* before he or she can move on. The idea here is a confirmation-of-rules page.

TABLE 8-16 THE TEXTBOX CONTROL

Setting Up the Control

```
<form id="Form1" method="post" runat="server">
  <P>
    <asp:Panel id="Panel1" runat="server">
    <asp:TextBox id="TextBox1" runat="server" />
    <BR>
    <asp:Button id="Button1" runat="server" Text="Button" />
    </asp:Panel>
  </P>
  <P>
    <asp:Label id="Label1" runat="server" />
  </P>
</form>
```

Working with the Control Programmatically

```
Private Sub Button1_Click(ByVal sender As System.Object, _
  ByVal e As System.EventArgs) Handles Button1.Click
    If TextBox1.Text = "yes" Then
        Panel1.Visible = False
        Label1.Text = "Congratulations."
    Else
        Label1.Text = "You must type in 'yes'."
    End If
End Sub
```

HTML Before Click

```
<form name="Form1" method="post" action="TextBox.aspx" id="Form1">
  <input type="hidden" name="__VIEWSTATE" value="dDwxOD...Q1E=" />
```

Continued

TABLE 8-16 THE TEXTBOX CONTROL *(Continued)*

```
<P><div id="Panel1">

  <input name="TextBox1" type="text" id="TextBox1" />
  <BR>
  <input type="submit" name="Button1" value="Button" id="Button1" />

</div></P>
<P><span id="Label1"></span></P>
</form>
```

HTML After Click

```
<form name="Form1" method="post"
  action="TextBox.aspx" id="Form1">
  <input type="hidden" name="__VIEWSTATE" value="dDwx...E04=" />
  <P><span id="Label1">Congratulations.</span></P>
</form>
```

Tables and other container controls

You use the second set of controls to create tables in your pages. As these controls do not make a great deal of sense by themselves, I am going to build complete tables. The controls I use are Table, TableRow, and TableCell.

BUILDING TABLES IN THE ASP.NET PAGE

You can build entire tables in ASP.NET using tags in HTML code. You start with an outer Table control, which has TableRows nested inside, which has TableCells. In other words, it is like really wordy HTML. Listing 8-10 shows a table built using tags in HTML code.

Listing 8-10: Writing a Table with ASP.NET

```
<asp:table id="Table1" runat="server"
    CellPadding="2" CellSpacing="2"
    GridLines="Both"
    HorizontalAlign="Center">
    <asp:tablerow BackColor=#000099 ForeColor=#ffffff>
       <asp:tablecell>Employee ID</asp:tablecell>
       <asp:tablecell>Name</asp:tablecell>
```

```
</asp:tablerow>
<asp:tablerow>
    <asp:tablecell>A635-24</asp:tablecell>
    <asp:tablecell>Gregory A. Beamer</asp:tablecell>
</asp:tablerow>
</asp:table>
```

 You can download the code in Listing 8-10 from the companion Web site (www.wiley.com/extras) in the file Ch08VS.zip (Visual Studio .NET) or Ch08SDK.zip (SDK version). The file to look at is Table.aspx.

BUILDING TABLES IN THE CODEBEHIND FILE

The next step is to build a table without placing it in the page first. The example in Table 8-17 shows how to populate a table programmatically with data from a database table.

TABLE 8-17 BUILDING A TABLE PROGRAMMATICALLY

Setting Up the Control

```
<asp:table id="Table2" runat="server"
    CellPadding="2" CellSpacing="2"
    GridLines="Both"
    HorizontalAlign="Center">
    <asp:tablerow BackColor=#000099 ForeColor=#ffffff>
        <asp:tablecell>
            Employee ID
        </asp:tablecell>
        <asp:tablecell>
            Name
        </asp:tablecell>
    </asp:tablerow>
</asp:table>
```

Working with the Control Programmatically

```
Private Sub Page_Load(ByVal sender As System.Object, _
        ByVal e As System.EventArgs) Handles MyBase.Load
```

Continued

TABLE 8-17 THE TEXTBOX CONTROL *(Continued)*

```vb
Dim strConn As String = _
    "Server=(local);Database=pubs;UID=sa;PWD=;"
Dim strSQL As String = "SELECT emp_id AS [Employee ID], " & _
        "fname+' '+lname AS [Name] FROM employee"
Dim intCounter As Integer

Dim objConn As _
    New System.Data.SqlClient.SqlConnection(strConn)
Dim objCommand As _
    New System.Data.SqlClient.SqlCommand(strSQL, _
    objConn)
  objConn.Open()
Dim objReader As System.Data.SqlClient.SqlDataReader
objReader = objCommand.ExecuteReader()

While objReader.Read()
  Dim objRow As New TableRow()
  For intCounter = 0 To objReader.FieldCount - 1
    Dim objCell As New TableCell()
    objCell.Text = objReader.Item(intCounter).ToString()
    objRow.Cells.Add(objCell)
  Next
  Table2.Rows.Add(objRow)
End While
  objConn.Close()
End Sub
```

Resulting HTML

```html
<form name="Form1" method="post" action="Table2.aspx" id="Form1">
  <input type="hidden" name="__VIEWSTATE" value="dDwtM...p8wI=" />
  <table id="Table1" cellspacing="2" cellpadding="2"
    align="Center" rules="all" border="1">
    <tr style="color:White;background-color:#000099;">
        <td>Employee ID</td><td>Name</td>
    </tr>
    <tr>
        <td>A-C71970F</td><td>Aria Cruz</td>
    </tr>
    <tr>
        <td>A-R89858F</td><td>Annette Roulet</td>
```

```
        </tr>
        <tr>
            <td>AMD15433F</td><td>Ann Devon</td>
        </tr>
        <!-- more rows here -->
    </table>
</form>
```

You have now created a table with code and a DataReader. Part III of our book covers this in more detail. Examine the code here closely, because the difference between this and the DataGrid is astounding.

PANEL

The Panel control acts as a container control. You can use it to show the next part of a form based on user input. In functionality, it is very similar to a Panel in Visual Basic. Table 8-18 shows a page that makes use of the Panel control.

TABLE 8-18 THE PANEL CONTROL

Setting Up the Control

```
<form id="Form1" method="post" runat="server">
  <P>
    <asp:panel ID="ShowMePanel" Runat="server"
      Visible="False">
    <p>Which of the following wars was not fought on
    American soil?</P>
    <P>
      <asp:radiobuttonlist id="RadioButtonList1" Runat="server">
        <asp:listitem Text="Revolutionary War" Value="1" />
        <asp:listitem Text="Civil War" Value="2" />
        <asp:listitem Text="World War I" Value="3" />
        <asp:listitem Text="World War II" Value="4" />
      </asp:radiobuttonlist>
    </P>
    </asp:panel>
  </P>
  <P>
    <asp:panel ID="HideMePanel" Runat="server" Visible="True">
```

Continued

TABLE 8-18 THE PANEL CONTROL *(Continued)*

```
      <asp:button id="SubmitButton"
        Runat="server" Text="Click To Show Form" />
    </asp:panel>
  </P>
</form>
```

Working with the Control Programmatically

```
Private Sub SubmitButton_Click(ByVal sender As System.Object, _
  ByVal e As System.EventArgs) Handles SubmitButton.Click
    HideMePanel.Visible = "False"
    ShowMePanel.Visible = "True"
End Sub
```

Resulting HTML Before Click

```
<form name="Form1" method="post" action="Panel.aspx" id="Form1">
  <input type="hidden" name="__VIEWSTATE" value="dDwt...+pyi8k=" />
  <P>
  <P></P>
  <P>
    <div id="HideMePanel">
      <input type="submit" name="SubmitButton"
        value="Click To Show Form" id="SubmitButton" />
    </div>
  </P>
  <P>
    <span id="Label1"></span>
  </P>
</form>
```

Resulting HTML After Click

```
<form name="Form1" method="post" action="Panel.aspx" id="Form1">
  <input type="hidden" name="__EVENTTARGET" value="" />
  <input type="hidden" name="__EVENTARGUMENT" value="" />
  <input type="hidden" name="__VIEWSTATE" value="dDwtN...2PAHQ==" />
```

```
<script language="javascript">
<!--
  function __doPostBack(eventTarget, eventArgument) {
    var theform = document.Form1;
    theform.__EVENTTARGET.value = eventTarget;
    theform.__EVENTARGUMENT.value = eventArgument;
    theform.submit();
  }
// -->
</script>
<P>
<div id="ShowMePanel">
  <P>Which of the following wars was not fought on American soil?</P>
  <P>
    <table id="RadioButtonList1" border="0">
      <tr>
       <td>
         <input id="RadioButtonList1_0" type="radio"
           name="RadioButtonList1" value="1"
           onclick="__doPostBack('RadioButtonList1_0','')"
           language="javascript" />
         <label for="RadioButtonList1_0">Revolutionary War</label>
       </td>
      </tr>
      <tr>
       <td>
         <input id="RadioButtonList1_1" type="radio"
           name="RadioButtonList1" value="2"
           onclick="__doPostBack('RadioButtonList1_1','')"
           language="javascript" />
         <label for="RadioButtonList1_1">Civil War</label>
       </td>
      </tr>
      <tr>
       <td>
         <input id="RadioButtonList1_2" type="radio"
           name="RadioButtonList1" value="3"
           onclick="__doPostBack('RadioButtonList1_2','')"
           language="javascript" />
         <label for="RadioButtonList1_2">World War I</label>
```

Continued

TABLE 8-18 THE PANEL CONTROL *(Continued)*

```
      </td>
      </tr>
      <tr>
       <td>
         <input id="RadioButtonList1_3" type="radio"
           name="RadioButtonList1" value="4"
           onclick="__doPostBack('RadioButtonList1_3','')"
           language="javascript" />
         <label for="RadioButtonList1_3">World War II</label>
       </td>
      </tr>
     </table>
    </P>
  </div>
  <P></P>
  <P></P>
  <P><span id="Label1"></span></P>
</form>
```

Data controls

The final set of controls simplifies data access. I could create samples that do not use real data, but it does not make much sense to show you how to create fake data sources in code; if you want to do this, you can find plenty of examples in the MSDN library for Visual Studio .NET and the .NET Framework SDK help files.

Because this section deals with heavier coding, I use CodeBehind files. If you are having difficulty with CodeBehind, see the section "CodeBehind: A Review," which directly follows this section. I don't go into detail about every aspect of the controls, because the Part III covers more of this.

Here are a few rules to follow with the various data controls:

◆ The DataGrid control is most useful for multiple columns. It is one of the easiest controls to use and provides a lot of options, including alternating line styles, header and footer styles, and most table options. To use DataGrid, you set your options and bind data. The control handles the rest.

◆ The DataList control is as simple to use as DataGrid, but it represents only a single field of data. Use this control when you have only one field to display.

◆ The Repeater control is the most flexible. You can take any HTML and place it to make the repeater look the way you would like. With this flexibility comes a bit more work.

DATAGRID

DataGrid is the control you use the most often in your work because it displays data in a common tabular format. You can set alternating lines to give the table a nicer look and feel, and it is a simple set-bind-and-forget control. Table 8-19 shows a simple DataGrid bound to the pubs database that ships with Microsoft database products, and Figure 8-2 shows a screenshot of the results. Note that the HTML produced is abbreviated. This example yields an almost identical table to the programmatic Table control example in Table 8-17.

TABLE 8-19 THE DATAGRID CONTROL

Setting Up the Control

```
<form id="Form1" method="post" runat="server">
  <h1>Employees</h1>
  <P>
    <asp:DataGrid id="DataGrid1" runat="server"
      BorderColor="#000099" BorderStyle="Dashed"
      BorderWidth="1" AlternatingItemStyle-BackColor="#9999ff"
      HeaderStyle-BackColor="#000099" HeaderStyle-
ForeColor="#ffffff" />
  </P>
</form>
```

Working with the Control Programmatically

```
Private Sub Page_Load(ByVal sender As System.Object, _
  ByVal e As System.EventArgs) Handles MyBase.Load

    Dim strConn As String = _
     "Server=(local);Database=pubs;UID=sa;PWD=;"
    Dim strSQL As String = "SELECT emp_id AS [Employee ID], " & _
     "fname+' '+lname AS [Name] FROM employee"

    ' Create and open Connection
```

Continued

TABLE 8-19 THE DATAGRID CONTROL *(Continued)*

```
Dim objConn As New System.Data.SqlClient.SqlConnection(strConn)
objConn.Open()

' Create a command and use it to fill a data adapter
Dim objCommand As _
  New System.Data.SqlClient.SqlCommand(strSQL, objConn)
Dim objDataAdapter As New _
System.Data.SqlClient.SqlDataAdapter(objCommand)

'*  Use the adapter to populate the data table
'*  employee in the data set
Dim objDataSet As New System.Data.DataSet()
```

Working with the Control Programmatically

```
objDataAdapter.Fill(objDataSet, "employee")

' Bind Data to the Data Grid
DataGrid1.DataSource = _
  objDataSet.Tables("employee").DefaultView
DataGrid1.DataBind()

End Sub
```

Resulting HTML

```
<form name="Form1" method="post" action="DataGrid.aspx" id="Form1">
  <input type="hidden" name="__VIEWSTATE" value="dDwtNT...J9jhg" />
  <h1>Employees</h1>
  <P>
    <table cellspacing="0" rules="all"
    bordercolor="#000099" border="1" id="DataGrid1"
    style="border-style:Dashed;border-collapse:collapse;">
      <tr style="color:White;background-color:#000099;">
        <td>Employee ID</td>
        <td>Name</td>
```

```
        </tr>
        <tr>
          <td>A-C71970F</td>
          <td>Aria Cruz</td>
        </tr>
        <tr style="background-color:#9999FF;">
          <td>A-R89858F</td>
          <td>Annette Roulet</td>
        </tr>
        <tr>
          <td>AMD15433F</td>
          <td>Ann Devon</td>
        </tr><tr style="background-color:#9999FF;">
          <td>ARD36773F</td>
          <td>Anabela Domingues</td>
        </tr>
        <tr>

          <td>CFH28514M</td>
          <td>Carlos Hernadez</td>
        </tr>
        <tr style="background-color:#9999FF;">
          <td>CGS88322F</td>
          <td>Carine Schmitt</td>
        </tr>
      <!-- ADDITIONAL ROWS HERE -->
      </table>
    </P>
</form>
```

DATALIST

The DataList control is similar to the DataGrid, except that it deals with one field from the DataTable. You can arrange this data into multiple columns and have the field repeat horizontally or vertically. The example shown in Table 8-20 uses the same Page_Load event as the DataGrid control, with one change: DataGrid1 becomes DataList1. The change is all that is highlighted in the "Working with the Control Programmatically" section of the table. Figure 8-3 shows the output of this control, which is a two-column list.

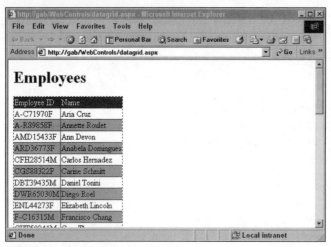

Figure 8-2: The DataGrid control in action.

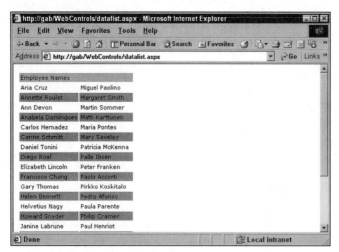

Figure 8-3: The DataList control in action.

TABLE 8-20 THE DATALIST CONTROL

Setting Up the Control

```
<form id="Form1" method="post" runat="server">
  <asp:DataList id="DataList1" runat="server"
    CellPadding="2" CellSpacing="2" Font-Name="Verdana"
```

```
    Font-Size="8pt" REPEATCOLUMNS="2">
      <HeaderStyle BACKCOLOR="#aaaadd" />
      <AlternatingItemStyle BACKCOLOR="#009999" />
      <HeaderTemplate>
        Employee Names
      </HeaderTemplate>
      <ItemTemplate>
        <%# DataBinder.Eval(Container.DataItem, "Name") %>
      </ItemTemplate>
  </asp:DataList>
</form>
```

Working with the Control Programmatically

```
DataList1.DataSource = objDataSet.Tables("employee").DefaultView
DataList1.DataBind()
```

Resulting HTML

```
<form name="Form1" method="post" action="DataList.aspx" id="Form1">
    <input type="hidden" name="__VIEWSTATE" value="dDwx...NSyA==" />
    <table id="DataList1" cellspacing="2"
      cellpadding="2" border="0"
      style="font-family:Verdana;font-size:8pt;">
      <tr>
        <td colspan="2" style="background-color:#AAAADD;">
          Employee Names
        </td>
      </tr>
      <tr>
        <td>
          Aria Cruz
        </td>
        <td>
          Miguel Paolino
        </td>
      </tr>
      <tr>
        <td style="background-color:#009999;">
```

Continued

TABLE 8-20 THE DATALIST CONTROL *(Continued)*

```
        Annette Roulet
      </td>
      <td style="background-color:#009999;">
        Margaret Smith
      </td>
    </tr>
    <tr>
<!-- MORE ROWS HERE -->
    </table>
</form>
```

REPEATER

The Repeater control is the most free form of the controls — it allows you to create templates to represent the data in any manner you want. With this flexibility comes a little bit of extra work. In the example in Table 8-21, I recreate the DataGrid from the DataGrid example (see Table 8-19). The output of this control is the same as the DataGrid output shown in Figure 8-2.

TABLE 8-21 THE REPEATER CONTROL

Setting Up the Control

```
<form id="Form1" method="post" runat="server">
  <asp:repeater id="Repeater1" runat="server">
    <HeaderTemplate>
      <table cellspacing="0" rules="all" bordercolor="#000099"
        border="1" style="border-style:Dashed;border-↵
collapse:collapse;">
        <tr style="color:White;background-color:#000099;">
          <td>
            Employee ID
          </td>
          <td>
            Name
          </td>
        </tr>
    </HeaderTemplate>
```

```
  <ItemTemplate>
    <tr>
      <td>
        <%# DataBinder.Eval(Container.DataItem, "[Employee ID]") %>
      </td>
      <td>
        <%# DataBinder.Eval(Container.DataItem, "Name") %>
      </td>
    </tr>
  </ItemTemplate>
  <AlternatingItemTemplate>
    <tr style="background-color:#9999FF;">
      <td>
        <%# DataBinder.Eval(Container.DataItem, "[Employee ID]") %>
      </td>
      <td>
        <%# DataBinder.Eval(Container.DataItem, "Name") %>
      </td>
    </tr>
  </AlternatingItemTemplate>
  <FooterTemplate>
    </table>
  </FooterTemplate>
</asp:repeater>
</form>
```

Working with the Control Programmatically

```
*    Changes in bold
Repeater1.DataSource = objDataSet.Tables("employee").DefaultView
Repeater1.DataBind()
```

Resulting HTML
```
... Source looks like Table 8-21
```

CodeBehind: A Review

CodeBehind is an important concept in .NET as it moves the developer to a place where code and User Interface are separate. The idea here is that HTML and DHTML, along with XML and JavaScript, are used to create the presentation layer. Any code that deals with data access or business rules should "run behind" the page in a separate file.

Setting up your page

To set up a CodeBehind file in ASP.NET, you simply add the CodeBehind property to your @ directive line, as shown in Listing 8-11. The current standard is to use the entire name of the ASPX file with the extension vb. You should also add the Inherits line for the class used in the CodeBehind file. The default is assemblyName.pageName, which is also shown in the listing.

Listing 8-11: Setting up CodeBehind

```
<%@ Page CodeBehind="ThisPage.aspx.vb"
Inherits="MyProject.ThisPage"%>
```

If you add the src (Source) property to the @ directive, the CodeBehind file compiles when the page is hit. If you use only CodeBehind, you have to compile the CodeBehind file before you access changes made to the file.

The CodeBehind file

The CodeBehind file consists of at least one class. By default, the file is only one class attached to a single ASPX page. You can, however, add multiple classes to a single file and have different pages inherit different classes in this file. Listing 8-12 shows a simple CodeBehind file. This one is empty because I pulled it from the ImageButton example shown previously in this chapter (refer to Table 8-9).

Listing 8-12: CodeBehind for ImageButton.aspx

```
Public Class ImageButton
   Inherits System.Web.UI.Page
   Protected WithEvents imagebutton1 As _
   System.Web.UI.WebControls.ImageButton

#Region " Web Form Designer Generated Code "

  This call is required by the Web Form Designer.
  <System.Diagnostics.DebuggerStepThrough()> _
  Private Sub InitializeComponent()
```

```
  End Sub

  Protected Sub Page_Init(ByVal Sender As System.Object, _
  ByVal e As System.EventArgs) _
  Handles MyBase.Init
InitializeComponent()
  End Sub

#End Region

  Private Sub Page_Load(ByVal sender As System.Object, _
ByVal e As System.EventArgs) _
Handles MyBase.Load
'Put user code to initialize the page here
  End Sub
End Class
```

Because Visual Studio .NET produced the code in Listing 8-12, the Page_Load event is already roughed in for your use. To use code from your ASP.NET pages, simply move the subroutines from your page to the CodeBehind file and either compile this project or use the src property in the @ directive for your page, which force the CodeBehind file to compile when it is next accessed.

Summary

In this chapter, you moved into the programming paradigm of ASP.NET. Although the HTML controls, covered in the Chapter 7, showed more interactivity than their HTML and ASP counterparts, Web controls are the meat and potatoes of your Web pages in ASP.NET.

I also covered CodeBehind again in this chapter. As Microsoft pushes deeper into n-tier development, separation of code and the User Interface becomes more and more important. In fact, in some builds of the .NET beta, code in the CodeBehind file would work, while the identical code in an ASP.NET page would fail. Although coding a CodeBehind file for your pages is a bit of a pain, unless you are using Visual Studio .NET, the separation of presentation and code is well worth the bother.

One thing you should be noticing by now is the strong dependency on objects in the .NET Framework base class library. If you have not taken time to look at the MSDN documentation that ships with both the Framework SDK and the Visual Studio .NET product, I advise you to become familiar with it now.

Chapter 9

Validation

IN THIS CHAPTER

- Understanding the concept of validation
- Using validation controls in ASP.NET
- Using regular expressions in validation
- Using the ValidationSummary control

IT'S EASY TO SET UP data validation with ASP.NET. Most of the work in this chapter deals with Web controls that you can add to your page and configure to set up validation on both client and server.

The Concept of Validation

Business acquires, utilizes, and disseminates enormous quantities of information every day. Simply managing the mass of information is a major undertaking.

In a modern-day application, a great deal of effort goes into making sure that the data in the enterprise stays clean. This is a concept known as *data integrity*. In a data-driven application, it is the duty of your relational database management system (RDBMS) to ensure the integrity of any data inserted into its databases. Through the use of data types, you can guarantee that character values are not inserted in a money field, and through the use of primary key/foreign key relations, you can guarantee that every record is properly linked.

In early Web applications, it was fairly common to rely on the database for validation as well as integrity of your data. The basic concept was that if the user entered invalid data, the application would attempt to insert that data into the database and, upon failing, would simply return an exception; and the user would have to figure out what was wrong. Unfortunately, there are two problems with this paradigm:

- **The burden is on performance and scalability.** Using the database as a data validator is an expensive proposition, performance-wise. This leads to applications that do not scale.

- **Validation and integrity are not the same thing.** Integrity deals with whether data is of the correct type, like a string, while validation deals with whether the actual data is valid for the application, such as an e-mail address. In the early days of the Web, for example, it was common for someone to mistake his America Online (AOL) logon for an e-mail address because he could send e-mail to other AOL members by ID alone. He therefore wouldn't enter the `@aol.com` part of the address. The AOL logon passes an integrity check because it is a valid string; it doesn't pass the validity check, though, because it isn't a real e-mail address, outside of AOL.

The Web programming community offered two alternatives to this paradigm. One side shifted to the creation of server-based Common Gateway Interface (CGI) applications, with compiled languages like C++ or scripted languages like PERL and PYTHON. The other side opted for JavaScript validation on the server side, a switch in thinking that was a boon for data validity, because you could create algorithms to catch improperly formatted e-mail addresses, for example. But it had its own share of problems, including a steeper learning curve that led to additional training and development expense, as well as additional expense for maintenance of code (lower maintainability).

Microsoft moved to a server-side paradigm, although it could implement client-side script. In many ways this was a compromise between both sides of the equation, as it could scale better than a database option, but had a shorter learning curve than the CGI or JavaScript option. If you did opt to include client-side script, which was an option, the benefit of the shorter learning curve was present only if you coded your applications for Internet Explorer.

ASP.NET has simplified the model tremendously. Through the use of validation controls, you can test for data validity through the use of an extremely simple programming model. This solves the maintainability and development issues. In addition, the validation code can be run on the client side for newer browsers, which aids in performance.

One thing that may seem like a bit of a downside should be mentioned: Whether or not the validation code is run on the client side, it is always run on the server side. The performance benefit of client-side validation is lessened a bit, although you still eliminate multiple round trips.

The server-side validation on every submission has a security benefit. One of the more common methods used by hackers who want to obtain items well below market value is form spoofing. The individual employing this technique creates his own form to submit values to the server, thus bypassing any client-side validation code. The result is that the target item's price is now much lower according to the application that provides pricing for the business. This should not be a great concern to those who do not place their final pricing validation in the presentation layer, but many companies have been burned by this practice.

Validation controls

The validation controls are part of the System.Web.UI.WebControls namespace, which was covered rather extensively in the last chapter. As with all other Web controls, each of the validation controls can use the properties, methods, and events of the classes they are derived from. All of the validation controls, except for the ValidationSummary control, which I cover in a separate section, are derived from the Label control, and can use those properties and methods, as well. Figure 9-1 shows a simplified hierarchy for the validation controls.

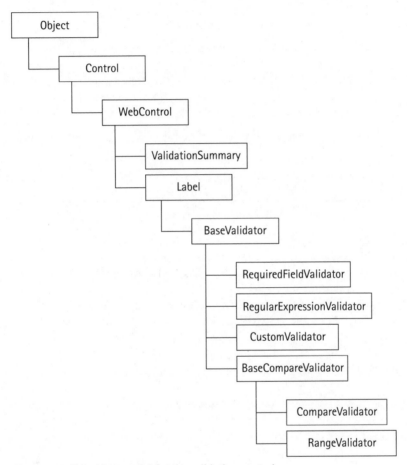

Figure 9-1: The object model for the validation controls.

By now you should be getting used to the idea that all classes derive from other classes and ultimately from System.Object. You should also be used to the concept of using the properties and methods of the classes from which a class is derived. So let's take a look at the BaseValidator control. The only class in this chapter that does not derive from the BaseValidator control is the Summary. Table 9-1 contains the most useful properties and methods of the BaseValidator control.

TABLE 9-1 PROPERTIES AND METHODS OF THE BASEVALIDATOR CLASS

Property or Method	Description
Display	Property to get or set the display behavior of the validator control.
Enabled	Property to get or set whether or not the validator control is enabled.
ErrorMessage	Property to get or set the error message displayed when the control being validated is invalid. This property always displays in the ValidationSummary control. Since the text property, from the label control, overrides this on the page, this property is useful to set a more complex message in the summary than on the page.
IsValid	Property to get or set whether the entry in the validated control is valid.
Validate	Method to evaluate the validity of the control being validated and update the IsValid property.

REQUIRED FIELD VALIDATOR

The required field validator ensures that there is an entry into a control, or, to be more precise, that the value of a control does not equal a preset value. This control is useful for controls that must be filled in prior to submitting a form. For example, it makes no sense to allow a user to set up an account without a logon ID and password. Listing 9-1 contains the ASP.NET code necessary to create a required field validator.

Listing 9-1: Required Field Validator

```
Logon ID:
<asp:TextBox id=strLogonID runat="server"></asp:TextBox>
<asp:RequiredFieldValidator
id=rfvLastName runat="server"
ErrorMessage="Logon ID is mandatory."
ControlToValidate="strLogonID">
</asp:RequiredFieldValidator>
```

To give you a better idea of how these controls work in HTML, Listing 9-2 shows the HTML that results from this required field validator.

Listing 9-2: HTML from Required Field Valuator

```
Logon ID:
<input name="strLogonID" type="text" id="strLogonID" />
<span id="rfvLastName" controltovalidate="strLogonID"
```

```
   errormessage="Logon ID is mandatory."
   evaluationfunction="RequiredFieldValidatorEvaluateIsValid"
   initialvalue="" style="color:Red;visibility:hidden;">
   Logon ID is mandatory.</span></P>
<P>
<input type="submit" name="Button1" value="Button" id="Button1" /></P>

<script language="javascript">
<!--
    var Page_Validators =  new Array(document.all["rfvLastName"]);
        // -->
</script>

<script language="javascript">
<!--
var Page_ValidationActive = false;
if (typeof(Page_ValidationVer) == "undefined")
    alert("Unable to find script library WebUIValidation.js.");
else if (Page_ValidationVer != "119")
    alert("This page uses an incorrect version of WebUIValidation.js.
    The page expects version 119. The script library is " +
    Page_ValidationVer + ".");else
    ValidatorOnLoad();

function ValidatorOnSubmit() {
    if (Page_ValidationActive) {
        ValidatorCommonOnSubmit();
    }
}
// -->
</script>
```

This code produces the error "Logon ID is mandatory" when the Logon ID field is left blank, as Figure 9-2 shows.

The InitialValue property is used to set the initial value for that control. This is not as useful on the first control of a page, like this example, because the entire text of the control will not be selected without some help (such as a JavaScript routine). Listing 9-3 shows the required validator with an initial value set.

Listing 9-3: Adding an Initial Value

```
<P><asp:TextBox ID="strLogonID" Runat="server">Fill in ID here</asp:TextBox>
<asp:RequiredFieldValidator ID="rfvLogonID" Runat="server"
ErrorMessage="Logon ID is mandatory" InitialValue="Fill in ID here"
ControlToValidate="strLogonID" Display="Dynamic" /><BR>
<asp:Button id="btnSubmit" runat="server" Text="Submit"></asp:Button></P>
```

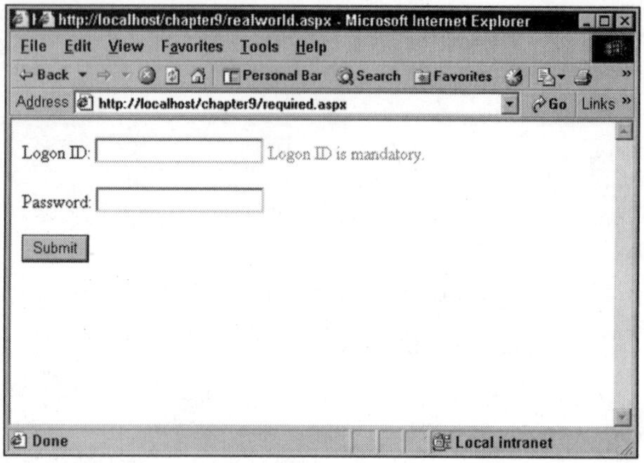

![Screenshot of Microsoft Internet Explorer showing a logon form. The address bar reads http://localhost/chapter9/required.aspx. The form has a "Logon ID:" text box with the text "Logon ID is mandatory." to its right, a "Password:" text box, and a "Submit" button.]

Figure 9-2: The required field validator control in action.

The page from Listing 9-3 can be found on the companion Web site (`www.wiley.com/extras`) in the file for this chapter: `Ch09SDK.zip` (SDK version) or `Ch09VS.zip` (Visual Studio .NET version). The page with the required field validator is named `RequiredFields.aspx`.

There is one downside to the required field validator. While it can determine if a field is filled in or not, it can't determine if the field is filled in with spaces only, which I have personally encountered with Web applications where a customer wants something but does not want to give information for it. I discuss a way to stop this in the "Regular Expression Validator" section later in the chapter.

COMPARE VALIDATOR

The compare validator has a dual purpose. It can be used to validate a control against a set value or it can be used to compare one control to another. The most common method of using this control is to compare confirmation entries, like e-mail addresses or passwords. If you have registered to join certain sites, you have probably seen the type of form that contains a confirmation field for one or both of these items.

Listing 9-4 presents a simple form with two e-mail address text boxes. The second e-mail address text box has a validator control to ensure that user input here exactly matches the first e-mail address text box input.

Listing 9-4: Using a Compare Validator to Confirm Password Entry

```
<P>Enter Email:
<asp:TextBox id=txtEmail runat="server"></asp:TextBox></P>
<P>Confirm Email:
```

```
<asp:TextBox id=txtEmail2 runat="server"></asp:TextBox>
<asp:CompareValidator id=CompareValidator1 runat="server"
ErrorMessage="Email Address must match."
ControlToValidate="txtEmail2"
ControlToCompare="txtEmail">
</asp:CompareValidator></P>
```

 The page from Listing 9-4 can be found on the companion Web site (www. wiley.com/extras) in the file for this chapter: Ch09SDK.zip (SDK version) or Ch09VS.zip (Visual Studio .NET version). The page with the required field validator is named CompareValidator.aspx.

This is great, except you can leave both controls empty and they will validate fine. Oops! Make sure you use a required field validator in conjunction with a compare validator if the fields must match and are required as well. Note that you can also use the compare validator to compare against a set value. Listing 9-5 shows an example of a compare validator to compare against a set value. My example is a bit inane, so I leave it up to you to come up with something more useful.

Listing 9-5: Using the Compare Validator to Compare against a Set Value

```
<P>If you agree to the terms, you must type "yes" in the box below:<BR>
<asp:TextBox id="txtConfirm" runat="server" Width="58px"></asp:TextBox> 
<asp:CompareValidator id="cvConfirm" runat="server"
ErrorMessage="You must type yes in the box." ValueToCompare="yes"
ControlToValidate="txtConfirm"></asp:CompareValidator></P>
<P>
<asp:Button id="btnSubmit" runat="server" Text="Submit"></asp:Button></P>
```

 The page for Listing 9-5 can be found on the companion Web site (www. wiley.com/extras) in the file for this chapter: Ch09SDK.zip (SDK version) or Ch09VS.zip (Visual Studio .NET version). The page with the required field validator is named CompareValidator2.aspx.

While this might seem like a nice way to validate, you cannot use this control to test to see if a check box is checked. This would be the primary reason I might want to use a compare validator against a set value, which makes this control largely useless against a set value.

One more note about using the compare validator against a set value: If the field is left empty, it validates fine, even though an empty field does not compare properly to the value you are trying to compare to. In one respect, this is good, since the required field validator should be the one that checks whether a required field is empty. On the other hand, an empty field compared against a value does not pass the compare test, either.

RANGE VALIDATOR

The range validator is used to ensure that an entry falls within a certain range. This is useful for situations in which you want to restrict certain types of input to a range of values. I am sure that one earned a "Well, duh" from the peanut gallery.

Overall, I believe this type of functionality is better served by a drop-down, unless the range is very large and could inhibit performance due to the large amounts of text that would have to be downloaded to the client to perform this type of range restriction. Why? Simple; I believe it is easier for end users to select a value from a list of valid ones than to correct the error raised later when they have entered an out-of-range value. Listing 9-6 shows the range validator used to ensure that a user chooses a number from 1 to 5.

Listing 9-6: Using the Range Validator

```
<P>Choose a number from 1 to 5:
<BR />
<asp:TextBox id="txtNumber" runat="server" Width="36px" /> 
<asp:RangeValidator id="rvNumber" runat="server"
ErrorMessage="Number must be between 1 and 5." MaximumValue="5"
MinimumValue="1" ControlToValidate="txtNumber"></asp:RangeValidator></P>
<P>
<asp:Button id="btnSubmit" runat="server" Text="Submit"></asp:Button></P>
```

The page for Listing 9-6 can be found on the companion Web site (www. wiley.com/extras) in the file for this chapter: Ch09SDK.zip (SDK version) or Ch09VS.zip (Visual Studio .NET version). The page with the required field validator is named RangeValidator.aspx.

REGULAR EXPRESSION VALIDATOR

The regular expression validator is used to compare the entry in a control to a regular expression. While this is not a book on regular expressions, per se, you really cannot use this validator without understanding at least the basics of regular expressions. I show you how to use this validator after I give you those basics.

REGULAR EXPRESSIONS   Regular expressions are statements that match a pattern of characters. They are useful for pattern matching when used with the regular expression validator, but they can also be used for search-and-replace functions in other languages, such as JavaScript. Since search-and-replace is out of context, I focus on the pattern-matching ability of regular expression. The following list details the basic rules of setting up a regular expression:

- A regular expression is delimited by forward slashes (/) that are called whacks. Here's a regular expression for any number of digits:

  `/\d*/`

- A statement is indicated by a caret (^) at the beginning and a dollar sign ($) at the end. Here's a regular expression that can take only the words true or false:

  `/^(true|false)$/`

- Each character represents itself, which is the reason that `true` and `false` work in the previous statement. You can also use ASCII numbers, at least in octal or hexadecimal, or even with control + letter, as these examples show:

  ```
  /\123/ -- octal
  /\xff/ -- hexadecimal
  /\cX/
  ```

There are some characters that have a purpose in regular expressions. In order to include these characters in your patterns, each of them must be escaped by placing an escape character immediately before it. The escape character in regular expressions is the backslash (\). The characters that must be escaped in this manner are

.	Period	(	Left parenthesis
*	Asterisk	)	Right parenthesis
/	Forward slash	[	Left bracket
\	Back slash	]	Right bracket
+	Plus sign	{	Left brace
?	Question mark	}	Right brace
|	Pipe		

Here's a regular expression that is used to check for http:// at the beginning of a statement, so the whacks (/) must be escaped:

`/^http:\/\//`

In addition, there are some characters such as a tab or carriage return (Enter) that cannot be expressed with letters or numbers. You can also use the escape character to specify characters through an octal or hexadecimal number. Table 9-2 shows some special characters used in regular expressions.

TABLE 9-2 CHARACTER ESCAPES

Expression	Value
\f	Form feed
\n	New line
\r	Carriage return
\t	Tab
\v	Vertical tab

The next concept to consider is character classes. Character classes are used to represent a group of characters. You can use a group of literals such as in [aeiou], which means any vowel that is lowercase, or you can use specific escaped letters that represent specific groups of characters. Table 9-3 shows the characters classes available in regular expressions.

TABLE 9-3 CHARACTER CLASSES

Expression	Value
[...]	Any character between the brackets. Example: [A-Z] equals any capital character A through Z, while [Aa] is upper- or lowercase a.
[^...]	Any one character not between the brackets. Example: [^A-Z] equals any character except for capitalized letters.
.	Any character except a new line.
\w	Any word character. This is equal to [a-zA-Z0-9_].
\W	Any non-word character. This is equal to [^a-zA-Z0-9_].
\s	Any white space character such as tab, new line, and so on. This is equal to [\t\n\r\f\v].
\S	Any non-white space character. This is equal to [^ \t\n\r\f\v].
\d	Any digit. This is equal to [0-9].
\D	Any non-digit. This is equal to [^0-9].

Quantifiers are another concept to consider. Quantifiers are pieces of a regular expression used to determine how many times a specific value is repeated. The basic syntax is {minimum, maximum}, where the maximum value is optional.

◆ Using {n,m} indicates at least n number of repeats with a maximum of m times. The m is optional. You can also specify a specific number of repeats with the format {n}.

◆ There are also a few special characters:

+ _ The same as {1,}, which means at least one time with no maximum

?: _ Equals {0,1}, which is either 0 or 1 repeats

* _ Indicates any number of characters and is equal to {0,}

Another key concept is grouping. While there are many grouping options, I am going to cover just one: any substring can be grouped using parentheses. Using brackets, which indicate options, you can get a lot of strength out of this part of regular expressions.

To give you an idea of how a regular expression is built, let me show you how to build an IP address step by step. It's a fairly simple example. With an IP address, there are three octets (8-bit numbers or bytes) separated by periods. This means each section can represent a number from 1–255. If this was 1–999, we could handle this quite easily with a digit \d and a quantifier {10}, like a regular expression for a phone number without special characters (/\d{10}/). The fact the number ends in 255 presents a bit of a problem here.

1. The first octet can be any number from 1 to 255. In the first octet, a 0 does not make sense. Therefore, we want to make a 1–9 as one of our options for this number:

   ```
   /^[1-9]$/
   ```

2. Now let's look at longer versions of the string. Two- and three-digit versions can be evaluated together. The following first line tests for 10–199, while the second is our string from 1– 199 because I added the [1-9].

   ```
   /^(1\d?\d)$/
   /^([1-9]|1\d?\d)$/
   ```

3. It takes two statements to get from 200 to 255. The first gets you from 200 to 249, and the second from 250 to 255.

   ```
   /^(\2[0-4]\d)$/
   /(25[0-5])$/
   ```

4. Now, put it all together with the period that follows the first octet.

```
/^([1-9]|1\d?\d|2[0-4]\d|25[0-5])\.$/
```

5. To get the second octet, the option of having a 0 is added. I also have the character for the period included at the end of the second octet. As a 0 is possible, the statement is simplified a bit, losing the [1-9] and changing the 1 in the second option to [0-1].

```
/^([0-1]\d?\d?|2[0-4]\d|25[0-5])\.$/;
```

6. The final octet is just like the first. Here's the entire regular expression:

```
/^([1-9]|1\d?\d|2[0-4]\d|25[0-5])\.([0-1]\d?\d?|2
[0-4]\d|25[0-5])\.([1-9]|1\d?\d|2[0-4]\d|25[0-5])$/
```

(Although this expression doesn't fit on one line in this book, it should be considered one long line with no spaces.)

Listing 9-7 shows some regular expressions that are useful to Web applications. To make this a bit more thorough, I have included a JavaScript routine using the regular expressions. You can include this script in your own applications if you're not interested in using the validators right now.

Listing 9-7: Common Regular Expressions

```
function checkEmpty(objControl,strControlName,intType) {
  var strObjValue objControl.value);
  var reEval;
  var blnEval;

  Switch(intType) {
    Case 1:
    // Social Security Number (with hyphens)
    reEval = /^\d{3}-\d{2}-\d{4}$/;
    blnEval = reEval.test(strObjValue)
    break;
    Case 2:
    // E-mail Address
    reEval = /^[\w\.=-]+@[\w\.-]+\.\w{2,3}$/;
    blnEval = reEval.test(strObjValue)
    break;
    Case 3:
    // URL in either http://mysite.com or mysite.com format (www optional)
    reEval = /^(http:\/\/\w*\.|\w*\.)(\w*\.\w{2,3}|\w{2,3})/;
    blnEval = reEval.test(strObjValue)
    break;
```

```
   Case 4:
   // Phone in 1234567890, (123) 456-7890 or (123)456-7890 format
   reEval = /^(\d{10}|\d{3}-\d{3}-\d{4}|\(\d{3}\)\s*\d{3}-\d{4})$/;
   blnEval = reEval.test(strObjValue)
   break;
   Case 5:
   // GIF and JPG files
   reEval = /^\w+\.(gif|jpg)$/;
   blnEval = reEval.test(strObjValue)
   break;
   Case 6:
   // IP Address
   reEval = /^([1-9]|1\d?\d|2[0-4]\d|25[0-5])\.([0-1]\d?\ ↵
d?|2[0-4]\d|25[0-5])\.([1-9]|1\d?\d|2[0-4]\d|25[0-5])$/;
   blnEval = reEval.test(strObjValue)
   break;
   default:
   // string of all spaces
      reEval = /(^\s+$)/;
   blnEval = !reEval.test(strObjValue)
   break;
   }

   if (blnEval) {
     return (true);
   } else {
     return (false);
   }

}
```

The page for Listing 9-7 can be found on this book's companion Web site (www.wiley.com/extras) in the file for this chapter: Ch09SDK.zip (SDK version) or Ch09VS.zip (Visual Studio .NET version). The file is called RegularExpression.html.

WORKING WITH THE REGULAR EXPRESSION VALIDATOR   Now that you have a rudimentary understanding of how to write a regular expression, the regular expression validator control is fairly simple to work with. I use the e-mail and the URL expressions in Listing 9-8. The button Web control in this example works with a validate event on the server.

Listing 9-8: Common Uses of the Regular Expressions Validator

```
<%@ Page Language="vb" AutoEventWireup="false"
  Codebehind="RegularExpression.aspx.vb"
  Inherits="Chapter09.RegularExpression"%>
<!DOCTYPE HTML PUBLIC "-//W3C//DTD HTML 4.0 Transitional//EN">
<HTML>
  <HEAD>
    <title>Regular Expression Validator</title>
  </HEAD>
  <body>
    <form id="Form1" method="post" runat="server">
      <P>
        Email:
        <asp:TextBox id="txtEmail" runat="server" />
        <asp:RegularExpressionValidator id="revEmail" runat="server"
         ErrorMessage="Email not formatted correctly."
         ValidationExpression="^[\w\.=-]+@[\w\.-]+\.\w{2,3}$"
         ControlToValidate="txtEmail" />
      </P>
      <P>
        URL: 
        <asp:TextBox id="txtURL" runat="server" />
        <asp:RegularExpressionValidator id="revURL" runat="server"
         ErrorMessage="URL is not formatted correctly."
         ValidationExpression="^(http:\/\/\w*\.|\w*\.)(\w*\.\w{2,3}|\w{2,3})"
         ControlToValidate="txtURL" />
      </P>
      <P>
        <asp:Button id="Button1" runat="server" Text="Submit" />
      </P>
    </form>
  </body>
</HTML>
```

The page for Listing 9-8 can be found on the companion Web site (www.wiley.com/extras) in the file for this chapter: Ch09SDK.zip (SDK version) or Ch09VS.zip (Visual Studio .NET version). The file is called RegularExpression.aspx.

CUSTOM VALIDATOR

The custom validator control is used when you need to validate a control with an algorithm that does not map to one of the common validators. A good example of this would be an enhanced e-mail validator that tests the e-mail address for validity. Weigh carefully the use of this type of control in your application. While bogus addresses are a problem, allowing the user to know that you know he has a bogus address may yield negative consequences of its own. Listing 9-9 shows a custom e-mail validator control. The e-mail script, to make things simple, uses the JavaScript regular expression for e-mail, shown in Listing 9-7.

Listing 9-9: An E-mail Custom Validator

```
<P>Email:
<asp:TextBox id="txtEmail" runat="server" /> 
<asp:CustomValidator id="cvEmail" runat="server"
ErrorMessage="Email must be in the format xxx@xxx.xxx."
ControlToValidate="txtEmail"
ClientValidationFunction="EmailValidator" /></P>
<P>
<asp:Button id="btnSubmit" runat="server" Text="Submit" /></P>
<script language="javascript">
function EmailValidator(source,arguments) {
  reEval = /^[\w\.=-]+@[\w\.-]+\.\w{2,3}$/;

  blnEval = reEval.test(arguments.Value)
  if (blnEval) {
    arguments.IsValid = true;
  } else {
    arguments.IsValid = false;
  }
}
</script>
```

The page for Listing 9-9 can be found on the companion Web site (www.wiley.com/extras) in the file for this chapter: Ch09SDK.zip (SDK version) or Ch09VS.zip (Visual Studio .NET version). The file is called CustomValidator.aspx.

Notice that just like server-side routines, you pass both a source object and an arguments object. You test the value of the arguments object and, if it is valid, you set the object's IsValid property to true.

Another good use of the custom validation is to create a validator to verify a credit card. While it is impossible, client side, to check whether a credit card number is bogus, you can check if the number checks out mathematically. Listing 9-10 has a credit card validator, with the validation routine on the server side.

Listing 9-10: A Credit Card Custom Validator

```
Sub CCValidate(source as object, args as ServerValidateEventArgs)
  Dim strCCValue As String = args.Value
  Dim intCounter As Integer
  Dim intHolder As Integer
  Dim intCCCheck As Integer

  intCounter = 1
  intHolder = 0

  strCCValue = Replace(strCCValue,"-","")

  If Not IsNumeric(strCCValue) then
      args.IsValid = False
      Exit Sub
  End If

  Do While intCounter <= Len(strCCValue)
   If IsEven(Len(strCCValue)) Then
     intHolder = Val(Mid$(strCCValue, intCounter, 1))
     If Not IsEven(intCounter) Then
       intHolder = intHolder * 2
       If intHolder > 9 Then intHolder = intHolder - 9
     End If
     intCCCheck = intCCCheck + intHolder
     intCounter = intCounter + 1
   Else
     intHolder = Val(Mid$(strCCValue, intCounter, 1))
     If IsEven(intCounter) Then
       intHolder = intHolder * 2
       If intHolder > 9 Then intHolder = intHolder - 9
     End If
     intCCCheck = intCCCheck + intHolder
     intCounter = intCounter + 1
   End If
  Loop

  intCCCheck = intCCCheck Mod 10

  If intCCCheck = 0 Then
 args.IsValid = True
  Else
 args.IsValid = False
  End If
```

```
End Sub

Function IsEven(ByRef lngNumber As Long) As Boolean

   If lngNumber Mod 2 = 0 Then
  IsEven = True
   Else
  IsEven = False
   End If

End Function
</script>
<asp:TextBox id=txtCreditCard runat="server">
</asp:TextBox>
<asp:CustomValidator id=CustomValidator1 runat="server"
  ErrorMessage="Invalid Credit Card Number"
  ControlToValidate="txtCreditCard"
  ClientValidationFunction=" CCValidate">
</asp:CustomValidator></P>
```

If you decide to enable validation on the client side, you should include a server-side validation routine (remember that you have the option to explicitly disable server validation), as well. If you don't do so, a malicious user could bypass your validation routine and wreak havoc.

ValidationSummary control

While individual validation of each control is a nice addition to your Web tools arsenal, there are many instances where you would much rather present the user with a summary of everything that is invalid in this form. This is the purpose of the ValidationSummary control.

The ValidationSummary control gathers information about each validation control in your form and retrieves the ErrorMessage for every control that failed validation. Listing 9-11 shows how to use this control.

Listing 9-11: The ValidationSummary Control

```
<asp:ValidationSummary id=ValidationSummary1
runat="server"></asp:ValidationSummary>
```

The code for the validation control is really simple. Every control that fails validation will show a message when validation fails for that control. Figure 9-3 shows the validation control results in a browser.

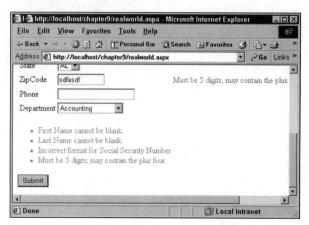

Figure 9-3: The ValidationSummary control results in a browser.

Final notes on validation

In order to protect you from having someone put together a page that submits to your site and gets around client-side validation, the validation controls always validate on the server side, even if the page has previously been validated on the client. As the practice of building forms to get around validation becomes more common in e-commerce, this is a good thing.

Putting It All Together

I want to take you through an employee form that validates input prior to inserting it into the database. The form takes information, like phone number, social security number, and birth date, as well as home address and e-mail. Each field is validated to attempt to ensure that the data is clean. Figure 9-4 shows the form built for user input.

If you would like to build the validation page yourself, there are two pages you can work with:

- ♦ `validationEmpty.aspx` — This page has no controls at all. You have to build from scratch to fill it in.

- ♦ `validationRaw.aspx` — This page has the form completed, but the validation controls and code to work with the validation controls has not been placed. If you want to skip placement of the form controls and start with validation, use this page and skip the section "Placing Web controls on the form."

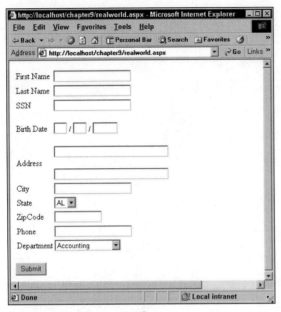

Figure 9-4: Employee entry form.

Placing Web controls on the form

The first step is to build the form. Table 9-4 has a list of controls necessary to add to the form, in the order of how they appear on the page. Use Figure 9-4 as a map for laying out the controls properly. If you use the grid layout in Visual Studio .NET, your layout will appear different from mine.

TABLE 9-4 WEB CONTROLS FOR THE EMPLOYEE PAGE

Control Type	Name	Notes
TextBox	FirstName	Max length 25.
TextBox	LastName	Max length 25.
TextBox	SSN	

Continued

TABLE 9-4 WEB CONTROLS FOR THE EMPLOYEE PAGE *(Continued)*

Control Type	Name	Notes
TextBox	BirthDateMonth	Max length 2.
TextBox	BirthDateDay	Max length 2.
TextBox	BirthDateYear	Max length 4.
TextBox	Address1	Max length 100.
TextBox	Address2	Max length 100.
TextBox	City	Max length 25.
DropDownList	State	Add states AL, GA, and TN.
TextBox	ZipCode	
TextBox	PhoneNumber	
DropDownList	Department	Add items for marketing, accounting, human resources and MIS.

Notice that I divided out the birth date into three boxes. In most applications, I would either have a single text box for birth date and then validate with regular expressions, or I'd use drop-downs in place of the text boxes. In this instance, however, I wanted something to use with a range validator.

Placing validation controls

The next step is placing the validation controls on the page. In general, I recommend placing the validation control next to the control being validated, which makes it easier for the user to understand what is needed to fill out the form correctly. For this page, I set up the controls as follows:

- ◆ Required field validators: First name and last name.

- ◆ Range validators: Birth date month, day, and year.

- ◆ Regular expression validators: Social Security number and ZIP Code.

- ◆ Custom validator: Phone number

In addition to the validation controls, you use a ValidationSummary control. The code necessary to set up the Web controls and validation controls is listed in Listing 9-12.

The validation control page from Listing 9-12 can be found on the companion Web site (www.wiley.com/extras) in the file for this chapter: Ch09SDK.zip (SDK version) or Ch09VS.zip (Visual Studio .NET version). The file is called ValidationControls.aspx.

If you are using the Visual Studio .NET IDE, you can easily drag and drop the controls onto a WebForm.

Listing 9-12: Code for Page

```
<form id="Form1" method="post" runat="server">
<table style="WIDTH: 632px; HEIGHT: 349px">
 <tr>
  <td>
   First Name
  </td>
  <td><asp:TextBox id="FirstName" runat="server" MaxLength="25" />
  </td>
  <td><asp:RequiredFieldValidator id="RequiredFieldValidator1"
  runat="server" ErrorMessage="First Name cannot be blank."
  ControlToValidate="FirstName" />
  </td>
 </tr>
</table>
<P>
 <asp:ValidationSummary id="ValidationSummary1"
   runat="server"></asp:ValidationSummary>
</P>
<P>
 <asp:Button id="Button1" runat="server" Text="Submit" />
</P>
</form>
```

Without doing anything else, you can now run the page and click the Submit button. Both the validation controls and the validation summary generate validation messages. Figure 9-5 shows the page after clicking Submit.

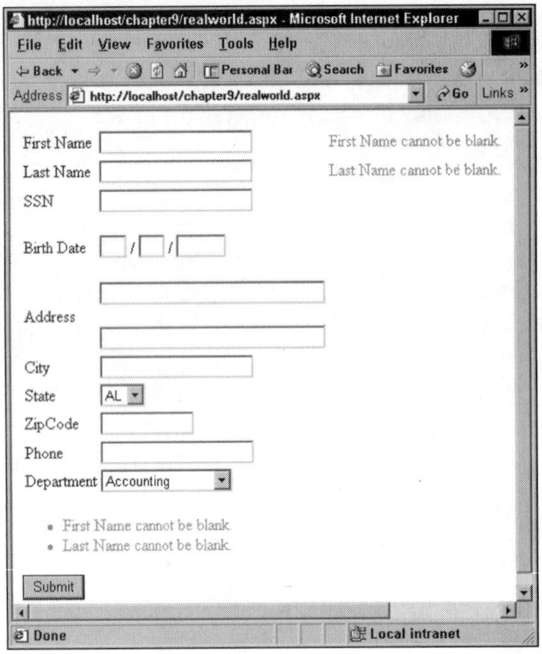

Figure 9-5: Validation controls on the page.

Since I cover ADO.NET and inserting data into a database in Part III, "Working with Data — ADO.NET," you are just going to prototype this form in this exercise. You have validation controls placed on the page, so the only thing left to do is check if it is valid and submit the information. The code in Listing 9-13 shows how to add an event handler to your validation routines.

Listing 9-13: Adding a Handler

```
Sub ValidateBtn_Click(sender As Object, e As EventArgs)
    If Page.IsValid Then
        'Load into database (covered under ADO.NET)
        blnOutputConfirm = True
    Else
        'Nothing to do here presently
    End If
End Sub
```

This code illustrates how easy it is to validate a page. Add a few controls, create a button click event handler, and check if the page is valid. If it is, you create a thank-you message. Otherwise, you show the form with the validation controls.

Summary

In this chapter, you were exposed to the concept of validation in ASP.NET. Each of the validation controls — the required field validator, the range validator, the regular expression validator, and the custom validation control — was given coverage.

In addition, I ran through a brief primer in regular expressions, showing a bit of favoritism to my personal favorite validator, the RegularExpressionValidator control. I also showed a brief example using the ValidationSummary control.

Finally, I took you through a small sample form designed to show a more real-world implementation of the controls. I cover placing data from the form into the database in Part III, "Working with Data — ADO.NET."

Chapter 10

Error Handling and Debugging

IN THIS CHAPTER, I COVER the lovely world of exceptions — errors to you and me. Well, not really, but I get to that soon. To make this discussion more useful, I deal with problem code by using comparison examples from both ASP and Visual Basic.

Exceptions?

They say there are only three sure things in life: death, taxes, and programming errors. Every program, at some point in its lifetime, encounters errors. Not your code or my code, of course, but that puts us in the minority that reach the Nirvana of programming bliss. For the rest of the programming world, errors are a part of everyday life.

Okay, you are probably saying, I understand the errors thing, but what about exceptions? Exceptions come from the C++ programming paradigm in which a return code was used to indicate that something was not quite perfect. In many cases, this was a full-blown error that, left unhandled, would foul up the application. In other instances, the exception was less-than-perfect execution. Essentially, the programming logic worked fine *except* for one thing — thus, an exception. Just like Billy Crystal's character in the movie *City Slickers,* it's your job to figure out what that one thing (the exception) is. If you have not seen the movie, just remember that your duty is to find the exception and handle it, rather than to allow the system to handle it for you.

In C++, one of the more common methods is to return a value rather than raise an error. A return code (value) of 0 means there are no exceptions, while any other number indicates that an exception occurred. (Pay attention, because the return

311

code rears its head again soon.) You examine the return code against a set of constants to determine which exception occurred and how critical it is. This, of course, is an oversimplification, because return codes can also indicate different types of successes. I am not concerned about non-exception return codes at present.

The problem, of course, is that you can ignore return codes and pretend like nothing happened. This would be the equivalent of a city using undersized water pipes and forcing enough water through the pipes that the pressure builds up and the water main explodes. Now I am going to assume you would never do this. I also know that ASP, Visual Basic, and even Visual Basic.NET do not allow this without additional effort on your part, so I feel safe in this assumption.

I personally believe that every exception should be handled in the procedure where it occurs. Even if the operation is not critical, something should be logged to show that the exception occurred. I have had arguments over this point, because some developers believe that logging every exception is unnecessary and adds bloat to code. My swan song was an assignment where my logging exceptions in a file delete routine turned up a problem in a file upload routine. Without my bloat, it would have taken quite a bit longer to find the problem in the code.

I had a friend in college who used to teach tailgaters a lesson by locking up his brakes. His justification was that it would be "the other guy's fault" if there was an accident. My retort was that death and injury are not concerned with fault. The upload exception would not have been my fault, but the developers were sure glad the exception was found before the car hit the highway. The analogy here is a bit flawed, of course, as exceptions are rarely intentional. The point, however, is still valid: Handling the exception is more important than whose fault the exception is.

Now that you know what exceptions are, I'll use the more familiar term *error* from here on out. Here are a couple of reasons for this decision:

1. I am used to using the word *error*. Although not all exceptions are errors in the strict sense, most exceptions I discuss are errors.

2. Terms such as *unstructured exception handler* sound strange. Microsoft also calls them *error handlers,* and that terminology may be easier for you, as well.

The one area in which I use *exception* — and it's the proper term in this case — is in dealing with the different exception objects in .NET.

Structured versus Unstructured Error Handling

You can handle exception errors in two ways. The first is through a structured error handler and the second through an unstructured error handler. The major difference between the two is that one has structure and the other doesn't.

Now that you have awarded me the "Well, duh" award for most inane statement in a programming book, I will digress and say that the statement is not completely true, as even unstructured error handling has some structure. Actually, the main difference is *where* the error handler is coded. In structured error handling, you surround the place in code where an error can occur with code to handle the error. In unstructured error handling, you either blow past errors or send them to a central location, where you test for return codes other than 0. As promised, the return code has returned.

If this doesn't make much sense, don't worry; it makes more sense when you see it in practice. The best way to understand the difference between the two is to compare them. So, it's off to the races.

Unstructured error handlers

Both Visual Basic and ASP use unstructured error handling. This form of error handling requires that you send all errors to a single point where you attempt to pull them apart to determine what happened. You use the statement On Error Goto Label and you handle the errors there.

This form of error handling is a step above the "ignore everything" approach to handling errors, which, unfortunately, is quite prevalent. Unfortunately, it's just a small step above and requires all sorts of kludgy code to test to see which type of error was thrown.

ERROR HANDLING IN ASP

ASP is at the bottom of the food chain when it comes to error handling. With ASP, the only type of error handling available is ignore and, hopefully, check. I dub this form of error handling "fire and forget," as it is just as easy to never go back and check. In this type of error handler, you ignore any error that occurs by using On Error Resume Next and then either forget it completely or check later to see what error code was returned.

To check the error in ASP, you use the number property of the Err object. Any number other than zero indicates an error. "Wow, Greg," you're thinking, "that sounds a lot like a C++ return code." And it is. To get a bit deeper into the concept, look at the code in Listing 10-1, which shows an ASP error handler.

Listing 10-1: Unstructured Error Handling in ASP (errorHandler.asp)

```
<%
On Error Resume Next

Private m_objConn       'As ADODB.Connection
Private m_objRS         'As ADODB.Recordset
Private m_strConn       'As String
Private m_strSQL        'As String
```

Continued

Listing 10-1 *(Continued)*

```
'This DSN does not exist
m_strConn = "DSN=testDSN;"

Set m_objConn = Server.CreateObject("ADODB.Connection")
'Error thrown here
Call m_objConn.Open(m_strConn)

If Err.number <> 0 then
    'TODO: Create a better error handler here
    Response.Write Err.Description
    Err.clear
End If
%>
```

This type of error handler may seem rather easy because you have the option of "blowing through" seemingly meaningless errors in your page. I do not recommend this practice, of course, although I do see it more often than I am comfortable with.

The downside is that you have to check for errors after each possible error-ridden statement, or you will not be able to track what went wrong. By using On Error Resume Next, each error that occurs nabs the Err object for itself, thus eliminating any record of earlier errors. To test this theory, I wrote a page (Listing 10-2) that includes more than one error. In this example, the second error is a simple typo.

Listing 10-2: More Than One Error in a Single Page (errorHandler2.asp)

```
<%@ Language=VBScript %>
<%
Option Explicit
    Private objConn     'As ADODB.Connection
    Private objRS       'As ADODB.Recordset
    Private strConn     'As String
    Private strSQL      'As String
On Error Resume Next

strConn = "{Connection String here}"
strSQL = "SELECT * FROM Customers"

Set objConn = Server.CreateObject("ADODB.Connection")

'Throws error
Call objConn.Open(strConn)

'Throws a second error (not declared)
intError = 0
```

```
%>
<HTML>
<HEAD>
<META NAME="GENERATOR" Content="Microsoft Visual Studio 6.0">
</HEAD>
<BODY>
<h1>More than one error</h1>
<p>No errors here either, but if there were, it might be:<br>
Error Number: <%=Err.number %> <br>
Error Description: <%=Err.description %><br>
Error Source: <%=Err.Source %>
<p>
</BODY>
</HTML>
```

Officially, the second error (the undeclared variable) is handled. The error you really needed to track, the error opening the database connection, was blown past and no longer exists. Well, that's not completely true — you can track it through the ADO errors collection. But the first error no longer exists inside the Err object. I see too few pages where the developer checked for ADO errors, so losing this error by the resetting of the Err object is a bad thing.

Now, this type of error handling can be improved in quite a few ways. The best option is to place your code with potential exceptions in its own routine. Then, you can catch the error very close to the place where it occurred. Listing 10-3 shows ASP code in which the code has been placed in routines where single types of errors can better be caught. Notice that I've also included Boolean return values for each of the functions here to ensure that any routine dependent on the success of another routine will not be run.

Listing 10-3: Encapsulating Error Handling in Routines (errorHandler3.asp)

```
<%
Option Explicit

Private m_objConn      'As ADODB.Connection
Private m_objRS        'As ADODB.Recordset

Private Function CreateConnection(objConn,strConn) 'As Boolean
  On Error Resume Next

  If not objCOnn is Nothing then
    Set objConn = Server.CreateObject("ADODB.Connection")
  End if
```

Continued

Listing 10-3 *(Continued)*

```
  If Err.number <> 0 then
    Err.clear
    CreateConnection = False
  Else
    CreateConnection = True
  End If
End Function

Private Function CreateRecordset(objConn,objRS,strSQL) 'As Boolean
  On Error Resume Next

  Set objRS = objConn.Execute(strSQL)

  If Err.number <> 0 then
    Err.clear
    CreateConnection = False
  Else
    CreateRecordset = True
  End If
End Function

Private Sub Main()
  Dim blnConnection     'As Boolean
  Dim strConn           'As String
  Dim strSQL            'As String

  strConn = "DSN=MyDSN"

  blnConnection = CreateConnection(m_objConn,strConn)

  If blnConnection = True then
    strSQL = "SELECT * FROM MyTable"
    blnRecordset = CreateRecordset(m_objConn,m_objRS,strSQL)
  End If
End Sub

Call Main()
%>
```

By encapsulating the error in routines, you have a bit more control over your errors, which brings ASP error handling closer to the way it's handled in Visual Basic. Unfortunately, even in routines, this "fire and forget" method of handling errors can be a performance pig. It is also very kludgy.

If you forget to handle all errors in ASP, you are greeted with the default error handler, which presents you with an error like the one shown in Figure 10-1.

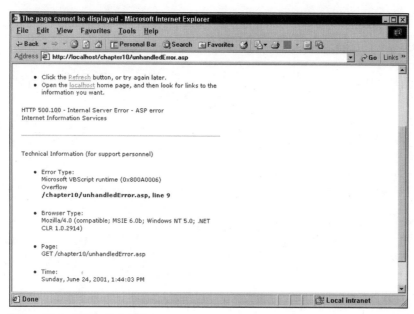

Figure 10-1: Unhandled ASP error.

ERROR HANDLING IN VISUAL BASIC

Error handling in Visual Basic is a slight improvement over error handling in ASP. When I say slight, I mean you are able to use `On Error Goto ErrorHandler` in place of `On Error Resume Next`. This indicates that you can send more than one error to the same error handler without resetting the error handler with `On Error Resume Next`. While this has made many Visual Basic developers scream "Woo Hoo!" over the years, it is really not much of an improvement, as you will see.

Listing 10-4 shows a routine with an error handler in Visual Basic. In this example, I purposefully throw an error.

Listing 10-4: Error Handling in Visual Basic (vberror.exe)

```
Private Sub cmdMakeError_Click()
  On Error GoTo CallErrorRoutine_Err

  CallErrorRoutine = ErrorRoutine(1000, 0)

  Exit Sub
```

Continued

Listing 10-4 *(Continued)*

```
CallErrorRoutine_Err:

  Err.Clear

  MsgBox "error cleared"
End Sub

Private Function ErrorRoutine(ByRef intNumber As Integer, _
            ByRef intDivisor As Integer) _
            As Boolean

  On Error GoTo ErrorRoutine_Err

  Dim intErrorValue As Integer

  intErrorValue = intNumber / intDivisor

  ErrorRoutine = True

  Exit Function
ErrorRoutine_Err:

  'Error number 11 is a divide by zero error
  If Err.Number = 11 Then
    Err.Raise Err.Number, "ErrorRoutine>" & Err.Source, _
            Err.Description
  End If
End Function
```

When intNumber is divided by intDivisor, a divide-by-zero error is thrown. To test for this type of error, you have to know which error number represents a divide-by-zero error. For those who have not memorized all of the numbers of errors thrown by Windows programs, this is number 11. You can then choose to either handle the error, or raise it again to pass it up to the calling procedure. I have chosen to throw the error up the stack.

This is a fairly common method of error handling in Visual Basic. The idea is that errors that can be solved should be corrected in the component, and the others should be passed up the call stack to inform the user. My method of concatenating the current routine to the source creates a complete call stack when the error is presented to the user. In a real-world application, I would use a centralized error handler to log these errors. Since this book is not about Visual Basic 6, I won't take the time to expound any further on this topic.

Error handling in Visual Basic is a fair bit more structured than it is in ASP, but it still requires knowing quite a bit about an error in order to test what type of error was thrown. I like to call this "paint-by-number" error handling. This type of error handling is not bad when the majority of your errors are handled in the same manner. It can be a research nightmare, however, when you have to handle each error a bit differently. This is most noticeable when a number is used to represent different types of errors in different objects, not that Microsoft would ever do that, right?

 You can find out the numbers for most errors in Microsoft products by consulting MSDN, either the CDs that ship with Visual Studio or online at http://msdn.microsoft.com.

Wouldn't it be nice if you could explicitly handle an error as it happens? How about if you could explicitly handle different types of errors easily through explicitly named exception objects? Hang on, Poncho, the train has just left the station.

Structured error handling

ASP.NET uses structured error handling as its methodology. By structured, I mean that ASP.NET has you surround potentially error-prone code to handle errors when they happen rather than send your code down a branch only when errors happen. Unlike fire-and-forget and paint-by-number error handling, you are going to catch an error at the spot where it happens.

The upside of this paradigm is you have to think through your code completely, and are, therefore, more likely to catch all of your errors. At least, this is the way it happens in my strange fantasy world; your results may vary. You may see this as a downside as fire-and-forget and paint-by-numbers error handling is fairly easy to institute without having to think through the code. I want to persuade those of you who are still skeptical that the new way is better.

TRY ... CATCH ... FINALLY

Structured error handling is achieved in ASP.Net with a `Try ... Catch ... Finally` code block. If you break down the keywords, it becomes quite evident what you need to do. You try to run some code; if it throws an error, you catch the error; finally, you run some additional code that occurs regardless of success or failure. This is one of those cases where the keywords do a good job of describing their function. To make sure that this chapter covers more than the blatantly obvious, here are a few rules for `Try ... Catch ... Finally` blocks:

- You place the code that might throw an error inside the `Try` section. Good candidates are calls to other objects. You can only have one `Try` section per each `Try ... Catch ... Finally` block.

- Any code you need in order to clean up problems you encounter in your `Try` section is placed in a `Catch` block. You can have multiple `Catch` blocks to catch specific types of errors. You'll see multiple `Catch` statements in Parts III and IV of this book.

◆ Any code that has to run regardless of the success or failure of the `Try` is placed in the `Finally` section. You can only have one `Finally` section per `Try ... Catch ... Finally` block.

To get a bit of practice with `Try...Catch...Finally`, envision your typical application. Where do most of your errors occur? If you follow the typical pattern, most errors occur when contacting other objects. This is generally due to either a misunderstanding of the interface(s) to the other object, or the object has changed and no one informed you. The second most common area for errors is mathematical computation. In Listing 10-5, I have a couple of structured error-handling blocks to catch these types of errors.

This project is adopted from Chapter 8's DataGrid Page, and can be found in the `chapter10.zip` file on the companion Web site (`www.wiley.com/extras`).

Listing 10-5: Structured Error Handling for Objects and Computation (raiseerror.aspx)

```
Private Sub Page_Load(ByVal sender As System.Object, _
    ByVal e As System.EventArgs) Handles MyBase.Load
  'Call the routine that writes the data grid
  WriteDataGrid()
End Sub

Private Sub WriteDataGrid()
  'Put user code to initialize the page

  Dim strConn As String = _
      "Server=(local);Database=NWind;UID=sa;PWD=0927Tiffy;"
  Dim strSQL As String = "SELECT emp_id AS [Employee ID],  " & _
      "fname+' '+lname AS [Name] FROM employee"

  Try
    '* Create and open Connection
    Dim objConn As New SqlConnection(strConn)
    objConn.Open()

    '* Create a command and use it to fill a data adapter
    Dim objCommand As New _
```

```
      SqlCommand(strSQL, objConn)
  Dim objDataAdapter As New _
      SqlDataAdapter(objCommand)

  '*  Use the adapter to populate the data table
  '*  employee in the data set
  Dim objDataSet As New System.Data.DataSet()
  objDataAdapter.Fill(objDataSet, "employee")

  '*
  '* Bind Data to the Data Grid
  DataGrid1.DataSource = objDataSet.Tables("employee").DefaultView
  DataGrid1.DataBind()
Catch objException As Exception
  'Print error to label control
  Label1.Text = objException.ToString()
End Try

End Sub
```

The error-handling routine in Listing 10-5 is very simple. I have purposefully changed the database from pubs to NWind to throw an error. When an error occurs, the routine sends the error to the user in the label control on the page. The error returned is shown in Figure 10-2.

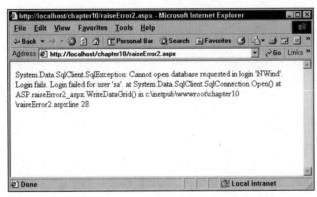

Figure 10-2: The error produced by code in Listing 10-5.

In real life, you would probably want to log this error and send a friendlier message to the user. Listing 10-6 shows changes to the Catch section necessary to add a user-friendly error message.

Listing 10-6: User-Friendly Errors (raiseError2.aspx)

```
Catch objException As Exception
   'TODO: Add ErrorLog() function
   'ErrorLog(objException)
   Label1.Text = "Cannot access data at this time."
```

You might be wondering how granular your error handler should be. For example, should you create a separate structured error-handling block for each call to an outside object? For database access, I would say no, although there are exceptions to this rule. For your own objects, the call is up to you. As a rule of thumb, I would treat everything that can make up a complete transaction in one block, as each transaction has to succeed or fail as a whole. By transaction, I mean a block of code that must fail or succeed as a whole. There are times you might want to take a more granular approach, but this rule of thumb should serve well for most applications.

On the other hand, granularity in catching errors is something you should strive for, especially if certain errors can be handled differently than others. For example, if the first object throws an error, but the second object can still complete its work, then a second Try ... Catch block is in order.

In Visual Basic 6 and traditional ASP, you have to test for errors by error number using either an If or a Select ... Case section. Fortunately, you can test each error differently in ASP.NET by adding additional catch statements. Listing 10-7 again shows the structured error-handler Catch section, only this time it is designed to capture the SQL error generated. The SQL errors should be logged, which is the purpose for the TODO.

Listing 10-7: Catching a Specific Error (raiseError3.aspx)

```
'Catch a SQL error
Catch objException as SQLException
   'TODO: Log the errors
      'Set the label with the specific error
   Label1.Text = "Cannot access the database."

'Catch any general errors
Catch objException as Exception
   Label1.Text = "An unknown error occurred."
```

The .NET help files contain exceptions that can be trapped for many of the Framework base class objects. I have highlighted a few of these exceptions in Table 10-1. You will want to use these in your programs, especially when you have more than one type of exception that can be thrown.

This is a small sampling of the exceptions that can be thrown. I discuss more exceptions in the Part III of this book.

Table 10-1 EXCEPTIONS IN THE .NET FRAMEWORK BASE CLASSES

Exception	Details
IndexOutOfRangeException	Used with arrays when code attempts to access an index of an array outside of the valid range. For example: ```\nDim Array(10) as String\nArray(99) = "My String"\n```
NullReferenceException	Occurs when code attempts to access properties of an object that is set to NULL. To avoid this type of exception, you can also check to see if the object is NULL prior to attempting access.
DivideByZeroException	Occurs when a number is divided by zero. This is a great exception to use against division mathematical operations. Note that floating-point numbers do not throw this exception.
InvalidCastException	Exception thrown when attempting to cast one simple type or object to an incompatible type or object.
OverflowException	This exception occurs when a variable is set outside of its legal range. For example, you place a value of 50,000 in a Short.
WebException	This exception occurs from the WebRequest and WebResponse classes. When this class is used, you will want to pull the status to determine the reason. For example, a ConnectFailure indicates the remote service could not be connected to at the Transport level of the TCP/IP stack.
DLLNotFoundException	This exception occurs when a DLL does not exist in either the application or the Global Access Cache (GAC). This exception has a partner that indicates an assembly entry point cannot be found: EntryPointNotFoundException.

THROW

The throw statement causes an error to be thrown up the call stack. If an error cannot be handled in the object where it's encountered, throwing the error up the call stack to a level where it can be displayed to the user is often the best option. This is similar to using an Err.Raise inside an error handler in COM components. Listing 10-8 shows an example of throwing an error up the stack.

Listing 10-8: Throwing an Error up the Call Stack (throwError.aspx)

```
Private Sub Page_Load(ByVal sender As System.Object, _
            ByVal e As System.EventArgs) Handles MyBase.Load
  Try
    ThrowError()
  Catch objError As System.Exception
    Dim objErrorThrow As New _
        System.Exception("This was caught in Page_Load")
    objErrorThrow.Source = "throwError.aspx.vb.Page_Load()>" & _
                          Err.Source
    Throw objErrorThrow
  End Try

End Sub

Private Sub ThrowError()
  Dim objError As New _
      System.Exception("This error is thrown in ThrowError().")
  objError.Source = "throw.Error.aspx.vb:ThrowError()"
  Throw objError
End Sub
```

When you run this code, you will find that the error handler in Page_Load catches the error thrown from ThrowError(). The throwError.aspx page serves no purpose other than to throw this error.

STRUCTURED ERROR HANDLING IN PRACTICE

As you can see, structured error handling is a shift from what you are used to with traditional ASP and previous versions of Visual Basic. If you have some exposure to C++ or Java, the methodology will certainly seem more familiar. Since I am assuming structured error handling is new to you, I want to mention some places where you should add error handling:

◆ **Instantiating other objects.** When you create an object from a class, you should put the code in an exception-handling block. A good example is instantiating database connection objects that use other resources outside of the scope of your Web server. Even your own objects, or perhaps especially your own objects, are prime spots for exceptions.

◆ **Working with system resources.** When you work with resources that may or may not be running, or even exist, you should make sure you have exception-handling code in place. A good example is using file system objects to manipulate files and folders that may not exist.

◆ **Using mathematical operations.** This is especially true with division and multiplication, which can produce divide-by-zero and overflow errors.

While addition and subtraction are not exempt from this type of exception, errors in these operations are less common.

Now for an example that is a bit more real world (not completely, as you will see, but you will have to live with it). The little application in Listing 10-9 is designed to figure out the percentage of your paycheck that you can put toward your 401K. For simplicity, and to ensure I can throw a divide-by-zero exception, I am only going to use integral types (long integers, to be exact). To make certain an exception can be thrown, I am not going to check whether a salary amount has been entered. If none is entered, a divide-by-zero exception will occur. Don't worry, someone will slap my wrist with a ruler later.

Listing 10-9: A More Realistic Structured Error–Handling Example

```
Public Function Get401kAmount(ByVal lngSalary As Long, _
    ByVal lngPercentageRate As Long) As Double

    Dim lngOutput As Long

    Try
        lngOutput = lngSalary/lngPercentageRate
    Catch objDBZError As System.DivideByZeroException
        'TODO: Log the exception
        lngOutput = 0
    Catch objError as System.Exception

        Dim objExceptionThrown as New _
            System.Exception(objError.Message)

        objExceptionThrown.Source = "MyClass>" &
        Throw objError
    End Try

    Return lngOutput

End Function
```

Why didn't I use floating-point numbers, like a real application? Simple; floating-point numbers do not err, but return NaN (not a number), negative infinity, or positive infinity instead of a divide-by-zero exception. For you trivia buffs, the reason is the IEEE 754 arithmetic, which dictates how floating-point numbers should behave when divided by zero. I also disagree that a real-world application would necessarily need dollars and cents, because rounding to an integral type most likely has enough precision, but that call has to be made on an application-by-application basis.

Note that I still have a catch statement with the generic `System.Exception` object. While absolutely unnecessary at this time, it is there for two reasons. First, it is likely that I will add additional code that could raise a different type of exception here. If the generic code is already in place, I do not have to worry about missing this new exception. Second, it is always good practice to include the generic exception. This is much like always including a `Case Else` in Visual Basic 6 and earlier VB.

In this application, I have chosen to not throw an exception up the call stack when there is a divide-by-zero. Instead, I return 0. Based on a salary of $0, the max contribution would be $0, regardless of the percentage rate. In a real-world application, I would probably throw an exception, but I wanted to show how you might handle one type of exception while throwing another. Since no generic exception should ever be encountered, throwing this exception up the stack made more sense. I also liked the idea of illustrating the Return Code again.

Tracking Errors

Now that you know how to throw exceptions and, more importantly, how to handle the exceptions thrown, you might be wondering how to get more information about the exceptions in your application. Since all I did was throw the current exception up the stack, how can I determine the exact location of the exception?

Tracing

Tracing is the process of determining exactly where an error occurred and what steps can be taken to reproduce the conditions that created the error. This has long been a weak point of the Microsoft programming languages. To be fair, however, it has been a weak point of programming in general, as I cannot think of a language that has had a really good stack trace. To get a better idea of how good having a trace is, another trek into the past is in order.

VISUAL BASIC AND ASP

In legacy code, if you consider .NET to be the only non-legacy code on the market, tracing is about as much fun as going to the dentist and finding out he has to drill. In all fairness, that might be fun for the dentist, but it's you I am talking about here. Legacy code has no built-in method to determine exactly where an exception occurred at each level in the stack in order to figure out how to correct these exceptions.

To solve this problem, the current module and routine is appended to the source property of the `Err` object and passed up the stack, as shown in Listing 10-10. In a true real-world application, I'd use constants for the module and function and add line numbers to determine the exact location of the exception in each object. In instances where exceptions are logged in each object (which is more my norm than my exception), I also generally add the routine parameters to the object to help determine where in the stack the exception actually began.

Listing 10-10: Including the Call Stack in Visual Basic 6.0

```
Public Function ThrowException() As Integer
  On Error Goto ThrowException_Err

      ThrowException = 1/0

  Exit Sub

ThrowException_Err:

  Err.Raise Err.Number, "MyClass.ThrowException>" & _
    Err.Source, Err.Description
End Sub
```

I can repeat this for every function called until I reach the user interface and spit out the errors for human consumption. For those not familiar with the highly technical "spit out" term, I mean "show to the user," which would actually be a bad thing. This technical term rides alongside its buddy "blew up," which describes what happens to an application when an unhandled exception is encountered.

Listing 10-11 contains the code for an ASP page that calls this method and returns an error message to the user. While the formatting is much nicer than the generic exception handler in ASP, this is still not the way I like to handle exceptions, which is to log the exception and show the users something more friendly, such as "The developer is an idiot, so your application does not work right now." After all, that is what the users are thinking, so why not humor them?

Listing 10-11: ASP Page to Display Divide-By-Zero Exception

```
<%
Option Explicit

On Error Resume Next

Dim objException

Set objException = Server.CreateObject("Chapter10.DivideByZero")
Call objException.ThrowException()

If Err.Number <> 0 Then
  Response.Write Err.Number & "<br>"
  Response.Write "----------------------<br>"
  Response.Write Err.Source & "<br>"
  Response.Write "----------------------<br>"
  Response.Write Err.Description
End If
%>
```

Since I am baring my soul a bit here, my personal preference would be to include line numbers in my Visual Basic COM components and use `erl` to add the line numbers to the error message. Yes, I know I am repeating myself here. While I am a firm advocate of keeping functions as short as possible, it is still nice to have a roadmap with an exact pointer to the line number where the exception occurred.

ASP.NET

Virginia Slims used to have an ad on television (boy, am I dating myself now) that stated, "You've come a long way, baby." This sentiment is applicable to tracing in ASP.NET. Tracing errors in the old Visual Basic/ASP days required a lot of code. No more. I have included a screenshot of a trace in ASP.NET in Figure 10-3.

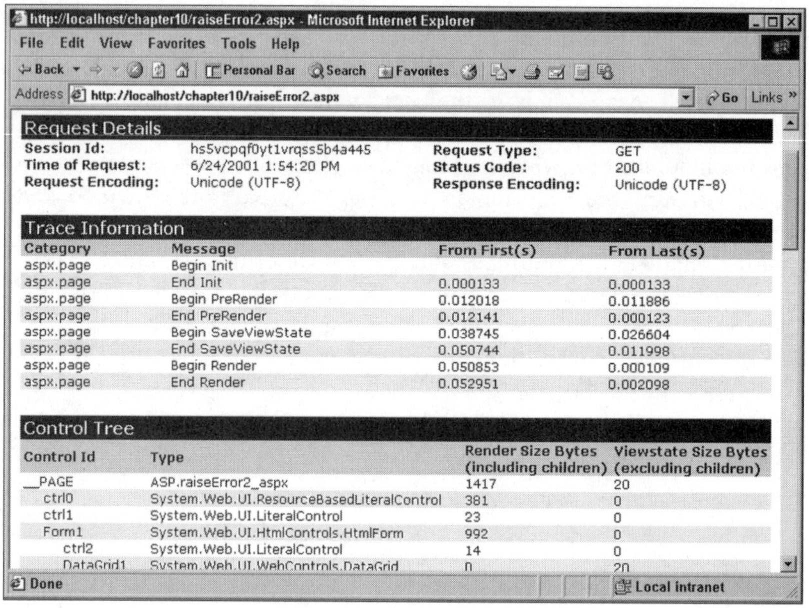

Figure 10-3: Tracing in ASP.NET.

The tracing mechanism in ASP.NET contains information including version information on the CLR and ASP.NET, the stack trace, timing on the trace, cookies, headers, and all server variables.

SETTING UP TRACING IN ASP.NET   So, how do you set up tracing on your ASP.NET application? Nothing could be easier. Listing 10-12 shows how to set up tracing on a single page. While this particular page is a bit too simple, you can set `TraceMode` to either `SortByCategory` or `SortByTime`. The default is `SortByTime`.

Listing 10-12: Setting Tracing for a Specific Page

```
<%@ Page Language="VB" Trace="True" TraceMode="SortByCategory" %>
<%@ Page Language="VB" Trace="True" TraceMode="SortByTime" %>
```

Of course, setting up tracing on every page can get a bit tedious. A better solution might be to set up a trace for every page in one place. Fortunately, this is easy to accomplish. In Listing 10-13, tracing is set for an entire application.

Listing 10-13: Setting Tracing for an Entire Application

```
<configuration>
 <system.web>
  <trace enabled="true" requestLimit="40" pageOutput="true"/>
 </system.web>
</configuration>
```

With one simple addition to web.config, all of your problems are available for the world to examine; the use of pageOutput="true" means the trace appears on the bottom of every page. You can avoid this by setting pageOutput to false and using the trace.axd file to examine the trace in privacy. Set the localOnly property to true to limit where the trace.axd file can be viewed from.

Here are the options you can use when setting up tracing in your application. All of these properties apply to the configuration file. I have noted the properties that apply to page level tracing (Listing 10-12).

- ◆ enabled: Specifies whether or not tracing is enabled in your application. If you plan to trace at an application level, set the other properties and change this one from true to false, as needed. The default is false.

- ◆ requestLimit: Specifies the number of trace requests to store on the server. The default is 10, which should be fine for most applications.

- ◆ pageOutput: Specifies whether the trace is shown at the bottom of the page. The default is false.

- ◆ traceMode: Can be set to either SortByTime or SortByCategory. With most simple exceptions, the output is the same regardless. Beyond this, the decision to choose one or the other is a matter of personal preference. You can set traceMode at page level.

- ◆ localOnly: Specifies whether you can view the trace viewer on the local server only. The default here is true, and that should suit most production environments.

For those of you who are full of questions, here's a little FAQ on tracing in ASP.NET:

What if you want to trace a page that is not throwing exceptions? No problemo! If you turn on tracing for an application, you get a trace for every page.

Can everyone see a trace if `pageOutput` is set to true? Yes, and this is the downside, but don't worry — see the next FAQ. For development, I recommend leaving `pageOutput` set to true, and then in production, change it to false.

Then how can I see a trace without everyone seeing it? When you set up tracing, the traces are stored on the server in cache (up to the `requestLimit`). As mentioned previously, you can go to a page called trace.axd to view traces. This is the reason for the `localOnly` property. When `localOnly` is set to true, you can only view this file on the local Web server. When set to false, it can be viewed anywhere.

I have a couple of recommendations at this point. First, keep tracing disabled except when you need to trace. Second, unless absolutely necessary to view the trace from other machines, keep the `localOnly` property set to true. While the information output in a trace should not expose any information that will help hackers, there is no reason to expose your call stack to anyone outside of your organization. Figure 10-4 shows the `trace.axd` file.

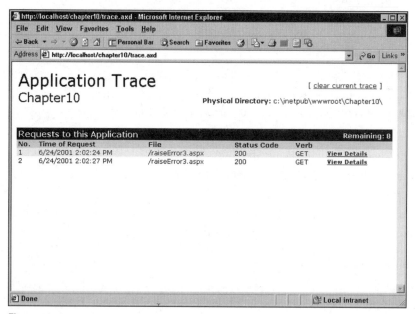

Figure 10-4: `trace.axd`.

You must have site-wide tracing turned on to use the trace.axd file. You cannot trace a single page and expect to find it. You can, of course, turn on tracing and set the page output to off, which is the suggested method of using the trace.axd file. I don't want to sound like a broken record, but I do believe that keeping the nature of your code hidden is paramount to security.

One final suggestion here: If you do not plan to use tracing on your production server, which I would advise, you can disable the trace.axd file altogether, as shown in Listing 10-14. This piece of code, adapted from an article by Microsoft's Rob Howard, can be seen in its entirety on the MSDN .NET site. With the changes instituted in Beta 2, this is most likely unnecessary, but I prefer knowing that my site is safe, even if Microsoft changes its mind on how tracing works.

Listing 10-14: Disabling trace.axd in web.config

```
<httphandlers>
  <configuration>
    <add verb="*" path="trace.axd"
        type="System.Web.Handlers.TraceHandler" />
      <remove verb="*" path="trace.axd"/>
  </configuration>
</httphandlers>
```

REAL LIFE TRACING   The default method of using a trace to track how a page runs is wonderful, but there has to be something more, right? I am so glad you asked.

Remember those little `Response.Write` statements you put in your ASP applications to figure out where an error occurred? If not, then either you were strictly a Visual Basic developer, or I was the only one fool enough to still use `Response.Write` in my applications rather than using the debugger in Visual InterDev 6.0. Those who have ever tried to debug (or even successfully debugged) in InterDev are laughing hysterically at my tongue-in-cheek humor; the rest of you will just have to trust that this is really funny.

Listing 10-15 shows the `Response.Write` method of debugging and tracing code. This was the only method in ASP 1.0 (Visual InterDev 1.0). It is still used in most ASP applications, because setting up debugging is a pain.

Listing 10-15: Using Response.Write to Find Errors (traceWithRW.asp)

```
<%
Option Explicit
Response.Buffer = False
  '... See file for rest
Private Sub Main()
  Call Response.Write("Entering Sub Main()<BR>")

  Dim objConn, objRS, intTraceCounter
  Dim strOut, strConn, strSQL, objField
```

Continued

Listing 10-15 *(Continued)*

```
    strConn = "Provider=SQLOLEDB.1;Server=(local);" & _
            "Database=Northwind;UID=sa;PWD=;"
    strSQL = "SELECT CustomerID, CompanyName, ContactName," & _
            "ContactTitle FROM Customers"

    Call Response.Write("  Connecting to Database<BR>")
    Set objConn = ConnectToDatabase(strConn)
    Call Response.Write("  Setting up Recordset<BR>")
    Set objRS = CreateRecordset(objConn, strSQL)

    strOut = "<table border=1>" & vbCrLf & "  <tr>" & vbCrLf

    Call Response.Write("  Setting up header row<BR>")
    For each objField in objRS.Fields
      strOut = strOut & "    <td>" & objField.Name & _
            "</td>" & vbCrLf
    Next

    strOut = strOut & "</tr>" & vbCrLf

    Do Until objRS.EOF
      strOut = strOut & "<tr>" & vbCrlf

      Call Response.Write(" Writing Row " & intTraceCounter)
      For each objField in objRS.Fields
        strOut = strOut & "    <td>" & objField.Value & _
              "</td>" & vbCrLf
      Next

      objRS.MoveNext
      strOut = strOut & "</tr>" & vbCrLf
      intTraceCounter = intTraceCounter + 1
    Loop

    strOut = strOut & "  </tr>" & vbCrLf
    strout = strOut & "</table>" & vbCrLf

    Response.Write strOut

    Call Response.Write("Exiting Sub Main()<BR>")
End Sub

Call Main()
%>
```

You notice that I have both `Response.Write` and `Call Response.Write` in this code. I use the `Call Response.Write` for tracing statements because it makes it easy to create a search-and-replace on just these `Response.Write` statements. This little technique saves tons of time in tracing errors, but it breaks my structure of using the keyword `Call` before every call to a routine that returns nothing. This applies to calls to subroutines, as well as functions when you are not using the return from the function. As a rule, I suggest retrieving the return value of every function, but I am a realist and realize this does not always work.

The `Response.Write` still exists in ASP.NET, but you can use it for its designed purpose, which is to output to the user rather than as a debugging aid. For debugging, use `Trace.Write()`. The benefit here is that you are not required to comment out `Trace.Write` after you uncover all of your bugs. Listing 10-16 shows the ASP.NET equivalent of `Response.Write` in debugging code.

Listing 10-16: Using Trace.Write to Find Errors

```
Private Sub Page_Load(ByVal sender As System.Object, _
            ByVal e As System.EventArgs) Handles MyBase.Load
  'Put user code to initialize the page here
  Dim strConn As String = "Server=(local);Database=Northwind;" & _
                   "UID=sa;PWD=;"
  Dim strSQL As String = "SELECT CustomerID, CompanyName, " & _
                   "ContactName, ContactTitle FROM Customers"
  Dim intTraceCounter As Integer = 1

  Trace.Write("Creating a Connection Object")
  Dim objConn As New SqlConnection(strConn)
  objConn.Open()

  Trace.Write("Creating Command Object")
  Dim objCommand As New SqlCommand(strSQL, objConn)

  Trace.Write("Creating Data Reader")
  Dim objReader As SqlDataReader
  objReader = objCommand.ExecuteReader()

  CreateHeader()

  While objReader.Read
    Trace.Write("Writing Line " & intTraceCounter)
    Response.Write("<tr><td>" & objReader.GetString(0) & "</td>")
    Response.Write("<td>" & objReader.GetString(1) & "</td>")
    Response.Write("<td>" & objReader.GetString(2) & "</td>")
```

Continued

Listing 10-16 *(Continued)*

```
    Response.Write("<td>" & objReader.GetString(3) & "</td></tr>")

    intTraceCounter = intTraceCounter + 1
  End While

  CreateFooter()
End Sub
```

There are a couple of notable advantages to using `Trace.Write` over using `Response.Write`. First, the `Trace.Write` can be written without the user seeing any of it. Just try that in a production ASP application having minor growing pains! Second, much like the `Debug` statements in Visual Basic, you can leave the `Trace` statements in your code, ready to use at the first hint of trouble.

Using a debugger

Remember my funny joke about debugging in Visual InterDev? Well, it isn't funny anymore. Debugging in Visual Studio.NET is a breeze. Debugging a Web application is as simple as debugging a desktop application in the Visual Basic 6.0. You simply click the Run button (or press the F5 key) and the page you have set as a start page pops up.

You have to ensure the solution is in debug mode (drop-down on the menu bar), but this is the default setting when you first start a new solution.

To get an idea of how easy debugging in Visual Studio.NET is, Table 10-2 shows how to debug an application is Visual InterDev, Visual Basic, and Visual Studio.NET.

TABLE 10-2 DEBUGGING THROUGH THE AGES

Visual InterDev	Visual Basic	Visual Studio.NET
Create new project.	Create new project.	Create new project,
Write code for page. Limited drag and drop for form creation.	Write code for form or class. Drag and drop elements on form.	Write code in `codeBehind` file. Drag and drop on Web Form.
Set Starting Page.	OPTIONAL: Set starting project if part of project group.	Set Starting Page.

Visual InterDev	**Visual Basic**	**Visual Studio.NET**
Click Run on Debug menu.	Click Run on Debug menu.	Click Run on Debug menu.
Program errors due to debugging not being set up for the application.		
Open Internet Services Manager and configure the application to allow server-side debugging.		
Click Run on Debug menu.		
* Debug errors out again. Find reason at support.microsoft.com.		
* Bind another IP address to the Network Interface Card (NIC).		
* Set up application to new IP address.		
* Click Run on Debug menu.		

It should be noted that the items with an asterisk are only supposed to occur when you are working with a remote server. You should avoid debugging ASP on a remote box whenever possible, so these steps shouldn't be necessary. Of course, I said, "only supposed to occur on a remote server," because I have seen these steps taken to solve errors on a local server. Isn't debugging traditional ASP a lot of fun? For those who have never tried this, you are beginning to get the joke I mentioned earlier.

The .NET Framework also ships with a debugger of its own, the CLR Debugger. Assuming a default install of Visual Studio .NET, you'll find the program DbgCLR.exe in the C:\Program Files\Microsoft Visual Studio.NET\FrameworkSDK\ GuiDebug folder. Figure 10-5 shows a screenshot of the debugger. To use the CLR debugger, choose a .NET executable to debug (Debug → *program to debug*) and then open the source files for the program.

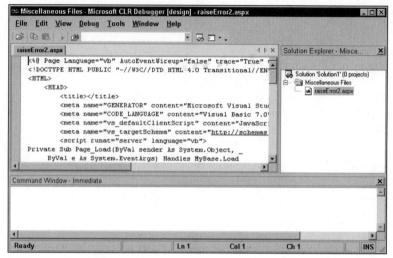

Figure 10-5: The CLR Debugger.

Summary

Finding problems in an application is an important aspect of all development efforts. In this chapter, I covered the methods of handling exceptions in .NET, including structured exception handling and how to throw exceptions up the call stack. I also covered how to trace exceptions that occur, as well as how to use tracing regardless of whether exceptions have occurred (to get timing of your page, for example). Finally, I briefly discussed using a debugger in .NET.

In Chapter 11 we'll take a look at application settings in ASP.NET.

Chapter 11

Sessions and Applications

IN THIS CHAPTER

- ◆ Application settings in ASP with global.asa
- ◆ Application settings in ASP.NET with global.asax
- ◆ Using the global.asax.vb CodeBehind file

APPLICATION SETTINGS IN ASP.NET are created either through events in a global.asax file or through application settings in a web.config file. In this chapter, I take you through the first of these files, the `global.asax` file. Those of you with ASP experience will feel at home with the basics of the file.

As I go through this chapter, remember that many of the practices here go against the grain in .NET. With application settings, overall, you want to move as much as possible into the configuration files, which are discussed in Chapter 12. I include some of the material in this chapter to help those who have to migrate, rather than rebuild, their ASP applications. Before you apply a lot of the material in this chapter, I advise seeing which settings you can set in the `web.config` file, because using that file is the preferred method.

Application Settings

When you design an application, especially an object-oriented application, the primary goal is to design in such a way that you do not repeat the same code over and over again. Rather than code a connection routine in each object, you want to create a connection object that can be used over and over again. This is not the best analogy for your software, because the connection object is already handled for you in ADO.NET, but it does illustrate reusability of software.

In the same manner, there are certain settings that apply for every page, or at least the majority of pages, in an application. It does not make sense to store these application settings in every page of the application. It's far more efficient (and logical) to store these settings in a central location.

Since the times of traditional ASP, Microsoft has decided that all common settings go in a central file called `global.asa`. With ASP.NET, the file has an x added to the end of the extension so that ASP and ASP.NET can continue to run side by side. The reasoning behind the separation of files is easy to understand if you just imagine the problems you'd have if both ASP code, written in VBScript, and ASP.NET code, written in Visual Basic .NET, were co-mingled in the same file with the same event name.

Since both ASP and ASP.NET have their roots in Visual Basic, the primary paradigm is event-driven programming. Unfortunately, most traditional ASP developers only see the event-driven paradigm in their application and session settings (the `Applicaton_Start`, `Application_End`, `Session_Start`, and `Session_End` events). If you only code ASP now, this chapter will expand your awareness.

Application settings in traditional ASP

Before I get started on traditional ASP, I want to warn you that I'm not going into a great amount of detail because this is not a book about ASP. I present just enough information to set up how things are done in ASP.NET and show you how things have changed.

In traditional ASP, application settings are stored in a file called global.asa. The primary use of the global.asa file is to put common application settings in a central location, so you do not have to hunt down application settings in every file. As such, it is an easily accessible place for connection strings, application names, and other global settings. Listing 11-1 shows application and session start events for an Intranet application. Please note that this code is only illustrative; there are security and scalability concerns with using a `global.asa` file in this manner.

Listing 11-1: A global.asa File

```
<script language="VBScript" runat="Server">
Sub Application_Start

  Application.Item("gabConnectionString") = _
     "Provider=SQLOLEDB.1;Server=(local);Database=dbLogon;UID=sa;PWD=;"

  Application.Item("Name") = "gabWeb"
  Application.Item("timeOut") = 600

End Sub

Sub Session_Start

  Dim objConn, objRS, strSQL, strAryLogon

  strAryLogon = Split(Request.ServerVariables("LOGON_USER"),"\")

  strSQL = "SELECT intUserID, strFirstName, strLastName " & _
           "FROM tblUser WHERE " & _
           "strNTUser='" & strAryLogon(1) & "'"
```

```
   Set objConn = Server.CreateObject("ADODB.Connection")
   Call objConn.Open(Application.Item("gabConnectionString"))

   Set objRS = objConn.Execute(strSQL)

   If not objRS.EOF then
     Session("intUserID") = objRS(0)
   End If

   Set objRS = Nothing
   Set objConn = Nothing
End Sub
</script>
```

There are only a couple of things you need to notice at this time.

- ◆ All of the code in the `global.asa` file is contained within `script` tags, which have `language` and `runat` attributes. The only change here moving forward is the choice of languages. (To compare, see Listing 11-3.)

- ◆ Each event handled takes the format of `FriendlyName_Event`. The major change here is going to be the addition of many new events.

EVENTS IN ASP

The event model in traditional ASP is very flat. The primary purpose of the files is to start and end applications and sessions. The events you commonly code for in traditional ASP are show in Table 11-1.

TABLE 11-1 APPLICATION AND SESSION SETTINGS

Event	Description
Application_Start	Create settings that are necessary for an application. Place settings here that are common to all users. Application settings apply to every user that visits your site; if you allow a user to change these settings, the changes apply to everyone across sessions, until the application is reset.
Application_End	Clean up any application settings, or use this event to save state when an application fails.

Continued

TABLE 11-1 APPLICATION AND SESSION SETTINGS *(Continued)*

Event	Description
Session_Start	Create settings that are necessary for an individual session in an ASP application. These settings are unique to an individual and are not shared. Session settings apply only to the single user session; if you allow a user to change these settings, the changes apply to that user, for that session, only.
Session_End	Clean up any session application settings.

OBJECTS IN ASP

In addition, you can also add objects to your application by including them to the global.asa. These objects hold the level of scope that you assign to them. Listing 11-2 shows an object tag with session scope.

Listing 11-2: Object with Session Scope in ASP

```
<OBJECT RUNAT="Server" SCOPE="Session" ID="Logon"
PROGID="gabWeb.Logon"><OBJECT>
```

Unfortunately, storing most custom COM objects in Application or Session is a very bad idea with ASP. There are some exceptions for C++ COM components created with a ThreadingModel of either both (pre-Windows 2000) or neutral (Windows 2000). If you program in Visual Basic, understand that putting your objects in Application or Session in ASP is a bad thing. Enough said!

Settings in ASP.NET

Your settings in ASP are stored in a global.asa file; in ASP.NET, they're stored in a global.asax file. There are a couple reasons for this. The first, and most important to the framework, is that ASP is unmanaged and ASP.NET is managed. The code in ASP.NET always runs in the CLR, while ASP code does not. The second, and most important to you, the developer, is that the separation allows you to develop new pages in ASP.NET and have them run in the same Web site as your old ASP pages.

While running ASP and ASP.NET pages might not instantly stand out as a major advantage, take a moment to picture an enterprise Web site. It is likely that some sections can benefit from ASP.NET and some wouldn't gain as much with the switch. Running ASP and ASP.NET side-by-side enables you to roll out the new pages that can take advantage of ASP.NET without having to recode the entire site first.

Of course, this is not the only change. In ASP, you are pretty much limited to four events (as detailed in Table 11-1). In ASP.NET, you still have these four events, but you can also handle any events raised by any object that implements

IHTTPModule. The Application and Session objects each implement this interface, allowing you to code the Start and End event of each. Listing 11-3 is an ASP.NET version of the global.asa file in Listing 11-1. Once again, the purpose here is only illustrative, because the preferred method is to code the connection in the web.config file. For an example of a connection string in web.config, examine Listing 12-2 in Chapter 12.

To compare setting a connection string in the global.asax file and in the web.config file, take a look at Listing 11-3 (in this chapter) and Listing 12-2 (in Chapter 12).

Listing 11-3: The global.asax File

```vb
<script language="VB" runat="server">
Sub Application_Start()
  Application.Item("ConnectionString") = _
      "Server=(local);Database=dbLogon;UID=sa;PWD=;"
  Application.Item("Name") = "gabWeb"
  Application.Item("timeOut") = 600
End Sub

Sub Session_Start()
  Dim strAryLogon(1) As String
  strAryLogon = Split(Request.ServerVariables("LOGON_USER"), "\")

  Dim strSQL As String = "SELECT intUserID, strFirstName, strLastName " & _
      "FROM tblUser WHERE strNTUser='" & strAryLogon(1) & "'"
  Dim objConn As New _
      System.Data.SqlClient.SqlConnection(Application.Item("ConnectionString"))
  objConn.Open()
  Dim objCommand As New System.Data.SqlClient.SqlCommand(strSQL, objConn)
  Dim objDataReader As System.Data.SqlClient.SqlDataReader

  objDataReader = objCommand.ExecuteReader(CommandBehavior.SingleRow)

  While objDataReader.Read()
    Session("intUserID") = objDataReader.GetInt32(0)
  End While

  objDataReader.Close()
  objConn.Close()
End Sub
</script>
```

The `Application_Start` event in the `global.asax` is pretty much the same as the way I coded the same event in the `global.asa` (Listing 11-1). If you use Access as your database, there are no changes at all, because the connection string has a provider. If you code for SQL Server, you will drop the `Provider=` portion of the connection string, because ADO.NET has a SQL Server namespace. The SQL Server namespace, or SQL Server .NET native provider, is covered in more detail in Part III of the book.

The `Session_Start` event is similar, although there are quite a few differences due to the disparity between VBScript and Visual Basic and between ADO and ADO.NET, which I discuss in Part III.

As you look at the `global.asax` file in Listing 11-3, remember that this is not the preferred method of setting up your `global.asax` file in the Visual Studio .NET IDE. Using the CodeBehind file is preferred, and I cover CodeBehind for the `global.asax` file shortly.

CODING GLOBAL.ASAX

The next three sections deal with coding the `global.asax` file as a tag-based file. Although CodeBehind (which I discuss later in the chapter) is the preferred paradigm in .NET, the tag-based example is included for easier transition for traditional ASP programmers. You cannot edit the global.asax file directly if you are using Visual Studio .NET, because the IDE forces you to code in the CodeBehind file.

I personally like the CodeBehind paradigm because it is a bit more akin to Visual Basic development model. If you are more familiar with tag-based languages such as HTML and ASP, you may feel more at home using the syntax found in the next three sections.

OBJECTS   When you set up an object tag in ASP.NET, the code looks similar to an object tag in ASP with a few additional attributes. Listing 11-4 shows a `global.asax` object tag.

Listing 11-4: Object Tag in global.asax

```
<object id="objConn" class="System.Data.SQLClient.SQLConnection"
scope="application" runat="server"/>
```

APPLICATION DIRECTIVES   With ASP.NET, you have the ability to add name-spaces to your global.asax file. Whether you use the `Import` tag in an ASPX file or in your `global.asax` file, it serves the same purpose: it allows you to import name-spaces so you do not have to type out the entire namespace to access these items.

As you'll see later in the "CodeBehind" section, you can also use the `Import` statement to import a namespace. Listing 11-5 shows a namespace `Import` tag in the `global.asax` file.

Remember, importing namespaces is not the same as adding references. If you import a namespace without adding a reference to the library (DLL) for the compiler, you will not be able to compile your application.

If you are an ASP developer, you may think that this warning does not apply to you; after all, in ASP you add a tag and the reference is taken care of. But everything you code in .NET is compiled; this includes ASP.NET.

Listing 11-5: Adding Namespaces

```
<%@ Import namespace="System.Data" %>
```

Adding a namespace creates a shortcut so that you no longer have to include the namespace in the name of the object. Once the System.Data namespace is imported, you can use the following line (in Listing 11-5) without putting the namespace System.Data in front of the declaration:

```
Dim objDataSet as DataSet() 'System.Data.DataSet()
```

If you want to use assemblies that aren't located in the bin directory of your application, you have to create a reference to the assembly. To do this, create an application directive using the keyword Assembly. The syntax is shown in Listing 11-6.

Listing 11-6: Adding Assemblies

```
<@ Assembly name="gabWeb" %>
<@ Assembly src="gabWeb.vb" %>
```

So, why do I have two tags here? The first tag contains the name of the assembly and is the only tag necessary to use the assembly. The second tag contains the source, using the keyword src. Using this attribute, I can dynamically compile the assembly with any changes I make. You must create two tags to dynamically compile an assembly by name.

If you have an application that inherits from another application, you use an Application tag, as shown in Listing 11-7. An optional description tells from which class the application will inherit. Once again, this is done fairly easily in the CodeBehind file, which is the preferred method to develop new applications.

Listing 11-7: Application Attributes

```
<%@ Application Inherits="gabWeb.App1" Description="Parent App" %>
```

SERVER-SIDE INCLUDES   Another new feature in the global.asax file, as compared to global.asa in ASP, is the ability to add server-side includes. I find it hard to get really excited over this, as I like the separation of code and tags, or user interface and code. On the other hand, I can acquiesce a bit here, because the idea of server-side includes is really nice if you are coding strictly from an ASP background.

As the `global.asax` file is the top of the food chain, separating code out probably has limited value, but just in case you find reuse of code between `global.asax` and one of your pages, the syntax is shown in Listing 11-8. I can only see you using server-side includes in `global.asax` if you have multiple applications with the same settings and want to use only one file.

Listing 11-8: Server-Side Includes

```
<!-- #include File="includes/common.inc" -->
<!-- #include Virtual="/gabWeb/includes/Logon.inc" -->
```

If you have never worked with server-side includes before, the `File` attribute points to a relative path, and the `Virtual` attribute points to a position off the root of the site. Using `Virtual` is a better option if you intend to copy a server-side include to multiple pages because the `File` include can change depending on how far your current page is from the root directory of the site. For those of you who have worked with either HTML or ASP in the past, the syntax here is identical to HTML standards.

CODEBEHIND

Now I'm going to turn a lot of what I have written here on its head. As with any other ASP.NET page, you can put the code from the `global.asax` page in a CodeBehind file For ASPX pages; the main reason is separation of code and user interface. This is not the case with `global.asax`, because there's no user interface. Therefore, the primary reason for moving to CodeBehind for the `global.asax` file is consistency.

If you have a copy of Visual Studio .NET, go ahead and take a look at the `global.asax` file. It opens to the designer, as shown in Figure 11-1. The view is the same you see if you open an ASMX (XML Web service page) because a Web service also has no user interface.

 XML Web services are covered in great detail in Chapter 14.

If you switch to Code view, you open the `global.asax.vb` file (the CodeBehind file), not the `global.asax` file. In fact, you cannot open the `global.asax` file in Code view in the IDE. You can drag items onto the designer, but the code shows up in the CodeBehind file, `global.asax.vb`, not the `global.asax` file. Listing 11-9 shows a `global.asax` file.

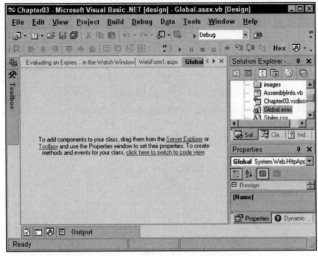

Figure 11-1: The global.asax file in Visual Studio .NET

 If you want to edit the `global.asax` file, as shown in the previous examples in this chapter, you have to use an ASCII text editor, like Notepad.

Listing 11-9: The global.asax File

```
<%@ Application CodeBehind="Global.asax.vb"
              Inherits="Chapter11.Global" %>
```

This line looks very similar to the @ directive in an ASPX page. Isn't object-oriented programming great? The downside is the same as for your ASPX pages: You have to either include a source attribute (`src`) or compile the `global.asax` file prior to use. Listing 11-10 shows a `global.asax.vb` CodeBehind file. This particular example was created in Visual Studio .NET.

Listing 11-10: The global.asax CodeBehind File (global.asax.vb)

```
Imports System.Web
Imports System.Web.SessionState

Public Class Global
    Inherits System.Web.HttpApplication
```

Continued

Listing 11-10 *(Continued)*

```
Public Sub New()
    MyBase.New()
    InitializeComponent()
End Sub

Private components As System.ComponentModel.IContainer

<System.Diagnostics.DebuggerStepThrough()> Private Sub
                InitializeComponent()
    components = New System.ComponentModel.Container()
End Sub


Sub Application_Start(ByVal sender As Object,
                ByVal e As EventArgs)
    ' Fires when the application is started
End Sub

Sub Session_Start(ByVal sender As Object,
            ByVal e As EventArgs)
    ' Fires when the session is started
End Sub

Sub Application_BeginRequest(ByVal sender As Object,
                    ByVal e As EventArgs)
    ' Fires at the beginning of each request
End Sub

Sub Application_AuthenticateRequest(ByVal sender As Object,
                        ByVal e As EventArgs)
    ' Fires upon attempting to authenticate the use
End Sub

Sub Application_Error(ByVal sender As Object,
                ByVal e As EventArgs)
    ' Fires when an error occurs
End Sub

Sub Session_End(ByVal sender As Object,
            ByVal e As EventArgs)
    ' Fires when the session ends
End Sub

Sub Application_End(ByVal sender As Object,
```

```
                         ByVal e As EventArgs)
       ' Fires when the application ends
    End Sub

End Class
```

> **TIP** If you would like to view the default events for the `global.asax.vb` file, create a new Web project in Visual Studio .NET. While using Visual Studio .NET to code your ASP.NET applications isn't mandatory, it does make things a lot easier, and it can be a great teacher if you are willing to poke around in the code that it creates for you.

Notice that the `global.asax.vb` file contains a constructor, the `Sub New()` routine. If you are rusty on constructors, revisit Chapter 2 for a refresher. The only thing currently in the routine is the default setup supplied by the Visual Studio .NET IDE. This changes in the next section.

SETTING UP OBJECTS IN GLOBAL.ASAX I've mentioned several times in this chapter that you shouldn't create your objects using tags in the actual `global.asax` file. Now I show you the better way to set up those objects. In this exercise, you use a combination of ASP and Visual Basic syntax.

If you remember, I told you that setting up objects in `Session` and `Application` was a bad thing. While this is certainly true for most, if not all, ASP applications; we are dealing with a whole new ballgame in .NET. As such, you can relax this rule a bit in ASP.NET, because the consequences are not nearly as dire.

Let's say you have a company that is an application service provider (ASP, part two). For security, you have every company's data segregated from other companies', but each has the same structure.

With this fictional application, a user can log in from your home page or from his application root. As before, I use the dbLogon database to check the user, but I then connect the user to his home database. The code for the `global.asax.vb` file is shown in Listing 11-11.

Listing 11-11: Working with the dbLogon Connection in the IntializeComponent Routine

```
Imports SQL = System.Data.SQLClient

...


Sub Application_Start(ByVal sender As Object, ByVal e As EventArgs)
    Application.Item("ConnectionString") = _
        "Server=(local);Database=dbLogon;UID=sa;PWD=0927Tiffy;"
```

Continued

Listing 11-11 *(Continued)*

```
        Application.Item("Name") = "gabWeb"
        Application.Item("timeOut") = 600


End Sub

Sub Session_Start(ByVal sender As Object, ByVal e As EventArgs)
    Dim strAryLogon(1) As String
    strAryLogon = Split(Request.ServerVariables("LOGON_USER"), "\")

    Dim strConn As String
    Dim strUser As String

    'error if anonymous access on
    Try
        strUser = strAryLogon(1)
    Catch
        Throw New Exception("You need to turn off anonymous access.")
    End Try

    'SQL statement to Pull database to log onto
    Dim strSQL As String = "SELECT u.intUserID, u.strFirstName, " & _
            "u.strLastName, c.strCompanyName, " & _
            "c.strServer, c.strDatabase, c.strUID, " & _
            "c.strPWD FROM tblUser u " & _
            "JOIN tblCompany c ON u.intCompanyID = c.intCompanyID " & _
            "WHERE u.strNTUser='" & strUser & " '"

    Dim objConn As New _
        SQL.SqlConnection(Application.Item("ConnectionString"))
    Dim objCmd As New SQL.SqlCommand(strSQL, objConn)
    Dim objDataReader As SQL.SqlDataReader

    objConn.Open()
    objDataReader = objCmd.ExecuteReader(CommandBehavior.SingleRow)
    objConn.Close()

    'Set up the Connection String
    While objDataReader.Read()
        Session("intUserID") = objDataReader.GetInt32(0)
        strConn = "Server=" & objDataReader.GetString(4) & _
                    ";Database=" & objDataReader.GetString(5) & _
                    ";UID=" & objDataReader.GetString(6) & _
                    ";PWD=" & objDataReader.GetString(7) & ";"
    End While
```

```
objDataReader.Close()

'Add a connection object to the application
Dim objLogonConn As New System.Data.SqlClient.SqlConnection(strConn)
Application.Add("objLogonConn", objLogonConn)

End Sub
```

 The code for the example in Listing 11-11 can be found on this book's companion Web site (www.wiley.com/extras) in the file ch11sdk.zip (SDK version) or ch11vs.zip (Visual Studio .NET version). Examine the global.asax.vb file.

If you download the code and take a look at it, you find that the connection string built aims toward the Northwind database if you are logged on as Administrator. If you don't log on as Administrator, you have to add an entry for your logon.

USING OBJECTS FROM THE GLOBAL.ASAX   In the last section, I set up some objects in the global.asax.vb file (Listing 11-11). To use these objects in your ASP.NET application, you apply the same methodology as your traditional ASP application.

When you add an object to the Application collection, you can access it using Application.Item("VariableName"). Using the Connection object in the hypothetical ASP application, I extract the Employee table from the Northwind database. Listing 11-12 shows you how to use the Connection object I set up in Listing 11-11.

Listing 11-12: Using the Connection Object from global.asax in an ASPX Page

```
Imports SQL = System.Data.SqlClient
...
Private Sub Page_Load(ByVal sender As System.Object,_
                      ByVal e As System.EventArgs) _
                      Handles MyBase.Load
    'Put user code to initialize the page here
    Dim objLogonConn As SQL.SqlConnection
    objLogonConn = Application.Item("objLogonConn")
    objLogonConn.Open()

    Dim strSQL As String = "SELECT LastName, FirstName FROM Employees"
```

Continued

Listing 11-12 *(Continued)*

```
    Dim objCommand As New SQL.SqlCommand(strSQL, objLogonConn)
    Dim objDataReader As SQL.SqlDataReader

    objDataReader = objCommand.ExecuteReader()

    DataGrid1.DataSource = objDataReader
    DataGrid1.DataBind()
End Sub
```

 The code for Listing 11-12 can be downloaded from the companion site (www.wiley.com/extras) in the file Ch11VS.zip (Visual Studio .NET version) or Ch11SDK.zip (SDK version). The files to look at are default.aspx and its CodeBehind page default.aspx.vb.

The page that results from running the ASPX page from Listing 11-12 is shown in Figure 11-2.

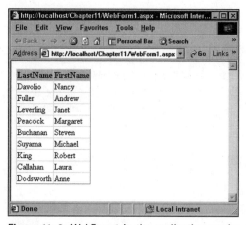

Figure 11-2: WebForm1 in the application service provider application.

Of course, setting objects is not the only thing you can accomplish with your global.asax file. Using CodeBehind, you can accomplish any task that you can envision in code. Overall, this gets beyond the scope of this book, but you're free to think about the opportunities available if you use this feature.

EVENTS IN THE GLOBAL.ASAX FILE   Earlier in the chapter, I covered the four events in the global.asa file in ASP: Application_Start, Application_End,

`Session_Start`, and `Session_End`. These events are still present in ASP.NET, although the syntax has changed slightly. In addition, the following events can be found in ASP.NET:

- ◆ `Application_BeginRequest`: This event fires at the beginning of every request to an application. This might be useful should you need to programmatically redirect a request if certain conditions apply.

- ◆ `Application_AuthenticateRequest`: This event fires when a secure application attempts to authenticate a user. One use could be a programmatic authentication routine. Because there are easier ways to handle authentication (see Chapter 13), I don't recommend this as a first choice.

- ◆ `Application_Error`: This event fires whenever an error occurs in an application. Since structured error handling gives you the ability to handle errors at the source (see Chapter 10), the primary use I can see for this event is adding an error log to every error without coding one in every `Try ... Catch ... Finally` block.

Note that you have the ability to code these events in either the `global.asax` file or its CodeBehind file (`global.asax.vb`).

Summary

In this chapter you learned to use the global.asax file and, more importantly, the CodeBehind file, `global.asax.vb`. You will use these files to work with Application and Session events in your application. In conjunction with the web.config file discussed in the next chapter, you will have all of the tools you need to set up your application.

In the next chapter, I discuss the configuration files in ASP.NET, especially the `web.config` file, which you use to set up your Web applications. The `web.config` file is coding using XML, and that makes it a much easier place to set application settings than the `global.asax` file.

Chapter 12

Configuring Web Applications

IN THIS CHAPTER

◆ A look at the web.config file

◆ A tag-by-tag run-through of the sections of the web.config file

CONFIGURATION FILES ENABLE YOU to set up the different aspects of your application in one convenient file. In this chapter, you learn the specifics of how to set up your Web application with configuration files. For the purposes of ASP.NET, you will set up configuration files at the Web site and subdirectory level through a file called `web.config`.

Using the web.config File

You may expect this to be the most boring chapter in this book. After all, configuring a Web site is not something that a developer does. It is something best left to an administrator, right?

That fits right in with the thinking of many IT professionals in the United States, where there is a definite rift between engineers and developers. On the other hand, how many frustrated developers have had to beg to get a Web setting changed because they never had the keys to the kingdom of IIS? Let's face it; an administrator's pessimistic security is a good thing until it's your deadline that's at stake.

If you are familiar with IIS, you will notice that many of the settings previously set in IIS can now be set with a simple XML file. This gives a lot of freedom to the developer (or admin), and perhaps a lot of extra responsibility.

There are a couple of really nice, positive consequences to moving these settings into a file. First, it is far easier to straighten out a human-readable file than a metabase, which is the configuration storage method for IIS 4 and 5. Second, Web changes can be done with a simple text editor, allowing easy access to all aspects of a Web site without jumping from screen to screen (or tab to tab). The negative consequences come from the fact that it's easier to mess up an XML file than it is to mess up a metabase, at least in theory, although the XML file can be fixed more easily, too.

353

From personal experience, I can tell you that you cannot copy the metabase from one server to another. No, I didn't do it, but I did not stop someone else from trying it, either, because I was curious. A co-worker thought it would be easier to copy the metabase from one server to another than it would be to set the settings in the other server. It didn't work.

You can, however, copy the web.config configuration file from server to server. If you like complicated setups, you can experiment on the development server and then move the changes to the production server without having to redo all of your work. This is what I call progress.

If you have set up a Web project in Visual Studio.NET, you can look at the default web.config file. It gives you a decent start on your configuration efforts. The basic skeleton of this file is shown in Listing 12-1.

Listing 12-1: Framework for web.config

```
<?xml version="1.0" encoding="utf-8" ?>
<configuration>
  <system.web>
    <!-- Other sections go here -->
  </system.web>
</configuration>
```

In this chapter, I am going to highlight the many tags you can place in a web.config file. Each of these tags adds a section of XML that sets different aspects of your application. From here on out, I call these tag snippets sections of the web.config file because that term fits best.

appSettings

The appSettings section is responsible for any customization you might need for your application to run. In the MSDN library, the example shows a key called "Application Name." This particular key sets the name of your application, so you can pull it up on any page that you want. The method of pulling the application setting and placing it in a variable is shown in Listing 12-2.

You can set application settings at a variety of levels, including the machine, site, application, and subdirectory levels. The level closest to the page overrides higher levels, giving you the capability to set different values for each subdirectory, application, or site. The basic purpose of the appSettings section is to add strings for your application. Listing 12-2 shows an application setting for a SQL connection, along with a bit of ASP.NET code to use this setting in your application.

Listing 12-2: Setting Up Your Application

```
<appSettings>
  <add key="SQLConn"
   value="server=(local);database=Northwind;UID=sa;PWD=;" />
</appSettings>
```

```
'Pull the application setting for the connection string
Dim strConn As String = ConfigurationSettings.AppSettings("SQLConn")
```

authentication

The authentication section is used to set up your authentication scheme. Authentication is use to check that a user is who he says he is, based on a set of credentials. It is not used to determine whether or not a user has rights to access items. That is authorization, which is covered next. I cover security in greater detail in the Chapter 13.

Briefly, there are three modes of authentication: forms, windows, and passport. Of these, forms authentication probably is the most used in ASP.NET applications, so I highlight it in Listing 12-3.

Listing 12-3: Forms Authentication Setup

```
<authentication mode="Forms">
  <forms name="MyCookie" loginUrl="/login.aspx"
    protection="All" timeout="10" path="/" />
  <credentials passwordFormat="Clear">
    <user name="gbeamer" password="MyPassword" />
  </credentials>
</authentication>
```

Fairly simple, yes? Since the configuration file is written in XML, the only challenge is learning the tags and their attributes. Here's is a breakdown of the tags in the authentication section:

◆ authentication: This tag is primarily concerned with the mode of authentication. As mentioned, the modes are forms, windows, and passport. Forms authentication directs an unauthenticated user to a form; after authentication, a cookie is placed on the user's machine to authenticate the user when he attempts to access other pages. Windows authentication uses IIS, in conjunction with Windows. Passport authentication uses the Microsoft Passport, a centralized, single sign-on method shared by a variety of vendors. You can also set the authentication mode to none, which means no authentication takes place.

◆ forms: The forms tag includes several attributes:

The name attribute is used to set the name of the cookie, so you can access it in code.

The loginUrl attribute sets the login URL; yes, this one is blatantly obvious.

The `protection` attribute can be set to `Encryption`, which is triple DES or DES); `Validation`, which adds a validation key to ensure that the cookie has not been altered; `All`, which does both; or `None`.

`Path`, which is best left at the default setting, specifies where the cookie is stored.

`Timeout` specifies the number of minutes the cookie lives after the last page access. The default for timeout is 30 minutes, which may be too long for a secure site.

◆ `credentials`: This tag (and its subtag `user`) is only used if you want to store authentication credentials in the config file. From a security standpoint, I can only see this as useful in a subdirectory to which few people have access. (This may change as Microsoft straightens out some of its security snafus.) You can choose to store unencrypted passwords in this file, as I have, or choose either a MD5 or an SHA1 hash, which encrypts the password string. If you find the need to store authentication credentials in this manner, I recommend encryption for an extra measure of safety.

◆ `user`: This tag stores the name and password of users for this site, section, or application. If you have chosen encryption, you have to place the encrypted string here instead of the cleartext password.

authorization

Authorization is the next step after authentication (by next step, I am not talking about the order of the tags, but the order for security). You must know who someone is before you give him access. Once you know who a user is, you need to check whether he has access, or authorize use. Authorization is also covered in Chapter 13. Listing 12-4 shows authorization set up for a subdirectory.

Listing 12-4: Allowing and Denying Users

```
<authorization>
    <allow roles="Admins" verbs="GET,POST" />
    <deny users="gbeamer" verbs="HEAD,DEBUG" />
</authorization>
```

In this example, I allow all administrators, but deny myself. As with NT permissions, the `deny` overrides the fact that I am an admin, and I am not allowed to use this subdirectory from the Web. Those administrators who can access the subdirectory can only `GET` or `POST`. The one exception is the wildcard (*), which will lose over more specific assignments. For example, if I had denied all users with `user="*"` and allowed `roles="Admin"`, a more realistic scenario, I would deny everyone except administrators.

The authorization section is useful in setting up department groups and allowing them access to their subdirectory through a Web interface. Of course, you would want to check if the user was in this role before even tempting him with a link.

browserCaps

If you have never used ASP, you probably aren't familiar with the `browserCaps` (browser capabilities) file. This file, from ASP 2.0 and later, contained a listing of all of the browsers that could hit your site, allowing you to tailor a site to a specific browser while still being able to set up pages for other, less fortunate browsers.

Microsoft has long since dropped support for the `browserCaps` file. For a while CyScape picked up browserCaps support but eventually dropped it because of its own product, BrowserHawk. Hopefully, browser capabilities are kept up to date in the .NET Framework. Listing 12-5 shows a sample of the browser capabilities for an imaginary browser called MyBrowser, which can render frames and tables, but little else.

Listing 12-5: Browser Capabilities

```
<browserCaps>
    <result type="class" />
    <use var="HTTP_USER_AGENT" />
        browser=MyBrowser
        version=1.0
        majorver=1
        minorver=0
        frames=true
        tables=true
    <filter>
        <case match="Windows 98|Win98">
            platform=Win98
        </case>
        <case match="Windows NT|WinNT">
            platform=WinNT
        </case>
    </filter>
</browserCaps>
```

The browser capabilities file is likely to be the most useful at the machine level, unless you really like having the same information in each of your sites. From experience, keeping up with browsers is a pain. Fortunately the browser field is a lot smaller these days, so there might not be a lot of use for this section going forward.

compilation

The compilation section is used to set up your compilers and add assemblies and namespaces to your Web sites. Most of you will likely stick with the default compilers and not need to touch this section of the file. If you are a Fujitsu COBOL or Eiffel developer, there might be a little bit of a call, especially if you do not use the language in the Visual Studio.NET IDE. Listing 12-6 highlights the compilation section.

Listing 12-6: Compilation Settings

```
<compilation defaultLanguage="VB" debug="false"
   strict="true" explicit="true">
   <compilers>
     <compiler language="VB;VBScript"
       extension=".cls"
       type="Microsoft.VB. VBCodeProvider,System" />
     <compiler language="C#;Csharp"
       extension=".cs"
       type="Microsoft.CSharp. CSharpCodeProvider,System" />
   </compilers>

   <assemblies>
     <add assembly="gbWebApp1" />
     <add assembly="*" />
   </assemblies>

   <namespaces>
     <add namespace="System.Web" />
     <add namespace="System.Web.UI" />
     <add namespace="System.Web.UI.WebControls" />
     <add namespace="System.Web.UI.HtmlControls" />
   </namespaces>
</compilation>
```

There are a couple of nice things about this section. First, it gives you a nice global spot to set namespaces used by all or most of the pages in your Web application. Second, it gives you the ability to add compilers. If you are running out of Visual Studio.NET, you will not likely add compilers, but it is nice to know you can add any new .NET compiler with a couple of tags. Here are some notes on the tags for this section:

- ◆ compilation: As Listing 12-6 shows, this tag enables you to set a default language and explicit and strict options for your application, as well as to create debug code. You can also allow batch compilation and a batch time limit (batchTimeout), and set a number of dynamic recompiles before the app restarts (numRecompilesBeforeApprestart).

- ◆ compilers, with compiler: Allows you to set compilers and compiler options. In addition to setting the language, extension(s), and the class and assembly (type), you can also set the warningLevel and add compilerOptions.

- ◆ assemblies: Allows you to add or remove assemblies from the Global Application Cache (GAC) or the bin directory in the Web for use in your pages. You use the assembly name you want to add. The * wildcard indicates you would like to add all assemblies from the application and the framework. Please think hard before doing this; while it makes your life a bit easier, I can think of few instances where you will use every assembly in one application. You can also use the `clear` tag to clear all assemblies inherited at this level; this is useful if the system administrator sets a `web.config` or `machine.config` file that uses the wildcard (*), and you do not need every assembly in your application.

◆ `namespaces:` The same `add`, `remove`, and `clear` tags apply here. Adding here eliminates the need for imports in your individual pages. You will want to add only the namespaces that are used by most pages in your application. For namespaces that are only used in a couple of pages, you are better off setting the namespace reference in the page, most likely as an `Imports` statement in the CodeBehind file.

customErrors

In IIS 4, and later, `customErrors` gives you the capability to set up custom pages for each error that occurs. This enables you to direct someone to a page of your choice when a page is missing or an unhandled exception is triggered. Listing 12-7 shows this useful section.

Listing 12-7: Setting Up a Custom Error Page

```
<customErrors defaultRedirect="error.aspx"
   mode="RemoteOnly">
     <error statusCode="500"
        redirect="serverError.htm"/>
</customErrors>
```

Custom error pages have always been nice, but there are a couple of enhancements here. You can now set up your default redirect page so it only shows up for clients. When you use the `RemoteOnly` option, running the same page on the server shows the standard ASP.NET error handler instead of the friendly page. This allows you to see the exception generated so you can solve the problem. The other options for `mode` are `On` and `Off`, which apply to everyone. In the `error` tag, you set up a page for different status codes (500, shown here, is a server error, which is what ASP and ASP.NET generate when they error out).

The mode here applies to `customErrors` only. If you have set redirect pages in Internet Information Server (IIS), they will still redirect, even when accessed locally. The 500 status code (server error) is the one you will be most concerned with, so this is not a problem. Note that I set up an ASPX page for the default redirector, but use a .htm page for the 500 error. If your page throws a 500 error, it is likely that the redirect to an ASPX page would error out as well.

Remember that you can also use the `Application_Error` event in your `global.asax` (see Chapter 11) if you want to handle custom errors through an event. I would still code any specific pages here, as well, because coding exceptions do not raise all the error codes you might encounter. A good example of this is the 404, page missing, error. If you are more comfortable setting these pages in IIS, this is certainly an option. Remember that both ASP and ASPX pages are handled by the same page if an error page for a standard error number is set in IIS, while only ASPX pages are handled by the `customErrors` section. This gives you the capability to set different pages for ASP and ASPX applications.

While the ability to redirect when you receive certain status codes is very powerful, I recommend that you employ a good error handler in your applications, because you do not want to rely on redirect pages to handle your errors.

For more information on error handling, see Chapter 10, "Error Handling and Debugging."

Globalization

Globalization, also known as internationalization, is the ability to code your page for residents of other countries around the world. In this section you can set up your application so all pages render in another language. The most common globalization setting for applications in the United States is shown in Listing 12-8.

Listing 12-8: Setting Up a U.S. English Page

```
<globalization requestEncoding="us-ascii"
responseEncoding="iso-8859-1" />
```

The request and response encoding is the only thing you really need to set with this section. You can also separately set the encoding of a file, using the `fileEncoding` attribute of the `globalization` tag. There are two other tags that deal with culture, which is not the same as encoding. Encoding has to do with the way the page is rendered. Culture deals with language, and regional coding of items such as dates and currency, as well as regional/language settings in Windows. Some of the options, like keyboard settings, are not likely to be useful in your Web applications. You can set both a `culture` tag (to handle Web requests) and a `uiculture` tag (to handle locale-specific requests).

httpHandlers

If you have seen some sites that use DLLs to process all incoming HTTP, you have at least some rudimentary experience with HTTP handlers. `httpHandlers` can either intercept specific types of requests or serve up all HTTP requests. In order to handle requests, you must use the `IHttpHandler` or `IHttpHandlerFactory` interface in the class you want to set up as a handler. Listing 12-9 shows how to set up a handler for put requests on an ASPX page.

Listing 12-9: Setting Up a Custom HTTP Handler

```
<httpHandlers>
 <add verb="PUT" path="*.aspx"
   type="SpecialHandler, PutHandler.dll" />
</httpHandlers>
```

Unless you are extremely serious about coding your own handler, it's unlikely that you'll ever use this section of your configuration files. This is really a shame, because httpHandlers give you the capability to handle your ASP.NET requests in the same manner as you would with a custom Internet Services API (ISAPI) application.

 The February 2002 edition of Visual Studio magazine (www.vbpj.com) shows a way to create hierarchical URLs using an httpHandler. The article is well worth a look. At the site, search for hierarchical URLs or browse to February 2002 to find the article. DevX often moves content from its free site to its premiere club, so the article may not be accessible for free in the future.

httpModules

HTTP Modules are those items that expose events to your Web applications. This is a rather simplistic explanation, but it should hold for now. HTTP Modules can be from the .NET Framework classes or can be custom classes you design using the IHttpModule interface. In Listing 12-10, I add a .NET Framework HTTP Module. Because most of the .NET Framework classes expose their methods, this is most useful for hardcore code pokers who want to implement their own HTTP Modules. While I would love to spend a chapter on this subject, it is far beyond the scope of this book.

Listing 12-10: The httpModules Section of the Configuration File

```
<httpModules>
   <add type="MyNamespace.MyModule" name="MyHTTPModule" />
</httpModules>
```

httpRuntime

The HTTP Runtime section sets up how your application handles HTTP requests and redirects. Listing 12-11 shows an example of using httpRuntime to set up for mobile applications.

Listing 12-11: Wireless Application Setup for HTTP Runtime

```
<httpRuntime maxRequestLength="4000"
    useFullyQualifiedRedirectUrl="true"
    executionTimeout="45"/>
```

The `maxRequestLengthSetting` specifies the file size; use a reasonable setting here to prevent denial-of-service (DOS) attacks from large files. The `useFullyQualifiedRedirectUrl` is a Boolean to specify whether or not the URL is fully qualified or relative; this should be set to true for mobile applications. Finally, `executionTimeout` specifies the number of seconds before ASP.NET shuts the request down, which helps stop a slow client from draining resources.

identity

The `identity` section is used primarily to set up impersonation or a user account for the application to run under. Listing 12-12 shows examples of two opposite settings for this tag — you cannot use both of these in the same `web.config` file.

Listing 12-12: Impersonation with the identity Section

```
<!-- Impersonation set to true -->
<identity impersonation="true" />

<!-- Impersonation set to false -->
<identity impersonation="false" username="webUser"
    password="password" />
```

`impersonation` (when the attribute is set to `true`) means that the application will take the user's credentials and impersonate the user in requests for other resources. This simplifies security in many ways, because a user needs only a single sign on for all applications. The opposite setting, `false`, requires a username and password that the application will use to run under.

You'll find more information about impersonation in Chapter 13, "Security and Authentication."

machineKey

`machineKey` is used to generate the keys used for forms authentication. It's used to encrypt cookies if you set the protection of the forms tag to `Encryption` or `All`. (See the "authentication" section of this chapter for information on the protection attribute.) Listing 12-13 shows an example of using `machineKey`.

Listing 12-13: Encryption Keys

```
<machineKey validationKey="AutoGenerate"
decryptionKey="AutoGenerate"
    validation="MD5"/>
```

If you want, you can set both keys to a specific value. You can also use 3DES, SHA1, or MD5 as your encryption scheme.

pages

In the `pages` section of the `web.config` file, you can make some global settings that affect all pages in your application. Let me show you an example (Listing 12-14) and explain the attributes afterward.

Listing 12-14: Page-Specific Configuration

```
<pages buffer="true" enableViewState="true"
enableSessionState="true" autoEventWireup="true"/>
```

The following list provides the details on the attributes. All of you ASP developers will feel at home with some of these attributes.

♦ `buffer`: Sets whether the response object will be buffered. In ASP, this is `Response.Buffer`. For those not familiar with the concept of buffering, this indicates whether the page should be written directly to the response stream or stored in a temporary memory space (the buffer) until the entire request can be served to the user.

♦ `enableSessionState`: For most applications, this is set to `true`, because you want to use state, especially since state can spread across a Web farm in ASP.NET. You can also turn this off, or set it to `ReadOnly`. When it is set to `ReadOnly`, you cannot set Session variables in your pages, which can be useful in some situations where you know the Session variables at the start.

♦ `enableViewState`: This attribute is new and is used to specify whether a particular view of a page is kept in state. Choose `true` or `false`. In most instances, you want ASP.NET pages to hold state, because this aids you in maintaining page values from request to request.

♦ `pageBaseType`: Another new attribute, this indicates the class in the CodeBehind file that pages will inherit from by default. This is useful in creating a single class to handle all page requests for all of your pages. While I am intrigued by this idea, especially the thought of a generic page processor for an application, I do not see this as being practical if you are using Visual Studio.NET, because Visual Studio .NET will handle all of this type of plumbing for you in each page.

♦ `userControlBaseType`: This attribute is also new. It indicates the class in the CodeBehind file that your user controls will inherit from by default. If you create your own user controls, `userControlBaseType` might come in handy, but it holds the same caveat as the `pageBaseType`: You have to be a bit more generic with your application for this to truly apply.

♦ autoEventWireup: This attribute is used to indicate whether page events are automatically enabled. In general, I leave this one set to true because I see little use in disabling page events.

processModel

The processModel section deals with applications settings having to do with the actual process of serving pages. You could also call this the IIS process. To get a better idea of processModel, take a look at the code in Listing 12-15.

Listing 12-15: IIS Settings

```
<processModel enable="true" timeout="10"
    idleTimeout="30" shutdownTimeout="5"
    requestLimit="2500" requestQueueLimit="1000"
    memoryLimit="50" cpuMask="16"
    webGarden="false" />
```

The most important settings for processModel settings are shown in Table 12-1. The term *worker process* in the table is used to distinguish between a client process (a worker process) and the IIS process itself. Different settings affect different processes.

TABLE 12-1 SETTINGS IN PROCESSMODEL

Attribute	Description
enable	Specifies whether the process model is enabled. Set this to true or false.
timeout	Number of minutes until ASP.NET creates a new worker process to replace the current process. The default setting is infinite.
idleTimeout	Number of minutes of inactivity before ASP.NET shuts down the current process. The default setting is infinite.
logLevel	Specifies the types of events that are logged. By default, only errors are logged. Valid settings are All, None, or Errors.
shutdownTimeout	Number of minutes allowed before the worker process shuts down. The timeout here is expressed in hours, minutes, and seconds. Default is 5 seconds (shown in Listing 12-15).
requestLimit	Number of requests before ASP.NET creates a process to replace the current one. The default is infinite.
requestQueueLimit	Number of requests in queue before the server uses a 503 error to tell users it is too busy.

Attribute	Description
memoryLimit	Maximum percentage of memory that a worker process can consume before a new worker process takes its place. The default setting is 40%.
cpuMask	A decimal number for a binary mask indicating which CPUs are used for ASP.NET requests in a multiple-processor machine. Because this is a bit mask, you convert the number to binary to see which processors are being used.
	With a four-processor machine, 1101, or 13, indicates that the first, third, and fourth processor (or 0, 2, and 3, because the system uses base 0) are set up to run ASP.NET applications. By default, all processors can run ASP.NET applications.
webGarden	If set to true, CPU usage is controlled by Windows. If set to false, the cpuMask tells which processors are eligible to be used by ASP.NET.
userName	The identity that the worker process runs under.
password	The password that the worker process runs under.

securityPolicy

The securityPolicy section sets policies for different levels of trust. You can set policies files for the levels none, low, high, and full. The full setting is set to internal while the rest of settings are set to point to configuration files. You can find the security policy configuration files in the directory C:\WINNT\Microsoft.NET\Framework\v1.0.3705\CONFIG if you use C:\ as your OS install drive.

Listing 12-16 shows how to point different security levels to security policy .config files. As you will see in Chapter 13, the system administrator normally uses these settings in the machine.config file.

Listing 12-16: Setting Up a Security Policy

```
<securityPolicy>
   <trustLevel name="Full" policyFile="internal" />
   <trustLevel name="High" policyFile="highTrust.config" />
   <trustLevel name="Low" policyFile="lowTrust.config" />
   <trustLevel name="None" policyFile="noTrust.config" />
</securityPolicy>
```

The security section is probably familiar to those of you who have done any administrative work on a Windows system, especially Windows 2000 or newer. If your job description is primarily development, this section may be of little use to you.

The securityPolicy section is covered in more detail in Chapter 13.

sessionState

This sets up the session state of ASP.NET by configuring the sessionState httpModule. Use the settings to set the mode (where state is stored), indicate whether cookies are used, and set a timeout value. When you set certain modes, you need to set some additional attributes.

When the mode is set to SqlServer, you specify a normal SQL Server connection string. When the mode is set to StateServer, you have to set a connectionString. The connectionString is specified as a server name and a port, such as 192.10.96.105:21075. Using a state server is useful for Web farms. This is a great advantage over ASP, which could not maintain state across a Web farm.

Listing 12-17 shows how to set up sessionState.

Listing 12-17: sessionState with a State Server

```
<sessionState mode="StateServer"
 cookieless="true" timeout="10"
 connectionString="192.10.96.105:21075" />
```

trace

The settings for trace can be set in the page or in the web.config file. The decision about where to set up trace depends on what you are tracing. My personal preference is to set tracing in the web.config file, since it gives you the ability to trace all pages. On a high-volume site, however, you might want to set up a trace on an individual page in production to track errors.

Listing 12-18, shows a sample trace tag. An explanation of the attributes of the tag follows in Table 12-2.

Listing 12-18: A Sample Trace Tag

```
<trace enabled="true" requestLimit="20"
  localOnly="true" pageOutput="false" />
```

Tracing is covered in more detail in Chapter 10, "Error Handling and Debugging."

TABLE 12-2 SETTINGS FOR TRACING

Attribute	Description
enabled	Specifies whether tracing is set up for the application.
requestLimit	Specifies how many traces are stored on the server. The default setting for the request limit is 10.
pageOutput	Specifies whether the trace should show up at the bottom of each page. If this is set to false, you have to use trace.axd to see the traces.
traceMode	The modes for tracing are sortByTime or sortByCategory.
localOnly	Specifies whether the trace.axd is only visible on the local server. The default setting is true.

webServices

The webServices section of the configuration file controls the settings of XML Web services created using ASP.NET. Listing 12-19 shows an example webServices section.

Listing 12-19: The webServices Section of the Configuration File

```
<webServices>
    <protocols>
        <add name="HttpSoap" />
        <add name="Documentation" />
    </protocols>
    <wsdlHelpGenerator href="MyWsdlGen.aspx" />
</webServices>
```

The most commonly used tags in the webServices section are

◆ protocols — There are four protocols acceptable for transmission of data from client to server in Web services: HttpGet, which puts information on the querystring; `HttpPost`, which puts information in a forms collection; `HttpSoap`, which uses SOAP; and, `Documentation`, which enables ASP.NET to create a documentation page for your .asmx pages.

♦ `wsdlHelpGenerator` — This is the help page that is generated when a user navigates to an .asmx page. When you create an XML Web service, a help file is automatically generated. Use this tag if you want to override the default behavior and create your own help page(s).

In addition, you can extend the capabilities of `webServices` by adding extension classes in one of four areas: serviceDescriptionFormatExtensionTypes, soapExtensionTypes, soapExtensionReflectorTypes, and soapExtensionImporterTypes. A discussion about these tag sections is beyond the scope of this book, but you are unlikely to need to extend XML Web Services in this manner in the foreseeable future.

Summary

In this chapter, you learned about the `web.config` file. While I doubt many of you will spend much time in this file, as coding is so much more fun, it is a good idea to familiarize yourself with `web.config`, because there are items you can solve more easily with this file than you can programmatically.

Of the sections covered in this chapter, I suggest spending the most time on authentication and authorization, which are also covered in Chapter 13, and `customErrors` and `trace`, which are covered in Chapter 10. These four sections will be the most useful in helping you set up your applications with the proper security and in finding errors.

In the next chapter, I cover security in ASP.NET. We'll focus on authentication, which is determining who the user is, and authorization, which is determining whether the authenticated user has access. In addition, I'll discuss some of the new security features particular to .NET, such as code access security, which determines whether your code is allowed to run at all, based on settings from your system administrator.

Chapter 13

Security and Authentication

IN THIS CHAPTER

- ◆ A brief overview of Windows Security
- ◆ Different types of authentication in ASP.NET
- ◆ Authorization in ASP.NET
- ◆ Code access security
- ◆ Encryption in .NET

SECURITY IS A SERIOUS ISSUE for Enterprise-level applications. In this chapter, you learn the basics of ASP.NET security and how to set up your own applications using a variety of authentication methods. Because security is primarily a declarative process, we'll deal mostly with settings instead of code.

Windows Security

Before I discuss how ASP.NET handles security, let's talk about how Windows handles security. In this section, I focus on the Windows NT system, which includes Windows 2000 and Windows XP. I am not going to be dealing with consumer Windows (Windows 95, Windows 98, and Windows Me), because ASP.NET is not currently supported on those versions of windows.

In the Windows NT basic security setup, a user logs in, providing a set of credentials. The credentials are authenticated, and the user is issued a security token that holds his identity. Any time a user attempts to access a resource, the security token is compared to a list of people authorized to use the resource. This list is called the Access Control List, or ACL. If the user is on the ACL, he can access the resource. This model is illustrated in Figure 13-1.

Figure 13-1 is a bit simple, of course, because there are ACLs on every object in the file system, including files. A file can even have a different ACL than the folder in which it's located. It is often easier, especially when building a Web application, to set the ACL on the folder(s) of your application to simplify administration.

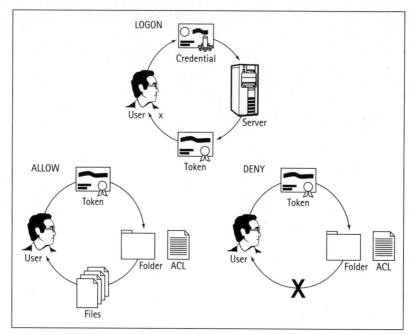

Figure 13–1: Windows NT security.

The primary concepts of security in Windows NT are authentication, authorization, and impersonation.

◆ **Authentication:** This is the question, "Who are you?" Every user has to have an identity to access resources on a Windows system. Authentication is the method of finding out the user's identity and setting up a method whereby that user can carry that identity with him.

◆ **Authorization:** Once a user's identity is established, there must be a method to find out if the user has the proper rights to access the resource requested. This process is known as authorization.

◆ **Impersonation:** Just like users, any process that runs independent of a user's context must have an identity. If a process has an identity that allows it greater access than the user, it may also have a method of mimicking a user to ask for items that the user wants to access. This is a process known as impersonation.

Authentication

Authentication is the process of determining who someone is, through a username and logon, domain account, digital client certificate, or any number of other means.

The basics of authentication are as follows:

1. The user requests some sort of access to an application (or a process on a Windows machine).

2. The machine or application asks for credentials to identify the user.

3. The user supplies his credentials. This might be in the form of a username and password (which can map to an application logon or a Windows account), a digital certificate, or even a retinal scan.

4. If the user's credentials are accepted, he is authenticated. At this point, the machine knows who the user states he is, but it does not yet give authority to run the application. That comes in the next section.

In the Windows NT world — which includes Windows NT, Windows 2000, Windows XP, and Windows .NET Server — everyone must be authenticated to run processes. There is no anonymous access in Windows. Oh, sure, you can set up IIS (Internet Information Server) to allow anonymous, but is it really anonymous?

When Internet Information Server is installed on a machine, a user account is created for anyone who accesses resources without a unique set of credentials. By default, this account takes on the name IUSR_ and the computer name. To see this information on your computer, follow these steps:

1. Open the Internet Services Manager by selecting Start → Run, typing **mmc** in the Run command window, and clicking OK. (This method is common to all versions of NT.)

   You can also use the Control Panel to open the Internet Services Manager. Select Start → Settings → Control Panel → Administrative Tools → Internet Services Manager. Alternatively, you can select Start → Programs → Administrative Tools → Internet Services Manager (for NT, it is NT Option Pack 4 instead of Administrative Tools). With Windows XP Professional, you have to use the Control Panel.

2. Right-click on the Default Web Site and choose Properties.

3. Click the Directory Security tab.

4. Click Edit under Anonymous Access and Authentication Control.

5. Click Edit under Anonymous Access.

6. The Anonymous User Account dialog box opens (see Figure 13-2), and you can change the username and/or password for the Anonymous User account.

Although you can alter this account by changing the username or the password, I generally recommend that you don't, because that serves no purpose and can have a detrimental effect, especially where security is concerned. If you want to change the password, you must uncheck the Allow IIS To Control Password box.

Figure 13-2: The Anonymous User Account in IIS.

Authorization

A user is only authorized to view items he is allowed to access in the ACL. The rule of thumb is that a user is allowed access as long as two criteria are met:

1. The user or one of the groups of which the user is a member is specifically allowed access to the resource.

2. The user and all groups of which the user is a member are not specifically denied access to the resource.

Basically, as long as a user is not explicitly denied access to a resource through any group memberships, he can access any item he is allowed to access through his memberships. The group that gives the user the broadest rights in any situation will win as long as there is not a deny in any of the lists.

This is, of course, a bit of an oversimplification, because there are times when these rules do not apply, especially when you start dealing with local permissions versus domain permissions. For the time being, I am just going to discuss the simplest permissions: disk access, or NT File System (NTFS), permissions.

To restrict access to a resource, the easiest method is to change the disk access, or NTFS, permissions. Alter the security for different users and groups by following these steps:

1. Open Windows Explorer. The easiest way is to use Run (Windows key + R), type in the command **explorer,** and click OK.

2. Find the file or directory to which you want to restrict access to, then right-click, select permissions, and move to the Security tab. This is where you set permissions. Figure 13-3 shows the Security tab of the Properties dialog box.

This section covers the basics of security in Windows NT, but there is one more concept to consider: impersonation.

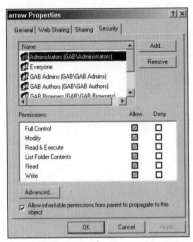

Figure 13-3: Setting NTFS permissions with Windows Explorer.

Impersonation

When a user logs on, he accesses resources with his own credentials. If another process takes over, there are two choices. You can either have the new process request resources with its own credentials, or have it pass on the user's credentials and act as if it is the user.

If I wanted to be technically correct, I'd state that passing on the user's credentials is called *impersonation,* whereas running a process under the same account for all users is called *proxying.* There is some difference of opinion on this, but I'm calling both methods impersonation, which is the normal use of the word in Microsoft documentation. Where applicable, I state which is being employed.

Security in ASP.NET

While it is interesting to understand the roots of a security model, it's more practical to see how it is employed. In this section, I discuss three authentication methods (Windows, Forms, and Passport) and then we move on to some other security topics.

Authentication in ASP.NET

As mentioned previously, there are three forms of authentication in ASP.NET: Windows authentication, Passport authentication and Forms authentication. You also can choose not to authenticate at all, which is only useful with anonymous access. Setting up authentication in the `web.config` file is shown in Listing 13-1.

Listing 13-1: Authentication Settings in web.config

```
<authentication mode= "Windows|Passport|Forms|None" />
```

This is a bit too generic, but it serves as a starting point. Each one of these forms of authentication has differing tags underneath, so I revisit this section of the web. config file with each type of authentication.

WINDOWS AUTHENTICATION

Windows authentication is performed in conjunction with IIS in ASP.NET. To use Windows authentication for your site, set the authentication method in IIS to Basic, Digest, or Windows Integrated (see Figure 13-4). If you've allowed Anonymous access, only items that you have restricted with NTFS permissions require further authentication. (See the "Authorization" section earlier in this chapter for information on setting NTFS permissions.) As long as the IUSR account or Everyone group has access, no dialog box appears for the user to log on.

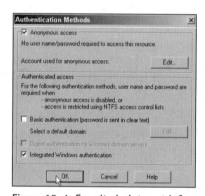

Figure 13-4: Security in Internet Information Server.

To set authentication methods in Internet Services Manager, right-click a site or folder in ISM and select Properties from the pop-up menu. Click the Directory Security tab of the Properties dialog box. Click the Edit button in the Anonymous Access and Authentication Control section. The Authentication Methods dialog box opens.

With the default settings shown in Figure 13-4, every request to the server is anonymous and is impersonated by the Anonymous account IUSR_ <ComputerName> if you have not edited it to specify another account. I have compiled some brief notes on each of the types of the authentication settings in IIS.

◆ **Basic authentication:** Basic authentication is used with most Internet applications that need some form of non-anonymous access. It is an insecure method of access, because all passwords are sent unencrypted. Unfortunately, you cannot get around this without forcing all users to use

Internet Explorer, since Netscape and other browsers do not implement Windows authentication. For secure Internet applications, basic authentication is normally used in conjunction with SSL (Secure Sockets Layer), which is activated using a certificate from an authority such as Verisign. When using basic authentication in conjunction with anonymous access, only items to which the anonymous account does not have access cause basic authentication to be employed. Basic authentication can be used with a proxy server.

◆ **Digest authentication:** Digest authentication is the newest addition to the Windows Web authentication model. It rolls the best of basic and Windows authentication into a new secure model. Digest authentication, unlike Windows authentication, can be used with a proxy. However, it does not send the passwords in cleartext, making it more secure than basic authentication. To gain this power, however, you make some sacrifices. Digest authentication requires Active Directory be installed on the server and is only supported in Internet Explorer 5 or greater. Realistically, this means digest authentication is most useful on Windows 2000 or Windows XP networks.

◆ **Integrated Windows authentication:** Windows authentication is implemented in Internet Explorer, and uses an encryption on the transmission of user logon and password information. As previously mentioned, you cannot use Windows authentication alone if you have users on browsers other than Microsoft browsers. When using Windows authentication in conjunction with anonymous access, only items to which the Anonymous account does not have access cause Windows authentication to be employed. When used in conjunction with basic authentication, Microsoft's browsers use Windows authentication, while other browsers use basic authentication. Windows authentication cannot be used through a proxy server.

USE OF WINDOWS AUTHENTICATION   Windows authentication is the easy method of authentication in ASP.NET because most of the security is declarative rather than programmatic. By declarative, I mean that you use the OS to restrict resources rather than program these restrictions. In Windows authentication, IIS passes the authentication information on to ASP.NET. Note, however, that these are two different systems. While the settings in IIS affect the ASP.NET authentication, changing the settings in ASP.NET has no effect on IIS.

Since Windows authentication uses windows accounts for authentication, you have to restrict resources by changing the NTFS permissions on the items. This is done with Windows Explorer and can be set on entire directory structures. Listing 13-2 shows the authentication section of the `web.config` file when Windows authentication is used.

Listing 13-2: web.config for Windows Authentication

```
<authentication mode="Windows" />
<identity impersonate="true|false" />
```

IMPERSONATION IN WINDOWS AUTHENTICATION   Remember that impersonation means that ASP.NET passes on each request under the user's identity. When you set identity impersonation to `true`, you continue to check for authorization using the user's credentials, and not the credentials of the ASP.NET process. If you set this to `false`, you also supply a username and password for the process to run under, as shown in Listing 13-3.

Listing 13-3: Adding an Identity When Impersonation Is False

```
<identity impersonate="false" username="gbeamer"
   password="cowboy" />
```

Since Windows authentication is more useful in an intranet situation, because every user is logged into the system, the choice of whether to impersonate or not really depends on how you have set up your Web application. For greatest security, impersonation is preferable, since a user cannot access any resource he is not authorized to use, even if you accidentally supply a link.

To summarize, every request must have some form of credentials in Windows. When you set for ASP.NET to impersonate, a user's credentials are sent for every request. When ASP.NET is not set to impersonate, you set up a single set of credentials for all users. Which of these you use depends on your needs. I advise using impersonation on any site where you need additional security. You can simplify this if the user's ID is only needed to gain access, and all pages in the Web are set up for any intranet user to see.

RESTRICTING ACCESS IN CONFIG FILES   I don't necessarily advocate using config files, but I offer it as another method to avoid setting up the ACLs for a lot of directories. Personally, I dislike leaving security in a text file that can be downloaded, although IIS 6.0 alleviates some of my concern.

If you are a developer, you can circumvent having to go to your system administrator by using `web.config` files. (I can see the veins in a few administrators' foreheads popping out at the thought of the developers taking over the ship.)

The basic format of using the configuration file is to either allow or deny roles or users. You can then restrict what these users can do with the application by using verbs for different HTTP actions. For example, Listing 13-4 shows settings for allowing everyone access, but permitting only Admins to `DEBUG`.

Listing 13-4: Restricting All But Administrators to a Section of a Web

```
<authorization>
    <allow users="*" verbs="GET,POST" />
    <allow roles="Admins" verbs="DEBUG" />
</authorization>
```

These are standard HTTP verbs used in Web applications:

- GET uses querystring arguments to configure your application.

- POST sends parameters in through the form collection (as if it was posted from a Web form).

- HEAD adds items to the headers collection, which is sent with every page sent across the Web.

- DEBUG is the ability to debug the application.

The right to run DEBUG should be as restrictive as possible, because debugging can give away some of the inner workings of your application.

SETTING UP WINDOWS AUTHENTICATION   There really isn't much to setting up Windows authentication, as most of it is declarative. I've already covered all of the steps necessary to work with Windows authentication on a basic level, but let's review them:

1. Check the proper authentication method(s) in IIS by setting the properties of the site in the Internet Services Manager. (Figures 13-2 and 13-4 can help you with this task.)

2. Set NTFS permissions on the directories that contain the files you want to protect. (Figure 13-3 can help you with this task.) You can also set up restrictions in web.config files for each directory.

3. Add a line to the web.config file to indicate the type of authentication is Windows authentication.

   ```
   <authentication mode="windows" />
   ```

4. Optionally, set up identity impersonation. In practice, this is a wise move as it allows the app to run under the user accessing it.

   ```
   <identity impersonate="true" />
   ```

5. If you are not using impersonation, remember to include an account for ASP.NET to run under.

   ```
   <identity impersonate="false" username="gbeamer"
     password="cowboy" />
   ```

PASSPORT AUTHENTICATION

One of Microsoft's visions with .NET is the ability to turn the Web into one gigantic set of applications. This vision is called Web services, which is the topic of Chapter 14. For this chapter, I discuss how the Web services model uses Passport authentication, where a user can be authenticated through a third party and remain anonymous to your site. The future of this type of authentication is still up in the air.

HISTORY OF SINGLE SIGN-ON   The idea of being able to authenticate a user once for all sites is not a new concept. One of the first forays into a single unique ID for a user was a digital signature, which grew out of encryption. Phil Zimmerman created a product called Pretty Good Privacy, which is better known by its acronym, PGP. PGP allows a user to create a set of keys, one private and one public. Documents encrypted with one key can only be opened with the other.

While the main use of this technology is to ensure that any private communication to the user was only opened with the private key, it also gives the user the ability to encrypt a digital signature with the private key. Users can check the signature by attempting to open it with the public key. If the message deciphers, it is authentic. There are still many businesses that rely on PGP to keep their communication safe and their identities validated.

The next idea to come down the pike was digital certificates. If you've ever worked with SSL, you know that this is not a novel concept, although it is hard to imagine that the original idea behind many of the digital certificate implementations was the concept of client certificates.

Unfortunately, client certificates never really flew. First, the Internet is known as a free medium, and the idea of paying anything to authenticate yourself is contra to Internet culture. Second, the Internet is thought of as an anonymous medium. If I want to buy, you can get some information; if I want to browse, I can say I am anyone I want to. A digital certificate that "proves" who I am seems very "big brother."

As such, digital certificates have taken off primarily for code signing, and little else. In order to build a business, companies like Verisign and Thawte (now Verisign owned) have shifted focus to secure server certificates instead.

Digital certificates are not a total bust. Many companies use them to secure their intranets. IIS has shipped with certificate server (now certificate services) since version 4, and many other companies have created their own implementations, so there is a large market for the heavy form of authentication that digital certificates provides. These certificates just have not gained much ground with the Internet community at large.

So, what does this have to do with Passport authentication? Nothing and everything! Microsoft saw a need for a single type of sign-on, but realized that it had to be the merchants, not the consumers, who would foot the bill. In the "Web as a service" model, the one who benefits from the service should pay to implement it. The primary concept here is a single sign-on that is used across multiple sites.

MICROSOFT'S SOLUTION   Passport is a centralized service where a user can sign up to access a variety of sites. The core of Passport was originally introduced as

Microsoft Wallet, which was designed as a way to store your financial information in a single location to safely purchase goods and services on the Web.

Wallet, which shipped free with Internet Explorer, fit the consumer model a bit better, but never really took off. There were many competing models, such as CyberCash, which had a better level of acceptance. Overall, however, the convenience of storing financial information with a third party was seen as more dangerous than convenient, and most consumers continued to pull out credit cards for each purchase.

Passport has evolved into an authentication model, with the financial aspect taking a back seat. I believe this is a temporary, but necessary move. If you sign up for MSN Messenger, which is part of the setup routine for Windows XP, you must get a Passport. (I now use Messenger daily, but I don't trust Passport with my financial information, because I still have security concerns about Microsoft.)

USE OF PASSPORT AUTHENTICATION   At one time, I thought Passport was primarily a tool for Microsoft sites and E-commerce, or a necessary evil in certain situations. Now that I have seen Microsoft's vision for MyServices (formerly known as Hailstorm), I see things a bit differently.

Imagine being able to access your calendar, contacts, and e-mail from anywhere in the world. Lose your pocket PC? No problem — you can easily pick up a new one and instantly get all of your information. The idea is both intriguing and a bit scary at the same time.

What if the system behind this was able to inform you of potential credit card fraud and asked you to approve whenever someone tried to access your information? You would be in control of every piece of information about you and could approve any attempt at access. Imagine that this could happen on your PC, your pocket PC, your cell phone, your X-Box, your television, or even your refrigerator. Now, say you have different levels of logon for different levels of information, whereby you could use a simple logon for e-mail, but require a stronger password, or encryption key, for your most private information.

What I have described is where Microsoft eventually sees MyServices going, with Passport as the primary authentication mechanism. Yes, I still have some reservations, but I must admit that the ability to retrieve my information anywhere, and having the ability to be informed before my information is accessed, is very interesting. And there are rumors that you and I will be allowed to choose from a variety of providers, not just Microsoft. Only time will tell if the MyServices vision becomes a reality.

Today, Passport is not much more than a tool to log into some sites and tools, like Hotmail, some E-commerce third-party sites and Messenger. In this state of its evolution, it is not worth spending a lot of time on Passport. I will, however, give you enough information to get started.

SETTING UP PASSPORT AUTHENTICATION   In order to set up Passport authentication, you need a copy of the Passport SDK. You can download it from either the MSDN download site at `http://msdn.microsoft.com/downloads/sample.asp?url=/MSDN-FILES/027/001/644/msdncompositedoc.xml` or the Passport site at www.passport.com/business. To implement this in your business, you have to pay a fee, but developers are allowed to play for free.

FORMS AUTHENTICATION

The most common form of authentication for most Internet applications is going to be Forms authentication (in beta 1, this was called Cookie authentication). While cookies are used, the name Forms authentication is a better explanation of what is going on.

With Forms authentication, a cookie is checked to see if a user is logged in. If the user is not logged in, he is forwarded to a page in which he can log on to the site. The user types in his name and password and, after authentication, a cookie is set.

INITIAL SETUP   To begin setting up Forms authentication, you need to set up the web.config file. The simplest way to set up is with usernames and passwords in the file. Listing 13-5 shows the basic setup of a web.config file for Forms security.

Listing 13-5: Setting Up for Forms Authentication in web.config

```
<authentication mode="Forms">
  <forms name="gabWeb" path="/" loginUrl="login.aspx"
     protection="All" timeout="10">
  <credentials passwordFormat="Clear">
    <user name="gbeamer" password="cowboy" />
  </credentials>
  </forms>
</authentication>

<authorization>
  <allow users="gbeamer" />
  <deny users="?" />
</authorization>
```

The code for Listing 13-5 is contained in the web.config file in this chapter's download: Ch13VS.zip (for Visual Studio .NET) or Ch13SDK.zip (for the .NET Framework SDK). You can find these files on the companion Web site at www.wiley.com/extras.

This is all that is necessary to redirect the user to the login page. The name of the cookie here is gabWeb and the path is the root of this application. I also set protection to use both validation and encryption on the cookie created (All), and I set a timeout of 10 minutes.

For credentials, I set up one user on this test Web application. This user is also the only one allowed. Note, however that I still have the default <deny users="?" />

because I want security to be checked. If I remove this tag, everyone is allowed regardless.

A word of warning here: Remember that words are case sensitive in the configuration file. If you use mode="forms", you will encounter an error.

LOGIN.ASPX   The next step is to create a login.aspx page for your Web application. Our login.aspx page is a simple username and password page. For an Internet application, you can also set a check box (preferable) or a radio button to have the user indicate whether he should be remembered. Let's examine the login.aspx page in Listing 13-6.

Listing 13-6: The HTML Portion of the login.aspx Page

```
<form id="Form1" method="post" runat="server">
  <table border="0">
    <tr>
    <td>
      <asp:Label id="Label2" runat="server">Password</asp:Label>
    </td>
    <td>
      <asp:TextBox id="strPassword" runat="server" />
    </td>
    <td>
      <asp:RequiredFieldValidator id="RequiredFieldValidator2"
runat="server" ErrorMessage="Password cannot be left blank."
ControlToValidate="strPassword" />
    </td>
    </tr>
    <tr>
    <td>
      <asp:Label id="Label1" runat="server"> Email</asp:Label>
    </td>
    <td>
      <asp:TextBox id="strEmail" runat="server">
    </td>
    <td>
      <asp:RequiredFieldValidator id="RequiredFieldValidator1"
runat="server" ErrorMessage="Email cannot be left blank."
ControlToValidate="strEmail" />
    </td>
    </tr>
  </table>
  <P>
```

Continued

Listing 13-6 *(Continued)*

```
  <asp:Button id="btnAuthenticate" runat="server"
    OnClick="btnAuthenticate_Click" Text="Authenticate" />
  </P>
  <P>
    <asp:Label id="lblMessage" runat="server"></asp:Label>
  </P>
</form>
```

If you try to hit the `default.aspx` page in this application, you are redirected to the `login.aspx` page, shown in Figure 13-5.

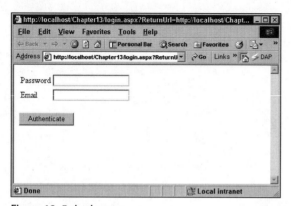

Figure 13-5: Login.aspx.

ADDING SECURITY CODE   You have now gone through most of the steps necessary to log on. When credentials are supplied in the `web.config` file, the final step is to add a simple authentication handler. As with all Web controls, the `onServerClick` event controls which event handles form submission. Listing 13-7 shows the authentication event.

Listing 13-7: Authenticating the User

```
Private Sub Page_Load(ByVal sender As System.Object, _
        ByVal e As System.EventArgs) Handles MyBase.Load
  'Put user code to initialize the page here
  If Page.IsPostBack Then
    If FormsAuthentication.Authenticate(strName.Text, _
            strPassword.Text) Then
      FormsAuthentication.RedirectFromLoginPage(strName.Text, False)
    Else
      lblMessage.Text = "<b>You are not allowed to use" & _
                    "this site!</b>"
    End If
```

```
      End If
   End Sub
```

 The page that contains the form logon (Listings 13-6 and 13-7) is contained in the download file for this chapter, Ch13VS.zip (for Visual Studio .NET) or Ch13SDK.zip (for the .NET SDK), on this book's companion Web site (www.wiley.com/extras). The file to look at is login.aspx.

All is well and good. When you attempt to log in with anything other than gbeamer with the password cowboy, you get a message letting you know you are not allowed to use this site. When you log in properly (case sensitive? You bet!), you are redirected to the page you wanted to access. A couple of notes:

◆ You do not have to write your own authentication routine. To authenticate, simply use the FormsAuthentication object's Authenticate method, and ASP.NET does the work of checking credentials for you.

◆ To redirect the user back to the page he was trying to access, use a RedirectFromLoginPage. (Try doing this in so few lines of code in traditional ASP or Visual Basic!)

HOW TO PROCEED WITH FORMS AUTHENTICATION   I have just scratched the surface of authentication and authorization in ASP.NET. I touch on this again in the Part III of this book.

Meanwhile, here are some recommendations:

◆ For higher security Web sites, do not use credentials in a configuration file. Create a data table in SQL Server, because you can control security better here. If you prefer XML, however, adding credentials to web.config might be your preferred method of setting up users.

◆ Setting up a click event for the button is preferable to using the Page_Load event. With this simple login example, this is fine, but a more elaborate login would be better served with its own event. (It would serve the ASP.NET paradigm better, anyway.)

◆ If you do slap in your own credentials, use some form of encryption on the password. I have included a small application (PasswordHasher) on this book's companion Web site that covers password hashing.

Authorization in .NET

Authorization (which is covered primarily in Chapter 12, "Configuring Web Applications") can be set through the web.config file. You can set who is authorized to view certain directories as well as entire applications. The two actions you can take at this level are `allow` and `deny`. Listing 13-8 shows a simple authorization section of a `web.config` file.

Listing 13-8: Authorization in web.config

```
<authorization>
    <allow verb="GET, POST" users=" *" />
    <allow verb="DEBUG" users="gbworld\administrators" />
</authorization>
```

The other way to set authorization in .NET is to set up Windows authentication and use NTFS (NT File System) permissions. When you set permissions in this manner, only those with the authorization to view the resource, whether it is a Web page or anything else, can view it.

I think of the file system as being similar to a database. Even if I have set authorization in a configuration file, I go ahead and set the ACL (Access Control List) for the resource. This is similar to the way I set permissions on objects in SQL Server to ensure that only those who have proper access can use these objects.

You can also work with authentication in a programmatic manner by using the principal classes, `WindowsPrincipal` and `GenericPrincipal`.

Code access security

If you own a Web Presence Provider (WPP), you are probably a bit concerned about the implications of .NET. After all, if you let your clients post .NET code, they have the keys to the kingdom. The full power of the Windows API is opened up to developers through .NET. Network administrators will have the same concerns; after all, the ability to map the network and find nuggets of gold is very tempting. What can you do to prevent this?

In traditional ASP, there was little you could do to stop code from using certain features other than to restrict compiled DLLs and put access rights on different system DLLs to restrict their use. Microsoft helps a bit by putting interfaces on dangerous components that cannot be accessed directly from ASP, but consider the danger that can be done with ASP and the `FileSystemObject`.

In ASP.NET, there is a much easier way to protect your system from errant users: code access security. To describe it in the simplest manner, it's similar to a log on for assemblies. When an assembly runs in the CLR, it is given a set of permissions by the runtime. By default, the permissions are fairly wide open, although different types of applications are defaulted to different levels of permissions. An admin, however, can override the default permissions to either give more access or less. And this can be done on-the-fly.

When an object is created, it is given rights based on the assembly to which it belongs. An admin can code a policy file that further restricts the rights, or that opens the rights up slightly. The combination of these rights, with the administrator's explicit decision to allow or deny being the deciding factor in gray areas, is applied to the object when it is created.

What about the case where an object calls an object that has greater rights? Can the developer circumvent the system in this manner? No! When an object asks for access, the entire call stack is checked to find a denial. In the case of an object that is refused, the object asking for rights would be denied since the object that called it is denied.

As with most issues in enterprise development, code access security can be approached programmatically or declaratively (through tools and or simple files).

WORKING WITH CODE ACCESS PROGRAMMATICALLY

I want to show you some tools you can use to view, update, add, and delete permissions in the .NET Framework. Then I'll tell you where to go for help if you want to explore the programmatic method of code access security, which is beyond the scope of this book.

There are two tools that you can use for code access security if you want to code security yourself. The first is `caspol.exe`, the code access security policy tool. This is a command-line tool that allows you to work with different security constructs in the .NET Framework. You can view, add, update, and delete permission sets, as well as do some basic configuration of assemblies. This is the more difficult of the tools to use.

The second, the Microsoft Management Control snap-in known as the .NET Framework Configuration tool, has a graphical user interface (GUI), so it's much better suited to our point-and-click world. You can access this tool through the Control Panel → Administrative tools (in Windows 2000 Server or Advanced Server, you can access it from Start → Programs → Administrative Tools).

I'm only going to cover the Runtime Security Policy section of this tool. There are many other tasks you can complete with this tool, but they deal with other aspects of .NET, and are best left alone in this context.

Figure 13-6 shows the Runtime Security Policy section of the .NET Framework Configuration tool. Under the Enterprise group, I've opened the Internet permissions set. The small window on the right side shows the security permissions for this permission set; you can see that code execution is the only security permission allowed. By default, other permissions, such as remoting, calls to unmanaged code, and extending the allowing any form of policy control, are turned off.

Contrast this set of security permissions with the Local Intranet permission set (see Figure 13-7), which allows both remoting and asserting permissions in addition to code execution.

In order to use code access at this level, you have to code your own permissions object and place an XML snippet into the runtime security policy using either `caspol.exe` or the .NET Framework Configuration tool. You add the `System.Security` and the `System.Security.Permissions` namespaces to your assembly in order to code security in your own applications. To create your own permission, you must implement the `IPermission` interface.

This is a huge subject better left to another book, but I want to show you an easy way to apply permissions already contained in the framework. This will fit a great majority, if not all, of your applications.

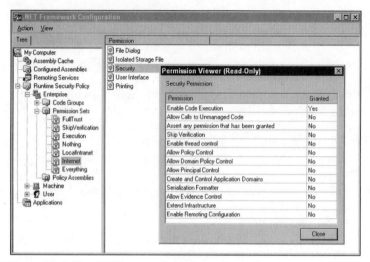

Figure 13-6: The .NET Framework Configuration tool.

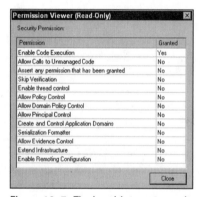

Figure 13-7: The Local Intranet security permissions.

WORKING WITH CODE ACCESS DECLARATIVELY

To configure code access security in a much easier manner, you can create configuration files for different levels of security. Remember the `web.config` files from Chapter 12? There is also a `machine.config` file, which is used to configure settings for an entire machine.

The `machine.config` file is located at <root>:\WINNT\Microsoft.NET\ Framework\<version number>\CONFIG. This file has the same sections as the `web.config` files, covered in Chapter 12.

The `<securityPolicy>` section of the config file points to a set of policy files and gives them a friendly name. By default, there are four levels of security in this file: `Full`, `High`, `Low`, and `None`. `Full` gives carte blanche to applications and is, therefore, contained in the framework itself (the internal designation). The other three have config files associated with them.

Listing 13-9 shows the default security setup in machine.config. This is how your file will look right after you install the .NET Framework.

Listing 13-9: The <securityPolicy> Section of machine.config

```
<securityPolicy>
    <trustLevel name="Full" policyFile="internal" />
    <trustLevel name="High" policyFile="web_hightrust.config" />
    <trustLevel name="Low"  policyFile="web_lowtrust.config" />
    <trustLevel name="None" policyFile="web_notrust.config" />
</securityPolicy>
```

To set which security policy I want for my users, I create a web.config file (see Listing 13-10) at a level above the users' Web directories. For all users, I can simply place this in <webDrive>:\Inetpub\wwwroot. Since I am envisioning an intranet, I probably start by giving full control. I have all of the users' webs located in a folder called users.

Listing 13-10: The web.config File for User Permissions

```
<?xml version="1.0" encoding="utf-8" ?>
<configuration>
    <location path="users" allowOverride="false">
        <system.web>
            <trust level="Full" />
        </system.web>
    </location>
</configuration>
```

Now, George in accounting is a bit disgruntled and decides to start using his knowledge of .NET to be a bit mischievous. He uses commands to access directories outside of his directory. The easiest way to stop this is to eliminate that right by changing George's trust level from Full to Low.

If you look again at Listing 13-8, you'll see that Low points to web_lowtrust. config. This file is also located in the CONFIG directory, next to machine.config. Rather than get bogged down in the details of the file, I examine just one portion.

Let's say we have certain users who use a system built by your developers to add content to their sites. Overall, the developers are given a high amount of trust, because this is an intranet site. One of the developers on this team decides to build a page that allows him to circumvent this system to add files. Under the web_high-trust.config file, he is given the right to do this. You want to take this right away. Here are the steps to take:

1. Open the web_hightrust.config file. Look for the following tag and delete the write="$AppDir$":

```
<IPermission class="FileIOPermission"
                        version="1"
                        Read="$AppDir$"
                        Write="$AppDir$"
                        Append="$AppDir$"
                        PathDiscovery="$AppDir$"/>
```

2. Save this file as `web_nowrite_hightrust.config` and save it in the
   directory C:\WINNT\Microsoft.NET\Framework\<version>\CONFIG.

3. Open `machine.config` and add the following line to the
   `<securityPolicy>` section:

   ```
   <trustlevel name="NoWrite"
   policyfile="web_nowrite_hightrust.config" />
   ```

4. Change the trust level in the `web.config` file in wwwroot:

   ```
   <trust level="NoWrite" />
   ```

5. Now go back and check the security permissions on the application to
   ensure your application has the right to write to the application directory,
   but not to any other directory.

 In the download for this chapter, I include a sample project,
`securityPermissions`, that accesses security permissions. It includes a
config file that goes into the directory path at C:\WINNT\Microsoft.NET\
Framework\<version>\CONFIG, as well as an application. Instructions for
running the project are included in the download. Go to this book's companion Web site (www.wiley.com/extras) and download either
`Ch13VS.zip` (for Visual Studio .NET) or `Ch13SDK.zip` (for the .NET
Framework SDK).

The changes take place immediately. Any code written to access a directory or
file outside of the application directory is instantly denied. This gives a lot of power
to the administrator.

For most applications, the preconfigured config files are more than adequate. If
you do need a custom configuration, I suggest you read a bit in the .NET
Framework.

Encryption in .NET

This section cannot, by any means, give you everything you need to know about code encryption but, without going into a lot of detail, I want you have an idea of how easy cryptography is in .NET.

If you coded encryption prior to .NET, you no doubt used the Microsoft Crypto API. Since API calls are largely foreign to Visual Basic and ASP developers, I am fairly certain that your encryption coding experience was not much fun.

Cryptographic objects and functions are quite a bit easier in .NET, although they take a bit of getting used to. Listing 13-11 shows a simple encryption routine, which is adapted from a Microsoft help file. If you'd like to build your own, the file is located at `http://support.microsoft.com/default.aspx?scid=kb;EN-US;q301070`. If the link breaks, you can go to the Microsoft support site and look up q301070.

Listing 13-11: Using Encryption in .NET

```
Public Sub EncryptFile(ByVal strInputFileName As String, _
                       ByVal strOutputFileName As String)
    'Create file streams and crypto provider
    Dim objInputFile As New SysIO.FileStream(strInputFileName, _
                          SysIO.FileMode.Open)
    Dim objEncryptFile As New SysIO.FileStream(strOutputFileName, _
                          SysIO.FileMode.OpenOrCreate)
    Dim objTripleDES As New SysCrypt.TripleDESCryptoServiceProvider()
    'Create key and IV byte arrays
    objTripleDES.GenerateKey()
    objTripleDES.GenerateIV()

    'Set up actual encryption objects
    Dim objTripleDESEncrypt As SysCrypt.ICryptoTransform = _
                              objTripleDES.CreateEncryptor()
    Dim objCryptoStream As New SysCrypt.CryptoStream(objEncryptFile, _
        objTripleDESEncrypt, SysCrypt.CryptoStreamMode.Write)

    'Encrypt and output
    Dim bytArrayInput(objInputFile.Length - 1) As Byte
    objInputFile.Read(bytArrayInput, 0, bytArrayInput.Length)
    objCryptoStream.Write(bytArrayInput, 0, bytArrayInput.Length)

    'Close all of your stream objects
    objCryptoStream.Close()
    objInputFile.Close()
    objEncryptFile.Close()
End Sub
```

Summary

The security model in ASP.NET is fairly simple. Most of the workings are declared rather than programmed, saving you a lot of time when creating your ASP.NET applications. This covers a great percentage of all ASP.NET applications. We'll discuss more about security in Part III, "Working with Data — ADO.NET," and in Part V, "Putting It All Together."

In this chapter, we covered the two primary subjects of security — authentication (who a user is) and authorization (what that user can access) — and also looked at code security and encryption.

Security is an important topic to me, and I could fill an entire book on security in .NET. This chapter serves as an introduction to get you started.

In the next chapter I discuss Web services. To many, Web services are the core of the .NET vision. You'll learn to build a basic Web service and how to adapt your current projects to turn them into Web services.

Chapter 14

Web Services

WEB SERVICES ARE A MAJOR PORTION of Microsoft's vision for .NET. The idea of setting up services that can be consumed across the Internet using standard Web protocols shows we have come a long way. This chapter discusses Web services, including how to set them up and how to consume them.

Web Services?

In the year 2000, I worked on an application that built Web sites for other businesses. The application made it quite simple for HTML-illiterate individuals to quickly create a robust portal site. They filled in some forms, clicked a button, and voilà, Web sites were born.

As good as we were at creating some content, it made no sense for us to build all aspects of the portals. Certain items such as health news and information were outside our realm of expertise, so we partnered with other businesses that could supply this information. To maintain the look and feel of the client sites, we sent the HTML and graphics to each partner site.

As you have probably discerned, this was a temporary fix. In time, our clients wanted to alter the look and feel of their sites and sending HTML with every change became overwhelming.

The next step was to create an interface to share the look and feel with our partner sites. The agreed-upon standard was XML for communication. I was tasked to build both the interface and the calling application, ensuring easy communication back and forth. A method of caching the HTML, XML, and XSL was created for the partner side and we were in business.

The change to a Web interface reduced time to market for a new client site with a new look to a matter of hours instead of days. Still, it took quite some time to bring a new partner up to speed. What I would have given for an easier method of discovery.

I have a dream

My dream is for a system that allows me to communicate using open standards to make my services easily accessible. I also dream that I can create a method whereby someone can query this service to figure out how to implement it in his business. It would also be nice if my service can help him create a proxy to contact my service. And, while I am dreaming, there is a directory where I can publish that my service is available to get the whole thing started.

If this were but a dream, the chapter would end here. It isn't a dream, however, because you can easily code Web services today that fit all of these ideals. And, the .NET Framework makes building these services a breeze. The basic outline of this Web services model is shown in Figure 14-1.

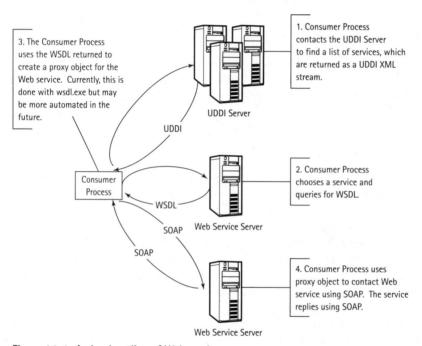

Figure 14-1: A visual outline of Web services.

In the Microsoft model, you contact a UDDI (Universal Description, Discovery, and Integration) server, which serves as a large yellow pages of services. From the listings, choose a service that you like. You can then contact the WSDL file on the server containing the service you are interested in to figure out how to code against it. Finally, you can contact the service with SOAP.

In the future, all of this can be done with a simple click of a button. For now, you have to, at minimum, get the WSDL file to create a proxy object. You then call the proxy object from your application and consume the service. If this sounds a bit too simple . . . well, it is.

Declaring a Web service

Theory and history are wonderful, but I bet you are ready to get into coding a Web service. To create a Web service, create a file with an .asmx extension. If you are using Visual Studio .NET, you can choose Web Service as a project type and have all of the plumbing created for you.

Listing 14-1 is a very simple Web service to say "Hello World." The first line is located in a file called HelloWorld.asmx, and the rest of the listing comes from the CodeBehind file. While you can code an entire Web service in an .ASMX page, you'll find that Visual Studio .NET fights you on every turn. That's why it is easier to code using the CodeBehind file.

Listing 14-1: A Simple Web Service

```
Imports System.Web.Services

<WebService(Namespace:="http://tempuri.org/")> _
Public Class HelloWorld
    Inherits System.Web.Services.WebService

    <WebMethod()> Public Function SayHello() As String
        Return "Hello, world!"
    End Function
End Class
```

The code for Listing 14-1 can be found on this book's companion Web site (www.wiley.com/extras) in the download file for this chapter: Ch14SDK.zip (SDK version) or Ch14VS.zip (Visual Studio .NET version). After unzipping, look for the file simple.asmx.vb.

This simple example will run and return an XML string that looks like this:

```
<?xml version="1.0" encoding="utf-8" ?>
<string xmlns="http://gbworld.com/">Hello, world!</string>
```

Because this is what you expect to be returned, you might assume that everything is correct. You would be wrong. From a technical standpoint, there are two problems with the code in Listing 14-1:

◆ There is no constructor. While not mandatory for every type of class, in classes that inherit from other classes, especially .NET Framework classes, I advise creating a constructor that calls the constructor of the base class, like so:

```
Public Sub New()
    MyBase.New()
End Sub
```

♦ There is no dispose method. Once again, this is not mandatory with most classes, but Web services are one of the areas where the Visual Studio .NET IDE considers this event absolutely imperative.

```
Protected Overloads Overrides _
  Sub Dispose(ByVal disposing As Boolean)
    If disposing Then
      If Not (components Is Nothing) Then
        components.Dispose()
      End If
    End If
    MyBase.Dispose(disposing)
End Sub
```

I don't include these methods in most of the code examples (listings) in this chapter for the sake of brevity and because these methods don't change in these Web service examples, but if you download the code, you'll notice that the New() and Dispose() methods are there.

The updated simple Web service file is called SimpleWebService-Corrected.asmx.vb and can be found on the companion Web site (www.wiley.com/extras) in the download file for this chapter: Ch14SDK.zip (SDK version) or Ch14VS.zip (Visual Studio .NET version).

The basic difference between a Web service file and another ASP.NET page that uses CodeBehind is the attribute <WebMethod()>, which tells the compiler that this method should be visible over the HTTP protocol. By adding this attribute alone, you can make any ASP.NET method a Web service, but it is much easier if the file that points to the service is an .ASMX page. To stay with convention, I code all of the examples in this chapter with an .ASMX page as the front end to the Web service.

When you hit this Web service with a browser, using the address http://localhost/Chapter14/simple.asmx for this example, you see the screen shown in Figure 14-2.

Don't worry about the default namespace here for a moment. This particular page tells me there is only one public Web method on this service, which is SayHello. For more information, I can click on this method, which takes me to the URL http://localhost/chapter14/simple.asmx?op=SayHello (see the output in Figure 14-3). If I had additional methods exposed, I could easily change the op parameter to the name of any other Web method.

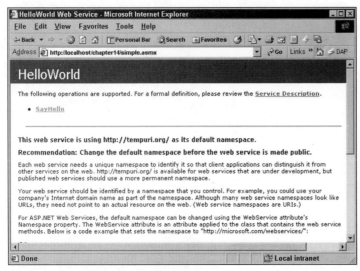

Figure 14-2: The HelloWorld Web service.

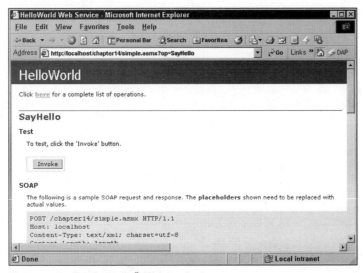

Figure 14-3: The SayHello() Web method.

The final step is to invoke the method by clicking on the invoke method or otherwise accessing the URL `http://localhost/chapter14/simple.asmx/SayHello?`. The return from this URL is shown in Figure 14-4.

Of course, very few Web services are quite this simple. What if I add a parameter? In Listing 14-2, I show a Hello World Web service with a single parameter. If you run this file in your browser and go to the page where you invoke the service, you'll see a single text box that allows you to enter a number for the `intTest` parameter.

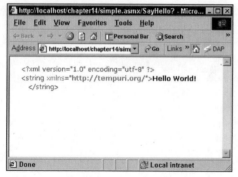

Figure 14-4: XML returned from the Web service.

Listing 14-2: Adding a Parameter

```vb
Imports System.Web.Services

<WebService(Namespace:="http://gbworld.com/webservices", _
Description:="Says Hello World.")>
Public Class helloParameter
    Inherits System.Web.Services.WebService

    <WebMethod(Description:="Different Hello Message.")> _
    Public Function _
    SayHello(ByVal intTest As Integer) As String
        Select Case intTest
            Case 1
                Return "Hello, World!"
            Case Else
                Return "Hello Something Else"
        End Select
    End Function
End Class
```

The code for Listing 14-2 can be found on the companion Web site (www.wiley.com/extras) in the download file for this chapter: Ch14SDK.zip (SDK version) or Ch14VS.zip (Visual Studio .NET version). After unzipping, look for the file helloParameter.asmx.vb.

With this declaration, using the URL http://localhost/chapter14/ helloParameter.asmx/SayHello? causes a server 500 error. You must add the parameter to the call string. The amended URL, when the value of intTest is 2, is

`http://localhost/chapter14/helloParameter.asmx/SayHello?intType=2`,
and its result is shown in Figure 14-5. The lesson here is that a Web service that
expects a parameter must receive a value for every parameter it expects.

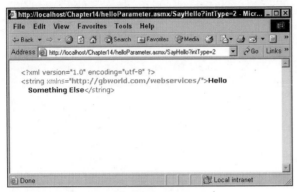

Figure 14-5: A Web service with a parameter.

CODEBEHIND

I'm sure you've caught on to the fact that I'm very fond of the `CodeBehind` file concept in .NET. The default behavior with `.ASMX` pages in Visual Studio .NET, as with
every type of page in ASP.NET except configuration files, is to separate code and
the user interface. This means moving your code into CodeBehind pages. (You can
circumvent this default behavior in .NET by hand-coding your pages outside of the
IDE, but I don't recommend this.)

With Visual Studio .NET, the default name of the CodeBehind page is the name
of your file with a `.vb` extension added. I follow this standard for all pages, even
those not created in Visual Studio .NET, and I advise following the same standard,
unless you have figured out a better method for your organization.

Note that you have to compile the CodeBehind page prior to running the Web
service. While it might be nice if you could dynamically compile with the `src`
attribute, the WebServices @ directive tag does not support this.

WEBMETHODS

Exposing a public method to a Web service is as simple as adding the tag
`<WebMethod>` to the front of any public function or subroutine you place in your
Web service class. This tag is a .NET attribute. While this book does not get into
attributes, I do want to explain at least a little about them.

An attribute is a tag added to a class or method that extends the metadata of that
item. If you have played around with Visual Studio .NET, you know that certain
methods, such `InitializeComponent()`, always have an attribute associated. This
attribute lets either Visual Studio .NET or the .NET runtime know that it is to handle this class or object in a special way.

The `WebMethod` attribute is added to tell the compiler that this particular routine is exposable through HTTP, which means exposed to the Web. When the `WebMethod` attribute is added to a Web service class, the method is exposed as part of the service. You do not have to create a large amount of code to create a service, because this attribute is included. The ability to expose a method to the Web by the addition of an attribute is very powerful. This does not mean that simply adding this tag to any class, for example a Windows Form, exposes the method as a Web service without any additional work.

With the `WebMethod` attribute, you can also add a description of your method to show up in the browser when the Web service is contacted. This is shown in Listing 14-3.

Listing 14–3: Adding to the WebMethod Attribute

```
<WebMethod(Description:="Different Hello Message.")>
```

WEBSERVICE

Just as `<WebMethod>` is an attribute, so is `<WebService>`. When you place a class into the @ directive of an `.ASMX` page, you do not need to explicitly use the `WebService` attribute. Listing 14-4 shows a `WebService` attribute added to the `HelloWorld` class. I recommend that you include the `WebService` tag for every class with methods you want to expose as part of the service. If you use Visual Studio .Net, this task is done for you with the default namespace pointer: `tempuri.org`.

Listing 14–4: Adding the WebService Attribute

```
<WebService(Namespace:="http://gbworld.com/webservices",
Description:="Says Hello World.")> Public Class HelloWorld
```

Note that I've changed the `Namespace` value in the `WebService` attribute from the default `tempuri.org`. I recommend that you provide your own schema for your services and change the namespace, as I have in Listing 14-4. The output is shown in Figure 14-6.

There is one other question that should be on your mind right now. Since the `WebService` attribute is not necessary, why use it? Why can't I name the namespace in the ASMX page and not have to worry about this attribute at all?

These are very good questions. The answer is flexibility. Any class you have already built can become a Web service by using the Web service attributes and importing the namespace (the latter being unnecessary if you do not mind typing System.Web.Services in front of every attribute). In order to use a class you have already built as a non-Web service class, you have to make the following changes.

♦ Make a project reference to the Web services DLL. If you are using Visual Studio, this is done for you.

♦ Add the `WebService` attribute to any class that will participate as a Web service.

♦ Add the `WebMethod` attribute to any method you want to expose.

♦ Create an ASMX page that points to the class you are exposing as a Web service.

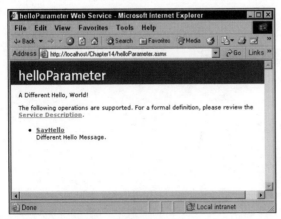

Figure 14-6: Web service with attributes set.

Let me recap: To make a Web service, you need an ASMX file with a class that is exposed as a Web service. When you code either in the ASMX file or the CodeBehind page, you do not need to explicitly declare the class as a Web service, using the `WebService` attribute, but I would suggest it. You do, however, have to declare all methods exposed to the Web as Web methods using the `WebMethod` attribute.

Using Web Services

Now that you have seen how to create a Web service, the next step is utilizing the service with a client. As stated in the "I have a dream" section, you can create a proxy object for the Web service without having to write any code. The tool that generates the proxy object is called `wsdl.exe`, which uses the WSDL generated by the Web service to create the proxy object.

When I covered Web services through a browser, I discussed how to get information on the Web service, the Web method(s), and the XML returned. The first two were human-readable descriptions, while the third showed how the service would be consumed. If you wanted to build your own objects to consume this XML, also known as reinventing the wheel, you could access the XML, place it in an XML document object, and go to town.

However, I am talking about the ability of the .NET tools to create a proxy object for you. You can use the `wsdl.exe` tool to have an object created that can access a Web service anywhere in the world. You don't have to write any code to accomplish this.

You must start out with a Web service and know where to access the WSDL. To return the WSDL from any Web service, you need only type the URL to the Web service with the ending `?WSDL`. For this example, I am going to show what happens when you use this against the `helloParameter.asmx` file. The complete URL to test is `http://localhost/Chapter14/helloParameter.asmx?WSDL`, and the result is shown in Figure 14-7.

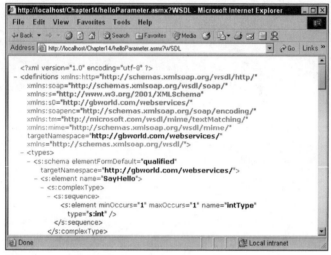

Figure 14–7: The WSDL from `helloParameter.asmx`.

Creating a proxy class

Now, let's get to it. There are two ways to produce a proxy object. You can open the WSDL file from the URL (`http://localhost/Chapter14/simple1.asmx?WSDL`) in your browser, save the file to your local hard drive, and then run WSDL against this file. The easier way is to run `wsdl.exe` against the URL and have the tool create the proxy object for you, which is the method shown in Figure 14-8. The statement run at the command line is `wsdl /l:VB http://localhost/Chapter14/simple1.asmx?WSDL`. To run this tool, I have included a batch file in the download that adds the path to `wsdl.exe`.

If you're using Visual Studio .NET for your development efforts, check out the sidebar "Working with Web Services in Visual Studio .NET" later in this chapter. It explains an easier way to work with Web services.

The code created from using `wsdl.exe` is shown in Listing 14-5. Notice that the main method, `SayHello()`, bears the same signature as the `WebMethod SayHello()`

in the original `helloParameter.asmx` file. To use the proxy object in your application, you simply call it in your code.

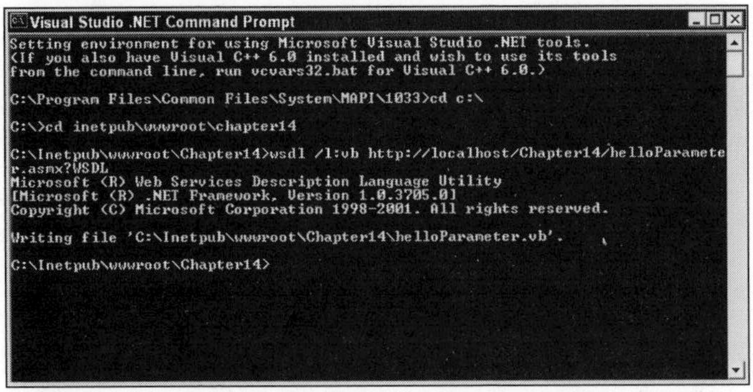

Figure 14-8: Creating the proxy class for a Web service.

Listing 14-5: Proxy Class Generated from WSDL

```
'-------------------------------------------------------------------
' <autogenerated>
'     This code was generated by a tool.
'     Runtime Version: 1.0.3705.0
'
'     Changes to this file may cause incorrect behavior and will
'     be lost if the code is regenerated.
' </autogenerated>
'-------------------------------------------------------------------


Option Strict Off
Option Explicit On

Imports System
Imports System.ComponentModel
Imports System.Diagnostics
Imports System.Web.Services
Imports System.Web.Services.Protocols
Imports System.Xml.Serialization

'
'This source code was auto-generated by wsdl, Version=1.0.3705.0.
'

'<remarks/>
```

Continued

Listing 14–5 *(Continued)*

```
<System.Diagnostics.DebuggerStepThroughAttribute(), _
 System.ComponentModel.DesignerCategoryAttribute("code"), _
 System.Web.Services.WebServiceBindingAttribute(Name:="helloParameterSoap", _
[Namespace]:="http://gbworld.com/webservices/")> _
Public Class HelloWorldConsume
    Inherits System.Web.Services.Protocols.SoapHttpClientProtocol

    '<remarks/>
    Public Sub New()
        MyBase.New()
        Me.Url = "http://localhost/Chapter14/helloParameter.asmx"
    End Sub

    '<remarks/>
    <System.Web.Services.Protocols.SoapDocumentMethodAttribute(_
    "http://gbworld.com/webservices/SayHello", _
    RequestNamespace:="http://gbworld.com/webservices/", _
    ResponseNamespace:="http://gbworld.com/webservices/", _
    Use:=System.Web.Services.Description.SoapBindingUse.Literal, _
    ParameterStyle:=System.Web.Services.Protocols.SoapParameterStyle.Wrapped)> _
    Public Function SayHello(ByVal intType As Integer) As String
        Dim results() As Object = Me.Invoke("SayHello", _
            New Object() {intType})
        Return CType(results(0), String)
    End Function

    '<remarks/>
    Public Function BeginSayHello(ByVal intType As Integer, _
     ByVal callback As System.AsyncCallback, _
     ByVal asyncState As Object) As System.IAsyncResult
        Return Me.BeginInvoke("SayHello", New Object() {intType}, _
            callback, asyncState)
    End Function

    '<remarks/>
    Public Function EndSayHello(ByVal asyncResult _
    As System.IAsyncResult) As String
        Dim results() As Object = Me.EndInvoke(asyncResult)
        Return CType(results(0), String)
    End Function
End Class
```

In order to consume a Web service in the same project using wsdl.exe, you have to change the name of the proxy class you created using wsdl.exe. I've already done this in the code in Listing 14-5: Note that the new class name, `HelloWorldConsume`, is bolded in the listing.

The code for Listing 14-5 is available on this book's companion Web site (www.wiley.com/extras) in the download file for this chapter: `Ch14SDK.zip` (SDK version) or `Ch14VS.zip` (Visual Studio .NET version). The name of the file is HelloWorldConsume.vb.

Using the proxy class

After generating the proxy class with `wsdl.exe`, you simply add the file to your project. You then create an object that uses this class and call the methods of this proxy class. The proxy class will connect to the Web service and call the same method across the Internet. As far as your local application is concerned, it is calling a local object rather than an application in some distant part of the world.

If you use the Visual Studio .NET Command Prompt to run `wsdl.exe`, you can create the proxy class `.vb` file in your solution directory. The command line directive is still the same as explained in the last section:

```
wsdl.exe /l:vb
http://localhost/Chapter14/helloParameter.asmx?WSDL
```

Running this command produces a file called `helloParameter.vb`. (The CodeBehind file for the `helloParameter.asmx` page is `helloParameter.asmx.vb`, so it's not affected by the new filename, although the class name will clash if you simply add the new file to your project.)

To follow along with the example in this chapter, click the Show All Files icon (second from the right) at the top of the Solution Explorer, right click on the `Simple1.vb` file, and select Include in Project. Change the name of the file to `HelloWorldConsume.vb`, open it, and change the class name to `HelloWorldConsume`.

To demonstrate how to use the proxy class, I change the name of the class in Listing 14-5 from `simple2` to `HelloWorld` to avoid having name collisions that would occur if I did not add another namespace. Then I test the service with a page called `default.aspx`. The page contains a text box to set the `intTest` parameter of the `SayHello()` method. Any postback to the form fires off the Web service. The code for the test page is shown in Listing 14-6, and the `CodeBehind` file is shown in Listing 14-7.

Listing 14-6: The Test Page

```
<%@ Page Language="vb" AutoEventWireup="false"
Codebehind="default.aspx.vb" Inherits="Chapter14._default"%>
<!DOCTYPE HTML PUBLIC "-//W3C//DTD HTML 4.0 Transitional//EN">
<HTML>
  <HEAD>
    <title>Test the Hello World Web Service</title>
  </HEAD>
  <body>
    <form id="Form1" method="post" runat="server">
      <P>
        Input a number:
        <asp:TextBox id="txtInput" runat="server" Width="50px" /></P>
      <P>
        <asp:Button id="btnCallService" runat="server" Text="Submit" /></P>
      <P>
        <asp:Label id="lblHello" runat="server" /></P>
    </form>
  </body>
</HTML>
```

You can download the code for Listings 14-6 and 14-7 from the book's companion Web site (www.wiley.com/extras) in the download file for this chapter: Ch14SDK.zip (SDK version) or Ch14VS.zip (Visual Studio .NET version). The files to look at are default.aspx and default.aspx.vb.

Listing 14-7: The CodeBehind File for the Test Page

```
Public Class _default
  Inherits System.Web.UI.Page
  Protected WithEvents lblHello As System.Web.UI.WebControls.Label
  Protected WithEvents txtInput As System.Web.UI.WebControls.TextBox
  Protected WithEvents btnCallService As System.Web.UI.WebControls.Button

    Private Sub Page_Load(ByVal sender As System.Object, _
      ByVal e As System.EventArgs) Handles MyBase.Load
        'Put user code to initialize the page here
    End Sub

    Private Sub btnCallService_Click(ByVal sender As System.Object, _
```

```
        ByVal e As System.EventArgs) Handles btnCallService.Click
          Dim objHello As New HelloWorldConsume()
        Dim intInput as Integer = txtInput.Text
          lblHello.Text = objHello.SayHello(intInput)
      End Sub
End Class
```

Now, here is a quick run through the code to understand what is happening. When the user clicks the button, the `blnCallService_Click` event is fired. Since the page is being posted, an Integer value (`intInput`) is created for the Web service by pulling the value of the text box. If the user puts a number in the text box (`txtInput`), the value is pulled and replaces the integer stored in `intInput`; otherwise the value is set to 0. The proxy object is then created, and the return value from the `SayHello()` method is placed in the label control (`lblHello`).

If you download the sample code, you can test out the Web service on your own machine by starting the `default.aspx` page. Figure 14-9 shows the `default.aspx` page when the number 2 has been placed in the text box and the button clicked.

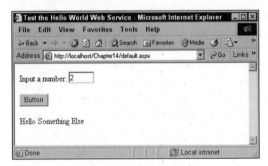

Figure 14-9: Testing the Web service.

Of course, you would never set up a Web service to run on the same machine. You would, instead, access the class directly if you need the message on your local server. The only modification to the code is changing `HelloWorldConsume` to `helloParameter`. This change is shown in Listing 14-8.

Listing 14-8: Using the Local Class

```
    Private Sub btnCallService_Click(ByVal sender As System.Object, _
      ByVal e As System.EventArgs) Handles btnCallService.Click
        Dim objHello As New HelloWorldConsume()
      Dim intInput as Integer = txtInput.Text
        lblHello.Text = objHello.SayHello(intInput)
      End Sub
```

The important point here is that using the `<WebMethod()>` attribute does not stop you from using the method locally. It just makes the method available for use in a Web service. If you have a Web service that contains code you need to use locally, don't create a proxy; use the local class instead.

Just because you've created a Web service doesn't mean your Web application has to access it as a Web service. It's better to access a class in your project as an object than as a Web service. If you don't, you'll needlessly degrade performance.

Marking a method as a `WebMethod` doesn't mean you have to access it via a Web service, if the class file is local. Making a class an XML Web service class adds a new method of contacting the class, but does not remove other ways.

At this point, you might be wondering if this is really all there is to Web services. The answer is a resounding yes. Sure, you can code much more complex examples, but the main point is that pretty much any function that you can code in your application can be exposed over the Internet.

While it's unlikely that you'd ever consume a Web service in the same project (except as a learning exercise), you must remember to alter the class name to avoid a name clash. By default, the proxy class bears the same name as the service, which means you'd end up with two classes with the same name.

There are two ways to solve this problem, should it occur. One is to rename the proxy class that is created through wsdl.exe, as I did in Listing 14-5. The other is to add a new namespace to the class file, so that the simple1 class in the proxy object exists in a different namespace. In this chapter, for example, I could have added a namespace `Chapter14Proxy` to the file containing the proxy class, like this:

```
Public Namespace Chapter14Proxy
  <System.Diagnostics.DebuggerStepThroughAttribute(), _
  System.ComponentModel.DesignerCategoryAttribute(_
"code"),System.Web.Services.WebServiceBindingAttribute(
  _
Name:="HelloWorld1Soap",_
[Namespace]:="http://gbworld.com/webservices/")> _
  Public Class simple1
    'rest of code in here
  End Class
```

```
End Namespace
```

I chose the first solution because it was an easier method to accomplish what I needed to show you: how to use a proxy object. Creating a separate namespace for your proxy objects is not a bad option, however, even if you are using Web services from a different solution, because you can use the namespace to distinguish your proxy objects from other objects in your solution. If you do not use aliases for namespaces, this is most likely a moot point.

Turning classes into Web services

If you think about it in the simplest of terms, a Web service is nothing but a piece of software with a method that is exposed, via Web interfaces, with SOAP. There are a couple of ways you can expose a class as a Web service. One way is completely programmatic. While this is certainly an option, and may actually perform slightly better, I want to focus on the easier way, which is to create an ASMX page to expose your Web service.

For this section, let's use a simple HelloWorld class. It has a method called SayHello() that returns a string. The code for this class is shown in Listing 14-9. The word Class, added to the end of the class name (HelloWorldClass) is to ensure that the class name does not clash with the items already in our Web application.

Listing 14-9: The HelloWorld Class

```
Public Class HelloWorldClass
    Public Function SayHello() As String
        Return "Hello, World!"
    End Function
End Class
```

The code for the HelloWorld console application from Listing 14-9 can be found on the companion Web site (www.wiley.com/extras) in the download file for this chapter: Ch14SDK.zip (SDK version) or Ch14VS.zip (Visual Studio .NET version). Look in the HelloWorld folder.

The original application is set up as a console application, so I have created both a class and a module. Listing 14-10 shows the module that instantiates the HelloWorld class.

Working with Web Services in Visual Studio .NET

Understanding how .NET works is of paramount interest to me, so I've purposely shown you how to consume a Web service using `wsdl.exe`. If you are using Visual Studio .NET, however, you can save a lot of time by using the tools included in the IDE.

It's quite simple to consume a Web service in Visual Studio .NET. Here are the steps:

1. In the solution explorer, right-click the folder icon labeled Web References.

2. Choose Add Web Reference from the menu.

3. A dialog box opens up. In the Address textbox, type **http://localhost/ Chapter14/simple1.asmx?WSDL**, and click Enter.

4. You should now see a screen like the one in the following figure. Click the Add Reference button at the bottom of the dialog box.

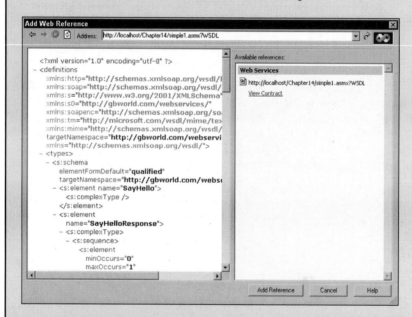

5. Right-click the Localhost icon, under the Web References icon in solution explorer, and click Rename. Rename this icon **HelloWorldService**.

6. You can now use this Web service in your application by coding against `HelloWorldService`, as the following shows:

```
Dim wsHelloWorld as New HelloWorldWebService()

Response.Write(wsHelloWorld.SayHello())
```

I've included a sample page in the `Ch14VS.zip` file called `ConsumeWebReference.aspx`. This file uses the Web reference to consume the Web service in `simple1.asmx`.

Listing 14-10: The Module File for the HelloWorld Application

```
Imports SysCon = System.Console

Module Module1
    Sub Main()
        Dim objHello As New HelloWorld()
        SysCon.WriteLine(objHello.SayHello())
        SysCon.Read()
    End Sub
End Module
```

TIP If you want to see the output of a Console application from inside the Visual Studio .NET IDE, you choose Debug → Start Without Debugging, or click Control + F5. When you use this command, the output of the console application halts at the end of execution, so you can see the output. This means the line `SysCon.Read()` is unnecessary in your code if you use the Start Without Debugging option.

If you are debugging, it is better to include a `SysCon.Read()` line to stop the execution of the program so you can read the output. If you don't, the console window opens and closes so fast, you can't read the output.

Of course, this is a console application, not a Web service. Now I'll show you two different methods of converting the console application to a Web service application.

USING A COMPILED EXECUTABLE

If you want to simply move the executable to the new application, you have to add a couple of items to the class file and recompile the class. First, add references to both `System.Web.DLL` and `System.Web.Services.DLL`. In Visual Studio .NET, you do this by right-clicking References in the Solution Explorer. If you are working with the SDK, you have to add the references when you compile.

The next step is to add the `Imports` statement for both the `System.Web` and `System.Web.Services` namespaces. I alias these with `SysWeb` and `SysWebSrv`, because, as you know, I believe every imported namespace should be aliased for easy maintainability. The class also has to inherit the Web service class: `System.Web.Services.WebService`. The final step is to add a couple of attributes, `WebService` and `WebMethod`. Since I have aliased the namespaces, the aliases have to be added to the Web service attributes. The changes in the class file are shown in Listing 14-11.

Listing 14-11: The Updated HelloWorld Class

```
Imports SysWeb = System.Web
Imports SysWebSrv = System.Web.Services

<SysWebSrv.WebService(Namespace:="http://gbworld.com/")> _
Public Class HelloWorldClass
    Inherits System.Web.Services.WebService

    Public Sub New()
        MyBase.New()
    End Sub

    <SysWebSrv.WebMethod()> Public Function SayHello() As String
        Return "Hello, World!"
    End Function
End Class
```

The code for Listing 14-11 is located on the companion Web site (www.wiley.com/extras) in the download file for this chapter: Ch14SDK.zip (SDK version) or Ch14VS.zip (Visual Studio .NET version). Look for the file HelloWorldClass.vb.

To run under IIS, you have to create a Web under IIS and move the content there. You can also create a new Web project in Visual Studio .NET, and copy the files to that Web project folder to include them in your project.

Now comes the easiest part. Copy HelloWorldClass.exe from the bin folder into the bin folder for your Web service project. Change the filename from HelloWorldClass.exe to HelloWorldClass.dll. This may seem strange, from a Visual Basic 6 point of view, but it really works — trust me!

You then have to add a file with an .asmx extension (a Web service). To match the code samples, simply call the service ConsumeHelloWorldClass.asmx and add a line to inherit the HelloWorld application. The code for the .asmx file is shown in Listing 14-12.

Listing 14-12: The Web Service File for the HelloWorld Class

```
<%@ WebService Language="vb" Class="HelloWorld.HelloWorldClass" %>
```

Prior to .NET, you could not make an executable (.exe) into a library (.dll) without changing the project type in Visual Basic. While the interfaces used to run the application under COM were identical, the compilation was quite a bit different, especially in the Visual Studio 6 IDE. In .NET, the executable is the same, whether it has a DLL or an EXE extension, because all code is compiled to the exact same MSIL, whether it is originally compiled as a DLL (class library project in Visual Studio .NET) or an EXE (console application or Windows application in Visual Studio .NET).

 The files `ConsumeHelloWorld.vb` and `HelloWorldClass.exe` can be found on the companion Web site (`www.wiley.com/extras`) in the download file for this chapter: `CH14SDK.zip` (SDK version) or `Ch14VS.zip` (Visual Studio .NET version). After compiling the project HelloWorldClass, drag the EXE to the bin folder in your Web project and change it to a DLL.

MOVING THE CLASS FILE

Your other option is just as simple. Make a copy of the class file and drop it in the Web services folder. If you are using Visual Studio .NET, refresh the project to see this new class file.

When you use the source file, you also have the option to include the CodeBehind attribute in your ASMX file. In this example, I have named the service `HelloWorld2`, so I don't interfere with the previous example, which is included in the same Web project. I make one other change. In this example, I create the class using Visual Studio .NET and move the Web method to this class. I still use the aliases. Listing 14-13 shows the full code for the class.

Listing 14-13: The HelloWorld2 Class

```
Imports SysWebSrv = System.Web.Services

<SysWebSrv.WebService(Namespace:="http://tempuri.org/")> _
Public Class HelloWorld2
    Inherits System.Web.Services.WebService

    Public Sub New()
        MyBase.New()

        InitializeComponent()
    End Sub

    Private components As System.ComponentModel.IContainer

    <System.Diagnostics.DebuggerStepThrough()> Private Sub InitializeComponent()
        components = New System.ComponentModel.Container()
    End Sub
```

Continued

Listing 14-13 *(Continued)*

```
Protected Overloads Overrides Sub Dispose(ByVal disposing As Boolean)
    If disposing Then
        If Not (components Is Nothing) Then
            components.Dispose()
        End If
    End If
    MyBase.Dispose(disposing)
End Sub

<SysWebSrv.WebMethod()> Public Function SayHello() As String
    Return "Hello, World!"
End Function
End Class
```

The code for Listing 14-3 is located on the companion Web site (www.
wiley.com/extras) in the download file: Ch14SDK.zip (SDK version) or
Ch14VS.zip (Visual Studio .NET version). Unzip the download and look in
the Chapter14WebService folder.

To run under IIS, create a Web under IIS and move the content there. Again,
you can also create a new Web project in Visual Studio .NET, copy the files to
the Web project folder, and include them in your project.

The main difference between the class in Listing 14-13 and the class in Listing
14-11 is the addition of the `InitializeComponent` and `Dispose` methods.

The final difference, as mentioned, is the addition of the CodeBehind attribute in
the ASMX file. Listing 14-14 shows the entire ASMX file for this Web service.

Listing 14-14: The ASMX File for the HelloWorld2 Web Service

```
<%@ WebService Language="vb" Codebehind="HelloWorld2.asmx.vb"
 Class="Chapter14WebService.HelloWorld2" %>
```

The last step in the process is consuming this Web service from another site. To
make things a bit more interesting, I'm going to accomplish this using a Visual
Basic 6 client and an ASP client.

Working with ASP and Visual Basic 6

What if you have clients that aren't using .NET? Can you still expose your .NET
classes as Web services for these clients? The answer is yes. While the implementation
is hidden from you, Web services are simply classes that respond to requests using

SOAP (the Simple Object Access Protocol). Any client that can use SOAP can utilize your Web service.

The steps for connecting to a Web service in ASP or Visual Basic are fairly straightforward. First, download the latest version of the SOAP toolkit from `http://msdn.microsoft.com/soap`. Then, create a SOAP client object and supply a URL to a WSDL (Web Services Description Language) file. Because this file is created on the fly in .NET, the URL will point to the Web service URL with a `?WSDL` at the end. For our example, the URL is

```
http://localhost/Chapter14WebService/HelloWorld2.asmx?WSDL
```

I use the `mssoapinit()` method of the SOAP client along with our `sayHello()` Web method. The code to connect from a Visual Basic 6 standard EXE is shown in Listing 14-15.

Listing 14-15: Connecting to a Web Service with SOAP Using Visual Basic

```
Option Explicit

Private Sub cmdRun_Click()
    Dim objSoapClient As MSSOAPLib.SoapClient
    Const WSDL_FILE As String = _
"http://localhost/Chapter14WebService/HelloWorld2.asmx?WSDL"

    Set objSoapClient = New MSSOAPLib.SoapClient
        Call objSoapClient.mssoapinit(WSDL_FILE)

        txtOutput.Text = objSoapClient.sayHello()
    Set objSoapClient = Nothing
End Sub
```

 The code for this application is located on the companion Web site (`www.wiley.com/extras`) in `Ch14SDK.zip` (SDK version) or `Ch14VS.zip` (Visual Studio .NET version). After you unzip the download, look in the `ConsumeHelloWorldVB` **folder**.

What about using .NET to consume a Web service, or SOAP class, created in Visual Basic 6? Here are the basic steps:

1. Create an ActiveX DLL project with at least one class with one method.

   ```
   Option Explicit

   Public Function SayHello() As String
   ```

```
        SayHello = "Hello, World!"
    End Function
```

2. Add a reference to the Microsoft SOAP Type Library: Project →
   References.

3. Compile the project.

4. Run the WSDL generator and store the WSDL file in a Web folder. In this
   example, I placed the file in the Chapter14WebService .NET project.

5. Run the wsdl.exe .NET tool to create a proxy object for the client you are
   going to create to consume this Web service. The entire proxy object is
   shown in Listing 14-16.

Listing 14-16: The Proxy Class for the Visual Basic 6 Web Service Using SOAP

```
Option Strict Off
Option Explicit On


Imports System
Imports System.ComponentModel
Imports System.Diagnostics
Imports System.Web.Services
Imports System.Web.Services.Protocols
Imports System.Xml.Serialization


<System.Diagnostics.DebuggerStepThroughAttribute(), _
 System.ComponentModel.DesignerCategoryAttribute("code"), _
 System.Web.Services.WebServiceBindingAttribute(Name:=_
    "clsSOAPInterfaceSoapBinding", _
    [Namespace]:="http://tempuri.org/wsdl/")> _
Public Class SayHelloSOAP
    Inherits System.Web.Services.Protocols.SoapHttpClientProtocol


    Public Sub New()
        MyBase.New
        Me.Url = "http://localhost/Chapter14WebService/SayHelloSOAP.WSDL"
    End Sub


    <System.Web.Services.Protocols.SoapRpcMethodAttribute( _
     "http://tempuri.org/action/clsSOAPInterface.SayHello", _
     RequestNamespace:="http://tempuri.org/message/", _
     ResponseNamespace:="http://tempuri.org/message/")> _
    Public Function SayHello() As _
     <System.Xml.Serialization.SoapElementAttribute("Result")> String
        Dim results() As Object = Me.Invoke("SayHello", New Object(-1) {})
```

```
        Return CType(results(0),String)
    End Function


    Public Function BeginSayHello(ByVal callback As System.AsyncCallback, _
                    ByVal asyncState As Object) As System.IAsyncResult _
        Return Me.BeginInvoke("SayHello", New Object(-1) {}, callback, _
                    asyncState)
    End Function


    Public Function EndSayHello(ByVal asyncResult As System.IAsyncResult)_
                            As String
        Dim results() As Object = Me.EndInvoke(asyncResult)
        Return CType(results(0),String)
    End Function
End Class
```

Now I simply have to create a page that uses this proxy class to call my Visual Basic 6 DLL via SOAP. No matter whether you're working in .NET or Visual Basic, you can both write and consume Web services. And each is fairly simple to utilize.

In the next section I address how to use UDDI to make Web services searchable on the Internet. A Web service becomes even more useful when it is available to client applications. UDDI provides the means to search for Web services on the Internet.

Using UDDI to publish the Web service

Publishing a Web service means providing enough information to a catalog that catalog users can tell if their applications would benefit from using your Web service. You also provide the information that enables the users to link their programs to your Web service. You make available the interface needed to call the Web service, not the source code needed to implement the Web service. There is already a standard that allows for the publication of Web service interfaces: Universal Description, Discovery, and Integration (UDDI) provides a way for a company to publish information about a Web service and enables that information to be queried both through a Web-based interface and programmatically. In this section I cover what it takes to publish the first simple service (Listing 14-1) created in this chapter.

UDDI provides for searches by the following criteria:

◆ Business name

◆ Business location

◆ tModel by name

◆ Business identifier

- ◆ Discovery URL

- ◆ GeoWeb Taxonomy

- ◆ NAICS Codes

- ◆ SIC Codes

- ◆ UNSPSC Codes

- ◆ ISO 3166 Geographic Taxonomy

- ◆ RealNames Keyword

UDDI is very extensive in the amount of information that can be supplied. UDDI provides standard ways for companies to describe themselves broken down into the following categories:

- ◆ White Pages: Includes basic information like the business name, contact information, and DUNS number.

- ◆ Yellow Pages: Contains the usual identifications for the type of business, such as standard industry codes, and the geographic location.

- ◆ Green Pages: Contains consumer-related information such as service descriptions and binding information.

UDDI also offers Service Type Registration, which allows you to provide detailed information about the Web service that you are providing. You can supply a URL to an access point, a site that you control where you publish specific information about your service.

To use the UDDI, you must register several pieces of information about both your company and your specific Web service. Let's look at how you can register a Web service that you want to deploy and have consumed by clients.

REGISTRATION DETAILS

To publish our simple interface, I'll use Microsoft's test UDDI service located at `http://test.uddi.microsoft.com`. Microsoft has provided both test and production UDDI servers. While learning how to register Web services, it's best to use the test UDDI server. Once you're comfortable, you can register your Web service on the production server. As will soon be evident, the majority of the work in registering a Web service involves the details about your organization or company. I'm covering only the registration details needed to get the Web service searchable and consumable by client applications. To learn more about the registration process, look at `http://uddi.microsoft.com`.

To get started, go to `http://test.uddi.microsoft.com/register.aspx`. This page requires a Microsoft Passport account. (You can use a Hotmail/MSN account if you have one; otherwise you need to sign up for a Passport account.)

Once you sign in, you're prompted to fill in registration information (shown in Figure 14-10).

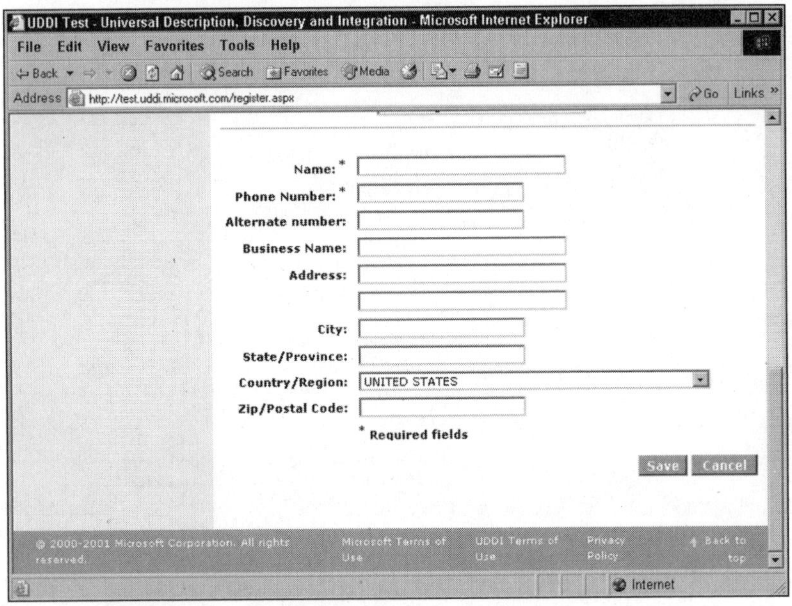

Figure 14-10: HTML form for filling in personal information.

Fill in the form, and click the Save button. The license agreement appears; click Accept to continue the registration process. The next screen indicates that you have completed the registration process, but actually this is only the start. At this point you have provided only a limited amount of information and certainly not enough to search for a Web service.

Click the Continue button, which brings up the Administer page, shown in Figure 14-11.

The Administer page enables you to add a new business, add a new tModel, and edit registration details. (tModel stands for type model.) Click the Add a new tModel link, and you are presented with a tModel Detail form like the one shown in Figure 14-12.

In the Service Name field, type in the name of our service structured as a Uniform Resource Name (URN). URNs fall under a larger grouping, Uniform Resource Identifiers (URI). They are similar to URLs in format but use colons instead of periods. The key point here is that the Service Name must be unique, and a URN is one way to provide this uniqueness. URNs are unique because they are registered with an Internet naming authority. Our example here is just for testing, so it isn't registered with an Internet naming authority. You can also fill in the description of the tModel in the Description field.

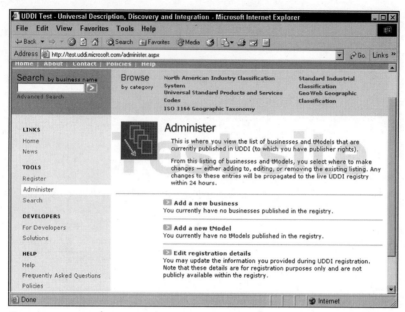

Figure 14-11: The main Administer screen for UDDI.

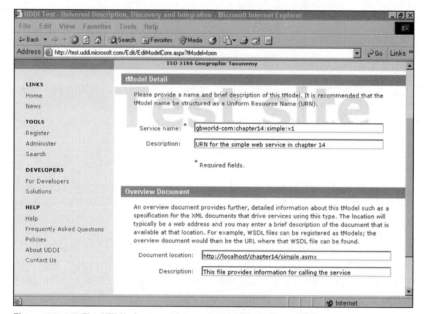

Figure 14-12: The HTML form used to enter tModel information.

For more information on Uniform Resource Identifiers (URIs) and Uniform Resource Names (URNs), go to `http://msdn.microsoft.com/msdnmag/ issues/01/07/xml/xml0107.asp.`

In the Overview Document section, enter the document location. This is where the WSDL is found or a page that contains a link to the WSDL file. In our case, I provide a link to the service located on the localhost. (I do this because it is easier to have a Web service deployed on a local system than on a Web server running the .NET Framework. In a production environment you would provide a legitimate address to the Web service.) Then enter a description about the document, and click the Continue button. The next page enables you to enter additional information about the tModel. At this point you could add a service classification and business identifiers. (I chose not to enter that information for this example). Click the Publish button, and an information screen appears indicating that the service has been published. Click Continue and you are sent back to the Administer page. This time, however, the page includes information about our first Web service. See Figure 14-13.

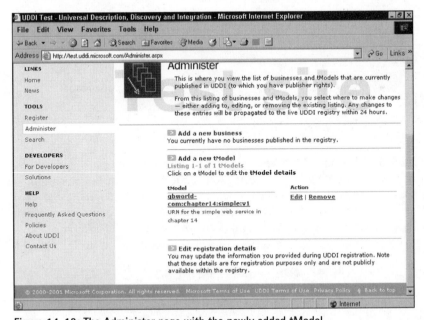

Figure 14-13: The Administer page with the newly added tModel.

Technically, that's all you need to do to register your Web service with UDDI. There are some details you have to fill out (about the business and contacts at the business), but that shouldn't be difficult. To prove that we now have a Web service that is searchable, let's search for our newly registered service. Click the Search link on the left side of the Administer page. Because we've entered such a small amount of information, I search for **chapter14** in **tModel by name**, as shown in Figure 14-14.

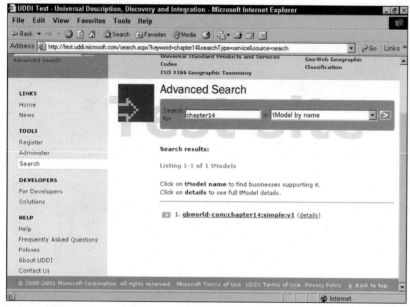

Figure 14-14: The search criteria and results.

Once the search is submitted in this example, it returns one result — our service. Click the **(details)** link, and you get information about the Web service and a link to the Overview URL (which we provided in the registration) that points to the local Web server. At this point our Web service can only be used by the system on which the service resides, but users on the Internet can still query the service.

The next step is to consume our service in a client-based application.

ADDING A WEB REFERENCE USING VISUAL STUDIO .NET

The easiest way to provide an application that will consume our published Web service is to create one in Visual Studio .NET. For this example, create a new Visual Basic Console Application by starting Visual Studio .NET, and clicking the New Project button. In the New Project dialog box, select Visual Basic Projects under the Project Types list box, and then select Console Application under the Templates list box. Enter **GetUDDIWebService** in the Name text box. (We only need a simple project that we can add a Web Reference to.) After clicking OK, right-click the project, and select Add Web Reference from the menu. The Add Web Reference dialog box (see Figure 14-15) opens.

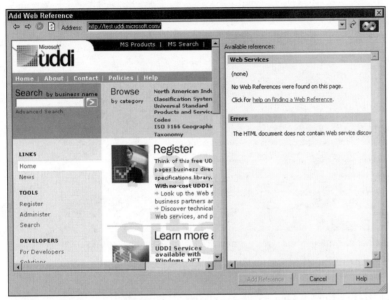

Figure 14-15: The interface used to search for a Web service from within Visual Studio .NET.

In the Address field at the top of the dialog box, enter the URL for the test UDDI Microsoft server (`http://test.uddi.microsoft.com`) where the service is registered. Click the Advanced Search link (under the Search text box) and specify that you want to search for **chapter14** in **tModel by name.** Submit the search. You get the same results as when we did our test search earlier. Clicking the **(details)** link of the returned result pulls up all of the information about the Web service. Now when you click the Overview URL under the Overview heading, you're redirected to the localhost of your system. In a production environment, you'd be directed to the public Web server where the service is hosted.

After clicking on the Overview URL, the Add Reference button is now enabled in the Add Web Reference dialog box. This means that Visual Studio .NET sees the WSDL file and can import it. Click the Add Reference button, and the interface reverts to the development environment. Now that the Web Reference is added, we can access the methods in our console application. The appearance of the IDE after adding the Web Reference is shown in Figure 14-16.

This small application just calls the Web service and prints out the Hello, World! message from the Web service.

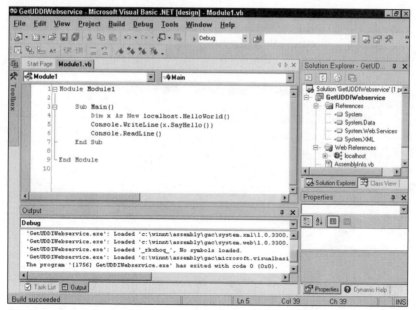

Figure 14-16: The console application, which references the Web service discovered on Microsoft's test UDDI site.

ADDITIONAL INFORMATION ABOUT UDDI

IBM provides a UDDI registry that you can use, too. The address is `www-3.ibm.com/services/uddi/protect/find`. IBM provides an interface similar to Microsoft's. Additionally XMethods also provides a site to register Web services: `http://uddi.xmethods.net`.

The future of UDDI seems somewhat uncertain. For example, of all of the entries that exist on both Microsoft's and IBM's production UDDI servers, it appears that only a fraction have actual working Web services that can be consumed by clients. This is somewhat disappointing because working with published Web services can be exciting once you find some that have practical value. A large number of the sites on the production servers refer you to a URL containing localhost, indicating that the host of the Web service is still testing, much like the example we created earlier in the chapter.

In the next section I'll briefly discuss Microsoft's DISCO standard, which relates to the UDDI standard used for publishing Web services. DISCO is an XML file that contains links to other supporting documents, such as WSDL files.

DISCO

Microsoft has introduced DISCO, a standard for discovering Web services. DISCO is a fairly simple standard, which requires an XML file to be stored with the Web service. The file is named with a `.disco` extension and contains links to other supporting documents for the Web service. The DISCO files themselves are XML documents containing pointers to WSDL documents or XSD schemas and can also contain links to other DISCO documents, creating a web of DISCO documents. When you build a Web service in Visual Studio .NET, Visual Studio .NET automatically creates the DISCO file for your service.

DISCO assumes that the client already knows how to find the Web service (usually done by searching the UDDI directories discussed in the previous section). Once the client has found the Web service, he can access the DISCO document to find additional information about the service. DISCO documents are not a necessity for a Web service — they are an extra convenience. UDDI provides sufficient information to consume a Web service (a link to the WSDL document); DISCO supplies additional documentation on top of the information UDDI provides.

To view a DISCO file, supply the querystring parameter ?DISCO to the end of the .asmx file (the main Web service file covered in the "Declaring a Web Service" section earlier in the chapter). By providing the ?DISCO at the end of the querystring the DISCO file is dynamically generated for the Web service. The result of trying this on the Web service from earlier in the chapter is shown in Figure 14-17.

Figure 14-17: The results of dynamically generating the DISCO file from the simple.asmx file.

You can create your own DISCO file, but it needs to be placed in the same directory as the .asmx file so that clients can locate it.

Microsoft has also provided a command-line-based utility, disco.exe, for retrieving the associated files listed in a DISCO file. disco.exe is located in the Bin folder of the .NET Framework installation directory. Running this utility against a Web service's URL provides all the associated resources for that service. I ran the DISCO utility against the simple.asmx file created earlier (Listing 14-1) using the following command:

```
disco http://localhost/chapter14/simple.asmx
```

Listing 14-17 shows the results.

Listing 14-17: Results of Executing the DISCO Command against the Web Service URL.

```
Microsoft (R) Web Services Discovery Utility
[Microsoft (R) .NET Framework, Version 1.0.3705.0]
Copyright (C) Microsoft Corporation 1998-2001. All rights reserved.

Disco found documents at the following URLs:
http://localhost/chapter14/simple.asmx?wsdl
http://localhost/chapter14/simple.asmx?disco

The following files hold the content found at the corresponding URLs:
  .\simple.wsdl <- http://localhost/chapter14/simple.asmx?wsdl
  .\simple.disco <- http://localhost/chapter14/simple.asmx?disco
The file .\results.discomap holds links to each of these files.
```

The DISCO utility created three files in the same directory where I ran the utility. As indicated by the output, it created `simple.wsdl`, `simple.disco`, and the `results.discomap` files, which can now be used for creating the client application.

Because DISCO is a Microsoft standard, it's hard to tell how well it will catch on in the industry. Additionally, because Web services work fine without DISCO, developers may stop using it altogether. For the time being, if you use Visual Studio .NET to create your Web services, Visual Studio .NET creates DISCO documents for them, an extra feature for documentation of your Web service.

Summary

This chapter covers how to build a Web service in ASP.NET, how you consume it with both ASP.NET and Visual Basic 6, and how easy it is to interact with legacy code, using SOAP, with a .NET Web service proxy class. I hope that I demystified the entire process and showed that Web services are just another interface for exposing the methods of classes you write. Any code you create in .NET can easily be altered to become a Web service, even if the original method is contained in a class that has been compiled into an `EXE` file. This is a powerful addition to every developer's arsenal.

You also saw how to register a Web service using Microsoft's UDDI registry and how to create a DISCO document used for documentation of your Web service.

This chapter is the end of Part II. In Part III, I cover ADO.NET and how to work with data in the .NET framework. Most of the chapters in Part III use SQL Server 2000 as a data source, because I deal primarily with Enterprise-level applications. While I do present a few examples using other databases, SQL Server is the standard.

Part III

Working with Data — ADO.NET

Chapter 15

Working with Provider Objects

IN THIS CHAPTER

◆ Working with data in ASP

◆ Using a DataReader with SQL Server

◆ Using a DataReader with OLE DB providers

◆ Using a DataReader with an ODBC data source

◆ Comparing a DataReader to a DataSet and when to use each

MUCH OF YOUR WORK IN ASP.NET can be accomplished by using objects in the provider namespaces `System.Data.SQLClient`, `System.Data.OleDb`, and `System.Data.Odbc`. This chapter takes a look at using a `DataReader` object to present data in an ASP.NET. It also gives a quick introduction to the `DataSet`, `DataTable`, and `DataView` objects, which are covered in greater detail in the next two chapters.

In this chapter, I use the full namespace of each of the objects to get you used to finding the objects.

The Way We Were

To understand where you are, you have to look back on where you have been. Where we have been, for the past few years, is in a data access model called ActiveX Data Objects, or ADO for short. I don't think there's a need to go back any further, but if you'd like to be really nostalgic, you can consult the MSDN documentation at `http://msdn.microsoft.com`; just look for DAO or RDO.

The basics of ADO are fairly simple. You have a connection object that represents the connection to the data source. I say data source instead of database here because ADO is designed to attach to non-traditional sources, such as an e-mail server or a text file. Using this connection, you create recordsets that contain the records with which you are going to work. In some instances, you may also want to use command objects to pass parameters to a preconfigured database query, such as a SQL Server stored procedure. Figure 15-1 shows the portion of the object model for ADO version 2.6 that is used in this chapter. While there are a couple of additional objects, such as the stream object, these are unimportant in comparing ADO to ADO.NET.

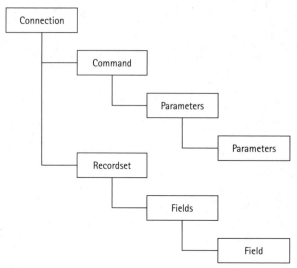

Figure 15-1: The ADO object model.

Rather than spend a lot of time going over the objects in a theoretical discussion, I think it would be much more useful to show you an example page. Listing 15-1 contains a rather simple page that pulls a list of employees linked by primary key (the EmployeeID field) to the same page to display details about a single employee.

Listing 15-1: A Simple Data Page

```
<%
Option Explicit

'Get the employeeID
Private m_intEmployeeID 'As Integer
m_intEmployeeID = Cint(Request("id"))

Private Function GetEmployee(intEmployeeID) 'As ADODB.Recordset
   Dim objConn 'As ADODB.Connection
   Dim strConn 'As String
   Dim strSQL 'As String

   'Open the Connection object
   strConn = "Provider=SQLOLEDB.1;Server=(local);" & _
      "Database=Northwind;UID=sa;PWD=;"
```

```
     Set objConn = Server.CreateObject("ADODB.Connection")
     Call objConn.Open(strConn)
   strSQL = "SELECT * From Employees"
     If intEmployeeID <> 0 then
       strSQL = strSQL & " WHERE intEmployeeID = " & intEmployeeID
     End If
   Set GetRecordset = objConn.Execute(strSQL)
End Function
%>
<html>
..<head>
   <Title>Employees</Title>
   </head>
   <body>
<%
  Dim objRS 'As ADODB.Recordset
  Set objRS = GetEmployee(m_intEmployeeID)
If m_intEmployeeID = 0 then
  'Make a listing
%>
<table>
  <tr>
    <td>Employee</td>
    <td>Title</td>
  </tr>
<% Do until objRS.EOF %>
  <tr>
    <td>
      <a href="employee.asp?id=<%=objRS("intEmployeeID")%>">
      <%=objRS("LastName")%>, <%=objRS("FirstName")%></a>
    </td>
    <td><%=objRS("Title")%></td>
  </tr>
<%
    objRS.MoveNext
  Loop
%>
</table>
<%
Else
  'Show an employee
%>
<h1><%=objRS("FirstName")%> <%=objRS("LastName")%></h1>
```

Continued

Listing 15-1 *(Continued)*

```
<p>Title: <%=objRS("Title")%><br />
Birth date: <%=objRS("BirthDate")%><br />
Hire date: <%=objRS("HireDate")%></p>
<p><%=objRS("Address")%><br />
<%=objRS("City")%>
<% If not IsNull(objRS("Region")) then
    Response.Write "," & objRS("Region")
  End If
End If
%>
  </body>
</html>
```

You can find the code for Listing 15-1 on this book's companion Web site (www.wiley.com/extras) in the download file `Ch15VS.zip` (**Visual Studio .NET** version) or `Ch15SDK.zip` (**SDK** version). The file is called `employee.asp`.

The steps to create this list are fairly simple. You create a connection object, open it using a connection string, and use it to fill a recordset. You then output the recordset by looping through the records.

To make the exercise a bit more complex, I include a method to use the same page to list the detail for a single record. If an ID is passed to the page, the detail for that employee is shown instead of the list of employees.

Traditional wisdom tells us that I am not supposed to write code that mixes ASP with HTML, especially in a loop. The rule for performance is to create a string and then use `Response.Write` to output to the browser. I have purposefully broken the rule of mixing HTML and ASP for three reasons:

1. The performance aspect is largely overrated. In tests I conducted with 2000 records for an article for ASPToday (www.asptoday.com) (January 2000), I found there was no real performance hit by mixing contexts until you got to the output of thousands of records. Since you won't be outputting this amount of data in one page, this is not a problem.

2. It is easier to maintain a page that mixes ASP with HTML because a Web author can edit it in FrontPage. While I know there is a contingency that abhors FrontPage, I believe a tool should be considered a tool, even one with such a nefarious history.

3. It is easier to follow code when it is in order.

Let's examine what this page does. When you first bring this page up, you create a table that makes a hyperlinked list of employees. Figure 15-2 shows this employee listing.

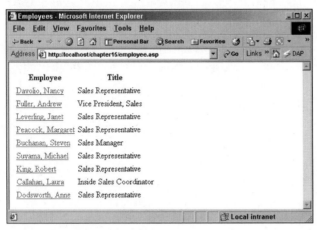

Figure 15-2: The employee list.

Since the output of the table includes a hyperlink for each record, which uses the primary key, it is fairly easy to pass this ID field back to the page. If the ID is present, a single record is displayed. I have also designed the recordset routine so it uses the same routine regardless of whether the page displays the entire list or just a single record. Figure 15-3 shows the single record after a user clicks on one of the names.

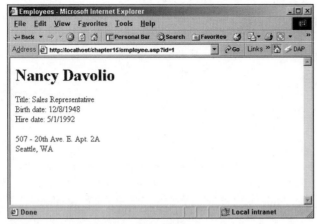

Figure 15-3: A single employee record.

The command object

While I won't go through every object in the ADO model, the command object is important to understand because the concepts behind it continue in ADO.NET.

The primary use of the command object is to attach to stored procedures in a variety of databases — that is, the command object nicely fits in with stored procedures enabling programmers to directly retrieve results from executing a stored procedure without writing complex code. Command objects fit well with stored procedures because the parameter objects connect to parameters in the stored procedure.

To illustrate the use of the command object, Listing 15-2 contains a stored procedure that does the same work as the SQL statement in the GetEmployee() routine in Listing 15-1.

Listing 15–2: A Stored Procedure to Return Employees

```
CREATE PROCEDURE sps_Employee
(
    @EmployeeID    int = 0
)
AS

IF @EmployeeID = 0
  BEGIN
     SELECT EmployeeID, FirstName, LastName, Title
     FROM Employees
  END
ELSE
  BEGIN
    SELECT EmployeeID, LastName, FirstName, Title,
        TitleOfCourtesy, BirthDate, HireDate, Address,
        City, Region, PostalCode, Country, HomePhone,
        Extension, Photo, Notes, ReportsTo, PhotoPath
    FROM Employees
    WHERE EmployeeID = @EmployeeID
  END
GO
```

 You'll find the script to recreate this stored procedure on the companion Web site (www.wiley.com/extras) in the download file for Chapter 15: Ch15VS.zip (Visual Studio .NET version) or Ch15SDK.zip (SDK version). Unzip the download and look for the sps_Employee.sql file in the Northwind folder.

To use this stored procedure with the connection and recordset objects alone, I can call the stored procedure with a space and then the integer value I want to call. This is fairly simple but does not really use the strength of ADO. Using the command object, I can attach parameters to the command to call the stored procedure. This is shown in Listing 15-3.

Listing 15-3: Using the Command Object

```
Private Function GetEmployee(intEmployeeID) 'As ADODB.Recordset
   Dim objConn 'As ADODB.Connection
   Dim objCmd 'As ADODB.Command
   Dim strConn 'As String
   Dim strSQL 'As String

   'Open the Connection object
   strConn = "Provider=SQLOLEDB.1;Server=(local);" & _
       "Database=Northwind;UID=sa;PWD=;"
     Set objConn = Server.CreateObject("ADODB.Connection")
     Call objConn.Open(strConn)

   SET objCmd = Server.CreateObject("ADODB.Command")

   With objCmd
      .ActiveConnection = objConn      'The connection object
      .CommandText = "sps_Employee"      'The stored procedure
      .CommandType = 4                 'adCmdStoredProc
      .Parameters.Refresh
   End With

   objCmd.Parameters.Item(1).Value = intEmployeeID
   Set GetEmployee = objCmd.Execute
End Function
```

The main strength of this method comes when you want to fire a stored procedure in a generic manner. Since ADO is not the focus of this book, it would not do well to include the routine here. I have, however, included an include file (dataRoutines.asp) in the download for this chapter, and it contains two routines: CallSprocWIthArray() and CallSprocWithDictionary(). I'm not as fond of the Dictionary object for this purpose, but it's easier to seed than the Array.

Connection strings

ADO has the capability to connect to any OLE DB data source. In addition, you can connect to any ODBC data source through the OLE DB ODBC provider. In this section, I connect to Access and SQL Server data sources using an ADO.NET managed provider, as well as the SQL Server .NET native provider.

With this in mind, I want to show you some connection strings in ADO. You use the same connection strings with ADO.NET. The first connection string is the same one used with our ASP application from the preceding section of this chapter. In Listing 15-4, I have presented two connection strings for connecting to SQL Server. Although the strings look different, they essentially do the same thing.

Listing 15–4: SQL Server Connection String

```
Provider=SQLOLEDB.1;Server=(local);Database=Northwind;UID=sa;PWD=;

Provider=SQLOLEDB.1;Data Source=(local);Initial Catalog=Northwind;
User Id=sa;Password=;
```

I use the first connection string not because of any inherent performance boost, but because it is easier to type in. The "SQLOLEDB.1" as a provider indicates that I want to use the latest SQL Server provider. Microsoft put in this shorthand for the eventuality that you might one day have to use an older driver. I have never had the opportunity to use anything other than SQLOLEDB.1 in my applications, so I do not think you can go wrong with it.

Moving to another database requires very few changes to the connection string. To move to Access, for example, you have to change the provider and point to either a DSN (Data Source Name) or a path to the Access database file. Because DSNs move you into the realm of ODBC, which adds another layer to the model, I do not recommend using them. Listing 15-5 contains the connection string for the default install of Visual Studio 6 Northwind Access database.

Listing 15–5: Access Connection String

```
Provider=Microsoft.Jet.OLEDB.4.0;Data Source=C:\Program ⏎
Files\Microsoft Visual Studio\VB98\NWind.mdb;
```

These are the only changes you need to make to switch from one provider to another when you are working with SQL statements. If you are working with stored procedures, it is better to stick with SQL Server. In the download, I include a file called employee3.asp that hooks up to the Access database to create the list. The list still points to the SQL Server stored procedure query for the detail page.

You can download the new version of the Northwind Access database that has the query to use with this page. The connection string is a bit different; it points to a directory named C:\Projects\Chapter15.

The customized Northwind database is included in the file Ch15SDK.zip (SDK version) or Ch15VS.zip (Visual Studio .NET version) on this book's companion Web site (www.wiley.com/extras). The name of the database is NWind.mdb.

As you move into ASP.NET, you find that these connection strings still work. There is one change if you use the native SQL Server provider, which I discuss later in this chapter.

Moving to ADO.NET

ADO.NET marks a departure from the standard ADO object model. The change is primarily to fit a disconnected paradigm. While you can create disconnected recordsets in ADO, it is more of an afterthought. ADO.NET was designed to be disconnected from the get-go. Figure 15-4 shows an object model for ADO.NET that you can compare to the ADO object model in Figure 15-1. This ADO.NET model is basically for comparison purposes. As you go forward, you'll see that this is not exactly how the model works, but it serves our purpose for now.

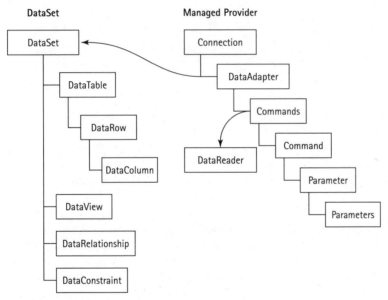

Figure 15-4: ADO.NET object model.

The object model in Figure 15-4 shows that there is a clear delineation between the objects that access the data source and the objects that consume the data. This is an important distinction. Note that the objects do not necessarily fall into this hierarchy; the command object, for instance, can be used outside of an explicit DataAdapter. Note, also, that this is an overly simplified model. ADO.NET can get quite complex. I build on this model throughout the next couple of chapters.

There are two important points you need to understand about the differences between ADO and ADO.NET:

1. The data access and consumption are done by two completely different sets of objects in ADO.NET. In ADO, the recordset derives directly from the connection object; in ADO.NET the `DataSet` is independent of the connection object.

2. In ADO, data was connected by default, and you had to work to disconnect a recordset. In ADO.NET, data is disconnected. You use a managed provider to get the data and then you fill a `DataSet`. The fact that the objects are in two different namespaces should help you remember this.

The core of the model is the .NET Data provider. There are currently three types of data providers in ADO.NET.

◆ ADO.NET managed providers: These providers connect to databases using OLE DB. ADO.NET managed providers use a standard connection string. You can connect to SQL Server using a managed provider, but there is a better way.

◆ SQL Server .NET native provider: SQL Server has its own provider in ADO.NET. The connection string using these objects does not require a provider object. In general, I run all SQL Server access through these objects.

◆ ODBC .NET providers: You connect to ODBC through a different set of providers if your database does not have an ADO.NET managed provider. At present, this is a separate download from the MSDN site (`http://msdn.microsoft.com/downloads/default.asp`). Note that you have to have MDAC 2.6 or greater to use ODBC.NET; this is not an issue because MDAC 2.6 is the minimum requirement to install both the .NET Framework SDK and Visual Studio .NET.

Whether you use ODBC .NET providers, OLE DB .NET managed providers, or the SQL Server.NET native provider, the objects you use are the same. The main difference is in the names of the objects and the namespace. Table 15-1 shows the namespace used for each and the prefix for the objects.

TABLE 15-1 ADO.NET PROVIDERS

Provider	Namespace	Prefix
OLE DB	System.Data.OleDb	OleDb
ODBC	System.Data.Odbc	Odbc
SQL Server	System.Data.SqlClient	Sql or SqlClient.

There are two basic methods of pulling data from ADO.NET. Forward only, you use a `DataReader`. If you need to update, insert, or delete data, and want to use the intrinsic abilities of ADO.NET rather than code it yourself, you have to use a `DataSet` instead. The basic architecture of ADO.NET is shown in Figure 15-5.

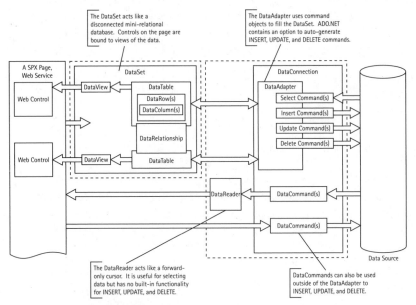

Figure 15-5: ADO.NET architecture.

Using a DataReader

When you want to pull data from a data source and show it in a page, you generally want to use a `DataReader`. The `DataReader` is part of the managed provider, meaning you have to change the prefix of the `DataReader` object if you want to change data sources. In this section, I recreate the page from the first part of the chapter.

The first few examples here are built using some bad coding habits. I do this on purpose not to make sure you read the entire chapter, but so you to can see a couple of sloppy habits that you can then spot in your own code. Don't spend too much time if it does not pop out at you immediately. This is a new paradigm, so you are going to have to get used to it.

FIRST PASS: SQL SERVER NATIVE .NET PROVIDER

Since I tend to build Enterprise applications, I am going to start with an Enterprise data source. My weapon of choice is SQL Server 2000, but this code works on SQL Server 7, as well. Most of the examples in this book use this provider, as it is the most efficient method of connecting with SQL Server.

If you do not have access to SQL Server and do not want to download a trial version, I use a couple of other providers in this `DataReader` section. You can alter the code samples to match the changes in this section if you want to use these databases to follow along.

If you aren't interested in SQL Server, I recommend joining the Oracle TechNet site (`http://technet.oracle.com`) so you can download Oracle instead. It's okay if you must use Access, but understand that Access is not meant to scale like SQL Server or Oracle. One last possibility is the Microsoft Data Engine (MSDE), which is a lightweight version of SQL Server, with a hard-coded limitation of five simultaneous connections. This is not as much of a limitation as it appears, because five connections can support a lot more than five users in an Internet application.

THE ASPX PAGE   To build the page, I use the `SqlDataReader`. The `DataReader` is used for forward-only result sets, which is fine for what we are doing here. In this example, I recreate the ASP example to show some differences between ASP and ASP.NET.

Remember one of the two changes you have to make to switch to another provider is changing the prefix here. Since data binding is the standard method of placing data on a page, I bind the `DataReader` object to a `DataGrid` and a `Repeater`.

First, I need to go through the ASPX page. This is the user interface for this section of the application. As with the earlier ASP example, the ASPX page displays a list of employees from employee table.

Listing 15-6 contains the code for the `employee.aspx` file. Note that there is no code in this page, just tags. I cover the CodeBehind page shortly.

Listing 15-6: Employee.aspx

```
<%@ Page Language="vb" AutoEventWireup="false" ↵
Codebehind="employee.aspx.vb" Inherits="Chapter15.employee"%>
<!DOCTYPE HTML PUBLIC "-//W3C//DTD HTML 4.0 Transitional//EN">
<HTML>
  <HEAD>
    <title>Employee List</title>
  </HEAD>
  <body>
    <form id="Form1" method="post" runat="server">
      <P>
        <asp:DataGrid id="DataGrid1" runat="server" CellPadding="2" ↵
CellSpacing="2" BorderWidth="0" AutoGenerateColumns="False">
          <Columns>
            <asp:HyperLinkColumn DataNavigateUrlField="EmployeeID" ↵
DataNavigateUrlFormatString="employee.aspx?id={0}" ↵
DataTextField="LastName" HeaderText="Name">↵
</asp:HyperLinkColumn>
            <asp:HyperLinkColumn DataNavigateUrlField="EmployeeID" ↵
```

```
DataNavigateUrlFormatString="employee.aspx?id={0}" ↵
DataTextField="FirstName">↵
</asp:HyperLinkColumn>
            <asp:BoundColumn DataField="Title" ↵
HeaderText="Title"></asp:BoundColumn>
          </Columns>
        </asp:DataGrid>
      </P>
      <asp:Repeater id="Repeater2" runat="server">
        <ItemTemplate>
          <h1>
            <%# Container.DataItem("LastName")%>
            ,
            <%# Container.DataItem("FirstName")%>
          </h1>
          <p>
            Title:
            <%# Container.DataItem("Title")%>
            <br>
            Birth Date:
            <%# FormatDateTime(Container.DataItem("BirthDate"), ↵
DateFormat.ShortDate)%>
            <br>
            Hire Date:
            <%# FormatDateTime(Container.DataItem("HireDate"), ↵
DateFormat.ShortDate)%>
            <br>
          </p>
          <p>
            <%# Container.DataItem("Address") %>
            <br>
            <%# Container.DataItem("City") %>
          </p>
        </ItemTemplate>
      </asp:Repeater>
    </form>
  </body>
</HTML>
```

The code for Listing 15-6 can be found on the companion Web site (www.wiley.com/extras) in the download file Ch15SDK.zip (SDK version) or Ch15VS.zip (Visual Studio .NET version). The file is named employee.aspx.

Let me run through this code quickly. I won't go through the header tags or any of the HTML, assuming that you are not lacking in either of these areas.

The @ directive tag is discussed in more detail in Chapter 3, in the CodeBehind section.

- DataGrid: The DataGrid is bound in the CodeBehind page, rather than with declarative binding. In Visual Studio, you can do a lot of your binding through properties; neat, yes; but not the focus of this book. Most important here is the fact that I have turned off the automatic generation of columns (I get back to this in Chapter 16).

  ```
  AutoGenerateColumns="False"
  ```

- Columns: The reason for turning off the automatic generation of columns is that I am going to create special columns to make the page similar to the ASP example. I have two types of columns: two hyperlink columns and one bound column. Each of the created columns much be contained here. Note: If you leave `AutoGenerateColumns` set to `True` (the default), you get both the columns you create in this section and the auto-generated columns, which is pretty messy. Try it, if you want; I'll wait.

- Hyperlink column: In the Hyperlink column, the `DataNavigateUrlField` attribute contains the field from the `DataReader` that fills the URL. This field replaces the `{0}` in the `DataNavigateUrlFormatString` attribute. The `DataTextField` attribute is the field from the `DataReader` that fills the column (the words for the hyperlink). The header cell for this column is filled with the word(s) in the `HeaderText` attribute.

- Bound column: The bound column is much simpler. The `DataField` attribute is the field in the `DataReader` that I am binding, while the `HeaderText` attribute once again is the word(s) in the header cell.

- Repeater: The Repeater Web control is fairly simple. The main point to note, for now, is the method of pulling fields out:

  ```
  <%# Container.DataItem("LastName")%>
  ```

  The Container here is the object that is bound to the Repeater. In this example, the `DataReader` is the bound object. The rest should be easy to break down. I display the `DataItem` (or column) "LastName" from the query.

- `<ItemTemplate>`: The `ItemTemplate` tag contains all of the HTML and bound items necessary to display the user chosen by a click on one of the hyperlink columns. Since this is a repeater, I can later decide to bind to a list control that allows more than one choice and then show each of the employees chosen on one page, using the format inside the Repeater Web control. Notice that I format the datetime returned from SQL Server to only display the date, as shown here:

```
<%# FormatDateTime(Container.DataItem("BirthDate"), ↵
DateFormat.ShortDate)%>
```

THE CODEBEHIND FILE I trust that you are now used to me using CodeBehind files, because I think the separation of code and user interface is one of the better features in ASP.NET. To complete our employee page example, the code for employee.aspx.vb is shown in Listing 15-7.

Listing 15-7: The CodeBehind File for the Employee List Page

```
Imports SQL = System.Data.SqlClient
...
Private Sub Page_Load(ByVal sender As System.Object, _
          ByVal e As System.EventArgs) Handles MyBase.Load
  Dim strConn As String = "Server=(local);Database=Northwind;UID=sa;PWD=;"
  Dim objConn As New SQL.SqlConnection(strConn)
  objConn.Open()
  Dim strSQL As String
  Dim intEmployeeID As Integer = 0
  If CInt(Request("id")) <> 0 Then
    intEmployeeID = CInt(Request("id"))
    strSQL = "SELECT * FROM Employees WHERE EmployeeID = " & intEmployeeID
  Else
    strSQL = "SELECT EmployeeID, LastName, FirstName, Title FROM Employees"
  End If
  Dim objCmd As New SQL.SqlCommand(strSQL, objConn)
  Dim objReader As SQL.SqlDataReader = objCmd.ExecuteReader()
  If intEmployeeID = 0 Then
    DataGrid1.DataSource = objReader
    DataGrid1.DataBind()
    Repeater2.Visible = False
  Else
    DataGrid1.Visible = False
    Repeater2.DataSource = objReader
    Repeater2.DataBind()
  End If
End Sub
```

When you run this page, notice that it looks exactly the same as the ASP page earlier in the chapter. Because the method is quite a bit different from the ASP example, here is a run-through of the code.

◆ Connection: Just like ASP, the first step is to create a connection to the database. The connection string is slightly altered, because you do not have to include the provider in the string. This only works when using the SQL Server native .NET provider. The connection needs to be opened just like the one in ASP.

◆ Command: Unlike ASP, you do not directly fill a recordset from a connection. Since ASP.NET is aimed toward a disconnected paradigm, you use a Command object. This may seem a bit strange at first, but it is much more flexible.

◆ Reader: Calling the ExecuteReader method on the command object fills the DataReader.

◆ Data binding: To bind the data to the control(s), I use the DataSource property of either the DataGrid or the Repeater control. I have explicitly set the other control's Visible property to false. In reality, this is not necessary because only one control is data bound at a time in this example, but I would rather explicitly hide the control I'm not using.

A QUICK NOTE ON THE DATAGRID   This particular example does not match the ASP example exactly because I have created two columns for the hyperlink. With the DataGrid control, it is much easier to have two hyperlink columns, because you don't have to code each column when you have two. Figure 15-6 shows the output of the page with the DataGrid.

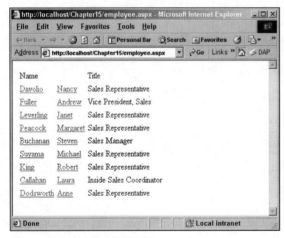

Figure 15-6: Using a DataGrid.

To create a custom output, I most likely would use a Repeater control instead. I do this in the second pass. However, I warn you that some of the code in the next example causes errors in the design view of Visual Studio .NET. This goes along with the CodeBehind paradigm, but is still a bit of a pain.

SECOND PASS: ORACLE 8I WITH A MANAGED PROVIDER

Since the DataGrid failed to reproduce the ASP.NET page verbatim, I am going to use a Repeater control instead. I still use the other Repeater for the detail output, because that was pretty much the same as the ASP output. The dual Repeater controls are shown in Listing 15-8.

Listing 15-8: Using a Repeater for the Employee List

```
<form id="Form1" method="post" runat="server">
  <asp:Repeater id="Repeater1" runat="server">
    <HeaderTemplate>
      <table cellpadding="2" cellspacing="2">
        <tr>
          <th>
            Employee
          </th>
          <th>
            Title
          </th>
        </tr>
    </HeaderTemplate>
    <ItemTemplate>
      <tr>
        <td>
<a href='employee2.aspx?id=<%# Container.DataItem("EmployeeID")%>'>
          <%# Container.DataItem("LastName")%>
            ,
          <%# Container.DataItem("FirstName")%>
        </a>
      </td>
      <td>
        <%# Container.DataItem("Title")%>
      </td>
    </tr>
  </ItemTemplate>
  <FooterTemplate>
    </table>
  </FooterTemplate>
</asp:Repeater>
<asp:Repeater id="Repeater2" runat="server">
  <ItemTemplate>
    <h1>
      <%# Container.DataItem("LastName")%>
        ,
```

Continued

Listing 15-8 *(Continued)*

```
        <%# Container.DataItem("FirstName")%>
    </h1>
    <p>
      Title:
      <%# Container.DataItem("Title")%>
      <br>
      Birth Date:
      <%# FormatDateTime(Container.DataItem("BirthDate"),
          DateFormat.ShortDate)%>
      <br>
      Hire Date:
      <%# FormatDateTime(Container.DataItem("HireDate"),
          DateFormat.ShortDate)%>
      <br>
    </p>
    <p>
      <%# Container.DataItem("Address") %>
      <br>
      <%# Container.DataItem("City") %>
    </p>
  </ItemTemplate>
 </asp:Repeater>
</form>
```

The main change is using the `Container.DataItem("ItemName")` syntax rather than binding a column to a field in the `DataReader`. One other thing to note here: since you cannot nest quotes, you have to use single quotes around the value for the `href` attribute of the `<a>` tag because of the double quotes around "EmployeeID". When the example is run, it works with double quotes in both places, because an ID is supplied. You can't use the Design view in Visual Studio .NET if you use double quotes in both places.

In the CodeBehind file, I also made a few changes. First, I switched to a .NET managed provider instead of the SQL native provider. Next, I switched databases. Listing 15-9 shows these changes.

Listing 15-9: Using Oracle with an OLE DB .NET Managed Provider

```
Imports OleDb = System.Data.OleDb
...
Private Sub Page_Load(ByVal sender As System.Object, _
        ByVal e As System.EventArgs) Handles MyBase.Load

    'Create a connection and open it
```

```
Dim strConn As String = "Provider=MSDAORA;UID=scott;PWD=tiger;"
Dim objConn As New OleDb.OleDbConnection(strConn)

'Declare variables
Dim strSQL As String
Dim intEmployeeID As Integer = 0

'Create a SQL Statement
If CInt(Request("id")) <> 0 Then
    intEmployeeID = CInt(Request("id"))
    strSQL = "SELECT * FROM Employees WHERE EmployeeID = " & intEmployeeID
Else
    strSQL = "SELECT EmployeeID, LastName, FirstName, Title FROM Employees"
End If

'Fill the Reader object with a Command Object

Dim objCmd As New OleDb.OleDbCommand(strSQL, objConn)

objConn.Open()


Dim objReader As OleDb.OleDbDataReader = objCmd.ExecuteReader()


'Bind the data
If intEmployeeID = 0 Then

    Repeater1.DataSource = objReader
    Repeater1.DataBind()

    Repeater2.Visible = False
Else
    Repeater2.DataSource = objReader
    Repeater2.DataBind()

    Repeater1.Visible = False

End If
objConn.Close()
End Sub
```

In Listing 15-9, all of the changes to the code to get this working with Oracle are in bold. (If I want to use a managed provider with SQL Server, I have to change each of these items as well, but the connection string change would be as simple as adding "Provider=SQLOLEDB.1;" to the beginning of the string.)

To accomplish these changes quickly, I did a couple of search-and-replace operations and one edit:

◆ OleDb replaces SqlClient

◆ .OleDb replaces .Sql

◆ Repeater1 replaces DataGrid1

◆ The connection string is edited to point to the Oracle database

A couple of notes: While I worked with Oracle on my home computer, I doubt all of you use Oracle, so I set the connection string in the examples in this chapter's download files to SQL Server. If you have access to Oracle, you have to modify the connection string. The user "scott" and password "tiger" are preconfigured logins that no self-respecting Oracle DBA would leave open on a production database. The connection string might also need to have a "data source" or "database" attribute to connect to a particular database.

THIRD PASS: MICROSOFT ACCESS

The third pass is the easiest of all. To use Microsoft Access, instead of Oracle with an OLE DB .NET managed provider, all you have to change is the connection string. This is very similar to using different data sources in ADO. Listing 15-10 highlights the single change to accomplish the move from Oracle, in Listing 15-9, to Access.

Listing 15-10: Switching to Microsoft Access

```
Imports OleDb = System.Data.OleDb
...
Private Sub Page_Load(ByVal sender As System.Object, _
           ByVal e As System.EventArgs) Handles MyBase.Load


    'Put user code to initialize the page here
    Dim strConn As String = "Provider=Microsoft.Jet.OLEDB.4.0;" & _
      "Data Source= " & Server.MapPath("NWind.mdb")
    Dim objConn As New OleDb.OleDbConnection(strConn)


    'Must declare strSQL and intEmployeeID outside of the If statement
    Dim strSQL As String
    Dim intEmployeeID As Integer = 0


    'Tailor SQL Statement based on ID input
    If CInt(Request("id")) <> 0 Then
```

```
        intEmployeeID = CInt(Request("id"))
        strSQL = "SELECT * FROM Employees WHERE EmployeeID = " & intEmployeeID
    Else
        strSQL = "SELECT EmployeeID, LastName, FirstName, Title FROM Employees"
    End If

    'Fill the Reader object with a Command Object
    Dim objCmd As New OleDb.OleDbCommand(strSQL, objConn)
    objConn.Open()
    Dim objReader As OleDb.OleDbDataReader = objCmd.ExecuteReader()

    'Determine whether to show list or detail
    If intEmployeeID = 0 Then
        Repeater1.DataSource = objReader
        Repeater1.DataBind()
        Repeater2.Visible = False
    Else
        Repeater2.DataSource = objReader
        Repeater2.DataBind()
        Repeater1.Visible = False
    End If
    objConn.Close()
End Sub
```

FOURTH PASS: STORED PROCEDURES

Now that you are used to working with a SQL query, I want to shake things up a bit. In a real-world application that connects to SQL Server, you would most likely use stored procedures for added security because you can limit the application user account to have no direct access to any tables.

THE STORED PROCEDURE   To make this shift, you have to code a stored procedure. Fortunately, I have already created one. The stored procedure in Listing 15-11 is the same stored procedure used in the ASP example, Listing 15-2. (It's repeated here so you don't have to flip back to the earlier page.)

Listing 15-11: A Stored Procedure to Return Employees

```
CREATE PROCEDURE sps_Employee
(
    @EmployeeID       int = 0
)
AS
```

Continued

Listing 15-11 *(Continued)*

```
IF @EmployeeID = 0
  BEGIN
     SELECT EmployeeID, FirstName, LastName, Title
     FROM Employees
  END
ELSE
  BEGIN
    SELECT EmployeeID, LastName, FirstName, Title,
       TitleOfCourtesy, BirthDate, HireDate, Address,
       City, Region, PostalCode, Country, HomePhone,
       Extension, Photo, Notes, ReportsTo, PhotoPath
    FROM Employees
    WHERE EmployeeID = @EmployeeID
  END
GO
```

THE CODEBEHIND FILE   Using this stored procedure, I have to make a couple of changes to the code. To make this easier to understand, I am highlighting only the changes to the command object rather than show all of the changes back to SQLClient objects (from OleDb objects). The CodeBehind file is shown in Listing 15-12.

Listing 15-12: CodeBehind File Using Stored Procedures

```
Imports SQL = System.Data.SqlClient
...
Private Sub Page_Load(ByVal sender As System.Object, _
          ByVal e As System.EventArgs) Handles MyBase.Load

       Dim strConn As String = "Server=(local);Database=Northwind;UID=sa;PWD=;"
       Dim objConn As New SQL.SqlConnection(strConn)


       'Use explicit casting on the Employee ID

       Dim strSQL As String = "sps_Employee"
       Dim intEmployeeID As Integer = CInt(Request("id"))

       'For maintainability, be explicit on command & parameter objects
       Dim objCmd As New SQL.SqlCommand(strSQL, objConn)

       objCmd.CommandType = CommandType.StoredProcedure

       Dim objParameter As SQL.SqlParameter
       objParameter = objCmd.Parameters.Add("@EmployeeID", SqlDbType.Int)
       objParameter.Direction = ParameterDirection.Input
```

```
      objParameter.Value = intEmployeeID

    objConn.Open()
    'ExecuteReader fills the DataReader object
    Dim objReader As _
        SQL.SqlDataReader = objCmd.ExecuteReader()

    'Show list or detail.
    If intEmployeeID = 0 Then
        DataGrid1.DataSource = objReader
        DataGrid1.DataBind()
        Repeater2.Visible = False
    Else
        Repeater2.DataSource = objReader
        Repeater2.DataBind()
        DataGrid1.Visible = False
    End If
    objConn.Close()
End Sub
```

Using a DataSet

While a `DataReader` is more efficient, there are certain times when you should use a `DataSet` instead. I explain my reasoning shortly. For now, I show you how to use a `DataSet` to create the same page that you've been working on in this chapter. You're probably tired of this page by now, but this is the last time. I promise!

The `DataSet` object, unlike the `DataReader`, is part of the System.Data namespace. You don't have to make any changes to a `DataSet` to change data sources. You change the provider objects, like the `Command` and `Connection`, but you leave the `DataSet` alone. Since this is the last employee table example for the chapter, go ahead and change the connection string and objects yourself.

The `DataSet` example is shown in Listing 15-13. The basic steps are these:

1. A connection object connects to the database.

2. A command object uses the connection to run a command and fill a `DataTable` in the `DataSet`. This is done through the `DataAdapter`.

3. `DataView`s are created on the `DataTable` for each of the controls.

Listing 15-13: Using a DataSet with SQL Server

```
Imports SQL = System.Data.SqlClient
...
Private Sub Page_Load(ByVal sender As System.Object, _
                ByVal e As System.EventArgs) Handles MyBase.Load
```

Continued

Listing 15-13 *(Continued)*

```
'******* Variables ************
Dim strConn As String = "Server=(local);Database=Northwind;UID=sa;PWD=;"
Dim intEmployeeID As Integer = CInt(Request("id"))

'******* Data Objects *********
Dim objConn As New SQL.SqlConnection(strConn)
Dim objAdapter As New SQL.SqlDataAdapter()
Dim objDataSet As New System.Data.DataSet("Northwind")

'Prepare the Adapter with a command object
'TODO: Change this to a stored procedure
Dim objCmd As New _
      SQL.SqlCommand("SELECT * FROM Employees", objConn)
objCmd.CommandType = CommandType.Text
objAdapter.SelectCommand = objCmd

Try
    'Keeping connection open as short as possible
    objConn.Open()
    objAdapter.Fill(objDataSet, "Employees")
    objConn.Close()

    'Create 2 views from a Single Table in a DataSet
    '    one will be filtered later to one record.
    Dim objDataView1 As New _
          System.Data.DataView(objDataSet.Tables("Employees"))
    Dim objDataView2 As New _
          System.Data.DataView(objDataSet.Tables("Employees"))

    'Filter the view for the Repeater control to avoid
    ' showing more than one record.
    objDataView2.RowFilter = "EmployeeID = " & intEmployeeID

    'Bind both views
    DataGrid1.DataSource = objDataView1
    DataGrid1.DataBind()
    Repeater2.DataSource = objDataView2
    Repeater2.DataBind()

    'Turn off the Repeater when it is empty
    If intEmployeeID = 0 then Repeater2.Visible = False
```

```
'TODO: Add a SQL Exception handler
'Catch objSQLException As SQLException

Catch objException As Exception
     'TODO: Make a more user-friendly error message and
     '      use the centralized error log routine.
     Label1.Text = "An Error Has Occured:<br>The text is " & _
                    objException.ToString()
   End Try
End Sub
```

This is not a great example from a UI standpoint. (I'd never bind a list to a table when the list could potentially take up a full page.) The reason for doing this was purely illustrative, to show that you can take two different views of the same data and put them on the same page. I cover this in more detail in the next chapter when I look at data binding. Then there will be many changes to the methodology used to work with a DataSet.

The following are the main objects used as conduits to get data from a data source to the page the user views. They include DataAdapter, which uses command objects to get data from the data source; DataSet, which holds the data in memory; and DataView, which provides a customized set of data to present to the end user:

◆ DataSet: The DataSet is the mini-relational database held in memory. It contains any number of tables, relations, and views. In this example, the DataSet is created, but never programmed against using the object itself. It is filled by the DataAdapter. Here's the code that creates the DataTable "Employees" in the DataSet named "Northwind":

```
Dim objDataSet As New System.Data.DataSet("Northwind")
objAdapter.Fill(objDataSet, "Employees")
```

◆ DataAdapter: The DataAdapter is the conduit for filling a DataTable from any number of command objects. In this example, SelectCommand is set to the command object and the Fill method is used to fill the DataSet. This action creates the DataTable "Employees":

```
objAdapter.SelectCommand = objCmd
...
objAdapter.Fill(objDataSet, "Employees"))
```

◆ DataView: Two DataViews are created off of the DataTable "Employees". The first DataView contains an unfiltered view of the table and is used to populate the DataGrid:

```
Dim objDataView1 As New _
   System.Data.DataView(objDataSet.Tables("Employees"))
...
```

```
DataGrid1.DataSource = objDataView1
DataGrid1.DataBind()
```

The second `DataView` is filtered to show only the current record. When the page initially comes up, this is Employee 0, which does not exist. This `DataView` is bound to the Repeater control:

```
Dim objDataView2 As New _
   System.Data.DataView(objDataSet.Tables("Employees"))
...
objDataView2.RowFilter = "EmployeeID = " & intEmployeeID
...
Repeater2.DataSource = objDataView2
Repeater2.DataBind()
```

To add additional tables to this example, simply change the command object to a different select statement and fill a different `DataTable` in the `DataSet`. This is covered in more detail in the next chapter. To whet your appetite, Listing 15-14 shows an example.

Listing 15-14: Adding More Tables to the DataSet

```
'Add Customers Table to the DataSet
objCmd.CommandText = "SELECT * FROM Customers"
objAdapter.Fill(objDataSet, "Customers")
```

As always, you can create a new command object to fill the second `DataTable`, but why add the additional overhead if you don't have to?

You probably thought that was a rhetorical question, but there is an answer. Command objects are cheaper than connection objects because they consume server resources only on the Web server. A connection object also consumes resources on the server that holds the data source.

The page coded in Listing 15-13 is quite efficient, because it opens only one table and turns around and closes the connection object rather quickly.

Fixing some bad habits

I told you earlier that some bad coding habits would be introduced in many of the examples in the chapter. Actually, the `DataReader` example in Listing 15-7 contains one or more bad coding practices. Listing 15-15 is a portion of the code in Listing 15-7. This example has every mistake in the book.

Listing 15-15: Bad Code Supreme

```
Imports SQL = System.Data.SqlClient
...
Private Sub Page_Load(ByVal sender As System.Object, _
```

```
         ByVal e As System.EventArgs) Handles MyBase.Load
Dim strConn As String = "Server=(local);Database=Northwind;UID=sa;PWD=;"
Dim objConn As New SQL.SqlConnection(strConn)
objConn.Open()
Dim strSQL As String
Dim intEmployeeID As Integer = 0
If CInt(Request("id")) <> 0 Then
  intEmployeeID = CInt(Request("id"))
  strSQL = "SELECT * FROM Employees WHERE EmployeeID = " & intEmployeeID
Else
  strSQL = "SELECT EmployeeID, LastName, FirstName, Title FROM Employees"
End If
Dim objCmd As New SQL.SqlCommand(strSQL, objConn)
 'TODO: Move objConn.Open() here
 'TODO: Add exception handler
Dim objReader As SQL.SqlDataReader = objCmd.ExecuteReader()
If intEmployeeID = 0 Then
  DataGrid1.DataSource = objReader
  DataGrid1.DataBind()
Else
  Repeater2.DataSource = objReader
  Repeater2.DataBind()
End If
End Sub
```

 You can find the code for Listing 15-15 on the companion Web site (www. wiley.com/extras) in the download file Ch15VS.zip (Visual Studio .NET version) or Ch15SDK.zip (SDK version). The file is named employee. aspx.vb.

Overall, this is not horrible, since it works, but there are things that can be done much better. In my book, about the only good thing I did was indent the code, but Visual Studio .NET does that for me, so I can't claim that one. Let's run through a list of the bad coding practices in the example:

1. **No error handler.** If this were a production application, I'd expect a firing squad. Just because this application was perfect when I left it does not mean it will stay in a state of perfection. The final error handler, used with the DataSet, is not perfect, but I included a TODO item to create a SQL specific exception handler.

2. **No comments in the code.** What the heck am I doing here? Maybe I figure I am maintaining my code so I do not need any comments. Besides,

this is a simple example. Of course the next page (`employee2.aspx` in Listing 15-9) contains comments that are not much better. Comments should explain the why, not the what.

```
'Create a connection and open it
Dim strConn As String = _
    "Provider=MSDAORA;UID=scott;PWD=tiger;"
Dim objConn As New OleDb.OleDbConnection(strConn)
objConn.Open()
```

If you are using Visual Studio .NET, I highly recommend that you use TODO: comments for anything you still have to do before the application goes into production. These comments automatically show up in your task list. Visual Studio also lets you create your own words to show up as tasks.

```
'TODO: Set connection to SQL Server after testing
```

If you know who is responsible for the work in the task, you can also add a keyword for that user to his Visual Studio .NET environment. (The "cowboy" in the following example comes from a nickname I got in Atlanta that has ridden with me for quite some years.) In your application, initials and/or names might work better. Of course, for hacks, the keyword HACK is included in Visual Studio .NET.

```
'COWBOY: Fix this hack.
'HACK: Quick fix to hold state
```

3. **Connection object open a lot longer than it needs to be.** In this example, you can open the connection just before filling the reader and close it just after. ADO.NET is a disconnected paradigm. In traditional ADO, except when using a disconnected recordset, you would have kept the connection open until you finished binding the data. Your code should look more like this example:

```
objConn.Open()
objAdapter.Fill(objDataSet, "Employees")
objConn.Close()
```

4. **Connection object left open.** Speaking of the connection object. I not only left it open too long, I never explicitly closed it. I can feel the ruler across my knuckles right now. Sure, it'll get cleaned up anyway, but how much time does it take to write

```
objConn.Close()
```

5. **DataGrid hidden.** The final faux pas is fairly minor. I did not set the visibility of the control that was not bound. Because it isn't bound, visibility means nothing (it won't show anyway). However, throwing in a

"`DataGrid1.Visible = False`" takes very little code and makes it clear that I intended to hide the control.

Should I use a DataReader or a DataSet?

Since there are two ways to return data, which should you use? A quick rule of thumb is to use a `DataReader` wherever possible, because it is more efficient. Here are a few other rules to help you decide which you should use:

♦ If you are using more than one table from your data source, use a `DataSet`. `DataReaders` use one result set. Although this result set can come from any number of tables, you cannot drill down through the data. A `DataSet` can contain multiple `DataTables`, each of which can contain multiple `DataViews`.

♦ When you need to use the data in a completely disconnected environment, use a `DataSet`. You can transfer a complete mini-relational database to a remote site using a `DataSet`.

♦ When you want to update data in your database using a declarative method, use a `DataSet`, which has built-in methods you can use for updating. With `DataReaders`, you need to build the methods to update data.

In summary, if your application deals primarily with displaying data, or you update data one row at a time, a `DataReader` to be much more efficient than a `DataSet`. If it is going to be more efficient to pass a small relational database, you should use a `DataSet`.

An Object Dictionary

I'm not going to simply repeat the MSDN library (even though I have seen other authors do that), but I do want to discuss the different objects used in this chapter because that will help going forward. In this section, I offer a lot of detail on the provider objects. I defer most of the conversation on the core data objects because they are used extensively in the next couple of chapters.

Provider objects

Provider objects interact with the data source, whether it is an OLE DB managed provider, an ODBC managed provider (through an additional download), or the SQL Server native .NET managed provider.

In this section, I present a set of objects that exist in every managed provider. When you see the objects at this high level, it is easier to understand how you can move from provider to provider with very few code changes.

CONNECTION OBJECTS

Connection objects (SqlConnection, OleDbConnection, and OdbcConnection) are used to set up a connection to a data source. Overall, the objects function the same no matter which namespace. There are some subtle differences with the different providers. Table 15-2 provides details of the Connection object.

TABLE 15-2 THE CONNECTION OBJECT

Property/Method	Description

ConnectionString	A property to set or retrieve the string necessary to connect to a data source. The strings are slightly different:
	
	`SqlClient:`
	`Server=(local);Database=Northwind;UID=sa;PWD=;`
	
	`OleDb:`
	`Provider=Microsoft.Jet.4.0;Data Source=C:\mydb.mdb`
	
	`ODBC:`
	`Driver={Microsoft ODBC for Oracle};`
	`Server=ORACLE8i7;UID=odbcuser;PWD=odbc$5xr`

ConnectionTimeOut	A read-only property to get the connection timeout value set in the connection string. You set the connection time-out value in the connection string rather than through this read-only property. The default is 15 seconds, but you can set this value to any time using the following code, where I have set the time to unlimited with a 0. (NOTE: Don't use 0 in your own code because you'll lock up an application.) `Connection Timeout=0;`
Database	A read-only property to get the name of the database you are connecting to. This property is also set in the connection string.
DataSource	Read-only. With SQL Server, this is the name of the instance of SQL Server. It is the location and filename of the data source in both OLE DB and ODBC. This property is also set in the connection string.
Driver	A read-only property to get the name of the driver for ODBC data sources. This property is also set in the connection string, but only with ODBC.

Property/Method	Description
PacketSize	A read-only property of the packet size used with SQL Server. This property is also set in the connection string, but only with SQL Server (through the SQL Server .NET native provider or with OLE DB).
Provider	A read-only property to get the name of the provider in OLE DB data sources. This property is set in the connection string except when using the SQL Server .NET native provider objects.
ServerVersion	A read-only property that shows the server version of the data source. This works with OLE DB, ODBC, and SQL Server.
State	A read-only property to get the current state of a connection.
WorkstationId	A read-only property to get the workstation ID from a SQL Server data connection.
Open	Method to open a connection to a data source.
Close	Method to close an open connection to a data source.
ChangeDatabase	Changes the database used in an open connection object.
CreateCommand	Method that returns a Command object. The following lines are functionally equivalent: ```'Initialize on creation
Dim objCmd as New SQLCommand(strSQL, objConn)``` ```'Use CreateCommand()
Dim objCmd As SQLCommand = _
objConn.CreateCommand()
SQLCommand.CommandText = strSQL```
BeginTransaction	Method used to begin a database connection. The method outputs a transaction object.

There are two ways to construct a connection object. You can either use an empty constructor or add a connection string. I most often use a connection string. If you prefer to set properties in your code, use an empty constructor instead. Here are my methods:

```
Dim strConn As String = "Server=(local);Database=Northwind;UID=sa;PWD=;"
Dim objConn As New SQL.SQLConnection(strConn)
```

COMMAND OBJECTS

Command objects (SqlCommand, OleDbCommand, and OdbcCommand) are used to run commands. The commands can be a complete table, a SQL statement, (text), or a stored procedure. Table 15-3 provides details of the Command object.

TABLE 15-3 THE COMMAND OBJECT

Property/Method	Description
CommandText	A property to get or set the text of the command that is run. This can be a SQL statement, table, or stored procedure. This can also be set in the constructor of the command object.
CommandTimeout	A property to get or set the timeout value for the command.
CommandType	A property to get or set the command type. The value comes from the CommandType enum: CommandType.TableDirect, CommandType.StoredProcedure, or CommandType.Text.
Connection	A property to get or set the connection object.
Parameters	A read-only property to retrieve the parameters collection. Because you can add to the parameters collection, you may believe this property is not read-only; however, you are adding to the collection, not the property.
Transaction	A property to get or set the transaction that the Command object runs under. By default, there transactions are NULL.
Cancel	Method to cancel the currently running command object.
ExecuteNonQuery	Designed for when you don't want data returned from the command object. This can be used for creating database objects or running UPDATE, INSERT, or DELETE queries when you are not using a DataSet (the DataSet has the ability to have different queries set for each type of operation). Note that ExecuteNonQuery returns the number of rows affected, when applicable, if you want to report on this information.
ExecuteReader	Used to create a DataReader object. This method is used a few times in this chapter.
ExecuteScalar	Runs the query and returns the first column of the first row. This can be used to return a single aggregate with much less code than a DataReader or DataSet object.

Property/Method	Description
| ExecuteXmlReader | SQL Server 2000-only method that is used with a FOR XML query. The XML returned can be placed in XML (for transfer across the Web, for example) or loaded into a DataSet:<br><br>```
Dim objDataSet as New DataSet()
objDataSet.ReadXml(objCmd.ExecuteXmlReader(),
    XmlReadMode.Fragment)
``` |
| Prepare | Used with text queries to prepare the statement with any parameters you have created. This method is useful with SQL Server when you want a prepared version of a query run, but do not want to create a stored procedure.<br><br>```
objCmd.CommandText = "INSERT INTO tblUser" & _
    " (UID,Name) VALUES (@ID,@Name)"
objCmd.Parameters.Add("@ID",1)
objCmd.Paramters.Add("@Name","Greg Beamer")
objCmd.Prepare()
objCmd.ExecuteNonQuery()
``` |
| ResetCommandTimeout | Resets the command timeout to the default value. |

There are four different constructors for the command object: empty, CommandText string, CommandText string with a connection object, and CommandText string with a connection object and a transaction object. I stick to the last two in the examples in this book. For now, the code I use is:

```
Dim objCmd As New SQL.SQLCommand("sps_StoredProc", objConn)
```

PARAMETER OBJECTS

Parameter objects (SqlParameter, OleDbParameter, OdbcParameter) act as parameters for a Command object. The most common use is to map to input and output parameters in a stored procedure. To use Parameter objects, add them to the Parameters collection of the Command object. Table 15-4 provides details of the Parameter object.

While parameters can be created via a constructor, I prefer using the Add method of the parameters collection. If you use the same parameter in a variety of queries, this is not the most efficient method, but here goes:

```
Dim objParameter As SQL.SqlParameter
objParameter = objCmd.Parameters.Add("@ParameterName",SqlDbType.Int)
```

TABLE 15-4 THE PARAMETER OBJECT

Property/Method	Description
DbType	A property to get or set the data type of the parameter. This is dependent on the data source being queried.
Direction	A property to get or set the direction of the parameter. Can be input, output, both, or a return value from a stored procedure.
IsFixedLength	A property of the Odbc namespace only. Gets or sets a Boolean to tell whether the parameter is a fixed length.
IsNullable	Gets or sets a Boolean saying whether the parameter accepts NULL values.
OleDbType/OdbcType/SqlDbType	A property to get or set the OleDbType/OdbcType/SqlDbType of the parameter. The OleDbType/OdbcType/SqlDbType and DbType must be compatible.
ParameterName	A property to get or set the name of the parameter.
Precision/Scale	Properties to get and set the precision (total number of digits) and scale (number of digits after the decimal) a numeric is set.
Size	Property to get or set the size of the parameter, in bytes.
SourceColumn	Property to get or set the column in a DataSet that the parameter is mapped to. This is useful with UPDATE, INSERT, and DELETE commands.
SourceVersion	Property to get or set the version of the source value to use. Normally, this is current with most queries, because you want to UPDATE, INSERT, or DELETE from the most current changes.
Value	Property to get or set the value of a parameter.

DATAREADER OBJECTS

DataReader objects (SqlDataReader, OleDbDataReader, OdbcDataReader) are quick, forward-only data objects. In many ways, they are similar to the default recordset in traditional ASP. In case you're wondering why the `DataReader` belongs here instead of with the core data objects, I have no clue either. I assume that at least one of the methods is overloaded in the SqlClient or Odbc namespace, but I have not found it yet. Table 15-5 provides details of the `DataReader` object.

TABLE 15-5 THE DATAREADER OBJECT

Property/Method	Description
Depth	Read-only property to retrieve the depth of nesting of the current row. Note that `Depth` always returns 0 for SQL Server, because the SQL Server .NET native provider does not support nesting.
FieldCount	Read-only property to retrieve the number of columns (fields) in the current row.
IsClosed	Read-only property that returns a Boolean to indicate if the `DataReader` is closed.
Item	Read-only property that returns the value of the current column in its native format. Note that this property is used as an indexer in C#, but not in Visual Basic .NET.
RecordsAffected	Read-only property to retrieve the number of rows inserted, updated, or deleted by the SQL statement.
Close	A method to close the current `DataReader` object.
Get[DataType]	Methods to retrieve the output of a certain column as a specific data type. The methods are `GetBoolean`, `GetByte`, `GetBytes`, `GetChar`, `GetChars`, `GetDateTime`, `GetDouble`, `GetFloat`, `GetGuid`, `GetInt16`, `GetInt23`, and `GetInt64`. In addition, there are these SQL Specific types: `GetSqlBinary`, `GetSqlBoolean`, `GetSqlByte`, `GetSqlDateTime`, `GetSqlDecimal`, `GetSqlDouble`, `GetSqlGuid`, `GetSqlInt16`, `GetSqlInt32`, `GetSqlInt64`, `GetSqlMoney`, `GetSqlSingle`, and `GetSqlString`.
GetDataTypeName	Method to get the data type of the current column.
GetName	Method to get the name of the current column.
GetValue	Method to get the value of the current column in its native format.

Continued

TABLE 15-5 THE DATAREADER OBJECT *(Continued)*

Property/Method	Description
IsDbNull	Method to test if the current column contains NULL values.
NextResult	Method to move the DataReader to the next result. Used with batch SQL statements.
Read	Method to advance the DataReader to the next value and read its result. Most often used in a while loop.

There is no constructor for a DataReader. Reader objects are made from methods of other objects. In this chapter, the reader has been made through the ExecuteReader method of the command object, as shown here:

```
Dim objReader As SQL.SQLDataReader = objCmd.ExecuteReader()
```

Core data objects

Core data objects sit in the System.Data namespace and are used no matter which data source is used. In this chapter, the core data objects center around the DataSet, which is a mini-relational database held in memory. As disconnected mode of operation is the paradigm for ADO.NET, DataSet objects stay disconnected by default. I expand heavily on core data objects in the next couple of chapters.

DATASET OBJECTS

DataSet object represents a mini-relational database in memory. It consumes more overhead than a DataReader, so use it wisely. I briefly showed the DataSet object, to compare it to a DataReader, in this chapter. There are some neat automated features of the DataSet that make it more attractive than the DataReader in many instances, despite the overhead. In the next two chapters, I cover the DataSet in great detail.

DATATABLE OBJECTS

If a DataSet is a mini-database, a DataTable object represents a single table. As you will learn in the next chapter, DataTables can be joined by DataRelationships to make a relational, in-memory database. I built one DataTable in this chapter; I build a complete DataSet with multiple tables in the next chapter.

DATAVIEW OBJECTS

Like DataTables represent tables, DataViews represent views in our mini, in-memory relational database. A view is a specific way of looking at data in a particular data table. The data in a DataView can be sorted and filtered in a manner different from the underlying `DataTable`. Any number of `DataViews` can be attached to a `DataTable`. I worked with two `DataViews` in this chapter and I expand on this topic in the next two chapters.

DATARELATION OBJECTS

A DataRelation is a way of relating two `DataTables` in a `DataSet`. I start discussing DataRelation objects in the next chapter.

Summary

I covered a lot of ground in this chapter. Beginning with a simple data page, I added a little bit with each example, so that you now know how to create a fairly simple page and submit it back to the server for further information. In the next chapter, I cover data binding and building a more complete `DataSet` for a real-world application.

Chapter 16

Data Binding with ADO.NET

IN THIS CHAPTER

- ◆ Simple binding of variables and functions
- ◆ Binding to a DataGrid, DataList, and Repeater
- ◆ Binding to simple Web and HTML controls

DATA BINDING IS THE PROCESS of attaching, or binding, data to your user interface, primarily through controls. In this chapter, we look at data binding with ASP.NET. While I throw in a variety of ways to work with DataSets and DataReaders, the primary focus is on binding the data from these objects to various types of controls on a page. Most of the examples in this chapter can easily be adapted to real-world situations. I do, however, take a few liberties with the Repeater control to illustrate its flexibility.

Data Binding

The concept of binding data to a control is not new. Prior to .NET, Microsoft used data binding for controls in Visual Basic 6, through both the DataEnvironment, which was a tool to easily bind data to a Windows application, and the ADO Data Control, which was a control for rendering data on a form. Many developers abandoned using data binding for custom ADO code for performance reasons. Had the data-binding paradigm made things a lot simpler, it might have caught on regardless.

Prior to ASP.NET, you could data bind in a Web application with RDS (Remote Data Service) or XML (eXtensible Markup Language). Both of these methods require Internet Explorer as a browser, so neither has caught on outside of intranet applications.

In ASP.NET, with ADO.NET, you bind to controls on the server side. The HTML sent can be rendered in any browser. In addition, data binding in ASP.NET greatly simplifies without degrading performance. Of course, you, the developer, can use the wrong data-access methodology and render non-degradation of performance null and void. An example of degrading performance, as mentioned in the last chapter, is using a DataSet when a DataReader would suffice.

465

Simple Data Binding

If you need a piece of information bound to a page, the easiest way is to place a tag for it. This can be a variable accessible to the page, or a function accessible from the page. If you place the code in your ASPX page, you can access all routines. From a CodeBehind page, all private functions and variables are inaccessible.

The term *simple data binding* is something I came up with. In reality, it is binding a single value (instead of binding to a list of values or using Web controls to bind data). Since it can be used with repetitive values, this is a bit of a simplistic explanation. Just remember that you deal with one value at a time with simple binding. Listing 16-1 provides the syntax for simple data binding in ASP.NET.

Listing 16-1: Basic Syntax for Simple Binding in ASP.NET

```
<%# variableName %>
<%# FunctionName(parameter1,parameter2) %>
...
Protected variableName As String = _
  "<p>This is the variable name variableName!</p>"

Private Sub Page_Load(ByVal sender As System.Object, _
  ByVal e As System.EventArgs) Handles MyBase.Load
    'This line is necessary to bind the page
    Page.DataBind()
End Sub

Protected Function FunctionName(ByVal parameter1 As String, _
  ByVal parameter2 As String) As String
    Return "<p>You sent in the following to FunctionName:" & _
      "<br />Parameter1 = " & parameter1 & _
      "<br />parameter2 = " & parameter2 & "</p>"
End Function
```

There is a sample illustrating the code in Listing 16-1 on the companion Web site (www.wiley.com/extras). Download the file Ch16VS.zip (Visual Studio .NET version) or Ch16SDK.zip (SDK version) and look for the file simpleBinding.aspx and its CodeBehind file simpleBinding.aspx.vb.

Single values

I'm going to digress a bit to show how you accomplish this in ASP and then move forward to the differences in ASP.NET. In ASP, to "bind" data (the quotes are present as you are not actually binding here), you have a small code block such as:

<%=variableName%>. When this code block is reached in the processing of the page, the variable name is written out to the HTTP stream to display to the user (realizing that, with buffering on, it writes to the buffer, which would later be written to the stream).

ASP

Listing 16-2 shows a simple ASP page that pulls a customer based on a customer ID. Note that I use ASP tags to pull values from both a variable and a function, both of which are set up in the code block at the top of the page.

Listing 16-2: Customer Page

```
<%@ Language=VBScript %>
<%
Option Explicit
Response.Buffer = True

Private m_strConn                'As String
Private m_strLastName    'As String
Private m_strSQL         'As String
Private m_intEmpID       'As Integer

'TODO: Migrate these from module level variable
m_intEmpID = CInt(Request("id"))
m_strConn = "Provider=SQLOLEDB.1;Server=(local);Database=Northwind;UID=sa;PWD=;"
m_strSQL = "SELECT LastName, FirstName FROM Employees WHERE EmployeeID = "

Function GetName(intUserID) 'As String
    Dim objConn      'As ADODB.Connection
    Dim objRS        'As ADODB.Recordset

    Set objConn = Server.CreateObject("ADODB.Connection")
    Call objConn.Open(m_strConn)

        Set objRS = objConn.Execute(m_strSQL & intUserID)

If not objRS.EOF then
    GetName = objRS("FirstName")
    m_strLastName = objRS("LastName")
Else
    GetName = "New"
    m_strLastName = "User"
End If
```

Continued

Listing 16-2 *(Continued)*

```
        Set objRS = Nothing
    Set objConn = Nothing
End Function
%>
<HTML>
  <HEAD>
    <Title>Welcome Page</Title>
  </HEAD>
  <BODY>
    <h1>Welcome <%=GetName(m_intEmpID)%> <%=m_strLastName%></h1>
    <P> </P>
  </BODY>
</HTML>
```

You can find the code in Listing 16-2 on the companion Web site (www. wiley.com/extras). Download the file for this chapter: Ch16VS.zip (Visual Studio .NET version) or Ch16SDK.zip (SDK version). The filename is simpleBindingData.asp.

The code you should focus on is bolded. To get the first name, the GetName() function is called, which also seeds the module level variable m_strLastName. Both use the same basic syntax. In this context the equals sign (=) is equivalent to Response.Write, just like ? means print in a Visual Basic 6 Immediate window. The output from this simple page is shown in Figure 16-1, which shows a page when there is no ID passed (bolded Else section in the code).

Figure 16-1: Simple binding in ASP.

ASP.NET

Now, let's move forward to ASP.NET. To get the same output in ASP.NET, the syntax is a bit different. Instead of using an equal sign (=), you will use the pound sign

(#), like `<%# variableName %>`. Listing 16-3 shows the differences in the ASP.NET page. Because ASP.NET does a better job of separating code and user interface (the tags), Listing 16-3 emphasizes the code in the actual ASP.NET page only.

Listing 16-3: The ASPX Page

```
<h1>Welcome<%# LastName(m_intEmpID) %> <%# m_strLastName %>
</h1>
```

To fill these values, we need to create a routine to populate the module-level variable and to return the last name. In addition, the page must be bound. Without the line `Page.DataBind()` (or `DataBind()` since the page is already referenced), you don't get an error, but no data displays. Listing 16-4 shows the CodeBehind file.

Listing 16-4: Simple Binding CodeBehind File

```
Imports SQL = System.Data.SQLClient
...
'The rest of this code block replaces Page_Load() in the CodeBehind file
Protected m_intEmpID As Integer = 0
Protected m_strLastName As String

Private Sub Page_Load(ByVal sender As System.Object, _
          ByVal e As System.EventArgs) Handles MyBase.Load
  m_intEmpID = CType(Request("id"), Integer)
  Page.DataBind()
End Sub

Protected Function LastName(ByVal intUserID As Integer) As String
  'Variables and objects used in routine
  Dim strConn As String = "Server=(local);Database=Northwind;UID=sa;PWD=;"
  Dim strSQL As String = "SELECT LastName, FirstName FROM Employees " & _
                     "WHERE EmployeeID = " & intUserID
  Dim objConn As New SQL.SqlConnection(strConn)
  Dim objCmd As New SQL.SqlCommand(strSQL, objConn)

  Try
    objConn.Open()
    Dim objReader As SQL.SqlDataReader = objCmd.ExecuteReader()

    'If you can read, there is a record
    '   If not: Return New User
    If objReader.Read() Then
      m_strLastName = objReader.Item("LastName")
      Return objReader.Item("FirstName")
```

Continued

Listing 16-4 *(Continued)*

```
    Else
      m_strLastName = "User"
      Return "New"
    End If


  objConn.Close()
Catch objException As System.Exception
  'TODO: Error handling code
End Try
End Function
```

 You can find the code in Listing 16-3 and Listing 16-4 on the companion Web site (www.wiley.com/extras). The download file for this chapter is Ch16VS.zip (Visual Studio .NET version) or Ch16SDK.zip (SDK version). The file to look at is simpleBindingData.aspx and its CodeBehind file is simpleBindingData.aspx.vb.

This is not the best code example because I'm returning some of the information from the function and assigning some to a variable. I'd generally regard this as bad code, but it's for illustration only, so it serves a purpose. What's important here is how similar the code in ASP.NET can be to ASP code.

This example illustrates how to use both a variable and a function from your CodeBehind file on your page. The syntax is more important than the methodology in this example. Just be aware that it is considered kludgy to use a module-level variable to return two values from a single function, as I have done here. The mappings you should get are shown here:

```
'Binding to a function
<%# LastName(m_intEmpID) %>
Protected Function LastName(ByVal intUserID As Integer)

'Binding to a variable
<%# m_strLastName %>
Protected m_strLastName As String = "User"
```

All functions and variables must be exposed to the page to use them. If you want to see how scope works, try setting these values to Private. I chose Protected to keep scope as narrow as possible while using the values in the page.

SIMPLIFYING THE METHOD FOR A SINGLE VALUE

In many ways, the DataReader is a bit of overkill to return a value. I've also coded an example that goes against the grain for many of you to show how to use both a variable and a function to bind data to a table. Since the first name and the last name can be retrieved as a single value in a SQL Statement, I can use the ExecuteScalar() method of the command object.

To use ExecuteScalar(), your query should only return one value. My example query uses the primary key to return a name. If it returns more than one value, you receive only the first column of the first row. Take this into account before using this method. Listing 16-5 shows the CodeBehind page using this simplified method. I also simplified the call to this method to <%# UserName(CInt(Request("id"))) %>. The main changes in the code are shown in bold.

Listing 16-5: Using ExecuteScalar to Return a Single Value

```
Protected Function UserName(ByVal intUserID As Integer) As String
    'Variables and objects used in routine
    Dim strConn As String = "Server=(local);Database=Northwind;UID=sa;PWD=;"
    Dim strSQL As String = "SELECT FirstName + ' ' + LastName as UserName" & _
                           " FROM Employees WHERE EmployeeID = " & intUserID
    Dim objConn As New SQL.SqlConnection(strConn)
    Dim objCmd As New SQL.SqlCommand(strSQL, objConn)
    Dim strReturn As String

    Try
        objConn.Open()
        strReturn = objCmd.ExecuteScalar()
        objConn.Close()

        If strReturn = "" Then
            strReturn = "New User"
        End If
    Catch objExeption As Exception
        'TODO: Create Error Handler
    End Try

    Return strReturn

End Function
```

You can download the code in Listing 16-5 from the companion site (www.wiley.com/extras). The download file for this chapter is Ch16VS.zip (Visual Studio .NET version) or Ch16SDK.zip (SDK version). The file to look at is simpleDataBinding2.aspx and its CodeBehind file is simpleDataBinding2.aspx.vb.

Repetitive simple binding

So far, I've been working with a single value with each item bound. How do I bind a list, like a DataReader, array, HashTable, or XML to a control? In the last chapter, I presented a few examples using the syntax `<%# Container.DataItem ("Itemname") %>`, which expands the paradigm for repetitive data for a Repeater control. Listing 16-6 shows repetitive binding to create a table of Customers in a Repeater control.

Listing 16-6: Simple Binding of Repetitive Values

```
<asp:Repeater id="Repeater1" runat="server">
<HeaderTemplate>
<table>
<tr bgcolor="#99ccff">
    <th>Company Name</th>
    <th>Contact</th>
    <th>Phone</th>
    <th>FAX</th>
</tr>
</HeaderTemplate>
<ItemTemplate>
<tr bgcolor="#ffffff">
    <td><%# Container.DataItem("CompanyName")%></td>
    <td><%# Container.DataItem("ContactName")%></td>
    <td><%# Container.DataItem("Phone")%></td>
    <td><%# Container.DataItem("Fax")%></td>
</tr>
</ItemTemplate>
<AlternatingItemTemplate>
<tr bgcolor="#ccffff">
    <td><%# Container.DataItem("CompanyName")%></td>
    <td><%# Container.DataItem("ContactName")%></td>
    <td><%# Container.DataItem("Phone")%></td>
    <td><%# Container.DataItem("Fax")%></td>
</tr>
</AlternatingItemTemplate>
<FooterTemplate>
</table>
</FooterTemplate>
</asp:Repeater>
```

In the CodeBehind page, you create the DataReader and make sure that the page is data bound while the reader is open, as in the following small code snippet:

```
Private Sub Page_Load(ByVal sender As System.Object, _
  ByVal e As System.EventArgs) Handles MyBase.Load
    Dim strConn As String = "Server=(local);Database=Northwind;UID=sa;PWD=;"
    Dim strSQL As String = "SELECT CompanyName,ContactName,Phone,Fax " & _
                "FROM Customers"
    Dim objConn As New SQL.SqlConnection(strConn)
    Dim objCmd As New SQL.SqlCommand(strSQL, objConn)

    Try
        objConn.Open()
        objReader = objCmd.ExecuteReader
        Page.DataBind()
        objConn.Close()

    Catch objException As System.Exception
        'TODO: Error handling code
    End Try

End Sub
```

The code for both Listing 16-6 and the small CodeBehind snippet that follows can be found on the companion Web site (www.wiley.com/extras) in the download file for this chapter: Ch16VS.zip (Visual Studio .NET version) or Ch16SDK.zip (SDK version). The name of the page is simpleBindingRepeater.aspx, and the CodeBehind file is simpleBindingRepeater.aspx.vb.

Can you hand code the table creation in the CodeBehind page and avoid using a repeater? Certainly, but you would begin to blur the line of separation of code and user interface. To illustrate, I'll take the page in Listing 16-6 and create a function that returns the table from the DataReader. To stick with the subject, data binding, I use "<%# CustomerList() %>" in the ASPX page. Listing 16-7 shows the code for this routine.

Listing 16-7: Hand Coding the Output with Simple Binding

```
Imports SQL = System.Data.SqlClient
...
Protected Function CustomerList() As String
  'Variables and objects used in routine
```

Continued

Listing 16-7 *(Continued)*

```vb
    Dim strConn As String = "Server=(local);Database=Northwind;UID=sa;PWD=;"
    Dim strSQL As String = "SELECT CompanyName,ContactName,Phone,Fax " & _
                "FROM Customers"
    Dim objConn As New SQL.SqlConnection(strConn)
    Dim objCmd As New SQL.SqlCommand(strSQL, objConn)
    Dim strColor As String = "#ffffff"
    Dim strOutput As String = "<table><tr bgcolor=""#99ccff"">" & _
      "<th>Company Name</th><th>Contact</th><th>Phone</th><th>FAX</th></tr>"

  Try
    objConn.Open()
    Dim objReader As SQL.SqlDataReader = objCmd.ExecuteReader()

    While objReader.Read()
      strOutput = strOutput & "<tr bgcolor=" & strColor & ">"
      strOutput = strOutput & "<td>" & objReader.Item("CompanyName") & "</td>"
      strOutput = strOutput & "<td>" & objReader.Item("ContactName") & "</td>"
      strOutput = strOutput & "<td>" & objReader.Item("Phone") & "</td>"

      If IsDBNull(objReader.Item("Fax")) Then
        strOutput = strOutput & "<td> </td>"
      Else
        strOutput = strOutput & "<td>" & objReader.Item("Fax") & "</td>"
      End If

      strOutput = strOutput & "</tr>"

      If strColor = "#ffffff" Then
        strColor = "ccffff"
      Else
        strColor = "#ffffff"
      End If
    End While

    objConn.Close()

  Catch objException As System.Exception
    'TODO: Error handling code
  End Try

  strOutput = strOutput & "</table>"
  Return strOutput
End Function
```

You can download the code in Listing 16-5 from the companion Web site (www.wiley.com/extras). The download file for this chapter is Ch16VS. zip (Visual Studio .NET version) or Ch16SDK.zip (SDK version). The file to look at is CreateTableInCodeBehind.aspx and its CodeBehind file is CreateTableInCodeBehind.aspx.vb.

There is one bit of code you should notice. If a query could return a NULL value from the database, I must remember to use the IsDbNull() function, or I'll get an invalid cast error due to the fact that DbNull is a type in .NET. There is no way to cast a DbNull to a String, either implicitly or explicitly, so you must test for a DbNull and set an empty value yourself. This means you cannot use a CType() function to cast a DbNull to a String value.

While there are instances where hand coding like this is a good experience, I advise using the Web controls whenever possible because they simplify coding your application. As long as the code you get is good code, you might as well take advantage of the shortcuts. I wasn't so eager to recommend the shortcuts in Visual InterDev, because I think Design Time Controls (DTCs) are performance pigs; I think differently in .NET. If I've impressed upon you that Web controls are the way to go, you'll love the next section.

Formatting output

In the last chapter, I formatted a date using the FormatDateTime() function (Listing 15-6). While this is a convenient way to format, there is a .NET way to do this with data binding.

The DataBinder class gives us the ability to format output via the Eval method. To format, you pass a DataItem object, the field to format, and a format to use. Listing 16-8 shows how to format a date using FormatDateTime(), and then the DataBinder Eval method.

Listing 16-8: Formatting a Date

```
<%# FormatDateTime(Container.DataItem("BirthDate"),
    DateFormat.ShortDate)%>
<%# DataBinder.Eval(Container.DataItem, "BirthDate", "{0:d}") %>
```

You can download the code that uses Listing 16-8 from the companion Web site (www.wiley.com/extras). The download file for this chapter is Ch16VS.zip (Visual Studio .NET version) or Ch16SDK.zip (SDK version). The file to look at is simpleBindingFormat.aspx and its CodeBehind file is simpleBindingFormat.aspx.vb.

While I haven't done exhaustive studies to test performance of the two methods under load, the methods seems to work about the same, which makes the output method largely a matter of programming style. Table 16-1 shows the different formatting strings you can use for a date, along with the `FormatDateTime` equivalent.

TABLE 16-1 FORMATTING A DATE

Date Format	DataBinder Character	DateFormat Enum
Friday, May 01, 2002	D	LongDate
5/1/2002	D	ShortDate
12:00:00 AM	T	LongTime
12:00 AM	T	ShortTime
Friday, May 01, 2002 12:00:00 AM	F	
Friday, May 01, 2002 12:00 AM	f	
5/1/2002 12:00:00 AM	G	
5/1/2002 12:00 AM	g	GeneralDate (varies by region)

In addition to dates, you can format numeric values as well. The basic set up of the string is the same as in Listing 16-8. Table 16-2 shows the format characters and what they represent. When you use the numeric formats, you can control the precision of the output by adding a number after the format type.

TABLE 16-2 FORMATTING A NUMERIC

Number Format	DataBinder Character	Sample
$1,234,567.89	C or c	{0:C} = $1,234,67.89
1234	D or d	{0:D} = 1234 {0:D6} = 001234 (padded)
1234E+56	E or e	{0:E} = 1.23456E+005 {0:E4} = 1.2346E+005
123.45	F or f	{0:F1} = 123.5 {0:F3} = 123.450

Number Format	DataBinder Character	Sample
Most compact of fixed . or scientific	G or g	{0:G} = 123245.6789 {0:G4} = 1.235E4
1,234.56	N or n	{0:N} = 1,234.56 {0:N4} = 1,234.5600
12.34%	P or p	Percent
0x1234	X or x	{0:X} = A1E4 {0:x} = a1e4

You can also place a mask for the format string in place of the simplified format. The masking format string goes in the place where the {0:D} would be:

```
DataBinder.Eval(Container.DataItem, "MyNumber", "#.#")
```

Use the following characters to mask:

◆ 0: Outputs either a digit or a 0. Useful when you want to ensure the output is always the same number of digits.

◆ #: Outputs nothing if there is not a digit in this place. You don't have to have a digit sign for every place if you are not using zeros. The format string "#.#" is perfectly legal.

◆ .: Put a period where you want a decimal point to go. To place a separator, use a comma in place of the period. You can also place a percent sign (%) to show a percentage.

I've just touched the basics here, of course. Before adding formatting to every item output on the page, consider the fact that using a DataBinder object brings added overhead to your page, as does any other formatting function. If you are outputting numbers, you may want to determine if using a DataBinder is necessary before applying it liberally to your page.

Binding to Web Controls

The easiest way to work with data in .NET is to use the data-binding capabilities of various Web controls. While you can bind data to the page directly (through "simple" binding, which I discussed earlier in this chapter), the various controls make your life so much easier. There are a few ways to bind, dependent on the control:

◆ Design time: Some controls can be bound to an object such as a
DataReader, DataTable, or DataView. You then bind individual columns in
the object to a specific part of the control. The DataGrid is a prime example of this type of binding, although it allows you to set both at runtime
and design time. Here's an example of binding the DataGrid to a
DataReader:

```
<asp:DataGrid id="DataGrid1" runat="server"
    DataSource="objReader">
<asp:BoundColumn DataField="Title" HeaderText="LastName" />
</asp:DataGrid>
```

I generally set some of the fields at design time and others at runtime
when using this type of control. With Visual Studio .NET, however, the
default is to drag your data on the page and then bind with syntax similar to the preceding example. All of these properties can be set in the
Property window of Visual Studio .NET when the control is highlighted
on the page.

◆ Simple binding: Some other controls allow for simple binding at design
time. You have seen this type of binding with the Repeater control. The
Repeater uses a template to determine how to render the data as it runs
through the records. To do this, you use the same syntax as simple binding a single value. Here's an example of binding one column from an
object, such as a DataReader, to a specific part of the Repeater control:

```
<%# Container.DataItem("LastName") %>
```

◆ Runtime: You can also set the properties of a control at runtime. This
method allows you to bind to some controls, such as HTML controls, that
do not have the ability to bind at design time. Here's an example:

```
ControlName.DataSource = objDataReader
ControlName.DataValueField = "EmployeeID"
ControlName.DataTextField = "LastName"
```

Web controls are designed to set properties at design time and runtime. Once you
set up the code in your ASPX page, you can decide whether design-time binding or
runtime binding is a better option. The decision is based on which is easier to code
and how much you want to customize the control. The DataGrid, which I discuss
next, can be set completely at runtime, after adding a single set of tags (or one tag,
if you use the XML /> ending to close the tag.). The Repeater, however, is easier to
use with a combination of runtime and design-time binding.

Throughout the rest of this section, I emphasize runtime implementations,
because Visual Studio .NET holds your hand if you decide to create a design-time
implementation. I also want to expose you to the code necessary to do this at
runtime.

Data binding with the DataGrid

Much of your work in ASP.NET will be done with a DataGrid control, so I am going to spend a fair amount of time discussing it. It has a lot of built-in features to make your coding life a lot easier. Perhaps management will now allow you time to design the technical specifications. I know, "The plane! The plane, Mr. Roarke!" For those of you too young to catch this one, there was once a television show called "Fantasy Island" where people got to live out their fantasies: My fantasy is to be able to design an application to a firm spec. .NET allows this time, but I bet management wants to see faster apps instead of properly designed apps.

SETTING UP THE DESIGN-TIME ASPECTS

I start out setting most of the properties of the DataGrid at runtime. There are, however, a few items, mostly event handlers, that are difficult to set in this manner.

My first example uses the automatic sorting feature of the DataGrid. The one portion that is difficult to set up at runtime is the command used to sort and page the data. In fact, a quick look at the object model shows you that this command is read-only. Rather than find a way to skirt around this, which would waste both your time and mine, I am going to set this at design time. The portion of the tag in question is bolded in the following code lines:

```
<asp:DataGrid id="DataGrid1" runat="server"
  OnSortCommand="DataGrid1_Sort" />
```

As you can see, there is not much to the DataGrid right now. If you were to start up the page, in fact, you would see nothing. I need a bit more information, which is what I set at runtime.

If you are using Visual Studio .NET, you can ignore the `OnSortCommand=` `"DataGrid1_sort"` portion of the `DataGrid` tag, as Visual Studio .NET will add the verbage `Handles DataGrid1.SortCommand` to the `DataGrid1_Sort()` event for you. I include both the tag and the `Handles` statement in the downloadable code to show the syntax of each.

You can follow either methodology if you are hand coding using the .NET Framework SDK. The decision is whether you want to memorize events or tag attributes. As including both is redundant, I would recommend using one or the other, not both.

SORTING A DATAGRID AT RUNTIME

The `Page_Load` event is the starting point. I first set up the look and feel of the DataGrid here. To initially seed the DataGrid, I check if this is a post back. If not, I bind the DataGrid to a DataView. For reusability, I create an event called CreateDataBindableView() to set up the DataView. Listing 16-9 shows the CodeBehind page.

Listing 16-9: Sorting a DataGrid Programmatically

```
Private Sub Page_Load(ByVal sender As System.Object, _
          ByVal e As System.EventArgs) Handles MyBase.Load

    'Code to set up a Unit for the Border Width
    Dim objBorderWidth As New System.Web.UI.WebControls.Unit(0)

    With DataGrid1
        .AutoGenerateColumns = True
        .AllowSorting = True
        .CellPadding = 2
        .CellSpacing = 2
        'This one should be set at design time if
        '     MS continues with this paradigm
        .BorderWidth = objBorderWidth
    End With

    'If PostBack, it will be through the sort field
    If Not Page.IsPostBack Then
        DataGrid1.DataSource = CreateDataBindableView("CustomerID")
        DataGrid1.DataBind()
    End If

End Sub

Private Function CreateDataBindableView(ByVal strSort As String) As ICollection
    'Create objects that will not error during creation
    Dim strConn As String = "Server=(local);Database=Northwind;UID=sa;PWD=;"
    Dim objConn As New SQL.SqlConnection(strConn)
    Dim objAdapter As New SQL.SqlDataAdapter()
    Dim objDataSet As New System.Data.DataSet("Northwind")

    Dim objCmd As New SQL.SqlCommand("SELECT CustomerID, CompanyName, " & _
    "ContactName, City, Region, PostalCode, Phone, Fax FROM Customers", objConn)

    objCmd.CommandType = CommandType.Text
    objAdapter.SelectCommand = objCmd

    Try
        'Fill a table for the DataView to sort
        objConn.Open()
```

```
    objAdapter.Fill(objDataSet, "Customers")
    objConn.Close()

    'Sorting done with a view
    Dim objDataView As New DataView(objDataSet.Tables("Customers"))
    objDataView.Sort = strSort
    Return objDataView

  Catch objException As Exception
      'TODO: Add error handler
  End Try

End Function

Protected Sub DataGrid1_Sort(ByVal sender As Object, _
        ByVal e As DataGridSortCommandEventArgs)
   DataGrid1.DataSource = _
      CreateDataBindableView(e.SortExpression.ToString())
   DataGrid1.DataBind()
End Sub
```

 You can download the code from Listing 16-9 from the companion Web site (www.wiley.com/extras). The download file for this chapter is Ch16VS. zip (Visual Studio .NET version) or Ch16SDK.zip (SDK version). The file to look at is DataGridSort.aspx.vb.

So far, so good! You recognize the method of filling a view. In order to sort, you need a DataView. Let's step through some code, okay?

1. Create a new Unit for the border width. I personally think this is rather silly, because CellPadding and CellSpacing can take integers. (I certainly hope the .NET design team is a bit more consistent on this in the future.) The code is as follows:

   ```
   Dim objBorderWidth As New System.Web.UI.WebControls.Unit(0)
   ```

   The fact that you have to use a unit object makes me prefer to set all of these items at design time. This, however, is a runtime demonstration.

2. Set all of the DataGrid runtime features. I autoGenerate the columns for simplicity. (I create columns from scratch in Listing 15-6 in Chapter 15 and Listing 16-12 later in this chapter.)

3. Use the `CreateDataBindableView()` command to set up the view that binds to the DataGrid. There is not much new here, except the `Sort` command. This value is passed in to the routine from either the `Page_Load` event, which takes a hard-coded default, or from the `DataGrid1_Sort` event. In the following code snippet, I show you how to set the field to sort on at runtime:

```
objDataView.Sort = strSort
```

4. Finally, the `DataGrid1_Sort` event, which is declared design time in the `<asp:DataGrid>` tag repeats the data binding code in the `Page_Load`. The main change is the fact that the sort comes from the `SortArgument` property of the `EventArgs` object.

Figure 16-2 shows the final result. Unfortunately, it is quite ugly at this time, but there is a lot of functionality built in. As the figure shows, I sorted the data with the City column.

 Microsoft set up the DataGrid with the .NET paradigm (UI in the ASPX page and code in the CodeBehind file). As such, it is difficult to beautify the output with code alone. The easiest method to beautify a DataGrid is setting all attributes that control the look of the control in the ASPX page and code everything else in the CodeBehind page.

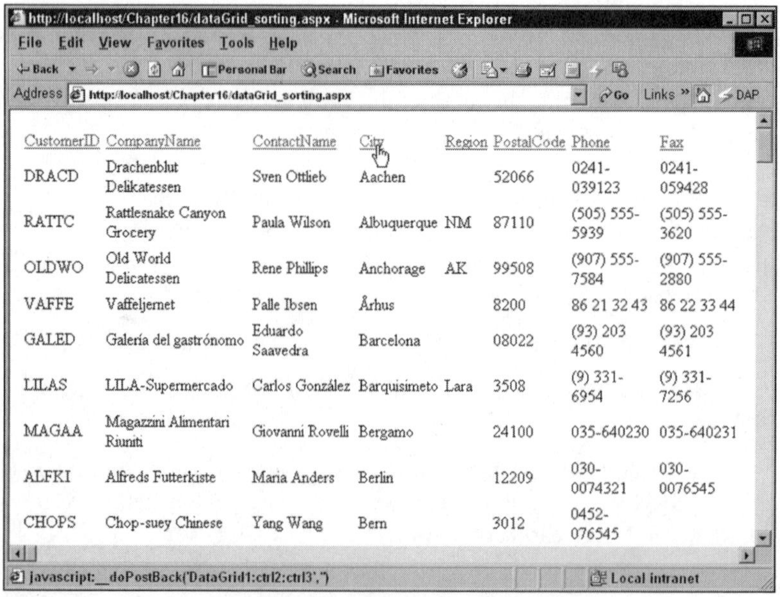

Figure 16-2: A plain DataGrid with sorting capabilities.

PAGING IN A DATAGRID

The Paging operation is very similar to sorting. You set up an event handler in the DataGrid tag for the `OnPageIndexChanged` event, as opposed to `onSortCommand`. In this example, I beautify the page a bit with styles.

Listing 16-10 shows the changes to the ASPX page — adding a set of styles and an `OnPageIndexChanged` event.

Listing 16-10: Setting Up Paging in the ASPX Page

```
<asp:DataGrid id="DataGrid1" runat="server"
    OnPageIndexChanged="DataGrid1_PageIndexChanged">
  <HeaderStyle BackColor="#000099"
     Font-Bold="True" ForeColor="#ffffff" />
  <ItemStyle BackColor="#ffffff" />
  <AlternatingItemStyle BackColor="#99ccff" />
</asp:DataGrid>
```

There are a few changes to the CodeBehind file, as well. I set up the code to allow paging instead of sorting and added a `DataGrid1_PageIndexChanged` event. The code is shown in Listing 16-11.

Listing 16-11: The CodeBehind Page for Paging

```
'This line replaces .AllowSorting = True from DataGridSort.aspx.vb
    .AllowPaging = True
...Protected Sub DataGrid1_PageIndexChanged(ByVal sender As Object, _
            ByVal e As DataGridPageChangedEventArgs)
    DataGrid1.CurrentPageIndex = e.NewPageIndex
    DataGrid1.DataSource = CreateDataBindableView()
    DataGrid1.DataBind()
End Sub
```

You can download the code from Listings 16-10 and 16-11 from the companion Web site (`www.wiley.com/extras`). The download file for this chapter is `Ch16VS.zip` (Visual Studio .NET version) or `Ch16SDK.zip` (SDK version). The file to look at is `DataGridPage.aspx` and its CodeBehind file is `DataGridPage.aspx.vb`.

It looks pretty similar to the last example, doesn't it? It just contains a slightly different routine. While this may seem like I'm beating a dead horse, take a look at the parameters of this routine (and the `DataGrid1_Sort` event, if you are so inclined), and notice the sender object and `EventArgs` parameters.

Figure 16-3 shows the beautified version of the page. The paging controls are the default supplied. The hand cursor sits on top of the next page hyperlink.

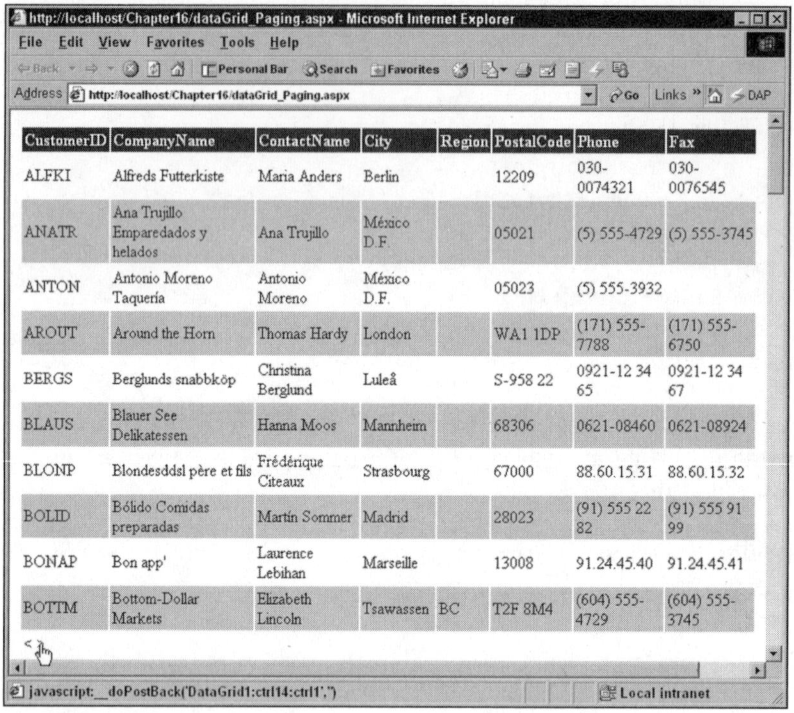

Figure 16-3: The more beautiful paging example of the customer page.

SORTING AND PAGING IN THE SAME PAGE

The code for this chapter, which you can download from this book's companion Web site, includes a page called `DataGrid_pageSort`, which uses both sorting and paging. While this is an interesting topic, I won't go into detail about it in this book. Here are a couple of basic changes necessary to do both sorting and paging:

◆ You bind a value for the sort in the page via hidden tags. This value is "simple" bound to the page using a `<%# %>` tag.

◆ You sort with the paging event using a `Request` on the bound value.

You can quickly get yourself into trouble when you mix sorting and paging, because the end user can get lost if he decides to page and sort at will. You can help him by adding numbers at the bottom of the page. As a rule, though, I do not recommend mixing paging and sorting, especially when you add editing capabilities to the mix.

EDITING DATA IN THE GRID

While sorting and paging are nice features to have, one of the real strengths you gain from using the DataGrid is the capability to edit data. This holds true for any of the Web controls that are used for advanced data binding (any control that starts with the word *Data*), but is especially true for the DataGrid.

In order to edit, you need to add an edit column and create template columns for every column you want to edit. In this example, I create a page where you can edit the contact name, phone number, and fax number for the customer table. While it might be nice to change all of the data, this example assumes this is a salesperson's view, which would likely require changes only to these few pieces of data. The code for the ASPX page is shown in Listing 16-12.

Listing 16-12: An Editable ASPX Page

```
<form id="Form1" method="post" runat="server">
  <asp:DataGrid id="DataGrid1" runat="server" DataKeyField="CustomerID"
   EditItemStyle-BackColor="#ffff99" AutoGenerateColumns="False"
   OnEditCommand="DataGrid1_Edit" OnCancelCommand="DataGrid1_Cancel"
   OnUpdateCommand="DataGrid1_Update">
    <HeaderStyle BackColor="#000099" Font-Bold="True"
      ForeColor="#ffffff" />
    <ItemStyle BackColor="#ffffff" />
    <AlternatingItemStyle BackColor="#99ccff" />
    <Columns>
      <asp:BoundColumn DataField="CustomerID"
        ReadOnly="True" HeaderText="Customer ID" />
      <asp:BoundColumn DataField="CompanyName"
        ReadOnly="True" HeaderText="Company Name" />
      <asp:BoundColumn DataField="ContactName"
        ReadOnly="False" HeaderText="Contact Name" />
      <asp:BoundColumn DataField="Phone"
        ReadOnly="False" HeaderText="Phone" />
      <asp:BoundColumn DataField="FAX"
        ReadOnly="False" HeaderText="Fax" />
      <asp:EditCommandColumn EditText="Edit"
        CancelText="Cancel" UpdateText="Update" />
    </Columns>
  </asp:DataGrid>
</form>
```

There are three basic areas of importance here:

1. **DataKeyField:** You must have a field for the edit to be run against. Without a key field, you resort either to editing every record, which is not too smart, or to writing a query that bombs out, which isn't too smart, either.

2. **Commands:** `OnEditCommand`, `OnCancelCommand`, and `OnUpdateCommand` point to an event that handles these events in the `EditCommandColumn`. You have to write some code to handle clicks that fire these events. Alternatively, you can use the `Handles` keyword in your CodeBehind file to handle these commands. Here's an example:

```
Handles DataGrid1.EditCommand
```

I include both in the source files to show the syntax. While this causes no problems, you should use one way or the other in your own files.

3. **ReadOnly:** The `ReadOnly` attribute of a `BoundColumn` determines whether or not the column will be editable when submitted back to the server. If you set `ReadOnly` to false, a text box will be rendered for this column when you click edit.

Now, you need to create code for each of the events that the different text items in the EditCommandColumn cover. Listing 16-13 shows this code, which includes handling `Edit`, `Cancel`, and `Update` events.

Listing 16-13: Handling Edit, Cancel, and Update Events

```
Imports SQL = System.Data.SqlClient


...


Protected Sub DataGrid1_Edit(ByVal sender As System.Object, _
  ByVal e As System.Web.UI.WebControls.DataGridCommandEventArgs) _
  Handles DataGrid1.EditCommand
    DataGrid1.DataSource = CreateDataBindableView()
    DataGrid1.EditItemIndex = e.Item.ItemIndex
    DataGrid1.DataBind()
End Sub

Protected Sub DataGrid1_Cancel(ByVal sender As System.Object, _
  ByVal e As DataGridCommandEventArgs) _
  Handles DataGrid1.CancelCommand
    DataGrid1.EditItemIndex = -1
    DataGrid1.DataSource = CreateDataBindableView()
    DataGrid1.DataBind()
End Sub

Protected Sub DataGrid1_Update(ByVal sender As Object, _
  ByVal e As DataGridCommandEventArgs) _
  Handles DataGrid1.UpdateCommand

    Dim ContactName As String = Request.Form.Item(3).ToString()
```

```
Dim Phone As String = Request.Form.Item(4).ToString()
Dim FAX As String = Request.Form.Item(5).ToString()

Dim strSQL As String = "UPDATE Customers SET ContactName = '" & _
        ContactName & "', " & _
        "Phone = '" & Phone & "', " & _
        "Fax = '" & FAX & "' " & _
        "WHERE CustomerID = '" & _
        DataGrid1.DataKeys(e.Item.ItemIndex) & "'"

Dim strConn As String = "Server=(local);Database=Northwind;UID=sa;PWD=;"
Dim objConn As New SQL.SqlConnection(strConn)

Dim objCmd As New SQL.SqlCommand(strSQL, objConn)

Try
    objConn.Open()
    objCmd.ExecuteNonQuery()
    objConn.Close()
Catch objException As Exception
    'TODO: Write exception handler
End Try

DataGrid1.EditItemIndex = -1
DataGrid1.DataSource = CreateDataBindableView()
DataGrid1.DataBind()

End Sub
```

The `Edit` and `Cancel` events are walks in the park:

- For the edit event, you set an `EditItemIndex` to display the editable column. This index comes from the item that was clicked and is part of your `DataGridCommandEventsArgs` collection. As with every event we have handled, you have to rebind the DataGrid to the data source.

- The second event is even easier. You simply set the `EditItemIndex` to -1, which resets the index. As always, rebind to a data source.

The `Update` event is a bit more complex, but easier to understand when you break it down into steps:

1. Create an object for each control in the edit row. The simplest way is to pull from the form item collection, as shown here:

```
Dim ContactName As String = _
Request.Form.Item(3).ToString()
```

The `Item` number is a bit strange. You see that our ContactName field is item number 3. This is because there are three arguments that belong to the form itself: `_EVENTTARGET`, `_EVENTARGUMENT`, and `_VIEWSTATE`.

2. Create your SQL statement. For this, you have to pull the `DataKey` of the `DataGrid`. You decide which field to use with the `DataKeyField` attribute of the `<asp:DataGrid>` tag, as shown here:

```
<asp:DataGrid id="DataGrid1" runat="server" ↵
DataKeyField="CustomerID">
```

To get the value of the selected row that you are editing, pass the current index of the Item in the DataGridEventArgs collection to the DataKeys collection of the DataGrid. Whew! That is a mouthful, but here is the result:

```
DataGrid1.DataKeys(e.Item.ItemIndex)
```

Without this key value, you update every row in the table.

3. Execute the query. Since there is no return value on this query, using the `ExecuteNonQuery` method of the command object is the most efficient manner. Once again, reset the edit index and rebind the data.

Figure 16-4 shows the page while it's being edited. Although it's hard to see in black and white, there is a major color shift in the editable row.

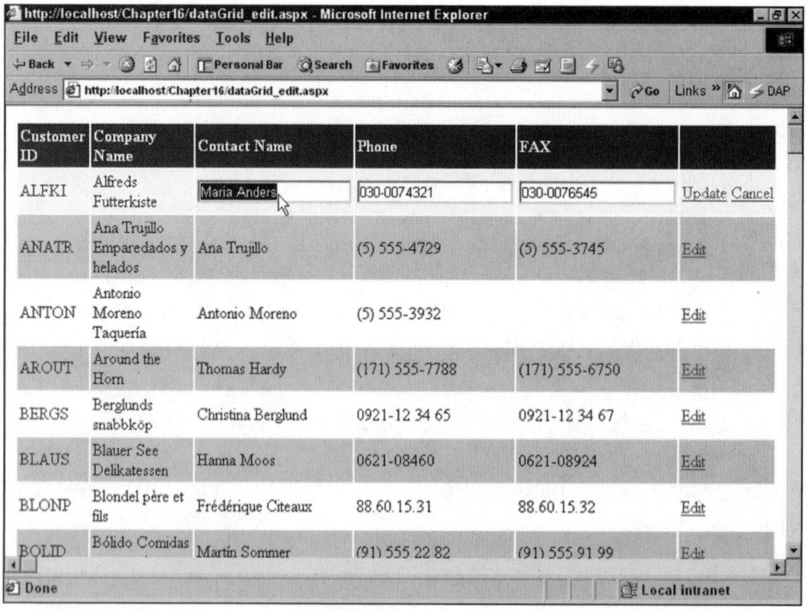

Figure 16-4: Editing with a DataGrid.

In case you are wondering if you can do the same thing with a DataReader, the answer is yes. I stuck with the DataSet because it leaves me a lot of leeway on where to go with this page. I can fairly easily set this to sort or page without much manipulation.

 You can view the code that was used to create the screen shot in Figure 16-4 by downloading `Ch16VS.zip` (Visual Studio .NET version) or `Ch16SDK.zip` (SDK version) from this book's companion Web site (`www.wiley.com/extras`). The page to look at is `DataGridEdit.aspx` and its CodeBehind file `DataGridEdit.aspx.vb`.

MAKING A DATAGRID IN VISUAL STUDIO .NET

I want to take a little time here to show you how Visual Studio .NET handles a DataGrid. To create the same look that I've been working on in the last few exercises, you follow these steps.

1. Open up the Server Explorer (left-hand side) and drag a table from the Northwind database onto the page. This creates both SQLConnection and SQLDataAdapter objects.

2. Drag an untyped DataSet (the wizard gives you a choice) and a DataView onto the page.

3. Drag a DataGrid onto the page and set the properties for the header, item, and alternating item templates in the property window.

4. Add the following code to the `Page_Load` event.

```
Me.SqlConnection1.Open()
Me.SqlDataAdapter1.SelectCommand = Me.SqlSelectCommand1()
Me.SqlDataAdapter1.Fill(Me.DataSet1, "Customers")
objDataTable = Me.DataSet1.Tables("Customers")
Me.DataView1.Table = objDataTable
Me.SqlConnection1.Close()

DataGrid1.DataSource = Me.DataView1
DataGrid1.DataBind()
```

 You may get an error with the page just created because SQL Connection is set up using integrated security and you are not logged onto a domain. There are two ways to fix this: Turn off anonymous access, or find the line that sets the `ConnectionString` and edit it to use a username and password.

The page created from this example can be found in the download file (dataGrid_edit2.aspx) for this chapter. The edit code is not yet placed in the page, but you can easily use it to practice your skills by simply following the examples from this chapter. A great deal of code is already created for you, if you opt to go this way. All in all, it took me about five minutes to complete the example. I've been hand coding instead of dragging and dropping, so the short time is a testimonial for the new tools.

Using DataList

The DataList is, in many ways, a simplified DataGrid that shows only one record. At least that is the DataList without using a template. In reality, you can bind multiple columns to a single list item, which is exactly what I intend to do now.

In this exercise, I create a page where the items can be edited by setting up a few templates. After the editable DataGrid exercise, this should be fairly simple. Listing 16-14 shows the page.

Listing 16-14: The Editable DataList ASPX Page

```
<asp:DataList Width="600" CellPadding="2" CellSpacing="2" id="DataList1" ↵
runat="server" DataKeyField="CustomerID" OnEditCommand="DataList1_Edit" ↵
OnCancelCommand="DataList1_Cancel" OnUpdateCommand="DataList1_Update" ↵
EditItemStyle-BackColor="#ffff99" AlternatingItemStyle-BackColor="#6699ff" ↵
HeaderStyle-BackColor="#0000cc" HeaderStyle-ForeColor="#ffffff">
    <HeaderTemplate>
        Customer List
    </HeaderTemplate>
    <ItemTemplate>
        <asp:Button CommandName="Edit" Runat="server" Text="Edit" />
          <b>
            <%# Container.DataItem("CompanyName") %>
        </b>
    </ItemTemplate>
    <AlternatingItemTemplate>
        <asp:Button CommandName="Edit" Runat="server" Text="Edit" ID="Button2" />
        <br>
        <%# Container.DataItem("CompanyName") %>
    </AlternatingItemTemplate>
    <EditItemTemplate>
        <%# Container.DataItem("CompanyName") %>
        <asp:Button CommandName="Update" Text="Update" Runat="server" />
        <asp:Button CommandName="Cancel" Text="Cancel" ↵
Runat="server" ID="Button1" />
        <br>
        Contact Name:
```

```
        <asp:TextBox ID="ContactName" Runat="server" ⏎
Text='<%# Container.DataItem("ContactName") %>' />
        <br>
        Phone:
        <asp:TextBox ID="Phone" Runat="server" ⏎
Text='<%# Container.DataItem("Phone") %>' />
        <br>
        Fax:
        <asp:TextBox ID="Fax" Runat="server" ⏎
Text='<%# Container.DataItem("Fax") %>' />
        <br>
    </EditItemTemplate>
</asp:DataList>
```

The CodeBehind file, shown in Listing 16-15, should look very familiar. Overall, the main change in the coding from the DataGrid example is changing the DataGrid1 to DataList1. Once again, note that while I set the commands in the ASPX page (Listing 16-14), I also add lines in the CodeBehind page (Listing 16-15) to indicate which event is being handled; as previously mentioned, you only have to do one or the other, not both.

Listing 16-15: The CodeBehind File with the Editable DataList

```
Imports SQL = System.Data.SqlClient
...
Private Sub Page_Load(ByVal sender As System.Object, ⏎
ByVal e As System.EventArgs) Handles MyBase.Load
    'Put user code to initialize the page here

    'Code to set a border width
    Dim objBorderWidth As New System.Web.UI.WebControls.Unit(0)

    With DataList1
        .CellPadding = 2
        .CellSpacing = 2
        'This one should be set at design time if
        '     MS continues with this paradigm
        .BorderWidth = objBorderWidth
    End With

    If Not Page.IsPostBack Then
        DataList1.DataSource = CreateDataBindableView()
        DataList1.DataBind()
```

Continued

Listing 16-15 *(Continued)*

```
        End If

    End Sub

    Private Function CreateDataBindableView() As ICollection
        'Create objects that will not error during creation
        Dim strConn As String = "Server=(local);Database=Northwind;UID=sa;PWD=;"
        Dim objConn As New SQL.SqlConnection(strConn)
        Dim objAdapter As New SQL.SqlDataAdapter()
        Dim objDataSet As New System.Data.DataSet("Northwind")

        Dim objCmd As New SQL.SqlCommand("SELECT CustomerID, " & _
          "CompanyName, ContactName, City, Region, PostalCode, " & _
          "Phone, Fax FROM Customers", objConn)

        objCmd.CommandType = CommandType.Text
        objAdapter.SelectCommand = objCmd

        Try
            'Fill a table for the DataView to sort
            objConn.Open()
            objAdapter.Fill(objDataSet, "Customers")
            objConn.Close()

            'Sorting done with a view
            Dim objDataView As New DataView(objDataSet.Tables("Customers"))

            Return objDataView

        Catch objException As Exception
            'TODO: Add error handler
        End Try

    End Function

    Protected Sub DataList1_Cancel(ByVal sender As Object, ByVal e As ↵
    DataListCommandEventArgs)
        DataList1.EditItemIndex = -1
        DataList1.DataSource = CreateDataBindableView()
        DataList1.DataBind()
    End Sub
    Protected Sub DataList1_Edit(ByVal sender As Object, ByVal e As ↵
    DataListCommandEventArgs)
```

```vb
        DataList1.EditItemIndex = e.Item.ItemIndex
        DataList1.DataSource = CreateDataBindableView()
        DataList1.DataBind()
End Sub
Protected Sub DataList1_Update(ByVal sender As Object, ByVal e As ↵
DataListCommandEventArgs)
        'First create controls to pull from
        Dim objContactName As TextBox = CType(e.Item.FindControl("ContactName"), ↵
TextBox)
        Dim objPhone As TextBox = CType(e.Item.FindControl("Phone"), TextBox)
        Dim objFax As TextBox = CType(e.Item.FindControl("Fax"), TextBox)

        Dim strSQL As String = "UPDATE Customers SET ContactName = '" & ↵
objContactName.Text & "'," & _
            "Phone = '" & objPhone.Text & "'," & _
            "Fax = '" & objFax.Text & "' " & _
            "WHERE CustomerID = '" & DataList1.DataKeys(e.Item.ItemIndex) & "'"

        Dim strConn As String = "Server=(local);Database=Northwind;UID=sa;PWD=;"
        Dim objConn As New SQL.SqlConnection(strConn)

        Dim objCmd As New SQL.SqlCommand(strSQL, objConn)

        Try
            objConn.Open()
            objCmd.ExecuteNonQuery()
            objConn.Close()
        Catch objException As Exception
            'TODO: Write exception handler
        End Try

        DataList1.EditItemIndex = -1
        DataList1.DataSource = CreateDataBindableView()
        DataList1.DataBind()

End Sub
```

The code from Listings 16-14 and 16-15 is included on the companion Web site (www.wiley.com/extras) in this chapter's download file: Ch16VS. zip (Visual Studio .NET version) or Ch16SDK.zip (SDK version). The page file is DataListEdit.aspx and its CodeBehind file is DataListEdit. aspx.vb.

Figure 16-5 shows the output of the DataList page when the Edit button is clicked.

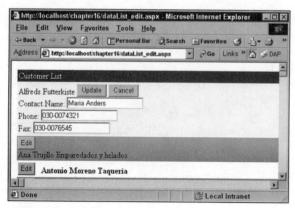

Figure 16-5: Editing in the DataList.

There is one other difference between the DataGrid and the DataList. If I were so inclined, I could place an extra step in the process to select the item prior to opening the edit form. To make this change, I'd have to add an event (`DataList1_Select`, for example) and a `<SelectTemplate>`. I think this extra step is unnecessary here, so I left it out. I can, however, see using a select template when you want to be able to provide a bit more information with a simple click.

Binding to a Repeater control

So far, I've been using the Repeater control in a way similar to a DataGrid. While this is nice enough, the power of the Repeater is not found in its capability to mimic other controls, but in its flexibility. Anything you can do in an HTML file can be done with a Repeater control.

The sample code for this chapter, which you can download from the companion Web site, includes the file `Repeater.aspx` and its CodeBehind file `Repeater.aspx.vb`. This example is definitely on the lighter side, so go ahead and fire up this page before you read any further. Don't worry; the book will be here when you get back.

Now that you've had a chuckle, I'll tell you that I just wanted to prove that a Repeater can do almost anything. I bound the employee first and last names to a marquee control. (I can't see a reason to ever use a marquee, except perhaps to annoy a customer. This is only an example of what you can achieve if you want to go to an extreme.) I use the EmployeeID to control the speed of each marquee. The ASPX page is shown in Listing 16-16.

Listing 16-16: A Unique Repeater Control

```
<asp:Repeater id="Repeater1" runat="server">
  <ItemTemplate>
```

```
      <marquee behavior="scroll"
        scrollamount='<%# Container.DataItem("EmployeeID")%>'>
        <%# Container.DataItem("EmployeeID")%>

        .
        <%# Container.DataItem("FirstName")%>
        <%# Container.DataItem("LastName")%>
      </marquee>
      <br>
    </ItemTemplate>
</asp:Repeater>
```

Listing 16-17 shows the code to fill this example page.

Listing 16-17: The CodeBehind File for the Repeater Page

```
Private Sub Page_Load(ByVal sender As System.Object, _
          ByVal e As System.EventArgs) Handles MyBase.Load
    'Variables and objects used in routine
  Dim strConn As String = "Server=(local);Database=Northwind;UID=sa;PWD=;"
  Dim strSQL As String = "SELECT EmployeeID, FirstName, LastName FROM Employees"
  Dim objConn As New SQL.SqlConnection(strConn)
  Dim objCmd As New SQL.SqlCommand(strSQL, objConn)

  Try
    objConn.Open()
    Dim objReader As SQL.SqlDataReader = objCmd.ExecuteReader()

    Repeater1.DataSource = objReader
    Page.DataBind()

    objConn.Close()
  Catch objException As System.Exception
    'TODO: Error handling code
  End Try
End Sub
```

 The code from Listings 16-16 and 16-17 can be downloaded from the companion site (www.wiley.com/extras). The download file is Ch16VS.zip (Visual Studio .NET version) or Ch16SDK.zip (SDK version). The page file is Repeater.aspx and its CodeBehind file Repeater.aspx.vb.

While this exercise is on the lighter side, the concept of being able to use a Repeater control in a variety of ways is serious.

Binding to Simpler HTML Controls

While the Web controls are far more easily configured, you may find reason to use an HTML control instead. The main reason I can think of right now is migrating code from ASP. The examples shown in this section apply to any control that contains a viewable text field and a value field.

Data binding with DataReaders

Let's look at an example that uses two DataReaders. (There is no real reason to use two DataReaders except to show you that DataReaders are disconnected. I could just as easily use a DataSet with a couple of DataTables, and perhaps some DataViews, but I cover setting up a DataSet as a mini-relational database in the next chapter.) First, look at the controls in Listing 16-18. I have also included a DropDownList to show that the method is the same.

Listing 16-18: Binding to an HTML Select Control

```
<form id="Form1" method="post" runat="server">
  <P>
    Company: <SELECT id="CustomerID" runat="server"></SELECT>
  </P>
  <P>
    Employee: 
    <asp:DropDownList id="EmployeeID" runat="server" />
  </P>
</form>
```

The basic method of binding these controls is setting properties of the control at runtime. Listing 16-19 shows the CodeBehind page. I bind Customer ID and Company name to one control and an Employee ID and name to another; I've bolded these sections of the code.

Listing 16-19: The CodeBehind Page Binding a Select Control

```
Imports SQL = System.Data.SqlClient
...
Private Sub Page_Load(ByVal sender As System.Object, _
           ByVal e As System.EventArgs) Handles MyBase.Load

  Dim strConn As String = "Server=(local);Database=Northwind;UID=sa;PWD=;"
  Dim strSQL As String = "SELECT CustomerID, CompanyName FROM Customers"

  'Build first DataReader for Customer Select Control
  CustomerID.DataSource = CreateDataReader(strConn, strSQL)
```

```
CustomerID.DataTextField = "CompanyName"
CustomerID.DataValueField = "CustomerID"
CustomerID.DataBind()

'Build second data reader for EmployeeID DropDownList control
strSQL = "SELECT EmployeeID, FirstName+' '+LastName As Name FROM Employees"
EmployeeID.DataSource = CreateDataReader(strConn, strSQL)
EmployeeID.DataTextField = "Name"
EmployeeID.DataValueField = "EmployeeID"
EmployeeID.DataBind()

End Sub

Private Function CreateDataReader(ByVal strConn As String, _
            ByVal strSQL As String) As SQL.SqlDataReader
    'Variables and objects used in routine

 Dim objConn As New SQL.SqlConnection(strConn)
 Dim objCmd As New SQL.SqlCommand(strSQL, objConn)

 Try
    objConn.Open()

    Dim objReader As SQL.SqlDataReader = objCmd.ExecuteReader()
    Return objReader

    objConn.Close()

 Catch objException As System.Exception
    'TODO: Error handling code
    Response.Write(objException.ToString())
 End Try
End Function
```

The code from Listings 16-18 and 16-19 can be downloaded from the companion site (www.wiley.com/extras). The download file is Ch16VS.zip (Visual Studio .NET version) or Ch16SDK.zip (SDK version). The file to look for is DropDowns.aspx and its CodeBehind file DropDowns.aspx.vb.

For both of the controls, you bind to a DataReader and then set the text and the value fields. The text field is what shows up in the drop-down list, while the value is the key you work with.

For good measure, I also included the code for creating a DataReader in a rather generic manner, in the function `CreateDataReader()`.

Quick trivia question: Why does Microsoft allow you to set the text and value fields at design time?

Answer: I don't have a clue. Perhaps it is to remain consistent with other controls that can. There are some controls that you cannot bind at design time, but they are few and far between. Because I prefer the CodeBehind paradigm, this is no skin off my nose.

Data binding with a DataSet

To do a quick comparison and to bait you into delving into the next chapter, Listing 16-20 shows the code for the same page as Listings 16-19 but with a DataSet instead of a DataReader. In the next chapter, I expand on this by making a DataSet that acts like a mini-relational database. For now, see how you can bind to multiple DataTables in one DataSet. I've bolded the differences in the way in which the CustomerID, Company name, Employee ID, and Name are retrieved and bound with a DataGrid.

Listing 16-20: Using a DataSet

```
Imports SQL = System.Data.SqlClient
...
Private Sub Page_Load(ByVal sender As System.Object, _
                      ByVal e As System.EventArgs) Handles MyBase.Load

  If Not Page.IsPostBack Then
    Dim objDataSet As New DataSet()
    objDataSet = CreateDataSet()

    CustomerID.DataSource = objDataSet.Tables("Customers")
    CustomerID.DataTextField = "CompanyName"
    CustomerID.DataValueField = "CustomerID"

    EmployeeID.DataSource = objDataSet.Tables("Employees")
    EmployeeID.DataTextField = "Name"
    EmployeeID.DataValueField = "EmployeeID"

    Page.DataBind()
  End If

End Sub


Private Function CreateDataSet() As DataSet
  Dim strConn As String = "Server=(local);Database=Northwind;UID=sa;PWD=;"
  Dim objConn As New SQL.SqlConnection(strConn)
```

```
Dim objAdapter As New SQL.SqlDataAdapter()
Dim objDataSet As New System.Data.DataSet("Northwind")

Dim objCustomerCommand As New SQL.SqlCommand("SELECT CustomerID, " & _
      "CompanyName FROM Customers", objConn)
objCustomerCommand.CommandType = CommandType.Text
Dim objEmployeeCommand As New SQL.SqlCommand("SELECT EmployeeID, " & _
      "Firstname+' '+LastName As Name FROM Employees", objConn)
objEmployeeCommand.CommandType = CommandType.Text

objAdapter.SelectCommand = objCustomerCommand

Try
  objConn.Open()
  objAdapter.Fill(objDataSet, "Customers")
  objAdapter.SelectCommand = objEmployeeCommand
  objAdapter.Fill(objDataSet, "Employees")
  objConn.Close()

  Return objDataSet
Catch objException As Exception
  'TODO: Add error handler
  Response.Write(objException.ToString())
End Try

End Function
```

You are now binding to individual tables. If you want to filter this, you could bind to DataViews instead. I wait to bind until every drop-down is set because I do not see any difference between page and individual control binding – at least not with only two controls – and to show that you can hold off the bind and bind the entire page. With so few controls, this just saves a bit of typing.

Summary

We've taken a long trip in this chapter so that you could see that binding your pages and controls to a data source is an easy endeavor in ASP.NET and a major improvement over both Visual Basic and ASP. In the next chapter, I work with more advanced ADO.NET.

Chapter 17

Advanced ADO.NET

IN THIS CHAPTER

- ◆ Reviewing relational databases
- ◆ Building a database in memory via a DataSet object.
- ◆ Binding a DataSet to a DataGrid and updating data through the DataAdapter
- ◆ Auto-generating of UPDATE, INSERT, and DELETE commands
- ◆ Using Transactions in ADO.NET

ADVANCED FEATURES OF ADO.NET include the auto-generation of data addition and alteration commands (INSERT, UPDATE, and DELETE) as well as coding to use transactions. I discuss the more important advanced features in this chapter. The information builds on what was presented in the last two chapters and relates ADO.NET to a relational database.

Relational Databases and DataSets

The concept of relational databases is largely rooted in mathematics. Dr. E. F. Codd created the relational model from set theory and first-order predicate logic. One of the misconceptions about relational databases is that the name is derived from the fact that different tables in a database are related. In reality, the word *relation* comes from set theory.

Under the relational model, each piece of data is stored in an attribute, more commonly called a field, with multiple fields comprising a tuple, or row, with multiple rows making up a relation, or table. As the individual rows (tuples) each have some unique method of identification, the actual order is unimportant.

From this point on, I use the term *record* to describe tuples. I would love to use the more correct term *tuple*, but you rarely hear this word used, even among database administrators. I also am using *column*, rather than *attribute*, and *table* rather than *relation*. If you see the word *field*, it describes the union of a column and a row. I reserve *relation*, or rather *relationship*, to describe how one table is connected to another.

501

Normal forms

In a database, the concept of normalization deals with the physical, or form, which is the method of storage, and the normal, which is how the items are identified and related. In simple terms, normalization is a set of database design rules that minimize data redundancy. The end result is a database in which both the database engine and application software can easily enforce data integrity.

The important point is that there is a set of well-defined rules, called normal forms, that are followed to ensure that data exists in only one place and is identifiable by a unique value (called a *key*), and that there is no place where many items from one table can directly be related to many items in another table.

FIRST NORMAL FORM

The first normal form ensures that there is only one value in each field and that the value cannot be further divided. A database breaks first normal form if a single field can be broken up into other forms to be useful as information. If a single customer in the Northwind database had two contacts, it would break first normal form. The fact that the contact has both a first and a last name in the same field follows first normal form since there is no need to further break down this information. If I had designed this for a business, however, I would have seriously considered making two fields, or better yet, moving contacts to another table.

SECOND NORMAL FORM

Second normal form ensures that each table describes only one object. In other words, all informational fields describe the object, and not some other information field or object. To better understand this, consider a table that has information about a car. The fields are Make, Model, Engine Size, Driver, and Driver Hair Color.

While it might be questionable that the Driver was placed in the Car table, there are certain situations this might work programmatically. However, there is no instance in which a driver's hair color has any bearing on the car. By the same token, a field containing the population of a city in an address table would be completely out of place. To get the database into second normal form, any table with informational fields that describe another object would necessitate another table.

THIRD NORMAL FORM

Third normal form states that there is one unique piece of information for each row in the table. This unique key helps us avoid redundancy of information.

NORMALIZATION IN PRACTICE

The easiest way to normalize is to first find the physical objects. For example, we have an employee, a customer, a city, a street address, a state, a county, and so on. These are each physical objects that I can touch or visit. The next step is to determine logical objects, such as orders or phone calls, which may or may not be represented physically. These are items my business is interested in tracking.

The next step is to figure out the attributes of the objects to ensure that there are no additional objects that have to be broken out. In this phase, I also need to determine if there are any objects that I only care about in context with other objects. An address, city, state, and phone number, for example, might be better stored in the Customer and Employee tables. It really depends on the needs of business.

In a completely normalized database, every object has its own table. In practice, however, not every real-world object has its own table, usually for space- and resource-saving reasons. It is also important to think about future uses of the data as you design your database, because you may later need specific objects separated out. A real-world need, for example, is demographics. To run efficient queries that determine a customer base by city, state, or ZIP Code, you would probably want these tables separated out. The process of moving away from the normal forms, which is done primarily for performance reasons, is called denormalization.

I then look at how the objects relate to other objects. If the relationship is always one-to-one, I need to examine whether the object should be an attribute of the other object. I am aiming for one-to-many relationships wherever possible.

In order to relate the objects and ensure that the relationship is not broken, I have to put in the following constraints:

◆ Every table has a primary key to uniquely identify each record.

◆ Each related table has this key value to be able to relate back to the original table.

◆ Each related table also has a foreign key constraint to ensure that a record cannot be entered if it does not have a value in the original table.

Some of you might think that this is a pain. After all, the likelihood of encountering an error is much higher if the constraint is there. You are right, of course, but it is much easier to uncover an error that tries to enter information that is not related than it is to find orphaned records. For more information on the details of database design, I recommend the book *Database Design for Mere Mortals* as a good starting point.

The primary type of constraint is a one-to-many constraint, where one row in a table links to many rows in a second table. Occasionally, however, you'll find that many rows in one table link to many rows in another. To make many-to-many relationships work, I add a table in the middle that serves as a junction between the two, creating two one-to-many relationships out of the many-to-many relationship that exists initially. Take, for example, a database with employees and tasks. Since an employee can have many tasks and tasks may require more than one employee, I would create a table called EmployeeTask to solve these many-to-many relationships.

The Northwind database

Because we are visual learners, the best way to understand the basic concepts of a relational database is by looking at a diagram. Figure 17-1 shows a diagram of the Northwind database taken from Visual Studio .NET Enterprise Architect. While you can use Northwind with any version, the SQL Server diagramming capabilities are not present in the Professional version. (If you do not have this version of Visual Studio .NET, you can get the same basic functionality through SQL Server Enterprise Manager or by examining relationships in Microsoft Access.)

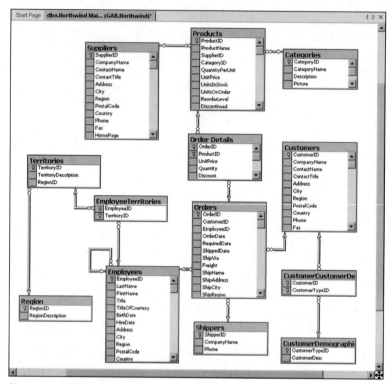

Figure 17-1: A diagram of the Northwind database.

Let's go through the Northwind database and to see how each concept is illustrated.

- **Primary key:** Each primary key is indicated by a key symbol. (The key symbol might be easier to see if you open the database yourself.) When you look at the Employees table, you will notice a unique EmployeeID for each row. There are a couple of composite keys — those that span more than one field — in this database. You can find them in each of the junction tables: EmployeeTerritories, OrderDetails, and CustomerCustomerDemographics.

- **One-to-many relationship:** Each of the relationship lines (the lines connecting the tables) is a one-to-many relationship in this database. The *one* side of the relationship is a key, while the *many* side is an infinity sign.

◆ **Many-to-many relationship:** If the EmployeeTerritories table did not exist here, there would be a many-to-many relationship between Employees and Territories tables. The EmployeeTerritories table serves as a junction between the other two tables.

◆ **Foreign key constraints:** You will notice that the table Orders contains EmployeeID and a CustomerID fields. These constrain the Orders table to only accept order records that contain both a valid employee and a valid customer.

The important concept missing from the diagram is that of a view. A *view* is a precompiled statement that acts as a virtual table. Views help you restrict data to only that which is important.

So, what does all of this have to do with ADO.NET? Nothing and everything! A DataSet is a relational set of objects. In ADO.NET, a DataSet represents the concept of a database. This is why I call a DataSet a mini-relational database. In order to build a useful DataSet, you need a good relational database to build from.

In the DataSet, DataTable objects represent tables. Each table contains multiple DataRow objects, which are comprised of DataColumn objects. If I want to view this information through different sortings or filters, I create DataView objects. So you can see that as you build up the DataSet, you use the same types of objects (DataTables for tables, DataViews for views) that you do for databases.

For a more advanced DataSet, you may also have DataRelations, which represent relationships, as well as DataConstraints, which represent different types of constraints. While you will most often be pulling from a single data source, the DataSet allows you to create a DataSet from more than one data source, enabling you to relate data from a variety of sources. Examples of this are relating users pulled from active directory to a WebDav folder in Exchange 2000, and having order information held in an Oracle SAP database, with additional customer information in a SQL Server database.

Building the Northwind DataSet

To illustrate how to set up a DataSet as a mini-relational database, I'm going to take a portion of the Northwind database and put it in a Web service. (While this can be accomplished using the entire Northwind database, it would run awfully slow, because the database is larger than 3MB.) I focus on presenting the products and their suppliers. The scenario assumes that this is something a buyer needs to negotiate with new-product suppliers in the field.

The main purpose of the following examples is to show how tables and relations are added to a DataSet, and how the entire DataSet is passed from server to client and reconstituted. Afterward we'll go to more real-world examples of DataSets.

CREATING THE WEB SERVICE

The first step is to create the XML Web service that creates the DataSet and exposes it to clients across the Web. The client application I create next will use this Web service to get its data.

SETTING UP THE DATACONNECTION, DATACOMMANDS, AND DATAADAPTER

Most of this section is a refresher course, because I set up a DataSet for ASPX pages earlier in the book. In this instance, each of the data objects can be created without worrying about an error handler, so I create the ADO.NET objects outside of the `Try ...Catch ... Finally` block. I use the exception handler once the connection object is opened, as this section may well error out. Listing 17-1 shows a small portion of the section.

Listing 17-1: Creating the DataSet Web Service

```
Imports SQL = System.Data.SqlClient
...
<WebMethod()> Public Function GetNorthwindSchema(ByVal blnSchema As Boolean) _
  As System.String
    Dim objDataSet As System.Data.DataSet = GetNorthwind()

    If blnSchema = True Then
        Return objDataSet.GetXmlSchema()
    Else
        Return objDataSet.GetXml()
    End If
End Function


<WebMethod()> Public Function GetNorthwind() As System.Data.DataSet
    'Connection
    Dim strConn As String = "Server=(local);Database=Northwind;UID=sa;PWD=;"
    Dim objConn As New SQL.SqlConnection(strConn)

    'Command Objects for each table
    Dim strSQL As String = "SELECT * FROM Products"
    Dim objProducts As New SQL.SqlCommand(strSQL, objConn)
    strSQL = "SELECT * FROM Suppliers"
    Dim objSuppliers As New SQL.SqlCommand(strSQL, objConn)

    'Create the Adapter and the DataSet objects
    Dim objAdapter As New SQL.SqlDataAdapter()
    Dim objDataSet As New Data.DataSet()

    Try
        'Fill the DataSet
        objConn.Open()
```

```
objAdapter.SelectCommand = objProducts
objAdapter.Fill(objDataSet, "Products")
objAdapter.SelectCommand = objSuppliers
objAdapter.Fill(objDataSet, "Suppliers")
objConn.Close()

Dim objDataRelation As New Data.DataRelation("SuppliersProducts", _
            objDataSet.Tables("Suppliers").Columns("SupplierID"), _
            objDataSet.Tables("Products").Columns("SupplierID"), True)

Catch objException As Exception
    'TODO:
End Try

'Output the DataSet
Return objDataSet

End Function
```

 You can download the code for Listing 17-1 from this book's companion Web site (www.wiley.com/extras). The download file is Ch17VS.zip (Visual Studio .NET version) or Ch17SDK.zip (SDK version). The file to look at is northwind.asmx.vb, which contains the code for the XML Web service.

In the GetNorthwind() Web method in Listing 17-1, the SqlConnection object takes a connection string as its only parameter. Each SqlCommand object takes the actual SQL command string and the connection object as parameters. The SqlDataAdapter then uses the SqlCommand objects to fill each DataTable in the DataSet. This is covered in the next section.

There are, of course, other ways to set up your objects in the DataSet. For example, you can hand-build the DataSet by creating each object, including DataColumns, DataRows, and DataTables. While building by hand is useful at times, it is not the easiest way to create a DataSet from an existing data source.

CREATING TABLES   To create the tables required for the page to work, I connect each Command object to the DataSet as a new DataTable by attaching the SqlCommand objects, one by one, to the DataAdapter and filling the table with the DataAdapter's Fill method. Because these commands are prone to error out, they are placed inside of a Try ... Catch block, as shown in Listing 17-2, which uses a small portion of Listing 17-1 to illustrate the point. Note that the Connection object is kept open only long enough to transfer the data from the data source to the DataSet object.

Listing 17-2: Filling the DataTables

```
Try
    'Fill the DataSet
    objConn.Open()

    objAdapter.SelectCommand = objProducts
    objAdapter.Fill(objDataSet, "Products")
    objAdapter.SelectCommand = objSuppliers
    objAdapter.Fill(objDataSet, "Suppliers")
    objConn.Close()

    Dim objDataRelation As New Data.DataRelation("SuppliersProducts", _
        objDataSet.Tables("Suppliers").Columns("SupplierID"), _
        objDataSet.Tables("Products").Columns("SupplierID"), True)

Catch objException As Exception
    'TODO: Add exception handling
End Try
```

CREATING RELATIONSHIPS   I can now add the relationships found in the database. If you are planning on sending a large amount of data to a client for processing, it's a good idea to create relations, because it is preferable to ensure that any new data does not break data rules rather than incur a round trip to the server to find out. Note, however, that XML Web services do not currently include `DataRelations` when a `DataSet` is serialized for consumption on the Web. For this reason, it's wise to create the relation code on the client side. Listing 17-3 uses a small portion of the code from Listing 17-1 to show how to create a `DataRelation`.

Serialization is the process of taking an object and turning it into a string of data (bytes). In the .NET world, objects are serialized into an XML document and streamed out to the client.

This is a bit of a simplification, because the XML document will have to be turned into bytes, but the important point is the object definition is serialized as XML so that it can be recreated on the client side. In the COM world, by contrast, the entire object would be pulled from memory and sent to the client, which is far less efficient.

Listing 17-3: Adding a Relationship

```
Dim objDataRelation As New Data.DataRelation("SuppliersProducts", _
        objDataSet.Tables("Suppliers").Columns("SupplierID"), _
        objDataSet.Tables("Products").Columns("SupplierID"), True)
```

First I create a name for the relation (SuppliersProducts), and then I add the parent column and the child column, as well as a Boolean to state that this relation should constrain the child table to the parent table. In this constructor, the parent column is named first and the child column is named second. If you download the code for this chapter, you'll see that I am constraining the tables on both the server and client. As mentioned previously, binding on the server is largely a waste of time if the class is only going to be used as a Web service.

CREATING THE OUTPUT   There are a couple of ways to output the data from the database. The best method is to output the DataSet directly. When the Web service outputs the DataSet, it creates the schema and the data XML as one large document. The data XML and the schema can also be output separately; this requires changing the output type of the function to a String. In Listing 17-1, this is accomplished by making a separate Web method to output the schema.

Listing 17-4 uses part of Listing 17-1 to show how to do each of the outputs. The first two lines are from the GetNorthwind() method, while the rest of the code shows the entire GetNorthwindXML() function.

Listing 17-4: Outputting the DataSet or Its XML Schema and Data Documents

```
'Output the DataSet
Return objDataSet

<WebMethod()> Public Function GetNorthwindXML(ByVal blnSchema As Boolean) _
  As System.String
    Dim objDataSet As System.Data.DataSet = GetNorthwind()

    If blnSchema = True Then
        Return objDataSet.GetXmlSchema()
    Else
        Return objDataSet.GetXml()
    End If
End Function
```

The GetNorthwindXML() Web method can return either the DataSet, as XML, or the XML schema, based on the value of the input parameter: blnSchema.

When the DataSet is output from the function, it is serialized into XML. If you examine the output in a browser, it looks like the output shown in Figure 17-2.

CREATING THE CLIENT APPLICATION

To create the client application, I use the WSDL command-line utility. (The WSDL.exe utility generates proxy clients for Web services and proxy classes for consuming Web services. It ships with the .NET Framework SDK and can be found, by default, in the directory <root>:\Program Files\Microsoft Visual Studio .NET\FrameworkSDK\Bin.) If you use the Visual Studio .NET command prompt, type **wsdl /l:VB http://localhost/Chapter17/northwind.asmx?WSDL.**

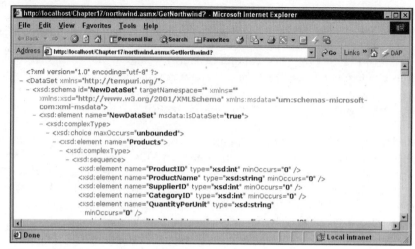

Figure 17-2: DataSet serialized as XML.

If you're using the SDK, rather than Visual Studio .NET, you have to use a Windows command prompt instead of the Visual Studio .NET command prompt. While functionally equivalent, the Visual Studio .NET command prompt contains the path to all .NET executables, while the Windows command prompt does not.

If you use a normal Windows command prompt, you have to either navigate to the Bin directory, located at `<root>:\Program Files\Microsoft Visual Studio .NET\FrameworkSDK\Bin`, or add this path to your Windows path. There is a batch file in the SDK download (`Ch17SDK.zip`) to create the proxy object, which contains the path alterations necessary. Open it if you need to employ this functionality in your own work.

The wsdl.exe command-line tool creates the proxy class in Listing 17-5. I make two alterations to the code, which I show in boldface. First, the name of the class is changed so the Web service can be consumed in the same project (this change is to avoid name clashes in the project, because I am creating one ASP.NET project per chapter. In a real-world situation, I do not see any need to change the name of the proxy class). Second, I turned option strict on. When the proxy class is created, option strict is off, which flies in the face of good programming practices.

Listing 17-5: The Proxy Class for the Northwind Web Service

```
Option Strict On
Option Explicit On

Imports System
Imports System.ComponentModel
Imports System.Diagnostics
Imports System.Web.Services
Imports System.Web.Services.Protocols
Imports System.Xml.Serialization


'
'This source code was auto-generated by wsdl, Version=1.0.3705.209.
'


'<remarks/>
<System.Diagnostics.DebuggerStepThroughAttribute(), _
 System.ComponentModel.DesignerCategoryAttribute("code"), _
 System.Web.Services.WebServiceBindingAttribute(Name:="northwindSoap", _
[Namespace]:="http://tempuri.org/")> _
Public Class NorthwindProxy
   Inherits System.Web.Services.Protocols.SoapHttpClientProtocol

   '<remarks/>
   Public Sub New()
     MyBase.New
     Me.Url = "http://localhost/Chapter17/northwind.asmx"
   End Sub

   '<remarks/>
   <System.Web.Services.Protocols.SoapDocumentMethodAttribute( _
    "http://tempuri.org/GetNorthwind", _
    RequestNamespace:="http://tempuri.org/", _
    ResponseNamespace:="http://tempuri.org/", _
    Use:=System.Web.Services.Description.SoapBindingUse.Literal, _
    ParameterStyle:=System.Web.Services.Protocols.SoapParameterStyle.Wrapped)> _
   Public Function GetNorthwind() As Object
     Dim results() As Object = Me.Invoke("GetNorthwind", New Object(-1) {})
     Return CType(results(0),Object)
   End Function

   '<remarks/>
   Public Function BeginGetNorthwind(ByVal callback As _
```

Continued

Listing 17–5 *(Continued)*

```
    System.AsyncCallback, ByVal asyncState As Object) _
    As System.IAsyncResult
     Return Me.BeginInvoke("GetNorthwind", New Object(-1) {}, callback, ↵
asyncState)
  End Function


  '<remarks/>
  Public Function EndGetNorthwind(ByVal asyncResult _
    As System.IAsyncResult) As Object
     Dim results() As Object = Me.EndInvoke(asyncResult)
     Return CType(results(0),Object)
  End Function
End Class
```

 You can find the code for Listing 17-5 on the companion Web site (www.wiley.com/extras) in this chapter's download file: Ch17VS.zip (Visual Studio .NET version) or Ch17SDK.zip (SDK version). The file to look at is NorthwindProxy.vb.

In this example, I add the class to my application. In the real world, the proxy class would be consumed from another system. The proxy class is responsible for deserializing the DataSet object and passing it on to other classes in the application.

Listing 17-6 is the CodeBehind page that fills a DataGrid with a list of suppliers. Users clicking on a supplier are shown the products that the supplier supplies to the Northwind company.

Listing 17–6: Consuming the Web Service

```
Private Sub Page_Load(ByVal sender As System.Object, _

            ByVal e As System.EventArgs) Handles MyBase.Load

  Dim objNorthwindProxy As northwind2 = New northwind2()
  Dim objDataSet As Data.DataSet = _
      objNorthwindProxy.GetNorthwind()

  If CInt(Request("SupplierID")) = 0 Then
   DataGrid1.DataSource = objDataSet.Tables("Suppliers").DefaultView
   DataGrid1.DataBind()
```

```
    DataGrid2.DataSource = objDataSet.Tables("Products").DefaultView
    DataGrid2.Visible = False
  Else
    Dim objDVSuppliers As New Data.DataView(objDataSet.Tables("Suppliers"))
    Dim objDVProducts As New Data.DataView(objDataSet.Tables("Products"))
    objDVSuppliers.RowFilter = "SupplierID=" & Request("SupplierID")
    objDVProducts.RowFilter = "SupplierID=" & Request("SupplierID")
    DataGrid1.DataSource = objDVSuppliers
    DataGrid1.DataBind()
    DataGrid2.DataSource = objDVProducts
    DataGrid2.DataBind()
  End If
End Sub
```

To consume the service, the DataSet is pulled from the Proxy object that has deserialized the XML from the Web service. The DataGrids are then bound to the DataTables in the DataSet. The fact that the data is coming from an XML Web service, which could be located anywhere in the world, is clear.

 You can find the code for Listing 17-6 on the companion Web site (www. wiley.com/extras) in this chapter's download file: Ch17VS.zip (Visual Studio .NET version) or Ch17SDK.zip (SDK version). The file to examine is NorthwindClient.aspx.vb.

What you should understand at this point is you can consume data from another Web site as easily as from your own database. The ADO.NET objects make working with disconnected data a breeze. You should also understand that DataSets are serialized as XML for use in a disconnected environment. Since it is XML, any application that utilizes XML can reconstitute the data. The XML of the serialized DataSet is wrapped inside of a SOAP package. Both XML and SOAP are covered in more detail in Chapter 18.

Using DataSets to Manipulate Data

Using DataSets to deliver data to an ASPX page is one of the smaller aspects of ASP.NET. After all, the ability to just view data is of limited value. Where you really get some benefit is by making data available to be edited.

In previous chapters, I have shown how you can set up DataGrids and DataList controls to edit data. While this is very impressive, you haven't yet seen the real strength of having a mini-relational database in memory.

Using Visual Studio .NET

While this book is designed to be used with or without Visual Studio .NET, I want to show you what is done for you within Visual Studio .NET. While the code generated by Visual Studio .NET is verbose and generic, you cannot beat the simplicity of the system. I don't ridicule anyone for using a tool, especially when it saves so much time. Listing 17-7 shows the massive amount of code automatically generated by Visual Studio .NET.

Listing 17-7: Manipulating Data with a DataSet

```
<System.Diagnostics.DebuggerStepThrough()> Private Sub InitializeComponent()
    Me.SqlSelectCommand1 = New System.Data.SqlClient.SqlCommand()
    Me.SqlInsertCommand1 = New System.Data.SqlClient.SqlCommand()
    Me.SqlUpdateCommand1 = New System.Data.SqlClient.SqlCommand()
    Me.SqlDeleteCommand1 = New System.Data.SqlClient.SqlCommand()
    Me.SqlConnection1 = New System.Data.SqlClient.SqlConnection()
    Me.SqlDataAdapter1 = New System.Data.SqlClient.SqlDataAdapter()
    '
    'SqlSelectCommand1
    '
    Me.SqlSelectCommand1.CommandText = "SELECT ShipperID, CompanyName, " & _
     "Phone FROM Shippers"
    Me.SqlSelectCommand1.Connection = Me.SqlConnection1
    '
    'SqlInsertCommand1
    '
    Me.SqlInsertCommand1.CommandText = "INSERT INTO Shippers " & _
     "(CompanyName, Phone) VALUES (@CompanyName, @Phone); SELECT Sh" & _
     "ipperID, CompanyName, Phone FROM Shippers WHERE (ShipperID = @@IDENTITY)"
    Me.SqlInsertCommand1.Connection = Me.SqlConnection1
    Me.SqlInsertCommand1.Parameters.Add(New _
     System.Data.SqlClient.SqlParameter("@CompanyName", _
     System.Data.SqlDbType.NVarChar, 40, _
     System.Data.ParameterDirection.Input, False, CType(0, Byte), _
     CType(0, Byte), "CompanyName", System.Data.DataRowVersion.Current, Nothing))
    Me.SqlInsertCommand1.Parameters.Add(New _
     System.Data.SqlClient.SqlParameter("@Phone", _
     System.Data.SqlDbType.NVarChar, 24, _
     System.Data.ParameterDirection.Input, True, CType(0, Byte), _
     CType(0, Byte), "Phone", System.Data.DataRowVersion.Current, Nothing))
    '
    'SqlUpdateCommand1
    '
```

```
Me.SqlUpdateCommand1.CommandText = "UPDATE Shippers SET CompanyName = " & _
 "@CompanyName, Phone = @Phone WHERE (ShipperID = " & _
 " @Original_ShipperID) AND (CompanyName = @Original_CompanyName) " & _
 "AND (Phone = @Original_Phone OR @Original_Phone1 IS NULL " & _
 "AND Phone IS NULL); SELECT ShipperID, CompanyName, Phone " & _
 "FROM Shippers WHERE (ShipperID = @Select_ShipperID)"
Me.SqlUpdateCommand1.Connection = Me.SqlConnection1
Me.SqlUpdateCommand1.Parameters.Add(New _
 System.Data.SqlClient.SqlParameter("@CompanyName", _
 System.Data.SqlDbType.NVarChar, 40, _
 System.Data.ParameterDirection.Input, False, CType(0, Byte), _
 CType(0, Byte), "CompanyName", System.Data.DataRowVersion.Current, Nothing))
Me.SqlUpdateCommand1.Parameters.Add(New _
 System.Data.SqlClient.SqlParameter("@Phone", _
 System.Data.SqlDbType.NVarChar, 24, _
 System.Data.ParameterDirection.Input, True, CType(0, Byte), _
 CType(0, Byte), "Phone", System.Data.DataRowVersion.Current, Nothing))
Me.SqlUpdateCommand1.Parameters.Add(New _
 System.Data.SqlClient.SqlParameter("@Original_ShipperID", _
 System.Data.SqlDbType.Int, 4, System.Data.ParameterDirection.Input, _
 False, CType(0, Byte), CType(0, Byte), "ShipperID", _
 System.Data.DataRowVersion.Original, Nothing))
Me.SqlUpdateCommand1.Parameters.Add(New _
 System.Data.SqlClient.SqlParameter("@Original_CompanyName", _
 System.Data.SqlDbType.NVarChar, 40, _
 System.Data.ParameterDirection.Input, False, CType(0, Byte), _
 CType(0, Byte), "CompanyName", System.Data.DataRowVersion.Original, _
 Nothing))
Me.SqlUpdateCommand1.Parameters.Add(New _
 System.Data.SqlClient.SqlParameter("@Original_Phone", _
 System.Data.SqlDbType.NVarChar, 24, _
 System.Data.ParameterDirection.Input, True, CType(0, Byte), _
 CType(0, Byte), "Phone", System.Data.DataRowVersion.Original, Nothing))
Me.SqlUpdateCommand1.Parameters.Add(New _
 System.Data.SqlClient.SqlParameter("@Original_Phone1", _
 System.Data.SqlDbType.NVarChar, 24, _
 System.Data.ParameterDirection.Input, True, CType(0, Byte), _
 CType(0, Byte), "Phone", System.Data.DataRowVersion.Original, Nothing))
Me.SqlUpdateCommand1.Parameters.Add(New _
 System.Data.SqlClient.SqlParameter("@Select_ShipperID", _
 System.Data.SqlDbType.Int, 4, System.Data.ParameterDirection.Input, _
 False, CType(0, Byte), CType(0, Byte), "ShipperID", _
 System.Data.DataRowVersion.Current, Nothing))
```

Continued

Listing 17–7 *(Continued)*

```
'SqlDeleteCommand1
'
Me.SqlDeleteCommand1.CommandText = "DELETE FROM Shippers WHERE "& _
 "(ShipperID = @ShipperID) AND (CompanyName = @CompanyName) " & _
 "AND (Phone = @Phone OR @Phone1 IS NULL AND Phone IS NULL)"
Me.SqlDeleteCommand1.Connection = Me.SqlConnection1
Me.SqlDeleteCommand1.Parameters.Add(New _
 System.Data.SqlClient.SqlParameter("@ShipperID", _
 System.Data.SqlDbType.Int, 4, System.Data.ParameterDirection.Input, _
 False, CType(0, Byte), CType(0, Byte), "ShipperID", _
 System.Data.DataRowVersion.Original, Nothing))
Me.SqlDeleteCommand1.Parameters.Add(New _
 System.Data.SqlClient.SqlParameter("@CompanyName", _
 System.Data.SqlDbType.NVarChar, 40, _
 System.Data.ParameterDirection.Input, False, CType(0, Byte), _
 CType(0, Byte), "CompanyName", _
 System.Data.DataRowVersion.Original, Nothing))
Me.SqlDeleteCommand1.Parameters.Add(New _
 System.Data.SqlClient.SqlParameter("@Phone", _
 System.Data.SqlDbType.NVarChar, 24, _
 System.Data.ParameterDirection.Input, True, CType(0, Byte), _
 CType(0, Byte), "Phone", System.Data.DataRowVersion.Original, Nothing))
Me.SqlDeleteCommand1.Parameters.Add(New _
 System.Data.SqlClient.SqlParameter("@Phone1", _
 System.Data.SqlDbType.NVarChar, 24, _
 System.Data.ParameterDirection.Input, True, CType(0, Byte), _
 CType(0, Byte), "Phone", System.Data.DataRowVersion.Original, Nothing))
'
'SqlConnection1
'
Me.SqlConnection1.ConnectionString = "data source=GAB;initial "& _
 "catalog=Northwind;integrated security=SSPI;persist securi" & _
 "ty info=True;workstation id=GAB;packet size=4096"
'
'SqlDataAdapter1
'
Me.SqlDataAdapter1.DeleteCommand = Me.SqlDeleteCommand1
Me.SqlDataAdapter1.InsertCommand = Me.SqlInsertCommand1
Me.SqlDataAdapter1.SelectCommand = Me.SqlSelectCommand1
Me.SqlDataAdapter1.TableMappings.AddRange(New _
 System.Data.Common.DataTableMapping() {New _
 System.Data.Common.DataTableMapping("Table", "Shippers", New _
 System.Data.Common.DataColumnMapping() {New _
```

```
System.Data.Common.DataColumnMapping("ShipperID", "ShipperID"), _
New System.Data.Common.DataColumnMapping("CompanyName", _
"CompanyName"), New System.Data.Common.DataColumnMapping("Phone", _
"Phone")})})
Me.SqlDataAdapter1.UpdateCommand = Me.SqlUpdateCommand1


End Sub
```

 You can find the code for Listing 17-7 on the companion Web site (www. wiley.com/extras) in this chapter's download file, Ch17VS.zip (Visual Studio .NET version) or Ch17SDK.zip (SDK version). Look at the file DataSet_mapped.aspx and its CodeBehind file, DataSet_mapped. aspx.vb.

I'll hand-code an example soon enough, but for now, let's quickly run though what is being created here. Remember, all I did to create this code was drag a table from the server explorer onto the Web form.

1. The first section is very similar to previous DataSet examples. A group of command objects are created, one for each type of SQL command. In addition, a DataAdapter and connection object are created.

```
Me.SqlSelectCommand1 = New System.Data.SqlClient.SqlCommand()
Me.SqlInsertCommand1 = New System.Data.SqlClient.SqlCommand()
Me.SqlUpdateCommand1 = New System.Data.SqlClient.SqlCommand()
Me.SqlDeleteCommand1 = New System.Data.SqlClient.SqlCommand()
Me.SqlConnection1 = New System.Data.SqlClient.SqlConnection()
Me.SqlDataAdapter1 = New

    System.Data.SqlClient.SqlDataAdapter()
```

2. Each command object is populated with a SQL command. With the select command, nothing else is necessary. With insert, update, and select commands, a parameterized command is created. Here's the creation of the insert command:

```
Me.SqlInsertCommand1.CommandText = "INSERT INTO " & _
    "Shippers(CompanyName, Phone) VALUES (@CompanyName, " & _

    "@Phone); SELECT ShipperID, CompanyName, Phone FROM " & _

    "Shippers WHERE (ShipperID = @@IDENTITY)"
```

A parameter object is created for each of the parameters in this query. Here's the parameter for the Company Name:

```
Me.SqlInsertCommand1.Parameters.Add(New _

    System.Data.SqlClient.SqlParameter("@CompanyName", _
    System.Data.SqlDbType.NVarChar, 40, _
    System.Data.ParameterDirection.Input, False, CType(0, _
    Byte), CType(0, Byte), "CompanyName", _
        System.Data.DataRowVersion.Current, Nothing))
```

3. After the command objects are created, the connection object command text is set, but the object is not opened — you have to do that in your own code.

```
Me.SqlConnection1.ConnectionString = "data source=GAB;" & _
    "initial catalog=Northwind;integrated security=SSPI;" & _
    "persist security info=True;workstation id=GAB;" & _
    "packet size=4096"
```

You can use the type of connection string shown here, or you can simplify this as I have done in earlier examples.

4. The commands are bound to the DataAdapter. This is where the magic begins to happen. The DataAdapter is set to have one command for each type of SQL command:

```
Me.SqlDataAdapter1.DeleteCommand = Me.SqlDeleteCommand1
Me.SqlDataAdapter1.InsertCommand = Me.SqlInsertCommand1
Me.SqlDataAdapter1.SelectCommand = Me.SqlSelectCommand1
Me.SqlDataAdapter1.UpdateCommand = Me.SqlUpdateCommand1
```

5. The table(s) and columns are mapped to the table(s) and columns in the database. This is what makes programming in Visual Studio .NET a breeze.

```
Me.SqlDataAdapter1.TableMappings.AddRange(New _
    System.Data.Common.DataTableMapping() {New _
    System.Data.Common.DataTableMapping("Table", "Shippers", _
    New System.Data.Common.DataColumnMapping() {New _
    System.Data.Common.DataColumnMapping("ShipperID", _
    "ShipperID"), New _
    System.Data.Common.DataColumnMapping("CompanyName", _
    "CompanyName"), New _
    System.Data.Common.DataColumnMapping("Phone", "Phone")}})})
```

As you know, this book can be used with or without Visual Studio .NET, but I do want to impress on you how much code is written for you when you use Visual

Studio .NET to build your pages. To finish off the Visual Studio .NET example, I
need only add a few lines of code and a DataGrid, as shown in Listing 17-8.

Listing 17-8: Binding to a DataGrid

```
Private Sub Page_Load(ByVal sender As System.Object, _
  ByVal e As System.EventArgs) Handles MyBase.Load

  Dim objDataSet As New System.Data.DataSet()

  Try
    'Open connection and fill DataSet
    Me.SqlConnection1.Open()
    Me.SqlDataAdapter1.Fill(objDataSet)
    Me.SqlConnection1.Close()
  Catch objException As Exception
    'TODO: Add exception handler here
  End Try

  DataGrid1.DataSource = objDataSet.Tables("Shippers").DefaultView
  DataGrid1.DataBind()
End Sub
```

If you get an error while running this code, it is most likely due to a login failure. To rectify this situation, you can either alter the connection string (auto-
generated by Visual Studio .NET to use integrated security) or set
anonymous access off on the project Web site in IIS.

If you examine the code from the download site, you'll see that I chose to
add a correct connection string rather than to alter security on the site. In a
real-world application, the choice of integrated security is largely dictated
by security needs.

Editing data in the grid

Let's build on the last exercise by using use the editable DataGrid from the last
chapter to edit the Shippers table in the database. Some of this will be old hat, but
none of the update code has to be rewritten for this exercise: it's all pulled directly
from Listings 17-7 and 17-8.

To have better code reuse, I change the Page_Load event to bind data to a
DataView created in a CreateBindableDataView() function. The code for these
routines is shown in Listing 17-9.

Listing 17-9: The CreateBindableDataView and Page_Load Routines

```
Private Sub Page_Load(ByVal sender As System.Object, _
   ByVal e As System.EventArgs) Handles MyBase.Load
      'Put user code to initialize the page here

      If Not Page.IsPostBack Then
          DataGrid1.DataSource = CreateDataBindableView()
          DataGrid1.DataBind()
      End If

End Sub

Private Function CreateDataBindableView() As System.Data.DataView
    Dim objDataSet As New System.Data.DataSet()

    Try
        Me.SqlConnection1.Open()
        Me.SqlDataAdapter1.Fill(objDataSet)
        Me.SqlConnection1.Close()
    Catch objException As Exception

    End Try

    Return objDataSet.Tables(0).DefaultView

End Function
```

 The code for Listings 17-9 and 17-10 is on the companion Web site (www. wiley.com/extras) in this chapter's download file: Ch17VS.zip (Visual Studio .NET version) or Ch17SDK.zip (SDK version). The file to look at is DataSet_MappedComplex.aspx.vb.

The CreateBindableView() is also used by the DataGrid1_Edit and the DataGrid1_Cancel events, as shown in Listing 17-10. If you've already read through Chapter 16, this will be a review, because I used the same logic there.

Listing 17-10: DataGrid Edit and Cancel Events

```
Protected Sub DataGrid1_Edit(ByVal objSender As Object, _
   ByVal objEventArgs As DataGridCommandEventArgs)
      Try
```

```
        DataGrid1.EditItemIndex = objEventArgs.Item.ItemIndex
        DataGrid1.DataSource = CreateDataBindableView()
        DataGrid1.DataBind()
    Catch e As Exception
        Response.Write(e.ToString())
    End Try

End Sub

Protected Sub DataGrid1_Cancel(ByVal objSender As Object, _
        ByVal objEventArgs As DataGridCommandEventArgs)
    DataGrid1.EditItemIndex = -1
    DataGrid1.DataSource = CreateDataBindableView()
    DataGrid1.DataBind()
End Sub
```

The DataGrid that this is being bound to (shown in Listing 17-11) is very similar to those in both Chapters 15 and 16.

Listing 17-11: The DataGrid Being Bound

```
<asp:DataGrid id="DataGrid1" runat="server"
      AutoGenerateColumns="False" OnEditCommand="DataGrid1_Edit"
      OnCancelCommand="DataGrid1_Cancel"
      OnUpdateCommand="DataGrid1_Update">
    <Columns>
    <asp:BoundColumn DataField="ShipperID"

        ReadOnly="True" HeaderText="Shipper ID" />
    <asp:TemplateColumn HeaderText="Company Name">
      <ItemTemplate>
        <%# Container.DataItem("CompanyName")%>
      </ItemTemplate>
      <EditItemTemplate>
        <asp:TextBox ID="CompanyName" Text='<%#

          Container.DataItem("CompanyName")%>' Runat="server" />
      </EditItemTemplate>
    </asp:TemplateColumn>
    <asp:TemplateColumn HeaderText="Phone Number">
      <ItemTemplate>
        <%# Container.DataItem("Phone")%>
      </ItemTemplate>
      <EditItemTemplate>
        <asp:TextBox ID="Phone" Text='<%#
```

Continued

Listing 17–11 *(Continued)*

```
        Container.DataItem("Phone")%>' Runat="server" />
    </EditItemTemplate>
  </asp:TemplateColumn>
  <asp:EditCommandColumn CancelText="Cancel"
        EditText="Edit" UpdateText="Update" />
  </Columns>
</asp:DataGrid>
```

The code for Listing 17-11 is on the companion Web site (www.wiley.
com/extras) in this chapter's download file: Ch17VS.zip (Visual Studio
.NET version) or Ch17SDK.zip (SDK version). The file to look at is DataSet_
MappedComplex.aspx.

As I mentioned, this code is old hat. The only real difference between the
examples here and the last chapter is that the setup is done for you by Visual
Studio .NET.

The DataGrid1_Update event is the first real change from the examples in the
last chapter. To update, the DataSet is created, the edit row is changed, and the
DataSet is updated. The code for this event is shown in Listing 17-12.

Listing 17-12: Updating the Shippers Table

```
Protected Sub DataGrid1_Update(ByVal objSender As Object, _
    ByVal objEventArgs As DataGridCommandEventArgs)
'First create controls to pull from
Dim objCompanyName As TextBox = _
    CType(objEventArgs.Item.FindControl("CompanyName"), TextBox)
Dim objPhone As TextBox = _
    CType(objEventArgs.Item.FindControl("Phone"), TextBox)

Dim objDataSet As New System.Data.DataSet()

Try
    Me.SqlConnection1.Open()
    Me.SqlDataAdapter1.Fill(objDataSet)

    Dim objTable As System.Data.DataTable = _

                objDataSet.Tables("Shippers")
    Dim objRow = objTable.Rows(DataGrid1.EditItemIndex)
```

```
    objRow("CompanyName") = objCompanyName.Text
    objRow("Phone") = objPhone.Text

    Me.SqlDataAdapter1.Update(objDataSet)
    Me.SqlConnection1.Close()

Catch objException As Exception
    'TODO: Write exception handler
    Response.Write(objException.ToString())
End Try

DataGrid1.EditItemIndex = -1
DataGrid1.DataSource = objDataSet.Tables("Shippers").DefaultView
DataGrid1.DataBind()

End Sub
```

The key to success here is pulling the `EditItemIndex` from `DataGrid1` to determine which row I am going to update. Updating the row is as simple as using the `Update` method of the DataAdapter. If you would like to test this, simply comment out the following line and try to run the page:

```
Me.SqlDataAdapter1.UpdateCommand = Me.SqlUpdateCommand1
```

 The code for Listing 17-12 is on the companion Web site (`www.wiley.com/extras`) in this chapter's download file: `Ch17VS.zip` (Visual Studio .NET version) or `Ch17SDK.zip` (SDK version). The file to look at is `DataSet_MappedComplex.aspx.vb`.

There are some upsides and downsides to this particular code exercise. Since the commands can be created by drag-and-drop through Visual Studio .NET, the initial coding is very simple. It is also quite easy to maintain the code. The downside, however, deals with the way ASP.NET works. Since each edit, update, delete, or cancel requires a trip to the server, the benefit of a DataSet is never realized when only one table is being edited. This is not as bad as it sounds, but you should be aware of the fact.

I advocate anything that speeds up development, so I'm not opposed to using the DataAdapter to its full potential. Be aware, however, that a DataReader would be more efficient here, with the downside being your having to code the update and delete events by hand. The trade-off is a bit of performance for ease of coding. My suggestion is to go the easy route first, and then tighten the code if you need to gain a few more cycles.

Auto-Generating Commands

Drag-and-drop is fairly easy, so you might feel compelled to use it for all of your pages. While there is nothing wrong with that, I urge you not to jump into a Visual Studio solution without considering some of the other additions to the .NET arsenal.

One thing that I find myself doing fairly often in applications is figuring out a way to render my code generically. In most instances, the generic code is designed to thin down my data layer. What I wouldn't give for an object that would generate my INSERT, UPDATE, and DELETE statements when I throw a SELECT statement at it.

Guess what? It's in there. With ADO.NET, you can use the drag-and-drop methodology without having to drag and drop code. The object you use is the CommandBuilder object (yeah, that should be hard to remember!). You will need to set up the select, but ADO.NET handles the rest.

Auto-generating commands and displaying them

Let's look at how we can use a SELECT query to pull data from an editable DataGrid and have ADO.NET create the rest of the queries for us. The code is very similar to Listing 17-11, but works with a much smaller table. To help you understand this process better, I start with code to create and display the auto-generated commands.

The snippet of code in Listing 17-13 shows how easy it is to use the CommandBuilder.

Listing 17-13: CommandBuilder Object

```
Dim objConn As New SQL.SqlConnection(Application("Northwind_SQL"))
Dim strSQL As String = "SELECT RegionID, RegionDescription FROM Region"
Dim objCmd As New SQL.SqlCommand(strSQL, objConn)

Dim objDataAdapter As New SQL.SqlDataAdapter(objCmd)
Dim objDataSet As New System.Data.DataSet()

objConn.Open()
Dim objCmdBuilder As New SQL.SqlCommandBuilder(objDataAdapter)

objDataAdapter.DeleteCommand = objCmdBuilder.GetDeleteCommand()
objDataAdapter.UpdateCommand = objCmdBuilder.GetUpdateCommand()
objDataAdapter.InsertCommand = objCmdBuilder.GetInsertCommand()
...
```

The code for Listings 17-13 and 17-14 is on the companion Web site (`www.wiley.com/extras`) in this chapter's download file: `Ch17VS.zip` (Visual Studio .NET version) or `Ch17SDK.zip` (SDK version). Look at `autoGenCommands.aspx` and its CodeBehind file, `autoGenCommands.aspx.vb`.

Now, that's certainly a lot less code than the drag-and-drop method produced. To view the text of these commands, simply use the `CommandText` property of the command you wanted to output. Listing 17-14 shows how to output these commands along with the SQL generated.

Listing 17-14: Outputting Auto-Generated Commands

```
'DELETE FROM Region WHERE ( RegionID = @p1 AND RegionDescription = @p2 )
Label1.Text = objDataAdapter.DeleteCommand.CommandText


'UPDATE Region SET RegionID = @p1 , RegionDescription = @p2 WHERE
'    ( RegionID = @p3 AND RegionDescription = @p4 )
Label2.Text = objDataAdapter.DeleteCommand.CommandText


'INSERT INTO Region( RegionID , RegionDescription ) VALUES ( @p1 , @p2 )
Label3.Text = objDataAdapter.InsertCommand.CommandText
```

Using the commands

Of course, it was probably not your lot in life to let an object create your code and marvel at the output. That being the case, you most likely will like to use the command to update the information in the table.

I've already covered the method of setting up editing in a DataGrid, so now I focus only on the update event. (You can consult Listing 16-12 in Chapter 16 if you need a reminder of how to create an editable DataGrid.)

Listing 17-15 shows the code for the update event. In it, I simply update a single value.

Listing 17-15: Updating a Single Row with an Auto-Generated Command

```
Protected Sub DataGrid1_Update(ByVal objSender As Object, _
    ByVal objEventArgs As DataGridCommandEventArgs)


    'First create controls to pull from
    Dim objRegionDescription As TextBox = _
        CType(objEventArgs.Item.FindControl("RegionDescription"), TextBox)
    Dim intItem As Integer = objEventArgs.Item.ItemIndex
```

Continued

Listing 17–15 *(Continued)*

```
Dim objConn As New SQL.SqlConnection(Application("Northwind_SQL"))
Dim strSQL As String = "SELECT RegionID, RegionDescription FROM Region"
Dim objCmd As New SQL.SqlCommand(strSQL, objConn)

Dim objDataAdapter As New SQL.SqlDataAdapter(objCmd)
Dim objDataSet As New System.Data.DataSet()

objConn.Open()

Dim objCmdBuilder As New SQL.SqlCommandBuilder(objDataAdapter)

objDataAdapter.DeleteCommand = objCmdBuilder.GetDeleteCommand()
objDataAdapter.UpdateCommand = objCmdBuilder.GetUpdateCommand()
objDataAdapter.InsertCommand = objCmdBuilder.GetInsertCommand()

objDataAdapter.Fill(objDataSet, "Region")

objDataSet.Tables("Region").Rows(intItem)("RegionDescription") = _

            objRegionDescription.Text

objDataAdapter.Update(objDataSet, "Region")
objConn.Close()

DataGrid1.DataSource = objDataSet.Tables("Region").DefaultView
DataGrid1.EditItemIndex = -1
DataGrid1.DataBind()
End Sub
```

 The code for Listing 17-15 is on the companion Web site (www.wiley.com/extras) in this chapter's download file: Ch17VS.zip (Visual Studio .NET version) or Ch17SDK.zip (SDK version). The file to look at is autoGenUpdate.aspx.vb.

The important part of the code is the portion where the single field **RegionDescription** is updated for the chosen row. Here is the step-by-step:

1. The current row is chosen by selecting ItemIndex from the DataGrid command event arguments:

   ```
   Dim intItem As Integer = objEventArgs.Item.ItemIndex
   ```

2. The value of the text box is then used to update the RegionDescription column in the row being edited:

```
objDataSet.Tables("Region").Rows(intItem)_
("RegionDescription") = objRegionDescription.Text
```

3. Finally, the `Update` method of the DataAdapter is called.

This technique, by itself, does not save you a whole lot of grief. Certainly, there must be more value to this, and there is, but not so much in a Web paradigm. If you code Windows Forms applications, you'll find the shortcuts of even greater value.

For instance, some developers use the update event to stop concurrency errors. I don't see this as a realistic methodology to follow in a Web environment because you do not open and hold the DataGrid in a Web environment, as you might in a desktop application. Instead, you open the database and send the DataSet to the client as HTML. The user edits the data and submits. You only have a fraction of a second to capture a concurrency error with the DataSet in this paradigm.

If you get lucky and have information submitted during the processing of the DataSet, you get a concurrency error. However, if someone changes the data while you are editing the page, you will overwrite the data without even realizing it has been done.

Transactions

ADO.NET has support for transactions, which should come as no surprise since ADO had a transaction model of its own. The main difference is the fact that you can now set up transactions the same way in your Visual Basic .NET desktop applications as you can in your ASP.NET code. While this may not seem like much, it does reduce the amount of code you have to learn.

Working with transactions in ASP.NET is very simple. Because most of your applications will probably use the edit capabilities of the DataGrid, most of your transaction-based code will be via forms that submit data back to multiple tables.

To illustrate this, I'll take a single item from the Products table and add the supplier into the mix. I am going to programmatically mess up one of the integer fields with a single character. If you attempt to submit the form back as it loads, you end up with a message due to the transaction failing. Figure 17-3 shows the page in a browser with the error message pointing out which text box is causing the problem.

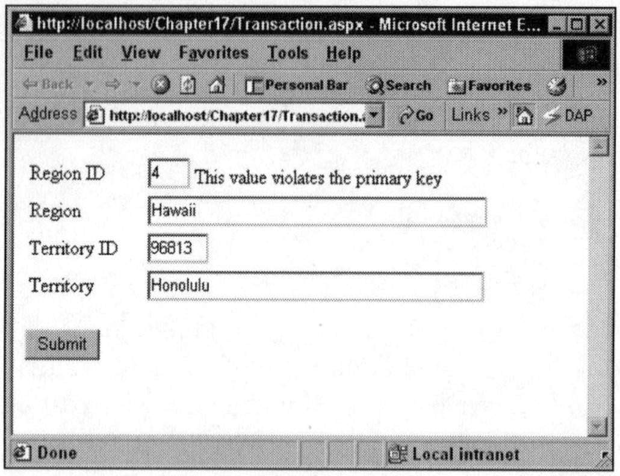

Figure 17-3: The transactional form.

To be complete, I've included the code for the form in the transactional page in Listing 17-16. You should be familiar with Web controls placed on a page by now, but one more look won't hurt.

Listing 17-16: The Transactional Form

```
<form id="Form1" method="post" runat="server">
  <p><asp:Panel id="Panel1" runat="server" Height="192px" Width="434px">
  <table width="400">
    <tr>
      <td style="WIDTH: 93px">Region ID</td>
      <td>
        <asp:textbox id="RegionID" runat="server" Width="36px"
            Height="24px">4</asp:textbox>
        This value violates the primary key
      </td>
    </tr>
    <tr>
      <td style="WIDTH: 93px">Region</td>
      <td>
        <asp:textbox id="RegionDescription" runat="server" Width="284px"

            Height="24px">Hawaii</asp:textbox>
      </td>
    </tr>
    <tr>
      <td style="WIDTH: 93px">Territory ID</td>
      <td>
        <asp:textbox id="TerritoryID" runat="server" Width="52px"
            Height="24px">96813</asp:textbox>
      </td>
```

```
      </tr>
      <tr>
        <td style="WIDTH: 93px">Territory</td>
        <td>
          <asp:textbox id="TerritoryDescription" runat="server" Width="282px"

              Height="24px">Honolulu</asp:textbox>
        </td>
      </tr>
    </table>
    <P>
      <asp:button id="Button1" runat="server" Text="Submit" /></asp:Panel>
    </P>
    <P>
    </P>
    <P>
       
      <asp:Label id="Label1" runat="server" />
    </P>
</form>
```

The only thing I added to this page is the panel control so I can hide the form if the submission is successful. The rest uses syntax similar to that found in Chapter 8. To handle the click of the Submit button, I have to write an event in my CodeBehind page that handles the click event of the button, which is labeled Button1.

The code for the click event is shown in Listing 17-17.

Listing 17-17: Code under the Submit Button

```
Protected Sub Button1_Click(ByVal sender As System.Object, _
  ByVal e As System.EventArgs) Handles Button1.Click
  Dim intRegionID As Integer = RegionID.Text
  Dim strRegionDescription As String = RegionDescription.Text
  Dim intTerritoryID As Integer = TerritoryID.Text
  Dim strTerritoryDescription As String = TerritoryDescription.Text

  Dim strConn As String = Application("Northwind_SQL")
  Dim objConn As New SQL.SqlConnection(strConn)
  Dim objTransaction As SQL.SqlTransaction

  'Set up Region Stored Procedure
  Dim objCmdRegion As New SQL.SqlCommand("spi_Region", objConn)
  With objCmdRegion
```

Continued

Listing 17–17 *(Continued)*

```
  .CommandType = CommandType.StoredProcedure
  .Parameters.Add(New System.Data.SqlClient.SqlParameter("@RETURN_VALUE", _
  System.Data.SqlDbType.Int, 4, _
  System.Data.ParameterDirection.ReturnValue, True, CType(10, Byte), _
  CType(0, Byte), "", System.Data.DataRowVersion.Current, Nothing))
  .Parameters.Add(New System.Data.SqlClient.SqlParameter("@RegionID", _
  System.Data.SqlDbType.Int, 4, _
  System.Data.ParameterDirection.Input, True, CType(10, Byte), _
  CType(0, Byte), "", System.Data.DataRowVersion.Current, intRegionID))
  .Parameters.Add(New System.Data.SqlClient.SqlParameter("@RegionDescription",

  System.Data.SqlDbType.NChar, 50, _
  System.Data.ParameterDirection.Input, True, CType(0, Byte), _
  CType(0, Byte), "", System.Data.DataRowVersion.Current, _
  strRegionDescription))
End With

'Set up Territory Stored Procedure
Dim objCmdTerritory As New SQL.SqlCommand("spi_Territories", objConn)
Dim objParameter As SQL.SqlParameter

With objCmdTerritory
  .CommandType = CommandType.StoredProcedure
  objParameter = .Parameters.Add("@TerritoryID", SqlDbType.Int, 4)
  objParameter.Value = intTerritoryID
  objParameter = .Parameters.Add("@TerritoryDescription", SqlDbType.NChar, 50)
  objParameter.Value = strTerritoryDescription
  objParameter = .Parameters.Add("@RegionID", SqlDbType.Int, 4)
  objParameter.Value = intRegionID
End With

Try
  objConn.Open()
  objTransaction = objConn.BeginTransaction

  'Add Command objects to the transaction
  objCmdRegion.Transaction = objTransaction
  objCmdTerritory.Transaction = objTransaction

  'Run both command objects
  objCmdRegion.ExecuteNonQuery()
  objCmdTerritory.ExecuteNonQuery()
```

```
    'No errors, so commit
    objTransaction.Commit()

    'Success message and no form
    Label1.ForeColor = System.Drawing.Color.Blue
    Label1.Text = "Record successfully added."
    Panel1.Visible = False

    objConn.Close()

  Catch objSQLException As SQL.SqlException
    objTransaction.Rollback()

    Label1.ForeColor = System.Drawing.Color.Red

    If objSQLException.Number = 2627 Then
      Label1.Text = "A record already exists with this number."
    Else
      Label1.Text = "An error occured inserting this record."
    End If
  Catch objException As Exception
    Label1.ForeColor = System.Drawing.Color.Red

    objTransaction.Rollback()
    Label1.Text = "An unknown error occured."
  End Try
End Sub
```

 The code for Listings 17-16 and 17-17 is on the companion Web site (www.wiley.com/extras) in this chapter's download file: Ch17VS.zip (Visual Studio .NET version) or Ch17SDK.zip (SDK version). The file to look at is Transaction.aspx and its CodeBehind file, Transaction.aspx.vb.

Look at the bolded code in Listing 17-17. To set up a transaction, I create a transaction object, in this case a SQLTransaction, from the SQLClient namespace. To set the transaction object up, I use the BeginTransaction method of the connection object. This transaction object is then set as the Transaction property of each command object:

```
objCmdRegion.Transaction = objTransaction
objCmdTerritory.Transaction = objTransaction
```

If I encounter any error, I roll the transaction back. Otherwise, I commit the transaction. I also have this set to roll back, just to keep the database clean, but you can set it to commit if you would like to test the data insert.

Summary

In this chapter you learned about relational databases and how the ADO.NET objects map to these items. You then learned how to use a DataSet to mimic a relational database, and how to use the DataAdapter to more easily update data in a relational database.

The DataAdapter, as you found out, can generate its own commands by using the select command as a model. It allows you to easily update the database by changing rows in the DataSet and issuing an Update against the DataAdapter.

Finally, the transaction processing aspect of ADO.NET was covered. In the next section of the book, I look at XML and how it is used in ASP.NET.

Part IV

Collaboration and Presentation — XML

Chapter 18

Working with XML

IN THIS CHAPTER

♦ Create a simple ASP.NET application to check for well-formed documents

♦ Introduce the Namespaces in the .NET Framework related to XML

♦ Use DataSets and DataGrids with XML

♦ Work with XML using .NET's Streams, Readers, and Writers

YOU'RE ALREADY FAMILIAR with the basics of XML and how to use it in your own applications (Chapter 4 is an XML primer of sorts). This chapter shows how to develop applications that access XML documents and how XML can be used with the .NET Framework. Among other things, I show you how to check for well-formed documents; we look at the core namespaces dedicated to XML; and I demonstrate how to return XML data from SQL Server 2000. Microsoft has gone out of its way to support XML across the board by including numerous namespaces that provide all of the functionality needed to create XML-based applications.

Valid versus Well Formed

The best way to understand how the .NET Framework interacts with XML is to create simple applications that read and write XML documents. To do this I start by creating a console application that makes sure that a given XML document is well formed. The .NET Framework provides several different classes that can be used to interact with XML documents. For this example I use the XmlDocument class which is part of the System.Xml namespace. The XmlDocument class provides the methods for opening an XML document and checks to make sure that the document is well formed as it is opened. Listing 18-1 shows the code for the console application.

Listing 18-1: Command-Line XML Application

```
Imports System.Xml
Module Module1

    Sub Main()
```

Listing 18-1 *(Continued)*

```
        Dim oXML As New XmlDocument()
        oXML.Load("c:\items.xml")
    End Sub

End Module
```

The first line in the simple application indicates that it will use the XML portion of the .NET Framework. All of the application is located in the Sub Main procedure. An instance of the XmlDocument is placed in the oXML variable. Next the Load method is called and loads the XML document from the path provided. In this case I've created an XML document and stored it on the c: drive in a file called items.xml, shown in Listing 18-2.

Listing 18-2: items.xml Used in the Console Application

```
<?xml version="1.0"?>
<Catalog>
    <item id="1">
        <color>Red</color>
        <size>Large</size>
    </item>
    <item id="2">
        <color>Blue</color>
        <size>Small</size>
    </item>
</Catalog>
```

 You can find the code from Listing 18-2 on the companion Web site (www. wiley.com/extras) in Ch18SDK.zip (SDK version) or Ch18VS.zip (Visual Studio .NET version). When you unzip the download, look for the file named items.xml.

The XML document shown in Listing 18-2 could be used to display some information about a catalog for a department store. If the code in Listing 18-1 compiles and the XML document in Listing 18-2 is placed in the correct location, the console application executes and runs without any problem. However, if any changes happen to the XML document to make it poorly formed, the console application throws an exception as shown in Figure 18-1.

To generate this type of exception I removed the letter e in size from the second record. The resulting error message is not very descriptive, however. The XML namespace includes a more descriptive error message that can be used when structured error handling is implemented. To get the more descriptive message, I alter the source code to look like Listing 18-3.

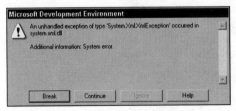

Figure 18-1: An XML document that is not well formed throws an exception.

Listing 18-3: Updated Source for Checking Well-Formed XML (Module1.vb)

```vb
Imports System.Xml
Module Module1

    Sub Main()
        Dim oXML As New XmlDocument()
        Try
        oXML.Load("c:\items.xml")
        Catch xErr As XmlException
            Console.WriteLine(xErr.Message)
            Console.ReadLine()
        End Try
    End Sub

End Module
```

You can find the code from Listing 18-3 on the companion Web site (www. wiley.com/extras) in Ch18SDK.zip (SDK version) or Ch18VS.zip (Visual Studio .NET version). When you unzip the download, look for the file named Module1.vb.

Listing 18-3 now produces a standard error message that helps determine where the error in the XML document occurs. Figure 18-2 shows the console screen and the new error message generated from the Console.WriteLine. Additionally I've included a Console.ReadLine so the actual error message can be read. Once an error occurs, the ReadLine method stops the application from executing until the user hits the Enter key.

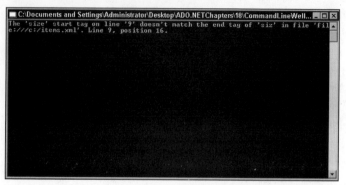

Figure 18-2: The new error message generated from the XML application.

That covers how to determine if an XML document is well formed and how to use the .NET classes to verify this. For a document to be well formed it needs to have closing and opening elements, a root element, and so on. But an XML document also needs to be *valid*, which means that, in addition to being well formed, it must conform to a document containing rules that indicate the appropriate values and constraints. The most basic of these types of documents is the document type definition (DTD). This technology was based on older technology and did not provide a great deal of flexibility, as discussed in Chapter 4. Realizing this shortfall, Microsoft introduced its implementation of a schema called XML Data Reduced (XDR). This provided something XML developers could use while the W3C worked on a specification for a standard schema. Once the W3C created the specification it was formally named XML Schema Definition Language (XSD). Microsoft provides excellent utilities with the .NET Framework for creating schemas based on these technologies. The topic of schemas is covered in detail in Chapter 19.

A Great Way to Express Data

Throughout the book the topic of XML keeps coming up, which indicates how integral XML is to the .NET Framework. XML has been integrated into almost all of Microsoft's technologies from Data Access to SQL Server 2000 to configuration files for ASP.NET. There are several reasons why XML is the choice for storing data:

◆ XML is text based. In the past, Web configuration information was stored in a binary file called the metabase. A great deal of information is now stored per application in the same directory as the Web application itself. This helps for migrating data and in day-to-day maintenance of a Web server.

◆ Because XML is text based, it is very portable, even between different operating systems. Initially this was the most compelling reason to use

XML, because there was there was no standard for interoperability between systems before XML.

◆ XML provides several standards that include the capability to query XML data, provide a way to validate data, and transform data into a different format.

The underlying format in ADO.NET is stored as XML. Microsoft has also provided specific methods, included with its Managed Provider for SQL Server 2000, which return XML, as shown later in the chapter in "Generating XML from SQL 2000."

The benefits up to this point are not enough to carry a technology. What makes XML even more powerful are all of the supporting technologies, from XPath for querying data from an XML document to XSLT for transforming data in an XML document. There are also very specific rules determining if a document is truly an XML document and ways to make XML documents fit a specification. All of these features and standards create a well-rounded technology for storing and manipulating data in the form of XML.

Over the next few sections and chapters I examine how Microsoft has implemented several of the technologies mentioned here. The .NET Framework is extensive when it comes to the support of XML and its supporting technologies.

The .NET XML Namespaces

Microsoft has provided a great deal of support for XML in the .NET Framework. The following section and the rest of the chapter are dedicated to the different areas that Microsoft has provided for in supporting this emerging technology.

 The examples in the rest of the chapter are ASP.NET pages, which are contained in a single project. While developing them, I created a new page for each example. From within Visual Studio .NET I was then able to right-click each file and set it as the start page for the project. I clicked the Run button and it executed the correct ASP.NET page. This made it convenient for developing the different pages in a single project. Alternatively, right-clicking the ASPX file and selecting Build and Browse also executes the file.

System.Xml

The System.Xml namespace is the fundamental namespace for dealing with XML. It provides the capability to read, write, and validate XML documents. System.Xml also provides sets of objects that represent different elements of an XML document.

Throughout the chapter I show examples of some of the more useful classes in this namespace. Additionally, Listing 18-3 earlier in this chapter demonstrated an example of using the `XmlDocument` class. The example in Listing 18-4 shows how to step through the `items.xml` file and display the values of the elements based on an XPath query. Using XPath expressions and its associated classes are discussed later in the chapter in the "System.Xml.XPath" section.

Listing 18–4: Code that Uses the XmlDocument and an XPath Expression (DisplayItemsWithXML.aspx)

```
Public Sub LoadData()
    Dim oXml As New XmlDocument()
    Dim oNodList As XmlNodeList
    Dim oNod As XmlNode
    oXml.Load("c:\items.xml")
    oNodList = oXml.SelectNodes("/Catalog/item/color")
    Response.Write(oNodList.Count & "<br>")
    For Each oNod In oNodList
        Response.Write(oNod.ChildNodes(0).Value & "<br>")
    Next
End Sub
```

You can find the code in Listing 18-4 on the companion Web site (www.wiley.com/extras) in `Ch18SDK.zip` (SDK version) or `Ch18VS.zip` (Visual Studio .NET version). When you unzip the download, look for the file named `DisplayItemsWithXML.aspx`.

This sample application first declares a variable of type `XmlDocument`. The document `items.xml` will be loaded into the variable. Next I declare the variables for the node list and the node itself. After loading the `items.xml` document, I execute the `SelectNode` method of the `XmlDocument` class. This returns a group of nodes that meet the criteria for the XPath expression. After getting the values back, I display exactly how many nodes were returned and iterate through the nodes displaying the value of a child element, the color. This application only requires that the `System.Xml` namespace be imported. The source code in Listing 18-4 is entered in the CodeBehind page and a call (`<%LoadData%>`) is added to the HTML source. The next section shows how to read and write a class to and from a file on the hard drive.

System.Xml.Serialization

In this section I create a sample application that demonstrates the capability of the `System.Xml.Serialization` namespace. The application utilizes the `XmlSerializer` object to serialize an object to an XML document. Generally speaking, serializing data means that the data in the XML document is being written to disk on the system. Serialization is not limited to writing data to a hard disk, however; it could also be written to memory. The `Serialization` namespace is very specialized and generally used in unique situations. The `Serialization` class in the .NET Framework writes the contents of a class to disk as an XML document. This is useful for disconnected applications that will eventually be reconnected to a server where the data can finally be saved. If a laptop user were traveling and could save his data to the home server, an XML document would make an excellent storage area. Listing 18-5 shows an example of how serialization could be employed.

Listing 18-5: ASP.NET Serializing an Object to an XML Document on the System Disk (UsingXMLSerialization.aspx)

```
Public Class Item
    Public id As Integer
    Public color As String
    Public size As String
End Class
Sub LoadData()
    Dim oItem As New Item()
    Dim oSerial As New XmlSerializer(GetType(Item))
    Dim oXml As New XmlTextWriter(Server.MapPath(".") & _
        "\ItemsSerial.xml", Nothing)

    oItem.id = 1
    oItem.color = "Red"
    oItem.size = "Large"

    oXml.Formatting = Formatting.Indented
    oSerial.Serialize(oXml, oItem)
    oXml.Close()
End Sub
```

You can find the code from Listing 18-5 on the companion Web site (www. wiley.com/extras) in Ch18SDK.zip (**SDK** version) or Ch18VS.zip (**Visual Studio .NET version).** When you unzip the download, look for the file named UsingXMLSerialization.aspx.

In this example, I first create a class that represents a general item. The class has three properties: id, color, and size. The LoadData subprocedure first creates an instance of one of these items. Next, I create an XmlSerializer object and pass it the type of Item. After creating the XmlSerializer object, I get an XmlTextWriter to write the XML document to and set the properties of the oItem object. I then set the format to use indentation on the XML document and execute the `Serialize` method of the `XmlSerializer` object. I pass the `Serialize` method the open `TextWriter` and also the object that I want to serialize. Finally I close the XML document and exit the application. (If the XML document is not closed, it cannot be viewed; the system will indicate that it is open by another process.)

 For this sample application to work correctly from the development environment, the user ASPNET on the system needs to be granted Write permission to the directory where the file will be written. If this is not done, an error is generated indicating that insufficient permissions exist to write the file to the directory. To check the necessary permission, right-click the folder and select Properties. Select the Security tab, click the Add button, select the ASPNET user in the list box, and click OK. Make sure the user has Write access to the directory, and click OK again.

The `System.Xml.Serialization` and the `System.Xml` namespaces need to be imported to this project for the application to work correctly. There is no real interface to the ASP.NET application so when it runs the browser won't display any information. The results of running this application are shown in Listing 18-6.

Listing 18-6: Results of Using an XmlSerializer.

```
<?xml version="1.0"?>
<Item xmlns:xsd="http://www.w3.org/2001/XMLSchema"
   xmlns:xsi="http://www.w3.org/2001/XMLSchema-instance">
  <id>1</id>
  <color>Red</color>
  <size>Large</size>
</Item>
```

The information in Listing 18-6 looks similar to the class that was included in the source for Listing 18-5, because Listing 18-5 is the XML version of the class from Listing 18-6.

Serialization is only good if the data can be reloaded into the application. This is where deserialization comes into play. Deserializing is almost the exact opposite of the serialization process. Listing 18-7 shows how the XML document in Listing 18-6 can be retrieved back into its original class.

Listing 18-7: Deserializing the Data Stored to Disk (UsingXMLDeserialization.aspx)

```
Public Class Item
    Public id As Integer
    Public color As String
```

```
        Public size As String
    End Class
    Sub LoadData()
        Dim oItem As New Item()
        Dim oXml As New XmlTextReader(Server.MapPath(".") & _
            "\ItemsSerial.xml")
        Dim oSerial As New XmlSerializer(GetType(Item))

        oItem = oSerial.Deserialize(oXml)
        Response.Write(oItem.id & "<br>")
        Response.Write(oItem.color & "<br>")
        Response.Write(oItem.size & "<br>")

        oXml.Close()
    End Sub
```

 You can find the code from Listing 18-7 on the companion Web site (www.wiley.com/extras) in Ch18SDK.zip (SDK version) or Ch18VS.zip (Visual Studio .NET version). When you unzip the download, look for the file named UsingXMLDeserialization.aspx.

The code for the deserialization is similar to the serialization. The same Item class is declared at the beginning. A new Item object is created and then, this time, I create an XmlTextReader instead of an XmlTextWriter, opening the file that was written to before. I declare the oSerial object again as an XmlSerializer. The oItem object is set to the value returned by the Deserialize method. I display the values pulled back by deserializing the document and then close the XmlTextReader. The resulting output looks like Figure 18-3.

Figure 18-3: The result of deserializing the XML document.

Serializing can be a difficult process, but Microsoft has provided an easy interface for reading and writing XML documents to disk. Other methods of reading and writing XML data to disk are discussed later in the section titled "Accessing XML Using Streams."

System.Xml.Schema

XML schemas, as discussed in Chapter 4, allow for the validation of an XML document. If an XML document is said to be valid, it means that the document has met all of the constraints defined in the schema. The System.Xml.Schema namespace includes all of the functionality to create and manipulate schemas. This topic is discussed in depth in Chapter 19.

System.Xml.XPath

XPath expressions are used for querying an XML document and returning a subset of the document based on the query. The example in Listing 18-8 uses four important classes from the XPath namespace:

- ◆ XPathDocument, which gets a handle to the XML document that we want to query.

- ◆ XPathNavigator, which allows for the navigation of the document.

- ◆ An XPathExpression object, which helps in the creation of the criteria for querying.

- ◆ XPathNodeIterator, which steps through the result set. It uses the Select method of the XPathNavigator and a passed-in XPath expression.

The entire application is shown in Listing 18-8. The application also requires that the System.Xml.XPath namespace be added.

Listing 18-8: Using the XPath Namespace for Requesting Data (ExecuteXPathExpression.aspx)

```
Sub LoadData()
    Dim oExp As XPathExpression
    Dim oDoc As New XPathDocument("c:\items.xml")
    Dim oNav As XPathNavigator = oDoc.CreateNavigator()
    oExp = oNav.Compile("/Catalog/item/color")

    Dim oItr As XPathNodeIterator = oNav.Select(oExp)
    While oItr.MoveNext
        Response.Write(oItr.Current.Value)
    End While

    oExp = oNav.Compile("/Catalog/item/@id")
```

```
        oItr = oNav.Select(oExp)
        While oItr.MoveNext
            Response.Write(oItr.Current.Value)
        End While
    End Sub
```

You can find the code from Listing 18-8 on the companion Web site (www. wiley.com/extras) in Ch18SDK.zip (SDK version) or Ch18VS.zip (Visual Studio .NET version)mpanion Web site. When you unzip the download, look for the file named ExecuteXPathExpression.aspx.

Listing 18-8 uses the same XML file, items.xml, that was used earlier in the chapter. The Select method of the XPathNavigator object accepts one of two potential parameters: a String, which represents the XPath expression to be executed against the document, or an XPathExpression object. The XPathExpression object contains a compiled version of an XPath expression. To populate the XPathExpression object I use the Compile method of the XPathNavigator object. Once the XPath expression is executed I use the MoveNext method of the XPathNodeIterator to step through the result set. The first XPath expression queries for the <color> element and the second XPath expression queries for the id attribute. The final result looks like Figure 18-4.

Figure 18-4: The results of the XPath queries.

System.Xml.Xsl

The System.Xml.Xsl namespace allows for XSL transformations. As discussed in Chapter 4, transformations work with XML documents to transform the data to a different format or a different layout. This topic is covered in detail in Chapter 20.

Generating XML from SQL Server 2000

With the .NET Framework, Microsoft has supplied a Managed Provider to access SQL Server. This affords added benefits, including speed, for accessing data that resides within SQL Server. Microsoft has also leveraged SQL Server's ability to return XML from queries. Listing 18-9 shows an ASP.NET page that accesses the example Northwind Database using the Managed Provider for SQL Server. The example uses the ExecuteXMLReader method of the SQLCommand object.

Listing 18-9: ASP.NET That Displays XML Results Returned from SQL Server 2000 (SQLData.aspx)

```
Public Sub LoadData()
    Dim oConn As New SqlConnection("server=localhost;" & _
        "User ID=sa;Password=asdf;Database=Northwind;")
    Dim oCmd As New SqlCommand("Select * from Customers for XML Auto", _
        oConn)

    Dim oXMLReader As XmlTextReader
    oCmd.Connection.Open()

    oXMLReader = oCmd.ExecuteXmlReader()

    While oXMLReader.Read
        If oXMLReader.HasAttributes Then
            Response.Write("<b>Attribute Count</b> ")
            Response.Write(oXMLReader.AttributeCount() & "<br>")
            While oXMLReader.MoveToNextAttribute()
                Response.Write("<b>" & oXMLReader.Name)
                Response.Write(" : </b>")
                Response.Write(oXMLReader.Value)
                Response.Write("<br>")
            End While
            Response.Write("<hr>")
        End If
    End While
    oConn.Close()
End Sub
```

In addition to the code in Listing 18-9, the following namespaces need to be included in the ASP.NET page in order for it to compile.

```
Imports System.Xml
Imports System.Data.SqlClient
```

You can find the code from Listing 18-9 on the companion Web site (www.
wiley.com/extras) in Ch18SDK.zip (SDK version) or Ch18VS.zip
(Visual Studio .NET version). When you unzip the download, look for the file
named SQLData.aspx.

The connection string to the database is specific to my installation of SQL
Server 2000. For the applications to function correctly, you may need to
change the server name, password, and username values to correspond to
the SQL Server you're using.

In Listing 18-9 I first generate the subprocedure declaration for the code in the
example. Once this sub is called, a SQLConnection is created, passing it a connection string to the database. After the connection is created, a SQLCommand object is
created and passed both the SQL query and the connection that the query is to execute against. Both the SQLConnection and the SQLCommand are part of the
SQLClient namespace included at the beginning of the ASP.NET page. The SQL
query that is passed to the SQLCommand object is different from a normal query
because of the for XML Auto appended to the end. This statement is what tells SQL
Server 2000 to pass back XML to the client. Besides Auto, Raw, and Explicit are
two other values for for XML. RAW returns each row returned from the query in a
single element with the values of each column mapped to an attribute. EXPLICIT
allows for greater flexibility by allowing the user to specify how the data is
returned to the client. There are more details regarding these values in the SQL
Server Books Online, which ships with SQL Server (for updates on SQL Server
Books Online, go to http://microsoft.com/sql/techinfo/productdoc/2000/
books.asp).

After the SQLCommand object is created, a new variable, oXMLReader, is created.
This variable is of type XmlTextReader that allows the application to read forward
through an XML document. oXMLReader will eventually hold the data returned
from the query. The connection to the database is then opened and the
ExecuteXMLReader method is called, which returns XML to the oXMLReader object.
The XmlTextReader, discussed in further detail in the "Readers and Writers" section, now contains the XML document returned from SQL Server.

The application then reads through the XML document in the XmlTextReader just as if it were a file. The Read method moves to the next element in the document. I check to see if the current element has attributes. If it does, I print the number of attributes the given element has and precede to iterate through each attribute. After all of the attributes and values have been printed to the browser and each element in the document has been traversed, the connection to the database is closed. The final output in the browser looks something like Figure 18-5.

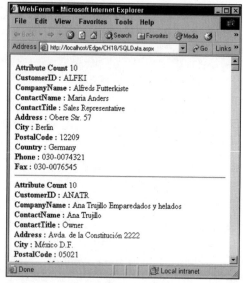

Figure 18-5: The output from retrieving data from SQL Server 2000 as XML.

The next section shows how XML can be generated from an ADO.NET DataSet.

XML from a DataSet

In the previous section I showed how SQL Server 2000 could return XML documents from a SQL query. While this is a nice feature of SQL Server 2000, not all applications are fortunate enough to have this flexibility. This section shows how to generate XML from a standard DataSet. Listing 18-10 shows an ASP.NET page that requests two fields from the Customers table from the Northwind Database.

Listing 18-10: ASP.NET Page That Exports Data in a DataSet to XML (PopulatingDataSet.aspx)

```
Public Sub LoadData()
    Dim oConn As New SqlConnection("server=localhost;User ID=sa;" & _
```

```
                "Password=asdf;Database=Northwind;")
        Dim oCmd As New SqlCommand("Select Address,City from Customers", _
        oConn)
        Dim oDs As New System.Data.DataSet()
        Dim oDa As New SqlDataAdapter(oCmd)
        oDa.Fill(oDs)
        oConn.Close()
        Response.Write(Server.HtmlEncode(oDs.GetXml))
    End Sub
```

 You can find the code from Listing 18-10 on the companion Web site (www.wiley.com/extras) in Ch18SDK.zip (SDK version) or Ch18VS.zip (Visual Studio .NET version). When you unzip the download, look for the file named PopulatingDataSet.aspx.

Once again, I include a subprocedure to do all of the work and call it from the ASP.NET page. I then instantiate a SQLConnection object just like the example in Listing 18-9. In this example the SQLCommand object is created with a standard SQL statement instead of one with the for XML clause. I use the DataSet and a SQLDataAdapter as discussed in Chapter 5. Executing the Fill method of the DataAdapter and passing it a DataSet fills the DataSet with the result of the query. I close the connection to the database and execute the GetXML method of the DataSet. The following are the namespaces needed for this example:

```
Imports System.Data
Imports System.Data.SqlClient
Imports System.Xml
```

Once the code executes, the browser should display something like Figure 18-6. While this isn't real pretty, it does show the representation of the DataSet as XML. In this example I used the Managed Provider for SQL Server 2000. I just as easily could have used a standard OLEDB Provider to get at the data from either Oracle or some other data source.

Finally, I use the HtmlEncode method of the Server object from within ASP.NET so that the actual text of the XML document will display. If I omit this, Internet Explorer won't display the XML tags. Instead, it tries to render the data leaving the tags out of the final output. Once the data has been placed in a DataSet it becomes easy to put the data in an ASP.NET DataGrid, which is discussed in the next section.

Figure 18-6: The results of generating XML from a DataSet.

XML into a DataGrid

In the preceding example I dumped the raw XML to the browser window. In this example I show you how to take an XML document and let the `DataGrid` parse it out and display it in the browser.

For this example I use the XML document shown in Listing 18-11. It's a simple XML document I stored in a text file called `cars.xml` in the same directory as the ASP.NET pages.

Listing 18-11: Cars.xml XML Document

```
<?xml version="1.0"?>
<Cars>
    <Car>
        <Make>Chevrolet</Make>
        <Model>S10</Model>
        <Year>2000</Year>
        <Color>Green</Color>
    </Car>
    <Car>
        <Make>Ford</Make>
        <Model>Escort</Model>
```

```
        <Year>1999</Year>
        <Color>Black</Color>
    </Car>
    <Car>
        <Make>Toyota</Make>
        <Model>Camry</Model>
        <Year>2001</Year>
        <Color>Red</Color>
    </Car>
    <Car>
        <Make>BMW</Make>
        <Model>328</Model>
        <Year>2003</Year>
        <Color>Blue</Color>
    </Car>
</Cars>
```

 You can find the code from Listing 18-11 on the companion Web site (`www.wiley.com/extras`) in `Ch18SDK.zip` (SDK version) or `Ch18VS.zip` (Visual Studio .NET version). When you unzip the download, look for the file named `cars.xml`.

Listing 18-11 is an XML document with makes and models of a few vehicles. I want to take the data from this XML document and format it using an ASP.NET `DataGrid`. To do this, I first need to set up a `DataSet`, which will eventually be bound to the `DataGrid`. To get started, I create a new Web Form and drag a `DataGrid` control (leaving the default name, `DataGrid1`) to the form as shown in Figure 18-7.

Once the form is set up, I place the code in the generic `LoadData` method used throughout the examples. The code in Listing 18-12 shows what it takes to bind the `DataGrid` to a `DataSet`, populated by the XML car document.

Listing 18-12: Populating the DataGrid (FillingDataGrid.aspx)

```
Public Sub LoadData()
    Dim ods As New DataSet()
    ods.ReadXml(Server.MapPath(".") & "\cars.xml")
    DataGrid1.DataSource = ods
    DataGrid1.DataBind()
End Sub
```

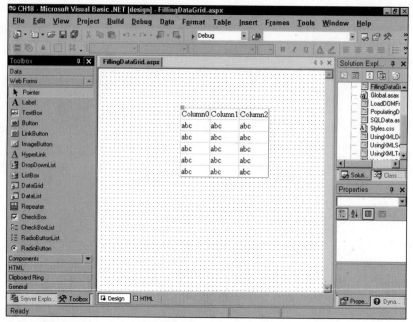

Figure 18–7: The layout for the DataGrid Web Form.

You can find the code from Listing 18-12 on the companion Web site (www. wiley.com/extras) in Ch18SDK.zip (SDK version) or Ch18VS.zip (Visual Studio .NET version). When you unzip, look for the file named FillingDataGrid.aspx.

I declare a DataSet object, which will hold the XML document. I execute the ReadXML method of the DataSet and pass in the path to the document that I want to load. After the document is loaded, I set the DataSource property of DataGrid1 to the newly created DataSet. Finally I execute the DataBind method to bind the data from the DataSet to the DataGrid itself. I used the MapPath method of the Server object to map the physical path of the document from the current virtual directory. When the application is executed, the results appear like Figure 18-8.

This section has shown you how to bind data to a DataGrid control on a Web Form. I used the ReadXML method of the DataSet object and passed it a physical path to a document. In the next section I load an XML document using a standard file stream.

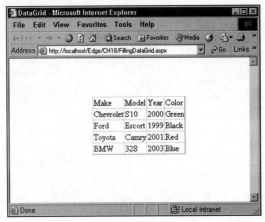

Figure 18-8: The resulting page after binding the DataGrid to a DataSet.

Accessing XML Using Streams

The XML namespace provides another object that can be utilized for interacting with XML documents. In the example in Listing 18-13, I use the XMLDocument object and the Node and NodeList objects to step through an in-memory XML document. The document is loaded using a file stream.

The listing shows the code for reading an XML document into a stream and then selecting and displaying some of the data to the browser.

Listing 18-13: Accessing the Cars XML Document as a Stream (LoadDOMFromStream.aspx)

```
Public Sub LoadData()
    Dim oXML As New System.Xml.XmlDocument()
    Dim oFil As New System.IO.FileStream(Server.MapPath(".") & _
        "\cars.xml", IO.FileMode.Open, IO.FileAccess.Read)
    Dim oNodeList As System.Xml.XmlNodeList
    Dim oNode As System.Xml.XmlNode
    oXML.Load(oFil)
    oFil.Close()
    oNodeList = oXML.GetElementsByTagName("Color")
    For Each oNode In oNodeList
        Response.Write(oNode.ChildNodes(0).Value & "<br>")
    Next
End Sub
```

You can find the code from Listing 18-13 on the companion Web site (www. wiley.com/extras) in Ch18SDK.zip (SDK version) or Ch18VS.zip (Visual Studio .NET version). When you unzip the download, look for the file named LoadDOMFromStream.aspx.

I first create a variable of type XmlDocument to be the in-memory representation of the cars.xml file. Next I declare a FileStream variable that will be used to hand the XML file off to oXML. This declaration actually loads the document into the stream. Then I declare both the NodeList and the Node variables. oNodeList is a collection of oNode objects. After the document is loaded, using the Load method, I close the file and fill the NodeList collection using the GetElementByTagName method. This method takes a string value indicating which elements in the document I want to step through. Because NodeList is a collection, I can use the For Each statement to iterate through each Node in the NodeList. I access the actual value of the <color> element by requesting value of the child element. ChildNodes is another collection that I access by using the index of the item that I want to access. The resulting page, shown in Figure 18-9, displays each of the colors in the XML document.

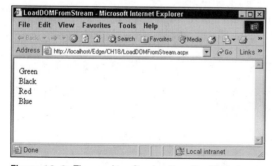

Figure 18-9: The results after loading the XML document from a file stream.

There are a few additional items to note in Listing 18-13. First, I did not import the namespaces that were required, but instead used the fully qualified variable types by including the namespace as part of the data type. This is just an alternative to importing each of the namespaces for the application. More interesting are the three additional parameters I need to pass to the FileStream constructor: the file name, the file mode, and the file access. If I just specify the file mode as IO.FileMode.Open and do not provide a third parameter, the system complains that the application does not have the appropriate rights to write to the folder, assuming the default permissions were left on the directory. In this case the application is trying to open the file with write access. In this example I did not need this type of access, so I explicitly indicated IO.FileAccess.Read as the file access.

Now let's look at how to use some basic XML readers and writers to work with XML documents.

Readers and Writers

The .NET Framework provides other ways to read and write XML data. The XmlReader and XmlWriter are both base classes that provide the base services for reading and writing XML.

Using XmlReader classes

The XmlReader class is implemented in the following classes:

- ◆ XmlTextReader: This class provides basic functionality for reading an XML document. It has the ability to determine if a document is well formed, but does not provide the ability to see if the document is valid against a schema.

- ◆ XmlValidatingReader: This class allows for validation against a schema; however, this reader is not as fast as XmlTextReader.

- ◆ XmlNodeReader: This class allows reading subsets of an XML document obtained by using an XPath expression. Once an XPath expression is executed, XmlNodeReader provides a way to iterate through the result.

Listing 18-14 is an example of an ASP.NET page that uses XmlTextReader to read through the cars.xml file used in the previous examples.

Listing 18-14: Utilizing the XmlTextReader (UsingXMLTextReader.aspx)

```
Public Sub LoadData()
    Dim oXml As New XmlTextReader(Server.MapPath(".") & _
    "\cars.xml")
    oXml.WhitespaceHandling = WhitespaceHandling.None
    While oXml.Read
        If oXml.HasValue Then
            Response.Write(oXml.Value & "<br>")
        End If
    End While

End Sub
```

You can find the code from Listing 18-14 on the companion Web site (www.wiley.com/extras) in Ch18SDK.zip (SDK version) or Ch18VS.zip (Visual Studio .NET version). When you unzip the download, look for the file named UsingXMLTextReader.aspx.

This example declares a variable as XmlTextReader and uses the constructor that accepts the path to the file. Again, I use the MapPath method of the Server object to get the actual path to the file and then append the actual file name to the path. I then tell the reader how it should address white space in the document. There are three possible values for WhitespaceHandling property:

◆ All: Returns all of the white space characters in the XML document.

◆ None: Returns none of the white space characters in the XML document.

◆ Significant: Returns only the characters that are significant, meaning that the white space characters returned are the ones that need to be preserved from the initial document to its final destination.

Next I read through the XML document checking each node to see if it has a value. If a value exists, I write it to the browser. Once the page runs, the results look like Figure 18-10.

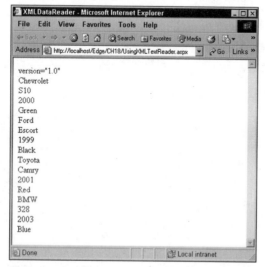

Figure 18-10: An example of the results of an XMLTextReader with no white space.

Additionally I imported the System.Xml namespace to this page so that the XML classes could be utilized.

Using XmlWriter

The counterpart to XmlTextReader is XmlTextWriter. XmlTextWriter is the only implementation of XmlWriter that Microsoft has shipped. Once a stream is available for writing to, the XML document is built using methods of XmlTextWriter. Listing 18-15 shows how XmlTextWriter is used to write an XMLDocument to a file.

Listing 18-15: The ASP.NET Page That Writes Out Part of the car.xml File (UsingXMLTextWriter.aspx)

```
Public Sub LoadData()
    Dim fil As New FileStream(Server.MapPath(".") & _
    "\carsout.xml", FileMode.Create, FileAccess.Write)
    Dim oXml As New XmlTextWriter(fil, Nothing)
    oXml.Formatting = Formatting.Indented
    oXml.WriteStartDocument()
    oXml.WriteStartElement("Cars")
    oXml.WriteStartElement("Car")
    oXml.WriteElementString("Make", "Chevrolet")
    oXml.WriteElementString("Model", "S10")
    oXml.WriteElementString("Year", "2000")
    oXml.WriteElementString("Color", "Green")
    oXml.WriteEndElement()
    oXml.WriteEndElement()
    oXml.Close()
End Sub
```

 You can find the code from Listing 18-15 on the companion Web site (www. wiley.com/extras) in Ch18SDK.zip (SDK version) or Ch18VS.zip (Visual Studio .NET version). When you unzip the download, look for the file named UsingXMLTextWriter.aspx.

To get the application to run correctly, add the following code to the application.

```
Imports System.Xml
Imports System.IO
```

The application in Listing 18-15 works similarly to the one in Listing 18-5, which also requires that a file be written to the file system. The user ASPNET on the system needs to be granted Write permission to the directory where the file will be written. If you didn't set the appropriate permissions before running the previous example, you'll need to do so now: Right-click the folder and select Properties. Select the Security tab, click the Add button, select the ASPNET user in the list box, and click OK. Make sure the user has Write access to the directory, and click OK again.

This example writes the `carsout.xml` file to the same directory as the script. For the sake of simplicity, I only include the first car in the listing. I first declare a variable for the file that will act as the stream for the `XmlTextWriter` object. I indicate that I want to create the file and open it for writing. Next I create an `XmlTextWriter`, passing it the stream object I just created and the type of encoding that I want to use on the file. In this case I passed it a value of `Nothing`, indicating that it should use the default of `UTF-8`. I also set the formatting so that the resulting data will be indented. After creating the `XmlTextWriter` object and setting the indentation, I'm ready to start writing elements to the text file as XML. First I write the XML declaration, the line that indicates the version of the XML file I am working with. To do this I use the `WriteStartDocument` method. After this I continue by writing the starting element, `<Cars>` and all of its associated elements with their values. Finally I call the `WriteEndElement` method for both the `<Cars>` and `<Car>` elements, which closes each of the opening elements, and then close the writer.

XML readers and XML writers are two excellent features of the .NET Framework when dealing with XML. They each provide a straightforward interface, and the `XmlWriter` makes it easy to create an XML document by calling intuitive methods for each of the possible entities in an XML document.

Summary

This chapter has been a summary of most of the technologies regarding XML in the .NET Framework. I addressed the `System.Xml` namespace, and included some interaction with SQL Server 2000 and how to display XML data in an ASP.NET `DataGrid`. You saw how the `XmlTextReader` and the `XmlTextWriter` allow for easy access to XML documents. Chapter 19 covers schemas and how the .NET Framework implements schema functionality.

Chapter 19

Schemas in the .NET Framework

SCHEMAS ARE USED to determine if an XML document is valid. Schemas dictate what data types are allowed and the overall flow of an XML document. If an XML document is associated to a schema, the XML document can be validated against the schema. Schemas, if compared to SQL Server, act as the constraints and properties that are set for a given field in a table. They indicate that a certain piece of data may be required or that a given piece of data may need to be a certain data type. Schemas can also indicate in which order items can appear.

The predecessors to schemas were Document Type Definitions (DTDs) and XML Data Reduced (XDR). Schemas, specifically XML Schema Definition (XSD) language, are a very new aspect to the entire XML environment. Chapter 4 introduced you to schemas; this chapter shows you how to address schemas in the .NET environment and briefly addresses DTDs.

The Predecessor to Schemas: DTDs

To start this section off on the right foot, I want to point out that DTDs are an older technology than schemas. Schemas present more defined standards than DTDs, such as being XML-based and providing clearly defined data types for implementing validation techniques. So why would anyone consider using DTDs in an environment? Here are a couple of reasons:

♦ DTDs are part of the World Wide Web Consortium (W3C) XML standard.

♦ Many existing applications have implemented DTDs.

DTDs have several shortcomings and have generally been replaced by XSD schemas. The following are some areas where DTDs suffer in functionality.

◆ **One DTD per XML document.** If you need to use multiple documents to make an XML document valid, you can't use DTDs. Schemas, on the other hand, allow for several namespaces to be specified for a single instance document.

◆ **DTDs have their own format.** Emerging schemas use XML as the syntax, and the actual schemas themselves are well-formed XML documents. By using XML syntax, the developer isn't required to learn a new language for describing XML documents.

◆ **DTDs lack true data types.** One of the most important aspects of describing data is classifying exactly what type of data it is. DTDs offer only primitive data types, the most prominent being CDATA, which translates into a text string. The schema specification allows for a multitude of data types, providing the capability to create more structured XML documents with tighter constraints. Additionally, XSD schemas can generate complex types, enabling the developer to create his own data types instead of relying on predefined types.

◆ **Emerging technologies, such as Visual Studio .NET, include functionality tailored toward schemas rather than DTDs.** As new standards appear, DTDs are viewed more as extra baggage, so developers are less likely to incorporate compatibility with them in applications.

DTDs were not initially designed to support such a detailed environment as XML. XML has become popular because of its functionality and flexibility, which has placed extra requirements on DTDs — requirements that DTDs can no longer reasonably support. Microsoft, realizing this, has incorporated the new, emerging technology of schemas into the .NET Framework and Visual Studio .NET.

XSD Schemas: A Better Way to Represent Data

Technically, both XSD and Microsoft's XML XDR fall under the category of *schema*. XSD schemas, however, are the W3C-supported standard, so this chapter focuses on how they work in the .NET Framework. An XDR schema, on the other hand, is a Microsoft standard that provides more flexibility than DTDs but came onto the scene before the official XSD schema standard. For this reason, I recommend that you use XSD schemas rather than XDR schemas.

Here are some reasons to consider moving to XSD schemas instead of looking into either DTDs or XDR schemas:

◆ **XSD schemas provide support for data types.** With DTDs, you define all of your data as a character data type. This makes it impossible to define something as a number or a date when you can only define the data as characters.

◆ **XSD schemas are XML documents.** DTDs use a proprietary format, which is difficult to read. XSD schemas are formatted as actual XML documents.

◆ **XML documents can draw from multiple schemas.** XML documents can use only one DTD, whereas multiple namespaces can be used when dealing with schemas.

◆ **XSD schemas are a W3C standard.** Microsoft's XDR standard is not supported throughout the industry.

These reasons alone provide a compelling case for using schemas exclusively, but the next section looks at how Visual Studio .NET provides even more benefits for using schemas.

Working with XML and schemas in Visual Studio .NET

Before Visual Studio .NET came along, you created XML documents and schemas by using either Notepad or a third-party tool such as XML Spy. (XML Spy helps with creating both XML documents and schemas and provides an entire suite of tools for working with XML.) Visual Studio .NET, however, makes a creating schema very easy.

If you don't have Visual Studio .NET, the .NET Framework provides an excellent utility for generating schemas from an XML document or additional sources. The xsd executable, located in the \Program Files\Microsoft Visual Studio .NET\FrameworkSDK\Bin of the .NET Framework installation, lets you produce a schema from several source types, including XDR files, XML documents, and assemblies such as DLLs or EXEs. You can access the utility's documentation by typing **xsd /?** at the command line and pressing Enter.

Visual .NET Studio includes the XML Designer, which enables you to work with XML documents and schemas in these three ways:

◆ Create new XML documents and their associated schemas

◆ Generate schemas from existing XML documents

◆ Validate an XML document against its schema

To start working with XML in Visual Studio .NET, follow these steps:

1. Choose File → New Project. The New Project dialog box opens, as shown in Figure 19-1.

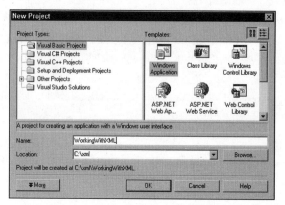

Figure 19–1: The New Project dialog box in Visual Studio .NET.

Visual Studio .NET doesn't provide an XML sample project, so I created a new Visual Basic Windows Forms project called WorkingWithXML. When you download and unzip `Ch19SDK.zip` (SDK version) or `Ch19VS.zip` (Visual Studio .NET version) from the companion Web site at `www.wiley.com/extras`, a WorkingWithXML folder is created on your system. I use this sample application to show you how to use the Visual Studio .NET environment to access XML functionality. The WorkingWithXML folder includes a file named `Paper.xml`, which contains the code shown in Listing 19-1. The project also contains `Paper.xsd`, which I use to `validate Paper.xml`. I have included both `Paper.xml` and `Paper.xsd` in the SDK download. This example uses Visual Studio .NET to show the functionality of the XML Designer.

2. Add an XML document to the project by choosing Project → Add New Item. This opens the Add New Item dialog box.

3. From the Add New Item dialog box, select the XML File template, as shown in Figure 19-2.

4. Name the document `Paper.xml` and click the Open button. The XML File template provides the following simple declaration:

```
<?xml version="1.0" encoding="utf-8" ?>
```

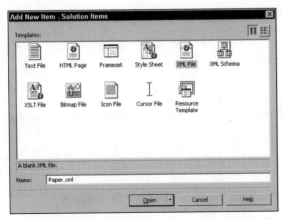

Figure 19-2: The Add New Item dialog box in Visual Studio .NET.

This is a standard XML declaration indicating the XML version and the way the file is encoded.

5. To add to the code, just start typing in the editor. Add the XML content shown in Listing 19-1 to the end of the XML document. As mentioned earlier in the On the Web paragraph, the code shown in Listing 19-1 can be found in the Paper.xml file included in the Ch19SDK.zip and Ch19VS.zip files that you can download from the companion Web site.

Listing 19-1: The Remaining Content for the XML Document (Paper.xml)

```
<Stock>
    <Paper height="11.0">
        <Cost>5.00</Cost>
        <Color>White</Color>
    </Paper>
    <Paper height="5.0" width="4.0">
        <Cost>3.00</Cost>
        <Color>Yellow</Color>
    </Paper>
    <Paper height="17.0" width="11.0">
        <Cost>10.00</Cost>
        <Color>White</Color>
    </Paper>
</Stock>
```

The document in Listing 19-1 uses both attributes and elements to describe the different kinds of paper stock a company might have on hand. After you add data to the document, the XML Designer makes it easy to add additional records to the original document.

6. To add additional records, click the Data tab at the bottom of the pane. The Designer displays a grid for entering information, based on how it understands the current structure of the document (see Figure 19-3). This makes it easier to enter data without having to remember element and attribute names.

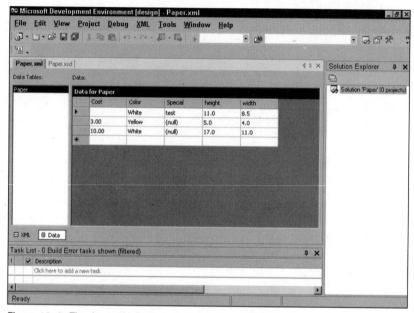

Figure 19-3: The data grid for entering data into the XML document.

7. To generate an XML schema from the XML document that you've created or opened, choose XML → Create Schema. An XSD document is created based on the current state of the XML document. In this case, Visual Studio .NET names the file Paper.xsd to match the original XML document. Besides creating the XML document, Visual Studio .NET alters the Stock element tag, changing it to the following:

```
<Stock xmlns="http://tempuri.org/Paper.xsd">
```

This code tells any applications that validate the XML document where to find the schema that the document is based on. Visual Studio .NET also adds the Paper.xsd file, shown in Listing 19-2, to the WorkingWithXML project.

Listing 19-2: The Schema Generated for the Paper.xml File (Paper.xsd)

```
<?xml version="1.0" ?>
<xs:schema id="Stock"
```

```
targetNamespace="http://tempuri.org/Paper.xsd"
xmlns:mstns="http://tempuri.org/Paper.xsd"
xmlns="http://tempuri.org/Paper.xsd"
xmlns:xs="http://www.w3.org/2001/XMLSchema"
xmlns:msdata="urn:schemas-microsoft-com:xml-msdata"
attributeFormDefault="qualified"
elementFormDefault="qualified">
    <xs:element name="Stock" msdata:IsDataSet="true"
      msdata:EnforceConstraints="False">
        <xs:complexType>
            <xs:choice maxOccurs="unbounded">
                <xs:element name="Paper">
                    <xs:complexType>
                        <xs:sequence>
                            <xs:element name="Cost" type="xs:string"
                                minOccurs="0"
                                msdata:Ordinal="0" />
                            <xs:element name="Color"
                                type="xs:string"
                                minOccurs="0"
                                msdata:Ordinal="1" />
                        </xs:sequence>
                        <xs:attribute name="height"
                            form="unqualified"
                            type="xs:string" />
                        <xs:attribute name="width"
                            form="unqualified"
                            type="xs:string" />
                    </xs:complexType>
                </xs:element>
            </xs:choice>
        </xs:complexType>
    </xs:element>
</xs:schema>
```

You can find the code for Listing 19-2 on the companion Web site (www.
wiley.com/extras) in Ch19SDK.zip (SDK version) or Ch19VS.zip
(Visual Studio .NET version). After you unzip the files, look for the file named
Paper.xsd in the WorkingWithXML folder.

8. To validate your XML document against the Designer-generated schema, switch back to the XML document, select XML view (instead of Data view), and select Validate XML Data. The result is a `No validation errors were found` message in the status line (see the lower-left corner in Figure 19-4).

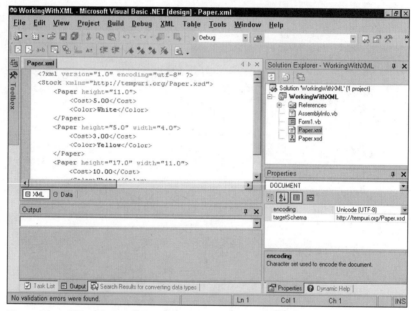

Figure 19-4: Visual Studio .NET indicating no validation errors in the XML document.

Now that you have a schema for your Paper XML document, you can put it to the test.

9. Make the following changes to the first record in the XML document:

```
<Cost>5.00</Cost>
<Color>White</Color>
<Available>Yes</Available>
```

Even before you finish typing, you can tell that this code is going to produce errors because a red line appears under the new (`<Available>`) attribute. The XML Designer also shows the available child elements for the Paper element (see Figure 19-5).

10. Even though the red lines indicate errors, go ahead and try to validate the document as you did before. Choose XML → Validate XML Data; the Task

List in the IDE fills with several errors. Each error is a result of the information that you added that goes against the schema generated for the
document.

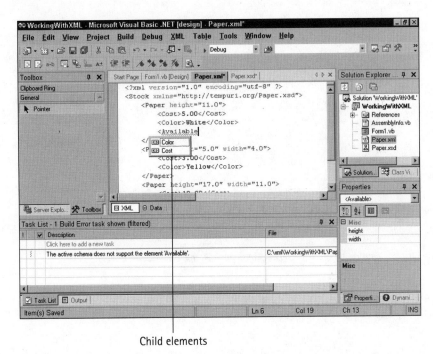

Child elements

Figure 19-5: The XML Designer shows the available child elements for the Paper
parent element.

11. To have the XML Designer create the schemas graphically, open
    Paper.xsd and click the DataSet tab instead of the XML tab (near the
    middle of the Visual Studio .NET IDE), as shown in Figure 19-6.

You've just seen how easy it is to work with XML in the Visual Studio .NET environment and to generate schemas for the data. In the next section, I discuss some
of the elements of an XSD schema.

A more detailed look at schemas

Let's look at some details about XSD schemas. I use the schema from Listing
19-2, duplicated here as Listing 19-3. Validating the document can either occur
in the XML Designer or by using the XML validator that I create in the next
example.

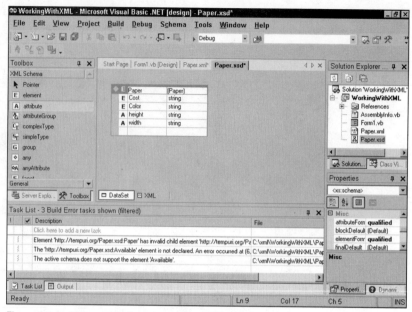

Figure 19-6: The graphical version of the XSD document.

Listing 19-3: The Schema from Listing 19-2, Repeated (Paper.xsd)

```
<?xml version="1.0" ?>
<xs:schema id="Stock" targetNamespace="http://tempuri.org/Paper.xsd"
xmlns:mstns="http://tempuri.org/Paper.xsd"
xmlns="http://tempuri.org/Paper.xsd"
xmlns:xs="http://www.w3.org/2001/XMLSchema"
xmlns:msdata="urn:schemas-microsoft-com:xml-msdata"
attributeFormDefault="qualified"
elementFormDefault="qualified">
    <xs:element name="Stock" msdata:IsDataSet="true"
    msdata:EnforceConstraints="False">
      <xs:complexType>
        <xs:choice maxOccurs="unbounded">
          <xs:element name="Paper">
            <xs:complexType>
              <xs:sequence>
                <xs:element name="Cost" type="xs:string" minOccurs="0"
                    msdata:Ordinal="0" />
                <xs:element name="Color" type="xs:string" minOccurs="0"
                    msdata:Ordinal="1" />
              </xs:sequence>
              <xs:attribute name="height" form="unqualified"
```

```
                    type="xs:string" />
            <xs:attribute name="width" form="unqualified"
                    type="xs:string" />
          </xs:complexType>
        </xs:element>
      </xs:choice>
    </xs:complexType>
  </xs:element>
</xs:schema>
```

The opening statement of Listing 19-3 is the same as the other XML documents that I've shown you up to this point. The statement indicates the version of XML used in the document:

```
<?xml version="1.0" ?>
```

The next section indicates the namespaces involved with this specific schema:

```
<xs:schema id="Stock" targetNamespace=
"http://tempuri.org/Paper.xsd"
xmlns:mstns="http://tempuri.org/Paper.xsd"
xmlns="http://tempuri.org/Paper.xsd"
xmlns:xs="http://www.w3.org/2001/XMLSchema"
xmlns:msdata="urn:schemas-microsoft-com:
xml-msdata"
attributeFormDefault="qualified"
elementFormDefault="qualified">
```

Notice that `http://tempuri.org/Paper.xsd` appears several places in these declarations; it's the default if a specific namespace isn't provided. In a production environment, I'd provide a domain over which I have control so that I can guarantee that the specific namespace is mine. The official W3C definition of the schema also is included in these declarations. Its namespace is defined as `http://www.w3.org/2001/XMLSchema`. Additionally, a Microsoft URN is included, which defines some specific Microsoft information for the document.

 Throughout this chapter, the XML documents — both the source documents and the schemas — utilize Uniform Resource Identifiers (URIs) to indicate where each documents is derived. A URI comes in two forms: a Uniform Resource Name (URN) and a Uniform Resource Locator (URL). Each of the URIs is used because it can guarantee uniqueness when identifying the schema for the document.

The next section of the XSD starts off with a declaration for an element:

```
<xs:element name="Stock"
msdata:IsDataSet="true"
msdata:EnforceConstraints="False">
```

This code draws from the W3C's definition of an element and includes IsDataSet and EnforceConstraints attributes from the Microsoft namespace. These attributes specifically relate to the DataSet class and to being able to load this data up in a DataSet. The <xs:complexType> element can contain additional elements and attributes, and choice in <xs:choice maxOccurs="unbounded"> indicates that the element can show up in the corresponding instance document maxOccurs times.

In the case of Paper.xsd, the Paper element can show up an unlimited number of times.

 Try out choice by changing the value from "unbounded" to "2". An error occurs at the third Paper element in the XML document because the choice element in the XSD file indicates that only two Paper elements can appear in the document.

The next element actually describes the Paper element:

```
<xs:element name="Paper">
```

After defining another complexType, the schema introduces the sequence element, which indicates that the Cost element needs to be before the Color element:

```
<xs:complexType>
    <xs:sequence>
    <xs:element name="Cost" type="xs:string" minOccurs="0"
        msdata:Ordinal="0" />
    <xs:element name="Color" type="xs:string" minOccurs="0"
        msdata:Ordinal="1" />
</xs:sequence>
<xs:attribute name="height" form="unqualified" type="xs:string" />
<xs:attribute name="width" form="unqualified" type="xs:string" />
```

If you switch the order of the elements, the document is no longer valid. The Cost and Color elements also contain data type information and the number of times the elements can appear in the XML document. Finally, the height and width attributes are defined. They are declared as string types. The remaining elements close the opening elements:

```
            </xs:complexType>
          </xs:element>
        </xs:choice>
      </xs:complexType>
  </xs:element>
</xs:schema>
```

Because the XML Designer generated this schema from an XML document that I created, it's lacking some of the additional constraints that might be included in a typical schema. The Designer was inferring what it could, based on the layout of the XML document. You usually create an XML document and then validate it against a schema. The schema may be one that you create or an existing schema that defines the layout and the types of data that are acceptable in an XML document.

In the next section, I show you how the .NET Framework provides functionality for validating XML documents against their associated schemas. I use the System.Xml.Schema namespace, which contains the functionality for validating XML documents.

Creating an XML validator using ASP.NET

In this section, I create an XML validator using ASP.NET. The validator uses an XML source document and ensures that the document is valid against an XSD schema. This example is useful when Visual Studio .NET is not available for developing XML documents and schemas. The .NET Framework includes the XmlValidaingReader for validating XML documents. I use a constructor that accepts an XmlTextReader (discussed in Chapter 18) as the only parameter. Listing 19-4 shows my sample ASP.NET XML validator.

Listing 19-4: The ASP.NET XML Validator (Validate.aspx)

```
<%@Import namespace="System.Xml"%>
<%@Import namespace="System.Xml.Schema"%>
<script language="vb" runat="server">

Public Sub ValidateData()
dim xmlTR as New XmlTextReader(Server.MapPath(".") & _
    "\" & txtXMLDocument.Text)
dim xmlVR as new XmlValidatingReader(xmlTR)

xmlVR.ValidationType=ValidationType.Schema

AddHandler xmlVR.ValidationEventHandler, _
    AddressOf ValidateHandler
```

Continued

Listing 19-4 *(Continued)*

```
Try
    While xmlVR.Read
        'Any processing that needs to be done.
    End While
Catch ex as xmlException
    Response.write("Xml Validation Error Occurred: " & _
        ex.Message & "<br>")
Finally
    xmlVR.Close
    xmlTR.Close
End Try

End Sub
Public Sub ValidateHandler(ByVal sender as Object, _
        ByVal e as ValidationEventArgs)
    Response.Write("Validation error: " & e.Message & "<br>")
End Sub

</script>

<html>
<head>
<title>
XML Validator
</title>
</head>
<body>
<form method="post" runat="server">
<table>
<tr>
<td><asp:Label id="lblXMLDocument" runat="server"
    text="XML Document Name:"/>
</td>
<td><asp:TextBox id="txtXMLDocument" runat="server"/>
</td>
</tr>
<tr>
<td colspan="2"><asp:button id="btnValidate"
        runat="server" text="Validate"/>
</td>
</tr>
</table>
</form>
<%If IsPostBack Then
```

```
    ValidateData()
End If%>
</body>
</html>
```

 You can find the code for Listing 19-4 on the companion Web site (www.wiley.com/extras) in Ch19SDK.zip (SDK version) or Ch19VS.zip (Visual Studio .NET version). After you unzip the files, look for the file named Validate.aspx in the folder named Validate.

This validator requires that the schema be identified in the XML document. Alternatively, the .NET Framework provides a way to cache schemas through the XmlSchemaCollection class. There are a couple of benefits to using a cached schema: faster performance and the fact that the namespace doesn't need to be identified in the XML source document.

The first few lines of Validate.aspx import both the System.Xml and System.Xml.Schema namespaces. I identify the script language for the ASP.NET page, declare the ValidateData() subroutine, declare an XmlTextReader and pass it the path to the file specified as txtXMLDocument.Text, and then declare an XmlValidatingReader passing it the XmlTextReader. The XmlValidatingReader is one of the implementations of the XmlReader class, as briefly discussed in Chapter 18. XmlValidatingReader extends the base class by incorporating the ability to validate XML documents.

After setting up the XmlValidatingReader, I set the ValidationType property, which has the following possible values.

◆ ValidationType.None: No validation is performed.

◆ ValidationType.DTD: Validates the document based on the DTD specified in the document.

◆ ValidationType.XDR: Validates the document based on the XDR specified in the document or the cached schema.

◆ ValidationType.Schema: Validates the document based on the schema specified in the document or the cached schema.

◆ ValidationType.Auto: Determines the best method for validation based on the information in the document.

In Listing 19-4 I use the Schema setting for the ValidationType property.

The next step is to add the event handler to be called if a validation error occurs. (The event handler won't be called if the ValidationType property is set to None.) Then, I create the error handler. If an exception occurs, the application displays the error information to the browser. The `Try` block is where all of the processing of the actual document takes place. I didn't put any exciting code in this section, but any of the properties for the `XmlValidatingReader` can be placed inside its `While` loop. The `Finally` block contains the `Close` methods for `XmlValidatingReader` and the `XmlTextReader` itself. This is the end of the `ValidateData()` subroutine.

The only other declaration is for the `ValidateHandler` event handler. This subroutine accepts two parameters, `sender` and `e`. The `e` parameter is defined as `ValidationEventArgs`, which has three properties:

♦ `Exception`: Returns the `XmlSchemaException` related to the error.

♦ `Message`: Gets the text of the error.

♦ `Severity`: Generates either an error or a warning. Errors generate an exception if the event handler is not defined; warnings do not.

In the `Validate.aspx`, I use only the `Message` property. At the bottom of the listing, a small HTML form is created with a text box and a Submit button. The text box is where the user enters the XML document to be validated. After the user specifies the XML document to validate, clicking the button creates a post back. The next time the page loads, it executes the `ValidateData()` call.

To run the application, I need both an XML document and a schema. For this example, I've created the XML document in Listing 19-5 and the associated schema shown in Listing 19-6. I'll show you several different scenarios based on these two documents.

Listing 19-5: The XML Source Document to Be Validated (Records.xml)

```
<?xml version="1.0"?>
<Records xmlns:xsi="http://www.w3.org/2001/XMLSchema-instance"
             xsi:noNamespaceSchemaLocation="Records.xsd">
    <Record id="1">
        <Band>Sheryl Crow</Band>
        <Title>C'mon, C'mon</Title>
        <Year>2002</Year>
        <Song Track="1">Steve McQueen</Song>
        <Song Track="2">Soak Up The Sun</Song>
        <Song Track="3">You're An Original</Song>
        <Song Track="4">Diamond Road</Song>
        <Song Track="5">It's So Easy</Song>
        <Song Track="6">C'Mon, C'Mon</Song>
        <Song Track="7">Safe and Sound</Song>
        <Song Track="8">Over You</Song>
        <Song Track="9">Hole In My Pocket</Song>
        <Song Track="10">Abilene</Song>
        <Song Track="11">Lucky Kid</Song>
        <Song Track="12">It's Only Love</Song>
```

```
        <Song Track="13">Weather Channel</Song>
    </Record>
    <Record id="2">
        <Band>Michael Jackson</Band>
        <Title>Thriller</Title>
        <Year>1982</Year>
        <Song Track="1">Wanna Be Startin' Somethin'</Song>
        <Song Track="2">Baby Be Mine</Song>
        <Song Track="3">The Girl Is Mine</Song>
        <Song Track="4">Thriller</Song>
        <Song Track="5">Beat It</Song>
        <Song Track="6">Billie Jean</Song>
        <Song Track="7">Human Nature</Song>
        <Song Track="8">P.Y.T. (Pretty Young Thing)</Song>
        <Song Track="9">The Lady in My Life</Song>
    </Record>
</Records>
```

You can find the code for Listing 19-5 on the companion Web site (www.
wiley.com/extras) in Ch19SDK.zip (SDK version) or Ch19VS.zip
(Visual Studio .NET version). After you unzip the files, look for the file named
Records.xml in the folder named Validate.

The document in Listing 19-5 is a list of records with several different elements
and attributes. Listing 19-6 is the schema that I will be validating the XML document in Listing 19-5 against.

Listing 19-6: The XSD Schema Used to Validate Records.xml (Records.xsd)

```
<?xml version="1.0" encoding="utf-8"?>
<xs:schema id="Records" xmlns:xs="http://www.w3.org/2001/XMLSchema">
  <xs:element name="Records">
    <xs:complexType>
      <xs:choice maxOccurs="unbounded">
        <xs:element name="Record">
          <xs:complexType>
            <xs:sequence>
              <xs:element name="Band" type="xs:string" minOccurs="0" />
              <xs:element name="Title" type="xs:string" minOccurs="0" />
              <xs:element name="Year" type="xs:string" minOccurs="0" />
```

Continued

Listing 19-6 *(Continued)*

```xml
                <xs:element name="Song" nillable="true"
                        minOccurs="0" maxOccurs="unbounded">
                  <xs:complexType>
                    <xs:simpleContent>
                      <xs:extension base="xs:string">
                        <xs:attribute name="Track" type="xs:string" />
                      </xs:extension>
                    </xs:simpleContent>
                  </xs:complexType>
                </xs:element>
              </xs:sequence>
              <xs:attribute name="id" type="xs:string" />
            </xs:complexType>
          </xs:element>
        </xs:choice>
      </xs:complexType>
    </xs:element>
</xs:schema>
```

 You can find the code for Listing 19-6 on the companion Web site (www.wiley.com/extras) in `Ch19SDK.zip` (SDK version) or `Ch19VS.zip` (Visual Studio .NET version). After you unzip the files, look for the file named `Records.xsd` in the folder named Validate.

I place `Records.xml`, the XML document (Listing 19-5), and `Records. xsd`, the schema (Listing 19-6), in the same directory as `Validate.aspx` (Listing 19-4). Then to ensure that things are working correctly, I load `Validate.aspx` specifying `Records.xml` as the document to validate. Figure 19-7 shows the results.

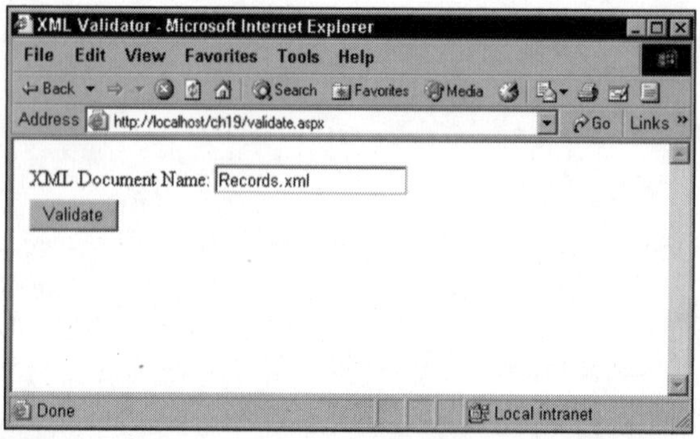

Figure 19-7: The results after validating Records.xml.

`Validate.aspx` only generates output to the browser if errors occur. To force an error to occur in the validation, I update the `maxOccurs` attribute of the `Song` element so that it can only contain a total of 10 songs. The first album fails this test as shown in Figure 19-8.

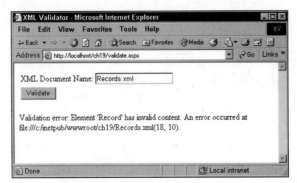

Figure 19-8: The results of the validation after updating the schema.

Additionally adjusting the data types from strings to something else, such as an integer, also generates an error. I adjusted the `id` attribute of the `Record` element, forcing it to an integer, to check that the validator would catch it. You can use any number of scenarios to test the example.

Now you've seen how to work with schemas and how to use the .NET Framework to validate an XML document against a schema. In the next section I demonstrate how to generate a schema from SQL Server 2000.

Generating Schemas from SQL Server 2000

At the beginning of this chapter, I alluded to the fact that schemas share similarities to tables in databases. I indicated that tables and schemas use techniques for describing the resulting structure of the data. Knowing this, Microsoft has provided the capability to create a schema based on a table in SQL Server. In this section, I show you how to generate a schema from an existing table in the Northwind database. After generating the schema, you populate an XML document using Visual Studio .NET.

You use the XML Designer discussed earlier in the chapter, take the Customers table from the Northwind example database, and create a schema based on its table structure. To do this, you first need to be running Visual Studio .NET. Then you create a new Visual Basic .NET Windows Application. You should also make sure that the Server Explorer is visible on the left side of the screen, as shown in Figure 19-9.

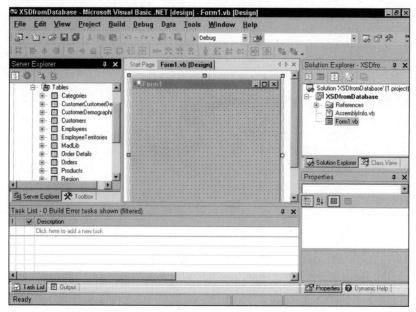

Figure 19-9: Setting up the interface to create the schema.

To generate a schema based on a SQL Server table, follow these steps:

1. Connect to your computer's local SQL Server by right-clicking the Data Connections icon and choosing Add Connection. The Data Link Properties dialog box opens, and you fill in the server name, the login information for the server, and select a database to connect to. In this case, I selected the Northwind database (Figure 19-10). After clicking OK, you are again prompted to log in. After logging in, the Northwind database connection is available for use.

You can find the code and project on the companion Web site (www.wiley.com/extras) under Ch19SDK.zip (SDK version) or Ch19VS.zip (Visual Studio .NET version). After you unzip the files, look for the files named Customers.xsd and Customers.xml in the folder named XSDfromDatabase.

2. Create a new file by choosing Project → Add New Item. You need to add a blank XSD document to host the schema generated from the table. The Add New Item dialog box opens.

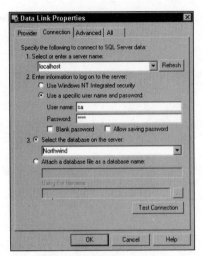

Figure 19-10: The Data Link dialog for connecting to the local server from within Visual Studio .NET's Server Explorer.

3. In the Add New Item dialog, select the XML Schema Template and type **Customers.xsd** in the Name text box to create a blank schema for the project. Then click the Open button. Visual Studio .NET opens a blank schema in the project.

4. With the blank schema open, drill down to the Customers table using the Server Explorer on the Northwind Database and drag the Customers table over to the graphical interface of the XML Designer. Visual Studio .NET creates the schema based on the table. The initial interface shows up as a graphical one, but you can click the XML tab at the bottom of the pane to toggle back and forth. The resulting schema provides all the information about the Customers table represented in a schema. This includes information about the data types and names allowed for the elements, which correspond to information in the original Customers table. Be sure to save the schema before continuing.

5. After you define the schema for the Customers table, you can create a corresponding XML document that validates against the Customers.xsd schema. First, add a blank XML document to the project by choosing Project → Add New Item, selecting the XML File Template, and naming it Customers.xml.

6. Click the Open button, and Visual Studio .NET adds to the project a blank XML document named Customers.xml.

7. Specify the schema that this XML document should be associated with by selecting http://tempuri.org/Customers.xsd from the targetSchema

property on the property sheet of the XML document. After you select the `Customers.xsd` schema, Visual Studio .NET adds the initial document element to the XML document.

8. Type a < character, and Visual Studio .NET provides a drop-down list box of the available elements that you can type (see Figure 19-11). After you associate the schema to the XML document, you can create an entire XML document based on the same layout as the Northwind `Customers` table.

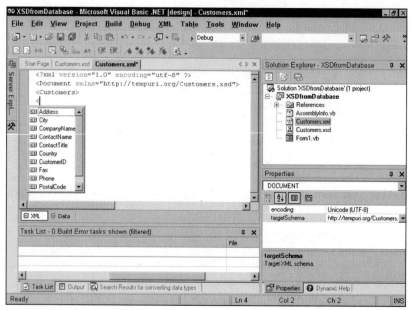

Figure 19-11: The Visual Studio .NET showing the available elements based on the XSD schema.

This section showed you how simple it is for Visual Studio .NET to generate a schema based on a table layout. In the next section, I show you how to programmatically generate schemas using the .NET Framework.

Working with Schemas in .NET

Microsoft has provided the Schema Object Model (SOM) in the .NET Framework for programmatically creating schemas or reading and adding to existing schemas. The Schema Object Model provides the same type of functionality as the `xsd` executable mentioned at the beginning of the chapter (see the Note in the section "Working with XML and schemas in Visual Studio .NET"). Each element defined in a schema is defined as an object in the SOM. The elements, such as the `element` and `complexType` tags shown in Listing 19-6, all have corresponding objects in the SOM.

The SOM also contains a `Compile` method, which can be used for checking a schema after it has been created or modified programmatically, to make sure that there are no errors. The `Compile` method should be called from the source code after the schema is built. Listing 19-7 is an ASP.NET page that builds the schema from Listing 19-6 using the SOM and then displays the results to the browser.

Listing 19-7: The Source Code for Creating the Schema Records.xsd (RebuildRecords.aspx)

```vb
<%@Import namespace="System.Xml"%>
<%@Import namespace="System.Xml.Schema"%>
<script language="vb" runat="server">

Public Sub RebuildRecords()
        Dim oXMLS As New XmlSchema()
        Dim oRecs As New XmlSchemaElement()
        Dim oRec As New XmlSchemaElement()
        Dim oComplexRecord As New XmlSchemaComplexType()
        Dim oComplexRecords As New XmlSchemaComplexType()
        Dim oComplexSong As New XmlSchemaComplexType()
        Dim oChoice As New XmlSchemaChoice()
        Dim oSeq As New XmlSchemaSequence()
        Dim oBand As New XmlSchemaElement()
        Dim oTitle As New XmlSchemaElement()
        Dim oYear As New XmlSchemaElement()
        Dim oSong As New XmlSchemaElement()
        Dim oRecAttr As New XmlSchemaAttribute()
        Dim oSimple As New XmlSchemaSimpleContent()
        Dim oTrackAttr As New XmlSchemaAttribute()
        Dim oSimpleExtension As New XmlSchemaSimpleContentExtension()

        '<xs:element name="Records">
        oRecs.Name = "Records"
        oXMLS.Items.Add(oRecs)
        '<xs:complexType>
        oRecs.SchemaType = oComplexRecord
        '<xs:choice maxOccurs="unbounded">
        oChoice.MaxOccursString = "unbounded"
        oComplexRecord.Particle = oChoice
        '<xs:element name="Record">
        oRec.Name = "Record"
        '<xs:complexType>
```

Continued

Listing 19-7 *(Continued)*

```
oRec.SchemaType = oComplexRecords

oChoice.Items.Add(oRec)
'<xs:sequence>
oComplexRecords.Particle = oSeq
'<xs:attribute name="id" type="xs:string">
oRecAttr.Name = "id"
oRecAttr.SchemaTypeName = New XmlQualifiedName _
    ("string", "http://www.w3.org/2001/XMLSchema")
oComplexRecords.Attributes.Add(oRecAttr)
'<xs:element name="Band" type="xs:string" minOccurs="0"/>
oBand.Name = "Band"
oBand.SchemaTypeName = New XmlQualifiedName _
   ("string", "http://www.w3.org/2001/XMLSchema")
oBand.MinOccurs = "0"
oSeq.Items.Add(oBand)
'<xs:element name="Title" type="xs:string" minOccurs="0"/>
oTitle.Name = "Title"
oTitle.SchemaTypeName = New XmlQualifiedName _
 ("string", "http://www.w3.org/2001/XMLSchema")
oTitle.MinOccurs = "0"
oSeq.Items.Add(oTitle)
'<xs:element name="Year" type="xs:string" minOccurs="0"/>
oYear.Name = "Year"
oYear.SchemaTypeName = New XmlQualifiedName _
   ("string", "http://www.w3.org/2001/XMLSchema")
oYear.MinOccurs = "0"
oSeq.Items.Add(oYear)
'<xs:element name="Song" nillable="true" minOccurs="0"
'  maxOccurs="0">
oSong.Name = "Song"
oSong.IsNillable = True
oSong.MinOccurs = "0"
oSong.MaxOccurs = "10"
oSeq.Items.Add(oSong)
'<xs:complexType>
oSong.SchemaType = oComplexSong
'<xs:simpleContent>
oComplexSong.ContentModel = oSimple
'<xs:extension base="xs:string">
oSimpleExtension.BaseTypeName = New XmlQualifiedName _
    ("string", "http://www.w3.org/2001/XMLSchema")
oSimple.Content = oSimpleExtension
```

```
       '<xs:attribute name="Track" type="xs:string"/>
       oTrackAttr.Name = "Track"
       oTrackAttr.SchemaTypeName = New XmlQualifiedName _
         ("string", "http://www.w3.org/2001/XMLSchema")
       oSimpleExtension.Attributes.Add(oTrackAttr)

       oXMLS.Compile(AddressOf eXmlValidationHandler)
response.ContentType="text/xml"
       oXMLS.Write(Response.Output)
    End Sub
    Public Sub eXmlValidationHandler(ByVal sender As Object, _
             ByVal e As ValidationEventArgs)
       Response.Write(e.Message)
    End Sub
</script>
<%If IsPostBack Then
    RebuildRecords
Else%>
<html>
<head>
<title>
Rebuild Records
</title>
</head>
<body>
<form method="post" runat="server">
<table>
<tr>
<td><asp:button id="btnRebuildRecords" runat="server" text="Rebuild Records"/>
</td>
</tr>
</table>
</form>
</body>
</html>
<%End if%>
```

You can find the code for Listing 19-7 on the companion Web site (www.
wiley.com/extras) in Ch19SDK.zip (SDK version) or Ch19VS.zip
(Visual Studio .NET version). After you unzip the files, look for the file named
RebuildRecords.aspx in the folder named RebuildRecords.

Listing 19-7 takes quite a bit of explaining. The first few lines indicate which namespaces to include in this ASP.NET page. To utilize the classes in the SOM, I need to include the `System.Xml.Schema` namespace. The `System.Xml` namespace is included only for the functionality provided by the `XmlQualifiedName` class. You use this functionality while declaring the data type of an attribute or element. The page then declares the `RebuildRecords` and `eXmlValidationHandler` subroutines, which I explain shortly. When the page first loads, it displays an HTML page with a button. After I click the button, the `RebuildRecords` subroutine is called. Instead of displaying the HTML, the schema is displayed (Figure 19-10).

The `RebuildRecords` subroutine is where all of the work in the ASP.NET page takes place. First, I declare all the variables for the page. The following list describes each type of variable:

- `XmlSchema`: Creating an instance of this class creates a blank XSD schema.

- `XmlSchemaElement`: The standard, fundamental schema element tag: `<xs:element>`.

- `XmlSchemaComplexType`: An object corresponding to the complex type: `<xs:complexType>`. A complexType is one that can contain both elements and attributes.

- `XmlSchemaChoice`: An object corresponding to `<xs:choice>`, the choice element in the XSD schema that forces only one element to appear within the group.

- `XmlSchemaSequence`: An object representing `<xs:sequence>`, the sequence element in the XSD schema that indicates that all of the elements in the group need to appear in a specified order.

- `XmlSchemaAttribute`: An object corresponding to `<xs:attribute>`, the attribute element in the XSD schema. An attribute is used to further define information about an element.

- `XmlSchemaSimpleContent`: An object corresponding to the `<xs:simpleContent>`, the simpleContent element in the XSD.

- `XmlSchemaSimpleContentExtension`: An object with no corresponding element in the XSD schema. It's used in conjunction with attributes and simple type content.

Throughout Listing 19-7, I use comments to indicate the element that the code is creating. Generally an element is created, some properties are set, and then the element is added to the schema. When a data type needs to be referenced, I use the `XMLQualifiedName`, passing it the type that I need and the namespace to which it is to be associated. Each of the elements in the Record group is declared as a type of string except for `Song`. `Song` is an element that can be repeated an infinite number of times and also contains the `Track` attribute.

Near the end of the subroutine, I call the `Compile` method and pass it the address of the event handler, which handles any error that occurs in the parsing of the schema during compilation. The `eXmlValidationHandler` subroutine merely prints the error message to the browser. I then set the content type to text/xml so that the browser displays the XML. Finally, I execute the `Write` method of the `XmlSchema` object and pass it the `Response.OutPut` stream. The final output of the application is shown in Figure 19-12.

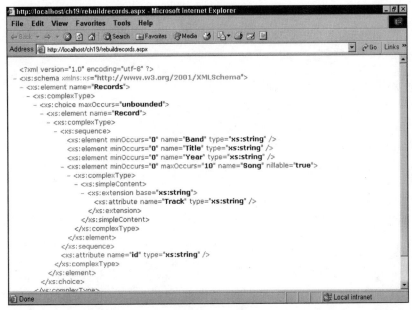

Figure 19-12: The resulting XSD schema generated using the Schema Object Model.

Here are a couple of tips for creating an application that creates schemas.

♦ Execute the `Compile` method often to see how the schema is going. To further troubleshoot, you can move the `Compile` method around in the source code. Compilation can take place several times throughout the creation process.

♦ It's possible to build the schema in almost any order. Moving the creation of the different elements around doesn't affect the building of the schema. I don't recommend building out of order, however; building the schema is difficult enough without adding this extra complexity. It's best to build the schema in the order in which it will eventually appear once it's output.

Summary

This chapter covered several topics regarding the .NET Framework and schemas. I made minor mention of both DTDs and XDR schemas because the future looks more and more like the XSD schema will be the standard of choice. I showed how to validate a schema using the .NET Framework, how the xsd executable can generate schemas from the command prompt, and how the XML Designer is a powerful tool for creating and validating XML documents and schemas. The XML Designer also enables you to validate both the schema and the actual XML document. I also covered how to generate a schema from a SQL Server 2000 table. Finally, I discussed how to generate schemas programmatically using the Schema Object Model.

In the next chapter, I discuss transformation using XSLT and show ways to query the XML document using XPath.

Chapter 20

Transformations and Navigation

IN THIS CHAPTER

- ◆ Understanding XPath and XPath expressions

- ◆ Creating an ASP.NET application to process XPath expressions

- ◆ Understanding the integration of XPath and XSL Transformations

- ◆ Navigate XML documents using XPath

- ◆ Discovering the classes used in the .NET Framework used for XSL Transformations

XML IS A KEYSTONE IN ADO.NET and the .NET Framework, as you've seen throughout this book. A hefty chunk of XML's power comes from its supporting technologies, including XPath, which is used to navigate to data in an XML document. This chapter covers XPath expressions and their uses, as well as XSL Transformations (XSLT), which take a source XML document and render it to some other form such as HTML. This chapter also shows you what the .NET Framework provides, and creates a simple application that executes XPath expressions. I then discuss XSLT and how it uses XPath, and the classes provided by the .NET Framework for dealing with XSL Transformations. Finally I create an application that processes XSLT files.

An Introduction to XPath

The analogy was made in Chapter 19 about how XML technology mimics database technology. A basic XML file acts like the standard table in a database. Schemas in XML are similar to the constraints and data types that monitor the integrity of a database. The only piece that I have not covered up to this point is a way to retrieve the data from an XML file and displaying it. SQL Server provides methods for querying data and returning a subset of the data for displaying. XML also provides XPath, a way to specify the location and retrieve data. XPath is a language used for querying data much like T-SQL for Microsoft's SQL Server. The syntax for XPath is different than standard SQL syntax, but it still provides a great deal of flexibility, much like SQL statements.

Basic XPath syntax

In this section I discuss how to navigate through an XML document by listing some short expressions that can eventually be executed. (I create an application that processes XPath queries in the section titled "XPath Query Application" later in the chapter). I detail the syntax used to return portions of an XML document and show how to navigate to certain pieces of data within the XML document.

Listing 20-1 is the sample XML document that I use for all of the examples in this chapter. (It's the same file I used in Chapter 19, although for the sake of simplicity, I've removed the namespace references from the top.)

Listing 20-1: The XML Record File (Records.xml)

```xml
<?xml version="1.0"?>
<Records>
    <Record id="1">
        <Band>Sheryl Crow</Band>
        <Title>C'mon, C'mon</Title>
        <Year>2002</Year>
        <Song Track="1">Steve McQueen</Song>
        <Song Track="2">Soak Up The Sun</Song>
        <Song Track="3">You're An Original</Song>
        <Song Track="4">Diamond Road</Song>
        <Song Track="5">It's So Easy</Song>
        <Song Track="6">C'Mon, C'Mon</Song>
        <Song Track="7">Safe and Sound</Song>
        <Song Track="8">Over You</Song>
        <Song Track="9">Hole In My Pocket</Song>
        <Song Track="10">Abilene</Song>
        <Song Track="11">Lucky Kid</Song>
        <Song Track="12">It's Only Love</Song>
        <Song Track="13">Weather Channel</Song>
    </Record>
    <Record id="2">
        <Band>Michael Jackson</Band>
        <Title>Thriller</Title>
        <Year>1982</Year>
        <Song Track="1">Wanna Be Startin' Somethin'</Song>
        <Song Track="2">Baby Be Mine</Song>
        <Song Track="3">The Girl Is Mine</Song>
        <Song Track="4">Thriller</Song>
        <Song Track="5">Beat It</Song>
        <Song Track="6">Billie Jean</Song>
```

```
        <Song Track="7">Human Nature</Song>
        <Song Track="8">P.Y.T. (Pretty Young Thing)</Song>
        <Song Track="9">The Lady in My Life</Song>
    </Record>
</Records>
```

 You can find the code from Listing 20-1 on the companion Web site in `Ch20SDK.zip` (SDK version) or `Ch20VS.zip` (Visual Studio .NET version). When you unzip the download, look for the file named `Records.xml` in the XPathQuery folder.

XPath expressions, in some cases, look a lot like paths to files on a hard disk. In XPath expressions, however, the paths are called *location paths*. The following location path would return each Band listed in the XML source document (we can test this later in the chapter).

`/Records/Record/Band`

This location path indicates that I want to start at the beginning of the document and select any Bands that are children of the Record element. Location paths are easier to define if they are built in reverse order. In the previous example I could start at the Band element and then add its parent (Record), and finally Record's parent (Records). This makes it a little easier to traverse the XML document. Additionally, I can request attribute values such as Track in the example XML document. To request a list all of the Tracks in the document, I specify the following expression:

`/Records/Record/Song/@Track`

This expression returns a list of the track numbers as they appear in the XML source document. When dealing with attributes in location paths, you need to use the @ symbol to identify the attribute you are searching for. XPath expressions can get considerably more complex, so let's look at one that searches for just a little more:

`/Records/Record[@id="1"]/Song/@Track`

The difference between this expression and the previous one is the brackets. Brackets are used to qualify the search criteria; specifically, this expression returns the entire set of Track numbers associated to the Record id attribute equal to 1. The lack of brackets in the previous example means that the query will return the values associated with every Track attribute.

Here's another example:

```
/Records/Record[@id="1"]/Song
```

This expression returns a list of all of the Song titles associated with Record id equal to 1. Note that I use double quotes to identify the value of the attribute that I'm looking for. You could switch between single and double quotes and the queries will work fine; however, it's in your best interest to be consistent.

These examples just scratch the surface of XPath expressions. In the "XPath Query Application" section later in the chapter, I create a simple XPath application that executes a given XPath expression using the .NET Framework. Now let's look at the XPath classes available in the .NET Framework.

XPath in the .NET Framework

The .NET Framework classes used with XPath are all included in the `System.Xml.XPath` namespace. You need to know the details of these classes in order to understand the discussion of XPath in relation to XSL Transforms later in the chapter. Chapter 18 briefly mentioned XPath and presented a simple XPath application, so you're already a little familiar with some of these classes.

The `System.Xml.XPath` namespace includes the following classes:

- ◆ `XPathDocument`
- ◆ `XPathNavigator`
- ◆ `XPathExpression`
- ◆ `XPathNodeIterator`
- ◆ `XPathException`

All of the classes combined provide the functionality required to process XPath expressions. The following sections discuss the details of these classes.

XPATHDOCUMENT

The `XPathDocument` class is the main class in the `XPath` namespace. It's used to store the XML document that will be queried. It has six different constructors, which accept readers, streams, and even paths to XML documents. In some cases, it accepts a second parameter indicating how to work with white space in a document. It has only one useful member, `CreateNavigator`, which returns an `XPathNavigator` object.

To find more information about the classes mentioned in the section, use Microsoft's MSDN Web site at `http://msdn.microsoft.com`. Search by specifying the class name.

XPATHNAVIGATOR

The XPathNavigator class contains the methods necessary for executing XPath expressions against the XML document. The class is created as a result of the CreateNavigator method of the XPathDocument class. Two of the important XPathNavigator methods are Select and Evaluate. Each of these methods accepts either a string as an XPath expression or an XPathExpression (discussed in the next section). If the expression evaluates to another set of nodes, a NodeIterator is returned; otherwise, a simple variable type is returned. If it's known that a node set will be returned — this can be determined programmatically using the XPathExpression object — the Select method should be used; if not, the Evaluate method should be used. The Evaluate method works on single values, such as the name of a single song. The Select method has the capability of returning a set of nodes, such as every song in the XML document.

The XPathNavigator also contains methods for navigating an XML document such as MoveToFirstChild and MoveToNextAttribute, just to name two. It also contains the properties HasChildren and HasAttributes, which indicate whether the current node has child nodes or attributes, respectively. Finally, the XPathNavigator includes the Compile method, which accepts a string as an XPath expression and returns an XPathExpression object.

XPATHEXPRESSION

After the XPathNavigator is set up, I can use the Compile method to check the XPath expression. Once compiled, the XPathNavigator returns an instance of the XPathExpression class. The XPathExpression object has two important properties, Expression and ReturnType. The Expression property returns the expression stored within the XPathExpression object. The ReturnType determines what type of data will be returned when the expression is executed. Table 20-1 shows some of the different values that can be returned.

TABLE 20-1 SOME OF THE RETURNTYPE PROPERTY VALUES

ReturnType Value	Description
Boolean	Evaluates to a Boolean value.
Error	Indicates that there was an error in the expression.
NodeSet	Indicates that a subset of the initial document will be returned as a set of nodes.
Number	Evaluates to a number.
String	Evaluates to a string.

Each of the values in Table 20-1 is part of the XPathResultType enumeration. To access a string value, use the following syntax:

```
XPathResultType.String
```

The example application in the "XPath Query Application" section later in the chapter shows how to utilize these values. If the return type of the expression evaluates to a node set, the XPathIterator class needs to be utilized to iterate through the results.

XPATHNODEITERATOR

The XPathNodeIterator enables me to step through a series of nodes. The most useful method of the XPathNodeIterator class is MoveNext, which allows for moving through the node set usually in conjunction with a While loop. The XPathNodeIterator is used in the sample application for this section.

XPATHEXCEPTION

The XPathException is similar to all of the other .NET Framework exception classes. It contains the standard members such as the Message and Source properties.

Now that you've looked at the XPath classes used from within the .NET Framework, I'll create a sample application that utilizes all of them.

XPath Query Application

The XPath application in Listing 20-2 will execute a query against the XML document from Listing 20-1. After I explain the application, I'll demonstrate some more of the capabilities of XPath.

Listing 20-2: The XPath Query Application (XPathQuery.aspx)

```vb
<%@Import namespace="System.Xml"%>
<%@Import namespace="System.Xml.XPath"%>
<script language="vb" runat="server">

Public Sub QueryXPath(strXPathQuery as String)
        Try
            Dim oXml As New XPathDocument(Server.MapPath(".") & _
                "\records.xml")
            Dim oNav As XPathNavigator = oXml.CreateNavigator
            Dim oExp As XPathExpression = oNav.Compile(strXPathQuery)

            Select Case oExp.ReturnType
                Case XPathResultType.Number
                    Response.Write("Query return type of: Number<br>")
                    Response.Write(oNav.Evaluate(oExp))
                Case XPathResultType.NodeSet
                    Dim oIter As XPathNodeIterator
```

```
                    Response.Write("Query return type of: Node Set<br>")
                    oIter = oNav.Select(oExp)
                    While oIter.MoveNext
                        Response.Write(oIter.Current.Value & "<br>")
                    End While
                Case XPathResultType.Boolean
                    Response.Write("Query return type of: Boolean<br>")
                    Response.Write(oNav.Evaluate(oExp))
                Case XPathResultType.String
                    Response.Write("Query return type of: String<br>")
                    Response.Write(oNav.Evaluate(oExp))
                Case XPathResultType.Error
                    Response.Write("Query return type of: Error<br>")
                    Response.Write("Error in expression<br>")
            End Select
        Catch eXPath As XPathException
            Response.Write(eXPath.Message & ":" & eXPath.Source)
        End Try
End Sub

</script>

<html>
<head>
<title>
XPath Query
</title>
</head>
<body>
<form method="post" runat="server">
<table>
<tr>
<td><asp:Label id="lblXPathQuery"
    runat="server" text="XPath Query:"/>
</td>
<td><asp:TextBox id="txtXPathQuery" runat="server"/>
</td>
</tr>
<tr>
<td colspan="2"><asp:button id="btnExecuteQuery"
        runat="server" text="Execute Query"/>
</td>
</tr>
</table>
```

Continued

Listing 20-2 *(Continued)*

```
</form>
<%If IsPostBack Then
        QueryXPath(txtXPathQuery.Text)
End If%>
</body>
</html>
```

You can find the code from Listing 20-2 on the companion Web site in `Ch20SDK.zip` (SDK version) or `Ch20VS.zip` (Visual Studio .NET version). When you unzip the download, look for the file named `XPathQuery.aspx` in the XPathQuery folder.

Listing 20-2 presents a standard Web page with a text box and a submit button. Entering an XPath expression into the text box and clicking the submit button invokes the `QueryXPath` subroutine, which accepts the XPath expression in the text box.

The top of the ASP.NET file indicates that both the `System.Xml` and the `System.Xml.XPath` namespaces are used in this page.

The entire `QueryXPath` subroutine is implemented within a `Try Catch` statement. The `Catch` section is invoked once an error occurs while trying to process the XPath expression. I declare a new variable to hold the instance of the `XPathDocument` object, and pass this object a path to the `Records.xml` file. Next I create an `XPathNavigator` object using the `CreateNavigator` method of the `XPathDocument` object. Finally I create an `XPathExpression` by using the `Compile` method of the `XPathNavigator` object. The `Compile` method accepts a string, which evaluates to an XPath expression.

The next section of the application uses a `Select Case` statement based on the `ReturnType` property of the `XPathExpression` object. The results of the query are displayed to the browser along with the kind of data (such as string or node set) that is returned. If the `ReturnType` is of type `NodeSet`, the `Select` method of the `XPathNavigator` is executed and the results are loaded into the `XPathNodeIterator` object. The node set is then stepped through, writing the results to the browser using the `MoveNext` method of the `XPathNodeIterator` object. For the simple data types, such as the string and number, the `Evaluate` method is called to execute the XPath expression. These values are printed directly to the browser along with an HTML break (`<br>`) to make the output readable.

The last section of the application is the `Catch` statement utilizing the `XPathException` class. If an error occurs, it displays the error message and the class where the error occurred.

This application is now ready to be tested. Entering the expressions discussed in the beginning of the chapter would be a good start. There are also several additional XPath functions that can be executed using the application. Table 20-2 provides some examples and the results of executing the expressions.

TABLE 20-2 SOME XPATH EXPRESSIONS TO ENTER INTO THE TEST APPLICATION

Expression	Result
`/Records/Record[@id="2"]/Song/@Track`	Returns all of the track numbers associated with song id 2.
`/Records/Record[@id="1"]/Song`	Returns all of the song titles associated with record id 1.
`/Records/Record/Song[position()=last()]`	Returns the last song in each of the Record elements.
`contains(/Records/Record[@id="2"]/Band,"Mich")`	Returns True.
`count(/Records/Record/Song)`	Returns the total number of Songs in the document.
`string-length(/Records/Record[@id="2"]/Band)`	Returns the number of characters in the name of the band from record id 2.

The examples in Table 20-2 show some of the querying functionality that the XPath expressions provide.

This section has shown a great deal of the flexibility that the .NET Framework supplies when working with XPath. I showed you how to create XPath expressions and how to step through the results of an XPath query, and I presented a simple XPath application that executes XPath queries and displays the return values. The next section addresses how XSL Transformations integrate with XPath expressions to alter XML documents in many different formats.

Transformations Using XSLT

The examples of XPath functionality that you've seen so far in this chapter really become beneficial once we tie them to eXtensible Stylesheet Language for Transformation (XSLT).

XML documents form the base set of data. The format of the data is usually readable by humans, but is not aesthetically appealing. Besides making an XML document readable by humans, XSLT provides methods for formatting data so other applications can read the data. If a client requires a document with only elements and you have a document with mixed elements and attributes, you can use XSLT to alter the document to contain only elements.

In a transformation there is usually one stylesheet that contains multiple templates. Each template may address a different area of the XML source document. In the first part of this section I use some sample transformations on the Records.xml file (Listing 20-1) to show you how to work with XSLT using Microsoft's Internet

Explorer. Internet Explorer provides a simple method for transforming XML documents and displays them all in the same interface. Later in this section I demonstrate the functionality that the .NET Framework provides for working with XSLT.

Transformations and Internet Explorer

Let me start by briefly discussing how XSLT and XML documents work together. First, there needs to be a processor that will combine the XML document and the XSLT document and produce a final result. Then, given an XML document and an XSLT document, there needs to be some way to associate the two, process, and return some type of result set. I use Notepad to create an XSLT document, and name it with the XSL extension (not to be confused with Excel's naming convention of XLS). Once the stylesheet is set up, the association can be made in the XML document by inserting the following line in the document right after the opening declaration:

```
<?xml-stylesheet type="text/xsl" href="MyRecords.xsl"?>
```

This example assumes that the XSL file has been named `MyRecords.xsl`. The type attribute indicates what type of stylesheet — in this case, an XSL stylesheet — to use. (A Cascading Style Sheet can be specified by setting the type to `"text/css"`.) Next I specify the location and name of the stylesheet. In this example, it's in the same directory as the source XML document, `Records.xml`, and is called `MyRecords.xsl`. Now when I click on the XML document, Internet Explorer looks for the stylesheet to execute the transformations.

For the purposes of the examples regarding transformations I copied `Records.xml` to `RecordsAssociated.xml` to indicate that the XML document is now associated to a stylesheet.

Listing 20-3 is a small XSL file that I'll use to demonstrate transformations. XSL is the usual file extension given to the file containing XSL Transformations. XSL files are also well-formed and valid XML documents.

Listing 20-3: An XSL Transformation That Displays the First Band in the
RecordsAssociated.xml File (MyRecords1.xsl)

```
<?xml version="1.0" encoding="utf-8"?>
<xsl:stylesheet version="1.0"
    xmlns:xsl="http://www.w3.org/1999/XSL/Transform">
<xsl:output method="html"/>

<xsl:template match="/">
<html>
<head>
```

```
</head>
<body>
   <xsl:value-of select="/Records/Record/Band"/>
</body>
</html>
</xsl:template>

</xsl:stylesheet>
```

 You can find the code from Listing 20-3 on the companion Web site in Ch20SDK.zip (SDK version) or Ch20VS.zip (Visual Studio .NET version). When you unzip the download, look for the file named MyRecords1.xsl in the Transformations folder.

This stylesheet starts out with the same line as the standard XML document. Next I indicate which version of stylesheet specification I'm using and the type of output for the resulting document (HTML, in this example). The other popular type of output is XML ("xml"), which is also the default if nothing is specified. I then specify the criteria for this specific template, indicating the root of the source document with the /, and start building a normal HTML document. The version and specification for the stylesheet is set by the W3C like all of the other specifications for XML. The namespace associates this document with the Transform specifications. In the body of the document I specify the xsl:value-of element and tell it to select the XPath expression that follows. In this case, the processor selects the first Band and displays it to the browser. I close the HTML document, template, and stylesheet. For this example to be very useful, I need some way to process the results found by an XPath query.

XSLT provides the xsl:for-each element for processing the results of a select statement. Listing 20-4 shows how for-each can be used to process the XML document.

Listing 20-4: Example of an XSLT Element For-Each Implementation (MyRecords2.xsl)

```
<?xml version="1.0" encoding="utf-8"?>
<xsl:stylesheet version="1.0"
    xmlns:xsl="http://www.w3.org/1999/XSL/Transform">
<xsl:output method="html"/>

<xsl:template match="/">
<html>
<head>
</head>
```

Continued

Listing 20-4 *(Continued)*

```
<body>
<xsl:for-each select="/Records/Record/Band">
    <xsl:value-of select="."/><br/>
</xsl:for-each>
</body>
</html>
</xsl:template>

</xsl:stylesheet>
```

You can find the code from Listing 20-4 on the companion Web site in
`Ch20SDK.zip` (SDK version) or `Ch20VS.zip` (Visual Studio .NET version).
When you unzip the download, look for the file named `MyRecords2.xsl` in
the Transformations folder.

This is similar to Listing 20-3, except I add the `xsl:for-each` syntax and indicate what part of the source document the `xsl:for-each` should iterate over. Once
`xsl:for-each` locates the path, it displays the current value, indicated by the `.`,
which is the name of the Band. I then append a break HTML tag, `<br>`, to the end
of this line so that each Band ends up on a new line. Note that I make the break
self-closing with the trailing `/`. If I don't do this, I receive the error message shown
in Figure 20-1.

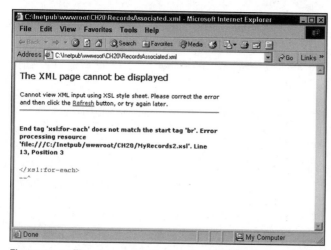

Figure 20-1: The error received when the HTML break tag is not closed.

The processor in this case is treating all of the HTML elements as standard XML elements. It understands that each opening element needs a closing element, and stops if one is missing.

Let's look at how attributes in the source document can be used in the select statement. Listing 20-5 shows how I can create a listing of all of the Tracks with the associated Songs.

Listing 20-5: XSLT Required to Generate a Listing of Songs and Tracks (MyRecords3.xsl)

```
<?xml version="1.0" encoding="utf-8"?>
<xsl:stylesheet version="1.0"
    xmlns:xsl="http://www.w3.org/1999/XSL/Transform">
<xsl:output method="html"/>


<xsl:template match="/">
<html>
<head>
</head>
<body>
<table>
<xsl:for-each select="/Records/Record/Song">
    <tr><td>
    <xsl:value-of select="@Track"/>: <xsl:value-of select="."/>
    </td></tr>
</xsl:for-each>
</table>
</body>
</html>
</xsl:template>


</xsl:stylesheet>
```

 You can find the code from Listing 20-5 on the companion Web site in Ch20SDK.zip (SDK version) or Ch20VS.zip (Visual Studio .NET version). When you unzip the download, look for the MyRecords3.xsl file in the Transformations folder.

I still use the xsl:for-each syntax but I change the select statement to check for the Song element in the source document. Once the Song element is located, I display the Track attribute by using the @ symbol, just like the examples from the section on XPath. I insert a colon and output the actual value of the Song listed. Instead of using the HTML break element this time, I choose to place the output in an HTML table. The output from this example is shown in Figure 20-2.

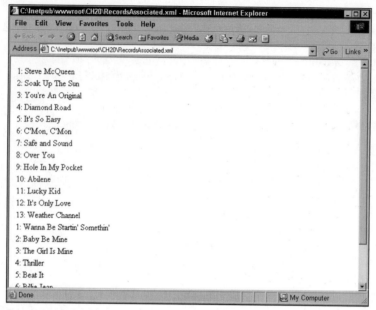

Figure 20-2: The output from the template displaying the Track and the title of the Song.

XSLT also contains If Then processing. Depending on a value, a different course of action can be taken. The source code in Listing 20-6 shows how to use the `xsl:if` statement within a template.

Listing 20-6: An Example Showing If Conditional (MyRecords4.xsl)

```
<?xml version="1.0" encoding="utf-8"?>
<xsl:stylesheet version="1.0"
    xmlns:xsl="http://www.w3.org/1999/XSL/Transform">
<xsl:output method="html"/>
<xsl:template match="/">
<html>
<head>
</head>
<body>

<xsl:for-each select="/Records/Record/Song">
   <xsl:if test="@Track>5">
     <b><xsl:value-of select="@Track"/>
     </b>:<xsl:value-of select="."/><br/>
   </xsl:if>
</xsl:for-each>

</body>
</html>
```

```
</xsl:template>
</xsl:stylesheet>
```

You can find the code from Listing 20-6 on the companion Web site in `Ch20SDK.zip` (SDK version) or `Ch20VS.zip` (Visual Studio .NET version). When you unzip the download, look for the `MyRecords4.xsl` file in the Transformations folder.

This example displays all of the Records that have a Track attribute greater than five. It accomplishes this by using the `test` attribute of the `xsl:if` element in which I indicate that the Track attribute of the Song element needs to be greater than 5. If the Track attribute is greater than 5, I bold the Track and print out the name of the Song. Figure 20-3 shows the output of this example.

In Listing 20-6, I used the greater than symbol (>) to evaluate the expression to see if it was greater than 5. This worked correctly. However, using the less than character (<) generates an error, because less than characters are not allowed in XML since they look like the beginning of an opening tag. To resolve this issue, use the `&gt;` and the `&lt;` characters for greater than and less than, respectively.

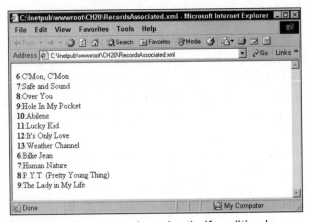

Figure 20-3: The output when using the If conditional.

The `xsl:if` conditional is similar to the `xsl:choose` element provided by XSLT and the `Select Case` statement within Visual Basic .NET. It allows for many possible values and can act on any of those values. Listing 20-7 shows how to utilize the `xsl:choose` statement inside an XSLT template.

Listing 20-7: Using the Choose Statement in XSLT (MyRecords5.xsl)

```
<?xml version="1.0" encoding="utf-8"?>
<xsl:stylesheet version="1.0"
    xmlns:xsl="http://www.w3.org/1999/XSL/Transform">
<xsl:output method="html"/>
<xsl:template match="/">
<html>
<head>
</head>
<body>

<xsl:for-each select="/Records/Record/Song">
   <xsl:choose>
      <xsl:when test="contains(.,'It')">
          <b><xsl:value-of select="."/>
          </b> is an It song<br/>
      </xsl:when>
      <xsl:otherwise>
          <b><xsl:value-of select="."/>
          </b> is not an It song<br/>
      </xsl:otherwise>
   </xsl:choose>
</xsl:for-each>

</body>
</html>
</xsl:template>
</xsl:stylesheet>
```

You can find the code from Listing 20-7 on the companion Web site in `Ch20SDK.zip` (SDK version) or `Ch20VS.zip` (Visual Studio .NET version). When you unzip the download, look for the `MyRecords5.xsl` file in the Transformations folder.

The example uses the `xsl:for-each` to process the document. I use the `xsl:choose` element, provide an `xsl:when`, and use the string function `contains` that checks for a substring within a string. In this case, I am looking for the word *It* anywhere within the title of the song. I also use the `xsl:otherwise` element for cases where the title does not contain the word *It*. Changing the case of *It* yields different values because of case sensitivity. The output for this example is shown in Figure 20-4.

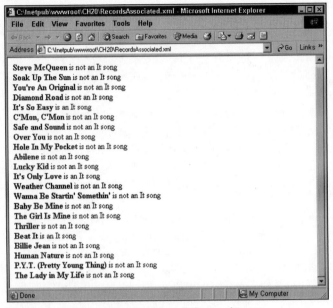

Figure 20-4: The output using the xsl:choose element.

The XSLT element `xsl:sort` sorts a set of elements based on the select criteria. The order in which they are sorted can be set along with the data types and the rules for the case. Setting the `select` attribute of the `xsl:sort` element determines what gets sorted. Listing 20-8 shows how to implement sorting in XSLT.

Listing 20-8: The Sorting Capabilities of XSLT (MyRecords6.xsl)

```xml
<?xml version="1.0" encoding="utf-8"?>
<xsl:stylesheet version="1.0"
    xmlns:xsl="http://www.w3.org/1999/XSL/Transform">
<xsl:output method="html"/>
<xsl:template match="/">
<html>
<head>
</head>
<body>

<xsl:for-each select="/Records/Record/Song">
  <xsl:sort select="." order="descending"/>
  <xsl:value-of select="."/><br/>
</xsl:for-each>

</body>
```

Continued

Listing 20-8 *(Continued)*

```
</html>
</xsl:template>
</xsl:stylesheet>
```

 You can find the code from Listing 20-8 on the companion Web site in `Ch20SDK.zip` (SDK version) or `Ch20VS.zip` (Visual Studio .NET version). When you unzip the download, look for the `MyRecords6.xsl` file in the Transformations folder.

In this example I step through all of the songs in the records XML document. I specify that I want to sort the songs in descending order, and then I display that result to the browser using the `xsl:value-of` XSLT element as I did in the previous examples. If I leave this out, the list sorts but does not display to the browser.

Finally, the XSLT `xsl:apply-templates` element is similar to the way subroutines are called in a standard programming language. A template is assigned a `select` attribute, which is the set of nodes that the template will affect. There can be multiple `xsl:apply-templates` per stylesheet, and they can all be nested. Figure 20-5 shows the kind of output that can be achieved using `xsl:apply-templates`.

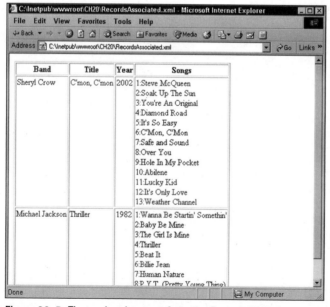

Figure 20-5: The rendered output from the Records XML document.

Listing 20-9 returns an HTML table. I created a new template for each of the columns. As each template is called using `xsl:apply-templates`, any nodes that equal the `match` attribute are applied to the resulting document.

Listing 20-9: Using the xsl:apply-templates Element to Create an HTML Document (MyRecords7.xsl)

```
<?xml version="1.0" encoding="utf-8"?>
<xsl:stylesheet version="1.0"
    xmlns:xsl="http://www.w3.org/1999/XSL/Transform">
<xsl:output method="html"/>
<xsl:template match="/">
<html>
<head>
</head>
<body>
<table border="1">
<tr><th>Band</th><th>Title</th><th>Year</th><th>Songs</th></tr>
<xsl:apply-templates select="/Records/Record"/>
</table>
</body>
</html>
</xsl:template>

<xsl:template match="Record">
  <tr><td valign="top">
   <xsl:apply-templates select="Band"/>
  </td>
   <td valign="top">
   <xsl:apply-templates select="Title"/>
  </td>
   <td valign="top">
   <xsl:apply-templates select="Year"/>
  </td>
   <td>
   <xsl:apply-templates select="Song"/>
  </td>
   </tr>
</xsl:template>

<xsl:template match="Band">
  <xsl:value-of select="."/>
</xsl:template>
<xsl:template match="Title">
  <xsl:value-of select="."/>
```

Continued

Listing 20-9 *(Continued)*

```
</xsl:template>
<xsl:template match="Year">
  <xsl:value-of select="."/>
</xsl:template>
<xsl:template match="Song">
  <xsl:value-of select="@Track"/>:<xsl:value-of select="."/><br/>
</xsl:template>
</xsl:stylesheet>
```

You can find the code from Listing 20-9 on the companion Web site in `Ch20SDK.zip` (SDK version) or `Ch20VS.zip` (Visual Studio .NET version). When you unzip the download, look for the `MyRecords7.xsl` file in the Transformations folder.

The first `xsl:apply-templates` element indicates that it needs a match against the /Records/Record context node. The only matching template for Record is the template that contains the `match` attribute set to `Record`. The Record template is responsible for invoking all of the other matching templates, including `Band`, `Title`, `Year`, and `Song`. For instance, once a Band element is found, the processor applies the Band template located at the bottom of the XSL file. The Record template contains an `xsl:apply-templates` for the Band, Title, Year, and Song element included in the original XML document. In this case I created templates to match each of the elements. Before applying the templates, I place the elements within the HTML table. Each of these four templates uses the `match` attribute to the appropriate element and then uses the `xsl:value-of` to get the value of the given element. The Song element gets both the Track attribute and the actual value of the element itself.

This section has covered some of the functionality provided by XSLT and shown how XPath expressions can be used in conjunction with XSLT and how transformations can select parts of an XML document to display to the user. In the next section you'll see how to use the .NET Framework to work with XSLT and XML documents.

Using the .NET Framework with XSLT

Microsoft provides the `System.Xml.Xsl` namespace for dealing with XSLT programmatically. This namespace contains all of the functionality for transforming XML documents. Table 20-3 lists the classes most commonly used for transformations.

TABLE 20-3 CLASSES IN THE SYSTEM.XML.XSL NAMESPACE

Class Name	Description
XsltArgumentList	A list of arguments that can be passed in to the Transform method of the XslTransform class.
XsltException	This exception is thrown if an error occurs while the transformation is occurring.
XslTransform	Contains the methods for actually producing an output document.

The example application in Listing 20-10 demonstrates the functionality of the XslTransform and the XsltException classes. It uses the stylesheets that were created earlier in the section.

Listing 20-10: A Sample Application That Processes XSLT Stylesheets (XSLTProcessor.aspx)

```vb
<%@Import namespace="System.Xml"%>
<%@Import namespace="System.Xml.XPath"%>
<%@Import namespace="System.Xml.Xsl"%>
<%@Import namespace="System.IO"%>

<script language="vb" runat="server">

Public Sub ProcessDocument(strXMLDocument as String,strXSLTFile as string)
    Try

        Dim oXsl As New XslTransform()
        Dim oXPath As New XPathDocument(strXMLDocument)

        oXsl.Load(strXSLTFile)

        oXsl.Transform(oXPath, Nothing, Response.output)
    Catch eXcpt as XsltException
        Response.Write("The following error occurred:" & eXcpt.Message)
    End Try
End Sub
Private Sub Page_Init(ByVal sender As System.Object, _
                ByVal e As System.EventArgs)
    Dim oDir As New DirectoryInfo(Server.MapPath("."))
    Dim oFil As FileInfo() = oDir.GetFiles("*.xsl")
```

Continued

Listing 20-10 *(Continued)*

```
        Dim oIterFil As FileInfo
        For Each oIterFil In oFil
            XSLTFiles.Items.Add(oIterFil.toString)
        Next
    End Sub
    </script>

    <html>
    <head>
    <title>
    XSLT Processor
    </title>
    </head>
    <body>
    <form method="post" runat="server">
    <table>
    <tr>
    <td><asp:Label id="lblXSLTFile"
        runat="server" text="XSLT File"/>
    </td>
    <td><asp:DropDownList id="XSLTFiles" runat="server">
        </asp:DropDownList></td>
    </tr>
    <tr>
    <td colspan="2"><asp:button id="btnProcessDocument"
            runat="server" text="ProcessDocument"/>
    </td>
    </tr>
    </table>
    </form>
    <%If IsPostBack Then
        Dim strXMLDocument as string=Server.MapPath(".") & "\Records.xml"
        ProcessDocument(strXMLDocument,Server.MapPath(".") & _
            "\" & XSLTFiles.SelectedItem.toString)
    End If%>
    </body>
    </html>
```

You can find the code from Listing 20-10 on the companion Web site in
Ch20SDK.zip (SDK version) or Ch20VS.zip (Visual Studio .NET version).
When you unzip the download, look for the XSLTProcessor.aspx file in
the XSLTProcessor folder.

This sample application includes all of the namespaces at the beginning of the script that are needed for the application. The `System.Xml.Xsl` namespace is the most important one here because it includes the classes capable of processing the XSLT stylesheets. The next section is the subroutine `ProcessDocument` that does the actual processing of the XSLT stylesheet. This subroutine takes two parameters, the path to the XML source document and the path to the XSLT stylesheet. I start by creating an instance of the `XslTransform` class. I then create an instance of the `XPathDocument` class and pass it the path to the XML document. I load the XSLT stylesheet and process the transformation. I pass the `Transform` method the `XPathDocument` variable, the `XsltArgumentList`, and the preferred output stream. I have no XSLT arguments to pass in, so I set this value to `Nothing`. By passing in the value of `Response.Output` as the third parameter, the data will be streamed directly out the `Response` object. The entire subroutine has the `Try Catch` block surrounding it. I am catching for the `XsltException` exception. I display the error message if an exception is thrown.

The next subroutine, `Page_Init`, loads a drop-down box located on the HTML form. It contains all of the files that have the .xsl extension in the directory. This makes it easy to test the application by just selecting which template to process against. `Page_Init` uses the `DirectoryInfo` object and the `FileInfo` object to get a listing of all of the files that match the criteria specified. Once I have an array of file names I can step through them using the `For Each` syntax and use the `Add` method of the `Items` collection to add the file names to the drop-down.

The rest of the example uses standard HTML form elements to present the interface to the user. Figure 20-6 shows the actual interface after a stylesheet is selected.

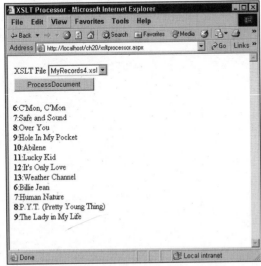

Figure 20-6: The rendered output after selecting an item from the drop-down list box.

The values that are returned from the example should look similar to the results returned earlier in the chapter when I was using Internet Explorer to process the

XML. The only issue with this application is that, in some cases, it returns a full HTML document to the browser. This is because the XSL files are designed to do that. Internet Explorer seems to handle the documents just fine.

In this section I've presented the different classes that are incorporated with the .NET Framework for working with XSLT stylesheets, as well as an example of using the classes to process the examples from earlier in the chapter.

Summary

This chapter has covered both XPath expressions and XSLT processing. I've demonstrated how the .NET Framework provides classes for working with XPath and XSLT and how Internet Explorer has its own XSLT processor, which works well for testing XSL transformations. The next chapter presents several applications which utilize the .NET Framework including XML.

Part V

Putting It All Together

Chapter 21

Designing an Intranet Using Forms Authentication

IN THIS CHAPTER

- ◆ Working with specifications
- ◆ Creating a database for an intranet
- ◆ Creating user- and role-based security from a database
- ◆ Creating the Daily Census, a user task

OVER THE NEXT THREE chapters, we are going to work with the Bedframer Corporation, a fictional company that runs rehabilitation facilities in some of the best communities in the United States. While the company is imaginary, the scenarios presented come from real-world situations I have encountered over the past few years.

In this chapter, we build the Bedframer intranet. In the next chapter, we deal with Bedframer's Internet Web site, and in the third, we create an XML Web service for Bedframer's partners that maintains the look and feel of the Bedframer intranet.

These chapters emphasize some of the high points of the Bedframer intranet application and how to map company goals to this application.

This chapter primarily deals with how to set up the security of an intranet site using forms authentication. We'll build the security around setting up a user table in a database rather than using Windows user accounts and groups.

Overview of the Bedframer Intranet

The first problem Bedframer needs to solve is putting up an intranet where its employees can record and track their moving of residents in and out of their rehabilitation facilities. The intranet replaces a paper-based system that was developed quite some time ago by the company from which Bedframer bought the facilities.

Initially, the marketing and accounting departments present the Information Services Department with a few demands for the new system:

◆ Replace all paper forms. This task includes forms for each task that occurs during a resident's stay, including move-in, move-out, and room change.

◆ Keep a daily census of all residents. Some residents are long-term, while others are only in the facility for a couple of days. Long-term residents often spend time away in a hospital or on vacation.

◆ Web-enable a set of reports that currently resides in Excel.

Ultimately, marketing would like to have the entire application moved to an OLAP database where serious analysis can be completed. In the interim, all residents are linked to demographic tables in the database.

The head of Information Services names the intranet site BOW (an acronym for Bedframer Operations Web). After examining the initial needs of the project, the Information Services creates the simple specifications shown in Table 21-1.

TABLE 21-1 SPECIFICATIONS OF THE NEW SYSTEM

Area	Needs
Forms	The following forms need to be created for the Web application: ◆ Daily Census check. ◆ Deposit and Resident Agreement. ◆ Forms to reserve a room, admit a resident, discharge a resident, and change a resident's room.
Reports	The specifications set down a requirement for move-in, move-out, and available-room reports.
Search	The user must be able to search for both resident and community information.
Security	The primary concern with the application is being able to authenticate a user: ◆ The user must be authenticated. ◆ The user must have authorization to use certain resources. ◆ The screen must timeout to accommodate privacy concerns.

In a real-world application, I'd create a full set of functional and technical specifications before moving ahead with the code. The functional specifications would contain use cases for each of the needs determined in Table 21-1. Before writing the full technical specifications, I settle on a platform (.NET), language (Visual Basic .NET), and database platform (SQL Server 2000).

Database Design

Bedframer has purchased a demographic database to use for its city, county, state, and MSA (Metropolitan Statistic Area) information. You can download a database with similar information from the book's companion Web site. If you want to design an application of this nature, consider purchasing this information. Because postal codes change, the data becomes out-of-date, but there are subscription services that can keep you up to date on every change. The data I've compiled for this project will likely be out of date a few months after you start working with it.

 You can download the database used in this chapter from this book's companion Web site (www.wiley.com/extras). The database file is called Ch21Data.zip. The database was culled from a variety of sources on the Internet and is useful as a starting point for your own demographic work. The code for this chapter, in the file Ch21VS.zip (Visual Studio .NET version) or Ch21SDK.zip (SDK version), contains a smaller subset of this data if you don't want to play with data from the entire United States.

As I mentioned earlier, the database design I'm using for this project is adopted from work I've done on a consulting assignment. Any of the sections of the database that seem a bit different from traditional design are probably rooted in the original project.

Let's first take a look at the demographics portion of the database, which is shown in Figure 21-1. The tables include City, County, State, Country, Metropolitan Statistical Area (MSA), and Nielsen Dominant Market Areas (DMA). The DMA is used to map out radio and television markets.

The main purpose of the demographic tables is for future analysis of data. At some point in time, Bedframer plans to build a data warehouse to aid in its marketing efforts, so these tables are included with this future use in mind. For example, this data might be used for the following:

◆ Linking a resident to a DMA can help Bedframer determine which radio and television markets might be useful for its advertising efforts.

◆ The postal code information is useful for mass mailing, as well as determining at which locations to hold seminars to get the best response.

◆ City data helps to determine newspaper advertising. Because many newspapers print editions tailored to certain areas of town, this can further be broken down using the postal code information.

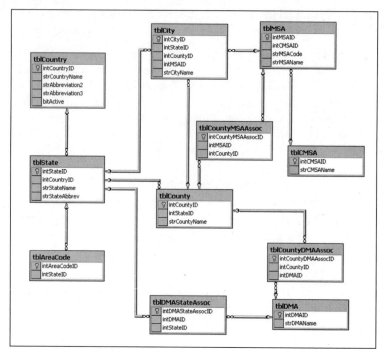

Figure 21-1: Demographics tables (and the tables that join these tables).

As mentioned, these are future uses of the data and not part of the current phase of the project.

The next portion of the database, shown in Figure 21-2, deals with the user and security sections. The center table is the Person table (tblPerson). Both the User and Employee tables are subtypes of the Person table. The User table is linked to the Menu tables to set permissions for each of the menu items (contained in tblSectionMenuItem and tblSideMenuItem). This ensures that the user cannot access menu items he does not have the proper permissions to view. Through the Employee table (tblEmployee), the person is linked to the community (tblCommunity) in which he works.

The Security and User tables (tblUser, tblSideMenuItem and tblSectionMenuItem) are designed to limit what a user can see based on his logon account. Using the User table (tblUser), the user logs on. Based on this logon and the type of user, the user's menu items are limited to only those items he can view (tblSideMenuItem and tblSectionMenuItem). Some accounts have more permissions than others. By linking the User table to menu tables, a user can be restricted without a lot of effort. Of course, an incorrect user and password combination result in no access to the site at all.

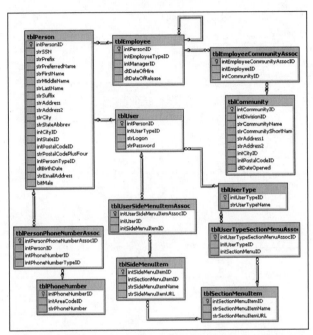

Figure 21-2: Security and User tables: tblCommunity, tblPerson, tblEmployee, tblUser, tblSideMenuItem, and tblSectionMenuItem (and the tables that join them).

The final section of the database, shown in Figure 21-3, deals with the people who stay in the communities and the communities they stay in. Once again the Person table is utilized to store the information about the person. The Resident table is also subtyped from the Person table, just like the User and Employee tables are.

The fact that so many tables are set up as subtypes of the Person table may seem a bit strange at first, but it does simplify a lot of queries because you can bypass tables in your joins. I thought this method of setting up a database was strange the first time I saw it, but I have come to like it in certain situations. This part of the database design is getting to a point where it's more object-oriented than relational; it can be very useful if you design objects for your users in your application.

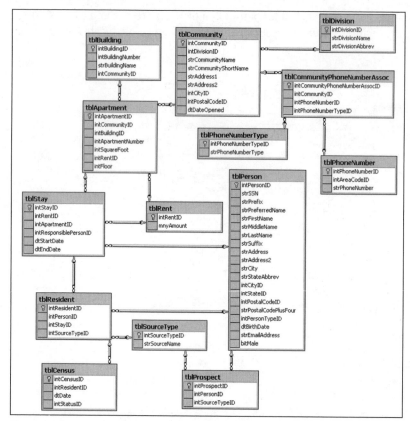

Figure 21-3: Resident and Community tables: tblResident, tblCensus, tblStay, tblApartment (and other supporting tables and join tables).

Security

The primary security method of the Bedframer intranet application is a database-driven logon using forms authentication. Since this is an intranet, Windows authentication was also a possibility but, because many users use the same workstation and do not always have time to completely log out of Windows, the IS staff opted to use forms authentication instead. This allows the ASP.NET application to time out, or the user to use a single-click logoff.

The logon page

The first step in authentication is to log the user into the application. There are two files that must be altered to accomplish this. The first is the web.config file, which is used to set the authentication method to forms authentication. The second is the logon.aspx file, which is used as the logon form.

Here's how our authentication process works:

1. A user attempts to access a page in the application.

2. The ASP.NET process detects the user is not authenticated and automatically directs the user to the logon.aspx file.

3. The user must log on and provide the appropriate password.

4. If the logon is successful, ASP.NET automatically redirects the user to the page he attempted to access. I assume that the user tried to access the home page in each of the examples in this chapter. Using forms authentication, a user can bookmark any page in the application and be redirected to that page, not the home page.

   If the logon fails, the user is denied access to the page he wanted.

Unlike in ASP, you don't have to create a custom redirect script to facilitate this in ASP.NET. To illustrate the point, Listing 21-1 presents a simple ASP script that is designed to direct a user to a logon.asp page. I use this to contrast the methodology employed in ASP.NET (Listings 21-2 through 21-4).

Listing 21-1: ASP Redirection

```
<%
  If Session("loggedon") <> True then
        Response.Redirect("logon.asp")
     End If
%>
```

In this scenario, the user logs on and the Session("loggedon") value is set to True. You can also facilitate this with cookies if you are using a Web farm for your application. As you will see, forms authentication handles this functionality, along with the redirect back to the page accessed, without any code on your part. You need only code whether a user successfully logged in.

THE WEB.CONFIG FILE

To set up forms authentication, you have to open the web.config file and make a few changes:

♦ Change the mode attribute of the authentication tag to read Forms.

♦ Add a forms tag that points to the URL (loginURL) you'll use for a logon page and set the path that uses this page. I use / as a path to ensure that all pages in the entire application redirect to this page.

The code snippet produced from these instructions is shown in Listing 21-2.

Listing 21-2: The web.config File for the Bedframer Operations Web

```
<authentication mode="Forms">
  <forms name="bow" path="/" loginUrl="logon.aspx"
         protection="All" timeout="10" />
</authentication>
```

The authentication method is set to `Forms`. The URL for the logon page is `logon.aspx`. The `protection="All"` is the default setting; it indicates that the cookie is encrypted and the data from the cookie is validated. The `timeout` setting here is 10 minutes.

In addition to `All`, other choices for `protection` are `Encryption` and `Validation`. These options, along with the options for all of the tags in the `web.config` file, are covered in much more detail in Chapter 12.

THE LOGON.ASPX FILE

The next step is to create a logon page. Figure 21-4 shows this Web page, which greets the user whenever he attempts to access any page in the Bedframer Operations Web. This page shows all but the menu system.

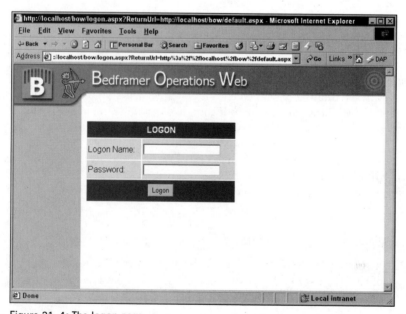

Figure 21-4: The logon page.

The ASPX page contains a couple text box controls, along with a label to tell the user that his username (Logon Name) and password combination were incorrect. The rest of the page is filled with the look and feel of the site. The code for the form is shown in Listing 21-3; the important portions are bold.

Listing 21-3: The logon.aspx Page

```
<form id="Form1" method="post" runat="server">
  <TABLE style="WIDTH: 300px; HEIGHT: 157px" cellSpacing="2" cellPadding="2"

        width="300" border="0">
    <TR>
      <TD colspan="2" bgColor="#333399" style="HEIGHT: 31px" align="middle">
        <font color="#ffffff"><STRONG>LOGON</STRONG></font>
      </TD>
    </TR>
    <TR>
      <TD style="WIDTH: 104px" bgColor="#99ff99">
        Logon Name:
      </TD>
      <TD bgColor="#99ff99">
        <asp:TextBox id="strLogon" runat="server" />
      </TD>
    </TR>
    <TR>
      <TD style="WIDTH: 104px; HEIGHT: 35px" bgColor="#99ff99">
        Password:
      </TD>
      <TD style="HEIGHT: 35px" bgColor="#99ff99">
        <asp:TextBox TextMode="Password" id="strPassword" runat="server" />
      </TD>
    </TR>
    <TR>
      <TD colspan="2" bgColor="#333399" align="middle">
        <asp:Button id="btnLogon" runat="server" Text="Logon" />
      </TD>
    </TR>
  </TABLE>
</form>
<P>
  <asp:Label id="lblLogonProblem" runat="server" />
</P>
```

The code for the `logon.aspx` file is included on the companion Web site (`www.wiley.com/extras`) in this chapter's download file: `Ch21-23VS.zip` (Visual Studio .NET version) or `Ch21-23SDK.zip` (SDK version).

The two text boxes, `strLogon` and `strPassword` are going to be used to input the logon name and password. The reason for using `str` instead of `txt`, which would be normal for a text box in Visual Basic 6, is to keep the names consistent from the page to the `dbBow` database field to which it will map. The button control, `btnLogon`, is used to submit the form, which I cover shortly. Finally, there is a label control, `lblLogonProblem`, which displays error messages when a user has problems logging on.

THE CODEBEHIND FILE: LOGON.ASPX.VB

The magic in the logon routine comes in the CodeBehind file. In this page, the user logon name and password are checked against values in the database. You can also stick these values into the `web.config` file, but I don't do this because I think it's more of a hassle to update a file than a database.

In order to use the database, I add a little bit of code to check the input from the form against the database and redirect the user. Listing 21-4 shows the `btnLogon_Click` event.

Listing 21-4: Logon Subroutine

```
Private Sub btnLogon_Click(ByVal sender As System.Object, _
          ByVal e As System.EventArgs) Handles btnLogon.Click
  'Values to store into Session
  Dim intPersonID As Integer
  Dim strFirstName As String
  Dim strLastname As String
  Dim intCommunityID As Integer

  Dim strConn As String = Application("ConnectionString")
  Dim objConn As New SQLData.SqlConnection(strConn)

  'Set up the command object to call the logon stored procedure
  Dim objCmd As New SQLData.SqlCommand()
  With objCmd
      .CommandText = "sps_UserLogon"
      .CommandType = CommandType.StoredProcedure
      .Connection = objConn
      .Parameters.Add(New SQLData.SqlParameter("@strLogon", SqlDbType.VarChar, _
                50, ParameterDirection.Input, False, 0, 0, "strLogon", _
```

```
                                DataRowVersion.Original, strLogon.Text))
        .Parameters.Add(New SQLData.SqlParameter("@strPassword", _
                        SqlDbType.VarChar, 15, ParameterDirection.Input, False, _
                        0, 0, "strPassword", DataRowVersion.Original, _
                        strPassword.Text))
End With


Dim objReader As SQLData.SqlDataReader


Try
    objConn.Open()
    objReader = objCmd.ExecuteReader

    'Get values from the reader
    While objReader.Read
     intPersonID = objReader.Item("intPersonID")
     strFirstName = objReader.Item("strFirstName")
     strLastname = objReader.Item("strLastName")
     intCommunityID = objReader.Item("intCommunityID")
    End While


    objConn.Close()

Catch objSQLException As SQLData.SqlException
    lblLogonProblem.Text = "Problem contacting database."
Catch objException As Exception
    lblLogonProblem.Text = "An unexpected error occurred."
End Try


'Set session objects (mirrors a current application in ASP)
Session.Add("intPersonID", intPersonID)
Session.Add("strFirstName", strFirstName)
Session.Add("strLastName", strLastname)
Session.Add("intCommunityID", intCommunityID)


If intPersonID <> 0 Then
    'Send the user ID to the application as a variable
    SysSecurity.FormsAuthentication.RedirectFromLoginPage(intPersonID, False)
Else
    lblLogonProblem.Text = "Either the logon or the password are incorrect."
End If


End Sub
```

I bolded the important parts of this routine in the listing, and want to take a little space to cover those sections:

◆ There are two `Catch` statements in the `Try ... Catch` block. The first is for SQL exceptions, and the second deals with generic exceptions. If you include an exception handler that catches specific exceptions, that `Catch` must come first. If it doesn't, you always get a generic exception message. Here's the syntax for using two `Catch` statements in a `Try ... Catch` block:

```
Try
    'Statements that might cause an error
Catch objSQLException as SQLData.SQLException
    'More specific exception
Catch objException as Exception
    'Less specific exception
End Try
```

◆ The individual pieces of information are added to the session object. The syntax is a bit different from the syntax in ASP.NET. To store values in `Session`, you use the `Add` method of the `Session` object:

```
Session.Add("intPersonID", intPersonID)
```

To retrieve the value, use the `Item` collection of the `Session` object:

```
intPersonID = Session.Item("intPersonID")
```

◆ To redirect to the page the user was attempting to access, use the `RedirectFromLogonPage` method of the `FormsAuthentication` object. You pass it a name to retrieve the cookie (you can also add additional information to the cookie) as well as a Boolean value to indicate whether this cookie should perpetuate beyond this session. In this application, it is assumed the cookie goes out of scope when the user logs off, as shown here:

```
SysSecurity.FormsAuthentication. _
    RedirectFromLoginPage(intPersonID, False)
```

If you only take one piece of information away from this section, it should be the `RedirectFromLoginPage` method.

If you want to create a site that perpetuates a user's credentials once she signs up on your site, you can use forms authentication. Just set the Boolean value for the `RedirectFromLoginPage()` to `True`. Because you can add any additional information you need to personalize your site, this is a rather effective way to set up an application that does not have great security needs. Here's the code snippet to cache a user's credentials in a cookie:

```
SysSecurity.FormsAuthentication. _
    RedirectFromLoginPage(intPersonID, True)
```

If you want to allow the user to decide if this information is persisted, set up a check box for the user to indicate if she'd like to be able to avoid logging in each time. Use this check box to set the Boolean value.

If you get nothing else from this section, you should realize that ASP.NET enables you to create a single logon page for the entire application, without having to create redirectors to the logon page from every other page in your Web site. Because the settings are set up in the `.config` file, you can also create this type of security on a directory-by-directory basis to easily set up public and private content.

Logoff page (logoff.aspx)

The logoff page is shown in Listing 21-5. To simplify this section, I've taken the `Page_Load` event and placed it in the ASPX page. In the actual application, this is not the case, because I stick to the CodeBehind paradigm.

Listing 21-5: The Logoff Page

```
<%@ Page Language="vb"%>
<script language=VB runat=server>
    Private Sub Page_Load(ByVal sender As System.Object, _

                    ByVal e As System.EventArgs) Handles MyBase.Load
        SysSecurity.FormsAuthentication.SignOut()
        Session.Abandon()
        Response.Redirect("default.aspx")
    End Sub
</script>
```

The code from Listing 21-5 is on the companion Web site (www. wiley.com/extras) in this chapter's download file: Ch21-23VS.zip (Visual Studio .NET version) or Ch21-23SDDK.zip (SDK version). Look for the file logoff.aspx.

Take a look at the code that is bolded in this listing. The first line — `SysSecurity.FormsAuthentication.SignOut()` — is used to delete the authentication cookie and end the session. Although not required, I also explicitly end the `Session` with the `Abandon` method. This is partially out of habit (from traditional ASP), partially due to my need to be explicit in my code, and partially due to my paranoia that there will be an exception somewhere that leaves a user logged in.

Finally, I redirect to the home page. As you should have guessed, this once again sends the user to the logon.aspx page with a redirect argument to return to `default.aspx` after the next user logs on. Since `default.aspx` is the home page, it is a good page to set this redirect to.

Menus

The final security measure is the way in which menus are built. The user ID is used on every page to build both the top and the side menus. Each of these menus is contained in a user control. Figure 21-5 shows the home page for the application (`default.aspx`) complete with menus.

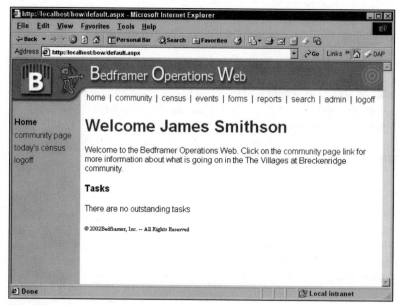

Figure 21-5: The home page with top and side menus.

The menu horizontally across the top is a sectional menu. It's the primary method of navigation from section to section in the site. The menu on the left side changes in context to the section.

The menus are included in the security section of the database so they can change depending on the user who logs on. Each menu is implemented as a user control to reduce repetitive code.

While not heavily covered in this book, because I consider them just another type of object, user controls are a very powerful tool in your ASP.NET arsenal. In addition to menus, there are a variety of snippets that you repeat from page to page throughout your application. User controls

◆ Enable you to cache the user control without caching the entire page as a single unit. This allows you to write applications that perform and scale better.

◆ Remove repetitive code from each page and place it in one central location. This helps with reuse and makes the site more maintainable.

◆ Allow you to share your controls with other ASP.NET developers. This reduces the amount of repeat code from a development team.

User controls are covered in Chapter 3, in the section "Creating Custom User Controls."

TOP MENU

The top menu is the sectional menu for the Bedframer intranet application. The application is divided into eight sections (home, community, census, events, forms, reports, search, and admin), whose links appear in the top menu. At the right end of the menu is a logoff button for the user to end his session.

The top menu spans across the top of the page. The ASPX page uses a `Repeater` control to make a simple list of hyperlinks, using a pipe character (|) as a separator. The code for this page is shown in Listing 21-6. Notice that the method of binding in a repeater template is through the use of the `Container.DataItem` (`"ItemName"`) lines of code.

The `Repeater` control is explained in Chapter 8, in the section "Data Controls," and is used in Chapter 15 in the section "Using a DataReader." Consult these chapters if you need a bit of guidance on this control.

Listing 21-6: The ASCX Page for the Sectional Menu

```
<table>
  <tr>
    <td>
      <asp:Repeater id="TopMenuRepeater" runat="server">
```

Continued

Listing 21-6 *(Continued)*

```
      <ItemTemplate>
        <a href='<%# Container.DataItem("strSectionMenuItemURL") %>'>
          <%# Container.DataItem("strSectionMenuItemName") %>
        </a>
      </ItemTemplate>
      <SeparatorTemplate>
         | 
      </SeparatorTemplate>
    </asp:Repeater>
  </td>
 </tr>
</table>
```

All of the code to fill this sectional menu is contained in the CodeBehind page. There's nothing really stellar about this page — you've seen this type of example numerous times in the Part III of this book. The only new item is pulling the user ID, which was placed in session in the logon page, and using it to create the menu. In this page, I've chosen to pull the user ID from session in the control. The CodeBehind file is shown in Listing 21-7. I bolded the line where I pull the user ID.

Listing 21-7: The CodeBehind File for the Top Menu

```
Private Sub Page_Load(ByVal sender As System.Object, _

                      ByVal e As System.EventArgs) Handles MyBase.Load
    Dim strConn As String = Application("ConnectionString")
    Dim objConn As New SQLData.SqlConnection(strConn)

    Dim strSQL = "sps_GetMenu"
    Dim objCmd As New SQLData.SqlCommand(strSQL, objConn)
    Dim intPersonID = Session.Item("intPersonID")

    With objCmd
        .CommandType = CommandType.StoredProcedure
        .Parameters.Add(New SQLData.SqlParameter("@intPersonID",

                        SqlDbType.Int, 4, ParameterDirection.Input, False, 0,

                        0, "intUserID", DataRowVersion.Original, intPersonID))
    End With

    Try
        objConn.Open()
        Dim objReader As SQLData.SqlDataReader = objCmd.ExecuteReader()
        TopMenuRepeater.DataSource = objReader
```

```
        TopMenuRepeater.DataBind()
        objConn.Close()
    Catch objSQLException As SQLData.SqlException
        'TODO: Handle SQL Exceptions
    Catch objException As Exception
        'TODO: Handle general exceptions
    End Try
End Sub
```

 You can find the code for Listings 21-6 and 21-7 on the companion Web site (www.wiley.com/extras) in this chapter's download file: Ch21-23VS.zip (Visual Studio .NET version) or Ch21-23SDDK.zip (SDK version). Look for SectionMenu.ascx and its CodeBehind file, SectionMenu.ascx.vb.

The procedure that fills this page is rather simple. It takes the user's ID, which is intPersonID (remember the subtyping of the Person table through any tables that have a persona?), and uses it to pull the menu items to which the user has access. The stored procedure is shown in Listing 21-8.

Listing 21-8: The sps_GetMenu Stored Procedure

```
CREATE PROCEDURE sps_GetMenu
(
    @intPersonID    int
)
AS

SELECT
        smi.strSectionMenuItemName,
        smi.strSectionMenuItemURL
FROM
        tblSectionMenuItem smi
JOIN
        tblUserTypeSectionMenuAssoc utsma
ON
        smi.intSectionMenuItemID = utsma.intSectionMenuID
JOIN
        tblUser u
ON
        utsma.intUserTypeID = u.intUserTypeID
WHERE
u.intPersonID = @intPersonID
```

The stored procedure from Listing 21-8 is on the companion Web site (www.wiley.com/extras) in this chapter's download file: Ch21-23VS. zip (Visual Studio .NET version) or Ch21-23SDDK.zip (SDK version). Look in the data directory. There are also SQL scripts to create the entire SQL database.

SIDE MENU

The side menu is almost identical to the sectional menu. One noticeable difference is that you need the section ID to put this menu in context. Since the user does not change, the side menu pulls the user ID from session. The section ID, however, does change with each page. To facilitate this, I create a `WriteOnly` property for the section in the user control. The value of this `WriteOnly` property is fed from a constant placed in the CodeBehind page for each ASPX page. Since the session ID is intimately joined with the page, this makes sense. There are a couple of other methods I could use to determine the section, but as much as I dislike hard coding, the simpler approach prevails here — I can't envision a place where the page and section would not be tightly linked.

The user control (ASCX page) for the side menu differs from the top menu pretty much in direction. I once again use a repeater control. For completeness, I include it here in Listing 21-9. I am using simple binding here to bind the section name and the links; these statements are highlighted in bold.

Listing 21-9: The Side Menu User Control

```
<asp:Repeater id="SideMenuRepeater" runat="server">
  <HeaderTemplate>
    <table cellpadding="2" cellspacing="2">
      <tr>
        <td>
          <strong>
            <%# SectionName %>
          </strong>
        </td>
      </tr>
  </HeaderTemplate>
  <ItemTemplate>
    <tr>
      <td>
        <a href='<%# Container.DataItem("strSideMenuItemURL") %>'>
          <%# Container.DataItem("strSideMenuItemName") %>
        </a>
      </td>
    </tr>
  </ItemTemplate>
```

```
<FooterTemplate>
  </table>
</FooterTemplate>
</asp:Repeater>
```

 The code for Listing 21-9 is on the companion Web site in this chapter's download file: Ch21-23VS.zip (Visual Studio .NET version) or Ch21-23SDDK.zip (SDK version). Look for the file SideMenu.ascx.

Looking at the code, you can see that I bound a property from the CodeBehind page to the HeaderTemplate section of the Repeater control. When I show you the CodeBehind page, you'll notice that I use the section ID to also set the section name.

Because the section ID changes from page to page, I have to use a property in the side menu user control. To set the properties in the page, I utilize a code line like this one taken from the home page (default.aspx):

```
<bow:SideMenu id="SideMenu" runat="Server" Section="<%# m_intSectionID %>">
```

The bolded section shows I am setting the Section property of the user control. To use this user control, as with all user controls, I have to register it on the page using a line like this:

```
<%@ Register TagPrefix="bow" TagName="SideMenu" src="SideMenu.ascx" %>
```

The @ Register line is located at the top of the page with other @ directives. Notice that the TagPrefix and TagName map to the tag used in the body of the page, <bow:SideMenu>. Listing 21-10 shows the Section property in the user control, which is set with the Section="" attribute of the user control tag.

Listing 21-10: Properties of the Side Menu User Control

```
Private m_intSection As Integer
Private m_strSectionName As String

Public WriteOnly Property Section() As String
    Set(ByVal Value As String)
        m_intSection = CType(Value, Integer)

        Select Case CType(Value, Integer)
            Case 1
                SectionName = "Home"
            Case 2
```

Continued

Listing 21-10 *(Continued)*

```
                SectionName = "Community"
            Case 3
                SectionName = "Census"
            Case 4
                SectionName = "Events"
            Case 5
                SectionName = "Forms"
            Case 6
                SectionName = "Reports"
            Case 7
                SectionName = "Search"
            Case 8
                SectionName = "Admin"
        End Select

    End Set
End Property

Public Property SectionName() As String
    Set(ByVal Value As String)
        m_strSectionName = Value
    End Set
    Get
        Return m_strSectionName
    End Get
End Property
```

"Okay, wait a second, Greg! You are hard-coding values in a page?" you ask, incredulous. Normally, I'd be as skeptical as you, but follow my logic for a second:

◆ Unless the entire application is data-driven (perhaps XML- and XSLT-driven), I am going to have more than one page in my Web application.

◆ It is unlikely the logon page will become a report page. The content may change, based on user input or data pulled from the database, but the page purpose is unlikely to change.

◆ If the page purpose is unlikely to change, why not have the page "tell" the application which page it is?

This methodology is a bit outside of the box, but it makes sense if you think about it. Since the Events page is always an Events page, and never a Reports page, why not let it help us render our side menu?

The Page_Load event is fairly similar to the Page_Load event in the sectional menu user control, so there's no need to elaborate here on how to fill a repeater.

MENUS AND SECURITY

To illustrate the security aspects of the top and side menus, you have to log in with two different user IDs. I've included an Excel file in the download file for this chapter; it has all of the users of the system and their logons and passwords. The file also tells their position in the company. In the system, users with the position "maintenance" are the most restricted.

The Excel file is called `users.xls`. You'll find it on the companion Web site (`www.wiley.com/extras`) in this chapter's download file: `Ch21-23VS.zip` (Visual Studio .NET version) or `Ch21-23SDK.zip` (SDK version).

For the first run, you will log in as William Charles, the president of Bedframer Corporation. In this database the logon is always first initial and last name, while the password is first name and last initials. The logon would therefore be WCharles with a password of WilliamC. When you log on as William Charles, you see the menus shown in Figure 21-6.

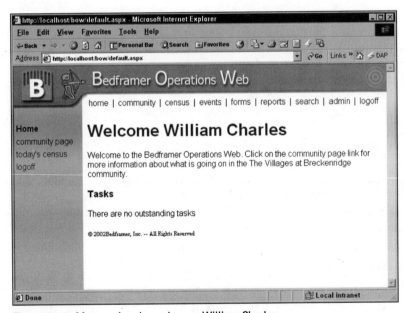

Figure 21-6: Menus when logged on as William Charles.

Now, log off and log on as Richard Grayson: logon is RGrayson with a password of RichardG. Notice the different menus (shown in Figure 21-7).

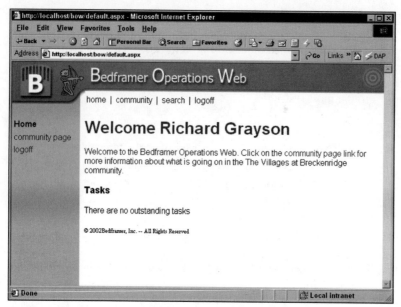

Figure 21-7: Menus when logged on as Richard Grayson.

When you are logged on as Richard Grayson, there are very few menu items that you have access to. If this were a real application, the maintenance man (Richard Grayson) would certainly be restricted more than the president (William Charles) of the company, but he would probably not be this restricted. The example is a bit exaggerated, but illustrates the point nicely.

The Census Page

One of the most important tasks for the Bedframer Operations Web is a daily accounting of all of the residents. This is done through the Daily Census. To ensure that the census is completed each day, every user is informed if the census for his or her primary community is still undone.

Showing the task

The Daily Census page is the page that most employees who regularly use the system will look at each day. It's where the status of the residents is placed. The first step is to look at the home page again. When the census is not done for the day, the home page has a Daily Census task, as shown in Figure 21-8.

The determination of whether the census has been done is made by running the Daily Census stored procedure to check for all items that have not been confirmed. If there are any that are unconfirmed, the Daily Census task shows up on the home page.

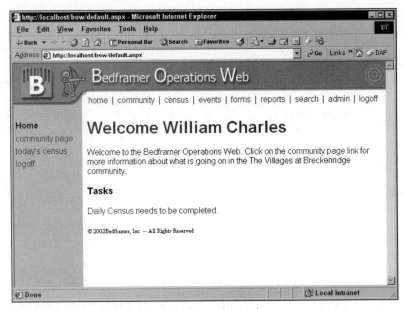

Figure 21-8: Home page when Daily Census is not done.

At some time in the future, other tasks will also appear on the front page, but the census is all for now. The code to determine if a census needs to be done for the day is shown in Listing 21-11. There are two bolded lines in the code sample. The first shows that I am using `ExecuteScalar()` to only return the first name of one of the residents, while the second shows where I test for NULL.

Listing 21-11: The Census Task Event

```
Protected Function GetTasks() As String

  Dim intCommunityID As Integer = Session("intCommunityID")
  Dim dtDate As Date = FormatDateTime(Date.Now, DateFormat.ShortDate)
  Dim strFirstName As String
  Dim bitConfirmed As Boolean = False

  Dim objConn As New SQLData.SqlConnection(Application("ConnectionString"))
  Dim objCmd As New SQLData.SqlCommand()

  With objCmd
    .CommandText = "sps_CensusByCommunity"
    .CommandType = CommandType.StoredProcedure
    .Connection = objConn
.Parameters.Add(New SQLData.SqlParameter("@intCommunityID", _
                SqlDbType.Int, 4, ParameterDirection.Input, False, _
```

Continued

Listing 21-11 *(Continued)*

```
    0, 0, "intCommunityID", DataRowVersion.Original, _
                intCommunityID))
    .Parameters.Add(New SQLData.SqlParameter("@dtDate", _
                SqlDbType.SmallDateTime, 4, ParameterDirection.Input, _
                False, 0, 0, "dtDate", DataRowVersion.Original, dtDate))
    .Parameters.Add(New SQLData.SqlParameter("@bitConfirmed", SqlDbType.Bit, _
                1, ParameterDirection.Input, True, 0, 0, "bitConfirmed",
                DataRowVersion.Original, bitConfirmed))
End With

Try
    objConn.Open()
    strFirstName = CType(objCmd.ExecuteScalar(), String)
    objConn.Close()

Catch objSQLException As SQLData.SqlException
    'TODO: Add SQL Server exception handler
Catch objException As Exception
    'TODO: Add generic exception handler
End Try

If IsDBNull(strFirstName) Then
    Return "There are no outstanding tasks."
Else
    Return "<a href=""census.aspx?dtDate=" & dtDate & """>Daily Census" & _
        "</a>" needs to be completed."
End If

End Function
```

The code from Listing 21-11 is on the companion Web site (www. wiley.com/extras) in this chapter's download file: Ch21-23VS.zip (Visual Studio .NET version) or Ch21-23SDDK.zip (SDK version). Look for default.aspx and its CodeBehind file, default.aspx.vb.

Here is a quick run-through of the code in Listing 21-11:

- I store today's date in a variable. I'll use this both for the stored procedure, as well as to create a link to the census if the stored procedure returns a value:

```
Dim dtDate As Date = FormatDateTime(Date.Now, _
DateFormat.ShortDate)
```

This format is a shortcut that is a throwback to Visual Basic 6 days. You can also use `Now()` method, which is an even greater throwback:

```
Dim dtDate as Date = FormatDateTime(Now, _
    DateFormat.ShortDate)
```

And, finally, you can actually create the `DateTime` structure and use the `Now` property:

```
Dim objDate as new System.DateTime(1,1,1)
Dim dtDate as Date = FormatDateTime(objDate.Now, _
    DateFormat.ShortDate)
```

In each case, I have added the `FormatDateTime()` function to make sure I am getting a short date returned. This is important since SQL Server returns nothing if I send the time in as well. Remember that a SQL Server datetime field stores a date sent in without a time as 1/1/01 00:00:00 AM, which equates to midnight on the date in question. When you send in a date without time to a stored procedure, it is converted in the same manner to compare against the field. Until Microsoft adds a separate date and time field, this is going to be the case.

◆ Create a connection object and a command object. In this example, I don't have to create a `DataAdapter`, `DataReader`, or `DataSet`, because only one value is returned.

```
Dim objConn As New _
  SQLData.SqlConnection(Application("ConnectionString"))
Dim objCmd As New SQLData.SqlCommand()
```

◆ Add parameters to the command object. In the stored procedure, I use the community ID, the date, and a Boolean for whether the census has been confirmed. In this instance, I only want to return those items that have not been confirmed, because the user confirms each person's status as he goes through the census. Here are the parameters:

```
With objCmd
  .Parameters.Add(New _
    SQLData.SqlParameter("@intCommunityID", _
    SqlDbType.Int, 4, ParameterDirection.Input, False, _
    0, 0, "intCommunityID", DataRowVersion.Original, _
    intCommunityID))
  .Parameters.Add(New SQLData.SqlParameter("@dtDate", _
    SqlDbType.SmallDateTime, 4, ParameterDirection.Input, _
    False, 0, 0, "dtDate", DataRowVersion.Original, dtDate))
  .Parameters.Add(New _
    SQLData.SqlParameter("@bitConfirmed", SqlDbType.Bit, _
    1, ParameterDirection.Input, True, 0, 0, _
    "bitConfirmed", DataRowVersion.Original, bitConfirmed))
End With
```

If I had written a separate stored procedure for this task, which I'd probably do except for the illustration of reuse of code, I'd only need the community ID passed, because the confirmation bit could always be set to 0 in the stored procedure (Boolean false in my Visual Basic .NET code) and the date could always be hard-coded to the current date.

◆ Because my only duty here is to check if there are any records, I use `ExecuteScalar` to return one value:

```
strFirstName = CType(objCmd.ExecuteScalar(), String)
```

◆ Finally, I check if the first name is empty. If it is, I add a link to the census page.

```
If IsDBNull(strFirstName) Then
  Return "There are no outstanding tasks."
Else
  Return "<a href=""census.aspx?dtDate=" & dtDate & """>" & _
          "Daily Census</a>" needs to be completed."
End If
```

As mentioned previously, the stored procedure used to create this page is not necessarily the most efficient. It would seem to be more efficient to write a stored procedure that simply returns a count of records. This is a fair assessment, but the code here was written to serve two purposes. The same stored procedure is used to create the complete census on the census page. With only one stored procedure to produce a census, or tell a user if there is a census, I have made an application that is easier to maintain. If I find I need a bit more performance, I can always alter this page to provide it.

Building the census page

It's fairly easy, following the logic in the home page, for you to develop your own census page, so I'm not going to take the time to explain everything about that page. I include this section to show how easy it is to reuse code by changing a couple of lines.

You already have a good deal of code for the census page. The stored procedure that creates the census page is the same stored procedure that helps you create the task hyperlink in Listing 21-11. The main difference here is you are going to use more than just a single value returned by `ExecuteScalar()`.

Listing 21-12 shows the code for the `RenderCensus()` subroutine. The changes from the `GetTasks` function are bolded.

Listing 21-12: The Routine to Render the Census

```
Protected Sub RenderCensus()

    Dim intCommunityID As Integer = Session("intCommunityID")
    Dim dtDate As Date = FormatDateTime(Date.Now, DateFormat.ShortDate)
    Dim strFirstName As String
```

```vb
Dim bitConfirmed As Boolean = False

Dim objConn As New SQLData.SqlConnection(Application("ConnectionString"))
Dim objCmd As New SQLData.SqlCommand()

With objCmd
    .CommandText = "sps_CensusByCommunity"
    .CommandType = CommandType.StoredProcedure
    .Connection = objConn
    .Parameters.Add(New SQLData.SqlParameter("@intCommunityID", _
    SqlDbType.Int, 4, ParameterDirection.Input, False, _
                  0, 0, "intCommunityID", DataRowVersion.Original, _
                  intCommunityID))
    .Parameters.Add(New SQLData.SqlParameter("@dtDate", _
                  SqlDbType.SmallDateTime, 4, ParameterDirection.Input, _
                  False, 0, 0, "dtDate", DataRowVersion.Original, dtDate))
    .Parameters.Add(New SQLData.SqlParameter("@bitConfirmed", SqlDbType.Bit, _
              1, ParameterDirection.Input, True, 0, 0, "bitConfirmed", _
              DataRowVersion.Original, bitConfirmed))
End With

Dim objDataReader As SQLData.SqlDataReader

Try
    objConn.Open()
    objDataReader = objCmd.ExecuteReader()
    objConn.Close()

Catch objSQLException As SQLData.SqlException
    'TODO: Add SQL Server exception handler
Catch objException As Exception
    'TODO: Add generic exception handler
End Try

dgCensus.DataSource = objDataReader
dgCensus.DataBind()


End Sub
```

You can find the code for Listing 21-12 on the companion Web site (www.wiley.com/extras) in the download file Ch21-23VS.zip (Visual Studio .NET version) or Ch21-23SDDK.zip (SDK version). Look for census.aspx and its CodeBehind file, census.aspx.vb.

As you can see in Listing 21-12, the only differences from the code in Listing 21-11 are as follows:

◆ I created a DataReader object to hold the data returned from the command object:

```
Dim objDataReader As SQLData.SQLDataReader
```

◆ I use ExecuteReader, as opposed to ExecuteScalar, to fill the DataReader object:

```
objDataReader = objCmd.ExecuteReader()
```

◆ The DataReader is bound to the DataGrid on the page, which I have named dgCensus:

```
dgCensus.DataSource = objDataReader
dgCensus.DataBind()
```

Summary

The intranet application for Bedframer Corporation centers on forms authentication, because different users use the same machine. In this chapter, I detailed the security model for the Bedframer. I also showed how each user is mapped only to sections he is able to see.

There is additional documentation for the Bedframer Operations Web, along with the code for the entire application, on this book's companion Web site.

In the next chapter, I expand on the Bedframer application by adding some XML and XSLT to render the look of the site. This functionality is then used in the extranet part of our project, in Chapter 23.

Chapter 22

Telling the World: An Internet Application

IN THIS CHAPTER

◆ Using XML, XSLT, and XHTML in .NET

◆ Adding content to a shell page using InnerXML and a Visual Basic Replace function

◆ Designing for reusability

THE PRIMARY FUNCTION OF THE INTERNET SITE for the Bedframer Corporation is to sell the company's services on the Web. Because each of Bedframer's facilities is a business, each facility has its own Web site. The purpose of this chapter is to show how a facility uses a template to build its site with XML and XSLT.

Building a Site with XSLT

The Bedframer Web sites are built using XML and XSLT. The XSLT for each site is stored in the database, and the menus are built using XML. The reasoning behind this architecture is largely driven by a desire to use one set of XSLT for both the facility site and for partner sites (covered in the next chapter). This chapter focuses on the Villages at Breckenridge, which is one of the many facilities that Bedframer owns.

Listing 22-1 shows the XSLT for this facility's Web site.

Listing 22-1: The XSLT for the Villages at Breckenridge

```
<xsl:stylesheet version="1.0" xmlns:xsl="http://www.w3.org/1999/XSL/Transform">
    <xsl:output method="xml" version="1.0" encoding="UTF-8" indent="yes"/>
<xsl:template match="/">
<html>
  <head>
    <!-- TODO: See if you can genericize the templates, by pulling
         title from XML -->
    <title>Villages at Breckenridge</title>
  </head>
```

Continued

Listing 22-1 *(Continued)*

```
<body topmargin="0" leftmargin="0" background="images/background.gif">
  <form id="Form1" method="post" runat="server">
<table border="0" cellpadding="0" cellspacing="0" width="100%">
  <tr>
    <td width="100%">
      <table border="0" cellpadding="0" cellspacing="0" width="100%">
        <tr>
          <td bgcolor="#637DC7" width="422" height="80">
            <img border="0" src="images/BreckenridgeLogo.gif" width="422"
            height="80" />
          </td>
          <td bgcolor="#637DC7" height="80"> </td>
        </tr>
      </table>
    </td>
  </tr>
  <tr>
    <td width="100%"><img border="0" src="images/clear.gif"
        width="100%" height="5" /></td>
  </tr>
  <tr>
    <td width="100%">
      <table border="0" cellpadding="2" width="100%">
        <tr>
          <td width="135">
    <xsl:for-each select="results/MenuItem">
      <A><xsl:attribute name="href">
            <xsl:value-of select="strMenuItemURL" />
        </xsl:attribute>
      <xsl:value-of select="strMenuItemName" />
      </A><br />
    </xsl:for-each>
    </td>
          <td id="content"><content /></td>
        </tr>
      </table>
    </td>
  </tr>
</table>
    </form>
  </body>
</html>
</xsl:template>
</xsl:stylesheet>
```

You can find the code for Listing 22-1 on the companion Web site (www.wiley.com/extras) in the file Ch22SDK.zip (SDK version) or Ch22VS.zip (Visual Studio .NET version). The name of the file to look at is test.xsl — it's the XSL that is loaded into the database for transformations.

As far as XSL goes, this is rather plain. To reiterate what you learned in Part IV of this book, let's run through a few points in the XSL:

◆ The first line of every XSL file is the `xsl:stylesheet` line. Presently, there is only one version: version 1.0. You must have a pointer to the namespace. Since this is an XSLT file, the namespace pointer is `http://www.w3.org/1999/XSL/Transform`. Here's the stylesheet tag:

```
<xsl:stylesheet version="1.0"
      xmlns:xsl="http://www.w3.org/1999/XSL/Transform">
```

◆ While not mandatory, it's a good idea to have an output tag. In this file, I set the output to `xml`, which will create an XHTML-compliant Web page. (I could have set this to `html` if I wanted a non-XHTML compliant Web page.) I also set the `indent` attribute to `yes` to make the output a bit easier to read. Here's the output line:

```
<xsl:output method="xml" version="1.0"
      encoding="UTF-8" indent="yes"/>
```

◆ I then start a template. I'd normally create a template for each branch, for finer-grained control of the elements, but there's only the root template in this document. Setting the match attribute to / indicates I am matching the root node in the XML document I'm transforming this XSL file against. Here's the template line:

```
<xsl:template match="/">
```

◆ The important part of the XSL is the portion that produces the side menu for this facility's site. Here's a snippet that produces one menu item:

```
<?xml version="1.0" encoding="UTF-8"?>
<results>
  <MenuItem>
    <strMenuItemURL>default.aspx</strMenuItemURL>
    <strMenuItemName>Home</strMenuItemName>
  </MenuItem>
</results>
```

The XSL that transforms this into a menu uses an `xsl:for-each` to traverse each `<MenuItem>` node and an `xsl:value-of` to output the value of each `<strMenuItemURL>` and `<strMenuItemName>` node:

```
<xsl:for-each select="results/MenuItem">
  <A><xsl:attribute name="href">
            <xsl:value-of select="strMenuItemURL" />
            </xsl:attribute>
  <xsl:value-of select="strMenuItemName" />
  </A><br />
</xsl:for-each>
```

As you look at the XSL, you'll notice a `<content />` tag in the middle of the page. This is going to be the focus of much of the remainder of this chapter. While the menu is part of the look of the site, the content changes from page to page and is dynamically rendered as each page is hit. The content for each page replaces the `<content />` tag. I'm going to show you a few ways to do this.

While spending an entire chapter on replacing a single tag may seem like overkill, I wanted to take time to contrast some methods to give you a bit of experience making architectural choices. Each of the choices presented here is a viable option in certain situations.

Version 1: Placing the contents inside the <content /> tag

The first method to place content into the Web page is to place the content inside of the `<content />` tag. To accomplish this, you programmatically retrieve the node for the `<content />` tag and use the `InnerXML` property to replace the text. As you'll see, this has some consequences, although it performs very well.

The reason for replacing the `InnerXML` of the `<content />` tag with our XML-driven content instead of the `InnerText` is that the text contains HTML markup, which is going set up as XHTML. If you use `InnerText`, the HTML tags are rendered as text, instead of as HTML, and show up in the page where the user can see them. This undesirable consequence is shown in Figure 22-1.

Oops! As you can see, this is not the effect we want, so I have to resort to using `InnerXML` to render the page properly. The code that produced this nightmare is shown in Listing 22-2. I am not going to explain the code now, because I break down the code to produce the content of the page completely as the chapter progresses. (The version of this code that uses `InnerXML` is in Listing 22-7. You might want to compare the two code listings.)

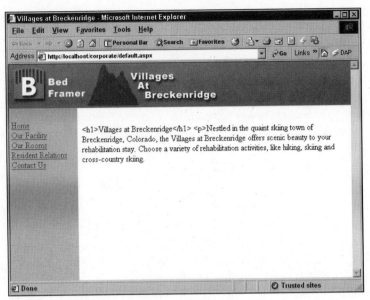

Figure 22-1: Using InnerText with HTML markup.

Listing 22-2: Code To Replace the <content/> Tag's InnertText

```
'Get the content node: node list to allow multiple content areas
Dim objNodeList As SysXML.XmlNodeList
objNodeList = objXSL.GetElementsByTagName("content")

'Replace the node
Dim objNode As SysXML.XmlNode = objNodeList.Item(0)
objNode.InnerText = strPageContent
```

For those of you who have never worked with InnerXML and InnerText before, here is a brief primer. (If you've worked with Dynamic HTML before, these two properties are pretty much identical to InnerHTML and InnerText in DHTML.)

InnerXML: The value you set this property to is assumed to be XML. Any markup tags are rendered as tags. In our example, these tags are treated as XHTML-compliant HTML tags.

InnerText: The value you set this property to is assumed to be text. Any markup tags are altered to render as text in the browser. For example, the < tag is changed to <.

The innerHTML (which is similar to InnerXML) and InnerText properties of container controls are explained in Chapter 7, in the section "Container Controls (HtmlContainerControl)."

Let's walk through the steps necessary to completely render the page using XML and replacing a tag with XHTML. I use XHTML here because any HTML I want to render must be able to pass through the XML parser. Remember that XHTML is always valid HTML, but not the other way around; the XML rules are stricter than the HTML rules.

GETTING THE XSL AND PAGE CONTENT

The first step in the process is retrieving the XSL (eXtensible Style Language), or rather XSLT (eXtensible Style Language for Transformations). In this application, the XSL is stored in a text field in the SQL Server database. If you're working with Access, a memo field is the same type of field.

I could, of course, get away with a very large varchar field, which would be more efficient. From experience, however, I find that the amount of XSLT stored in the database tends to grow rather than shrink. By starting with a text field to begin with, I don't have to worry about changing the database in the future. While the text data type is not as efficient as a varchar data type, the downside here is very small, because it's unlikely the XSLT will change.

To retrieve the XSL from the database, I use the same techniques you saw in the Part III of the book. The DataReader object, in this case a SQLDataReader, is used, because the site URL is being read as well. The same reader object will be reused to pull the XHTML page content.

In addition to reading the XSLT, I read the page content that will replace the content tag. The page content, as XSL, is placed into the database by whoever creates the page content. Listing 22-3 shows the portions of the code to retrieve the XSLT and page content XHTML.

Listing 22-3: Retrieving the XSL and the Page Content

```
Dim strChrome As String
Dim objConn As New SQLData.SqlConnection(Application("ConnectionString"))
Dim objCmd As New SQLData.SqlCommand()

With objCmd
    .CommandText = "sps_GetChrome"
    .CommandType = CommandType.StoredProcedure
    .Connection = objConn
    .Parameters.Add(New SQLData.SqlParameter("@intSiteID", SqlDbType.Int, _
                4, ParameterDirection.Input, False, 0, 0, "intSiteID", _
                DataRowVersion.Original, m_intSiteID))
End With
```

```vb
Dim objReader As SQLData.SqlDataReader
Dim strPageContent As String

Try
    objConn.Open()
    objReader = objCmd.ExecuteReader()

    'Get the chrome (XSLT) and the site URL
    While objReader.Read
        strChrome = objReader.GetString(0)
        strSiteURL = objReader.GetString(1)
    End While

    objReader.Close()

    objCmd.CommandText = "sps_PageContent"
    objCmd.Parameters.Add(New SQLData.SqlParameter("@intMenuItemID", _
                        SqlDbType.Int, 4, ParameterDirection.Input, False, _
                        0, 0, "intMenuItemID", DataRowVersion.Original, _
                        m_intPageID))
    objReader = objCmd.ExecuteReader()

    While objReader.Read
        strPageContent = objReader.GetString(0)
    End While

    'Load XSL from String
    Dim objXSL As New SysXML.XmlDocument()
    objXSL.LoadXml(strChrome)

    objReader.Close()
    objConn.Close()

Catch
    'TODO: Add error handler here
End Try
```

 You'll find the code for Listing 22-3 on the companion Web site (www.wiley.com/extras) in the file Ch22SDK.zip (SDK version) or Ch22VS.zip (Visual Studio .NET version). The code in Listing 22-3 is the core of the routines in each of the pages used for this chapter. Look for the file chrome.vb.

RETRIEVING THE XML

The next step is to retrieve the XML. This section is a bit more involved as some of the newer features of SQL Server 2000 are implemented. This portion cannot be done with an Access database, or at least not directly. If you have not used XML with SQL Server 2000, a bit of background is in order.

SQL Server is Microsoft's Relational DataBase Management System (RDBMS). Originally created in conjunction with Sybase, SQL Server became a Microsoft-only creation with SQL Server 7. With SQL Server 2000, Microsoft added XML select, insert, update, and delete capabilities to its flagship data server. Unfortunately, most of these features were poorly implemented when the product was released, which led to updates to the XML capabilities that have continued through the recent SQL Server XML release 2.

If you want to use XML with SQL Server, I recommend downloading the latest version of SQL XML. I have SQL XML version 2.0 loaded on my development machine, but SQL XML 3.0 should be out shortly after this book is released.

The basic retrieval of XML is done through the use of FOR XML keywords, as shown in Listing 22-4.

Listing 22-4: The XML Stored Procedure

```
CREATE PROCEDURE sps_MenuBySite_XML
(
    @intSiteID    int
)
AS

SELECT
    strMenuItemName,
    strMenuItemURL
FROM
    tblMenuItem MenuItem
JOIN
    tblSiteMenuItemAssoc smia
ON
    MenuItem.intMenuItemID = smia.intMenuItemID
WHERE
    smia.intSiteID = @intSiteID
ORDER BY
    smia.intOrder
FOR XML AUTO, ELEMENTS

GO
```

You can find the code for Listing 22-4 on the companion Web site (www.wiley.com/extras) in the download file Ch22SDK.zip (SDK version) or Ch22VS.zip (Visual Studio .NET version). After unzipping, open the file sps_MenuBySite_XML.sql. Running this query returns the results from Listing 22-5, shown later in the chapter.

Looking at the code, you can see that the stored procedure looks pretty much the same as a stored procedure to return data for a dataset. The major difference here is the last line of the SELECT statement: FOR XML AUTO, ELEMENTS.

When you use FOR XML AUTO, the tags are named after the objects in the query, namely the table(s) and column(s). If you drop the ELEMENTS keyword, all of the columns will be attributes instead of elements.

Although FOR XML SQL clause was covered in detail in Part IV, a bit of a review is in order to better understand the choices made in this chapter. For each of the examples in the list, I use the Northwind database. I'll use the following query:

```
SELECT CustomerID, CompanyName, ContactName, Phone FROM Customers
 WHERE CustomerID LIKE 'AN%'FOR XML [AUTO|RAW]
```

The only thing that changes from item to item is the FOR XML portion of the query.

◆ **FOR XML RAW:** If you want a consistent output format to your queries, use FOR XML RAW. Regardless of the table you are pulling your output from, the output always uses the tag name row:

```
<row CustomerID="ANATR"
CompanyName="Ana Trujillo Emparedados y helados"
ContactName="Ana Trujillo" Phone="(5) 555-4729"/>
<row CustomerID="ANTON" CompanyName="Antonio Moreno Taquerкa"
ContactName="Antonio Moreno" Phone="(5) 555-3932"/>
```

◆ **FOR XML AUTO:** If you want to label your output with the name of table it comes from, use FOR XML AUTO. I personally find this option more useful than FOR XML RAW in most queries, because it's difficult to create a truly generic routine to handle all of your XML needs. The only difference between the FOR XML AUTO and the FOR XML RAW examples is the tag name the rows are contained in: row versus Customers. Here's the output of FOR XML AUTO:

```
<Customers CustomerID="ANATR"
CompanyName="Ana Trujillo Emparedados y helados"
ContactName="Ana Trujillo" Phone="(5) 555-4729"/>
<Customers CustomerID="ANTON"
CompanyName="Antonio Moreno Taquerka"
ContactName="Antonio Moreno" Phone="(5) 555-3932"/>
```

◆ ELEMENTS: The ELEMENTS keyword can only be used with a FOR XML AUTO query; you cannot use ELEMENTS with FOR XML RAW. I find elements the most useful, because it's human readable. The output of FOR XML AUTO, ELEMENTS is shown here:

```
<Customers>
  <CustomerID>ANATR</CustomerID>
  <CompanyName>Ana Trujillo Emparedados y
helados</CompanyName>
  <ContactName>Ana Trujillo</ContactName>
  <Phone>(5) 555-4729</Phone>
</Customers>
<Customers>
  <CustomerID>ANTON</CustomerID>
  <CompanyName>Antonio Moreno Taquerka</CompanyName>
  <ContactName>Antonio Moreno</ContactName>
  <Phone>(5) 555-3932</Phone>
</Customers>
```

As previously mentioned, I like to make XML a bit more human-readable (and therefore easier to maintain), so I prefer to stick with elements. Note, however, that using attributes gives a slight performance advantage over elements, at least for the time being. If you are using elements and find that your application needs a slight boost, try using attributes instead and then compare the amount of load the application can bear.

The output of this stored procedure, shown in Listing 22-5, illustrates how SQL Server 2000 is geared toward XML templates under IIS. Check out the XML returned; see if you notice anything wrong.

Listing 22-5: The XML Output of the Stored Procedure

```
<MenuItem>
    <strMenuItemName>Home</strMenuItemName>
    <strMenuItemURL>default.aspx</strMenuItemURL>
</MenuItem>
<MenuItem>
    <strMenuItemName>Our Facility</strMenuItemName>
    <strMenuItemURL>facility.aspx</strMenuItemURL>
</MenuItem>
```

```
<MenuItem>
    <strMenuItemName>Our Rooms</strMenuItemName>
    <strMenuItemURL>rooms.aspx</strMenuItemURL>
</MenuItem>
<MenuItem>
    <strMenuItemName>Resident Relations</strMenuItemName>
    <strMenuItemURL>resident.aspx</strMenuItemURL>
</MenuItem>
<MenuItem>
    <strMenuItemName>Contact Us</strMenuItemName>
    <strMenuItemURL>contact.aspx</strMenuItemURL>
</MenuItem>
```

Did you catch anything wrong with the XML returned? Here's a hint: Think about the root element.

In XML, you can have only one root element, but the XML output shown in Listing 22-5 has five (or none, if you don't consider MenuItem a root element). If you were to run this XML through an XML validator, you would find that it is not well formed. You have to add some form of root tags to the XML string released by SQL Server, as shown in Listing 22-6. There are other ways to do this as well, but this method is rather simple to implement.

Listing 22–6: Placing XML into the String

```
objCmd.CommandText = "sps_MenuBySite_XML"
objReader = objCmd.ExecuteReader()

While objReader.Read
    strXML = "<results>" & objReader.GetString(0) & "</results>"
End While
```

I added a <results> tag to each end of the XML string produced by the stored procedure to make a valid XML string and allow this string to be loaded into an XML Document object.

If you're asking, "What's up with that?" I reiterate: Microsoft seems to have focused XML retrieval toward Internet Information Server (IIS) and templates instead of retrieval through components. After I finish with the rest of the code for this page, I'll cover retrieval of well-formed XML using IIS. While you can opt to use the IIS method of XML data retrieval in your application, the addition of a root tag is, in many ways, more efficient, because it does not require retrieval from a Web server.

REPLACING THE <CONTENT /> TAG

After retrieving the XSLT, XHTML page content, and the XML for the menu, the only thing left to do is work with the XML objects is to render the page. Since the page content is XHTML, it makes much more sense to replace the content prior to transforming the XML with XSLT.

To do this, I use an XML node list. As I only have one node to replace, I could have chosen to retrieve a single node instead. The reasoning for not doing this, however, is to maintain the ability to have multiple content tags, each with a different ID attribute. While I have not implemented multiple content sections in this application, there is a possibility, especially with partners involved. I cover partner implementation, through Web services, in the next chapter.

Listing 22-7 shows the code to fill the single content tag with the XHTML page content.

Listing 22-7: Merging XHTML and XSLT

```
'Get the content node: node list to allow multiple content areas
Dim objNodeList As SysXML.XmlNodeList
objNodeList = objXSL.GetElementsByTagName("content")

'Replace the node
Dim objNode As SysXML.XmlNode = objNodeList.Item(0)
objNode.InnerXml = strPageContent
```

 You can find the code for Listing 22-7 on the companion Web site (www.wiley.com/extras) in the file Ch22SDK.zip (SDK version) or Ch22VS.zip (Visual Studio .NET version). After unzipping, open the file InnerXML.aspx.vb.

As mentioned earlier, I simply replace the InnerXML of the `<content />` tag. Since there is only one `<content />` tag in the XSLT for this exercise, I simply grab Item(0) of my node list. Overall, this is a fairly simple solution that works well as long as the HTML used to replace the tag is well-formed XHTML.

TRANSFORMING THE XML WITH XSLT

The next step to render the page is taking the XML and XSLT and transforming to create well-formed HTML (XHTML). To transform the XML, the XSL object is placed into an XML node reader object, which is then loaded into a transform object. The XML object is loaded into the same transform object along with a string writer object that will contain the transformed XHTML.

Now all I need to do is create the output string. This is unnecessary for this particular example, but will make the next version much easier to create. I could have used the objStringBuilder.ToString() in the Write method of the Response object. Instead, I put the output into a variable, strOutput, because I am going to want to replace the `<content/>` tag at some point; replacing this tag is a more straightforward if I use a variable for the result of the transformation. Listing 22-8 shows the code for this transformation.

Listing 22-8: Transforming XML with XSLT

```
'Create a Reader for XSL and a Navigator for XML
Dim objXSLReader As New SysXML.XmlNodeReader(objXSL)

'Create a tranform object
Dim objXSLTransform As New SysXSL.XslTransform()
objXSLTransform.Load(objXSLReader)

'Set up String Builder and String Writer for Output
Dim objStringBuilder As New SysText.StringBuilder()
Dim objStringWriter As New SysIO.StringWriter(objStringBuilder)

objXSLTransform.Transform(objXML, Nothing, objStringWriter)

Dim strOutput As String
strOutput = objStringBuilder.ToString()

Response.Write(strOutput)
```

 You can find the code for Listing 22-8 on the companion Web site (www.wiley.com/extras) in the file Ch22SDK.zip (SDK version) or Ch22VS.zip (Visual Studio .NET version). After unzipping, open the file Default.aspx.vb.

There are other ways — in fact, a great many ways — to work with XML in .NET. Most of the methods of working with XML, however, require saving the result out to a file. While this is certainly useful in some situations, I find streaming the output directly to the client browser to be more the norm. The fully rendered page is shown in Figure 22-2.

Version 2: Using a Replace method

I prefer version 1 as the primary method of placing the page content inside of the pages of the Bedframer site. The one potential downside I can see is when someone creates non-XHTML–compliant HTML, such as that in Listing 22-9, to place into the page.

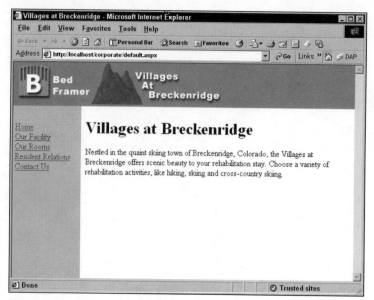

Figure 22-2: The page fully rendered.

Listing 22-9: Non-XHTML–Compliant HTML

```
<h1>Villages at Breckenridge</h1>
<p>Nestled in the quaint skiing town of Breckenridge,
Colorado, the Villages at Breckenridge offers scenic
beauty to your rehabilitation stay. Choose a variety
of rehabilitation activities, like hiking, skiing and
cross-country skiing.
```

The problem with the HTML is the lack of the </p> tag. Most browsers overlook this oversight and render the page. An XML application, however, must conform to the rules. The missing </p> tag should cause an error to be thrown when the transformation is attempted. When it is run, you get the page shown in Figure 22-2.

Wait, there is no error there; the page looks exactly the same way it did in the prior example. Listing 22-10 shows why.

Listing 22-10: Outputting the <content> Section

```
<content>
  <h1>Villages at Breckenridge</h1>
  <p>Nestled in the quaint skiing town of Breckenridge, Colorado, the Villages
    at Breckenridge offers scenic beauty to your rehabilitation stay. Choose a
    variety of rehabilitation activities, like hiking, skiing and cross-country
    skiing.</p>
</content>
```

What happened is that Microsoft, in its wisdom, saw fit to close out the <p> tag, and mess up what otherwise would have been a great example.

Now, while this may seem wonderful, it is "foresight" like this that leads developers into a false sense of security. It also can potentially lead to bad output. Table 22-1 highlights a few examples that I have seen placed into applications of this nature. Most of these examples of bad HTML render without problems in Internet Explorer, but produce horrible HTML.

TABLE 22-1 BAD HTML AND INNERXML

Test	HTML	Output

Image Tag	```<img src="images/```
	```freedom.gif">```
	```<p>This is a sample```
	```paragraph</p>```
		```<img src="images/```
		```freedom.gif">```
		```<p>This is a sample```
		```paragraph</p>```
		```</img>```

List	```<ul>```
	```<li>List Item 1```
	```<li>List Item```
	```</ul>```
		```ERROR:```
		```System.Xml.XmlException:```
		```This is an unexpected token.```
		```Expected 'EndElement'.```

Table	```<table><tr>```
	```<td>This is a test</td>```
	```</tr>```
		```ERROR:```
		```System.Xml.XmlException:```
		```This is an unexpected token.```
		```Expected 'EndElement'.```

Break #1	```<p>This is line 1
	``
	```This is line 2</p>```
		```ERROR:```
		```System.Xml.XmlException: The```
		```'br' start tag on line '1'```
		```does not match the end tag```
		```of 'p'.```

Break #2	```<p>This is line 1
	``
	``<p>This is line 1
	``
		```This is line 2```
		```This is line 2</br></p>```

One of three things happens when you place bad HTML into the application:

1. The page errors out. This, in my opinion, is the only proper response because there is no way, without over-engineering .NET, to cover every applicable error condition. To attempt to "correct" the XML leads to inconsistency. It also paints the developer into a box.

2. The resulting HTML is incorrect. You can see this in the image tag output example in Table 22-1. The paragraph is completely contained inside of the image tag. While this is not a problem with Internet Explorer, it is not the desired result.

3. The XML parser gets lucky and produces correct HTML. This is what happened in the paragraph tag example (Listing 22-9).

Since the output of the Microsoft .NET XML components is inconsistent, you should think twice before developing this type of application without extensive error handling. Any time a content developer creates non-XHTML–compliant HTML, you'll probably end up with errors.

I mentioned this to a colleague who stated that you could just make sure that the HTML from the content writers was produced using a tool rather than by hand: The content writer creates the copy, places it in FrontPage, and FrontPage straightens out the code. I see two problems with this suggestion:

◆ The only version of FrontPage that produces well-formed HTML is FrontPage 2002 (or XP). In order to get this level of compliancy, you have to tell the program you want XHTML, because this is not a default way in which FrontPage handles HTML.

◆ This could potentially lead to some very heavy code. If you haven't copied from Microsoft Word to FrontPage lately, you should try it. All of the XML coding to render properly in Word is copied to FrontPage. Here's our simple paragraph when taken from Word:

```
<h1>Villages at Breckenridge<o:p></o:p></h1>
<span style="font-size:12.0pt;font-family:&quot;
Times New Roman&quot;;mso-fareast-font-family:
&quot;Times New Roman&quot;;mso-ansi-language:
EN-US;mso-fareast-language:EN-US;
mso-bidi-language:AR-SA">Nestled in the quaint skiing town
of Breckenridge, Colorado, the Villages at Breckenridge
offers scenic beauty to your rehabilitation stay. Choose
a variety of rehabilitation activities, like hiking,
skiing and cross-country skiing.</span>
```

In case you're wondering, this example is very light on XML compared to many of the samples I've seen since Office 2000 hit the scene.

Now that I have carried on for a while on the dangers of HTML that is not well formed, I have to show the solution to this problem. To avoid XML errors, or bad XHTML output, strip out the section that replaces the InnerXML of the <content> tag and replace the content tag instead. Listing 22-11 shows the line of code necessary.

Listing 22-11: Altered Code to Use the Replace Method

```
strOutput = Replace(strOutput, "<content />", strPageContent)
```

You can find the code for Listing 22-11 on the companion Web site (www.wiley.com/extras) in the file Ch22SDK.zip (SDK version) or Ch22VS.zip (Visual Studio .NET version). After unzipping, open the file ReplaceMethod.aspx.vb.

This is not necessarily the best way to handle every situation, but it works well when you cannot ensure that the person responsible for the content will always produce XHTML-compliant content. The downside of this method is that it is not the most efficient routine. However, it is unlikely it will rock your world too much if you can replace one string, as Listing 22-11 shows.

The code in Listing 22-11 is nothing new. Unlike the XML <content /> replacement example (Listing 22-7), you can accomplish the same thing in traditional ASP or Visual Basic 6.

Version 3: Coding in a function

Since the same logic is going to be used for each page, it makes sense to move the code for the rendering of a page to a function. Then each page can call the same method to render the page through the use of a couple of parameters.

As you think about the application, you can easily determine which items should be parameters for your new class. Site ID and Page ID are obvious choices, because you will alter the look and content based on these two items. To make the function a bit more generic, I also pass in the connection string.

The only other change that needs to be made so that the method can be used on each page is to return the string created instead of writing it out to the HTTP string. The resulting function is shown in Listing 22-12.

Listing 22-12: The GetLook() Method

```
Public Function GetLook(ByVal intSiteID As Integer, _
    ByVal intPageID As Integer, _
    ByVal strConn As String) As String

    Dim strChrome As String
```

Continued

Listing 22–12 *(Continued)*

```vb
Dim objConn As New SQLData.SqlConnection(strConn)
Dim objCmd As New SQLData.SqlCommand()

With objCmd
    .CommandText = "sps_GetChrome"
    .CommandType = CommandType.StoredProcedure
    .Connection = objConn
    .Parameters.Add(New SQLData.SqlParameter("@intSiteID", SqlDbType.Int, _
                    4, ParameterDirection.Input, False, 0, 0, "intSiteID", _
                    DataRowVersion.Original, intSiteID))
End With

Dim objReader As SQLData.SqlDataReader
Dim strSiteURL As String
Dim strXML As String
Dim strPageContent As String
Dim strHTML As String

Try
    objConn.Open()
    objReader = objCmd.ExecuteReader()

    While objReader.Read
        strChrome = objReader.GetString(0)
        strSiteURL = objReader.GetString(1)
    End While

    objReader.Close()

    objCmd.CommandText = "sps_MenuBySite_XML"
    objReader = objCmd.ExecuteReader()

    While objReader.Read
        strXML = "<results>" & objReader.GetString(0) & "</results>"
    End While

    objReader.Close()

    objCmd.CommandText = "sps_PageContent"
    objCmd.Parameters.Add(New SQLData.SqlParameter("@intMenuItemID", _
                    SqlDbType.Int, 4, ParameterDirection.Input, _
                    False, 0, 0, "intMenuItemID", _
                    DataRowVersion.Original, intPageID))
    objReader = objCmd.ExecuteReader()
```

```vbnet
While objReader.Read
    strPageContent = objReader.GetString(0)
End While

objReader.Close()
objConn.Close()

'Load XML from String
Dim objXML As New SysXML.XmlDocument()
objXML.LoadXml(strXML)

'Load XSL from String
Dim objXSL As New SysXML.XmlDocument()
objXSL.LoadXml(strChrome)

'Create a Reader for XSL and a Navigator for XML
Dim objXSLReader As New SysXML.XmlNodeReader(objXSL)

'Create a tranform object
Dim objXSLTransform As New SysXSL.XslTransform()
objXSLTransform.Load(objXSLReader)

'Set up String Builder and String Writer for Output
Dim objStringBuilder As New SysText.StringBuilder()
Dim objStringWriter As New SysIO.StringWriter(objStringBuilder)

objXSLTransform.Transform(objXML, Nothing, objStringWriter)

'To use outside of the If, must be declared outside
Dim strOutput As String

If intPageID <> 0 Then
    strOutput = Replace(objStringBuilder.ToString(), _
                        "<content />", strPageContent)
End If

GetLook = strOutput

Catch objXMLException As SysXML.XmlException
    GetLook = objXMLException.ToString()
Catch objSQLException As SQLData.SqlException

Catch objException As Exception
```

Continued

Listing 22-12 *(Continued)*

```
      'TODO: Add error handler
      GetLook = objException.ToString()
   End Try


End Function
```

 You can find the code for Listing 22-12 on the companion Web site (www.wiley.com/extras) in the file Ch22SDK.zip (SDK version) or Ch22VS.zip (Visual Studio .NET version). After unzipping, open the file usingFunction.aspx.vb.

I expand this example in the next chapter, when I move the GetLook() method to a class of its own.

Notice that I made the Replace so it happens only if the page ID does not equal 0. The reasoning behind this will make more sense in the next chapter when the look of the Web site is fed to a partner site through a Web service.

Summary

In this chapter, I took you through methods whereby you can easily change the look of a site, and showed you two methods of adding content to the rendered page using XML, XSLT, and XHTML.

Chapter 23 builds on this by revealing a method to share a Web site's look with partner sites. In order to accomplish this, all of the code is migrated to a class file.

Chapter 23

Partnering and Portals: An Extranet through XML Web Services

IN THIS CHAPTER

◆ Creating a portal interface

◆ Offering the look of a site as a Web service.

◆ Creating partner pages in ASP.NET

WEB PORTALS ALLOW A SITE to offer a user a variety of products and services without having to create all of the content. This is wise, because a company cannot be expert in all fields.

The Bedframer corporation has been working hard with a variety of partners to add content to its facilities' Web sites. The only item of concern is informing the users of which partner site they are actually on. To solve this problem, I'm taking the concept of creating the look of a site dynamically and expanding it to an extranet situation. I'll use a Web service to deliver the look and feel of the Bedframer facility sites to a partner site. With the look maintained, the average user won't realize he has switched sites.

Making a Portal

As the Internet grows, more and more companies are building portal sites. This includes businesses partnering with companies that can provide additional services to their clients. In some instances, a company purchases other companies outright. It is more common, however, to either purchase services from companies or send your users to their sites, which maintain the look and feel of your site.

Prior to the advent of the Simple Object Access Protocol (SOAP), maintaining the look and feel was a matter of sending a file to your partner site every time you made a significant change to the look, and coordinating with the partner when the site change went live. While this system works, it gets more and more time consuming as you pick up additional partners.

Overview of Bedframer's partnering

A few months ago, Bedframer foresaw the potential of the Internet to expand into new avenues of commerce through its Web site. Because its residents routinely receive gifts from friends and relatives around the world, Bedframer figured it could tap into the get-well gift and flower market. The company had already planned to introduce the capability for friends and family to send messages to residents, so flowers and gifts seemed like a perfect tie-in.

Unfortunately, Bedframer's own gift and flower operation was not a great success. Unprepared for the waste, and because it was not a core business, management determined that it was better to outsource the flowers and gifts rather than continue to pour money into a losing venture. Bedframer picked a partner that was willing to work with the company to maintain the look and feel of each of its sites.

The problem with outsourcing became apparent very quickly. Every time Bedframer updated the look of its Web sites, its partner's Web site was out of sync until it also updated the HTML that comprised this look. This was further compounded when facilities convinced corporate management that the Bedframer look did not work with all sites. With the addition of a new look for each facility's site, trying to coordinate changes in the look was becoming painful.

Recently, William Charles, the Bedframer president, went to the IT department to see if something could be done to reduce the costs associated with changing the look of a facility site. He wanted a system that automated the change on both the Bedframer and the partner sites.

The implementation

The Bedframer implementation of a partner interface is designed so that when a partner URL is accessed, a last-updated date and a site ID (for the facility) are passed to the partner site on the query string. The partner site then compares these to a database cache on its side. If the date passed is newer than the cached date, the partner application contacts the Bedframer site to request the latest look.

To get the latest look, the partner site passes the date it last cached the look, along with the partner ID it is associated with and the ID of the site it wants to retrieve. The Bedframer site then returns the newer look as an XHTML file.

CREATING A CLASS LIBRARY

To best utilize the code we developed in the last chapter, I put the code for the transformation into a class library project. If you would like to follow the same steps, create a new project and choose Class Library. The code for the transformation, minus the replace() function, is moved to this new class library inside a method called GetLook(), as shown in Listing 23-1. Name this class Chrome, to match the naming convention used throughout this chapter.

Listing 23-1: The Method inside the Class Library (Chrome.vb)

```vb
Public Function GetLook(ByVal intSiteID As Integer, _
                        ByVal intPageID As Integer, _
                        ByVal strConn As String) As String
    Dim strChrome As String
    Dim objConn As New SQLData.SqlConnection(strConn)
    Dim objCmd As New SQLData.SqlCommand()

    With objCmd
        .CommandText = "sps_GetChrome"
        .CommandType = CommandType.StoredProcedure
        .Connection = objConn
        .Parameters.Add(New SQLData.SqlParameter("@intSiteID", SqlDbType.Int, _
                        4, ParameterDirection.Input, False, 0, 0, "intSiteID", _
                        DataRowVersion.Original, intSiteID))
    End With

    Dim objReader As SQLData.SqlDataReader
    Dim strSiteURL As String
    Dim strXML As String
    Dim strPageContent As String
    Dim strHTML As String

    Try
        objConn.Open()
        objReader = objCmd.ExecuteReader()

        While objReader.Read
            strChrome = objReader.GetString(0)
            strSiteURL = objReader.GetString(1)
        End While

        objReader.Close()

        objCmd.CommandText = "sps_MenuBySite_XML"
        objReader = objCmd.ExecuteReader()

        While objReader.Read
            strXML = "<results>" & objReader.GetString(0) & "</results>"
        End While

        objReader.Close()

        objCmd.CommandText = "sps_PageContent"
```

Continued

Listing 23-1 *(Continued)*

```
        objCmd.Parameters.Add(New SQLData.SqlParameter("@intMenuItemID", _
                         SqlDbType.Int, 4, ParameterDirection.Input, _
                         False, 0, 0, "intMenuItemID", _
                         DataRowVersion.Original, intPageID))
        objReader = objCmd.ExecuteReader()

        While objReader.Read
            strPageContent = objReader.GetString(0)
        End While

        objReader.Close()
        objConn.Close()

        'Load XML from String
        Dim objXML As New SysXML.XmlDocument()
        objXML.LoadXml(strXML)

        'Load XSL from String
        Dim objXSL As New SysXML.XmlDocument()
        objXSL.LoadXml(strChrome)

        'Create a Reader for XSL and a Navigator for XML
        Dim objXSLReader As New SysXML.XmlNodeReader(objXSL)

        'Create a tranform object
        Dim objXSLTransform As New SysXSL.XslTransform()
        objXSLTransform.Load(objXSLReader)

        'Set up String Builder and String Writer for Output
        Dim objStringBuilder As New SysText.StringBuilder()
        Dim objStringWriter As New SysIO.StringWriter(objStringBuilder)

        objXSLTransform.Transform(objXML, Nothing, objStringWriter)

        'To use outside of the If, must be declared outside
        Dim strOutput As String

        If intPageID <> 0 Then
            strOutput = Replace(objStringBuilder.ToString(), "<content />", _
                         strPageContent)
        End If

        GetLook = strOutput
```

```
    Catch objXMLException As SysXML.XmlException
        GetLook = objXMLException.ToString()
    Catch objSQLException As SQLData.SqlException
        'TODO: Handle SQL exception
    Catch objException As Exception
        'TODO: Add error handler
        GetLook = objException.ToString()
    End Try
End Function
```

 You can find the code for the Chrome class on this book's companion Web site (www.wiley.com/extras) in the file Ch21-23SDK.zip (the SDK version) or Ch21-23VS.zip (the Visual Studio .NET version). The code is contained in the file Chrome.vb.

In all likelihood, knowing that the code would be implemented as a Web service, I would have created a Web service project instead of a class library, but I wanted to illustrate how easy it is to create a Web service from any class you create.

THE WEB SERVICE

The implementation of the interface is through a Web service. The actual routine is the same routine used to create the Web site. The only difference is that the XHTML produced is for external rather than internal consumption. You'll recall from the last chapter that a variable named strURL was presented in the GetLook() method, but never used. The internal workings of this method have to be changed slightly to use this URL (strURL) now. In order to facilitate the use of the URL, the GetLook() method of the Chrome class has to be altered to become a Web method, and there are a couple of ways to do that. The easiest is to create a Web service that calls the class created in the last chapter.

OPTION 1: CALL THE CHROME OBJECT   To create the Web service in the quickest manner, copy the function declaration for GetLook() from the Chrome class in the Chrome.vb file; get rid of the Connection string argument. The method of calling the Chrome class is shown in Listing 23-2.

Listing 23-2: The GetLook() Web Service (Simple)

```
<WebMethod()> Public Function GetLook(ByVal intSiteID As Integer, __
ByVal intPageID As Integer) As String
    'Call the Chrome.GetLook method
    Dim objLook As New Chrome()
    Return objLook.GetLook(intSiteID, intPageID, _
```

Continued

Listing 23-2 *(Continued)*

```
                    Application("ConnectionString"))

End Function
```

 You can download the code for the page in Listing 23-2 from this book's companion Web site (www.wiley.com/extras). Choose the file Ch21-23SDK.zip (the SDK version) or Ch21-23VS.zip (the Visual Studio .NET version). The implementation of this page is found in the file ChromeService.asmx.vb.

Those of you familiar with Visual Basic most likely have experience building a class, followed by a test standard EXE, and finally by an ASP page that calls the component. ASP.NET uses a compiled language, so you don't have to bounce back and forth between tools. The following steps show you how to create the Web service in ASP.NET:

1. Build the page with the code. This page is responsible for grabbing the look from the database and rendering it for the user. Chapter 22 was devoted to creating a page that accomplishes this.

2. Migrate the code to render the look to function in a vb class file. This migration provides a lot of flexibility, because the class can be moved to any number of project types. (We accomplished this step with the Chrome.vb file in the last chapter—see Listing 22-11.)

3. Create a Web service (ASMX page) and migrate the code from the Listing 23-2 to the Web service. If you download the code from the companion site, there is a code snippet for Listing 23-2 in the snippets directory.

Another way to create the Bedframer Web service is to create a new Web service file and copy the code to this file.

OPTION 2: A WEB SERVICE WITHOUT A SEPARATE CLASS LIBRARY   If you're not going to use the function in other applications, there is a better option. Rather than create a separate class file to hold the GetLook() method and calling it from a page, place the GetLook() method in a Web service from the start.

Now, you may be wondering, "If I build a Web service, how do I contact it from my ASPX page?" Remember that everything in .NET is an object. The Web service is nothing but a class file that has a bit of special plumbing. This means you can call a Web method from your local application without calling it as an XML Web service. Because ASP.NET compiles all files, you can call the GetLook() function locally no matter where you place it.

In Listing 23-1, I placed the GetLook() method in a class file and later called it from a Web service. Listing 23-3 shows the only change I make for that method to be placed directly in a Web service. The bolded attribute is the change necessary to make a Web method out of a subroutine or function.

Listing 23-3: The LookService Web Service

```
<WebMethod()> Public Function GetLook(ByVal intSiteID As Integer, _
                            ByVal intPageID As Integer) As String
    'Snipped rest of code from list 23-1
End Function
```

 You can download the code for the LookService Web service from this book's companion Web site (www.wiley.com/extras). Look for the file Ch21-23SDK.zip (the SDK version) or Ch21-23VS.zip (the Visual Studio .NET version). The implementation for this page is in the file LookService.asmx.vb.

As you can see, this function is nearly identical to the function in Listing 23-1. The only exception is that the connection string is pulled from an application variable instead of being passed in as a parameter. Because this is a Web service, it should be fairly obvious why I would do this: who would want to reveal the keys to his database to each person who consumed his service?

The only other change is that the GetLook() method now has the <WebMethod()> attribute. The code in Listing 23-4 is exactly like Listing 23-2 except it calls the Chrome class instead of the LookService class to finish its work.

To get the information out of the Web service without creating a class to consume the service, you simply instantiate the LookService class in the application and call the GetLook() method, as shown in Listing 23-4.

Listing 23-4: Calling the GetLook() Method

```
Private m_intSiteID As Integer = 1
Private m_intPageID As Integer = 1

Private Sub Page_Load(ByVal sender As System.Object, _
        ByVal e As System.EventArgs) Handles MyBase.Load
    Dim objChrome As New LookService()

    Response.Write(objChrome.GetLook(m_intSiteID, m_intPageID))
End Sub
```

In the "Consuming the Web Service" section later in this chapter, I cover the steps necessary to consume the Web service across the Internet.

The most important thing for you to understand at this point is that a Web service is nothing more than a normal class with some plumbing built in so it can be used as a Web service.

OPTION 3: CHANGING THE CLASS INTO A WEB SERVICE   The final method is a bit of a bastardization of the previous two methods. As you know, you can turn any method, in any component, into a Web method by adding a single attribute. In addition, you have to make a couple of changes to your class file to accomplish this:

◆ Inherit the WebService class in the System.Web.Services namespace.

◆ Add a constructor, or a `New()` method, which calls `MyBase.New()`.

While Microsoft has pushed out some press on how every method can easily become a Web method, there are dangers in this method (as shown in this section). Since the Web service file is compiled, you should not see a lot of additional weight if you go this route. And, it is quite a bit safer.

The changes to the `Chrome.vb` class file are shown in Listing 23-5.

Listing 23-5: Changes Made to the Chrome.vb File

```
Inherits System.Web.Services.WebService

Public Sub New()
    MyBase.New()
End Sub
```

If you are using the `Chrome` class in other pages or applications, you will still be able to use this class. The fact that the `GetLook()` method is now a Web method does not change its accessibility by other means, nor does the addition of the preceding code. This may sound like a broken record, but it is important to understand that adding additional means of accessing the methods in a class doesn't mean you cannot access it through "normal" means.

Now you have created the Web method and built the application. You type in **http://localhost/corporate/bin/corporate.dll?WSDL** and you end with the screen shown in Figure 23-1.

A read error? Okay, that one is easy to solve. Browse to the directory in the Internet Services Manager and allow read access, right? Wonderful solution, if you want to expose your code. Take a look at Figure 23-2 to see what I mean.

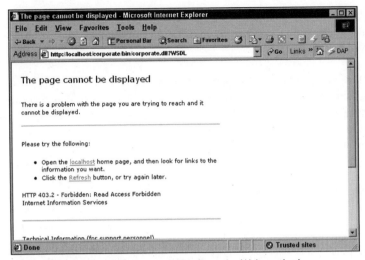

Figure 23-1: Error trying to get WSDL from the Web method.

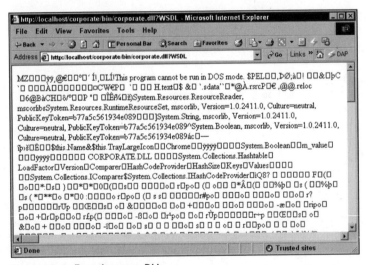

Figure 23-2: Exposing your DLL.

The better way to solve this error is to create a simple ASMX file (Web service) that uses the Chrome class (see Listing 23-6). This in and of itself is a bit of fun if you're using Visual Studio .NET. By default, the new Web service file has no user interface, so you can't open the code in a designer and change the single tag in the Web service (the actual ASMX file). Instead, you open the ASMX file in Notepad and edit the top line, as shown in Listing 23-6.

Listing 23-6: The ASMX File That Calls the Web Method

```
<%@ WebService Language="vb" Codebehind="Chrome.vb"
Class="corporate.Chrome" %>
```

If you want to have a bit of fun, you can work on doing all of this programmatically. Personally, I find typing (or altering) one line and allowing .NET to handle the plumbing to be a much easier method.

CONSUMING THE WEB SERVICE

The final step in the process is consuming the Web service on the partner side. Because you cannot guarantee that all partners employ .NET, I am going to cover two methods of consuming this Web service: one using ASP.NET and the other using traditional ASP and/or Visual Basic.

CONNECTING WITH ASP.NET   The easiest method to consume the Web service was covered in the Part II of the book, so this is just a very short refresher. If you need more help, turn back to Chapter 14. Here is a quick step-by-step:

1. Connect to the WSDL for the page, using the `wsdl.exe` framework tool.

   ```
   wsdl.exe /l:VB ⏎
   http://localhost/corporate/lookService.asmx?WSDL
   ```

2. Compile the proxy class. In this case, copy the proxy class to a new Visual Basic object. In the download, I call this proxy class. In a real-world situation, this would be on a partner site and not in the same project. You can move the code to another site if you want to prove that the Web service is actually reaching out across the Web.

You can download the code for the proxy class from this book's companion Web site (`www.wiley.com/extras`). Look for the file `Ch21-23SDK.zip` (the SDK version) or `Ch21-23VS.zip` (the Visual Studio .NET version). The partner proxy implementation is contained in the file `proxyClass.vb`.

3. Because the class is named `LookService` (as is the class in the WSDL), you have to change the name of the Visual Basic .NET file created, as well as the class name in the file. I have chosen, for simplicity, the name `ProxyClass` for each.

Creating a proxy class using the WSDL.exe tool is covered in much greater detail in Chapter 14.

Listing 23-7 contains the proxy class code. If you compare the code in this listing with the code in Listing 14-5 you will find the only differences to be the names of the functions and the parameters. I've also added aliases for each of the namespaces to shorten the names and turned option `Strict` on.

Listing 23-7: The Proxy Functions of the Proxy Class

```
Option Strict On
Option Explicit On

Imports System
Imports SysDiag = System.Diagnostics
Imports SysWebServ = System.Web.Services
Imports SysWebProtocol = System.Web.Services.Protocols
Imports SysXMLSerial = System.Xml.Serialization

<SysWebServ.WebServiceBindingAttribute(Name:="LookServiceSoap", _
    [Namespace]:="http://tempuri.org/")> _
Public Class ProxyClass
  Inherits SysWebProtocol.SoapHttpClientProtocol

  <SysDiag.DebuggerStepThroughAttribute()> _
  Public Sub New()
      MyBase.New()
      Me.Url = "http://localhost/corporate/lookservice.asmx"
  End Sub

  <SysDiag.DebuggerStepThroughAttribute(), _
   SysWebProtocol.SoapDocumentMethodAttribute("http://tempuri.org/GetLook", _
   Use:=SysWebServ.Description.SoapBindingUse.Literal, _

   ParameterStyle:=SysWebProtocol.SoapParameterStyle.Wrapped)> _
  Public Function GetLook(ByVal intSiteID As Integer, _
                          ByVal intPageID As Integer) As String
      Dim results() As Object = Me.Invoke("GetLook", New Object() _
                              {intSiteID, intPageID})
      Return CType(results(0), String)
  End Function

  <SysDiag.DebuggerStepThroughAttribute()> _
  Public Function BeginGetLook(ByVal intSiteID As Integer, _
                          ByVal intPageID As Integer, _
                          ByVal callback As System.AsyncCallback, _
                          ByVal asyncState As Object) As System.IAsyncResult
      Return Me.BeginInvoke("GetLook", New Object() _
```

Continued

Listing 23-7 *(Continued)*

```
                 {intSiteID, intPageID}, callback, asyncState)
End Function

<SysDiag.DebuggerStepThroughAttribute()> _
Public Function EndGetLook(ByVal asyncResult As System.IAsyncResult) As String
    Dim results() As Object = Me.EndInvoke(asyncResult)
    Return CType(results(0), String)
End Function

End Class
```

 You can download the code for the proxy class from the companion Web site (www.wiley.com/extras) in the file Ch21-23SDK.zip (the SDK version) or Ch21-23VS.zip (the Visual Studio .NET version). The partner proxy implementation is contained in the file proxyClass.vb.

To call this class, I have to create either a Visual Basic .NET component or an ASPX page. In this instance, I've chosen an ASPX page. In this page, I use the same database code as in Chapter 22 (Listing 22-3) to pull the content of the page. In a normal partner situation, the content would, of course, be different.

To call the component, I simply call the proxyclass GetLook() method. I then use the code from the page that utilizes the replace() method (replaceMethod.aspx) to place the content in the page. Listing 23-8 shows the code that creates the page.

Listing 23-8: Creating the Page

```
Private Sub Page_Load(ByVal sender As System.Object, _
                      ByVal e As System.EventArgs) Handles MyBase.Load
    Dim objProxy As New ProxyClass()
    Dim objReader As SQLData.SqlDataReader
    Dim strPageContent As String

    Dim objConn As New SQLData.SqlConnection(Application("ConnectionString"))
    Dim objCmd As New SQLData.SqlCommand()

    With objCmd
        .CommandText = "sps_GetChrome"
        .CommandType = CommandType.StoredProcedure
        .Connection = objConn
        .Parameters.Add(New SQLData.SqlParameter("@intSiteID", SqlDbType.Int, _
                    4, ParameterDirection.Input, False, 0, 0, "intSiteID", _
                    DataRowVersion.Original, m_intSiteID))
```

```
                objCmd.Parameters.Add(New SQLData.SqlParameter("@intMenuItemID", _
                                SqlDbType.Int, 4, ParameterDirection.Input, _
                                False, 0, 0, "intMenuItemID", _
                                DataRowVersion.Original, m_intPageID))
        End With

        Try
            objConn.Open()
            objReader = objCmd.ExecuteReader()

            While objReader.Read
                strPageContent = objReader.GetString(0)
            End While

            objReader.Close()
            objConn.Close()

        Catch objException As Exception
            'TODO: Add error handler
        End Try

        'Retrieve the content for the page
        Dim strOutput As String = Replace(objProxy.GetLook(m_intSiteID, _
                                m_intPageID), "<content />", _
                                strPageContent)

        'Output the page
        Response.Write(strOutput)

End Sub
```

 You can download the code for the proxy class from the companion Web site (www.wiley.com/extras) in the file Ch21-23SDK.zip (the SDK version) or Ch21-23VS.zip (the Visual Studio .NET version). The partner page implementation is contained in the file partner.aspx.vb.

What's important here is how simple it is to create this type of proxy in .NET. If you have never had to work with the Win Inet API to achieve the same functionality, you may not even realize how much Microsoft has done to make your life easier. Of course, you can still do things the hard way if you want (or if you need the additional functionality that you get by hand-coding the plumbing).

If you are particularly adventurous, you can create an object that generates the proxy object for you, compiles it, and enables you to dynamically connect to the object. If you would like to see an example of this type of project, you can go to www.eyesoft.com/dotnet and download the dynamic Web service proxy project.

The results of this transformation are shown in Figure 23-3. Note that there's currently no content added, because this is just a test from the partner side.

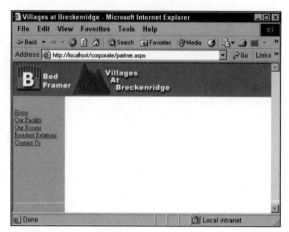

Figure 23-3: Testing the code to ensure the Web service works.

CONSUMING A WEB SERVICE WITH TRADITIONAL ASP   What if someone needs to attach to a Web service with a VB 6 COM object or ASP? It is fairly simple. First, you must have the SOAP Toolkit installed on the client. Then, you need to use the SOAP Client object, as shown in Listing 23-9.

Listing 23-9: Using an ASP Client with a Web Service

```
'Create a SOAP object
Dim objSoapClient          'As MSSOAPLib.SoapClient
Dim strChrome     'As String
Dim strContent    'As String
Dim strConn               'As String
Dim strSQL                'As String
Dim objConn               'As ADODB.Connection
Dim objRS                 'As ADODB.Recordset

Const intPageID = 1
Const intSiteID = 1

strConn = "Provider=SQLOLEDB.1;Server=(local);Database=dbBow;UID=sa;PWD=;"
strSQL = "sps_PageContent " & intSiteID & "," & intPageID

Set objSoapClient = Server.CreateObject("MSSOAPLib.SoapClient")
```

```
'Attach to the WSDL file created by the service
Call  objSoapClient.mssoapinit("http://localhost/corporate/" & _
                               "useChromeVB.asmx?WSDL")
    strChrome = objSoapClient.GetLook(intSiteID, intPageID)
Set objSoapClient = Nothing

Set objConn = Server.CreateObject("ADODB.Connection")
Call objConn.Open(strConn)

'Assumption here that the code will not fail. Add error handling to live code
Set objRS = objConn.Execute(strSQL)
StrContent = objRS(0)

strChrome = Replace(strChrome,"<content />", strContent)
```

 You can download the code for the ASP consumer from the companion Web site (www.wiley.com/extras) in the file Ch21-23SDK.zip (the SDK version) or Ch21-23VS.zip (the Visual Studio .NET version). The file to look at is partner.asp.

The code here is also very simple, thanks to the SOAP Toolbox 2.0. If you were to code the interface on your own, you'd have a much more difficult row to hoe. If you want to experiment further with the SOAP toolkit, you can download it from http://msdn.microsoft.com/soap.

Completing the portal

Of course, one partner site does not create a portal, but it is a very good start. The Bedframer site is now linked to a single partner, but adding additional partners is as easy as telling them where to point to the WSDL file for the service(s) created for this chapter.

To see an example of a portal site created using a similar methodology, point your browser to www.ehc.com. This site, along with the sites developed for EHC's clients, is built from a tool that allows the person running the tool to pick and choose a variety of types of content. Some of the content comes from partner sites. In order to maintain the look and feel of the site (with most of the partners, at least), an interface similar to the Web service(s) in this chapter was built.

Once the interface was built, the time necessary to add a new partner was greatly reduced, saving both time and money.

In the Bedframer application, I assume that more partners will come online. Some might have a need for information that Bedframer stores in its database, such as room inventory. The possibilities are endless.

Summary

In this chapter, I covered the method of creating a portal interface using Web services. By sharing the look of a Web site with partner sites, a uniform look can be presented to users despite the fact they have been sent to a partner site.

To create the interface, I created a Web service that called a Visual Basic .NET class, created a Web service that contained all of the code for the service, and, altered the Visual Basic .NET class to use it as a Web service. In the end, each of these implementations worked pretty much the same way, but the methodology employed to get there was a bit different.

On the partner side, I utilized the WSDL generation tool (`wsdl.exe`) to create a proxy object for use with .NET. I also created a Web service consumer in traditional ASP, using the SOAP Toolkit to simplify connection with the service.

What a ride this has been! I hope you've gained as much out of reading this book as I have writing it.

Index

Symbols

continued

continued

continued

continued

continued